MANAGEMENT SKILLS
FOR EVERYDAY LIFE

The Practical Coach

SECOND EDITION

MANAGEMENT SKILLS FOR EVERYDAY LIFE

The Practical Coach

Paula J. Caproni, Ph.D.

Director
Executive Skills Program
University of Michigan Business School
Ann Arbor, Michigan

PEARSON

Prentice
Hall

Upper Saddle River, New Jersey 07458

Library of Congress Cataloging-in-Publication Data
Caproni, Paula J.
   Management skills for everyday life / Paula J. Caproni.
     p. cm.
   Revised ed. of the author's The practical coach.
   Includes index.
   ISBN 0-13-143968-5
    1. Management. 2. Interpersonal communication.   I. Caproni, Paula J. Practical coach.
   II. Title.

HD31.C3434 2004
658—dc21   2004053499

VP/Editorial Director: Jeff Shelstad
Project Manager: Ashley Santora
Editorial Assistant: Denise Vaughn
Marketing Manager: Shannon Moore
Marketing Assistant: Patrick Danzuso
Managing Editor: John Roberts
Production Editor: Suzanne Grappi
Manufacturing Buyer: Michelle Klein
Production Manager: Arnold Vila
Cover Design Manager: Jayne Conte
Cover Design: Bruce Kenselaar
Composition/Full-Service Project Management: Progressive Publishing Alternatives
Printer/Binder: Phoenix Book Tech

Credits and acknowledgments borrowed from other sources and reproduced, with permission, in this textbook appear on appropriate page within text.

Pearson Education LTD.   Pearson Education Australia PTY, Limited
Pearson Education Singapore, Pte. Ltd   Pearson Education North Asia Ltd
Pearson Education, Canada, Ltd   Pearson Educación de Mexico, S.A. de C.V.
Pearson Education–Japan   Pearson Education Malaysia, Pte. Ltd

PEARSON
Prentice
Hall

10 9 8 7 6 5 4 3 2 1
ISBN 0-13-143968-5

For Charlie, Julia, and Leah with love

BRIEF CONTENTS

Chapter 1   What Predicts Success?   1

Chapter 2   Developing Self-Awareness   31

Chapter 3   Building Trust   86

Chapter 4   Communicating Effectively   113

Chapter 5   Gaining and Using Sustainable, Ethical Power and Influence   157

Chapter 6   Managing Relationships with Your Bosses, Subordinates, and Peers   212

Chapter 7   Managing Cultural Diversity   269

Chapter 8   Creating High-Performing Teams   311

Chapter 9   Diverse Teams and Virtual Teams: Managing Differences and Distances   349

Chapter 10   Crafting a Life   390

CONTENTS

Preface   xv

CHAPTER 1   What Predicts Success?   1

Managerial Derailment   3

Why Managers Derail   3

Intelligence isn't enough   4

Early success can lead to failure   6

A flaw now matters   8

What Predicts Success?   9

Proactivity   10

Learning goal orientation   11

Creative and practical intelligence   13

Emotional intelligence   13

Positive emotions   13

Why We Hold Onto Past Behaviors That No Longer Serve Us Well   15

Steps toward personal change   16

The New Rules   17

Investing in lifelong learning and critical thinking   20

Developing self-awareness   21

Creating a broad and diverse network of high-quality relationships   21

Designing a workplace that brings out the best in others   22

Crafting a meaningful life   22

How This Book Is Organized   23

Chapter Summary   25

Food for Thought   26

Endnotes   27

CHAPTER 2   Developing Self-Awareness   31

Barriers to Self-Awareness   33

The Brand Called You   34

So what's a well-intentioned manager to do?   35

The Self-Concept: I Think, Therefore I Think I Am   37

What is the self-concept?   37

Cultural Influences on the Self-Concept: The Independent and Interdependent Self   38

The independent self-concept   39

The interdependent self-concept   40

Advantages of a cultural view of the self-concept   41

Social Influences on the Self-Concept: Seeing Ourselves as Others See Us   43
   Family influences on the self-concept   44
   Other people's expectations on our self-concept   46
   Group influences on the self-concept   46
Why the Self-Concept Is Important   47
The Self in Contemporary Organizations   49
   The challenges for managers today   50
   A day in a saturated life   52
   Identity in the age of the internet   54
   Identity in the age of mass media and celebrities   56
The Promise, Perils, and Self-Concept of the Postmodern Manager   58
   The updated managerial self-concept   59
   Managers as bricoleurs   60
   Managers as meaning makers   60
   Managers as multiple selves   61
   Managers as self-monitors   65
Managerial Growth and Development   67
Chapter Summary   68
Food for Thought   69
Endnotes   79
Case 1: Self-Awareness   85

CHAPTER 3   Building Trust   86
Why Trust Matters   86
What Is Trust?   89
Why Should I Trust Thee? Let Me Count the Reasons   91
   Personality and trust   91
   Assessment of another person's trustworthiness   93
   Optimum trust: Is there such a thing as trusting too much?   94
Creating Trust: Interpersonal Strategies   94
   How to repair trust once it is broken: The art of the apology   96
Creating Trust: Organizational Strategies   98
   Organizational structure and swift trust   99
Beyond Trust: The Relationship Between Positive
  Emotions and Success   101
   How positive emotions and behaviors lead to professional success and well-being   101
   How positive emotions lead to organizational effectiveness   102
   Positive emotions and organizational crises   102
Conclusion   104
Chapter Summary   105
Food for Thought   106
Endnotes   107

CHAPTER 4 Communicating Effectively   113

Active Listening   115

Giving and Receiving Feedback   119

Creating a feedback-friendly work environment   120
Giving feedback   120
Receiving feedback   122
The effectiveness of multirater feedback   123
Managerial language that motivates employees   125
Are you getting enough bad news?   125

Communicating Across Cultures   128

Culture, language, and power   130

Communicating to Mobilize Action   132

Using inspiring language   134
Telling stories   135
Be wise when listening to stories   139

Talk and Technology   140

Rules for effective e-mail communication   142

Conclusion   146

Chapter Summary   148

Food for Thought   149

Endnotes   150

Case 2: Communicating   156

**CHAPTER 5 Gaining and Using Sustainable, Ethical
                    Power and Influence   157**

Foundations of Sustainable, Ethical Power and Influence   159

Why we need power and influence skills   159
Characteristics of people with power   160

Developing Interpersonal Power: Reading and Adapting to Other People's
Interests and Styles   163

The social styles model   163

Using the Six Universal Forms of Influence   169

The reciprocation rule   171
The scarcity rule   174
The authority rule   175
The rule of social proof   177
The commitment and consistency rule   178
The liking rule   179

Developing Political Savvy   184

Characteristics of politically savvy people   186
Minimizing dysfunctional organizational politics   192

Conclusion   194

Chapter Summary   195

Assessment 5-1: Social Styles   200

Food for Thought   203
Endnotes   204

**CHAPTER 6   Managing Relationships with Your Bosses,
                Subordinates, and Peers   212**

Authority Relations at Work   213
  Organizational structure and authority relations   214
  Personality and authority relations   215
Managing Subordinates   217
  The situational leadership model   219
  The denison leadership development model   221
  A note on empowerment: It's more than a feeling   224
A Cautionary Note: Obedience to Authority   227
  Lessons for everyday work life   230
Managing Your Boss   233
  Managing abrasive bosses   235
Managing Mentor-Protégé Relationships   239
  Diversity and mentoring   241
  How to make the most of mentoring relationships   242
  Advice for protégés   242
  Advice for mentors   244
Networking   244
  Characteristics of effective networks   247
  Diversity and networks   248
  Networking advice   251
Impression Management   254
Conclusion   257
Chapter Summary   257
Food for Thought   259
Endnotes   259
Case 3: Relationships: Gaining Power and Motivating   268

CHAPTER 7   Managing Cultural Diversity   269

Part 1 What Is Culture?   270
Dimensions of Culture   273
  Who am I?   274
  How do I relate to others?   277
  How do I communicate with others?   278
  How do I deal with time?   280
  What is truth?   282
  How do I relate to the environment?   283
  What is the relationship of work to life?   284
  A note on cultural differences   285
Part 2 Why Managing Diversity Effectively Is a Competitive Advantage   286
If Diversity Is So Good for Organizations, Why Does Progress Seem to Lag
  Behind the Promise?   289

Given These Hurdles, What's a Manager to Do?   291
Enhancing Your Personal Multicultural Competence   292
   Culture-specific skills   294
   Culture-general skills   295
   Developing multicultural competence   296
Creating Cultural Synergy   297
Summary   302
Chapter Summary   303
Food for Thought   304
Endnotes   306

CHAPTER 8   Creating High-Performing Teams   311
Beyond the Team Hype   312
What Is a Team?   313
Criteria for Judging Team Effectiveness   314
Foundations of High-Performing Teams: Purpose, Performance Measures,
   People, Process, and Practice   316
   Foundation 1: Clear, engaging purpose   316
   Foundation 2: Performance goals and measures   317
   Foundation 3: People   318
   Foundation 4: Results-driven processes   319
   Foundation 5: Preparation and practice   323
Team Leadership: Creating a Context for High-Performing Teams   325
   Team leadership skill 1: Invest in ongoing personal development   326
   Team leadership skill 2: Provide team direction, structure, and resources   327
   Team leadership skill 3: Help the team manage boundaries   329
   Team leadership skill 4: Manage the type and timing of interventions   335
The Team Life Cycle   336
   Forming   336
   Storming   339
   Norming   340
   Performing   340
   Adjourning   341
Creating and Managing High-Performing Teams: The Bottom Line   342
Chapter Summary   343
Food for Thought   344
Endnotes   345

**CHAPTER 9   Diverse Teams and Virtual Teams: Managing
              Differences and Distances   349**
Part 1 Diverse Teams   351
   The diversity dilemma   351
   Potential advantages and disadvantages of diverse teams   352
   Now the hurdles   355
   Additional factors to consider   357

Leading diverse teams   *358*
Conclusion   *361*
Part 2 Virtual Teams: Working Together Apart   361
Why virtual teams?   *361*
Differences Between Co-Located and Distributed Teams   363
Social Dynamics in Distributed Teams   364
Communication   *365*
Belonging and cohesion   *367*
Social influence   *368*
Status and power   *370*
Managing Distributed Teams   371
Determine the appropriate level of technology for the team task   *372*
Manage the technological environment   *373*
Develop work processes that enhance team performance   *374*
Cohesion   *374*
Communication   *375*
Coordination   *376*
Virtual teams: The bottom line   *376*
Chapter Summary   379
Food for Thought   381
Endnotes   382
Case 4: Building Teams   389

CHAPTER 10   Crafting a Life   390
Happiness   391
Happiness, Work, and Flow   394
Optimism and Success   397
The role of explanations in optimism   *400*
When optimism is overrated   *401*
Work and Health   402
Perfectionism   *404*
Type A behavior   *405*
*What are the organizational consequences of
   perfectionism and Type A behavior?*   *406*
Integrating Work and Family   407
Who works?   *409*
What is the impact of working parents on organizations?   *412*
What is the impact of children on working parents' careers?   *412*
What is the impact of working parents on children?   *413*
What do children say about their working parents?   *417*
Conclusion   420
Chapter Summary   421
Food for Thought   422
Endnotes   427
Case 5: Managing Stress   434

Index   437

PREFACE

This book, now in its second edition, is designed to translate the science of success (what researchers know about success) into the practice of success (what you should know about success). My goal in this book is to provide ideas, techniques, and best practices that will help you achieve the success that you desire—*however you define success*. Specifically, this book can help you improve your effectiveness at work, advance your career (marketability, promotions, salary increases, job satisfaction and job flexibility), and enhance your general well-being (happiness and health). Let me say this up front: If you are effective at your job but your family and friends cannot remember the last time you paid attention to them, if you never take a vacation without worrying about your work, if you do not have a moment to spare to contribute to your community, and if you are headed for poor health or an early death because of the stress of your job, that is not a strategy for success that will serve you, others, your organization, or society well.

As with the previous edition, this second edition is based on the assumption that the most successful people achieve their goals by working *smarter*, not necessarily harder, than less successful people. People who achieve the success that they desire do not necessarily have the highest IQs, degrees from top-rated universities, well-connected families, or the full support of devoted bosses and mentors. Rather, successful people earn their success by focusing on goals that are meaningful to them and others, learning the perspectives and skills that will help them reach these goals, understanding themselves (their styles, strengths, and weaknesses, as well as how others perceive them), developing a broad and diverse network of high-quality and mutually supportive relationships, and—if they are managers—creating a work context that brings out the best in others.

This book assumes that you are—or want to be—a manager. So what is management? Management textbooks say it is about getting things done through others, but it is more than that, much more. For many of us, being a manager is an important part of our identity. It is how we spend our days, it is what we do with and to others, it is how we express (or suppress) our competence, it can be our best selves or worst selves, and it offers us the opportunity to make a contribution to our organizations and society's future.

ASSUMPTIONS OF THIS BOOK

Several themes are woven throughout this book. The first is that managing in a diverse, global, technologically driven, and fast-changing economic environment requires a more complex set of skills than those needed by managers in the past. Unfortunately, even as we enter the twenty-first century, many management books and magazines are implicitly (if not explicitly) being written for the organizational man (with a spouse at home) in a gray flannel suit (except on casual Fridays, when he wears khaki) who works in a brick-and-mortar organization. However, today's manager is just as likely to be a man or woman in a dual career relationship who works in a brick-and-click (or just click) organization that advocates work-life balance and simultaneously expects a 24/7 commitment to work (in other words, being available 24 hours a day, 7 days a week). This book is designed to help you navigate the opportunities and hurdles of today's and tomorrow's social and economic environment.

The second theme is that one of the biggest mistakes managers can make is to assume their technical skills and cognitive intelligence are enough to ensure their professional effectiveness and success. Professor John Tropman, my colleague at the University of Michigan, says that when people become managers, they tend to think of their new job as being "the same as their old job only bigger." In other words, they try to use the skills that worked for them as individual contributors even though their primary responsibility as managers is to create a context in which others can do their best work. This book is designed to help you move from an individual contributor mindset to a managerial mindset.

The third theme is that the ability to manage professional relationships is one of the most important skills that managers can have. Indeed, substantial research suggests that people with a broad and diverse network of relationships inside and outside of their work organization tend to be more effective in their jobs, have more successful careers, and lead happier and healthier lives than those who do not. Not surprisingly, the ability to manage professional relationships becomes increasingly important as one climbs the organizational hierarchy. Yet even though building effective relationships is critical to managerial and organizational success, many managers mistakenly categorize relationship-building skills as "nice to have" rather than "need to have." Consequently, they miss out on daily opportunities to build trust, respect, support, and influence, all of which can enhance their effectiveness, career success, and general well-being. This book is designed to help you develop relationship-building skills that will serve you well regardless of your professional and personal goals.

The fourth theme is that today's managers are becoming saturated with information and are being exposed to a seemingly endless parade of management theories, fads, and gurus. Consequently, they need to become more critical consumers of managerial knowledge. Indeed, *The Futurist* magazine wisely warns that this deluge of information can actually "decrease our thinking skills" and "future generations may be more easily led astray." I took this warning seriously when I wrote this book. I present what I believe are some of the most insightful and useful theories and research studies available to managers today. My purpose is to provide you with food for thought, trigger your imagination, and offer useful frameworks and techniques. As social psychologist Kurt Lewin once said, "There is nothing so practical as a good theory."

But keep in mind that few, if any, theories work for all people and all situations all of the time; theory should not replace thinking. Too often, management theorists, researchers, and educators present their ideas as universally applicable, even when these ideas are culturally biased and when their effectiveness is limited to particular situations. This is particularly important to keep in mind when a theory promotes one way of seeing or acting as universally normal, effective, or moral. When presenting theories and research studies in this book, I have used phrases such as "research suggests that" and "researchers have concluded that" to avoid falling into the "theory is truth" trap and to leave room for alternative views. When I have forgotten to do so, I hope that you continue to keep the theories, research conclusions, and advice in their place, as useful conceptual tools that enable you to respond thoughtfully and quickly to the routine and complex situations that you face in everyday work life. The words of Maya Lin, architect and designer of the Vietnam memorial in Washington, DC, best express the spirit of this book: "I create places in which to think, without trying to dictate what to think."

NEW INFORMATION IN THIS SECOND EDITION

Although the characteristics that predict success are no different today than they were when the first edition of this book was published, the context in which we live and work has changed significantly. Indeed, the ancient curse "May you live in interesting times" seems disturbingly relevant today. The dot.com boom turned into the dot.com bust (although the use of information and communication technologies remains central to the success of organizations that use these technologies wisely). Many high-profile organizational leaders and executives who were stars in the 1990s became known as scoundrels only a few years later for lying, looting, and engaging in a variety of other self-serving misdeeds that harmed their employees, customers, shareholders, and organizations. Terrorism gave citizens worldwide a stark reminder of the instability of the world order, as well as the compassion and resilience that can emerge from heartbreak.

Regardless of the events that dominated much of our attention these past few years, the lessons from the first edition of the book remain timeless. However, I have added new material to this second edition to reflect some lessons learned from these and other recent events. I have also added practical ideas from useful research that has emerged since the first edition was written.

- The first chapter title was changed from "The New Rules" to "What Predicts Success" because the characteristics that predict success in work and life are similar regardless of the issues and challenges people face in a particular point in time. In addition, I added a comprehensive section about the characteristics that predict success to this chapter. Because of the recent organizational scandals, I also added a section on why smart executives do stupid things as a warning that many of the same qualities that lead an executive to success also can lead to failure when taken to extremes.
- I have integrated useful ideas from the most recent research into each chapter. I have also introduced new self-assessments, best-practices, and end-of-chapter questions that will help you to put into practice the skills that you learn in each chapter.
- I have added a new section on the power of positive emotions to the chapter on developing trust. Every now and then, a new line of research emerges that has a far reaching impact on management theory and practice. *The Harvard Business Review* acknowledged the Positive Organizational Scholarship Group at the Michigan Business School as one of the most important new ideas of 2003 for its contribution to our knowledge of how positive emotions enhance individual, team, and organizational performance, as well as personal well-being. Although I had introduced some of these ideas in the first edition of the book (e.g., trust, happiness, and flow), I expanded these ideas based on this new research.
- I have added a new chapter on developing sustainable, ethical power and influence. Successful people know how to gain power, influence others, and engage in appropriate organizational politics so that they can achieve goals that would otherwise be beyond their reach. Successful people also know how to identify and avoid unethical forms of power, influence, and politics that can derail their careers and harm the people and organizations who depend on them.
- For instructors, I have revised the comprehensive instructor manual to include more supporting materials, as well as recommendations for useful resources such as Web sites, videos, simulations, short exercises, and additional readings that will help bring the materials to life and make teaching these materials a pleasure. The

sample syllabi, chapter outlines, test item files, and slides have also been revised to reflect the changes that I made to this second revision.

ACKNOWLEDGMENTS

In addition to the many researchers and theorists cited throughout this book, I am indebted to many people at Prentice-Hall. David Shafer, former management editor, and Leslie Oliver, former sales associate, who enthusiastically and persistently encouraged me to write the first edition of the book. Michael Campbell, Michele Foresta, Kim Marsden, Kelly Warsak, and many others skillfully nurtured the first edition of this book through the production process. For this second edition, I thank Jeff Shelstad, Editorial Director, and Mike Ablassmeir, Acquisitions Editor, who believed the positive response to the first edition warranted this revision. I also thank Ashley Santora, Project Manager, Suzanne Grappi, Production Editor, and Lisa McClanahan for their persistent and expert roles in bringing this second edition to market. Working with them was a pleasure.

I offer a special thanks to my friend and colleague Maria Eugenia Arias who I had initially hoped would be a co-author of this book. Unfortunately for me, she decided that her heart is in consulting. However, she continues to offer me valuable advice and encouragement. I am also thankful to Clayton Alderfer, Ella Bell, David Berg, and Linda Smircich, my early mentors at Yale University and the University of Massachusetts who inspired me to think critically about managerial knowledge and practice and to encourage others to think critically as well. Although my early mentors may not agree with everything I wrote in this book, I believe they would agree with my reasons for writing it.

I owe sincere thanks to the many people who stimulated and clarified my thinking, recommended books and articles, read and edited chapters, and provided technical and emotional support, especially Roann Altman, Joy Beatty, Julia Davies, Gelaye Debebe, Deb Mondro, Dan Denison, Jane Dutton, Jane Fountain, Joe Garcia, Suzanne C. de Janasz, Ellen Kossek, Graham Mercer, Karen Newman, Dina Pasalis, Gene Penner, Lance Sandelands, Robert Sternberg (for his insightful research on successful intelligence), Barbara Tag, Ollie Thomas, Dave Ulrich, the members of the Organizational Behavior Teaching Society and the Academy of Management learning and education division, and the many reviewers of the first edition. I am particularly indebted to Gene Anderson, Susan Ashford, Jerry Davis, Bob Dolan, Jim Walsh, Joe White, and my colleagues in the Management and Organizations department at the University of Michigan who provide me with an awesome job and an intellectually stimulating work environment.

I am also grateful to the students and executives who have attended my courses in many countries, Brazil, China, Finland, Germany, Nigeria, Poland, Sweden, South Korea, and the United States, to name a few. I have learned much from them. Their wisdom, warmth, and good humor have made teaching a joy and a privilege.

In the first edition of this book, I offered many thanks to the staff at Community Day Care and in particular to Trudi Hagen, the director, and Tara Sturgeon, who was our babysitter when our children were younger. I was able to focus on the first edition of this book only because I knew that our daughters, Julia and Leah, were safe and happy in their loving and competent care. Although our children are now older, I will always be indebted to the day care providers and teachers who contributed so much to our children's lives and helped them grow into the wonderful young people that they are today.

I am deeply thankful for the support that my family has given me throughout the years. I am appreciative of the many sacrifices that my parents and grandparents made so that their children and grandchildren could have a better life (I have a great life). I thank my husband, Charlie Penner, for being a fantastic father to our two daughters. And I remain in awe of our wonderful daughters, Julia and Leah. They are the light of my life. They are also a constant reminder that the work we do is important because it shapes the world for our children and for future generations. Finally, I must note that Julia, when she was eight years old, suggested that I call this book Management Skills for Smarty Pants. I only wish I had been courageous enough to use her clever title.

Paula J. Caproni
Ann Arbor, Michigan
October 2004

ABOUT THE AUTHOR

Paula J. Caproni teaches in the Management and Organizations Department at the Stephen M. Ross School of Business at the University of Michigan. She received her MBA from the University of Massachusetts and her Ph.D. in Organizational Behavior from Yale University. In addition to teaching in the University of Michigan MBA and Executive Programs, Professor Caproni is Director of the Executive Skills Program and the Executive MBA Professional Development Program. She has also taught for the Helsinki School of Economics, for the Catho Group (Brazil), for the University of Michigan's global MBA programs in Hong-Kong, Brazil, and South Korea, and for Management Sciences for Health in Nigeria. In addition to *Management Skills for Everyday Life: The Practical Coach*, she is currently writing a new book called *What Predicts Success*. In addition to teaching courses in leadership, interpersonal skills, and team-effectiveness, Professor Caproni consults to organizations in both the public and private sector, including Avon, Dartmouth College, Exxon, Ford, Internal Revenue Service, Mead-Johnson, Nokia, Onninen, Philips, Phelps-Dodge, Stora-Enso, and Management Sciences for Health. She is a reviewer for several academic journals, including the *Academy of Management Review, Human Resource Management Journal,* the *Journal of Management Inquiry, Journal of Management Education,* and the *Journal of Business Ethics.* She has served on the Editorial Board of the Journal of Applied Behavioral Science and the Academy of Management Journal of Learning and Education, and has served on the Teaching Committee of the Academy of Management Organizational Behavior Division and the Board of Directors of the Organizational Behavior Teaching Society.

Contact Information
2607 Executive Education
University of Michigan Business School
Ann Arbor, Michigan 48109-1234

Phone: (734) 763-1010
Fax: (734) 615-4323
E-mail: pcaproni@umich.edu

CHAPTER

1

What Predicts Success?

This chapter will help you:

■ Understand the changes that are affecting managerial work today

■ Learn why many high-potential managers derail

■ Learn why IQ is not a strong predictor of managerial success

■ Learn what characteristics and skills predict success in a diverse, global, technologically driven, and fast-changing economic environment

■ Learn strategies for changing your behavior so that you can have the success that you desire

> *It's not the strongest of the species that survive,*
> *nor the most intelligent, but the one most*
> *responsive to change.*
> —CHARLES DARWIN

For people who thrive on challenge and making a difference in organizations, the managerial profession is one of the most fulfilling avenues to personal growth, organizational change, and social contribution. More than 25 years ago, management theorist Henry Mintzberg stated what is still timely today: "No job is more vital to our society than that of the manager. It is the managers who determine whether our social institutions serve us well or whether they squander our talents and resources."[1] Certainly, there are other professions that are equally vital to any society. But the fact remains that managers in private, public, and nonprofit organizations significantly influence whether their organizations' and societies' resources are well-used or wasted.

Despite managers' importance to organizational and societal advancement, many talented people are promoted to managerial positions with little more than a congratulatory pat on the back, a salary increase, and many new responsibilities. Too often, newly promoted managers are left to figure out for themselves how to move from their role as successful individual contributors to their new roles as managers who are responsible for creating a work environment in which *others* can do their best work. Even experienced managers often hit a wall when they are promoted to the next managerial level, especially when many of the skills that made them successful in their previous jobs are insufficient for the demands of their new jobs.

This book is designed to help you achieve three goals, regardless of whether you are a new manager, experienced manager, or professional who wants to develop a more well-rounded skill set. First, it will provide you with skills that will help you enhance your own performance, create work contexts in which others can do their best work, and add greater value to your organizations. Second, it will help you achieve the career success that you desire, however you define success. Third, it will help you enhance your well-being. It may come as a surprise to you to learn that many of the skills that enhance your work effectiveness and career success also help you have a longer, healthier, and happier life.

These are lofty goals but not impossible ones. Although there are no guarantees in life, the advice given in this book is based on decades of practical research about what predicts success in work and life. One of the most important lessons that you will learn from this book is that the most effective people—those who bring significant value to their organizations and who obtain the professional and personal success that they desire—don't necessarily have higher IQs, bigger budgets, or higher-status educations than others. They do not necessarily work more hours than those who are less effective, although they do tend to be more focused and work harder, work smarter, and are more disciplined toward their goals. They do not follow the same path to success (e.g., they do necessarily climb the organizational or professional ladder in predictable stages), nor do they define success in the same way. They do not necessarily have the best bosses, nor are they all blessed with brilliant mentors devoted to their success. They are not born leaders or heroic figures, nor are they perfect. They do not share the same personality style. Some are big-picture oriented, whereas others are detail oriented. Some are extroverts and others are introverts. Some are fast on their feet, whereas others are slow and steady. Some are charismatic, and others prefer to avoid the spotlight. But successful people do tend to share certain characteristics, and you will learn about these characteristics later in this chapter.

I've got my faults, but living in the past isn't one of them. There's no future in it. *Sparky Anderson, Former Manager of the Detroit Tigers*

Another important lesson that you will learn from this book is that significant social and economic trends such as increased diversity, globalization, and technological advances have fundamentally changed the nature of managerial work. Indeed, many managerial behaviors that were used in the past—and are still firmly entrenched in many organizations today—are no longer adding value (and some didn't add much value in the past either). Therefore, all managers must take a serious look at the larger social, cultural, economic, and technological context in which they live and work—what *Wall Street Journal* columnist Hal Lancaster calls the "defining issues of their time"[2] and determine how these issues affect their clients, employees, and organizations.

This book is not about quick fixes, easy answers, and one-size-fits-all truths. Roger Enrico, former CEO of PepsiCo, described the inadequacy of one-size-fits-all managerial advice: "Somewhere along the way we either told people or they surmised . . . that it was a paint by number system. That if you used these tools in this sequence in this way, success is inevitable. . . . [If it were that easy] I wouldn't need a manager, I'd have a machine."[3] Rather than provide quick fixes, easy answers, and one-size-fits all advice, this book will (1) help you think in broader and more complex ways about what successful managers do and (2) develop the skills and flexibility that will serve you, your organizations, and your communities well regardless of the defining issues of your time.

Despite the changes that will continue to affect organizations and societies, managerial work will always have some common themes across time, place, and culture. Managers will always be human and, thus, imperfect. Consequently, self-awareness—an understanding of one's styles, strengths, and weaknesses, as well as how one is perceived by others—will always be a hallmark of successful managers. Managers will always work with others, so the ability to build trust and respect with a broad and diverse group of people will always be the foundation on which enduring and effective work relationships are built. Managers will always need to gain the support of others, so the ability to communicate effectively, influence people, and manage organizational politics will always be critical to success. Teams will always be a building block of most organizations, so the ability to design a work context that enables people working in teams to achieve their collective goals will always be in demand. Social, cultural, and technological forces will continue to transform the nature of work, so the willingness to engage in ongoing learning and change will always be essential characteristics of successful people. And because there is more to life than work, the ability to integrate the dual themes of love and work, intimacy and mastery, will always be at the heart of our humanity.

This is an exciting time to be a manager—full of challenges and opportunities. But challenges and opportunities do not come without hurdles, so let's first look at some of these hurdles. For most people, the first hurdle to confront is oneself.

MANAGERIAL DERAILMENT

Most managers come to an organization with a strong intellect, solid education, substantial technical skills, desire to be competent, motivation to work hard, and the aspiration to succeed. Yet according to research conducted by the Center for Creative Leadership, almost half never reach their full potential, shortchanging themselves and their organizations.[4] This phenomenon is called derailment.

Derailment occurs when a high-potential manager expects to advance in an organization and was judged initially to have the ability to do so, yet is fired, demoted, or plateaued below anticipated levels of achievement. Derailment does not refer to individuals who, by their own choosing, change jobs, decline promotions, or quit their jobs to pursue other careers or life interests. Rather, derailment is involuntary and frequently preventable.[5]

Derailment is costly to individuals, organizations, and society. Derailed managers and their families suffer emotionally and financially. Organizations lose their financial and intellectual investment in derailed managers and must invest substantial recruitment and development costs to replace them. And if an organization has high levels of managerial derailment, highly talented people may avoid joining the organization because they may fear that they, too, may face the same fate.

WHY MANAGERS DERAIL

Derailment often comes as a surprise to unsuspecting managers who see themselves as intelligent, well-educated, and technically competent. They learn too late that these assets are necessary but insufficient characteristics for long-term productivity and

Fortunately, people's beliefs about intelligence—and thus their potential for success—can change. Researchers have found that teaching young students the "malleable theory of intelligence" increases their persistence and commitment and consequently enhances their grades, scores on achievement tests, and performance on tasks.[17] Researcher Yin-Yi Hong and colleagues, in a study of college students at a top university in Hong Kong, conducted a study in which they gave students purported "academic" articles that promoted either a fixed or fluid view of intelligence. In other words, one group of students was taught that intelligence is a fixed trait, and the other group was taught that intelligence is fluid and often can be changed if one puts in more effort and persists. The researchers then gave students from each group a challenging task. The students who read the articles that proposed that intelligence is fluid persisted more at the challenging task and thus were more likely to succeed at the task.[18]

Successful mechanical engineer Carolyn Turk describes the link between perceptions of intelligence and success in a *Newsweek Magazine* article: "In eighth grade I took algebra. On one test I got only 36 percent of the answers correct. I failed the next one, too. I started to think, 'Maybe I'm just no good at this.' I was lucky enough to have a teacher who didn't take my bad grades as a judgment of my abilities, but simply as an indication that I should study more. He pulled me aside and told me he knew I could do better. He let me retake the tests, and I pulled my grade up to an A." Turk explains further that when she went to college for her engineering degree, this early lesson reminded her "that no one was ever born knowing calculus" and that her success would depend more on her willingness to persist and study hard rather than possessing an innate engineering ability.[19]

The point being made here is this: Managers derail not because they don't have the intelligence to succeed, but because they may rely too much on their cognitive intelligence and fail to develop other skills and beliefs (such as a fluid view of intelligence) that will serve them well when the challenges they face exceed their current abilities. As Sternberg explains, "the true measure of your intelligence is not in a test score; it is in your willingness to develop your own talents."[20]

Early Success Can Lead to Failure

Managers who derail learn the hard way that the skills that led to their previous success may not bring them future success, particularly when the current and future environment no longer look like the past. Lois Frankel, Ph.D., in her consulting work with employee development, found that managers who continue to invest in skills and routines that brought them success in the past—and who forego learning new skills that may serve them better in the future—are often unable to "overcome their strengths":[21]

> The common thread for people who derail is that they exhibit superior skill in a particular area to the exclusion of developing complementary ones. Even when a change in a job assignment requires them to apply a different skill set, or when they see people around them develop in diverse areas, they fail to notice that they're limiting themselves and turn up the volume on those behaviors that they already do well, hoping that doing more of the same will save them!

Robert Sternberg and psychologist Peter Frensch illustrated how being an expert can be detrimental under certain circumstances, particularly under conditions

Old	*New*	*Consequences for Managers*
Knowledge and product stability	Knowledge and product obsolescence; mass customization	From routinization to improvisation, adaptability, and flexibility
Knowledge in the hands of a few	Knowledge in the hands of many (in large part due to advances in information and communication technologies)	From manager as expert and information broker to manager as a creator of a context that enhances collective learning
Stability of managerial knowledge and practices	Escalation of new managerial knowledge and practices	From a focus on learning to a focus on learning and unlearning; from uncritical acceptance of managerial knowledge to becoming wise consumers of managerial knowledge
Technology as a tool for routine tasks (data processing era)	Escalating information and communication technologies (knowledge and relationship era)	From using technology primarily for routine tasks to using technology as a key leadership resource for wide-scale organizational and societal changes
Economies of scale	Mass customization, cycle time, speed	From routinization to improvisation, adaptability, and flexibility
Local focus	Local and global focus	From one-size-fits-all styles and standards to multiple styles and standards
Bureaucracy	Networks	From command and control to relationship building; from autonomy to interdependence; from clear to permeable boundaries inside and outside the organization
Managers as fixed cost	Managers as variable cost	From security to pay for performance
Predictable, trajectory careers	Multiple careers	From employment to employability
One-breadwinner families	Dual and triple career families	From an emphasis on traditional family and work roles to an emphasis on fluid family roles, flexible work schedules, and work/life integration

How do you operate successfully in such a complex and ever-changing environment? The skills that are the hallmarks of effective managers today fall into five categories. Each enables managers to become faster, more flexible, and—most importantly—more thoughtful. Managers must have the willingness and ability to:

- Invest in lifelong learning and critical thinking
- Develop self-awareness

- Create a broad and diverse network of high-quality relationships
- Design a workplace that brings out the best in individuals and teams
- Craft a meaningful personal and professional life

Investing in Lifelong Learning and Critical Thinking
Lifelong Learning

If there is one thing on which management educators, researchers, and executives agree, it is that the willingness and ability to engage in lifelong learning is one of the most important skills you can have. Dr. Nancy Dixon (whose consulting firm helps organizations create learning organizations.) explains: "We have entered the Knowledge Age, and the new currency is learning it is learning, not knowledge itself, which is critical. Knowledge is the result of learning and is ephemeral, constantly needing to be revised and updated." Quoting Thurber, she continues: "In times of change learners shall inherit the earth, the learned are beautifully equipped for a world that no longer exists."[46]

Stand on my grave and tell me the news of the world. *Inscription on eighteenth century tombstone found by anthropologist Jennifer James*

Lifelong learning goes far beyond the willingness and ability to adopt new techniques. Harvard professor Linda Hill, in her book *Becoming a Manager*, argues that managers need "the sort of learning after which an individual conceives of something in a qualitatively different way, and which has lasting influence."[47] Lifelong learning refers to an ongoing process of discovery and innovation through which we achieve a wisdom that enables us to make decisions for which there are no precedents; draw on our own life experience and take seriously the life experience of others; see the relationships between seemingly independent ideas, contradictions, and skills; and make sense out of the ambiguity and multiple agendas inherent in managerial work.

Critical Thinking

The proliferation of management gurus and consultants, the seduction of "instant answer" fads,[48] and the escalating forms of mass communication (popular press books and magazines, research journals, management training, and the Internet) make it essential for managers to be able to sort through and thoughtfully assess the value of new information and advice. In short, managers need to become critical thinkers and wise consumers of managerial knowledge.[49]

Yet for many people, learning means "to thoroughly grasp what an expert knows . . . finding and comprehending someone else's answer."[50] Most of us were taught to believe from a young age that what teachers tell us is true and useful. But claims to one-right-way and one-size-fits-all answers, although comforting, are naive and misleading in unstable times, when problems can be defined in multiple ways, when new problems arise that have never been faced before, and when problems are too complex for any one person or perspective to understand and resolve.

Two assumptions are at the heart of critical thinking. First, much of our knowledge is socially constructed, and there are many perspectives on what is true, useful, and good. Second, power relations in a society affect what kind of knowledge is pursued and promoted, so much of what managers and professionals need to know is yet unstudied. Therefore, it is up to managers to develop their own managerial knowledge,

I developed the idea very early that if there were rules that didn't make sense, you had to think carefully about how you broke them. If you got caught, well, OK, you got caught, but that was not a reason to stop thinking. *Mary Catherine Bateson quoting "Alice d'Entremont" in "Composing a Life"*

in large part through trial and error. Critical thinking involves four basic steps: understanding the assumptions on which managerial knowledge is built; considering the cultural relativity of all managerial knowledge; considering whether some organizational and societal groups gain from a particular form of knowledge while others lose; and thinking creatively about alternative ways of seeing, thinking, and acting. Critical thinkers not only ask "What is?" but also "Who said so?" "Why?" and "What if?"[51]

Developing Self-Awareness

Studies of managerial development have consistently concluded that self-awareness is a core managerial competency. In many studies of the characteristics of successful executives, researchers found that successful executives tend to seek out honest feedback about their strengths and weaknesses and have a relatively accurate sense of how they are perceived by others. They give serious thought to how their styles, strengths, and weaknesses affect their ability to solve problems, build relationships, gain support, and achieve the results they desire. Furthermore, effective managers are able to change their ways of thinking and behaving based on what they learn about themselves, the perceptions of others, and the consequences of their actions.

Self-awareness can significantly enhance managerial performance, career success, and personal satisfaction.[52] The more you know about yourself, the better able you are to choose fulfilling jobs, make informed decisions about life and work, make the most of your strengths, target and compensate for your weaknesses, learn from past mistakes and failures, and develop productive and mutually supportive relationships with others.

Self-awareness also requires an understanding of how the cultures we belong to influence our ideas about ourselves and others. A critical lesson for managers is that what is considered the ideal self, ideal manager, and ideal employee in one culture may be considered inappropriate, unappealing, and ineffective in another. For example, some cultures promote individualism and others collectivism; some cultures promote formality and others informality; some cultures promote hierarchy and others egalitarianism. Many organizational theorists, educators, and executives have learned the hard way that practices that are developed by and for one culture may be built on assumptions that are not as relevant to other cultures.

Creating a Broad and Diverse Network of High-Quality Relationships

The most important single ingredient in the formula of success is knowing how to get along with people. *Theodore Roosevelt, Former U.S. President*

Relationship skills are particularly important today. Organizational structures are moving from the rigid bureaucratic pyramids that characterized the industrial age to the fluid networks that characterize the postindustrial information age. Researchers Nitin Nohria and Robert Eccles describe the network organization as "consisting of a fluid, flexible, and dense pattern of working relationships that cut across various intra- and interorganizational boundaries."[53] To be effective, managers must proactively manage their relationships with their bosses, subordinates, peers, customers, suppliers, distributors, community leaders, and so on. They must know how to build trust, communicate effectively, influence others, and build relationships with an increasingly diverse network.

Researcher and consultant Jay Conger explains that managers "need to become diversity experts . . . The more a leader represents the interests and goals of a single group or faction, the greater the resistance from the other groups . . . [Lack of awareness and insensitivity] will no longer be acceptable and may raise serious questions about a manager's credibility."[54] And managing relationships in a global environment "rarely means mastering twenty-two ways to shake hands in Romania. More often, it's a true appreciation of how differently—and equally well—things get done in other parts of the world and how you had better take steps to understand this deeply, should step in to help."[55]

Advances in information and communication technologies make relationship skills more important and complex than ever before. Today, managers' relationships are often coordinated, expanded, adapted, and sustained through a variety of information and communications technologies. New technologies create new forms of relationships to be managed, such as telecommuters, virtual teams, and virtual organizations. Therefore, managers must be able to use communication and information technologies not only to manage information but also to create, sustain, and nurture effective organizational relationships.

It is of interest that recent research conducted with young and old people in several countries found that engaging in relationships is good for the brain. Specifically, the researchers found that the more socially engaged participants in the study were, the lower their cognitive impairment over time, the greater their memory function, and the better their working memory performance. Researcher Oscar Ybarra explains: "To some extent, the human mind evolved to deal with social problems, so it's not surprising that exercising that aspect of our minds has downstream benefits . . . In fact, it may be that our technical prowess depends on our social intelligence. In studies of primates and other mammals, the size of the brain has been correlated with the size of the social group the animals typically form."[56]

Designing a Workplace That Brings Out the Best in Others

Managers are responsible not only for their own work but for creating a work environment in which individuals and teams can do their best work. To do so, managers need to inspire employees and teams with meaningful goals and give them the support they need to achieve these goals. They need to develop clear performance measures and feedback mechanisms that guide employees' behavior toward these goals and help employees understand whether their day-to-day efforts are making a difference. Managers need to motivate and empower employees working independently and in teams to think creatively, solve problems, and make quick decisions. And managers need to know when they should step in and help individuals and teams do their work and when they should stay out of the way to enable employees and teams to solve their own problems.

Crafting a Meaningful Life

Writers, poets, and psychologists have come to the same conclusion: The ability to engage in both love and work, mastery and intimacy, are at the heart of psychological well-being.[57] Regardless of our culture, we all share the drive to fulfill and align dual needs: to have a sense of contribution and accomplishment that comes from what we do (our work) and to enjoy the intimacy that comes from being appreciated for who we are. It is not surprising that satisfaction with our work enhances our satisfaction with our personal lives, and vice versa.[58]

Never mistake motion for action. *Ernest Hemingway*

For managers, satisfying our needs for both intimacy and mastery can be difficult. Henry Mintzberg's classic observation that "managers work at an unrelenting pace, that their activities are characterized by brevity, variety, and discontinuity, and that they are strongly oriented to action . . ." is no less true today.[59] What has changed, however, is that the increase in competition, risk of downsizing, flattening of hierarchies, decentralization of decision making, broader spans of control, and pay for performance mean that many managers are feeling squeezed with too many expectations, too few employees, and too little time. Although the proliferation of managerial "how to do it better and faster" books and new communication and information technologies promise to show managers how to get more done with less, many managers seem to be getting less done with more.

For many of us, our tendency is to respond to increasing demands by trying harder, working faster, working longer, cutting more out of our private lives, and reducing sleep time so that we can focus more on our work. Indeed, several studies suggest that far too many professionals are willing to trade their personal well-being for success at work.[60] But this strategy often backfires because, as philosopher Rollo May cautioned, "It is an old and ironic habit of human beings to run faster when we have lost our way."[61]

Learn as if you were going to live forever. Live as if you were going to die tomorrow. *Mahatma Gandhi*

Frankly, working more and faster rather than thinking smarter is a form of laziness. Robert Kiyosaki and Sharon Lechter, in their best-selling book *Rich Dad, Poor Dad*, call this "laziness by staying busy." They make the compelling case that many people are too lazy to take the time to identify what's truly important to them, to learn strategies for working smarter rather than harder, and too lazy to do the hard work of changing bad habits that are slowing them down even though they're working harder than ever.[62]

As you will read in the last chapter of this book, I'm not a believer that we can balance our lives, nor do I believe that striving for balance is a useful strategy because attempting to do so may be an impossible attempt at perfection that can only leave us feeling increasingly frustrated. Instead, I believe that we can create engaging, meaningful lives in which we do work that we believe makes a difference. We can create a career that satisfies our needs. And we can enjoy the well-being that comes from having fulfilling relationships, good health, and time to be with the people we love and contribute to the communities of which we are a part. Crafting a meaningful life involves thinking carefully about what success means to you both professionally and personally, understanding the trade-offs you are willing to make to achieve that success, living with the consequences, and being willing to adapt your choices as your life and needs change over time.

HOW THIS BOOK IS ORGANIZED

This book has nine more chapters: "Developing Self-Awareness"; "Building Trust"; "Communicating Effectively"; "Developing Sustainable, Ethical Power and Influence"; "Managing Relationships with Your Subordinates, Bosses, and Peers"; "Managing Cultural Diversity"; "Creating High-Performing Teams"; "Diverse Teams and Virtual Teams: Managing Differences and Distances"; and "Crafting a Life." Each chapter provides practical research-based advice that will help you increase your immediate and long-term effectiveness, career potential, and general well-being. Each chapter also includes self-assessments that will help you increase your self-knowledge, end-of-chapter questions that will help you reflect on what you learn, and guided activities for applying what you learn to your everyday life.

As the author of this book, I see myself as a provocateur. Throughout this book, I encourage you to hold on to the timeless lessons of the past, unlearn those that are no longer useful, and learn new lessons that will help you succeed in today's organizational environment. I intentionally push the boundaries of what traditionally has been considered normal, desirable, and effective managerial thinking and behaving. I encourage you to use common sense and think critically about what you learn in each chapter and how it applies—and doesn't apply—to your own life. I encourage you to look for the explicit and implicit assumptions in each chapter and consider whether you agree with them or not. Which materials are and are not relevant to your cultures, work environments, and personal goals? Under what conditions is the knowledge useful and when might it be problematic? Are any perspectives excluded, misrepresented, or disadvantaged in any way by any of the theories, ideas, and recommendations presented in this book? Are there alternative ways of thinking that are not presented in the book that could enrich individuals, organizations, and society? In short, I want you to think of this book as a conversation rather than a monologue and a work in progress rather than the final word on immutable and universal truths.

FIGURE 1-2   Organization of Book

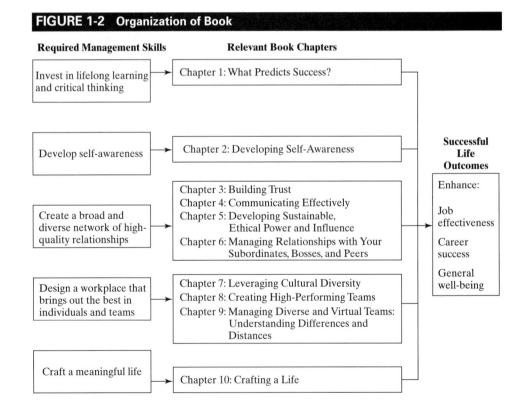

Ultimately, my goal in writing this book is to help you make a contribution in the world through work that you truly enjoy, achieve the career success that you desire, have time to spend with the people that you care about, and lead a long, happy, and healthy life.

CHAPTER SUMMARY

This is an exciting time to be a manager— full of challenges and opportunities. Today's organizations are increasingly complex, unpredictable, and fast-paced. Significant social and economic trends such as diversity, globalization, and technological advances have fundamentally changed the nature of managerial work. In such an environment, the ability to have a learning orientation, to think broadly from a wide variety of perspectives, and the willingness to learn new skills are some of the most important skills a manager can have.

Derailment occurs when a high-potential manager expects to advance in an organization, and was judged initially to have the ability to do so, yet is fired, demoted, or plateaued below anticipated levels of achievement. Derailment does not refer to individuals who, by their own choosing, change jobs, decline promotions, or quit their jobs to pursue other careers or life interests. Rather, derailment is involuntary and frequently preventable.

When derailed managers reflect on their experience, they learn three important lessons. First, intelligence isn't enough for long-term success. Second, the same talents that once brought them early success can later lead to failure. Third, flaws and blind spots that seemed insignificant earlier in their careers suddenly matter.

Research suggests that successful people share several characteristics: conscientiousness (hard work, thoroughness, efficiency, reliability, and ambition), a belief that intelligence is fluid rather than fixed, proactivity, a learning goal orientation, creative intelligence, practical intelligence, emotional intelligence (self-awareness and

social skills), positive emotions, and the ability to unlearn ineffective perspectives and behaviors and learn new ones.

Although people may resist change, they can change. Steps to behavioral change include believing that you can change; understanding the beliefs, characteristics, and skills that lead to success; assessing your personal strengths and weaknesses through self-assessment and feedback from others; practicing new skills by taking the small-wins approach; obtaining feedback on your progress from people who are affected by the changes you are making; and overlearning new behaviors so that you don't fall back on old habits, especially when under stress.

The skills that are the hallmarks of effective managers today fall into five categories. Each enables managers to become faster, more flexible, and—most importantly—more thoughtful. To be an effective manager, you must be willing and able to:

- Invest in lifelong learning and critical thinking
- Develop self-awareness
- Create a broad and diverse network of high-quality relationships
- Create an environment that brings out the best in others
- Craft a meaningful personal and professional life

Invest in lifelong learning. The proliferation of management gurus and consultants, the seduction of "instant answer" fads, and the escalating forms of mass communication (popular press books and magazines, research journals, management training, the Internet) make it essential for managers to be able to sort through and thoughtfully assess the value of new information and advice. In short, managers need to become wise consumers of managerial knowledge.

Develop self-awareness. Successful people understand their strengths, weaknesses, and behavioral styles, as well as how they are perceived by others. They use this self-understanding to select fulfilling work and adapt their behavior to bring out the best in others. They also understand that the images of the ideal manager and employee differ from culture to culture.

Create a broad and diverse network of relationships. Your ability to effectively develop, nurture, and leverage an extensive network of high-quality relationships depends on having several social skills, including the ability to communicate and develop trust and respect with a diverse group of people; the ability to communicate effectively across many cultures; the ability to manage relationships up, down, and sideways; the ability to influence others; and the ability to use new technologies to expand and enhance organizational relationships.

Creating a workplace that brings out the best in others. Managers create this context by providing clear and engaging goals, designing a workplace that provides employees with the support and resources they need to achieve these goals, and coaching employees so that they develop the perspective and skills needed to achieve their personal, professional, and organizational goals.

Crafting a meaningful life. Regardless of our culture, we all share the drive to fulfill and align dual needs: to have a sense of contribution and accomplishment that comes from what we do (our work) and to enjoy the intimacy that comes from being appreciated for who we are. Crafting a meaningful life means integrating these needs in ways that enhance our effectiveness, career development, and personal well-being.

FOOD FOR THOUGHT

1. What is the one most useful thing you learned in this chapter and why?
2. Based on what you learned in this chapter, what is the one most important thing about yourself that you want to change? What would the benefits be to you, others, and/or your organizations if you succeeded in making this change? In the spirit of small wins, practice making this change this week, beginning today if possible. Then reflect on what you learned and gained (and perhaps lost) by doing so.
3. In *FastCompany* magazine, well-known executive coach Marshall Goldsmith wrote a column titled, "Making a Resolution That Matters." In this column, he asked readers the following question: "I want you to imagine that you're 95 years old. Before taking your last breath, however, you're given a great gift: the ability to travel back in time—the ability to talk to the person who is reading this column, the ability to help this person be a better professional and lead a better life. The 95-year-old understands what was really important and what wasn't, what mattered and what didn't, what counted and what really didn't count. What advice would this wise 'old you' have for the 'you' who is reading this page?" Answer Goldsmith's question, focusing on the personal and professional advice you would give yourself, as well as how you would define success.
4. What characteristics predict success? Of these, which are your strengths? Which of these do you still need to develop to enhance your job effectiveness, career potential, and general well-being—and to achieve the success you described in question 3 above.
5. What characteristics predict derailment? Do you have any of these characteristics? If so, what do you need to do to avoid derailment in your professional and personal life?
6. What are the three most critical changes that are transforming the environment in which you work? What new skills do you need to develop to succeed in this environment?

7. What did you learn about yourself based on taking the assessments in this chapter? Specifically, describe your styles, strengths, and weaknesses. How do you think you are perceived by others, for better and worse?

8. Describe three changes you made in your life since you were in high school. What motivated them? What were the consequences? What "heavy tools" did you drop? What have you learned about what motivates you to change and your strategies for personal change?

9. Imagine you work for a magazine called *The Smart Manager's Guide to Management Theory*. The purpose of this magazine is to help managers wade through the escalating number of management theories that come off the press every day and judge their usefulness. Similar to *Consumer Reports, The Smart Manager's Guide to Management Theory* has developed a set of criteria against which it judges each theory. What criteria would you use to assess the usefulness of a management theory, and why?

10. Imagine that you could have three people throughout history, living or dead, to be your management consultants for a day. Who would these people be, and why? What kinds of lessons would you want to learn from them?

ENDNOTES

1. Mintzberg, Henry. "The Manager's Job: Folklore and Fact." 1975. *Harvard Business Review*, 1990 republished, March–April: 163–176.

2. Lancaster, Hal. 1997. *The Wall Street Journal*, May 6: B1.

3. Tichy, Noel. 2002. *The Leadership Engine*, Harper Business: 8.

4. Lombardo, Michael, and Robert Eichinger. 1991. *Preventing Derailment Before It's Too Late*. Greensboro, NC: *Center for Creative Leadership*.

5. Ibid., p. 1.

6. Church, Allan. 1997. "Managerial Self-Awareness in High-Performing Individuals in Organizations." *Journal of Applied Psychology,* 82(2): 281–292.

7. Finklestein, Sydney. 2003. *Why Smart Executives Fail: And What You Can Learn from Their Mistakes*. New York: Portfolio, 237.

8. Shipper, Frank, and John Dillard Jr. 2000. "A Study of Impending Derailment and Recovery of Middle Managers Across Career Stages." *Human Resource Management*, 39(4): 331–345; Atwater, L.E., and F. J. Yamminanno. 1992. "Does Self-Other Agreement on Leadership Perceptions Moderate the Validity of Leadership and Performance Predictions?" *Personnel Psychology,* 45: 141–164; Hogan, Robert, Gordon Curphy, and Joyce Hogan. 1994. "What We Know About Leadership: Effectiveness and Personality." *American Psychologist* June: 493–504; Bass, Bernard and Francis Yamminarino. 1991. "Congruence of Self and Others' Leadership Ratings of Naval Officers for Understanding Successful Performance." *Applied Psychology: An International Review,* 40(4): 437–454; Vancouver, Jeffrey B., Charles M. Thompson, Casey Tischner, and Dan Putka. 2002. "Two Studies Examining the Negative Effects of Self-Efficacy on Performance." *Journal of Applied Psychology,* 83(3): 506–516.

9. Lombardo, Michael, and Robert Eichinger. 1991. *Preventing Derailment Before It's Too Late*. Greensboro, NC: Center for Creative Leadership.

10. O'Reilly, Brian. 1994. "Reengineering the MBA." *Fortune*, January 24: 37–47.

11. Ibid. O'Reilly, Charles, and Jennifer Chatman. 1994. "Working Smarter and Harder: A Longitudinal Study of Managerial Success." *Administrative Science Quarterly,* 39(4): 603–628; Kotter, John. 1995. *The New Rules: Eight Business Breakthroughs to Career Success in the 21st Century*. New York: Free Press.

12. Sternberg, Robert J. 1996. *Successful Intelligence: How Practical and Creative Intelligence Determine Success in Life*. New York: Simon and Schuster, 224.

13. Sternberg, Robert. 1996. *Successful Intelligence: How Creative and Practical Intelligence Determine Success in Life*.

Plume; Wagner, Richard. 2002. "Smart People Doing Dumb Things: The Case of Managerial Incompetence." In Robert Sternberg (ed.). *Why Smart People Can Be So Stupid.* New Haven: Yale University Press, 24–41. Goleman, Daniel. 1998. *Working with Emotional Intelligence.* Bantom Doubleday Dell, 1998.

14. Dweck Carol S. 2002. "Beliefs That Make Smart People Dumb." In Robert Sternberg (ed.). *Why Smart People Can Be So Stupid.* New Haven: Yale University Press, 24–41.

15. Ibid., 29.

16. Grant, Heidi, and Carol S. Dweck. 2003. "Clarifying Achievement Goals and Their Impact." *Journal of Personality and Social Psychology,* 85(3): 541–553.

17. Aronson, J. 1998. "The Effects of Conceiving Ability as Fixed or Improvable on Responses to Stereotype Threat." Unpublished manuscript, University of Texas. Dweck, Carol, and L. Sorich. 1999. "Mastery Oriented Thinking." In C. R. Snyder (ed.). *Coping.* New York: Oxford University Press.

18. Hong, Yin-Yi, C. Chiu, Carol S. Dweck, D. Lin, and W. Wan. 1999. "A Test of Implicit Theories and Self-Confidence as Predictors of Responses to Achievement Challenges." *Journal of Personality and Social Psychology,* 77: 588–599.

19. Turk, Carolyn. 2004. "A Woman Can Learn Anything A Man Can." *Newsweek,* April 4: 12.

20. Sternberg, Robert. 1997. *Successful Intelligence: How Creative and Practical Intelligence Determine Success in Life.* Plume.

21. Frankel, Lois P. 1997. *Overcoming Your Strengths.* New York: Harmony Books, 3–4

22. Sternberg, Robert J. 1996. *Successful Intelligence: How Practical and Creative Intelligence Determine Success in Life.* New York: Simon and Schuster, 216–217.

23. Lombardo, Michael, and Robert Eichinger. 1991. *Preventing Derailment: What to Do Before It's Too Late.* Greensboro, NC: Center for Creative Leadership.

24. Caproni, Paula, and Joycelyn Finley. 1997. "When Organizations Do Harm: Two Cautionary Tales. In Pushkala Prasad, Albert J. Mills, Michael Elms, and Anshuman Prasad (eds.). *Managing the Organizational Melting Pot: Dilemmas of Workplace Diversity.* Sage Publications, 255–284.

25. "Executives on Trial: Scandals from A to W." 2004. *Wall Street Journal.* March 30: C1.

26. Finklestein, Sydney. 2003. *Why Smart Executives Fail and What You Can Learn From Their Mistakes.* Portfolio. Roderick Kramer. 2003. "The Harder They Fall." *Harvard Business Review,* 81(10): 58.

27. Staw, Barry, and Jerry Ross. 1987b. "Knowing When to Pull the Plug." *Harvard Business Review,* March–April: 68–74; Whyte, Glen, Alan Sakes, and Sterling Hook, 1997. "When Success Breeds Failure: The Role of Self-Efficacy in Escalating Commitment to a Losing Course of Action." *Journal of Organizational Behavior,* 18: 415–432.

28. Roderick Kramer. 2003. "The Harder They Fall." *Harvard Business Review,* 81(10): 58.

29. Toobin, Jeffrey. 2004. "A Bad Thing: Why Did Martha Stewart Lose?" *The New Yorker,* March 22: 60–72.

30. Bandler, James. 2004. "Report Cites 'Virus of Fear' at USA Today." *Wall Street Journal,* April 23: B1–B2.

31. Seibert, Scott, Michael Crant, and Maria Kraimer. 1999. "Proactive Personality and Career Success." *Journal of Applied Psychology,* 84: 416–427.

32. Bateman, Thomas, and J. Michael Crant. 1993. "The Proactive Component of Organizational Behavior." *Journal of Organizational Behavior,* 14: 103–118; Crant, J. Michael. 1995. "The Proactive Personality Scale and Objective Job Performance among Real Estate Agents." *Journal of Applied Psychology,* 80: 532–537; Seibert, Scott, Michael Crant, and Maria Kraimer. 1999. "Proactive Personality and Career Success." *Journal of Applied Psychology,* 84: 416–427.

33. Eby, Lillian, Marcus Butts, and Angie Lockwood. 2003. "Predictors of Success in the Era of a Boundaryless Career." *Journal of Organizational Behavior,* 24: 689–708.

34. Schibert, Scott, Maria Kraimer, and Michael Crank. 2001. "What Do Proactive People Do: A Longitudinal Model Linking

Proactive Personality and Career Success." *Personnel Psychology,* 54(4): 845–874.

35. VandeWalle, Don. 2001. "Goal Orientation: Why Wanting to Look Successful Doesn't Always Lead to Success." *Organization Dynamics,* 30(2): 162–171; Grant, Heidi. 2003. "Clarifying Achievement Goals and Their Impact." *Journal of Personality and Social Psychology,* 85(3): 541–553.

36. Sternberg, Robert. 1996. *Successful Intelligence: How Practical and Creative Intelligence Determines Success in Life.* New York: Simon and Schuster.

37. Bar-On, Reuven. 1997. *Bar-On Emotional Quotient Inventory: Technical Manual.* Toronto: Multi-Health Systems. Goleman, Daniel, Richard Boyatzis, and Annie McKee. 2001. "Primal Leadership." *Harvard Business Review,* December: 43–51; Goleman, Daniel. 1998. *Working with Emotional Intelligence.* New York: Bantam. Mayer, J. D., Salovey, P., Caruso, D. "Models of Emotional Intelligence." In Robert J. Sternberg (ed.). *The Handbook of Emotional Intelligence* 2nd ed. New York: Cambridge University Press, 396–420.

38. Shipper, Frank, Denise Rotondo, and Richard C. Hoffman. 2003. "A Cross Cultural Study of Linkage Between Emotional Intelligence and Managerial Effectiveness." Presented at the Academy of Management Meeting, Seattle, Washington, August 1–6, 2003; Meer, Hogan, Robert, Gordon Curphy, and Joyce Hogan. 1994. "What We Know About Leadership Effectiveness and Personality." *American Psychologist,* 49(6): 493–503.

39. Frederickson, Barbara. 2002. "Positive Emotions." In C. R. Snyder, and Shane J. Lopez. *Handbook of Positive Psychology.* Oxford: Oxford University Press, 120–134.

40. Weick, Karl E. 1996. "Drop Your Tools: An Allegory for Organizational Studies." *Administrative Science Quarterly,* 41: 301.

41. U.S. Forest Service. 1994. *1994 Report of the South Canyon Fire Accident Investigation Team,* August 17, 1994, pp. A3–5. Washington, DC: U.S. Forest Service.

42. Brookfield, Stephen. 1986. *Understanding and Facilitating Adult Learning.* San Francisco: Jossey-Bass; Whetton, David,

and Kim Cameron. 2005. *Developing Managerial Skills.* New Jersey: Prentice Hall; Dweck, Carol S. 2002. "Beliefs That Make Smart People Dumb." In Sternberg, Robert J. (ed.). 2002. *Why Smart People Can Be So Stupid.* New Haven: Yale University Press, 24–41; Kolb, David. 1984. *Experiential Learning: Experience the Source of Learning and Development.* Upper Saddle River, NJ: Prentice Hall.

43. Weick, Karl. "Small Wins." *American Psychologist,* 39: 40–49.

44. O'Reilly, Brian. 1994. "Reengineering the MBA." *Fortune,* January 24: 39.

45. Denison, Daniel. 1984. "Bringing Corporate Culture to the Bottom Line." *Organizational Dynamics* 5–22; Kim S. Cameron, and Robert E. Quinn. 1999. *Diagnosing and Changing Organizational Culture.* Reading, MA: Addison Wesley.

46. Dixon, Nancy. 1996. *The Organizational Learning Cycle: How We Can Learn Collectively.* New York: McGraw-Hill Book Company, 1.

47. Hill, Linda. 1993. *Becoming a Manager: Mastery of a New Identity.* Boston: Harvard Business School Press, 7.

48. Shapiro, Eilene. 1995. *Fad Surfing in the Boardroom: Reclaiming the Courage to Manage in the Age of Instant Answers.* Reading, MA: Addison-Wesley Publishing Co.

49. Caproni, Paula, and Maria Eugenia Arias. 1997. "Managerial Skills from a Critical Perspective." *Journal of Management Education,* 21(3): 292–308.

50. Dixon, Nancy. 1996. *The Organizational Learning Cycle: How We Can Learn Collectively.* New York: McGraw-Hill Book Company.

51. Prasad, Pushkala, and Paula Caproni. 1997. "Critical Theory in the Management Classroom: Engaging Power, Ideology, and Praxis." *Journal of Management Education,* 21(3): 284–291.

52. Goleman, Daniel. 1998. *Working with Emotional Intelligence.* New York: Bantam Books.

53. Nohria, Nitin and Robert Eccles (eds.). *Networks and Organizations: Structure, Form, and Action.* Boston, MA: Harvard Business School Press, 289.

54. Conger, Jay. 1993. "The Brave New World of Leadership Training." *Organizational Dynamics,* 21(3): 46–59.

55. O'Reilly, Brian. 1994. "Reengineering the MBA." *Fortune,* January 24: 42.

56. *Schmoozing is Good for the Brain.* University of Michigan News Service, Press Release, Institute for Social Research, October 22, 2002.

57. Csikszentmihalyi, Mihaly. 1990. *Flow: The Psychology of Optimal Experience.* New York: HarperPerennial; Erikson, Erik H. 1963. *Childhood and Society.* 2d ed. New York: Norton; Kofodimos, Joan. 1990. "Why Executives Lose Their Balance." *Organization Science,* 58–73.

58. Judge, T. A., and S. Watanabe. 1993. "Another Look at the Job Satisfaction-Life Satisfaction Relationship." *Journal of Applied Psychology,* 78: 939–948; Heller, Daniel, Timothy Judge, and David Watson. 2002. "The Confounding Role of Personality and Trait Affectivity in the Relationship Between Job and Life Satisfaction." *Journal of Organizational Behavior,* 23: 815–835.

59. Mintzberg, Henry. 1975. "The Manager's Job: Folklore and Fact." *Harvard Business Review,* March–April: 163–176. 1990 republished.

60. Abraham Korman, Ursula Witteg-Berman, and Dorothy Lang. 1981. "Career Success and Personal Failure: Alienation in Professionals and Managers." *Academy of Management Journal,* 24(2): 342–360.

61. May, Rollo. 1969. *Love and Will.* New York: Dell Publishing Co., 15.

62. Kiyosaki, Robert, and Sharon Lechter, 1998. *Rich Dad, Poor Dad.* New York: Time Warner.

CHAPTER

2

Developing Self-Awareness

This chapter will help you:

■ Understand why self-awareness is important to managerial effectiveness and well-being

■ Learn about your self-concept and how it is constructed through everyday life at home, at work, and in society

■ Consider whether you should create "the brand called you"

■ Understand how having high self-esteem can backfire

■ Understand how diversity, globalization, and new technologies are changing the ways we think about ourselves, others, and relationships

■ Understand the postmodern manager and implications for the managerial self-concept

■ Learn why some people benefit from having multiple selves rather having a solid, stable sense of self

> *I've always wanted to be somebody. Now*
> *I realize I should have been a little more specific.*
>
> —PLAYWRIGHT JANE WAGNER
> *The Search for Signs of Intelligent Life in the Universe*

Self-awareness is a hallmark of effective managers. Successful managers know what they want, understand why they want it, and have a plan of action for getting it. They also know how their styles, strengths, and weaknesses influence their ability to achieve their goals. Furthermore, they understand how they are perceived by others and how these perceptions affect their ability to gain support.[1] And they have a special combination of self-confidence, humility, and adaptability that enables them to appreciate the views and styles of others and to thrive in the ambiguous, imperfect, and often stressful world of management.

Walter Kiechel, columnist for *Fortune*, contrasts effective managers with what he calls "empty suits." He describes empty suits as having "much form, style and dress-for-success dash; little substance, skill or managerial accomplishment."[2] Although such managers emphasize form over substance and self-promotion over self-understanding, they are not necessarily without competence. Researcher David Campbell of the Center for Creative Leadership explains that some of these managers "might be bright and effective, but in a very predictable, very cubbyholed way,"[3] hardly a formula for success in today's complex and fast-changing environment. But it is not only empty suits who lack self-awareness.

Researchers Robert Kaplan, Wilfred Drath, and Joan Kofodimos studied "expansive executives" who, like empty suits, don't place self-awareness high on their list of leadership skills.[4] But unlike empty suits who look out for themselves, expansive executives are genuinely committed to the success of their organizations. They set high standards for their work and the work of others. They make heroic efforts to meet their own high standards, typically working longer and faster than others. Expansive executives tend to be very competent, ambitious, and successful in conventional terms—high salaries, high-level positions, and substantial organizational power. Yet beneath their success lie serious problems.

According to Kaplan and his colleagues, expansive executives gain their sense of self-worth primarily through their unconscious needs for control, mastery, and professional success. They pursue these goals at all costs, often sacrificing their health and personal relationships. Yet despite these sacrifices, their goals are always beyond their reach. After all, total control is an illusion in today's complex and unpredictable environment, and mastery is fleeting in an era of rapid changes in knowledge and technology. Consequently, expansive executives are always performing below the impossible standards they set for themselves, faithfully (and desperately) running a race that never ends and that they cannot win.

> **Mastery of others is strength; mastery of yourself is true power.**
> *Lao-Tzu*

On the surface, it would seem that executives who set such high standards and endure such sacrifices would be beneficial to their organizations, but that is often not the case. Expansive executives are driven primarily by their unconscious needs for control, perfection, and status rather than the needs of the organization.[5] Despite their commitment to the success of the organization, their lack of self-awareness prevents them from seeing the consequences of their behavior. For example, they may become overly critical micromanagers who resist delegating to others. Or they may avoid taking risks because risk taking involves giving up control, which makes expansive executives particularly uncomfortable.

Although empty suits and expansive executives are common in organizations, most managers are less extreme in their behaviors. Yet both empty suits and expansive executives hold important lessons for us all. Like empty suits and expansive executives, we are all, to some degree, unaware of how our ways of thinking, feeling, and behaving affect our decisions, actions, and relationships—and ultimately our personal well-being, professional effectiveness, and the success of our organizations. But the simple fact is that we can't manage others effectively unless we learn how to manage ourselves first.

BARRIERS TO SELF-AWARENESS

Unfortunately, lack of self-awareness may be an occupational hazard of managerial work. Long work hours and the fast pace of work make it difficult for managers to take time out for thoughtful self-reflection. Managers routinely face the pressures of tight deadlines, workflow interruptions, unexpected crises, and the threat of being "dejobbed" in an era of downsizing, mergers, and acquisitions. Although the ability to learn new ways of seeing, thinking, and behaving are most valuable during stressful periods, most managers' "ability to learn shuts down precisely at the moment they need it most."[6] Indeed, during times of stress, most people fall back on their habitual ways of thinking and acting, even though these ways of thinking and acting probably contributed to their predicament in the first place.

In addition to job pressures, there are many other obstacles to managerial self-awareness. People typically get promoted to managerial positions because of their past achievements. Thus, a "leading reason for resisting attempts at inner-directed change is the fear of losing effectiveness by tampering with a 'winning formula.'"[7] In addition, because of the status differences between managers and subordinates, many managers do not make themselves accessible to the people who work for them. Consequently, they deny themselves the opportunity to receive useful advice and feedback. Furthermore, managers "hire people in their own image" and are thus more likely to receive reinforcement for their decisions and actions rather than useful constructive criticism from those they hire.[8]

Managers' busy personal lives also leave little time for self-reflection. Although home life traditionally has been viewed as a retreat from job pressures, many managers today take their work home with them to keep up with the escalating work responsibilities. Many managers are also balancing the demanding schedules of dual (or triple) career couples, often while caring for dependent children and aging parents. Indeed, given the multiple pressures of coordinating and caretaking in the home, as well as the lack of immediate feedback (one doesn't know how well one is raising children until the children grow up), many managers find the workplace to be a welcome escape from the emotional and physical demands of home life.[9] As a colleague recently told me on a Monday morning, "I've had a very busy weekend at home and it's time for a work break."

Despite these hurdles to managerial self-awareness, many managers make good-faith efforts to increase their self-knowledge. Although some people are "developmental couch potatoes" who avoid the challenges of personal growth,[10] the proliferation of self-help books and professional development workshops suggest that many managers actively invest their time and money in their quest for self-understanding and personal growth. Steven Covey's book *The Seven Habits of Highly Effective People*, for example, has sold more than 10 million copies in 70 countries and is translated into 28 languages. *Fortune* notes that the managerial coaching business—designed to help managers better understand how their attitudes, thinking patterns, and interpersonal styles affect their well-being and professional effectiveness—is "thriving at American Express, AT&T, Citibank, Colgate, Levi Strauss, Northern Telecom, Procter & Gamble, and many other major companies . . . Fees range from $1,500 for a single day (which is never enough) to $100,000 or more for a coaching program that lasts several years."[11]

THE BRAND CALLED YOU

Recently, management gurus in the United States have been offering a new kind of advice: To be successful, today's managers must think of themselves as a one-person enterprise.[12] Popular management author and consultant Tom Peters, in his controversial Fast Company article called "The Brand Called You," boldly advises managers and professionals to know themselves, understand their customers, develop unique and marketable competencies that help them stand out from the crowd, reinvent themselves if necessary, and then package and sell their personal brand. "To be in business today," says Peters, "your most important job is to be head marketer for the brand called You . . . You're every bit as much a brand as Nike, Coke, Pepsi, or the Body Shop."[13]

Seeing oneself as a unique, marketable, and portable product may be a reasonable survival strategy in an era where the psychological contract between individuals and organizations no longer promises the security of lifetime employment. But seeing oneself as a product to be bought and sold comes with a price. It can leave one feeling alienated from one's self, estranged from others, and of questionable loyalty to one's current organization. And in cultures that are based on an ideology of collectivism and loyalty to one's group and organization, promoting oneself can be a lonely, difficult, and ultimately unrewarding enterprise.

Whether you want to consider yourself a brand is, of course, your own decision depending on whether you find this a compelling or distasteful idea. But one thing is certain. You should not assume that people will simply notice your hard work and contributions without some assistance from you. Frankly, if you have something of value to offer, you probably don't want to be the best kept secret in your organization or profession. Says communications coach Peggy Klaus, "It's stunning to me how many people think that if they keep their heads down and work hard, their boss 'will just know' what they're contributing and how valuable they are, as if there were some kind of psychic connection there . . . You have to let the people above you know what you're doing, what skills you're developing, which goals you're achieving . . . Don't make them guess." And if you want to be noticed, be sure you notice others. Klaus also advises, "Listen [to others] . . . Showing a genuine interest in other people's goals really floors them . . . They're just not used to it."[14] Tom Peters suggests that you build your brand around the following questions:

- What do I do that I'm most proud of?
- What do I do that adds remarkable, measurable, distinguished, distinctive value?
- What do my colleagues and customers say is my greatest and clearest strength . . . [and] most noteworthy personal characteristic?
- What have I done lately—this week—that added value to the organization (and that was noticed by others)?
- In what ways is what I do difficult to imitate?

Peters also recommends that you become "a broad-gauged visionary" who understands the bigger issues, challenges, and opportunities that face your organization; anticipate problems before they become crises; become an expert in an area that is not easy to copy and that adds real value to the organization; be a dependable and supportive colleague and team member; think of your job as a compilation of distinct projects, each of which adds measurable value to the organization; consistently deliver high-quality work on time; and complete projects within or under budget. In short, your brand must have substance.

As every manager who seeks self-awareness and professional development and success sooner or later realizes, there are no shortcuts. It takes commitment, time, and effort to identify your brand, styles, strengths, and weaknesses. Furthermore, it's not easy to understand how you are perceived by others, as well as the consequences of these perceptions on your ability to be effective. There are many long and winding paths to personal and professional growth, and each comes with its own possibilities, limitations, and trade-offs.

So What's a Well-Intentioned Manager To Do?

It's hard to imagine that our self-improvement efforts will be successful without considering what is this "self" that we want to improve (and brand, if we choose to do so). Most of us couldn't imagine trying to fix a car without understanding how it works, yet many of us routinely engage in self-development efforts without understanding how marvelously complex we are as human beings and how we got to be who we are. In the following sections, I define the self-concept, explore the many different ways that we develop our self-concept, and consider the kind of self-concepts that are most likely to enhance our professional effectiveness and personal well-being in today's diverse, global, and technologically driven organizational environment.

BOX 2-1

The Costs of High Self-Esteem

"Self-esteem" refers to one's general feelings about his or her self-worth. Many parents and teachers, particularly in the United States, have become preoccupied with the development and benefits of high self-esteem. They assume that the payoffs of high self-esteem include greater happiness, personal success, and contributions to one's organizations and communities. Recent research, however, is challenging the widely believed assumption that high self-esteem is inevitably a positive characteristic. People who have high self-esteem do tend to be happier, have more self-confidence, and expect to have a good future, in part because they have self-enhancing biases (e.g., they think they have more positive characteristics than many other people have). But their high self-esteem doesn't necessarily translate into higher grades, more kindness toward others, better job performance, greater leadership ability, or positive citizenship behavior. Indeed, gang members often have high self-esteem, and they often pursue that self-esteem through destructive behaviors. Furthermore, compared with people with high self-esteem, people with low self-esteem are not more prone to behaviors that are destructive to oneself or others.

(continued)

Box 2-1 (*cont.*)

Researcher Jennifer Crocker and her colleagues argue that it's how one *pursues* self-esteem, rather than whether one has high or low self-esteem, that determines whether high self-esteem will benefit oneself, others, organizations, and one's communities. For example, if one overly links his or her self-worth to high academic achievement, looking good to others, or having abundant material success, these goals can backfire by creating excessive stress, physical problems, and even increased drug and alcohol use. People with these goals can use unethical or destructive means to achieve these goals. People can cheat on exams to do well at school, take drugs to maintain the high energy it may take to work excessive hours, get into extreme debt to have a lot of material possessions, or sunbathe because they believe the sun tan will make them look good, despite ample medical evidence that doing so increases one's chances of getting cancer.

Notably, Crocker and her colleagues found that students who base their self-esteem on grades do not necessarily get better grades than those who do not, but they do tend to feel worse when they receive poor grades and show "greater drops in self-esteem, positive emotions, and more detachment from their majors when they received poor grades." Furthermore, researchers Harry Wallace and Roy

Baumeister argue that high self-esteem can turn into narcissism, and some research suggests that narcissists are more likely to put considerable effort into highly visible projects in which their efforts will be admired by others, yet are more likely to reduce their effort when the spotlight isn't on them.

The lesson here is that if we want to achieve greater benefits and fewer costs associated with high self-esteem, we should focus not only on whether one has high or low self-esteem but also on how one pursues feelings of self-worth. Strategies based on achieving external standards, such as how one appears to others (grades, physical appearance, or material possessions), are less likely to bring benefits than are strategies based on contributing to others, living in accordance with personal values, and having the desire and ability to control one's behaviors when these behaviors may be harmful to oneself or others.

Crocker and her colleague, Lora Park, remind well-intentioned parents and teachers that ". . . attempts to raise children's self-esteem by teaching them that they are 'special,' 'fabulous,' or 'unique' may be teaching narcissism rather than self-worth and self-respect." Instead, positive self-esteem "requires the strong motivation that results from having goals that are larger than the self."

SOURCE: Baumeister, Roy F. 1999. "Aggression and Self Esteem." *American Psychological Association Monitor,* 30(1). Crocker, Jennifer, and Lora E. Park. 2004. "The Costly Pursuit of Self-Esteem." *Psychologial Bulletin,* 130(3): 2004: Crocker, Jennifer, Diane Quinn, Andrew Karpinski, and Sara Chase. 2003. "When Grades Determine Self-Worth: Consequences of Contingent Self-Worth for Male and Female Engineering and Psychology Majors." *Journal of Personality and Social Psychology,* 85(3): 507–516; Crocker, Jennifer, and Connie T. Wolfe. 2001. "Contingencies of Self-Worth." *Psychological Review,* 108(3): 593–623; Wallace, Harry, and Roy Baumeister. 2002. "The Performance of Narcissists Rises and Falls With Perceived Opportunity for Glory." *Journal of Personality and Social Psychology,* 82(5): 819–834.

THE SELF-CONCEPT: I THINK, THEREFORE I THINK I AM

Researchers agree that individuals differ from each other in many ways, including (but not limited to) worldview, skills, abilities, learning styles, problem-solving styles, and interpersonal styles. Researchers disagree, however, about the degree to which these personality differences are created by nature or nurture. There is compelling and controversial evidence that certain characteristics, such as tendencies toward introversion and extroversion, risk seeking and risk aversion, optimism and pessimism, desire for dominance, and vulnerability to anxiety, may be shaped, in part, by our genetic programming.

Yet despite considerable evidence that some tendencies may be inherited, researchers agree that our genes are not our destiny.[15] Whether genes account for 5 percent or 50 percent of our personality, that still leaves a large percentage of who we are and how we behave to be shaped by our experiences in our environments and our willingness to learn from our experiences.[16] Enriching environments that inspire us to have confidence in ourselves, pursue our dreams, and develop the skills that will enable us to achieve our goals increase the possibility that we will make whatever genetic tendencies we have serve us, others, and our communities well. An important lesson, of course, is to put yourself in environments that bring out the best in you. Indeed, our social environment—and how we interpret and interact with our social environment—is one of the most powerful influences on our behavior: our self-concept.

What Is the Self-Concept?

The self-concept is an internalized set of perceptions that each of us has about ourselves that are relatively stable over time, consistent across situations, resistant to change, and of central importance to us.[17] Our self-concept is made up of our beliefs about our personalities, interests and skills, strengths and weaknesses, what makes us similar to others, and what makes us unique. Our self-concept influences our everyday thoughts and actions, including how we see the world, what we perceive to be threats and opportunities, how we make decisions, how we cope with stress, how we define success, and how we behave toward others. Perhaps most importantly, our self-concept influences our fundamental beliefs about who we are, who we should be, who we can be, who we can never be, and who we are afraid of becoming.[18]

People seldom improve when they have no other model but themselves to copy themselves after.
Oliver Goldsmith,
Cited in www.
greenleafenterprises.
com/quotes/s.html

Our self-concept is, in large part, socially constructed throughout our lives in our families, schools, workplaces, communities, and other social institutions. Social psychologists Hazel Markus and Shinobu Kitayama explain that these institutions socialize us into ways of thinking, feeling, and acting that enable us "to function well—naturally, flexibly, and adaptively—in the types of situations that are fairly common and recurrent in [our] cultural context."[19] In short, we develop our beliefs about who we are, who we should be, who we can be, and who we can never be through taken-for-granted social practices such as the media, language, norms, rituals, and reward and punishment systems (which may include formal means such as laws or informal means such as peer pressure).

In the following sections, I discuss how our cultures, families, interpersonal relationships, and groups influence our self-concept and how our self-concept, in turn, influences our day-to-day thoughts and actions. See Figure 2-1 for a summary of these influences on the self-concept.

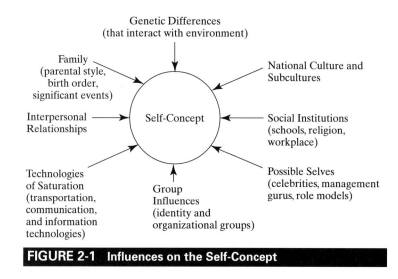

FIGURE 2-1 Influences on the Self-Concept

CULTURAL INFLUENCES ON THE SELF-CONCEPT: THE INDEPENDENT AND INTERDEPENDENT SELF

The most simple but powerful understanding of all is the understanding that every successful and happy "me" is dependent upon the establishment of an operationally sound, effective, and successful "us." James Musgrave and Michael Anniss, Authors of Relationship Dynamics

If our self-concept is, in large part, socially and culturally determined, then it follows that our beliefs about the ideal self—and ideal manager—vary across cultures.[20] From the moment we are born and first reach out to other human beings, we begin the lifelong process of trying to make sense of ourselves, others, and our relationships. One of the most fundamental lifelong challenges we face is to reconcile our basic needs to be both connected to and separate from others, to be both "a part" of others and "apart" from others.[21] We learn how to reconcile these basic needs for separateness and connectedness through our informal cultural norms and formal cultural institutions. Different cultures provide their members with different ways to reconcile these needs. Some cultures (often labeled individualistic) emphasize independence from others, and other cultures (often labeled collectivist) emphasize interdependence with others. Each is described below.

As you read the following sections, keep the following in mind: (1) The descriptions of independent and interdependent conceptions of the self do not imply that either one is better or worse than the other—simply different with different implications for how people think, feel, act, and interpret the behavior of others; (2) Any references to national cultures are generalizations and not all people in a particular culture will reflect that culture's tendencies, especially because each nation has many subcultures; (3) Descriptions of the independent and interdependent self are described as extremes on a continuum, although all individuals and nations have a blend of the characteristics of independent and interdependent self-concepts;[22] and (4) Culture is one of many influences on the self-concept. Despite these caveats, the following descriptions are useful for understanding many subtle, yet significant, differences among people.

The Independent Self-Concept

You are what you think.
Buddha

Cultures that promote an independent self-concept encourage individuals to see themselves as separate from others and to be unique, self-sufficient, self-promoting, and, ideally, free from social constraints.[23] Cultures that favor an independent view of the self tend to value self-actualization and individual freedom over social obligations, personal rights over mutual obligations, and the pursuit of personal happiness over personal sacrifice.[24] An ideal life in these cultures is one in which one is able to be true to oneself, express oneself honestly to others, follow one's dream, aspire to be the best one can be, and achieve personal success and self-fulfillment. In individualistic cultures, people who fail to separate from others, who are easily influenced by others, who prefer to go unnoticed, and who don't stand out from the crowd are often encouraged to be more independent, think more for themselves, make themselves heard, and find (and promote) their unique qualities.

In such cultures, one's behavior is assumed to be largely independent of outside influences such as the social and cultural context, driven instead by one's personality, internal motivations, and personal skills and abilities. Consequently, the "private self" ("Who am I and what do I need and want?") tends to be more developed and more complex than the "public self" ("What do other people think of me?") and the "collective self" ("I am a member of this community.").[25] People who emphasize the private self try to differentiate themselves from others in many ways, including through their clothing, material possessions, communication patterns, personal styles, and so on.[26]

Researchers Sheena S. Iyengar and Mark R. Lepper found in their studies of Anglo American and Asian American children that the Anglo American children (who tend to be influenced by independent cultures) were more likely to be motivated and perform better when they were able to make choices for themselves because, for them, "making a personal choice offers not only an opportunity to express and receive one's personal preference, but also a chance to establish one's unique self-identity." In contrast, the Asian American children (who tend to be influenced by interdependent cultures) were more likely to be motivated and perform better when they were given specific instructions (rather than personal choice) by "valued in-group members" (e.g., mother or peers) because, for them, following instructions from a trusted in-group member provided "a greater opportunity to provide harmony and to fulfill the goal of belonging to the group."[27]

In independent cultures, feelings of self-worth come from being able to express oneself and confirm that one has positive characteristics.[28] People from such cultures tend to have what is called a "uniqueness bias."[29] They tend to see their strengths as unique talents ("I received a top grade on the exam because I'm smart.") and their weaknesses as common limitations that are shared by others or as caused by external factors such as poor training, problematic team members, or ineffective management ("I did poorly on the exam because the professor is a poor teacher.", "Most people people found this exam exceptionally difficult."). People from cultures that promote an independent sense of self also tend to have what is called a "self-enhancement bias" in which they tend to see themselves as better than the average person on important positive characteristics such as intelligence, motivation, or interpersonal skills. In one study, for example, more than 50 percent of a sample of North American college undergraduates reported that they were in the top 10 percent in "intergroup sensitivity."[30]

It should come as no surprise that many management development programs in the United States refer to what were once called personal "weaknesses" as "developmental opportunities," which is a more palatable phrase in a culture that promotes self-enhancement.

Recent research suggests that people from independent cultures are more likely to believe that talking out loud is a positive act because it is a form of individual expression. They also are more likely to believe that talking is associated with thinking and learning. In contrast, people from interdependent cultures are more likely to believe that one may think and learn better while staying silent. For example, in one study, researcher Heejung S. Kim found that thinking out loud while trying to solve reasoning problems hampered Asian Americans' performance but did not affect the performance of European Americans. This difference in perceptions is important because a person who believes that talking is related to thinking may misinterpret silence as lack of interest or motivation rather than a problem-solving strategy that can enhance a person's performance. And someone who believes that one can solve problems better when one is concentrating silently may think that people who talk while they are solving problems may be immature, distracting, and lacking in focus.[31]

Why are some cultures more individualistic than others? Research suggests that cultures that have significant affluence, diversity, and mobility are more likely than others to promote an independent self-concept. Affluence decreases one's dependence on others. Acceptance of diversity enables one to belong to multiple groups and reduces one's dependence on any one group. And mobility (such as moving geographically to take new jobs) requires self-reliance and the willingness to psychologically and physically join and leave groups quickly.[32]

The Interdependent Self-Concept

Cultures that promote an interdependent self-concept encourage individuals to fit in with others, to attend to the needs of others, and to create and fulfill mutual obligations. People with an interdependent self-concept tend to be motivated by a desire to be connected to others and a willingness to sacrifice their own needs, wants, and opportunities for the welfare of the groups to which they belong. In such cultures, fundamental values are belonging, reciprocity, empathy, dependence on others, group cohesion, interpersonal harmony, and occupying one's proper place. In Japan, for example, where connectedness to the group is central to one's identity and sense of self-worth, the word for "self" is "jibun," which refers to "one's share of the shared life space."[33]

People with an interdependent self-concept are likely to be uncomfortable when they feel disconnected from others, stand out from the group, are inattentive to the needs of others, act in ways that are inappropriate for their social role, and fail to fulfill their social obligations. Maturity in these cultures is seen as the ability to voluntarily control one's personal emotions, needs, and goals to advance significant relationships and the community as a whole. It is viewed as immature and irresponsible to express oneself freely without considering the needs of others or the social context. Thus, in these cultures, the public self ("What do other people think of me?") and collective self ("I am a member of this community.") tend to be more developed and complex than the private self ("Who am I and what do I need and want?").[34] Consequently, people from collectivist cultures are likely to develop a wide range of skills that enable them to fit in with others and focus on the overall success of the groups to which they belong. These skills include the willingness to pay attention to others, the perceptual acuity to notice subtle patterns and changes in behaviors and social contexts, and the insight to interpret and respond to these subtle cues in socially appropriate ways.

You don't want to be the fattest pig in the pen. You will be the first to be slaughtered.
Indian Proverb

People from interdependent cultures tend to derive feelings of self-worth from the their ability to control themselves in social situations, maintain harmony, and adjust and contribute to the group.[35] Research suggests that although people from individualistic cultures tend to have uniqueness and self-enhancement biases, people from collectivist cultures are more likely to have self-critical and self-improvement biases. In other words, they are more likely to attribute their success to luck or the effort of the group as a whole ("I received a high grade because I had a great study group.") and attribute their weaknesses to a lack of personal ability or talent ("I received a poor grade because I didn't study hard enough.").[36] In collectivist cultures, this self-critical bias serves several purposes. By focusing on fixing their personal shortcomings, group members work toward improving the overall capability of the group.[37] In addition, by taking personal responsibility for errors, they enable other group members to save face, and by doing so, show loyalty to the group and enhance their relationship to the group.

Certainly, people from all cultures recognize that individual and collective survival depends on both independence and interdependence. There are times when we must do things ourselves and times when we must depend on the group. However, cultures differ in the degree to which they emphasize one over the other. For example, people from Western nations are more likely to emphasize an independent self-concept. People from Eastern societies are more likely to emphasize an interdependent self-concept. Researchers Hazel Markus and Shinobu Kitayama describe this difference as follows: "In America, the squeaky wheel gets the grease" and in Japan, "The nail that sticks out gets pounded down."[38]

Table 2-1 summarizes differences between independent and interdependent self-concept. Cultural researcher Geert Hofstede, in his classic studies of more than 116,000 (primarily male) employees in 40 nations, categorized these nations based on their tendencies to promote individualism or collectivism.[39] Table 2-2 summarizes Hofstede's research. You can take the "Twenty Questions: I Am" assessment in Box 2-5 at the end of this chapter to better understand your own orientation toward independence or interdependence.

Advantages of a Cultural View of the Self-Concept

In today's diverse and global economic environment, a cultural perspective on the self-concept has many advantages for managerial effectiveness. A cultural perspective:

- encourages us to look outward to our cultures in order to better understand who we are and how we got to be that way, which gives us a more complex understanding of ourselves and others;
- makes us more inclined to try to understand and respond to others on their terms rather than as variations of or deviations from ourselves, which makes us better able to create relationships based on mutual understanding and respect;
- broadens our ways of thinking about what constitutes normal and effective behavior, which expands our ways of seeing the world and our repertoire of behaviors;

TABLE 2-1   Differences between the Independent and Interdependent Self-Concept

Feature Compared	*Independent*	*Interdependent*
Relationship to others	Separate	Connected
Focus	Internal, private self (e.g., own thoughts, feelings, and behavior)	External, public self (e.g., status in group, roles, relationships)
Personal goals	To be unique, express oneself, promote own needs	To belong, conform, occupy one's place, promote others' needs
Basis of self-esteem	Ability to understand, express, and validate one's self	Ability to understand and adjust to others, control oneself, maintain harmony
Types of emotions	Self-focused emotions (e.g., pride, anger, frustration)	Other-focused emotions (e.g., shame, sympathy, interpersonal connectedness)
How emotions are expressed	Publicly expressed	Emotions that may negatively affect relationships are kept private
Credit for success and blame for failure	Self-serving bias: takes the credit for success and blames others or the situation for failure	Other-serving bias: gives the group credit for one's success and takes personal responsibility for failure
Self-expression	Confidently display and express one's own strengths (e.g., self-enhancement and self-promotion)	Show humility and modesty (e.g., self-critical and self-improvement)

Source: Adapted from Markus, Hazel, and Shinobu Kitayama. 1991. "Culture and the Self: Implications for Cognition, Emotion, and Motivation." *Psychological Review,* 98(2): 224–253.

- enables us to be wise consumers of managerial knowledge because we become more skeptical of "one-size-fits-all" theories;
- enables us to implement management practices that are respectful of the ways of thinking, feeling, and acting that are considered normal and effective in the particular culture in which we are working at any given time, thus increasing our individual and organizational effectiveness.

For example, empowerment programs that are highly acclaimed in the United States may not work the world over (and don't always work in the United States, either).[40] Empowerment may be more desirable in cultures that promote an independent self-concept that emphasizes individual choice, personal control, and equality over hierarchy. Yet empowerment programs based on individualism may be less desirable in cultures that promote a collectivist orientation, which emphasizes adherence to the established order and dependence on authority figures (the boss) rather than equality. Certainly, empowerment programs may work in collectivist cultures, but the success of these programs depends on the degree to which managers consider the cultural context and integrate cultural values, beliefs, and norms when designing, implementing, and evaluating the program.

TABLE 2-2 Hofstede's Country Individualism Index			
Country	*Ranking*	*Country*	*Ranking*
U.S.A.	91	Argentina	46
Australia	90	Iran	41
Great Britain	89	Brazil	38
Canada	80	Turkey	37
Netherlands	80	Greece	35
New Zealand	79	Philippines	32
Italy	76	Mexico	30
Belgium	75	Portugal	27
Denmark	74	Yugoslavia	27
Sweden	71	Hong Kong	25
France	71	Chile	23
Ireland	70	Singapore	20
Norway	69	Thailand	20
Switzerland	68	Taiwan	17
Germany (FR.)	67	Peru	16
South Africa	65	Pakistan	14
Finland	63	Colombia	13
Austria	55	Venezuela	12
Israel	54		
Spain	51		
India	48		
Japan	46		

Source: Hofstede, Geert. *Culture's Consequences: International Differences in Work-Related Values.* Newbury Park, CA: Sage Publications, 1984, p. 158.

Remember that cultures are constantly changing. As people from one culture are exposed to other cultures, they inevitably compare their own perceptions of the world and cultural norms with those of others. For example, in the 1980s, North American businesses became enthralled with the success of Japanese work teams and, as a consequence, became more team-oriented. As Southeast Asia faced severe economic turbulence in the late 1990s, many Asian businesspeople, now faced with the threat of losing their jobs, grappled with how to integrate traditionally Western values of self-reliance and reduced organizational loyalty into more traditional collectivist values. Furthermore, people from younger generations typically grow up more exposed to outside cultures than did their parents and are more likely to be influenced by cultures outside their own.

SOCIAL INFLUENCES ON THE SELF-CONCEPT: SEEING OURSELVES AS OTHERS SEE US

Our self-concept is developed, sustained, and changed through our day-to-day interactions with others.[41] Each time we interact with people who are significant to us—parents, children, friends, partners, spouses, teachers, students, colleagues, bosses, subordinates—they send us signals about how they perceive us. These signals may be descriptive ("You completed the task on time and under budget.") or evaluative ("You have the skills to be an excellent manager."). Consciously and unconsciously, we interpret their words, tone of voice, gestures, and body language to make inferences about whether they see us as interesting ("Is that a yawn I see?"), competent ("Why did she ignore my last comment?"), worthy ("Why didn't the boss return my phone call?"), and influential ("Why wasn't I invited to the meeting?"). The signals we receive from others, as well as our interpretations of these signals, affect our perceptions of ourselves. As organizational scholar Karl Weick explains: "How can I know who I am until I see what they do?"[42]

Family Influences on the Self-Concept

Our early relationships within our families significantly influence our self-concept. Childhood experiences within our families—particularly parental style, pleasurable family experiences, early losses and tragedies, birth order, and sibling relationships—influence many aspects of our self-concept, including our sense of competence, feelings of belonging, and willingness to trust ourselves and others. For example, through our early social interactions within our families, we determine whether we can depend on others or must be self-reliant, whether emotional attachments are fulfilling or threatening, and whether the authority figures in our lives will be benevolent or harsh. The degree to which parents show love and affection (whether they are accessible or distant, whether love is unconditional or conditional), how they discipline their children (whether they are authoritarian or democratic), and the moral lessons they pass on to their children through words and deeds (whether they treat all people as equals or treat some people better than others) powerfully influence their children's developing self-concept and their behavior as adults.

Parental Style

Jack Welch, former CEO of General Electric, attributes much of his success to his late mother:

> Like I've said many times, my mother was the greatest leadership teacher I ever had, even though she was never in a formal leadership position herself. (The truth was, she did 'run' the neighborhood). My mother taught me about unconditional love and, at the same time, set very tough standards for achievement. That combination . . . brought out the best in me, and I used it myself to bring out the best in others.[43]

Rajat Gupta, worldwide managing director of McKinsey & Co, discussed the importance of his father's teachings about Hinduism's karma yoga:

> 'You have a right only to work, never to the results of that work.' To me that means that not only must you do the right thing, but you must do it with the right motives. And you must always do your very best. It was my father who first taught me this idea. He never worried about what the results would be but always did the right thing. If I was disappointed about something, he would ask only: 'Did you do your best?'[44]

Ann Fudge, CEO of advertising giant Young & Rubicam, attributes her stellar success as an African American woman, in part, to having had strong parental role models (her mother worked as a manager at the National Security Agency and her father worked with the U.S. Postal Service) and a tight and supportive community when she was growing up that outweighed the societal messages of racism.[45]

Early Losses

For some people, the early loss of a parent or other family tragedy can create a drive to succeed. People who lose a parent at a young age may believe that their life, too, may be cut short and may strive to achieve as much as they can early in life. Their sense of security may be shaken and may want to achieve financial success for the security it can offer. They may want to live up to their perceptions of the lost parent's expectations or they may want to "right a wrong" by making a mark on the world in memory of the people who can no longer do so themselves. And they may develop characteristics such as compassion, resiliency, and risk taking that help them persist in the face of personal hardship. Says Global Crossing entrepreneur and billionaire Gary Winnick, "No professional adversity can ever reach the pain I suffered when my father died. Any obstacle thrown in my path becomes a challenge and another hurdle to climb over . . . [I am] willing to take more risks. As long as it's not fatal, so what? You're still alive to try again. So you go for it and go for it."[46]

Investing wholeheartedly in work can help some people cope with loss. At age 13, Morrison and Foerster Law Firm partner Linda Shostake lost her mother to cancer. Says Shostake, "I just immersed myself in my work so I didn't have to think about it . . . On the one side I developed an incredible work ethic, but I also compartmentalized my emotions. Yet I know I am not alone. When I went to Harvard Law, only a handful of women were graduates, and the majority had only one parent. I never believed that was a coincidence."[47] Known for having had a stellar career and a reputation for reviving brands at Kraft Foods, Ann Fudge left the organization to take a two-year sabbatical shortly after being promoted to a $5 billion division just before she turned 50 years old. Despite the gratification she received from her work, she made this decision not to link her life too closely to her professional identity and to have the option to take an early retirement. Her decision to take the sabbatical was in part influenced by her sister-in-law's earlier diagnosis of multiple sclerosis and the realization that—despite her success—there was more to life than climbing the corporate ladder.[48] Fudge joined Young and Rubicam as CEO after her sabbatical.

Birth Order

Historian Frank Sulloway makes the controversial argument that birth order (whether we are born first, second, third, etc.) significantly influences our personalities, particularly with regard to whether we are likely to become conservative or radical, leaders or innovators. He contends that children compete for the love and attention of their parents in different ways. In particular, firstborns try to earn their parents' attention by following the rules and, thus, are more likely to become rule followers (conservative) when they grow up. Laterborns try to earn their parents' attention (which is now more scarce because it is divided among more than one child) by rebelling against these rules and, thus, are more likely to become more rebellious when they grow up.[49] Says Sulloway:

> [M]ost individual differences in personality, including those that underlie the propensity to rebel, arise within the family . . . Siblings raised together are almost as different in their personalities as people from different families . . . It is natural for firstborns to identify more strongly with power and authority.

They arrive first within the family and employ their superior size and strength to defend their special status. Relative to their younger siblings, firstborns are more assertive, socially dominant, ambitious, jealous of their status, and defensive. As underdogs within the family system, younger siblings are inclined to question the status quo and in some cases to develop a "revolutionary personality." In the name of revolution, laterborns have repeatedly challenged the time-honored assumptions of their day.[50]

Of course, Sulloway's theory is much more complex and controversial than is represented here, but the point is that family dynamics and the early lessons we learn about our place in the world often continue to get unconsciously played out throughout our lives in our roles as friends, partners, parents, direct-reports, and managers.

Other People's Expectations of Our Self-Concept

People's expectations of us can powerfully influence our self-concept. For example, our sense of competence tends to rise or fall to other people's expectations, a phenomenon that is often referred to as the self-fulfilling prophecy. In the 1960s, researchers Robert Rosenthal and Lenore Jacobson conducted one of the most well-known studies of the self-fulfilling prophecy. They wanted to determine whether a teacher's expectations of students could influence the students' performance on cognitive tests. They randomly selected 20 percent of the children in the teachers' classes and told the teachers that these children showed "unusual potential for intellectual growth." At the end of the school year, these randomly chosen students showed greater improvement on cognitive test scores than did the other children.

The teachers did not know that these students were randomly chosen. Furthermore, they were told not to say anything to the students or the students' parents about their perceived superior intellectual potential. What, then, made the difference in the students' performance? The researchers concluded that "the change in the teachers' expectations regarding the intellectual performance of these allegedly 'special' children had led to an actual change in the intellectual performance of these randomly selected children."[51] Because the teachers had high expectations of the "high-potential" students, they gave them subtle but powerful cues that enhanced the students' actual performance, including more positive responses, more challenging work, and more feedback.

This study powerfully illustrates how people's expectations for another person's behavior can result in a self-fulfilling prophecy in which the person begins to act as expected, for better or worse. It is not surprising that managers, through their expectations and the subtle (and not so subtle) assumptions about and behaviors toward others, may influence the effectiveness of others.

Group Influences on the Self-Concept

Our group memberships also shape our developing self-concept. We all belong to many identity groups (such as gender, race, nationality, and religion) and organizational groups (such as profession, organization, and hierarchical level).[52] Through socialization within our groups, we come to believe that our groups are distinctive and meaningful, become emotionally attached to our groups, and learn to take on many of the values, perspectives, and behaviors that we believe are characteristic of our groups.[53]

Our group memberships affect us in several ways. We tend to see ourselves as having more in common with people from our identity and organizational groups than with other people. We also tend to see people from our own groups as more competent and trustworthy. Consequently, we may be more cooperative, empathic, and trusting toward them. Depending on the degree to which we feel emotionally connected to our groups, we may actively advocate on their behalf, as women and African Americans did so passionately (together with many men and non-African Americans) during the women's and civil rights movements in the United States in the 1960s.[54] Indeed, our identity and organizational group members may expect us to act on behalf of the group and may be disappointed with us when we do not do so.

Even if we do not have a sense of connection to a particular social or organizational group, we may be seen by others as having more in common with people from our identity and organizational groups than with people from other groups. For example, we may expect people from North America to be assertive, people from Japan to be team-oriented, engineers to be logical, and so on. Consequently, even if we don't feel attached to a particular group, other people may see us as members of that group and encourage us to behave in ways that reinforce their perceptions and stereotypes of those groups.

In short, our group memberships influence our self-concept by (1) our personal regard for and loyalty to our groups, (2) internal group pressure to conform, and (3) external pressures to conform to what are perceived by others as our group memberships.

WHY THE SELF-CONCEPT IS IMPORTANT

Not only do we see different things, but we see the same things differently. *Mihnea Moldoveanu and Ellen Langer, Social Pychologists*

Our self-concept is important because it influences how we think, feel, and act in everyday organizational life. Understanding the self-concept is particularly important for managers because self-knowledge helps managers understand why they do the things they do and how their beliefs and behaviors affect themselves, others, and the organization—for better and worse. The self-concept is, of course, only one of many factors that affect managerial thinking, feeling, and behavior, but it is undoubtedly one of the most powerful influences on many important behaviors.[55] Specifically, the self-concept influences the following:

- *Attention.*   Our self-concept acts like a filter that lets some information in and keeps other information out. We tend to notice things that are important to our self-concept, things that are novel, and things that challenge our self-concept.[56] In addition, we tend to "see and find sensible those things [we believe we] can do something about."[57]
- *Memory and speed of attention.*   We tend to remember and process information that is consistent with our self-concept more quickly. For example, in one study, individuals were asked to read a story that was congruent with high Machiavellianism (a tendency to be "opportunistic, manipulative, and motivated by a need for power"). People who rated themselves high on a Machiavellianism scale read the story more quickly than did people who rated themselves low on the Machiavellianism scale.[58]

- *Interpretations and decision making.* Our self-concept provides us with a frame of reference for making sense of what we notice. It affects whether we interpret what we see as relevant or irrelevant, interesting or boring, and threatening or opportune. It provides us with the logic we use to understand our world, particularly the categories we use to organize our world and the connections we make among these categories. University of Virginia professor Celia Harquail explains: "For example, to a Muslim diplomat choosing a menu for a state dinner, a categorization system that distinguishes among Jews, Christians, and Muslims and thus distinguishes among religious dietary restrictions will be more appropriate for her situation than a system which categorizes diplomats, politicians, and journalists."[59]

- *Social relations.* Our self-concept significantly influences who we view as similar to and different from us, who we judge as trustworthy and competent, and who we seek out and who we avoid. Consequently, it affects the breadth, diversity, and quality of our network of relationships. It also affects our assumptions about how we should relate to others and how we handle important interpersonal challenges of the managerial job such as cooperation and competition, power and influence, and authority and delegation.

- *Moral decision making.* Our self-concept influences our assumptions about right and wrong, ethical and unethical, and how we should resolve moral dilemmas. The research of Harvard psychologist Carol Gilligan and her colleagues suggests that people who emphasize an independent self-concept are more likely to make moral decisions based on a universal set of standards of right and wrong. In other words, they are likely to believe that the same set of rules should apply to all people, regardless of the circumstances. For example, someone with an independent self-concept may feel that all people who come to work late, regardless of the reasons, should be subject to the same penalty. In contrast, people who emphasize an interdependent self-concept are more likely to make moral decisions in response to the particular person and circumstances involved.[60] From this perspective, whether one is penalized for coming in late depends on their reason for being late. Someone who overslept may be penalized, whereas someone who was caring for a sick parent may be given an opportunity to make up for the lost time rather than be penalized.

- *Ability to cope with stress.* Our self-concept helps us deal with the challenges of managerial work. A healthy self-concept gives us the psychological resources we need to find meaning among the chaos, complexity, and contradictions of contemporary organizational life; confidence during times of change; integrity during periods of moral ambiguity; and a sense of identity in a vast and largely anonymous world. In addition, a healthy self-concept helps us cope with the frequent interruptions that are common to managerial work and, in doing so, gives us a sense of personal control that enables us to take organized action.[61]

In short, our self-concept is important because it significantly influences our effectiveness in our managerial and professional roles. It shapes what we notice and ignore, how we interpret what we notice, how we make decisions, how we manage our work relationships, how we make moral decisions, and how we cope with the ambiguity and complexity of organizational life.

THE SELF IN CONTEMPORARY ORGANIZATIONS

Regardless of our culture or the defining issues of our time, we all share five fundamental needs: the need to find meaning in our lives, the need to belong, the need to feel
competent, the need for control, and the need for consistency.

Meaning

We all need to make sense of ourselves, the world, and our place in it. We all strive to
answer the questions "Who am I?", "What is true and real?", "What are my values?",
"What is worth doing?", and "What are my goals?" The need to find meaning in our
life is particularly important during difficult times of disruption, change, and loss.[62]

Belonging

We all need to be appreciated not only for what we do but for who we are. As social
beings, we want to create and maintain "lasting, positive, and significant interpersonal
relationships" that are characterized by mutual caring, emotional connection, and frequent interaction.[63] Our effectiveness and well-being depend on our ability to form
what psychiatrist John Bowlby calls "a secure base," unconditional emotional attachments to others that enable us to go out into the world knowing that we will be wel-
comed home again where we will be "nourished physically and emotionally, comforted
if distressed, reassured if frightened."[64]

Competence

We all need to feel competent at something that we value. This need to believe that we
can be successful at what we do is called the "self-efficacy" motive.[65] Our work and
achievements are important to us because they help us define our identity, stretch our
skills, challenge us, and build self-confidence.

Control

We all need to believe that we have some control over our lives. Research suggests that
having a sense of control over our work gives us a sense of ownership of our work,
inspires us to be more problem-focused and proactive in solving work problems, and
enhances our work satisfaction and our health.[66]

Consistency

We all need to believe that the world is coherent, orderly, and bounded and that tomorrow will be somewhat similar to today. A consistent and predictable environment
enables us to to learn from our experiences, have an impact on our environment, and
maintain the delicate balance between the need for stability and adaptability.
Consistency helps us understand cause-and-effect relationships, identify deviations
from the norm, anticipate situations, process information efficiently, make decisions
quickly, develop shared understandings, and build connections with others that
enhance coordination.[67]

Managers who understand these fundamental human needs will be better able to
create relationships and work environments that support these needs. By doing so, they
are more likely to create a workplace that brings out the best in themselves, others, and
the organization.

BOX 2-2

Clean Homes, Organization, and Success

Does a sense of order early in life predict success later in life? A study of 3,395 young adults conducted by researchers at the Institute for Social Research at the University of Michigan suggests that it does. The researchers found that young adults who grew up in orderly households tended to stay in school longer and earn more money than did those who grew up in less orderly households. After controlling for parental education, income, socioeconomic background, cognitive ability, and other factors, the researchers found that the children who grew up in homes that were rated "clean" to "very clean" completed an average of 13.6 years of school and earned an average of $14.17 as young adults, compared with 12 years of school and $12.60 an hour for those whose childhood homes were rated as "not very clean" to "dirty". Why this difference? Researcher Rachel Dunifon explains that, "Parents who keep their homes clean may be more organized and efficient than others and these characteristics may carry over to other aspects of their lives such as parenting . . . Keeping a clean and organized home reflects an overall ability and desire to maintain a sense of order in a wide range of life activities . . . These are qualities that also seem to be important in predicting intergenerational success."

SOURCE: The University of Michigan News and Information Services News Release, March 5, 2001. "Clean Homes Can Boost Children's Adult Education and Earnings." http://www.umich.edu/~newsinfo/Releases/2001/Mar01/r030501f.html.

The Challenges for Managers Today

Profound societal changes—including new technologies, globalization, and the increasingly diverse workforce—are challenging our feelings of belonging, competence, control, and consistency as well as our ability to make sense of ourselves, the world, and our place in it. These changes are also fundamentally shifting the means by which we construct our self-concept. As mentioned earlier in this chapter, we develop our beliefs about who we are and who we should be in large part through our families, neighborhoods, group memberships, and stable cultural institutions such as our schools, religious institutions, and work organizations. However, today's families come in many forms, our neighborhood is a global village that often connects through cyberspace, and many of us identify with an increasing number of groups. Furthermore, our cultural institutions are mired in heated debates about who does and doesn't belong, the standards for excellence, and the truths and moral foundations upon which social institutions should be built.

These changes in the social context in which we construct our identities are due, in large part, to the rapid development of new technologies throughout the past century. Psychologist Kenneth Gergen,[69] in his book *The Saturated Self: Dilemmas of Identity in Everyday Life*, explains:

As a result of advances in radio, telephone, transportation, television, satellite transmission, computers, and more, we are exposed to an enormous barrage of social stimulation. Small and enduring communities, with a limited cast of significant others, are being replaced by a vast and ever-expanding array of relationships ... [T]his massive increment in social stimulation—moving toward a state of saturation—sets the stage for both radical changes in our daily experiences of self and others ... Beliefs in the true and good depend on a reliable and homogeneous group of supporters who define what is the reliable "there," plain and simple. With social saturation, the coherent circles of accord are demolished, and all beliefs thrown into question by one's exposure to multiple points of view.[70]

Cars, trains, airplanes, telephones, cellular phones, telefaxes, pagers, mail services, radios, television, motion pictures, commercial publishing, electronic communication, and other technologies are bringing us all closer to each other, faster and more often, and exposing us to new perspectives, choices, and ways of acting. These communication, information, and transportation technologies result in what Gergen calls "social saturation"—personal feelings of overload and confusion as well as excitement and opportunity. Of course, everyone is not equally affected by technologies of saturation. Some of us are affected more, some less, yet few of us can escape the effects of technology altogether.

A Day in a Saturated Life

To get a picture of how new technologies and social trends are changing our lives, consider an average day in the life of a management educator and consultant in North America's Midwest. As you read this, consider the following questions: (1) How has technology affected her professional and personal life? (2) How have living and working in a multicultural society, largely made possible by modern technology, affected her life? (3) What do you think about her lifestyle? She's happy with it. Would you be? (4) How have technology and associated social changes—multiculturalism, the increasingly fast pace of life, and so on—affected your life?

At 5:30 A.M., my husband and I wake up. I go into my home office, turn on my computer, and check my e-mail to see if I have received any new messages since yesterday. Meanwhile, my husband, a management consultant, gets ready for work. At 6:00 A.M., I skim my favorite sections of *The Wall Street Journal* (which I have delivered to my home) as I eat breakfast and then watch the Cable News Network on television as I get dressed for the day. My husband leaves for his office at 7:00 A.M. At 7:30 A.M., I wake up our two young daughters, help them eat their breakfast and get ready for school, start my car from the living room by remote control, and then drive the children to their schools, where they interact with a vibrant group of teachers and children from many races, classes, and national cultures. They will not read the same books, learn the same history, or learn reading, writing, and arithmetic the same way that I did.

At 9:00 A.M. I get back to work. My home office has all that I need to get much of my work done—computer, printer, cell phone, fax, copier—so most days I work from home. On days when I go to my office, I first check my telephone messages, mail, and faxes. Throughout the day, I determine what information needs to go to whom and how I should send it—telephone, fax, e-mail, snail mail (regular post), two-day delivery, or overnight delivery with either a 10:00 A.M. or 2:00 P.M. guaranteed delivery time.

Later in the morning, I teach an MBA class that is approximately 20 percent African American, 4 percent Latin American, 6 percent Asian American, 40 percent European American, and 30 percent non-U.S. citizens. At lunch, I have Italian food with my friend from Kenya. In the afternoon, I conduct a leadership seminar with a group of South Korean executives, all men, and then attend a provocative lecture on the impact of feminism on organizational work. Before I leave the office at 5:00 P.M., I check my mailbox, telephone messages, e-mail, and fax machine one more time. I then telephone a local restaurant to order a dinner that faintly resembles Chinese food, charge it, and ask that it be delivered to my home around 5:30.

When I arrive home about 5:15 P.M., I quickly read, sort, and recycle the mail. I turn off the volume on the telephone and answering machine so that we can spend our evening as a family undisturbed. While waiting for the food to arrive, I light a fire in the fireplace and set the table (sometimes with paper plates to minimize cleanup). Shortly after the food arrives, my husband arrives home with the children, and we all sit down for our family dinner.

At the dinner table, we discuss everyone's day. Our kindergartner has been studying Native American and Middle Eastern cultures. Our blond-haired, blue-eyed preschooler, who is of Polish-Italian-Austrian descent, enthusiastically announces that tomorrow she wants to wear her hair in many tiny braids with colorful beads and barrettes just like her friend Syrah who is of African American descent. We reminisce about how much we miss the children's grandparents, aunts, uncles, and cousins who live in California, Florida, Maine, Massachusetts, New York, and Italy. We look at the calendar and make plans to visit our families throughout the next year.

After dinner, we log on to the computer and send an e-mail message to grandparents in Florida, play CD-ROM Barbie fashion designer, order a few books and music CDs through one of our favorite Web sites (these books will arrive at our door within 3 days), and order electronic airplane tickets for a business trip to Finland and a family vacation to California. Later in the evening, we turn off the computer and read a few books in front of the fire or watch a DVD on television.

At 8:00 P.M., we help the children get ready for bed and read to them their favorite book about how Louis Pasteur developed vaccinations. We then tell them their often-requested story about the "olden days" when we were little and didn't have many of the vaccinations that keep our children healthy today. We talk about how our children's children will have vaccinations and cures for diseases that still hurt people around the world today. Then we kiss our children goodnight, knowing that we love them more than life itself. Before going to bed, I put the ingredients for a loaf of organic whole grain raisin bread in the bread machine and program it to be ready when the children wake up in the morning.

Every weekend, our children attend religious school in a house of worship that is shared by both Jewish and Christian congregations. On Saturdays in this house of worship, the Jews face an ark. On Sundays, the ark mechanically rotates to the back and a Christian altar appears in its place. On Saturdays, the Christians baby-sit the Jewish children and on Sundays the Jews baby-sit the Christian children. A few times a year, the Jewish and Christian congregations share a common religious service.

My husband and I are happy with our lives, and we believe our children are too. We try to make careful choices about how we live, although we know that it's too soon to tell if we're making the right choices. We have been steadily adjusting our dual-career lives over the past 2 years so that we can enjoy more time together as a family. We work quite a bit less than many of our friends. Despite our busy schedules, we are the slackers among many of our professional friends. We keep our evenings and weekends free to spend with our family and our friends. Twice a month, my husband and I count on our trusted baby-sitter Tara, a very responsible young single mother with a happy and confident son, to take care of our children so that we can go out to dinner and a movie so that we can keep the spark alive in our marriage.

Admittedly, this is a privileged life. It is not like the life that I was born into in the 1950s, a life that I look back on with nostalgia. My grandparents came to this country to give their descendants a better life. I was raised in a Polish-Italian immigrant family. My father and mother owned and operated a luncheonette that served the local community in a primarily White Christian town in New England. I was 30 before I used my first computer. Our children began using our home computer when they were toddlers. I took my first airplane ride at 18; our daughters each took their first airplane rides before they were 4 months old and are seasoned travelers at ages 4 and 6. I had my first child when I was 38 and my second at 40. My mother had her first child at 21 and had sent her firstborn child off to college by the time she was 40. Despite our busy days, I often feel that I work less than my parents did as owners of a busy luncheonette. Most days, I feel very fulfilled. I'm certainly never bored!

For some, this story represents the promise of technology, a utopia of rich cultural experiences, multiple choices, a variety of time-saving conveniences, and social progress. For others, the story represents the decline of what some feel was once a more civilized society. For my family, it is simply the life that we take for granted.

Everybody must learn this lesson somewhere— that it costs something to be what you are.
Shirly Abbot,
Womenfolks: Growing Up Down South

For the purposes of this management skills book, the story illustrates how radically technology and cultural diversity have changed our everyday lives in less than half a century. It also shows that we are not passive recipients of technology, but that we make choices about how much technology we will use and in what ways. This story also raises two important questions for managers that we will address in the next sections. How do information, communication, transportation, and other technologies influence our sense of ourselves, as well as the means by which we construct our identities? What kind of self-concept can enhance our managerial effectiveness and psychological well-being in a global, diverse, and technologically driven social and economic environment? To arrive at some answers to these questions, let us focus on two technological forces that are profoundly affecting our identities: the Internet and the mass media.

Identity in the Age of the Internet

Ego surfing: The practice of scanning the Net, databases, print media, and so on, looking for references to one's own name.
New Management Words for the 1990s, http://www.lc21.com/ humor9.html

In her compelling book *Life on the Screen: Identity in the Age of the Internet*, Massachusetts Institute of Technology sociologist Sherry Turkle argues that the Internet is transforming the computer from an efficient calculator used for organizing and processing large amounts of data to a "gateway of communication" through which we are redefining human identity and relationships. Through the Internet, we can converse with people we may never meet face-to-face, take on multiple identities, participate in virtual communities, and "form on-line relationships that can be more intense than real ones."[71]

Turkle argues further that increasingly we are using the computer as a flexible toy to experiment, play, and learn with, not as a rigid machine that requires sophisticated technical expertise. Indeed, most of us don't try to decipher the detailed and complex technical manuals that come with our computers. Rather, we are more likely to solve our computing problems by talking to friends and colleagues, experimenting, and improvising solutions as we go along.

Turkle uses the term bricolage to characterize on-line tinkering with the computer environment. People who engage in bricolage challenge the belief that there is one true way to think about problems and that step-by-step logic is the quickest and most effective way to solve them. Bricoleurs play with the different conceptual and material resources they have, combining them in different ways—often by trial and error—to see what happens. Bricoleurs are sophisticated, experienced "problem-solvers who do not proceed from top-down design but by arranging and rearranging a set of well-known materials."[72]

Human beings' taste for bricolage can be illustrated by the blockbuster success of "The Sims," which in 1994 was the "most popular PC game ever," having sold more than 12 million copies, according to the *Wall Street Journal*.[73] In this PC game, players create characters, everyday actions and life events, and the spaces in which they live out these actions and events. Indeed, some research suggests that playing such video games may enhance children's problem-solving capabilities. Playing video games like "The Sims" (note that not all video games are educational and some may have adverse consequences) encourages children to plan ahead and make thoughtful decisions by anticipating the many possible outcomes of their decisions, tinker with the online characters and environment, evaluate the outcomes (as well as unintended consequences) of their choices, and design their next steps in response to what they have learned.[74]

To illustrate the use of bricolage in cyberspace, Turkle describes multiuser domains (MUDs) in which people jointly create virtual spaces with virtual characters whose virtual lives are entwined in virtual ongoing sagas that engage the mind with real problems and evoke real emotions. She explains:

> MUDs are a new kind of virtual parlor game and a new form of community. In addition, text-based MUDs are a new form of collaboratively written literature. MUD players are MUD authors, the creators as well as consumers of media content. In this, participating in a MUD has much in common with script writing, performance art, street theater, improvisational theater—or even commedia dell'arte. But MUDs are something else as well.
>
> As players participate, they become authors not only of text but of themselves, constructing new selves through social iteration . . . The anonymity of MUDs—one is known on the MUD only by the name of one's character or characters—gives people the chance to express multiple and often unexplored aspects of the self, to play with their identity and to try out new ones.[75]

One does not have to participate in MUDs to experience how cyberspace is influencing everyday life. Electronic mail enables us to create and sustain relationships with a broader and more diverse range of people than ever before possible, and to do so faster, from any place (including from a cybercafe), in real or delayed time. As our personal networks change, our self-concept may change as well.

Self-knowledge comes too late and by the time I've known myself I am no longer what I was.
Ademola Reflections: Nigerian Prose and Verse

When we tinker with life on the screen, we tinker not only with technology, but also with our selves, our relationships, and our organizations. As we pretend to be someone else on the screen, we may get a better view of who we are and who we could be. As we reach out to others around the world, we expose ourselves to different worldviews and ways of acting in the world and often change ourselves in the process. As we create and participate in virtual communities, we consider how we can use what we learn from our virtual communities to create new kinds of relationships, organizations, and societies.

As we make information and communication available to more people in more places, we challenge traditional bases of power in organizations and societies. Computer savvy 12-year-olds may have faster access to more people and information than seasoned 50-year-old executives. Someone who is silenced in one's home, workplace, or country can send a message to thousands of people in seconds and be heard around the world. And people learn that they can do the impossible, as a father in China learned when his son, Shao-Shao, was born with a congenital heart defect. Doctors in China told him that his son's heart condition was incurable and that the child would die. The father posted a message on a Web page created in Sweden by a human rights activist, asking for assistance, saying, "To all the kind people of the world, please help me save my son." A woman in the United States responded and enlisted others on the Web to find a physician to donate surgery for the child; raised $100,000 in donations to help the family with expenses; and found a family to host Shao-Shao and his parents during the successful surgery and recuperation period.

Certainly, life on the screen has risks as well as rewards. The Internet has increased our concerns about privacy, identity theft, and our ability to protect ourselves and our children from people who use cyberspace to harm others. As we search for solutions to the very real problems of our virtual worlds, we will continue to change ourselves, relationships, organizations, and societies in the process.

Identity in the Age of Mass Media and Celebrities

Futurists Jim Taylor and Watts Wacker argue that we live in an age of celebrity perpetuated by our broad exposure to mass media.[76] Television, motion pictures, and commercial publishing are exposing us to a growing number of superstars, management gurus, and role models who are shaping our beliefs about who we are, who we should be (a highly effective person), who we can be (a millionaire), who we can never be (Bill Gates), and who we are afraid of becoming (you fill this in). This exposure to celebrities, management gurus, and role models is important to our self-concept because we develop our self-concept, in part, by comparing ourselves to others.[77] This tendency to compare ourselves with others is known as the "looking glass self."[78] Social psychologists Penelope Lockwood and Ziva Kunda explain:

> The superstar illustrates the wonderful heights of accomplishment one can hope to achieve, encourages and motivates one to strive for this now all the more palpable success, indicates particular goals to aim for along the way, points to the road one should follow to achieve them, and makes one feel more competent and capable of such achievement. On the other hand, if the superstar's success seems unattainable, one will be discouraged and demoralized. The superstar's success highlights one's own failures and shortcomings. One realizes that one can no longer hope for comparable stardom, one's own lesser achievement seems paltry by comparison, and one feels disheartened and inferior.[79]

In addition to inflating and deflating our egos, superstars increase our "pool of possible selves,"[80] both those we strive to become and those we don't want to become. Hazel Markus and Paula Nurius make a compelling case that our awareness of possible future selves may be more important to our well-being and effectiveness than our current self-concept for several reasons. First, possible selves can influence our satisfaction with our current self and guide our aspirations for our future self. Second, possible selves can be liberating because exposure to a possible self helps us believe that we can change and that there is always a different and potentially better future self.[81] Third, possible selves can inspire us to create new identities for which our society has no previous models, such as Madelyn Albright did when she became the first woman Secretary of State in the United States during the Clinton and Gore administration. When Henry Kissinger, former U.S. Secretary of State during the Nixon and Ford administration, congratulated Albright by saying, "You're number 64 [U.S. Secretary of State]. Welcome to the fraternity," Albright replied, "Henry, it's no longer a fraternity."[82] Each time someone pursues and achieves a possible self that is not the norm for their organization and society, they change not only themselves but also their organizations and societies in the process.

Management Gurus and the Managerial Self-Concept

Management gurus play a critical role in the development of the managerial self-concept. Since the early 1980s, particularly in the United States, we have seen an increasing number of management gurus writing books, appearing on television, conducting seminars, appearing as keynote speakers at conferences, and consulting to organizations. These gurus have achieved celebrity status within the managerial and professional community and are able to charge up to $50,000 a day for their advice.

The popularity of management gurus cannot be explained solely by their ability to solve managerial problems. Most of us are well aware that it's risky business to put too much faith in the newest management consultants, theories, or trends.[83] Yet we continue to buy their books, watch their videos, go to their seminars, and hire them to help us fix our organizations. Researcher Bradley Jackson explains that we do so, in large part, because management consultants help managers "make sense of their own lives and their place in the scheme of things."[84]

Management gurus help us feel important and proud of our managerial work by giving us a sense of purpose and emphasizing the moral imperative of managerial work (e.g., "Managers must solve organizational problems or people will lose their jobs."). In addition, management gurus respond to our "need for a measure of predictability in an increasingly uncertain world" and "reduce the feeling of insecurity that is an inevitable fact of managerial life."[85] They offer us simple and straightforward ways of framing and solving complex problems, give us an opportunity to "stand back from [our] everyday pressures and encourage [us] to reflect on what [we] are doing,"[86] and provide us with hope for a better future. Finally, management gurus motivate us with their enthusiastic can-do delivery (often called edutainment) and engage us in ways that our day-to-day jobs often don't. Although management gurus may not solve all of our business problems, they help us fulfill our fundamental needs to be somebody, to feel competent at our work, to feel like we have control over our increasingly complex environment, to find meaning in our everyday lives as managers, and to enjoy the pleasure that comes from watching an engaging presentation.

In short, celebrities and management gurus give us alternative ways to construct our selves and enact our managerial, professional, and personal roles. We can be happy slackers with time on our hands or fast-trackers with money in our pockets. We can choose upward mobility or downward nobility.[87] We can work for large organizations or become entrepreneurs. We can be working parents, stay-at-home parents, or stay-at-home-working parents. We can manage by walking around (as recommended by Tom Peters) or clowning around (as recommended by Herb Kelleher, founder and former CEO of Southwest Airlines). Each choice has its own costs and benefits. Although our increased awareness of possibilities offers us more opportunities than ever before, it also opens the door to self-doubt (Did I make the right decision?), regret (I could have been a contender.), and a paralyzing lack of focus given all the perceived opportunities before us.

THE PROMISE, PERILS, AND SELF-CONCEPT OF THE POSTMODERN MANAGER

Technology—from the Internet to the mass media—can broaden our perspective, increase our speed and capacity for learning, help us develop a broader and more diverse network of relationships, and expand our intellectual, emotional, and behavioral repertoire—all of which enable us to become more effective and responsible managers, professionals, and world citizens. But living in such a stimulating and information-rich world can also increase our concerns about the gaps "between what we understand and what we think we should understand"[88] and who we think we are and who we think we should be. These are just a few of the dilemmas of today's manager, whom we shall refer to as the postmodern manager.

The postmodern manager must try to make sense of a world that is increasingly difficult to understand, make decisions even though many of today's problems are too complex to anticipate all the consequences, and feel a sense of control in a world that is in continuous flux. Today's manager must be both high tech and high touch; manage both global and local interests; create unity while promoting diversity; reach across organizational and social boundaries that have traditionally divided people, organizations, and nations; and help people find meaning among the chaos and confusion that are the hallmark of our time. This world of the postmodern manager is both exciting and nerve-racking. Psychologist Robert Doan explains:

> Being part of the postmodern age can have its advantages. It offers the potential of less restrictions and intolerance than preceding years. It promises flexibility, diversity, and the space to author a story that is primarily informed by one's own perceptions, memories, and meanings. It challenges the weight of undisputed authority and is, perhaps, the inevitable result of trusting a single informing metaphor for too many years, that is, assuming the world can be best understood as a machine that can be reduced to its various parts.

It has, of course, an equal potential for the opposite. The same aspects that make the aforementioned claims possible can also be experienced as a state of psychological free fall, with no parachute or net. One can be left without a foundation on which to base life's decisions and a gnawing sense of being lost with no map within reach.[89]

Doan's words remind us that despite all the changes that we face today, some things stay the same. Our fundamental needs to make sense of our world and to find our place in it haven't changed, nor have our basic needs for belonging, competence, control, consistency, and pleasure. For many of us, fulfilling these needs today, however, requires a more fluid and sophisticated way of understanding ourselves and our roles as managers and professionals.

The Updated Managerial Self-Concept

Today's managers are being asked to sail into the future without a map. To be effective, it's less likely that they will be able to fall back on "the one best way," "that's the way it should be," or "that's the way it has always been done" to solve problems. And having a rock-solid identity and one-size-fits-all approaches to solving problems may be more constraining, less effective, and more frustrating than ever before. To be effective, managers must be at least as complex as their environment, and they must see themselves as being:

- Bricoleurs who are able to combine taken-for-granted resources in novel ways to address novel situations.
- Managers of meaning who can unite diverse employees toward common goals by helping employees make sense of the organization and their role in it.
- Multiple selves who are comfortable with a multifaceted, sometimes conflicting self-concept rather than a stable, unified self-concept.

Of course, there are times when there will be one right answer and one best way to accomplish a task. And there are some parts of our identities that will always be precious to us and that we will hold onto regardless of how our world changes. But the need for consistency in managerial identity and behavior has been overstated in most management books, and broadening our view of the managerial self-concept can enhance our professional effectiveness and personal well-being. Table 2-3 constrasts the traditional and postmodern view of the manager.

TABLE 2-3 Contrasting the Managerial Self-Concept in the Industrial and Postmodern Ages		
	Self in Industrial Age *"I think, therefore I am"*	*Self in Post-Modern Age* *"I think, therefore* *I think I am"*
Work environment	Concrete, stable, homogeneous, predictable	Virtual, fluid, heterogeneous, unpredictable
Characteristics of identity	One fixed identity	Multiple selves
Alignment	Well-integrated, bounded, and aligned identity	Shifting, less bounded, and sometimes contradictory identities
Consistency	Stable self across time and place "To thy own self be true"	Adaptable, flexible self "To thy own selves be true"
Problem solving	Fact-finders and planners	Meaning makers and bricoleurs
Purpose of self-development	Self-discovery: finding one's "true self"	Self-expansion: developing, making sense of, and leveraging multiple identities

Managers as Bricoleurs

> To be someone ... is one of the deep urges of the human heart ... [It] is a need that becomes more intensely felt—and also more difficult to satisfy—as the course of history carries us all further away from the old realities that structured our identities and life experiences for us.
>
> *Political Scientist Walter Truett Anderson, Author of Reality Isn't What It Used to Be*

Political scientist Walter Truett Anderson argues that an organism's survival depends on its conformity to "the 'law of requisite variety,' meaning that an organism, if it is to survive, must be at least as complex as its environment."[90] In an age in which exceptions increasingly are becoming the norm, today's managers must become comfortable tinkering with ideas about themselves, others, and their environment and improvising new ways of thinking and behaving on the spot. Effective tinkering involves changing habitual routines, breaking traditional boundaries, and using taken-for-granted resources (ideas, materials, and people) in new ways.[91] In short, today's managers must think of themselves as bricoleurs.

Sherry Turkle explains that bricoleurs "tend to try one thing, step back, reconsider, and try another. For planners, mistakes are steps in the wrong direction; bricoleurs navigate through midcourse corrections."[92] Organizational Scholar Karl Weick echos this view, saying that bricoleurs:

> . . . remain creative under pressure, precisely because they routinely act in chaotic conditions and pull order out of them. Thus, when situations unravel, this is simply normal natural trouble for bricoleurs, and they proceed with whatever materials are at hand. Knowing these materials intimately, they then are able, usually in the company of other similar skilled people, to form the materials or insights into novel combinations.[93]

Managers as Meaning Makers

In a world with shifting meanings, multiple realities, and conflicting yet equally reasonable ideas, managers must not only try harder to make sense of themselves, the world, and their place in it, but they must help others to do the same. Consequently, say organizational scholars Linda Smircich and Gareth Morgan, managers must see themselves as "managers of meaning" whose primary task is "framing experience in a way that provides a viable basis for action, e.g., by mobilizing meaning, articulating and defining what has previously remained implicit or unsaid, by inventing images and meanings that provide a focus for new attention, and by consolidating, confronting or changing prevailing wisdom."[94] Smircich and Morgan explain:

> The person that is most easily recognized as an organizational leader is one who rises above and beyond the specification of formal structure to provide members of the organization with a sense that they are organized, even amidst an everyday feeling that at a detailed level everything runs the danger of falling apart.[95]

To be credible and effective managers of meaning, managers must learn to think of themselves as "homo narratus"[96] and become storytellers who can focus and energize their constituents. Good stories are important to individual and organizational well-being and effectiveness because they help people make sense of who they are by enabling them to find their place in the story. Good stories hold the organization together by pulling seemingly disparate parts of the organization together, articulating both a shared past and future, and sometimes creating common enemies. Good stories are engaging to listen to, creating heroes and hurdles that challenge people to stretch their goals and skills. And, many good stories have moral lessons that help people identify and resolve moral dilemmas that are a part of everyday organizational life.

Managers of meaning do not deny that the world consists of immutable facts, concrete realities (bodies, buildings, and natural resources), and real events (people get hired, promoted, demoted, and fired). However, they also realize that human beings interpret these facts, concrete realities, and events through the filters of their cultures, organizations, and self-concept. Consider the following example. Financial data may show that an organization's profits have decreased in the last quarter by 4 percent, but whether this is viewed as a threat or an opportunity (or both) depends on how we interpret the situation.

In short, managers of meaning take seriously the critical role they play in helping others interpret facts and events and use these interpretations to motivate organized action that adds value to the organization. Managers of meaning realize that some of the most important human concepts—love, morality, effectiveness, happiness, and success—are always ambiguous and open to interpretation. Perhaps most importantly, managers of meaning pay attention to what psychoanalysts M. Knight and Robert Doan refer to as "stories that have gone awry or outlived their usefulness and stories [that] are in collision,"[97] as well as "the inherent danger of the one story that has no room for alternative accounts."[98]

Managers as Multiple Selves

Twentieth-century management literature promoted the image of an effective manager as someone with a unified, stable, and predictable self-concept. From this perspective, the goal of self-awareness and professional development is to know one's "true self," to be "centered," to be well integrated, and to be consistent across a variety of situations. This view of the self fits with the Latin root of the word identity—idem—which means "the same." But as author Adolf Huxley once said, "The only completely consistent people are the dead."

No sooner do we think we have assembled a comfortable life than we find a piece of ourselves that has no place in it.
Gail Sheehy, Passages

It's not a stretch to imagine that today's managerial self-concept must be more complex than that of the past. In the industrial age, organizations were often described as machines in which well-tuned, solid, and stable parts fit precisely together and worked together through predictable routines to create a consistent product. In such a context, a well-defined, clearly bounded, stable, and predictable managerial self-concept was considered to be the hallmark of professional effectiveness and psychological well-being. However, this solid, stable, and consistent self-concept may be out of date and overrated for many people in today's fast-changing, multicultural, and technologically driven social and economic environment in which we are routinely exposed to new people and ideas, novel situations, and increasingly complex problems with no clear solutions.

Today, many managers are likely to find it more difficult to be centered, well integrated, and consistent. In contrast to the model of the "rock solid" ideal manager of the industrial age, many managers today must develop a self-concept that is more complex, more open to experience, more fluid, more dependent on others, more comfortable with change, and less sure of oneself but more certain that what one does matters. In short, many managers are likely to find it more effective and psychologically fulfilling to see themselves as having fluid, often fragmented multiple selves. Although the notion of multiple selves is relatively new to the management literature, it is not a new concept. More than 40 years ago, sociologist Erving Goffman argued that the self is a collection of roles that a person turns on and off depending on the characteristics of the situation.[99]

For many people—particularly those who routinely interact across multiple cultures, cross organizational boundaries, or manage complex personal and professional lives (e.g., working parents who engage fully in both their parental and professional roles)—the ability to develop multiple selves and shift among these selves as appropriate is a necessary and effective survival skill. Historian W. E. B. Dubois, the first African American to receive a Ph.D. from Harvard University and cofounder of the National Association for the Advancement of Colored People in 1910, coined the term "double consciousness" to refer to the need and ability to live in multiple worlds simultaneously. Scholar Aida Hurtado, describing the experience of women of color, uses the phrase "shifting consciousness" to refer to the ability "to shift from one group's perception of social reality to another, and, at times, to be able simultaneously to perceive multiple social realities without losing their sense of self-coherence."[100] In the management literature, organizational researchers Ella Bell and Mary Yoko Brannen use the term "biculturalism" to refer to individuals who are members of, and accountable to, at least two significant identity groups simultaneously, each with their own worldviews, values, norms, and expectations.[101]

Yet having multiple selves is most often framed as a problem to be fixed rather than a skill to be developed. Hurtado argues that "nonconflictual and monocultural social identities are [considered] superior and desirable" and that the "dominant paradigm emphasized in mainstream scholarship for understanding 'biculturality' is the pain and stress of transitioning from one 'cultural world' to another . . . marginality, alienation, acculturation stress, and so on."[102] She notes that when having multiple selves is viewed as a problem, people are encouraged to integrate these selves, a strategy that requires diluting or disowning one or more treasured selves. Similarly, terms such as "role overload" (the stress placed on a person when one has to manage too many roles) and "role conflict" (when the demands of one role prevents one from meeting the demands of other roles) are well-known concepts in the psychology and management literature,[103] whereas the healthy functions of multiple roles are less known.

Yet recent research is focusing on how many people develop and use multiple roles to enhance their peace of mind, well-being, and professional success. When having multiple selves is viewed as a normal, desirable, and effective adaptive mechanism, people actively cultivate different selves, learn to shift among these selves, and are able to leave one self aside for a while, only to pick it up later when the situation is more appropriate. Researcher Iris Settles and colleagues call this "high self-complexity."[104]

Although living in multiple worlds and having multiple selves can be frustrating, even painful at times, there are advantages for many people. Hurtado explains that people with multiple selves reap the rewards of the "unique knowledge" that is gained by membership in multiple groups, the freedom that is gained by being able to "rise above the restrictions defined by these memberships," and the value of being able to bring both an insider's and outsider's perspective and knowledge to one's multiple groups. People who cultivate multiple selves may be better able to resist categorization and "avoid polarization," accept their own and others' "inconsistent personae,"[105] and acknowledge and accept diversity in general.

Speaking to me from his own experience, a Japanese MBA student explained: "The benefits of having multiple selves are the quick assimilation into different environments, the ability to influence a group from inside instead of outside, and the satisfaction of being effective in different settings. With multiple selves between home and work, I can easily separate the two worlds, so that the frustration and stress that I might experience in one tend not to be carried over to the other."

Many research studies support the view that people with "high self complexity" can reap many personal and professional rewards, including greater job effectiveness, as well as greater psychological and physical well-being.[106] Specifically, researchers have found

- People with highly complex selves may have more diverse resources, such as skills, knowledge, experience, and relationships, to draw on to enhance their performance, especially when facing complex problems.
- People who sometimes keep their roles separate may be better able to turn off the demands of one role while focusing on another, which can lead to better performance. When people are unable to separate and "turn off" their different roles at times, they may find themselves constantly multitasking and unable to concentrate on the responsibilities of one role because of their attention to the other.
- People who are willing to try on new possible selves may be better able to find a greater variety of jobs, as well as succeed in the jobs they obtain because they may be better able to see themselves in different roles (and thus think more broadly about job possibilities), test out new ways of behaving that may be inconsistent with prior selves, and adopt new characteristics and skills that can make them more effective in new roles.
- When things are going well with many of the multiple selves in one's life, people can have even greater feelings of happiness because they can experience well-being on many fronts.
- The pleasure people experience through one role may balance the pain experienced in another role. When one is having problems in one role, one may still derive pleasure from other selves, thus sustaining well-being despite life's challenges. And if one loses an important part of his/her identity, one still has other identities from which to draw fulfillment.

In short, having multiple identities can be replenishing rather than draining, clarifying rather than confusing, and opportunity-enhancing rather than constraining.[107] The following studies illustrate these benefits.

I'm the kind of woman who wants to enjoy her-selves in peace. **Alice Walker,** **The Temple of My Familiar**

In a study of experienced engineers and other professionals, Simon Fraser researchers Janice Beyer and David Hannah found that people with more complex identities were better able to adjust when they took on new jobs because they had more "cognitive materials and personal resources" from which to draw.[108] In a different study of 61 women between the ages of 26 and 57 who were managers and executives, researcher Marian Ruderman and colleagues found that women who managed multiple roles were rated more highly by their managers and peers on interpersonal skills and task performance. They explain:[109]

> [The] roles women play in their personal lives provide psychological benefits, emotional advice and support, practice at multitasking, relevant background, oppportunites to enrich interpersonal skills and leadership practice that enhances effectiveness in the management role. Multiple role commitment positively relates to life satisfaction, self-esteem, and self-aceptance. Commitment to multiple roles was also related to interpersonal and task-related managerial skills . . . Work-family conflict may be overstated for some women . . . because as one accumulates additional roles in life, they also accumulate additional skills and mechanisms (e.g., support systems) for travelling between and integrating roles.

Wharton professor Nancy Rothbard explains that women such as these are not portraying the superwoman syndrome, but rather have learned a more sophisticated way of taking advantage of the benefits of having multiple roles. Rothbard adds that this is "good news because 72 percent of female vice presidents and top leaders in Fortune 1000 companies are married, and 64 percent have children."[110] Of course, even for people with high levels of self-complexity, the different parts of one's selves are integrated in part by some deeply held common beliefs and values that are consistent over time and place. Furthermore, having multiple selves is likely to have greater benefits when one chooses one's identities (e.g., choosing to be both a working professional and a parent) and sees them as a desirable part of oneself rather than a burden or a façade.

On the basis of her research on job transitions, Insead professor Herminia Ibarra argues that having "provisional selves" can help us find and adapt to new work roles. In one study, she asked men and women who were consultants and investment bankers about their career development (e.g., she asked, "What does it take to be successful and effective in your current job?" "Tell me a bit about your career to date. What are the key events of your years at the firm?"). Many of these consultants and investment bankers told stories about how they transitioned to new roles, such as when one moved from being an individual contributor to a boss by trying on new practice or trial selves to see if these new identities fit or if they could grow into them. Ibarra says, "By rehearsing these clumsy, often ineffective, sometimes inauthentic selves, they learned about the limitations and potential of their repertoires and thus began to make decisions about what elements to keep, refine, reject, or continue to search for."[111] To illustrate, she quotes the words of a participant in Harvard professor Linda Hill's study on new managers' career development:

> I even dressed like him [a favorite boss], to look like an authority figure . . . [He] always kept people up. You enjoyed coming to the office, because he always had fun up his sleeve. I wanted to create that kind of atmosphere. But guess what

I found out? I don't have much of a sense of humor and I'm not spontaneous like him. If you have to work at making something funny, it falls flat. I had to come up with another way that fit who I am to create the right office atmosphere. I could keep his concepts but I had to put my own words and form around them.[112]

When stuck on a hard problem (MIT-educated invester) Levy tries a mental trick he invented in the third grade. He asks himself, "How would I answer this if I were a smart person?" *Fortune*

In another study, Ibarra interviewed managers and professionals during career transitions. She found that many people did not find new jobs by undertaking a systematic process of identifying their "true calling" ("Who am I and what's the perfect job for me?"). Rather, Ibarra found that many successful job searches began with a broader question: "Among the many possible selves that I might become, which is most intriguing to me now?" She concluded that many successful job searchers succeed through a "process of tinkering with a whole set of possibilities: imagining new ones, trying them on for size, elaborating on some, dropping others, getting rid of outdated images, coming to grips with the fact that some might languish."[113]

Note that marketers have also recognized the importance of mutliple selves. A recent *Fast Company* article quotes the advice of Melinda Davis, founder and CEO of the Next Group marketing firm which helps companies such as AT&T, Corning, Merck, and Viacom anticipate the future:[114]

... what's going on inside our heads keeps getting more complicated. There's a new fascination with the Sybil syndrome—not as a psychiatric disorder, but as an aspirational value. People are dividing themselves into multiple, virtual identities as a way to handle an increasingly complex, chaotic world. Consumers are enthusiastic about products that allow them to switch identities at will ... At the 2002 World Economic Forum, one of the most popular seminars was called "How to Become Someone Else." The implications for marketers: Each of your customers is actually many customers fitting into multiple segmentation models.

In short, many people today are finding that having multiple selves (rather than an integrated self) helps them be more effective at their jobs, more successful in their careers, and happier and healthier as well. Indeed, for many people, having multiple selves is a creative adaptive mechanism that can open up new opportunities that would be closed if they clung to a solid, stable sense of self.

Managers as Self-Monitors

Be careful of what you pretend to be because you may become what you pretend to be. *Kurt Vonnegut, Jr., Author*

Self-monitoring refers to a person's willingness and ability to be attentive to "social and interpersonal situational cues" and to adapt one's behavior to these cues.[115] High self-monitors are highly sensitive to social and interpersonal cues in their environment and are willing and able to modify their behavior in response. Low self-monitors are less sensitive to social and interpersonal cues and less willing and able to adapt their behaviors in response.[116] "In a social situation, high self-monitors ask the following: 'Who does this situation want me to be and how can I be that person?' By contrast, low self-monitors ask, 'Who am I and how can I be me in this situation?'"[117] Self-monitoring appears to be a relatively stable personality character-istic, and research suggests that about 60 percent of people in the United States are low self-monitors and 40 percent are high self-monitors.[118]

As you read the following paragraphs, keep in mind that neither high or low self-monitoring is inherently better or worse than the other—it depends on what you want to accomplish. Furthermore, remember that each of us has characteristics that are associated with both high and low self-monitoring, although we tend to use one style more often than the other. Whether you should learn to be more or less self-monitoring depends on what you want to achieve in your professional and personal life. To enhance your effectiveness, it makes sense to understand your self-monitoring style and the impact it has on your behavior, how others perceive you, and the ways in which it is helping and hindering you from achieving your professional and per-sonal goals.

How do high and low self-monitors differ? In their study of 139 graduates of a nationally ranked MBA program, researchers Martin Kilduff and David Day found that the high self-monitors were more likely than the low self-monitors to change employers and move geographic locations. High self-monitors also had a slight edge at achieving internal and cross-company promotions. They found no sig-nificant differences between the effects of self-monitoring behaviors on men and women. In their review of the research on self-monitoring behavior, Kilduff and Day found that:

> High self-monitors perform better than lows in boundary-spanning jobs that require incumbents to be sensitive to a variety of social cues. Further, high self-monitors tend to emerge as the leaders of work groups and are more likely than low self-monitors to resolve conflicts through collaboration and compro-mise. In addition, high self-monitors, faced with the failure of a project for which they have personal responsibility, are better than low self-monitors at rationalizing their actions and managing the information others receive about the situation. Finally, as Snyder and Copeland pointed out, high self-monitors "may be particularly willing and able to tailor and fashion an image to match the position into which they hope to be promoted."[119]

In addition, high self-monitors are more likely to seek out prestigious work, rely more on their social networks to make career decisions, have more central positions in organizational networks, have more instrumental relationships, be less committed to current relationships, and be more "flexible about the possibility of forming new rela-tionships elsewhere."[120]

Adaptable as human beings are and have to be, I sometimes sympa-thize with the chameleon who had a nervous breakdown on a patch-work quilt. *John Stephen Strange*

In contrast, low self-monitors tend to be more committed to current employers, friends, and geographic locations; "tend to invest emotionally in particular relationships so that they can be them-selves;"[121] "tend to value the freedom to pursue work compatible with their own interests rather than work that is prestigious or well-defined;"[122] and "may not need to gather so much information from external sources concerning diverse career opportunities because they appear to have a greater self-knowledge concerning career preferences than high self-monitors."[123]

The late Akio Morita, CEO of Sony, may have been a high self-monitor. In his book *Sony: The Private Life*, author John Nathan says: "What accounted for Akio Morita's unique ability as a Japanese businessman to establish and sustain beneficial relationships with the most important Western business and political leaders? There is striking agreement among those who knew him over time that he was special because he was someone who seemed to understand them, and, as important, whom they could understand." Morita's self-monitoring may not have come without effort and some personal costs, however. Says Nathan:

> But was he really as effortlessly at ease in the company of his foreign friends as he appeared, as familiar and at home with their way of perceiving the world and acting in it? . . . [T]here is evidence to suggest that Morita had to labor hard to achieve what may have been the illusion of familiarity . . . There is even room for speculation that Morita's lifelong, tireless campaign to install Sony in the West required a painful personal struggle to reconcile a foreign sensibility with his own . . . and he was never able to resolve that tension satisfactorily.[124]

Research on the influence of self-monitoring behavior on managerial careers and performance is relatively new, and there is still much to be learned. For example, we don't know if certain jobs lend themselves better to high or low self-monitoring. We also don't know how high or low self-monitoring behavior affects a manager's mental health; for example, who tends to be happier, high or low self-monitors? New research on self-monitoring behavior promises to give us important insights into how particular characteristics of both high and low self-monitoring can enhance and inhibit our effectiveness, careers, and well-being. For now, it's worth thinking about your self-monitoring behavior and whether it's helping you achieve the goals you want. You can assess your self-monitoring style by completing the self-monitoring assessment in Box 2-6.

MANAGERIAL GROWTH AND DEVELOPMENT

Undoubtedly, developing self-awareness is essential to our long-term work effectiveness, career development, and personal well-being. Many of us are drawn to go beyond who we currently are toward who we are capable of becoming. Yet leadership researcher and consultant Wilfred Drath explains that personal growth can be disconcerting as well as exhilarating because "to grow personally, [we] must give up a deeply personal meaning, a fundamental way of understanding the self and relating the self to the world," that gives our lives coherence and predictability.

You've got to do your own growing, no matter how tall your grandfather was. *Irish Proverb*

Growth does not simply mean moving in logical, concrete steps toward a particular direction, nor does it imply constant change. We grow and develop, not steadily, but by advancing a little and then plateauing or even retreating. What looks like regression may actually be a necessary retreat or plateau that gives us the time we need to assimilate important changes. Sometimes growth occurs in spurts and sometimes very slowly. Sometimes we are aware that we are learning something new and at other times our learning is unconscious—all we feel is the tension that often accompanies personal growth.[125]

But, despite the ambiguity and anxiety that often accompanies personal growth, remember that our self-concept will always be a work in progress, and our personal growth will always be, in part, under our control. We can promote personal growth by taking time out for self-reflection, putting ourselves in challenging situations that require us to go beyond our current ways of thinking and behaving, developing relationships with a diverse range of people who can provide us with alternative ways of being, and asking others for feedback on how we are perceived and how our behavior affects other people and organizations.

Chapter Summary

Our self-awareness contributes to our managerial success. The more we know about ourselves and how we are perceived by others, the better we can understand how our ways of seeing, thinking, feeling, and acting affect our work effectiveness and psychological well-being.

Some management gurus advise managers and professionals to think of themselves as "the brand called you" and "me, inc." They warn that it is misleading to assume that others will see, understand, and reward our contributions. Rather, it's important to identify, develop, and "market" our strengths and contributions.

The self-concept refers to an internalized set of perceptions that each of us has of ourselves that are relatively stable over time, consistent across situations, resistant to change, and of central importance.

The self-concept is, in large part, socially and culturally constructed through our families, interpersonal relationships, identity and organizational group memberships, and social institutions.

Understanding our self-concept is important because it influences what we pay attention to, how we interpret what we see, how we make decisions, who we interact with and how we interact with them, how we make moral choices, and how we cope with the stress and complexity of managerial work.

One of the most important lifelong challenges we face is to reconcile our basic needs to be both connected to and separate from others. We learn how to reconcile these basic needs for separateness and connectedness through our culture. Different cultures provide their members with different ways to reconcile these needs. Some cultures (often labeled individualistic) emphasize independence from others, and other cultures (often labeled collectivist) emphasize interdependence with others. These different conceptions of the self have implications for how we see the world, make sense of what we see, interpret the behavior of others, and behave in our everyday life.

Despite cultural differences in the construction of the self-concept, people the world over share universal human needs: meaning, belonging competence, control, and consistency. These needs become more relevant in times of change or adversity.

Today's managers live and work in a multicultural, technology-driven, fast-paced, fast-changing, and unpredictable environment. This environment exposes us to an increasing number of possible selves, which expands our assumptions about who we are, who we should be, who we can be, and who we can never be.

Today's manager can be described as a postmodern manager. Postmodern managers have a self-concept that is more complex, more culturally aware and responsive, more open to experience, more relational, more comfortable with change, more fragmented, and less sure of oneself, but more certain that what one does, matters.

In today's complex work environment, effective managers see themselves as:

- Bricoleurs who are able to combine taken-for-granted resources in novel ways to address novel situations.
- Managers of meaning who can bring a community together by helping people make sense of the organization and their role in it.
- Having multiple selves who are comfortable with a multifaceted, sometimes conflicting self-concept rather than a stable, unified self-concept.

Self-monitoring refers to one's willingness and ability to be attentive to interpersonal and contextual cues and to adapt one's behavior in response. High self-monitors ask themselves, "What does this situation want me to be and how can I be that person?" Low self-monitors ask themselves "How can I be myself in this situation?" Although each of us has characteristics associated with high and low self-monitoring, we tend to prefer one style of self-monitoring over the other and use this style more often. These styles have implications for how we choose jobs, behave in those jobs, whether we are drawn to status, whether we prefer to have deep personal relationships or many relationships that may be more superficial, and many other behaviors associated with organizational life.

Personal growth is not always a logical, linear process. We learn some things quickly, some things slowly, and sometimes we're not even aware that we're learning at all. However, we can control our growth to some degree by creating a context that promotes our personal and professional development.

FOOD FOR THOUGHT

1. What is the one most useful thing you learned in this chapter, and why?
2. Based on what you learned in this chapter, select one behavior to do differently this week. Practice this behavior and note any benefits and progress you make.
3. Do you agree with the idea that you should develop "Me, Inc" or "The Brand Called You" as described in the beginning of this chapter? Why or why not?
4. Answer the five questions posed by Tom Peters in his article, "The Brand Called You," and summarized at the beginning of this chapter. These include: What do I do that I'm most proud of?; What do I do that adds remarkable, measurable, distinguished, distinctive value?; What do my colleagues and customers say is my greatest and clearest strength . . . [and] most noteworthy personal characteristic?; What have I done lately—this week—that added value to the organization (and that was noticed by others)?; In what ways is what I do difficult to imitate? What do your answers tell you about your brand as it stands now? What do you need to do to enhance and market your brand?
5. Complete the "I am" assessment at the end of this chapter. Does your self-concept emphasize independence or interdependence? Under what conditions is this self-concept (independence or interdependence) useful and under what conditions is it a problem?
6. What forces (such as family, group membership, social institutions) most shaped your self-concept to date, and in what ways? How does your current self-concept affect your work style, work effectiveness, career potential, and psychological well-being?
7. Draw a "lifeline" that includes critical periods of your life, influential events and people, and discuss the effects that they had on your worldview and behavior today.

8. Research suggests that we often underestimate the degree to which we change over time. List five things that have changed about yourself since you were in high school. Why did these changes occur and what benefits and/or costs have they created?

9. How have technology, globalization, and diversity changed your personal and professional life? What have you gained from these changes, and what have you lost?

10. Think of a time when you solved a problem in a novel way. What were you trying to accomplish, and how did you do it?

11. Do you have multiple selves? If not, why not? If so, why and in what ways are they helpful and in what ways are they problematic? How do you manage your multiple selves?

12. Are you a low or high self-monitor? What are the consequences of your self-monitoring style on your effectiveness, career, and well-being? Remember that both high and low self-monitoring styles bring advantages and disadvantages. Based on what you learned about your self-monitoring style, which behaviors would you want to change and which would you want to keep the same? Why?

13. Visit someone's office and look around. What assumptions do you make about the person based on their office? Ask the person what the office says about them. What did you learn about that person's sense of self or selves?

14. Complete the personality Box 2-4 included in this chapter. What did you learn from it? How might your styles influence how you solve problems and how you are perceived by others? Under what conditions might you be more or less effective? Do you agree with the way this assessment categorizes you? Why or why not?

BOX 2-3

A Note on Personality Assessments

Self-assessments traditionally have been an important cornerstone of managerial development. The use of self-assessments is based on the reasonable assumptions that (1) people have habitual ways of seeing and acting in the world, (2) different people have different ways of seeing and acting in the world, (3) these different ways of seeing and acting have consequences on our effectiveness and well-being, (4) these differences can be identified through self-assessment instruments, and (5) personal change is possible and desirable. Furthermore, personality assessments assume that if we understand the different ways people see and behave—and their reasons for doing so—we can better understand the world from multiple perspectives, appreciate the value that these perspectives bring, understand our strengths and weaknesses, and learn to be more flexible. There are hundreds of instruments designed to assess a variety of personality characteristics, including learning style, problem-solving style, interpersonal style, self-monitoring tendencies, locus of control, moral development, creativity, multicultural competence, emotional intelligence, and stress management, to name just a few. Some assessments, including one similar to the popular Myers-Briggs Assessment (Box 2-4), are included at the end of this chapter. There are other self-assessments throughout this book as well. Many self-assessments are also available through the Internet.

Developing self-awareness through personality instruments has several advantages, including encouraging personal and professional growth, increasing our self-awareness and our understanding of how we are perceived by others, helping us make career choices, enhancing our decision making, and helping us improve our interpersonal relationships through better communication, conflict management, and increased acceptance of people who differ from us in thinking and behavioral styles.

Although personality assessments can enhance individual and organizational performance, they have limitations as well. Although many personality assessments are often (though not always) based on well-developed theories of human behavior and are often (though not always) well researched, they are often (some would argue always) biased. Assessments are often presented as universally applicable, yet many tend to reflect the cultural biases of the researcher(s) who created the assessments and the segments of the population that the researcher studied. In addition to these limitations, people who put too much emphasis on personality assessments may compartmentalize people into rigid categories, may underestimate the degree to which people's "styles" change over time and place, and may overemphasize the impact of personality characteristics and underemphasize the impact of situational variables on our behavior.

Despite these limitations, self-assessments can significantly contribute to individual and organizational effectiveness when used wisely. To enhance the usefulness of assessments, take a variety of self-assessments and look for patterns across them. Have other people assess you and compare your self assessment with their perception of you. When interpreting results, carefully consider how the assessment may reflect cultural biases. This is especially important when the assessment claims universal applicability or when certain "styles" are claimed to be generally more normal, moral, or effective than others. In addition, although people's ways of perceiving and acting tend to be somewhat consistent over time, people do change as a consequence of training, significant emotional experiences (e.g., births, deaths, illness, travel, or job termination), or socialization into a profession or culture. Finally, remember that personality assessments can give you pieces of data about yourself, and only you can make sense of this data based on your knowledge of your life history, cultural group memberships, and future career and life goals.

BOX 2-4

Self-Assessment Personality Inventory

WHAT IS MY PERSONALITY TYPE?

For each item, select either a or b. If you feel both a and b are true, decide which one is more like you, even if it is only slightly more true.

1. I would rather
   a. Solve a new and complicated problem.
   b. Work on something I have done before.

2. I like to
   a. Work alone in a quiet place.
   b. Be where the action is.

3. I want a boss who
   a. Establishes and applies criteria in decisions.
   b. Considers individual needs and makes exceptions.

4. When I work on a project, I
   a. Like to finish it and get some closure.
   b. Often leave it open for possible changes.

5. When making a decision, the most important considerations are
   a. Rational thoughts, ideas, and data.
   b. People's feelings and values.

6. On a project, I tend to
   a. Think it over and over before deciding how to proceed.
   b. Start working on it right away, thinking about it as I go along.

7. When working on a project, I
   a. Maintain as much control as possible.
   b. Explore various options.

8. In my work, I prefer to
   a. Work on several projects at a time, and learn as much as possible about each one.
   b. Have one project that is challenging and keeps me busy.

9. I often
   a. Make lists and plans whenever I start something and may hate to seriously alter my plans.
   b. Avoid plans and just let things progress as I work on them.

10. When discussing a problem with colleagues, it is easy for me to
    a. See "the big picture."
    b. Grasp the specifics of the situation.

11. When the phone rings in my office or at home, I usually
    a. Consider it an interruption.
    b. Do not mind answering it.

12. Which word describes you better?
    a. Analytical.
    b. Empathetic.

13. When I am working on an assignment, I tend to
    a. Work steadily and consistently.
    b. Work in bursts of energy with "down time" in between.

14. When I listen to someone talk on a subject, I usually try to
    a. Relate it to my own experience and see if it fits.
    b. Assess and analyze the message.

15. When I come up with new ideas, I generally
    a. "Go for it."
    b. Like to contemplate the ideas some more.

16. When working on a project, I prefer to
    a. Narrow the scope so it is clearly defined.
    b. Broaden the scope to include related aspects.

17. When I read something, I usually
    a. Confine my thoughts to what is written there.
    b. Read between the lines and relate the words to other ideas.

18. When I have to make a decision in a hurry, I often
    a. Feel uncomfortable and wish I had more information.
    b. Am able to do so with available data.

19. In a meeting, I tend to
    a. Continue formulating my ideas as I talk about them.
    b. Only speak out after I have carefully thought the issue through.

20. In work, I prefer spending a great deal of time on issues of
    a. Ideas.
    b. People.

21. In meetings, I am most often annoyed with people who
    a. Come up with many sketchy ideas.
    b. Lengthen meetings with many practical details.

22. I am a
    a. Morning person.
    b. Night owl.

23. What is your style in preparing for a meeting?
    a. I am willing to go in and be responsive.
    b. I like to be fully prepared and usually sketch an outline of the meeting.

24. In a meeting, I would prefer for people to
    a. Display a fuller range of emotions.
    b. Be more task oriented.

25. I would rather work for an organization where
    a. My job was intellectually stimulating.
    b. I was committed to its goals and mission.

26. On weekends, I tend to
    a. Plan what I will do.
    b. Just see what happens and decide as I go along.

27. I am more
    a. Outgoing.
    b. Contemplative.

28. I would rather work for a boss who is
    a. Full of new ideas.
    b. Practical.

In the following, choose the word in each pair that appeals to you more:

29. a. Social.
    b. Theoretical.

30. a. Ingenuity.
    b. Practicality.

31. a. Organized.
    b. Adaptable.

32. a. Active.
    b. Concentration.

SCORING KEY AND ANALYSIS

This assessment classifies people as extroverted or introverted (E or I), sensing or intuitive (S or N), thinking or feeling (T or F), and perceiving or judging (P or J). These classifications can then be combined into sixteen personality types (e.g., INTJ, ENTP). Score your responses as follows: Count one point for each item listed below that you have marked in the inventory.

Scoring Key

Score for I	Score for E	Score for S	Score for N
2a	2b	1b	1a
6a	6b	10b	10a
11a	11b	13a	13b
15b	15a	16a	16b
19b	19a	17a	17b
22a	22b	21a	21b
27b	27a	28b	28a
32b	32a	30b	30a

Total

Identify the one with the more points— I or E.

Identify the one with the more points— S or N.

(*continued*)

Box 2-4 (*cont.*)

Score for T	Score for F	Score for J	Score for P
3a	3b	4a	4b
5a	5b	7a	7b
12a	12b	8b	8a
14b	14a	9a	9b
20a	20b	18b	18a
24b	24a	23b	23a
25a	25b	26a	26b
29b	29a	31a	31b

Total

Identify the one with the more points— T or F.

Identify the one with the more points— J or P.

ANALYSIS

This assessment is similar to the popular Myers-Briggs Type Indicator and Keirsey Bates personality assessments. It classifies people as extroverted or introverted (E or I), sensing or intuitive (S or N), thinking or feeling (T or F), and perceiving or judging (P or J). These classifications can then be combined into sixteen personality types (for example, INTJ, ENTP).

This assessment is based on the assumption that different people have different ways of seeing the world and solving problems. It is designed to assess your tendencies toward:

- Introversion or extroversion. The tendency to get energized by focusing inward (introversion) or to the outer world (extroversion)

- Sensing or intuition. The tendency to see the world and acquire information by focusing on details (sensing) or by focusing on the big picture (intuition)

- Thinking or feeling. The tendency to make decisions based on systematic logic (thinking) versus values (feeling)

- Judging or perceiving. The tendency to take a planned, orderly approach to the world, and come to closure quickly (judging) or a flexible spontaneous approach and a tendency to leave decisions open as long as possible (perceiving)

No one preference is better than the others. Rather, your effectiveness depends on your ability to be aware of the impact of your preferences on your behavior, being able to use the most appropriate way of thinking and acting for each particular situation, and respecting and leveraging different styles when they are expressed by others.

Knowing your preferred ways of interacting with the world and solving problems is useful for several reasons. It helps you be aware of the different ways that people make sense of and interact with their environment. This awareness can make you more accepting, even encouraging, of these differences. Being able to understand and respect differences in styles can also help you become a more effective communicator, negotiator, conflict manager, and team leader.

SOURCE: D. Marcic and P. Nutt. 1989. "Personality Inventory." In D. Marcic, ed. *Organizational Behavior: Experiences and Cases*. St. Paul, MN: West. Reprinted with permission.

BOX 2-5

Self-Assessment 20 Questions: "I Am"

Complete the following sentences, all of which begin with "I am . . .," to describe yourself. You do not have to show your answers or discuss your results with anyone. This is for your use only. Do not turn the page until you have completed the sentences.

1. I am _____
2. I am _____
3. I am _____
4. I am _____
5. I am _____
6. I am _____
7. I am _____
8. I am _____
9. I am _____
10. I am _____
11. I am _____
12. I am _____
13. I am _____
14. I am _____
15. I am _____
16. I am _____
17. I am _____
18. I am _____
19. I am _____
20. I am _____

Please turn the page for a discussion of your responses.

(*continued*)

Box 2-5 (*cont.*)

"I Am" Interpretation of Responses: The Private, Public, and Collective Self-Concept

How you completed these sentences gives you some insights into your self-concept. Your responses reflect your tendencies to emphasize a private, public, or collective self-concept.

- *Private self-concept.* Responses that emphasize your personal traits, states, or behaviors (e.g., I am creative, I am a big thinker, I am introverted, I am kind, I am competitive, I am conscientious) and do not make reference to connections to others, perceptions of others or your membership in specific groups. These responses are more aligned with an independent self-concept than with an interdependent self-concept.

- *Public.* Responses that emphasize your relationships, connection to others, or perceptions of others (e.g., I am respected by others, I am trusted, I am loved). These are associated with a tendency to emphasize your public self and a concern with how others view and experience their relationship with you. These responses are more associated with an interdependent self-concept than with an independent self-concept.

- *Collective.* Responses that mention specific social groups or cultural institutions (e.g., I am Asian American, or I am an MBA) or your role in the group (I am a parent, I am a manager, or I am an engineer). These are associated with a tendency to emphasize group memberships that have value and emotional significance to you. These responses are more associated with an interdependent self-concept than with an independent self-concept.

Analysis: Count your responses for each of the categories. Your responses will probably include private, public, and collective responses, but you may have emphasized some over others. Do your responses suggest that you emphasize a private, public, or collective self? Do you agree? Why or why not? What implications does this have for your effectiveness in different types of situations?

SOURCE: Adapted from Triandis, H. C. 1989. "The Self and Social Behavior in Different Cultural Contexts." *Psychological Review,* 96: 506–520. Copyright ©1989 by the American Psychological Association. Reprinted with permission.

BOX 2-6

Self-Monitoring Assessment

The statements on this page concern your personal reactions to a number of different situations. If a statement is TRUE or MOSTLY TRUE as applied to you, circle "T". If a statement is FALSE or NOT USUALLY TRUE as applied to you, circle "F". Answer honestly.

T   F   1.   I find it hard to imitate the behavior of other people.

T   F   2.   At parties and social gatherings, I do not attempt to do or say things that others will like.

T   F   3.   I can only argue for ideas which I already believe.

T   F   4.   I can make impromptu speeches even on topics about which I l information.

T   F   5.   I guess I put on a show to impress or entertain others.

T   F   6.   I would probably make a good actor.

T   F   7.   In a group of people, I am rarely the center of attention.

T   F   8.   In different situations and with different people, I often act like persons.

T   F   9.   I am not particularly good at making other people like me.

T   F   10.   I am not always the person I appear to be.

T   F   11.   I would not change my opinions (or the way I do things) in order to please someone.

T   F   12.   I have considered being an entertainer.

T   F   13.   I have never been good at games like charades or improvisational acting.

T   F   14.   I have trouble changing my behavior to suit different people and different situations.

T   F   15.   At a party, I let others keep the jokes and stories going.

T   F   16.   I feel a bit awkward in public and do not show up quite as well as I should.

T   F   17.   I can look anyone in the eye and tell a lie with a straight face (if for a right end).

T   F   18.   I may deceive people by being friendly when I really dislike them.

Please see next page to determine your style.

_____

SOURCE: Snyder, Mark and Steve Gangestad. 1986 "On the Nature of Self Monitoring." *Journal of Personality and Social Psychology*, 51(1). Copyright © 1986 by the American Psychological Association. Reprinted with permission.

(continued)

Box 2-6 (*cont.*)

Self-Monitoring: Interpretation of Responses

Circled responses indicate high self-monitoring responses. If you have eleven or more responses that match those circled below, this indicates you may have a high self-monitoring orientation. If you have ten or fewer responses that match those circled below, this indicates you may have a low self-monitoring orientation. Remember that one style (low or high self-monitoring) is not generally better than the other. Each style has benefits and costs.

T (F)   1. I find it hard to imitate the behavior of other people.

T (F)   2. At parties and social gatherings, I do not attempt to do or say things that others will like.

T (F)   3. I can only argue for ideas which I already believe.

(T) F   4. I can make impromptu speeches even on topics about which I have almost no information.

(T) F   5. I guess I put on a show to impress or entertain others.

(T) F   6. I would probably make a good actor.

T (F)   7. In a group of people, I am rarely the center of attention.

(T) F   8. In different situations and with different people, I often act like very different persons.

T (F)   9. I am not particularly good at making other people like me.

(T) F   10. I am not always the person I appear to be.

T (F)   11. I would not change my opinions (or the way I do things) in order to please someone.

(T) F   12. I have considered being an entertainer.

T (F)   13. I have never been good at games like charades or improvisational acting.

T (F)   14. I have trouble changing my behavior to suit different people and different situations.

T (F)   15. At a party, I let others keep the jokes and stories going.

T (F)   16. I feel a bit awkward in public and do not show up quite as well as I should.

(T) F   17. I can look anyone in the eye and tell a lie with a straight face (if for a right end).

(T) F   18. I may deceive people by being friendly when I really dislike them.

ENDNOTES

1. Church, Allan. 1997. "Managerial Self-Awareness in High-Performing Individuals in Organizations." *Journal of Applied Psychology*, 82(2): 281–292; Ashford, Susan, and Ann Tsui. 1991. "Self-Regulation for Managerial Effectiveness: The Role of Active Feedback Seeking." *Academy of Management Journal*, 34, 251–280.

2. Kiechel. 1989. "How to Spot an Empty Suit." *Fortune.* November 20: 22.

3. Ibid., p. 23.

4. Kaplan, Robert, Wilfred Drath, and Joan Kofodimos. 1991. *Beyond Ambition: How Driven Managers Can Lead Better and Live Longer*. San Francisco, CA: Jossey-Bass Publishers.

5. Kofodimos, Joan. 1993. *Balancing Act: How Managers Can Integrate Successful Careers and Fulfilling Personal Lives*. San Francisco, CA: Jossey-Bass Publishers.

6. Argyris, Chris. 1991. "Teaching Smart People How to Learn." *Harvard Business Review*, 69(3): 99–110.

7. Kaplan, Robert, Wilfred Drath, and Joan Kofodimos. 1985. *High Hurdles: The Challenge of Executive Self-Development* (Technical Report No. 125). Greensboro, NC: Center for Creative Leadership.

8. Ibid.

9. Hochschild, Arlie Russell. 1997. *The Time Bind: When Work Becomes Home and Home Becomes Work*. New York: Holt and Company.

10. Reuter, Anne. 2004. "Professor Puzzles Over Why Some Grow and Some Falter," citing Neal Krause. *Ann Arbor News*, pp. E1–E2.

11. Smith, Lee. 1993. "The Executive's New Coach." *Fortune.* December 27: 126.

12. Bridges, William. 1997. *Creating You & Co.: Learn How to Think Like the CEO of Your Own Career*, Reading, MA: Addison-Wesley Longman; MA; Peters, Tom. 1997. "The Brand Called You." *Fast Company. August/September.*)

13. Peters, Tom. 1997. "The Brand Called You." *Fast Company.* August/September: 84.

14. Fisher, Ann. 2004. "Show Off, without Being a Blowhard." *Fortune.* March.

15. Johnston, Timothy, and Laura Edwards. 2002. "Genes, Interactions, and the Development of Behavior." *Psychological Review,* 109(1): 26–34; Olson, James, Philip A. Vernon, Julie Aitken Harris, and Kerry L. Jang. 2001. "The Heritability of Attitudes: A Study of Twins." *Journal of Personality and Social Psychology,* 80(6): 845–860; Borkenau, Peter, Rainer Miemann, Alois Angletner, and Frank M. Spinath. 2001. "Genetic and Environmental Influences on Observed Personality: Evidence from German Observational Study of Adult Twins." *Journal of Personality and Social Psychology,* 80(4):655–668; Dickens, William, and James R. Flynn. 2001. "Heritability Estimates Versus Large Environmental Effects: The IQ Paradox Resolved." *Psychological Review,* 108(2).

16. Hollister, Anne, and George H. Colt. 1998. "Were You Born That Way?" *Life Magazine.* April: 39–50.

17. Athos, Anthony, and John Gabarro. 1978. *Interpersonal Behavior: Communication and Understanding in Relationships.* Upper Saddle River, NJ: Prentice Hall, 4.

18. Markus, Hazel, and Paula Nurius. 1986. "Possible Selves." *American Psychologist,* 41: 954–969.

19. Kitayama, Shinobu, Hisaya Matsumoto, Hazel Rose Markus, and Vinai Norasakkunkit. 1997. "Individual and Collective Processes in the Construction of the Self: Self-Enhancement in the United States and Self-Criticism in Japan." *Journal of Personality and Social Psychology,* 72(6): 1245.

20. Sedikides, Constantine, Lowell Gaertner, and Yoshiyasu Togushi. 2003. "Pancultural Self-Enhancement." *Journal of Personality and Social Psychology,* 84(1): 60–79.

21. Tillich, Paul. 1952. *The Courage to Be*. New Haven, CT: Yale University Press: Berg, David, and Kenwyn Smith. 1997. *Paradoxes of Group Life*. New Lexington 1977.

22. Oyserman, Daphna, Heather Coon, and Markus Kemmelmeier. 2002. "Rethinking Individual and Collectivism: Evaluation of Theoretical Assumptions and Meta-Analysis." *Pyschological Bulletin*, 128(1): 3–72; Fiske, Alan Page. 2002. "Using Individualism and Collectivism to Compare Cultures—A Critique of the Validity and Measurement of the Constructs: Comment on Oyserman et al." *Psychological Bulletin*, 128(1): 78–88.

23. Sedikides, Constantine, Lowell Gaertner, and Yoshiyasu Togushi. 2003. "Pancultural Self-Enhancement." *Journal of Personality and Social Psychology*, 84(1): 60–79.

24. Spence, Janet T. 1985. "Achievement American Style: The Rewards and Costs of Individualism." *American Psychologist*, 40(12): 1285–1295.

25. Triandis, Harry C. 1989. "The Self and Social Behavior in Differing Cultural Contexts." *Psychological Review*, 96: 507.

26. Ibid.

27. Iyengar, Sheena, and Mark R. Lepper. 1999. "Rethinking the Value of Choice: A Cultural Perspective on Intrinsic Motivation." *Journal of Personality and Social Psychology*, 76(3): 349–366.

28. Sedikides, Constantine, Lowell Gaertner, and Yoshiyasu Togushi. 2003. "Pancultural Self-Enhancement." *Journal of Personality and Social Psychology*, 84(1): 60–79.

29. Marks, Gary. 1984. "Thinking One's Abilities Are Unique and One's Opinions Are Common." *Personality and Social Psychology Bulletin*, 10(2): 203–208.

30. Kitayama, Shinobu, Hisaya Matsumoto, Hazel Rose Markus, and Vinai Norasakkunkit. 1997. "Individual and Collective Processes in the Construction of the Self: Self-Enhancement in the United States and Self-Criticism in Japan." *Journal of Personality and Social Psychology*, 72(6): 1246.

31. Kim, Heejung S. 2002. "We Talk, Therefore We Think? A Cultural Analysis of the Effect of Talking on Thinking." *Journal of Personality and Social Psychology*, 83(4): 828–842.

32. Triandis, Harry C. 1989. "The Self and Social Behavior in Differing Cultural Contexts." *Psychological Review*, 96: 510.

33. Markus, Hazel, and Shinobu Kityama. 1991b. "Culture and the Self: Implications for Cognition, Emotion, and Motivation." *Psychological Review*, 98: 224–253.

34. Triandis, Harry C. 1989. "The Self and Social Behavior in Differing Cultural Contexts." *Psychological Review*, 96: 507.

35. Sedikides, Constantine, Lowell Gaertner, and Yoshiyasu Togushi. 2003. "Pancultural Self-Enhancement." *Journal of Personality and Social Psychology*, 84(1): 60–79.

36. Kitayama, Shinobu, Hisaya Matsumoto, Hazel Rose Markus, and Vinai Norasakkunkit. 1997. "Individual and Collective Processes in the Construction of the Self: Self-Enhancement in the United States and Self-Criticism in Japan." *Journal of Personality and Social Psychology*, 72(6): 72.

37. Ibid.

38. Markus, Hazel Rose, and Shinobu Kitayama. 1991b. "Culture and the Self: Implications for Cognition, Emotion, and Motivation." *Psychological Review*, 98(2): 224.

39. Hofstede, Geert. 1984. *Culture's Consequences: International Differences in Work-Related Values*. Newbury Park, CA: Sage Publications.

40. Klidas, Antonios. October 31-November 2, 2002. "The Cultural Relativity of Employee Empowerment: Findings From the European Hotel Industry." The Netherlands: Institute for Research on Intercultural Cooperation.

41. Gilligan, Carol. 1982. *In a Different Voice*. Cambridge: University Press.

42. Weick, Karl. 1996. *Sensemaking in Organizations*. Thousand Oaks, CA: Sage Publications, 23.

43. 2001. "Personal Histories: Leaders Remember the Moments and People Who Shaped Them." *Harvard Business Review*, 34: 27–38.

44. Ibid.

45. 2004. Brady, Diane. Act II *BusinessWeek*, 72–82.

46. Brooke, Jill. 2001. "Grief and Greatness." *Forbes* 182–186.

47. Ibid.

48. 2004. Brady, Diane. Act II, *BusinessWeek*, 72–82.

49. Sulloway, Frank J. 1996. *Born to Rebel: Birth Order, Family Dynamics, and Creative Lives*. New York: Pantheon Books.

50. Ibid., xiii.

51. Rosenthal, Robert, and Lenore Jackson. 1968 and 1992. *Pygmalion in the Classroom: Teacher Expectations and Pupils' Intellectual Development.* New York: Irvington Publishers, vii–viii.

52. Alderfer, Clayton. 1983. "Intergroup Relations and Organizations." In J. Richard Hackman, Edward W. Lawler, and Lyman W. Porter (eds.). *Perspectives on Behavior in Organizations.* 408–416.

53. Harquail, Celia Virginia Felicia. 1996. "When One Speaks for Many: The Influence of Social Identification on Group Advocacy in Organizations." Unpublished dissertation. Ann Arbor, MI: University of Michigan, 29.

54. Ibid.

55. Markus, Hazel, and E. Wurf. 1989. "The Dynamic Self-Concept: A Social Psychological Perspective." *Annual Review of Psychology,* 38: 307–308.

56. Markus, Hazel, and E. Wurf. 1989. "The Dynamic Self-Concept: A Social Psychological Perspective." *Annual Review of Psychology,* 38: 299–337; Weick, Karl E. 1995. *Sensemaking in Organizations.* Thousand Oaks, CA: Sage; Fiske, Susan T., and Shelley E. Taylor. 1991. *Social Cognition*, 2nd ed. New York: McGraw-Hill.

57. Weick, Karl E. 1996. *Sensemaking in Organizations.* Thousand Oaks, CA: Sage.

58. Druian, P., and R. Catrambone. 1966. "Cognitive Accessibility of the Self Concept in Person Perception." Behavioral Science Research Foundation. Unpublished.

59. Harquail, Celia Virginia Felicia. 1996. "When One Speaks for Many: The Influence of Social Identification on Group Advocacy in Organizations." Unpublished dissertation, Ann Arbor: University of Michigan, 270.

60. Gilligan, Carol. 1992. *In a Different Voice.* Cambridge, MA: Cambridge University Press.

61. Weick, Karl E. 1995. *Sensemaking in Organizations.* Thousand Oaks, CA: Sage.

62. Albert, Stuart, Blake Ashforth, and Jane Dutton. 2002 "Organizational Identity and Identification: Charting New Waters and Building New Bridges." *Academy of Management Review,* 25(1): 13–18; Frankl, Viktor. 1959. "Man's Search for Meaning. New York: Simon and Schuster.

63. Baumeister, Roy, and Mark Leary. 1995. "The Need to Belong: Desire for Interpersonal Attachments as a Fundamental Human Motivation." *Psychological Bulletin,* 117(3): 497.

64. Bowlby, John. 1988. *A Secure Base: Parent-Child Attachment and Healthy Human Development*. New York: Basic Books, 11.

65. Bandura, Alfred. 1986. *Social Foundations of Thoughts and Action: A Social Cognitive Theory*. Upper Saddle River, NJ: Prentice Hall.

66. Ashforth, Blake, and Alan M. Saks. 2000. "Personal Control in Organizatons: A Longitudinal Investigation with Newcomers." *Human Relations,* 53(3): 311–339; Bandura, A. 1995. *Self-Efficacy in Changing Societies*. New York: Cambridge University Press; Krause, Neal, and Benjamin Shaw. 2000. "Role-Specific Feelings of Control and Mortality." *Psychology and Aging,* 15(4): 617–626.

67. Feldman, Martha, and Anat Rafaeli. 2002. "Organizational Routines as Sources of Connections and Understandings." *Journal of Management Studies*, 39(3): 309–329; Kelvin, Peter. 1977. "Predictability, Power and Vulnerability in Interpersonal Attraction." In Duck, Steven (ed.). *Theory and Practice in Interpersonal Attraction*, London: Academic Press, 355–378.

68. Frankl, Viktor E. 1984. *Man's Search for Meaning: An Introduction to Logotherapy,* 3rd ed. (originally published in 1959). New York: Simon and Schuster, 88.

69. Gergen, Kenneth. 1991. *The Saturated Self, Dilemmas of Identity in Contemporary Life*. New York: Basic Books.

70. Ibid.

71. Judge, Paul. 1997. "Is the Net Redefining Our Identity?" *Business Week.* May 12: 100–102.

72. Turkle, Sherry. 1995. *Life on the Screen: Identity in the Age of the Internet.* New York: Simon and Schuster, 51.

73. Delaney, Kevin. "Play it Again: Sims Game is Hard to Trump." *Wall Street Journal.* B1 and B4.

74. Subrahmanyam, Kaveri, Robert E. Kraut, Patricia M. Greenfield, and Elisheva F. Gross. 2000. "The Impact of Home Computer Use on Children's Activities and Development." http://www.futureofchildren.org 10(2).

75. Turkle, Sherry. 1995. *Life on the Screen: Identity in the Age of the Internet.* New York: Simon and Schuster.

76. Taylor, Jim, and Watts Wacker with Howard Means. 1997. *The 500 Year Delta: What Happens after What Comes Next.* New York: HarperBusiness. 1997.

77. Festinger, Leon. 1954. "A Theory of Social Comparison Processes." *Human Relations,* 7: 117–140.

78. Cooley, C. H. 1956. *Human Nature and the Social Order.* New York: Free Press.

79. Lockwood, Penelope, and Ziva Kunda. 1997. "Superstars and Me: Predicting the Impact of Role Models on the Self." *Journal of Personality and Social Psychology,* 73(1): 93.

80. Markus, Hazel, and Paula Nurius. 1986. "Possible Selves." *American Psychologist,* 41: 954, 965–966.

81. Ibid.

82. 1997. "Perspectives." *Newsweek* October 13: p. 27.

83. Shapiro, Eileen. 1995. *Fad Surfing in the Boardroom: Reclaiming the Courage to Manage in the Age of Instant Answers.* Reading, MA: Addison-Wesley.

84. Jackson, Bradley. 1996. "Reengineering the Sense of Self: The Manager and the Management Guru." *Journal of Management Studies,* 33(5): 571–590.

85. Ibid., p. 572.

86. Ibid.

87. Taylor, Jim, and Watts Wacker with Howard Means. 1997. *The 500 Year Delta: What Happens after What Comes Next.* New York: HarperBusiness.

88. Gergen, Kenneth. 1991. *The Saturated Self, Dilemmas of Identity in Contemporary Life.* New York: Basic Books, 34.

89. Doan, Robert E. 1997. "Narrative Therapy, Postmodernism, Social Constructionism, and Constructivism: Discussion and Distinctions." *Transactional Analysis Journal: Special Theme Issue on Transactional Analysis and Constructivism,* 27(2): 128.

90. Anderson, Walter Truett. 1997. *The Future of the Self: Exploring the Post-Identity Society.* New York: Tarcher Putnam, xvi.

91. Dougherty, Deborah, and Cynthia Hardy. 1996. "Sustained Product Innovation in Large, Mature Organizations: Overcoming Innovation-to-Organization Problems." *Academy of Management Journal,* 30(5): 1120–1153.

92. Turkle, Sherry. 1995. *Life on the Screen: Identity in the Age of the Internet.* New York: Simon and Schuster, 51.

93. Weick, Karl E. 1993b. "The Collapse of Sense-making in Organizations: The Mann Gulch Disaster." *Administrative Science Quarterly,* 38: 628–652.

94. Smircich, Linda, and Gareth Morgan. 1982. "Leadership: The Management of Meaning." *Journal of Applied Behavioral Science,* 18(3): 258.

95. Ibid., p. 260.

96. Knight, M., and Robert Doan. 1994. *The Stories We Tell Ourselves: I-Spi: A Technique for Narrative Assessment.* Orlando, FL: Harcourt Brace.

97. Doan, Robert E. 1997. "Narrative Therapy, Postmodernism, Social Constructionism, and Constructivism: Discussion and Distinctions." *Transactional Analysis Journal: Special Theme Issue on Transactional Analysis and Constructivism,* 27(2): 131.

98. Ibid., p. 129.

99. Goffman, Erving. 1959. *The Presentation of Self in Everyday Life,* New York: Anchor Books; Andrzej Nowak, Robin Vallacher, Abraham Tesser, and Wojceich Borkowski. 2000. "Society of Self: The Emergence of Collective Properties of Self-Structure." *Psychological Review,* 107(1): 39–61.

100. Hurtado, Aida. 1996. "Strategic Suspensions: Feminists of Color Theorize

the Production of Knowledge." In Nancy Goldberg, Blythe Clinchy, Mary Belenky, and Jill Mattuck Tarule (eds.). *Knowledge, Difference and Power.* New York, New York, 384.

101. Bell, Ella. 1990. "The Bicultural Life Experiences of Career-Oriented Black Women." *Journal of Organizational Behavior,* 11: 459–477; Brannen, Mary Yoko. 2000. Your Next Boss is Japanese: Recontextualization, Negotiated Culture, and Organizational Change. New York: Oxford University Press.

102. Hurtado, Aida. 1996. "Strategic Suspensions: Feminists of Color Theorize the Production of Knowledge." In Nancy Goldberg, Blythe Clinchy, Mary Belenky, and Jill Mattuck Tarule (eds.). *Knowledge, Difference and Power.* New York, New York.

103. Settles, Iris, Robert Sellers, and Alphonse Damas, Jr. 2002. "One Role or Two? The Function of Psychological Separation in Role Conflict." *Journal of Applied Psychology,* 87(3): 574–582.

104. Ibid.

105. Ibid., p. 387.

106. Beyer, Janice, and David R. Hannah. 2002. "Building on the Past: Enacting Established Personal Identities in a New Work Setting." *Organization Science,* 13(6): 636–652; Ruderman, Marian, Ohlott, Patricia; Kate Panzer, and Sara King. 2002. "Benefits of Multiple Roles for Managerial Women." *Academy of Management Journal,* 45(2): 369–386; Settles, Iris, Robert Sellers, and Alphonse Damas, Jr. 2002. "One Role or Two? The Function of Psychological Separation in Role Conflict." *Journal of Applied Psychology,* 87(3): 574–582, 57; Rothbard, Nancy. 2001. "Enriching or Depleting? The Dynamics of Engagement in Work and Family Roles." *Administrative Science Quarterly,* 46(4): 655–685; Ibarra, Herminia. 2003. *Working Identity: Unconventional Strategies for Reinventing Your Career.* Boston: Harvard Business School Press, 35; Moen, Phyllis, Donna Dempster-McClain, and Robin M. Williams Jr. 1992. "Successful Aging: A Life Course Perspective on Women's Multiple Roles and Health." *American Journal of Sociology*, 97(6): 1612–1638.

107. Rothbard, Nancy. 2001. "Enriching or Depleting? The Dynamics of Engagement in Work and Family Roles." *Administrative Science Quarterly,* 46(4): 655–685.

108. Beyer, Janice, and David R. Hannah. 2002. "Building on the Past: Enacting Established Personal Identities in a New Work Setting." *Organization Science,* 13(6): 636–652.

109. Ruderman, Marian, Patricia Ohlott, Kate Panzer, and Sara King. 2002. "Benefits of Multiple Roles for Managerial Women." *Academy of Management Journal,* 45(2): 369–386.

110. Rothbard, Nancy. 2001. "Enriching or Depleting? The Dynamics of Engagement in Work and Family Roles." *Administrative Science Quarterly,* 46(4): 655–685.

111. Ibarra, Herminia. 1999. "Provisional Selves: Experimenting with Image and Identity in Professional Adaptation." *Administrative Science Quarterly,* 1999: 764–791.

112. Hill, Linda. 1992. *Becoming a Manager: Mastery of a New Identity.* Boston: Harvard Business School Press, 173–174. Cited in Ibarra, Herminia. 1999. "Provisional Selves: Experimenting with Image and Identity in Professional Adaptation." *Administrative Science Quarterly,* December: 764–791.

113. Ibarra, Herminia. 2003. *Working Identity: Unconventional Strategies for Reinventing Your Career.* Boston: Harvard Business School Press, 35.

114. Breen, Bill. 2003. "Desire, Connecting with What Customers Want." *Fast Company*, 86–89.

115. Blustein, David L. 1994. "Social Cognitive Orientations and Career Development: A Theoretical and Empirical Analysis." *Journal of Vocational Behavior,* 31: 63–80. Cited in Martin Kilduff and David Day. 1994. "Do Chameleons Get Ahead? The Effects of Self-Monitoring on Managerial Careers." *Academy of Management Journal,* 37(4): 1047–1060.

116. Snyder, Mark, and S. Gangestad. 1982. "Choosing Social Situations: Two Investigations of Self-Monitoring Processes." *Journal of Personality and Social Psychology,* 43: 123–135. Cited in

Martin Kilduff and David Day. 1994. "Do Chameleons Get Ahead? The Effects of Self-Monitoring on Managerial Careers." *Academy of Management Journal,* 37(4): 1047–1060.

117. Ibid.

118. Gangestad, Steven, and Mark Snyder. 2000. "Self-Monitoring: Appraisal and Reappraisal." *Psychological Bulletin,* 126(4); Snyder, Mark. 1987. Public Appearances, Private Realities: The Psychology of Self-Monitoring. New York: W. H. Freeman & Co.

119. Snyder, Mark. 1979. "Self-Monitoring Processes." In L. Berkowitz (ed.). *Advances in Experimental Social Psychology,* Vol. 12, New York: Academic Press, 35–128. Cited in Martin Kilduff and David Day. 1994. "Do Chameleons Get Ahead? The Effects of Self-Monitoring on Managerial Careers." *Academy of Management Journal,* 37(4): 1047–1060.

120. Mehra, Ajay, Martin Killduff, and Daniel J. Brass. 2001. "The Social Networks of High and Low Self-Monitors: Implications for Workplace Performance." *Administrative Science Quarterly*, 46: 121–146; Gangestad, Steven, and Mark Snyder. 2000. "Self-Monitoring: Appraisal and Reappraisal." *Psychological Bulletin,* 126(4).

121. Snyder, Mark, and J. Copeland. 1989. "Self-Monitoring Effects in Organizational Settings." In R. A. Giacoalone and P. Rosenfeld (eds.). *Impression Management in the Organization.* Hillsdale, NJ: Erlbaum, 16. Cited in Martin Kilduff and David Day. 1994. "Do Chameleons Get Ahead? The Effects of Self-Monitoring on Managerial Careers" *Academy of Management Journal,* 37(4): 1047–1060.

122. Mark Snyder. 1987. 68–69. Cited in Martin Kilduff and Daniel Day. 1994. 1049; Snyder, Mark. 1987. *Public Appearances/Private Realities: The Psychology of Self-Monitoring.* San Francisco: Freeman, 68–69. Cited in Martin Kilduff and David Day. 1994. "Do Chameleon's Get Ahead? The Effects of Self-Monitoring on Managerial Careers." *Academy of Management Journal,* 37(4): 1049.

123. Kilduff, Martin. "The Friendship Network as a Decision-Making Resource: Dispositional Moderators of Social Influences on Organizational Choice." *Journal of Personality and Social Psychology,* 62: 168–180.

124. Nathan, John. 1999. *Sony: The Private Life.* Boston: Houghton-Mifflin.

125. Knowles, Malcolm. 1990. *The Adult Learner: A Neglected Species,* 4th ed. Houston, TX: Gulf Publishing.

-------------------------V I D E O   C A S E-------------------------

Case 1   Self-Awareness

Sweeping changes in our social and economic environment have fundamentally changed the nature of work, and of managing in particular. It is the job of every manager today to take a serious look at the new social, economic, and cultural context in which we live and work and to determine how these changing environments affect the nature of the job and the skills needed to thrive both professionally and personally in this environment.

The postmodern manager, operating in today's rapidly evolving world, must achieve a sense of control in situations that are too complex to fully understand, defy prediction, and constantly change. Challenging and intimidating at once, this new world forces us to find meaning amid confusion, reach across organizational and cultural boundaries that have traditionally divided us, and maintain our humanity in a world that is increasingly, and irrevocably, high tech. The postmodern manager clearly needs a more sophisticated way to understand him- or herself, and to continually reinvent the role of the manager.

Although diversity, globalization, and technology have transformed the organizations in which we work, one thing has not changed and will never change: Managers today—and in the future—will always get their work done with and through others, making the quality of relationships with others of primary importance. Effective relationship skills begin with self-awareness and a continuing effort to seek honest feedback about personal strengths and weaknesses. This effort to achieve self-awareness and to understand how we are perceived by others is what helps us make the most of our strengths, target weaknesses we can correct, and learn from our past successes and failures to build a better future for others, the organization, and ourselves.

In this video segment, Mia Cipirano, founder of a Web site for working women called allaboutself.com, confronts the fact that her bank is considering withholding the financing Mia needs to expand the business through new marketing efforts. Joe, the bank's representative, suggests that Mia needs to show the site is holding its own before the bank will invest more money in it. In response to his suggestion that she needs to find out more about how well the site is doing, Mia believes that she can take one of two actions: quiz some friends who visit the site or hire an outside consultant to evaluate it. ■

DISCUSSION QUESTIONS

1. Do you think Mia is aware of her strengths and weaknesses, as well as how she is perceived by others?
2. Do you think Mia is a high or low self-monitor? Why?
3. How do you think her self-monitoring style influences her effectiveness?
4. Do you think Mia has the skills of a postmodern manager? Why or why not?
5. What kinds of information and links would you include in allaboutself.com

to appeal to today's working woman? Would you recommend that Mia take the advice of Melinda Davis of the Next Group who suggests that marketers think of each of their customers and potential customers as having several different selves? If so, how would you integrate this idea into the Web site?
6. Would you want to work for Mia? Why or why not?

CHAPTER

3

Building Trust

This chapter will help you:

■ Understand how trust contributes to individual and organizational effectiveness

■ Develop a working definition of trust

■ Learn how to build trust

■ Learn how to repair trust once broken

■ Learn how to create "swift trust" when needed

■ Learn how positive emotions and behaviors build trust and enhance personal and organizational effectiveness

> *The importance of trust becomes clear when we try to imagine a world without it.*
>
> —ROBERT BRUCE SHAW
> *Author of Trust in the Balance*

WHY TRUST MATTERS

> In the office in which I work there are five people of whom I am afraid. Each of these five people is afraid of four people (excluding overlaps), for a total of twenty, and each of these twenty people is afraid of six people, making a total of one hundred and twenty people who are feared by at least one person. Each of these one hundred and twenty people is afraid of the other one hundred and nineteen, and all of these one hundred and forty-five people are afraid of the twelve men at the top who helped found and build the company and now own and direct it.[1]

So begins the chapter "The Office in Which I Work" in Joseph Heller's classic book, *Something Happened.* I begin this chapter with Heller's words not because they necessarily reflect everyday work life today (although they do for some people and ring true, at least in part, for many others). Rather, I begin this chapter with Heller's words because they illustrate the fundamental importance of trust in our lives.

Why is trust so important to human beings? We need trust because we must live in a complex world that we cannot fully understand, depend on people whom we can never completely know, and rely on organizations that do not exist for the sole purpose of meeting our personal needs. Therefore, we must rely on trust—essentially a leap of faith—that "some things will remain as they are or ought to be,"[2] that other people will not take unfair advantage of us,[3] and that we will not be harmed by the organizations in which we invest our future. In short, trust helps us face the inevitable risks of everyday life so that we can rise above our fears, take productive action, and experience tranquillity and happiness in a complex, unpredictable, and sometimes threatening world.

Despite the importance of trust in everyday work life, many managers see it as a luxury rather than a necessity. In her study of new managers, Harvard professor Linda Hill found that "most new managers put their efforts into demonstrating their technical competence" rather than building trust. One of the managers in her study explained:

> The first thirty days were critical . . . I had to demonstrate that I had ability. I kept looking for a big win, picking the right stock, stealing a big producer from the competition. I had to demonstrate that I worked hard. I stayed late and came in on weekends. It was hard to get relief from the pressure of it all.

However, Hill found that employees "were making judgments using a different set of standards. They wanted to find out if the new manager deserved their trust and respect. Staff members were clearly sizing up the new boss—and their criteria weren't always fair." By emphasizing their technical competence and ignoring trust-building activities, managers often "missed opportunities for building goodwill among their subordinates, just when they needed it most."[4]

Bosses also make judgments about the trustworthiness of the managers who work for them. In a study of middle- and upper-level executives, researchers found that executives who derailed were viewed by their managers as less trustworthy and as having less integrity than were their more successful peers. What criteria did these bosses use to determine trustworthiness? The bosses focused on whether the manager blamed others or took personal responsibility for mistakes, put personal desires over organizational needs, and denied or admitted personal shortcomings.[5]

It is not surprising that managers who inspire trust—both in themselves and in the organization—tend to have better job performance, have more committed employees, have stronger networks, get more challenging job assignments, and get promoted more often than those who don't inspire trust.[6] Specifically, they are better able to:

- Attract and retain followers because employees prefer to work with people who they believe are trustworthy.
- Promote a sense of belonging because employees are more likely to identify with organizational goals and values, invest psychologically in their jobs, and feel pride, loyalty, and affection toward their managers and organizations.[7]
- Build support for their goals because employees who trust their managers are less likely to question managers' competence, goodwill, direction, and intentions.[8]

- Develop more productive employees because people in trusting relationships tend to exhibit increased emotional stability, self-control, creativity, and flexibility as well as less stress and defensiveness.[9]
- Inspire employees to go "beyond the call of duty" and contribute to the organization in ways that add value but that are not in their job descriptions.[10]
- Enhance the quality of customer service because employees who trust their managers are more likely to engage in the kinds of helping behaviors that result in high-quality service.[11]
- Focus on value-added work because they do not need costly employee control systems that can consume both managers' and employees' time, distract them from focusing on fundamental work objectives,[12] and reduce innovation and cooperation.[13]
- Enhance communication because employees are more likely to speak openly and honestly, listen carefully, and give bad news upward if they trust the boss.[14]
- Increase the "speed and efficiency in the creation and transfer of knowledge" because employees are more willing to cooperate with each other in the sharing of information.[15]
- Reduce conflict and the costs of negotiation because employees are more likely to give each other the benefit of the doubt and be open-minded, flexible, and willing to be influenced by each other.[16]
- Have more effective group decision-making processes because group members feel free to focus on organizational tasks and goals rather than defend themselves from what they perceive to be threatening. Some researchers have concluded that members of low-trust groups are more likely to have difficulty concentrating on their tasks; are more likely to engage in self-protecting and low-risk behaviors; have more difficulty dealing with uncertainty; are less able to accurately interpret the words, motives, values, and emotions of others; are less likely to accept each other's ideas; and are less likely to support and implement the ideas of their leaders.[17]
- Promote organizational change because employees are more likely to feel secure, be flexible, take risks, and cope productively with complexity, ambiguity, and uncertainty.[18]
- Collaborate more across organizational boundaries.[19]
- Survive organizational crises because they are more likely to receive undistorted information from employees, enable decentralized decision making that allows employees to react quickly to crises, and encourage collaboration with and across organizations affected by the crisis.[20]
- Help employees accept unfavorable information and decisions that adversely affect them because employees who trust their managers are more likely to assume that their managers did the best that they could under the circumstances, were fair in their decision-making process, and will do whatever it takes to turn the situation around. The more unfavorable and unexpected the situation, the more important trust becomes.[21] For example, researchers Aneil Mishra and Gretchen Spreitzer found that employees who trust their organizations are more likely to cope effectively during downsizings.[22]

For all of these reasons, trust has been called a "social lubricant,"[23] "invisible asset,"[24] "collaborative capital,"[25] "hidden source of wealth,"[26] and the "heart of relationships."[27]

Rather than being a nice-to-have luxury, trust in organizations is increasingly being viewed as a source of competitive advantage. This is because high-quality relationships—those built on trust—provide economic value to the organization, take a long time to develop, and cannot be easily copied by other organizations.[28]

For example, at this writing, Southwest Airlines ranks among the most successful airlines today. The company has consistently been on *Fortune* magazine's annual lists of the ten most admired companies, and the company's stock has been among the best performing stocks for decades. The success of the company has been attributed in large part to founder and former CEO Herb Kelleher's outstanding "people skills" and his ability to build trust among employees and customers.[29] When asked about the secrets to the company's success, describing the company's success, Herb Kelleher explained:

> The intangibles are more important than the tangibles. Someone can go out and buy airplanes from Boeing and ticket counters, but they can't buy our culture, our esprit de corps. We've had people come in to see how we turn around planes. (Southwest's time to get planes in and out of gates is about half the industry average.) They keep looking for gimmicks, special equipment. It's just a bunch of people knocking themselves out.[30]

Herb Kelleher stepped down from his position as CEO of Southwest Airlines in 2001. Time will tell if the new leadership will be able to maintain Southwest Airlines' unique culture.

A *Fortune* magazine article explains how recent scandals have increased the importance of trust in organizations: "Thanks to the Enron implosion and the subsequent rash of accounting and corporate governance scandals, the credibility of any organization is no longer assumed. It must be earned. It's not enough to have a great brand, dazzling returns, and a charming CEO. Now more than ever, trust is the sine qua non of reputation."[31] Yet research suggests that organizations have a long way to go toward building trust. Walker Information Global Network and the Hudson Institute recently conducted a study of more than 9,700 employees in 32 countries and found that "only 34% of worldwide employees are truly loyal to their organizations." Based on employee responses, the researchers concluded that "fairness at work, care and concern for employees, and trust in employees are the three areas that neeed the greatest attention from employers worldwide."[32]

Trust is a particularly important competitive advantage for companies that try to sell products and services on-line. An article in *Marketing Management* magazine cites several studies that highlight the importance of building trust on-line and concludes that "Web users will become buyers only when marketers overcome the lack of trust that paralyzes would-be shoppers."[33]

WHAT IS TRUST?

Researchers John Cook and Toby Wall define trust as "a willingness to ascribe good intentions to and have confidence in the words and actions of other people."[34] This willingness will, in turn, affect the way in which one behaves toward others. Three characteristics are fundamental to our understanding of trust: uncertainty, risk, and perceptions.

Uncertainty

We need to depend on trust—a leap of faith—only if we do not have all information about a person or situation and if we cannot completely control the outcome. If we have complete knowledge and control of a situation, we have no need to trust because we can anticipate and ensure the outcome that we desire. For example, if we are willing and able to monitor all aspects of an employee's work-related behavior (e.g., through videotaping, electronically counting computer keystrokes, or monitoring phone calls), then we do not need to rely on trust to ensure that the employees are doing their jobs. However, if we choose to delegate or create self-managing teams, then we must trust that employees are focusing on their tasks and working together toward organizational goals.

Risk

When we trust a person or organization, we assume that the benefits of our relationship with them will outweigh any costs to us. Indeed, trust is only necessary if the costs of a loss will be greater than the possible gain.[35] To illustrate this point, researcher Dale Zand provides this fine example:

> [A] parent is exhibiting trusting behavior in hiring a baby-sitter so he can see a movie. The action significantly increases his vulnerability, because he cannot control the baby-sitter's behavior after leaving the house. If the baby-sitter abuses that vulnerability, the penalty may be a tragedy that may adversely affect the rest of his life; if the baby-sitter does not abuse that vulnerability, the benefit will be the pleasure of seeing a movie.[36]

Thus, when we decide to give our boss bad news, we trust that our boss will not kill the messenger. When we give employees confidential organizational information that enables them to make appropriate decisions quickly, we trust that they will not give this information to our organization's competitors.

Perception

Trust is necessary in situations in which we do not have complete information about another person's intentions. Therefore, our trust in someone is based in large part on our perceptions of that person's trustworthiness. We base our perceptions of a person's trustworthiness on several factors, including the person's reputation,[37] our prior experiences with the person,[38] and our stereotypes about that person's identity group memberships (such as gender, race, religion, and nationality)[39] and organizational group memberships (such as department or hierarchical level).[40] Massachusetts Institute of Technology Researcher Michele Williams notes that we are more likely to believe someone is trustworthy and cooperate with them when we see them as belonging to the same group(s) that we do. Furthermore, we are more likely to rely on stereotypes when we are under time pressure.[41]

The importance of perception in the development of trust and mistrust cannot be overstated because our perceptions often turn into self-fulfilling prophecies. Researcher Sandra Robinson explains that we tend to look for and focus on information that confirms our prior perceptions about a person's trustworthiness and ignore or minimize information that disconfirms our prior perceptions. Consequently, when we mistrust someone, we are "more likely to look for, find, and remember incidents of breach, even in the absence of an objective breach" because it is consistent with our prior perceptions.[42] We are also less likely to invest emotionally in the relationship because we may doubt that there will be a payoff for our investment. Consequently, the relationship is likely to be characterized by avoidance, conflict, or a "veneer of civility," each of which can increase mutual mistrust.[43] In contrast, when we trust someone, we are "more likely to overlook, forget, or not recognize an actual breach when it does occur" and invest more emotionally in the relationship. Trust, it seems, is a cognitive and emotional "filter" that influences our interpretations of another person's behavior, as well as our expectations of how we believe the person will act in the future.[44]

In short, if we have complete information about a person or organization, if we can completely control a situation, if we can perfectly predict an outcome, and if we have nothing or little to lose, then trust is not necessary. However, such situations are rare—perhaps nonexistent—in our everyday work life, so the ability to trust and to be trustworthy is essential to managerial effectiveness. The antecedents and consequences of trusts are described in more detail on the following pages and are summarized in Figure 3-1.

WHY SHOULD I TRUST THEE? LET ME COUNT THE REASONS

If trust is based on our willingness to put ourselves in a vulnerable position in situations in which we have limited control and in which the hazards of a broken trust will be greater than the potential gains, then how do we determine whom we should trust? Our decision to trust or mistrust is both a rational decision and an emotional reaction. As researchers Gary Fine and Lori Holyfield explain, "... one not only thinks trust, but feels trust."[45]

Substantial research suggests that our tendency to trust or mistrust another person has two roots: our personality (our general tendency to trust or mistrust others) and our assessment of the trustworthiness of the other person.

Personality and Trust

Some people, it seems, are simply more—or less—trusting than others. Indeed, many psychologists believe that our tendency to trust or mistrust others is a personality characteristic rooted, in part, in our early childhood experiences. For example, psychiatrist John Bowlby argues that through our infant and childhood experiences with our parents and other early "attachment figures," such as grandparents and day-care providers who act as primary caretakers, we develop a general "working model of others" that affects how willing we are to trust others throughout the rest of our lives.[46]

If our earliest experiences with the significant others on whom we depend for our survival are consistently loving and dependable, then we develop a "secure base" from which we develop a comfort with close relationships and believe that we "can confidently take the risks" associated with depending on others. When we begin our lives with a secure base, we are more likely to grow up believing in the goodwill of others, remembering more positive than negative experiences in our relationships with others, and having confidence in the competence of others. Consequently, we are more likely to engage in constructive coping behaviors when under stress (e.g., giving our boss bad news rather than hiding it, providing our colleagues with useful information rather than hoarding it, or speaking openly to people whom we believe have violated our trust rather than avoiding them).[47]

FIGURE 3-1 **Framework for Understanding the Antecedents and Consequences of Trust**

However, if our earliest experiences with significant attachment figures are inconsistent (e.g., if a parent sometimes responds to our needs in a loving way and at other times in an angry or aloof way) or undependable (e.g., a parent is consistently distant or punitive toward us), we are more likely to develop an insecure or avoidant working model of others. Consequently, we are more likely to grow up believing that we generally cannot rely on the goodwill of others or their willingness and ability to take care of our needs. Thus, when in relationships, we are likely to engage in self-protective behaviors such as trying too hard to please others or dismissing the importance of relationships altogether, becoming overdependent on others in our effort to gain their approval or distancing ourselves from others in an effort to avoid the risk of being let down, avoiding confrontation or challenging consistently, and under- or over-controlling our environment.[48]

Furthermore, people with insecure or avoidant working models of others tend to have "more rigid and narrow expectations" of relationships and, through their behavior, tend "to provoke the very reactions they fear."[49] For example, managers who do not trust their employees may micromanage their employees and encourage dependency, lack of initiative, increased resentment, and decreased commitment to the task. This leads the managers to believe that these employees indeed cannot be trusted, and then they micromanage these employees even more, which creates an escalating cycle of mutual mistrust. In contrast, managers who trust their employees are more likely to give them the information, training, resources, and emotional support that they need to act independently and successfully accomplish their tasks, which creates a virtuous cycle of mutual trust.

In short, the seeds of our tendency to trust or mistrust may be sown early in our lives. Furthermore, our decisions to trust others may be based as much in our emotional reactions to past experiences as they are based in the particular circumstances of the current situation.

Assessment of Another Person's Trustworthiness

In an ideal world, there would be a "person who was trusting and a second person who was worthy of that trust."[50] What do people look for to determine whether you are worthy of their trust?[51]

- *Competence.*   Are you effective at your work?
- *Consistency.*   Is your behavior predictable over time and across situations?
- *Communication.*   Are you accessible, willing to share accurate information freely, open to the opinions of others, and willing to give explanations for your decisions?
- *Caring.*   Do you have their best interests at heart?
- *Reliability.*   Do you follow through on your commitments?
- *Fairness.*   Do you make decisions based on fairness rather than favoritism?
- *Integrity.*   Are you honest, moral, and consistent in your words and deeds?

The relative importance of each of these characteristics in determining whether one should trust another person is situation-specific. For example, if I'm going to a physician for lifesaving surgery, then I'm likely to base the choice of physician primarily on the physician's reputation for technical competence and a consistent record of success. However, if I'm choosing a day care for my child, then I'm likely to base my choice of day care on its reputation for being a caring and responsive place as much as for its technical expertise.

Optimum Trust: Is There Such a Thing as Trusting Too Much?

If you asked his favorite color, he'd say plaid.
Anonymous

It is naive and ineffective to break our social world into either/or categories of people that we trust and people that we do not trust. Trusting too much can lead us to harm our own and our organization's performance by taking unnecessary risks, unwittingly ignoring or discounting information that suggests that our trust has been misplaced, saying more than is politically wise, misusing organizational resources, failing to monitor people and situtions closely when appropriate, and ignoring our own judgment. Trusting too little can cause us to be overly suspicious, miss out on opportunities that require risk, limit our sphere of relationships to a chosen few, minimize our dependence on others, resist others' attempts to influence us, withhold or distort information, develop a defensive orientation to the world, engage in costly monitoring activities to ensure compliance, and make us generally unpleasant to be around. In short, trusting too much leads to blind faith and gullibility; trusting too little leads to cynicism and suspicion. Both diminish our effectiveness. Researcher Andrew Wicks and his colleagues recommend that managers develop "optimal trust," which they describe as "knowing whom to trust, how much to trust them, and with respect to what matter."[52]

One of the biggest mistakes many managers make is to invest too much trust in too few people. We tend to trust people with whom we have frequent positive interactions and with whom we share significant similarities, yet these criteria can significantly limit our circle of trusted people.[53] One problem with trusting too few people too much is that we may become overdependent on their interpretations and advice and fail to reach out to others who can provide a more complex view of the situations that we face and the problems we must solve. Asking a few trusted confidants for advice may be fine when trying to understand a simple situation or solve a straightforward problem. However, limiting input to that which is provided by a few trusted colleagues can be a recipe for disaster when trying to solve more complex problems.[54]

Researchers Gabriel Szulanski, Robert Jensen, and Rossella Cappetta explain that the problem with trusting too few sources is that "we take far too much for granted with a trustworthy source . . . We assume that the source knows the many factors related to the situation, understands all the interconnections that influenced the results, and comprehends the whole interplay of subtle actions by many people leading to decision making . . . With a trustworthy source, we may unwittingly suspend our own power of observation and judgment." These tendencies can lead to simplistic and misguided interventions to complex problems.[55]

How can you avoid trusting too much in too few sources? You should approach complex problems with a systematic decision-making process that involves the input of many people who represent different perspectives. And you should take time to informally develop relationships with a broad and diverse group of people so that they are willing to provide you with honest and useful input when you need it.

CREATING TRUST: INTERPERSONAL STRATEGIES

Effective managers see building trust as a critical part of their everyday work life. They realize that, although trust is critical to managerial effectiveness, it cannot be enforced,[56] cannot be created instantaneously,[57] takes ongoing effort to maintain,[58] and is difficult to rebuild once broken. We build interpersonal trust in two ways: by developing personal credibility and by creating a work environment that promotes trust throughout the organization. To develop a personal reputation for being trustworthy:

- *Be competent at what you do.*   Make sure employees know what you are good at and find opportunities to show your competence.
- *Be clear about what values are important to you and model these values.* Employees want to know that you stand for something beyond self-interest and instrumental concerns.[59]
- *Have frequent positive interactions with employees.*   The more positive contact you have with employees, the more opportunity you have to build familiarity and mutual understanding—both of which help to build mutual trust.[60]
- *Communicate regularly.*   Be accessible to employees and provide ongoing information, status reports, and feedback. Keep employees informed of decisions and the processes by which decisions are made.
- *Listen to employees and take their opinions seriously.*   Employees who feel that they can voice their opinions and believe that these opinions are taken seriously are more likely to trust their leaders, have greater commitment to the leader's decisions, and are more likely to implement these decisions.[61] Don't "kill the messenger" of bad news.
- *Be predictable and consistent.*   Abrupt and arbitrary changes in behavior confuse people, make it difficult for people to know what you want, and increase anxiety.[62]
- *Provide unsolicited help.*   Take time to listen to others' problems, give useful information to others, help others even at some cost to you, and take others' needs into account when making decisions.[63]
- *Show understanding and concern for employees.*   Respect style and cultural differences. Recognize employees' needs to take care of family obligations. Says Amazon's founder and CEO Jeff Bezos, "I try to use Tuesdays and Thursdays to say thank-you to people. I still don't do that nearly enough. It's a classic situation of something that's never the most urgent thing to do. But it's actually very important, in a soft way, over a long period."[64]
- *Follow through on commitments.*   Don't promise more than you can deliver.

People with humility don't think less of themselves, they just think of themselves less.   *Ken Blanchard and Norman Vincent Peale in the Power of Ethical Management*

In short, effective managers see every encounter—large or small—as an opportunity to build or break trust. The most common ways to break trust are advancing your own interests at the expense of others, being blatantly and pompously self-promoting, using inconsistent standards to evaluate employees, allowing some people to break rules while expecting other people to follow the rules, not taking care of performance problems quickly, enabling employees who continue to perform poorly to stay with the organization, not giving employees opportunties to grow, taking credit for employees' work, withholding information, being close-minded, acting disrespectful toward others, lying, breaking promises, betraying confidences, consistently underperforming, and acting inconsistently in what you say and do.[65]

How to Repair Trust Once It Is Broken: The Art of the Apology

Apology is a lovely perfume; it can transform the clumsiest moment into a gracious gift.
Margaret Lee Runbeck, *Time for Each Other*

Despite our best efforts, sooner or later we all do something that breaks someone's trust in us. Sometimes it is intentional, and we regret it afterward. Sometimes it is unintentional, and we may not even notice our transgression until it is pointed out to us. But regardless of whether our transgression is intentional or not, it can undermine our relationship with a person who loses faith in us or feels harmed by our actions. Therefore, it is important to take steps to rebuild the trust that has been broken.

To rebuild trust, both parties must believe that the relationship is worth saving and must be willing to invest the time and emotional energy into repairing the relationship.[66] However, organizational researchers Roy Lewicki and Barbara Benedict Bunker recommend that the "perpetrator" of the broken trust—the person who has done the real or perceived misdeed—take the first step toward rebuilding trust. They explain:

> If the victim has to do the confrontation, the victim bears a double burden: the consequences of the trust violation and the social awkwardness and embarrassment that may be entailed with confronting the other about his or her actions. In addition, if the victim has to do the work, it may imply that the violator is insensitive and out of touch with his or her actions and the consequences . . . Denying that the act happened, claiming that there weren't any consequences, denying any responsibility for it, or claiming that the act was unimportant and should have no impact on the trust level will likely intensify the others' anger and contribute to further trust deterioration rather than to trust repair. If trust has been broken "in the eye of the beholder," it has been broken.[67]

Psychiatrist Aaron Lazare says that the apology is critical because it is "at the heart of the healing process."[68] Lazare explains that when we apologize, we take the shame off the person that we hurt by our actions and put the shame on ourselves for having hurt that person. When we admit to someone that we did something inappropriate, we are saying to the person, "I'm the one who was wrong, mistaken, insensitive, or stupid" and "You were not wrong or stupid for having trusted me." By acknowledging that we caused the problem and are taking responsibility for the harm that we caused, we give the offended person "the power to forgive."[69]

Although apologies are critical for maintaining relationships, many people find it difficult to apologize. Says Lazare:

> Despite its importance, apologizing is antithetical to the ever-pervasive values of winning, success, and perfection. The successful apology requires empathy and security and the strength to admit fault, failure, and weakness. But we are so busy winning that we can't concede our own mistakes.[70]

When we do something that breaks someone's trust in us, how we describe our wrongdoing and the sincerity of our apology and our offer to make amends influence that person's willingness to forgive.[71] If the apology is not seen as sincere, then the person who felt harmed by us may be hypervigilant in future interactions with us, and the road to rebuilding trust will be steep.[72] For your apology to be viewed as sincere:

- You should acknowledge that a breach of trust has occurred. People who feel harmed and who can clearly place responsibility on the transgressor are more likely to forgive than are people who feel the attribution of harm-doing is more ambiguous.[73]
- Your apology should be specific rather than general ("I'm sorry that I didn't give you credit for all the work that you did on the project" rather than "I'm sorry for what I did."). By being specific, you acknowledge that you understand what you did that hurt the other person.
- Your apology should acknowledge that you know that you hurt the other person by your actions ("I'm very sorry that I hurt you by not acknowledging your contribution to the success of the project at the meeting.") and that you are troubled by your actions ("It bothers me that I could have been so insensitive, especially after all the work you did on the project."). By doing so, you assure the other person that you share a common moral ground and are disappointed that you have not lived up to your mutual moral standards. Never trivialize the transgression by saying or implying that "it was nothing" or "no harm was done."
- Explain why you did what you did ("I wasn't thinking" or "I was in a hurry."). Doing so tells the other person that you are not an untrustworthy person by character but that you acted that way in a specific situation.
- Say that you are willing to do what it takes to repair the trust, even at some discomfort to yourself ("At the next meeting, I'll be sure to publicly acknowledge your contributions. I already mentioned them to the boss and noted my oversight."). Doing so lets the other person know that you are willing to endure personal hardship on his or her behalf.

By taking the preceding steps in your apology, you assure the other person that you have empathy for his or her feelings, that you are genuinely sorry, that the other person and the relationship are important to you, that you share similar moral values, and—most importantly—that the person can feel safe with you in the future.

Lazare warns that "pseudoapologies" are unlikely to work. In a pseudoapology, the wrongdoer fails to show empathy for those who feel harmed or to take responsibility for what he or she has done. Saying "I'm sorry that you feel that way" is less likely to incur forgiveness than saying "I'm sorry I've broken your trust in me by my actions." Former U.S. Senator Robert Packwood gave a pseudoapology when Packwood was accused of sexually harassing several women while in office. His apology: "I'm apologizing for the conduct that it was alleged that I did."[74]

Forgiveness

> The weak can never forgive. Forgiveness is the attribute of the strong.
> *Mahatma Gandhi*

Forgiveness also rebuilds trust and restores relationships. Forgiveness is defined as the willingess to rise above negative feelings associated with a person who we believe has harmed us and instead view the person with goodwill.[75] In short, forgiveness is a "cancellation of debt."[76]

Notably, forgiveness is associated with greater well-being for the forgiver as well as the forgiven. People who are willing to forgive others tend to have better social relationships, fewer illnesses, less stress, and lower rates of depression.

For example, in his studies of how stresses throughout life influenced the health of approximately 1,500 older people, gerontologist Neal Krause found that older people who unconditionally forgave others (and themselves) and made peace with their past tended to have better mental health (e.g., less depression, fewer anxieties about death, and greater life satisfaction) than did those who held grudges or forgave reluctantly.[77]

Forgiveness liberates us from anger and the desire for revenge and helps us see the world in more sophisticated ways rather than in black and white. People who don't forgive may use less effective coping strategies such as distancing themselves from others, engaging in "pity parties," and relatiating.[78] It is not surprising that the more important the relationship is, the more important it is to forgive.[79]

CREATING TRUST: ORGANIZATIONAL STRATEGIES

Interpersonal trust is necessary but insufficient for creating high-trust organizations. In addition to trusting their peers, subordinates, and bosses, employees must also trust their organizations. To build a foundation of trust, employees must believe that their organization's strategies are appropriate, that the people in charge know what they are doing, that the organizational policies and processes are fair and ethical, and that the work is designed to help employees achieve organizational goals.[80] Effective managers create trust-sustaining mechanisms—institutional norms, policies, procedures, and structures—that promote trust throughout the organization.[81] To create a work climate that fosters trust:

- *Develop a collective identity.*   Bring employees together psychologically by articulating a common vision, promoting shared values, creating joint products, emphasizing similarities among employees and departments and the benefits of the differences that exist, giving employees opportunities to interact with each other, developing feelings of mutual obligation and dependence, and encouraging norms that promote cooperation.[82]
- *Provide clear goals, job expectations, standards, and performance measures.* Employees need to know how they create value, what is and is not in their job descriptions, how they will be evaluated and on what criteria, and the consequences of their behavior.
- *Provide predictable routines.*   Employees need shared routines, habits, and rituals that they can count on in their everyday work life. Particularly during times of change, employees need a "safe haven of predictability"[83] that provides feelings of stability, promotes a collective memory, and enables cooperation and coordination among employees.[84]
- *Communicate consistent messages.*   Consistency in words and deeds in good times and in bad times minimizes confusion, cynicism, and rumors.
- *Encourage employee participation in decision making.*   When employees feel that they are involved in decision making and that their input is taken seriously, they are more likely to believe that the decision-making process is fair and are thus more likely to be committed to the leader, the organization, and the decisions that are made.[85]
- *Enable employees to control their work and their time.*   After the boundaries of their jobs and the performance expectations have been made clear, give employees the freedom, information, and training to make many of their

own decisions about the day-to-day details of their work, including how they will manage work-life balance issues. Remember that trust begets trust.

- ***Watch for employees who undermine trust.***   These include people who are incompetent, unmotivated, unethical and deceptive, as well as people who are micromanagers and cynics who promote negative attitudes toward the organizations. Offer training to employees who undermine trust. If they don't change, remove them from the organization or at least get them out of the way of employees who are trying to move the organization forward.[86]

- ***Rebuild organizational trust once broken.***   When something happens that damages employee trust, immediately work to rebuild trust by identifying the source of the mistrust, owning up to being part of the problem if that is the case, identifying what you and others will do to rebuild trust, and replacing people who were involved in creating the mistrust.[87]

In short, work environments that promote trust are those that provide employees with a common direction, competent and dependable colleagues, opportunities to interact with each other, clear work structures and task expectations, predictable routines, and some freedom to control their own environment within these boundaries. A work climate that is unpredictable or consistently out of control will undermine trust because it threatens employees' basic human needs to predict and control their environment. When these needs aren't met, employees are more likely to react defensively rather than productively to their managers, each other, their customers, their tasks, and their organizations.

How can you tell if mistrust is festering? In his article "Nobody Trusts the Boss," researcher Fernando Bartoleme provides several questions that can help you determine whether trust is waning: Are employees communicating with you or each other less often? Do employees avoid giving you bad news? Do employees avoid meetings? Do some employees rarely speak up at meetings? Does morale seem to be deteriorating? In particular, do employees lack enthusiasm and increasingly complain about their workload? Is there an increase in absenteeism and turnover? Are employees blaming other people and departments for problems?[88]

If your answers to these questions are "yes," then you may want to consider that you or the work climate (rather than the employees themselves) may be at fault. Then consciously intervene by changing your own behavior or the work environment by heeding the advice in the previous sections.

Organizational Structure and Swift Trust

In today's organizations, organizational members are becoming more dispersed; work assignments are becoming more project-based; short-term work relationships are becoming more common (such as relationships with subcontractors, consultants, and temporary workers); and temporary task teams are becoming the norm rather than the exception. Consequently, our professional effectiveness and success depend on our ability to work quickly and competently on complex problems with people whom we don't know very well and with whom we have never worked before.

In such situations, we must depend on what organizational researchers Debra Meyerson, Karl Weick, and Rod Kramer call "swift trust." This is a kind of trust that is developed when "there isn't time to engage in the usual forms of confidence-building activities that contribute to the development and maintenance of trust in more traditional and enduring forms of organization."[89]

Consider the case of temporary groups such as new product development teams, emergency room medical teams, and airplane cockpit crews. A temporary group is a collection of individuals with diverse skills who have never worked together before (and may not work together in the future) and who must depend on each other to accomplish a complex task successfully and quickly. A high degree of mutual trust is necessary because the outcome of their work is uncertain, group members must depend on each other for a successful outcome, and people risk serious consequences if the group fails.[90] For example, if all group members do not work together effectively, a new product development team's products may never get launched, an emergency medical team's patients may die, and an airplane cockpit crew's plane may crash.

However, members of temporary groups do not have time to develop a history of shared experiences that can lead to trust. Instead, to be successful, they must presume that each member of the group is trustworthy. On what bases do members of temporary groups presume trust? Rather than rely on personal relationships and a common history with each other, members of temporary groups base their mutual trust on the system in which the group does its work. Researcher Robyn Dawes explains:

> We trust engineers because we trust engineering and believe that engineers are trained to apply valid principles of engineering; moreover, we have evidence every day that these principles are valid when we observe airplanes flying. We trust doctors because we trust modern medicine, and we have evidence that it works when antibiotics and operations cure people.[91]

In short, temporary groups depend on "depersonalized trust."[92] Members of effective temporary groups trust each other because they trust that they share a set of standard operating procedures and expectations about how to define and solve problems, what information and tools are needed to solve problems, who has the authority to make certain decisions and take particular actions, how to deal with routine and nonroutine events, what behaviors are appropriate and inappropriate, what accountability measures should be used, and how to define success. Such trust is developed not through interpersonal relationships, but through the cultures, policies, and procedures of the institutions of which they are a part.[93]

Researcher Robert Ginette illustrates the importance of institutional trust-building mechanisms using airplane cockpit crews as an example:

> Even though the particular members of a given crew may never have worked together as a team before, when they come together, they step into a preexisting "shell" (Hackman, 1986a; Ginette, 1987) that defines much of what is expected of them as a team. This shell includes not only the context and design factors . . . but also a set of expectations about the roles of each individual in the crew. It is as if the definitions of the captain, the first officer, the engineer, and the rest of the crew (and, to some degree, the boundaries of the group as a whole) are already in place before any individual enters the setting.[94]

In short, trustworthy systems are as important as trustworthy interpersonal relationships, particularly when employees need to quickly develop into fast-moving temporary teams that can handle both the day-to-day routines as well as the unexpected emergencies that may arise.

BEYOND TRUST: THE RELATIONSHIP BETWEEN POSITIVE EMOTIONS AND SUCCESS

As mentioned in the previous chapter, researchers are coming to the same conclusion that it pays to feel good and to do good. People who feel and express positive emotions tend to be more effective at their jobs, have more successful careers, and lead happier, healthier, and longer lives. You may be thinking, "Sure, if I had a job that I enjoyed, made more money, and had perfect health, I'd feel pretty positive, too." However, researchers have found that it's not what you have that counts, but whether you appreciate what you have and share your goodwill with others. After all, many people have similar jobs, incomes, material belongings, health status, blessings, and tragedies. However, some of these people wake up each morning thankful for what they have, whereas others wake up miserable despite what they have. To make this point, researcher Barbara Fredrickson quotes John Milton: "The mind is its own place, and in itself can make a heaven of hell, a hell of heaven."

How Positive Emotions and Behaviors Lead to Professional Success and Well-Being

Positive feelings, such as joy, hope, love, compassion, generosity, gratitude, optimism, pride, serenity, and forgiveness, serve many purposes.[95] When we feel these positive emotions, we tend to think more broadly and creatively, seek out new information and experiences, behave more flexibly, have more confidence in our abilities and the abilities of others, be more persistent, get over bad experiences and negative emotions more quickly, and give and get the social support we need to solve problems and implement solutions. We are also better able to both engage in the moment and plan for the future. In contrast, negative emotions, such as fear, anger, envy, resentment, frustration, worry, guilt, and shame, tend to narrow our focus and flexibility, often limiting our options just when we need them most. For example, fear tends to lead to the desire to escape or to hoard resources, anger can lead to the desire to attack or take revenge, and guilt and shame can result in the desire to withdraw rather than engage. Frederickson explains that although negative emotions narrow our ability to think and act in complex ways, positive emotions broaden these abilities and create an upward spiral that increases our effectiveness and well-being in the short and long term.[96]

To understand how positive emotions affect our problem-solving abilities, researcher Alice Isen and colleagues designed a simple experiment to see how positive emotions might influence physicians' decision-making abilities. They gave some physicians a small bag of candy and asked them to think out loud as they tried to understand a case of a patient with liver disease. The physicians who received the bag of candy were able to integrate facts faster and were less likely to get stuck with premature conclusions. Other studies have shown that employees who express positive emotions tend to be evaluated more highly by their supervisors, receive greater pay increases, and receive more support from their supervisors and coworkers. In one study of MBAs, those who reported that they experience more positive emotions tended to be more careful during a decision-making simulation and were perceived to be more effective interpersonally in team discussions.[97]

In addition to contributing to our effectiveness and career success, many studies have shown that positive emotions can help us bounce back from adversity and live longer, healthier lives.[98] People who experience positive emotions, especially during the most difficult periods of life, tend to tolerate pain better, cope with and recover from illness faster, and experience less depression. For example, people who experience the death of a loved one and yet find positive meaning amidst their suffering are more likely to create long-term plans and have greater well-being a year after their loss. In a landmark study of aging nuns, researchers found that nuns who had expressed positive emotions in essays they wrote when they were young had a lower incidence of Alzheimer's disease decades later and lived up to 10 years longer than nuns who expressed fewer positive emotions through their writing.[99] For more information about this fascinating study, go to www.nunstudy.com.

Despite the emphasis on positive emotions, we should not assume that positive emotions always lead to success. For example, there is considerable research that suggests that although self-enhancing beliefs and optimism lead to higher performance and success for some people, they do not bring out the best in all people. In her research, Julie Norem found that some people—particularly people who tend to be more anxious than others—use a strategy called "defensive pessimism" to enhance their performance. They worry about what might go wrong, overprepare, and fret over the smallest details. Although pessimism can be paralyzing for some people, defensive pessimists harness their anxiety in ways that lead to higher performance. They seem to prepare for the worst and hope for the best. Therefore, advising them to relax or "look on the bright side" may undermine, rather than enhance, their performance.[100]

How Positive Emotions Lead to Organizational Effectiveness

Positive emotions are not only good for individuals; they are good for organizations. Researchers have found that organizational leaders who express positive emotions encourage their organizational members to feel positive emotions as well. When employees feel positive emotions, they are more likely to set higher goals, see and fix mistakes, feel more competent and empowered, have greater problem-solving capabilities, act more flexibly, feel more job satisfaction and loyalty to their organizations, go above and beyond the call of duty, interact with each other more frequently, give and get social support, share resources, resolve conflict and negotiate more reasonably, and rebound from hurdles and crises more quickly.[101]

In a recent study, University of Michigan professor Kim Cameron found that when employees in recently downsized organizations viewed their leaders as "virtuous" ("compassionate, forgiving, trusting, and optimistic"), the organization ". . . had significantly higher productivity, higher quality outputs and lower employee turnover." Employees in virtuous organizations also believed their organizations were more profitable, offered higher quality products or services, were better able to retain customers, and paid employees more than the competition.[102] How important is organizational loyalty? As noted in an MIT Sloan Review article about loyalty in organizations worldwide, "the truly loyal exhibit the kinds of behaviors that make business successful—they work hard, stay late, go the extra mile to delight the customer, and recommend the company to their friends as a good place to work . . . High risk employees are spending their working hours clicking through Monster.com."[103]

Positive Emotions and Organizational Crises

It is not surprising that positive emotions are particularly critical during a crisis because they enable employees to be mindful of what is happening around them, improvise behaviors that increase their chances for success in the crisis, broaden rather than constrain their perceptions of available options, and—rather than focus only on themselves—take care of others who are also affected by the crisis.[104] Managers' and employees' reactions during a crisis are often a moment of truth for organizations. Especially during a crisis, positive emotions such as compassion and empathy enoble as well as enable.

After the Twin Towers toppled on September 11, 2001, employees at a Starbucks located near the Towers were told by their manager that they could leave to protect their own safety. Instead, employees and the store manager compassionately chose to stay and literally pull stunned people passing by into the store, giving them food and drink, shelter from falling debris, and emotional support.[105] During the September 11 crisis, says Sue Shellenbarger of the *Wall Street Journal*, "Employees . . . believed they were seeing their bosses' true colors. Their conclusions about what they saw either deepened their commitment or damaged it beyond repair . . . At a Chicago consulting firm, a senior supervisor ordered employees on September 11 to return to business as usual. A consultant who worked at the firm said, "What we needed was to stop and say, 'OK, we're going to take a deep breath and think about this . . . I will remember this situation and how my firm dealt with it . . .'" Shellenbarger concludes: "Embedded in a crisis is an opportunity for employers to rebuild damaged loyalty. Loyalty shapes people's choices not only about where to work, but also about how long, hard, and wholeheartedly to apply their mental energies."[106]

Note that positive emotions are not always happy ones. Kenneth Chenault, CEO of American Express Co., ensured that employees and customers felt the care and concern they needed during the September 11 crisis. *BusinessWeek* described Chenault's leadership:[107]

> AmEx helped 560,000 stranded cardholders get home, in some cases chartering airplanes and buses to ferry them across the country. It waived millions of dollars in deliquent fees on late-paying cardholders and increased credit limits to cash-starved clients . . . Most telling, Chenault gathered 5,000 American Express employees at the Paramount Theater in New York on September 20 for a highly emotional "town hall meeting." During the session, Chenault demonstrated the poise, compassion, and decisiveness that vaulted him to the top. He told employees that he had been filled with such despair, sadness, and anger that he had seen a counselor. Twice he rushed to spontaneously embrace grief-stricken employees. Chenault said he would donate $1 million of the company's profits to the families of the AmEx victims. "I represent the best company and the best people in the world," he concluded. "In fact, you are my strength, and I love you." It was a poignant and unscripted moment. Says AmEx board member Charlene Barshefsky, a partner at Wilmer Cutler & Pickering, who viewed a video of the event, "The manner in which he took command, the comfort and direction he gave to what was obviously an audience in shock was of a caliber one rarely sees."

In good times and in bad times, positive emotions and behaviors create positive upward spirals in organizations because they can create a "contagion effect" in which people copy each other's emotions. Furthermore, when employees feel gratitude for the goodwill they receive, they want to repay this goodwill with greater loyalty and effort and pass this goodwill on to others such as coworkers and customers. Consequently, positive emotions in organizations can be a competitive advantage that is not easily copied by competitors. How can you cultivate positive emotions in your workplace?

- Express positive emotions—gratitude, generosity, optimism, trust—regularly at work. Start meetings with sincere words of appreciation. Walk around the hallways and notice who is there, what they are doing, and why you should be thankful. Be appreciative to the clients that you serve. Help other people. Remember that positive emotions are contagious, especially when expressed by direct supervisors and organizational leaders.
- Engage in positive deviance. Give unexpected kindnesses and reach out to others when it is least expected. When you engage in positive emotions and behaviors when it goes against the norm, the element of surprise and courage becomes a powerful example to others, both strengthening people's trust in you and role-modeling behavior for others to follow.[108]
- Help people find positive meaning in their day-to-day work lives, including in the mundane, the sad, and the crises. Help employees see how their work contributes to a greater good and whom they are helping through their efforts.
- Provide opportunities for people to help each other and to express appreciation for the help they receive from others.
- Celebrate small wins so that employees experience ongoing success and the associated positive emotions.
- In a crisis, enable employees to experience and express what it feels like to rise to the occasion and find the strength and resources they never knew they had.
- And the next time someone says, "have a nice day," you'd be wise to heed their advice.

CONCLUSION

Effective managers realize that one of their most important jobs is to earn the trust of their employees, colleagues, bosses, customers, and other constituents. They also realize that it is equally important to create organizational structures and processes that promote trust at all levels of the organization. They know that trust is necessary for managing the routine interactions of everyday life and vital for initiating organizational change and responding to crises. Most importantly, says ethics researcher LaRue Hosmer, they recognize that people in organizations pay attention to issues concerning "what is right, just, and fair as well as what is efficient, effective, and practical."[109]

The ability to earn trust and create work environments that promote trust throughout the organization is becoming increasingly valuable in today's global, diverse, and technology-driven economic environment. Managers must be able to help people who don't share a common culture (and whose cultural groups may share a history of animosity and distrust toward each other) learn to work together productively to serve organizational goals. They must be able to help employees involved in alliances, mergers, and acquisitions build trust and interdependence quickly. They must be able to develop trust and respect among employees who work in virtual teams and who rarely, if ever, see each other. They must be able to create conditions that empower employees to take independent action so that their organizations can be responsive, flexible, and fast. And because of the executive and organizational scandals that have dominated the media in recent years, managers must work harder than ever to build trust. Undoubtedly, in today's work environment, trust is a must-have, not a nice-to-have.

Chapter Summary

Trust in organizations is a source of competitive advantage. A high-quality network of internal and external relationships that is built on trust provides economic value to the organization, takes a long time to develop, and cannot be easily copied by other organizations.

Managers who are able to inspire trust tend to be more effective, have stronger networks, and get promoted more often than those who do not inspire trust. They are better able to attract and retain followers, promote loyalty and a sense of belonging, build support for their goals, develop more productive employees, focus on value-added work rather than costly employee control systems, enhance communication, reduce conflict, reduce the costs of negotiation, inspire employees to go beyond their job descriptions to serve organizational goals, enhance group decision making, encourage cooperation across boundaries, promote organizational change, survive organizational crises, and help employees accept unfavorable decisions.

When we trust someone or an organization, we are willing to ascribe good intentions to that person or organization and have confidence in their ability to act on these intentions. Our belief in a person's trustworthiness will influence how we behave toward that person, the task, and organization.

Trust is only necessary in conditions of vulnerability, risk, and uncertainty. If we can perfectly predict and control a situation, or if we have nothing to lose if our assumptions about the person's or organization's good intentions or actions are wrong, then trust is not necessary.

Our willingness to trust is based on our perceptions of a person's or organization's trustworthiness. These perceptions are based on the person's or organization's reputation, our past experiences with the person or organization, and our stereotypes about that person. Perceptions are important because they can turn into self-fulfilling prophecies.

We determine whether to trust another person based on our assumptions about whether that person is competent, reliable, predictable over time and across situations, open to communication, fair in his or her decision making, concerned about our welfare, and morally correct.

When we break someone's trust in us, we may be able to rebuild that trust by offering a sincere apology and making amends. Apologies are important because they assure the person who feels harmed that we are genuinely sorry, share similar moral values, and can be counted on to be trustworthy in the future. Forgiveness is also important because it enables the relationship to move forward and it increases the psychological and physical well-being of the forgiver.

Our willingness to trust—or mistrust—others may be a personality trait rooted in our early childhood experiences. If our earliest experiences with "attachment figures" (parents, day-care providers, and significant others) are consistently loving and dependable, we are more likely to become comfortable trusting and depending on others. If our earliest experiences with attachment figures are inconsistent or undependable, we are more likely to grow up believing that we cannot rely on the goodwill of others and their ability to take care of our needs.

Our willingness to trust is also based in the organizational environment in which we work. High-trust organizations create a collective identity among employees, opportunities for employees to interact, clear job structures and processes, predictable routines, and opportunities for employees to control their own work environment and make their own decisions about their day-to-day work.

Clear structures and processes are particularly critical in organizations that routinely depend on temporary teams because members of such teams tend not to know each other very well and do not have the time to build interpersonal trust. Therefore, they must rely on "depersonalized trust"—shared goals, knowledge, operating measures, and performance standards—to become an effective team quickly.

It is possible to trust too much, especially when we have too much trust in the ideas of too few people. When we have too few people to count on for ideas and support, we narrow our perception of problems and solutions and thus inhibit our ability to make and implement high-quality decisions. Effective problem-solvers develop a broad network of people they can trust so that they can see their problems and solutions from many different perspectives.

In good times and in bad times, positive emotions and behaviors create positive upward spirals in organizations because they can create a "contagion effect" in which people copy each other's emotions. Positive emotions broaden people's perspectives, enhance decision-making abilities, and increase flexibility. Furthermore, when employees feel gratitude for the goodwill they receive, they want to repay this goodwill with greater loyalty and effort and pass this goodwill on to others, such as coworkers and customers. Consequently, positive emotions in organizations can be a competitive advantage that is not easily copied by competitors.

FOOD FOR THOUGHT

1. What is the most useful thing you learned in this chapter, and why?
2. Based on the personal strategies described in this chapter, what can you do to increase your own trustworthiness? Practice this behavior and note any benefits and progress you make.
3. How does trust contribute to individual and organizational success?
4. Think of two people, one that you trust and one that you don't trust. List the reasons that lead to your trust or distrust of each person. What are the three most important lessons about gaining and losing trust that you learned from these people? What, if anything, could the person you don't trust do to earn your trust?
5. If you are a manager, what kinds of specific organizational interventions can you make to create a more trustworthy organizational environment (i.e., one that enhances trust among employees, clients, and other constituents)?
6. Imagine the following situation. Last week, you inadvertently mentioned at a meeting that a colleague was undergoing chemotherapy for cancer. Your colleague had told you about the illness and the chemotherapy in confidence just a few weeks ago. Your colleague heard that you had mentioned the illness at a meeting and was angry that you did so, particularly in such a public way. Today, your colleague came to your office to discuss this breach of confidence and mentioned several concerns, not the least of which was that his or her own children did not know about the illness and were likely to hear of it from other employees who knew the family personally. You feel that an apology is necessary. Describe how you would apologize. Specifically, what would you say to your colleague who is undergoing cancer treatment? What else can you do to rebuild trust with this person?
7. Think about someone from your past to whom you are grateful. Write a note of appreciation to that person, explaining what they did and why you are thankful.
8. Write down five things that you are thankful for today. Do this for the next week and see if it enhances your general mood and behavior.

ENDNOTES

1. Heller, Joseph. 1966. *Something Happened.* New York: Alfred A. Knopf, Scapegoat Productions, 13.

2. Hosmer, Larue. 1995. "Trust: The Connecting Link between Organizational Theory and Philosophical Ethics." *Academy of Management Review,* 20(2): 379–403.

3. McAllister, Daniel J. 1995. "Affect- and Cognition-Based Trust as Foundations for Interpersonal Cooperation in Organizations." *Academy of Management Journal,* 38(1): 24–59.

4. Hill, Linda. 1992. *Becoming a Manager: Mastery of a New Identity.* Cambridge, MA: Harvard Business School Press.

5. Lombardo, Michael, Marian Roderman, and Cynthia McCauley. "Explanations of Success and Derailment in Upper Level Managerial Positions." *Journal of Business and Psychology,* 2(3): 199–216.

6. Hosmer, Larue. 1995. "Trust: The Connecting Link between Organizational Theory and Philosophical Ethics." *Academy of Management Review,* 20(2): 379–403; Dirks, Kurt, and Donald L. Ferrin. 2001. "The Role of Trust in Organizational Settings." *Organizational Science,* 12(4): 450–467.

7. Cook, John, and Toby Wall. 1980. "New Worker Attitude Measures of Trust, Organizational Commitment and Personal Need Nonfulfillment." *Journal of Occupational Psychology,* 53: 39–52; citing Buchanan, B. 1974. "Building Organizational Commitment: The Socialization of Managers in Work Organizations." *Administrative Science Quarterly,* 19: 40, 533–546.

8. Podsakoff, Philip, Scott MacKenzie, Robert Moorman, and Richard Fetter. 1990. "Transformational Leaders Behaviors and Their Effects on Followers' Trust in Leader, Satisfaction, and Organizational Citizenship Behaviors." *Leadership Quarterly,* 1: 107–142.

9. Rogers, Carl. 1961. *On Becoming a Person.* Boston MA: Houghton Mifflin.

10. Konovsky, Mary, and S. Douglas Push. 1994. "Citizenship Behavior and Social Exchange." *Academy of Management Journal,* 37: 656–669; Organ, Dennis. 1988. *Organizational Citizenship Behavior: The Good Soldier Syndrome.* Lexington, MA: Lexington Books; Dirks, Kurt, and Donald L. Ferrin. 2001. "The Role of Trust in Organizational Settings." *Organizational Science,* 12(4): 450–467; Yoon, Mahn Hee, and Jaebeom Buh. 2003. "Organizational Citizenship Behaviors and Service Quality as External Effectiveness of Contact Employees." *Journal of Business Research,* 56: 597–611.

11. Yoon, Mahn Hee, and Jaebeom Suh. 2003. "Organizational Citizenship Behavior and Service Quality as External Effectiveness of Contact Employees." *Journal of Business Research,* 56: 597–611.

12. McAllister, Daniel. 1995. "Affect- and Cognition-Based Trust as Foundations for Interpersonal Cooperation in Organizations." *Academy of Management Journal,* 38(1): 24–59.

13. Hosmer, Larue. 1995. "Trust: The Connecting Link between Organizational Theory and Philosophical Ethics." *Academy of Management Review,* 20(2): 379–403.

14. Mishra, Aneil. 1996. "Organizational Responses to Crises: The Centrality of Trust." In Kramer, Roderick, and Tom Tyler eds.). *Trust in Organizations: Frontiers of Theory and Research.* Thousand Oaks, CA: Sage Publications, 261–287.

15. Nahapiet, Janine, and Sumantra Goshal. 1998. "Social Capital, Intellectual Capital, and the Organizational Advantage." *Academy of Management Review,* 23(2): 242–266.

16. Butler, John K. 1995. "Behaviors, Trust and Goal Achievement in a Win-Win Negotiating Role Play." *Group and Organization Management,* 20(4): 486–501.

17. Zand, Dale E. 1971. "Trust and Managerial Problem Solving." *Administrative Science Quarterly,* 17: 229–239; Dirks, Kirk. 1999. "The Effects of Interpersonal Trust on Work Group Performance." *Journal of Applied Psychology,* 84(3): 445–455.

18. Nahapiet, Janine, and Sumantra Goshal. 1998. "Social Capital, Intellectual Capital, and the Organizational Advantage." *Academy of Management Review,* 23(2): 242–266.

19. Vangen Siv and Chris Huxham. 2003. "Nurturing Collaborative Relations: Building Trust in Interorganizational Collaboration." *The Journal of Applied Behavioral Science,* 39(1): 5–31.

20. Mishra, Aneil. 1996. "Organizational Responses to Crises: The Centrality of Trust." In Kramer, Roderick, and Tom Tyler (eds.). *Trust in Organizations: Frontiers of Theory and Research.* Thousand Oaks, CA: Sage Publications, 261–287.

21. Korsgaard, M. Audrey, David M. Schweiger, and Harry Sapienza. 1995. "Building Commitment, Attachment, and Trust in Strategic Decision-Making Teams: The Role of Procedural Justice." *Academy of Management Journal,* 38(1): 60–84; citing Folger, Robert, and Mary Konovsky. 1989. "Effects of Procedural and Distributed Justice on Reactions to Pay Raise Decisions." *Academy of Management Journal,* 32: 115–130; McFarlin, Dean, and Paul Sweeney. 1992. "Distributive and Procedural Justice as Predictors of Satisfaction with Personal and Organizational Outcomes." *Academy of Management Journal,* 35: 626–637.

22. Mishra, Aneil, and Gretchen M. Spreitzer. 1998. "Explaining How Survivors Respond to Downsizing: The Role of Trust, Empowerment, Justice, and Work Redesign." *Academy of Management Review,* 23(3): 567–588.

23. Gambetta, Diego. 1988. "Can We Trust Trust?" In Gambetta, Diego G. (ed.). *Trust.* New York: Basic Blackwell, 213–237.

24. Nooteboom, Bart, Hans Berger, and Niels G. Noorderhaven. 1997. "Effects of Trust and Governance on Relational Risk." *Academy of Management Journal,* 40(2): 308–338.

25. Shaw, Robert. 1997. *Trust in the Balance.* San Francisco, CA: Jossey-Bass.

26. Lipnack, Jessica, and Jeffrey Stamps. 1997. *Virtual Teams: Reaching across Time,* *Space, and Technology.* New York: John Wiley, 228–229.

27. Robinson, Sandra. 1996. "Trust and the Breach of the Psychological Contract." *Administrative Science Quarterly,* 41: 574–599.

28. Barney, Jay, and M. Hansen. 1994. "Trustworthiness as a Source of Competitive Advantage." *Strategic Management Journal,* 15: 175–190.

29. Serwer, Andy, and Kate Bonamici. 2004. "The Hottest Thing in the Sky." *Fortune* 86–94.

30. Lancaster, Hal. 1999. "Herb Kelleher Has One Main Strategy: Treat Employees Well." *The Wall Street Journal.* August 31: B1.

31. Boyle, Matthew. 2002. "The Right Stuff." *Fortune* 85–86.

32. Commitment in the Workplace: The 2000 Global Employee Relationship Report. Walker Information Fact Sheet.

33. Dayal, Sandeep, Helen Landesberg, and Michael Zeisser. 1999. "How to Build Trust On-Line." *Marketing Management.* Fall 64–69.

34. Cook, John, and Toby Wall. 1980. "New Work Attitude Measures of Trust, Organizational Commitment and Personal Need Nonfulfillment." *Journal of Occupational Psychology,* 53: 39–52.

35. Deutsch, Mortin. 1958. "Trust and Suspicion." *Journal of Conflict Resolution,* 2: 26–279.

36. Zand, Dale E. 1971. "Trust and Managerial Problem Solving." *Administrative Science Quarterly,* 17: 229–239.

37. Burt, R., and M. Knez. 1995. "Kinds of Third-Party Effects on Trust." *Rationality and Society,* 7: 255–292.

38. Bartolome, Fernando. 1989. "Nobody Trusts the Boss, Now What?" *Harvard Business Review,* 67: 135–143.

39. Williams, Michele. 1999. "In Whom We Trust; Social Categorization, Affect and Trust Development." Unpublished paper. Ann Arbor, MI: University of Michigan; citing Cox and Taylor. 1993. *Cultural Diversity in Organizations.* San Francisco, CA: Berrett-Koehler; Adler, Nancy. 1997. *International Dimensions of*

Organizational Behavior 2nd ed. Cincinnati, OH: South-Western College Publishing.

40. Smith, Kenywn. 1982. *Groups in Conflict: Prisons in Disguise.* Dubuque, IA: Kendall Hunt.

41. Williams, Michele. 2001. "In Whom We Trust: Social Group Membership as an Affective-Cognitive Context for Trust Development. *Academy of Management Review,* 26(3): 377–396.

42. Robinson, Sandra. 1996. "Trust and the Breach of the Psychological Contract." *Administrative Science Quarterly,* 41: 574–599.

43. Ross, Michael, and John G. Holmes. 2001. "Trust and Communicated Attributions in Close Relationships." *Journal of Personality and Social Psychology*, 81(1): 57–64.

44. Ross, Michael, and John G. Holmes. 2001. "Trust and Communicated Attributions in Close Relationships." *Journal of Personality and Social Psychology*, 81(1): 57–64; Kurt T. Dirks, and Donald L. Ferrin. 2001. "Trust in Organizational Settings." *Organizational Science*, 12(4): 450–467.

45. Fine, Gary, and Lori Holyfield. 1996. "Secrecy, Trust and Dangerous Leisure: Generating Group Cohesion in Voluntary Organizations." *Social Psychology Quarterly,* 59: 22–38.

46. Mikulincer, Mario. 1998. "Attachment Working Models and the Sense of Trust: An Exploration of Interaction Goals and Affect Regulation." *Journal of Personality and Social Psychology,* 74(5): 1209–1225; Bowlby, John. 1988. *A Secure Base: Clinical Applications of Attachment Theory*. London: Routledge.

47. Mikulincer, Mario. 1998. "Attachment Working Models and the Sense of Trust: An Exploration of Interaction Goals and Affect Regulation." *Journal of Personality and Social Psychology,* 74(5): 1209–1225; Holmes, John G., and John K. Rempel. 1989. "Trust in Close Relationships." In C. Hendrick (ed.). *Review of Personality and Social Psychology*, 10: 187–220.

48. Mikulincer, Mario. 1998. "Attachment Working Models and the Sense of Trust:

An Exploration of Interaction Goals and Affect Regulation." *Journal of Personality and Social Psychology,* 74(5): 1209–1225.

49. Holmes, John G., and John K. Rempel. 1989. "Trust in Close Relationships." In C. Hendrick (ed.). *Review of Personality and Social Psychology,* 10: 187–220.

50. Barber, Bernard. 1983. *The Logic and Limits of Trust.* New Brunswick, NJ: Rutgers University Press; cited in Hosmer, Larue. 1993. "Trust: The Connecting Link between Organizational Theory and Philosophical Ethics." *Academy of Management Review,* 20(2): 379–403.

51. Mayer, Roger, James H. Davis, and F. David Schoorman. 1995. "An Integrative Model of Organizational Trust." *Academy of Management Journal,* 20(3): 709–734; Clark, Murray, and Roy L. Payne. 1997. "The Nature and Structure of Workers' Trust in Management." *Journal of Organizational Behavior,* 18: 205–224; Whitener, Ellen, Susan Brodt, M. Audrey Korsguaard, and Jon Werner. 1998. "Managers as Initiators of Trust: An Exchange Relationship Framework for Understanding Managerial Trustworthy Behavior." *Academy of Management Review,* 23(3): 513–530.

52. Wicks, Andrew C., Shawn L. Berman, and Thomas M. Jones. 1999. "The Structure of Optimal Trust: Moral and Strategic Implications." *Academy of Management Review,* 24(1): 99–116.

53. Cialdini, Robert. 2001. Influence: Science and Practice. Allyn & Bacon: Needham Heights, MA; McAllister, Daniel. "Affect and Cognition Based Trust as Foundations for Interpersonal Cooperation in Organizations." *Academy of Management Journal,* 38(1): 24–59.

54. Sweetman, Kathrine. 2001. "The Perils of Trusting Too Much." *MIT Sloan Management Review*, Spring: 10.

55. Szulanski, Gabriel, Rossella Cappeta, and Robert Jensen. 2002. "When Trustworthiness Matters: Knowledge Transfer and the Moderating Effect of Causal Ambiguity." Working Paper. Wharton School.

56. Hosmer, Larue. 1995. "Trust: The Connecting Link between Organizational Theory and Philosophical Ethics." *Academy of Management Review,* 20(2): 379–403.

57. Nooteboom, Bart, Hans Berger, and Niels G. Noorderhaven. 1997. "Effects of Trust and Governance on Relational Risk." *Academy of Management Journal,* 40(2): 308–338.

58. Nahapiet, Janine, and Sumantra Goshal. 1998. "Social Capital, Intellectual Capital, and the Organizational Advantage." *Academy of Management Review,* 23(2): 242–266.

59. Clawson, James. 1987. "The Role of Trust and Respect in Developmental Relationships." Charlottesville, VA: Teaching Note, Colgate Darden Graduate Business School.

60. McAllister, Daniel. 1995. "Affect- and Cognition-Based Trust as Foundations for Interpersonal Cooperation in Organizations." *Academy of Management Journal,* 38(1): 24–59; Nooteboom, Bart, Hans Berger, and Niels G. Noorderhaven. 1997. "Effects of Trust and Governance on Relational Risk." *Academy of Management Journal,* 40(2): 308–338.

61. Korsgaard, M. Audrey, David M. Schweiger, and Harry J. Sapienza. 1995. "Building Commitment, Attachment, and Trust in Strategic Decision-Making Teams: The Role of Procedural Justice." *Academy of Management Journal,* 38(1): 60–84; Zaheer, Akbar, Bill McEvily, and Vincenzo Perrone. "Does Trust Matter?" *Organization Science.* March–April, 9(2): 1998.

62. Stevenson, Howard H, and Mihnea Moldoveanu. 1995. "The Power of Predictability." *Harvard Business Review.* July–August: 140–143.

63. McAllister, Daniel. 1995. "Affect- and Cognition-Based Trust as Foundations for Interpersonal Cooperation in Organizations." *Academy of Management Journal,* 38(1): 24–59.

64. *Wall Street Journal.* 1999. B1.

65. Bartoleme, Fernando. 1989. "Nobody Trusts the Boss Completely, Now What?" *Harvard Business Review;* Galford, Robert, and Ann Seibold Drapeau. 2003. "The Enemies of Trust." *Harvard Business Review,* 89–95.

66. Lewicki, Roy, and Barbara Benedict Bunker. 1996. "Developing and Maintaining Trust in Work Relationships." In Kramer, Roderick, and Tom R. Tyler (eds.). *Trust in Organizations: Frontiers of Theory and Research.* Thousand Oaks, CA: Sage Publications, 114–139.

67. Ibid., p. 132.

68. Lazare, Aaron. 1995. "Go Ahead, Say You're Sorry." *Psychology Today.* January/February: 40–78.

69. Ibid.

70. Ibid., p. 40.

71. Lewicki, Roy, and Barbara Benedict Bunker. 1996. "Developing and Maintaining Trust in Work Relationships." In Kramer, Roderick, and Tom R. Tyler (eds.). *Trust in Organizations: Frontiers of Theory and Research.* Thousand Oaks, CA: Sage Publications, 114–139.

72. Ibid.

73. McCullough, Michael, Frank Fincham, and Jo-Ann Tsang. 2003. "Forgiveness, Forbearance, and Time: The Temporal Unfolding of Transgression Related Interpersonal Motivations." *Journal of Personality and Social Psychology,* 84(3): 540–557.

74. Lazare, Aaron. 1995. "Go Ahead, Say You're Sorry." *Psychology Today.* January/February: 40–78.

75. McCullough, Michael, Frank Fincham, and Jo-Ann Tsang. 2003. "Forgiveness, Forebearance and Time: The Temporal Unfolding of Transgression-Related Interpersonal Motivations." *Journal of Personality and Social Psychology,* 84(3): 540–557.

76. Exline J. J., and R. F. Baumeister. "Expressing Forgiveness and Repentance: Benefits and Barriers." In I. M. E. McCullough, K. I. Pargament, and C. E. Thoresen (eds.). *Forgiveness: Theory, Research, and Practice.* New York: Guilford Press, 133–155.

77. Rueter, Anne. 2002. "Prescription for Health: Forgive Freely." *Ann Arbor News* E1–E2.

78. McCullough, M. E., K. C. Rachal, S. J. Sandage, E. Worthington, S. W. Brown, and T. L. Hight. 1998. "Interpersonal Forgiving in Close Relationships: Theoretical Elaboration and Measurement." *Journal of Personality and Social Psychology*, 75: 1586–1603.

79. Karremans, Johan, and Paul Van Lange. 2003. "When Forgiving Enhances Psychological Well-being: The Role of Interpersonal Commitment." *Journal of Personality and Social Psychology*, 84(5): 1011–1026.

80. Galford, Robert, and Anne Seibold Drapeau. 2003. "The Enemies of Trust." *Harvard Business Review*, 89–95.

81. Shaw, Robert. 1997. *Trust in the Balance*. San Francisco, CA: Jossey-Bass.

82. Lewicki, Roy, and Barbara Benedict Bunker. 1996. "Developing and Maintaining Trust in Work Relationships." In Kramer, Roderick, and Tom Tyler (eds.). *Trust in Organizations: Frontiers of Theory and Research*. Thousand Oaks, CA: Sage Publications, 114–139; Nahapiet, Janine, and Sumantra Goshal. 1998. "Social Capital, Intellectual Capital, and the Organizational Advantage." *Academy of Management Review,* 23(2): 242–266.

83. Stevenson, Howard H., and Mihnea Moldoveanu. 1995. "The Power of Predictability." *Harvard Business Review.* July–August: 140–143.

84. Nahapiet, Janine, and Sumantra Goshal. 1998. "Social Capital, Intellectual Capital, and the Organizational Advantage." *Academy of Management Review,* 23(2): 242–266.

85. Korsgaard, Audrey M., David Schweiger, and Harry Sapienza. 1995. "Building Commitment, Attachment and Trust in Strategic Decision-Making Teams: The Role of Procedural Justice." *Academy of Management Journal*, 38(1): 60–64.

86. Galford, Robert, and Anne Seibold Drapeau. 2003. "The Enemies of Trust." *Harvard Business Review*, 89–95.

87. Galford, Robert, and Anne Seibold Drapeau. 2003. "The Enemies of Trust." *Harvard Business Review*, 89–95.

88. Bartoleme, Fernando. 1989. "Nobody Trusts the Boss: Now What?" *Harvard Business Review.* March–April: 135–142.

89. Meyerson, Debra, Karl Weick, and Roderick Kramer. 1996. "Swift Trust and Temporary Groups." In Kramer, Roderick, and Tom R. Tyler (eds.). *Trust in Organizations: Frontiers of Theory and Research*. Thousand Oaks, CA: Sage Publications, 166–197.

90. Ibid.

91. Meyerson, Debra, Karl Weick, and Roderick Kramer. 1996. "Swift Trust and Temporary Groups." In Kramer, Roderick, and Tom R. Tyler (eds.). *Trust in Organizations: Frontiers of Theory and Research*. Thousand Oaks, CA: Sage Publications, 166–197; citing Dawes, Robyn. 1994. *House of Cards: Psychology and Psychotherapy Built on Myth*. New York: Free Press, 24.

92. Brewer, M. B. 1981. "Ethnocentrism and Its Role in Interpersonal Trust." In M. Brewer, and B. Collins (eds.). *Scientific Inquiry and the Social Sciences.* San Francisco, CA: Jossey-Bass.

93. Zucker, Lynn. 1986. "Production of Trust: Institutional Sources of Economic Structure, 1840–1920." In Barry Shaw, and Larry Cummings (eds.). *Research in Organizational Behavior*. Greenwich, CT: JAI Press, 53–111; Meyerson, Debra, Karl Weick, and Roderick Kramer. 1996. "Swift Trust and Temporary Groups." In Kramer, Roderick, and Tom R. Tyler (eds.). *Trust in Organizations: Frontiers of Theory and Research*. Thousand Oaks, CA: Sage Publications, 166–197.

94. Ginette, Robert. 1990. "Airline Cockpit Crew." In J. Richard Hackman (ed.). *Groups That Work (and Those That Don't)*. San Francisco, CA: Jossey-Bass, 427–448.

95. Isen, Alice. 2003. "Positive Affect as a Source of Human Strength." In Aspinwall, Lisa, and Ursula Staudinger (eds.). *A Psychology of Human Strengths*. Washington, D.C.: American Psychological Association, 179–195; Cameron, Kim, Jane E. Dutton, and Robert Quinn (eds.). 2003. *Positive Organizational Scholarship*:

Foundations of a New Discipline. San Francisco: Berrett, 263–278; Snyder, C. R., and Shane J. Lopez (eds.). 2002. *Handbook of Positive Psychology.* Oxford: Oxford University Press.

96. Fredrickson, Barbara. 2003. "Positive Emotions and Upward Spirals in Organizations." In Cameron, Kim, Jane E. Dutton, and Robert Quinn (eds.). *Positive Organizational Scholarship: Foundations of a New Discipline.* San Francisco: Berrett Koehler, 163–175.

97. Staw, Barry, Robert Sutton, and Lisa Pelled. 1994. "Employee Positive Emotion and Favorable Outcomes at the Workplace." *Organization Science,* 5(1): 51–72; Staw, Barry, and Sigal Barsade. 1993. "Affect and Managerial Performance: A Test of the Sadder-but-Wiser and Happier-and-Smarter Hypothesis." *Administrative Science Quarterly,* 38(2): 304–332.

98. Taylor, Shelly. 1991. *Positive Illusions*: *Creative Self-Deception and the Healthy Mind.* Basic Books.

99. Danner, D. D., D. A. Snowdon, and W. V. Friesen. 2001 "Positive Emotions Early in Life and Longevity: Findings from the Nun Study." *Journal of Personality and Social Psychology,* 80: 804–813.

100. Norem, Julie. 2001. *The Positive Power of Negative Thinking: Using Defensive Pessimism to Harness Anxiety and Perform at Your Peak.* New York: Basic Books.

101. Cameron, Kim, Jane Dutton, and Robert E. Quinn (eds.). 2003. *Positive Organizational Scholarship: Foundations of a New Discipline.* San Francisco: Berrett-Koehler Publishers.

102. Cameron, Kim S. 2003. *Organizational Virtuousness and Performance.* In Cameron, Kim, Jane E. Dutton, and Robert Quinn (eds.). *Positive Organizational Scholarship: Foundations of a New Discipline.* San Francisco: Berrett-Koehler, 48–65.

103. Sweetman, Katherine. 2001. "Employee Loyalty Around the Globe." *MIT Sloan Management Review,* Winter: 16.

104. Sutcliff, Kathleen, and Timothy Vogus. 2003. "Organizing for Resilience." In Cameron, Kim, Jane E. Dutton, and Robert Quinn (eds.). *Positive Organizational Scholarship*: *Foundations of a New Discipline.* San Francisco: Berrett-Koehler, 94–110.

105. Argenti, Paul. 2002. "Crisis Communication: Lessons from 9/11." *Harvard Business Review* 103–109.

106. Shellenbarger, Sue. 1999. "Some Bosses Fumbling in Crisis Have Bruised Loyalty of Employees." *Wall Street Journal.* B1.

107. Byrne, John, and Heather Timmons. 2001. "Tough Times for a New CEO." *Business Week Online.*

108. Spretizer, Gretchen, and Scott Sonenshein. 2003. "Positive Deviance and Extraordinary Organizing." In Cameron, Kim, Jane E. Dutton, and Robert Quinn (eds.). *Positive Organizational Scholarship*: *Foundations of a New Discipline.* San Francisco: Berrett-Koehler, 207–224.

109. Hosmer, Larue. 1995. "Trust: The Connecting Link between Organizational Theory and Philosophical Ethics." *Academy of Management Review,* 20(2): 379–403.

CHAPTER

4

Communicating Effectively

This chapter will help you:

■ Understand how communication influences managerial effectiveness

■ Learn techniques for active listening

■ Learn how to give and receive effective feedback

■ Learn how to make 360-degree feedback effective

■ Enhance your cross-cultural communication

■ Understand how language reflects and perpetuates status and power differences in organizations and learn techniques for inclusive communication

■ Understand why stories are one of the most effective ways to mobilize action and learn how to tell a motivating story

■ Learn how to use electronic mail and other communication technologies effectively

Have I reached the party to whom I am speaking?
—GERALDINE, THE TELEPHONE OPERATOR
Character Created by Lily Tomlin

ommunication is a contact sport. We communicate to comfort and hurt, influence and resist, coordinate and create chaos, bring people together and pull them apart, make ourselves known and hide behind our words. Yet we often worry so much about speaking clearly and concisely that we overlook the power of language to transform ourselves, our relationships, and our organizations.

Not that speaking clearly and concisely isn't important. Indeed, researchers and businesspeople agree that people who communicate clearly tend to be more effective and more valued in organizations than those who do not.[1] Our efforts to communicate clearly and concisely help us organize our thoughts, avoid misunderstandings, and focus employees' attention on important organizational goals and issues. But the ability to articulate a clear and concise message is only one of many communication skills that we can use to enhance our personal and organizational performance. To better understand the power of language in organizations, consider the following assumptions.

Communication creates, as well as reflects, reality. Great leaders communicate in ways that change people's view of what is real, true, right, worthy, and possible. Steven Jobs of Apple Computer and Pixar Films, the Reverend Martin Luther King of the civil rights movement, and Gloria Steinam of the women's movement all used the power of words to create new realities and convince others that these new realities were worth pursuing.

Language. I loved it. And for a long time I would think of myself, of my whole body, as an ear. Maya Angelou in *the New York Times*

Communication is the real work of managers. In a study of *Fortune* 1,000 workers commissioned by Pitney Bowes, "84 percent of the employees polled [said they] were interrupted more than three times an hour by messages; 71 percent said that they feel 'overwhelmed' by the onslaught. Each employee in the survey said that he or she receives an average of 178 messages and documents every day. Because of the deluge of communications, many of the workers said that 'real work' often has to wait until after hours or weekends."[2] Although communication may distract some employees from their "real work," it *is* the real work of managers. Researchers have concluded that effective managers spend much of their time in informal and unplanned communication. Rather than viewing this as a distraction, they depend on this communication to obtain timely information, build relationships, and develop support for their ideas.[3]

Communication is not a predictable, controllable process. Many of us have been taught that communication is a linear process in which our goal is to get a clear message to the listener and to have this message understood in the way it was intended. But Robert Holland, information manager of the Micro-Electronics Unit of Lucent Technologies, gives a more realistic picture of communication in complex organizations:

> As long as communication is a human activity, there will be chaos in communication. The fact is that we cannot control information, and those who try will be frustrated. The only sane alternative is to manage information and the communication of it. . . . Management is all about creating the message, evaluating the media at your disposal, assessing the benefits and risks of using each, deciding which media to use, and then closing the loop by monitoring the results and responding to them. It sounds like it will work, but as we all know, there are hundreds of variables that can throw our best plans into chaos.[4]

In short, organizational communication lies somewhere between order and chaos, requiring continuous adjustment and adaptation.[5] Even if we could make everything perfectly clear, would we want to? Not always: Ambiguity in communication leaves room for new interpretations, creative thinking, and experimentation, all of which are fundamental to personal and organizational innovation, change, and growth.

But even though communication cannot be controlled, it can—and should—be managed. In this chapter, I focus on five communication skills that can increase your effectiveness. I begin with two classic communication skills that are as relevant today as they were when they were introduced decades ago: active listening and giving and receiving feedback, including 360-degree feedback. I then move to three communication skills that are getting increasing attention in organizations today: communicating across cultures, telling stories that create meaning and mobilize action, and communicating through electronic media, particularly through electronic mail.

ACTIVE LISTENING

The Swiss psychiatrist Paul Tournier wrote that "it's impossible to overemphasize the immense need human beings have to be really listened to, to be taken seriously, to be understood."[9] Yet in a "Brand Called You" economy in which being able to sell oneself is fast being seen as the mother of all skills, the value of listening does not seem to get the respect it deserves. Indeed, the old saying that "the opposite of talking isn't listening, it's waiting to talk"[10] seems increasingly relevant. However, the *Wall Street Journal* columnist Hal Lancaster warns:

> It's time to stop promoting yourself and start listening. . . . To get what you want in your career, stop talking and start listening and observing. Instead of aggressively selling yourself, learn how others communicate, how they process information, and what their needs are.[11]

The act of listening is often confused with the exercise of waiting for one's turn to speak. *Anonymous* Whether starting your career or standing on the pinnacle of success, the ability to listen to others in ways that make them feel heard and understood is a critical managerial skill. The more you listen to others, the more likely you are to hear what employees need to do their jobs, learn what customers want, hear good ideas, receive bad news, avoid mistakes, and build stronger relationships. People who don't listen are unlikely to hear important information or earn the support of others.

Everything that needs to be said has already been said. But since no one was listening, everything must be said again. Andre Gide, Nobel Laureate in Literature

In the late 1980s, for example, disgruntled Yale University employees publicly chastised the university's president Benno Schmidt by creating this unflattering ditty: "Benno doesn't listen; and when he listens, he doesn't hear; and when he hears, he doesn't understand; and when he understands, he's against it."[12] In a more recent example, critics blamed Jill Barad, former CEO of Mattel, for the company's steep decline in shareholder earnings in the late 1990s. Although they credited Barad's marketing savvy and persistence with building Barbie from a $250 million brand in the mid-1980s to a $1.7 billion brand a decade later, they also argued that her ego was too caught up in the Barbie brand, that she suffered from "an inability to accept an alternative point of view," that executives at Mattel were afraid to contradict her, and that customers and dealers felt that they weren't being listened to.[13] In contrast, when Ann Fudge took the CEO position at Young & Rubicam, Inc., she was asked what she would do when she stepped into the role. "The first thing I'm going to do is listen," said Fudge who, according to the *Wall Street Journal*, is "known as a coalition builder with the ability to rally loyal troops around her."[14]

Why is listening so hard to do? There are several opinions on this. Harvard's John Kotter says that "the problem with people who are very successful is that they suffer ego expansion. It crushes everything in its path. It also becomes a wall."[15] The Brazilian educator Paulo Freire put it this way: "Dialogue cannot exist without humility. How can I [talk developmentally with others] if I always project ignorance onto others and never perceive my own?"[16] Psychologist Carl Rogers argued that listening to others is difficult because it takes courage: "If you really understand another in this way, if you are willing to enter his [sic] private world and see the way life appears to him [sic], without any attempt to make evaluative judgments, you run the risk of being changed yourself."[17]

When we're in everyday conversation with another person, how do we block active listening? Sometimes our impressions or stereotypes of a person shape how we interpret his or her comments. We may emphasize certain things the person says and downplay other things the person says. Sometimes we get carried away with our own ideas and start thinking about how we will respond (while the other person is speaking) rather than really listening to what the other person is saying. Sometimes our emotions get in the way, especially during difficult conversations. And sometimes we just let our mind drift while the other person is speaking. As one manager recently told me, "If I had a dollar for every time I nodded my head at someone without having heard most of what he or she said, I'd be a millionaire today."

Our meeting had that quality of sweetness that lasts for a lifetime; even if you never speak to the person again, see their face, you can always return in your heart to that moment when you were together to be renewed. bell hooks, *Teaching to Transgress*

"Active listening" refers to listening to understand another person's point of view without evaluating or judging the other person or his or her views. It requires empathy, which is both a perception and behavioral skill. As a perception skill, empathy means understanding that each person views the world from his or her own perspective, accepting that this perspective may be different from one's own, and respecting that difference. As a behavioral skill, empathy means responding to another person in ways that validate that person's perspective.[18] Nearly 40 years after psychologist Carl Rogers coined the term "active listening," Steven Covey, author of the book *Seven Habits of Highly Effective People*, explains: "Seek first to understand, then to be understood . . . when others feel

FIGURE 4-1   Active Listening

understood first, they feel affirmed and valued, defenses are lowered, and opportunities to speak openly and to be understood come much more naturally and easily."[19]

In their wonderful book *Difficult Conversations*, Douglas Stone and his colleagues at the Harvard Negotiation Project explain that most conversations, especially difficult ones, are really three conversations happening at once. Some of these conversations are happening out loud, but the others are happening inside the participants heads and hearts. The "*what happened conversation*" focuses on perceptions of the facts—who did what to whom, when, why, who is right, what was meant, who gets credit, and who's to blame? The "*feelings conversation*" focuses on emotions—how do I feel about this, how does the other person feel, how much should I protect the other person's feelings, and do I show or hide my feelings. The "*identity conversation*" focuses on the impact of the discussion on the participants' identity and self-esteem—am I competent or incompetent, how am I being perceived by the others, what impact will how I handle this conversation have on my future? By listening actively to the other person, you may gain valuable insights at each of these levels of conversation, which can help you and the other person identify the best outcomes.[20]

To listen actively:

1. *Listen with intensity.*   Give the person speaking your full attention. This means:
   - Don't get distracted. Turn off the phone, ignore the computer screen, and don't look at your watch.
   - Don't assume that the issue is uninteresting or unimportant.
   - Don't listen only for what you want to hear.
   - Don't think ahead to what you plan to say next.
   - Don't interrupt, talk too much, or finish people's sentences for them.
   - Don't engage in fake listening techniques such as nodding your head, saying "I see," or smiling even though you aren't really paying attention.
   - Don't let the person's status, appearance, or speaking style distract you from hearing the message.

2. *Listen with empathy.*   Try to understand the message from the speaker's point of view. Empathy does not mean agreeing with the other person, but it does mean respecting the person's perspective and feelings.
   - Suspend thoughts (such as counterarguments, stereotypes, and preconceptions) and feelings (such as defensiveness) that can distract you from hearing the speaker's perspective.

- Don't relate everything you hear to your own experience, such as "That reminds me of the time. . . ."
- Listen for feeling as well as content.
- Pay attention to body language that can provide clues to the speaker's concerns and emotional state.

3. *Demonstrate acceptance.*   Show that you are listening with an open mind.

   - Avoid killer phrases such as "You've got to be kidding," "That will never work," and "Yes, but. . . ." These responses belittle and discount what the other person thinks and feels. See Box 4-2 for a list of other killer phrases.
   - Avoid judgmental body language. Condescending grins and rolling one's eyes can have the same affect as killer phrases.
   - Use encouraging language and body language.

4. *Take responsibility for completeness.*   Encourage the speaker to give complete information.

   - Ask open-ended questions, such as "What do you think the critical issues are?" "Why do you think so?" "What do other people think about this?" and "What other choices do you have?" "How do you think this will affect your future choices?" "Do you have any more concerns?"
   - Confirm your understanding by paraphrasing what you heard, summarizing the main points, and asking if what you summarized was the message that the speaker intended. Doing so ensures that you understood the message, gives the speaker an opportunity to clarify his or her ideas, and let's the speaker know that you are sincerely interested in understanding the key issues.

5. *Be yourself.*   Be natural and don't come across as a compulsive, artificial, or overly trained active listener.[21] Remember that active listening is based more on a sincere attitude of openness, respect, and learning than on a set of rigid techniques.

A new idea is delicate. It can be killed by a sneer or a yawn; it can be stabbed to death by a joke or worried to death by a frown on the right person's brow.   *Charles Brower, U.S. advertising executive*

How important is it to develop a reputation for being a good listener? In one study of executive promotion, researcher Peter Meyer and his colleagues concluded that "the most common factor that differentiated the successful candidates for promotion was this: The executive was seen as a person who listens."[22] In other words, successful people "get caught listening." Both Benno Schmidt of Yale University and Jill Barad of Mattel may have been listening to their constituents, but some of their most important constituents didn't think that they were.[23]

How do people determine whether someone is listening? They consider how much time the person spends listening, whether the person asks questions about what they're hearing, whether they interrupt when others are speaking, whether they use body language that suggests they are listening, and whether they actually do something about what they hear.

BOX 4-2

Killer Phrases

You can't teach an old dog new tricks.
Don't rock the boat.
It will never work.
Don't be silly.
The boss (or employees) will never go for it.
People don't want to change.
We tried that before.
You've got to be kidding.
Prove it.
If it ain't broke, don't fix it.
You must be kidding.
Be realistic.
Yes, but . . .

Fill in other killer phrases:

_____

_____

_____

GIVING AND RECEIVING FEEDBACK

Simply stated, feedback is "any information that answers the question 'How am I doing?'"[24] At its best, feedback answers employees' questions, sets clear expectations, reduces uncertainty, encourages desired behaviors, helps employees learn new skills, enhances employee performance, and is a necessary part of coaching.

Researchers have found that although receiving feedback is an important developmental opportunity, managers often resist giving feedback. A conference board study found that 60 percent of the U.S. and European companies that participated in the study "identified improper or insufficient performance feedback [as] a primary cause of deficient performance."[25] Why do managers resist giving feedback? Says Harvard professor Lou Barnes:

> The biggest problem usually found in organizations is the problem of excess caution. All too often people are not told things that would help them behave more effectively because of our fear of "not wanting to hurt them." As a result, the problem is perpetuated, and people get hurt later when . . . they are fired, demoted, or suddenly told that they are worth far less to the organization than they had thought.[26]

How can you promote effective feedback in your organization? First, you can create a feedback-friendly work environment. Second, you can promote effective feedback techniques.

Creating a Feedback-Friendly Work Environment

Remember that employees are more likely to seek out feedback if they feel that they will not be negatively evaluated for doing so and that it will help improve their performance.[27] To create such a work environment:

- Set clear, measurable performance standards so that people can judge for themselves when they are and are not meeting performance standards.
- Give ongoing feedback rather than only during performance reviews or when something goes wrong.
- Find opportunities to give positive feedback. Spencer Johnson and Ken Blanchard, authors of the book *The One-Minute Manager*, call this "catching people doing something right."[28]
- Set a tone of openness. Let employees know that giving feedback—not only from managers to subordinates but also from subordinates to managers and peers to peers—is an important part of their job.
- Make sure that organizational managers and leaders are role models of feedback seeking and feedback giving.
- Make sure that managers know the feedback policies concerning potential discrimination, sexual harassment, or other activities that may be illegal. The way such feedback is given (or not given) has legal implications.
- Institutionalize feedback by providing employees with ongoing feedback regarding unit, industry competition, and industry performance. This can be provided through an organization's Intranet.

Giving Feedback

Effective feedback is motivated by the desire to genuinely help another person, a relationship, or an organization. To be most helpful, feedback should enable the receiver to understand the information, accept the information, and do something about the information. The following advice can increase your effectiveness in giving feedback:[29]

- Choose the right moment. In general, feedback is most useful when the person is ready to hear it (when the person is not too busy, tired, or upset); when the recipient has solicited the information; and as soon as possible after the event that triggers the feedback.
- Choose the right place. A useful, though not universal, rule of thumb is to praise in public and criticize in private. Remember, however, that in some cultures people enjoy receiving positive feedback in public, and in other cultures they prefer receiving positive feedback in private.
- Choose an appropriate communication style. Know your own communication style as well as the receiver's style, and adapt your message to the style of the receiver as much as possible.
- State the purpose of the feedback session and where it fits into the broader organizational goals. For example, say, "I've had two complaints from customers this month, and I want to discuss these complaints with you. As you know, customer satisfaction is one of our top five quality indicators for your department" or "I've noticed that profits in your area have increased by 5 percent since last quarter. Because profitability is an important measure of

success in our company, I want to let you know how much I appreciate your efforts and the efforts of the employees who work for you." If it's a delicate issue and you are uncertain how to frame it, be honest and say, "I don't know how to say this, and. . . ."[30]

- Focus on key performance issues, behavior that the receiver can do something about, and only one or two issues at a time. Frustration is only increased when the receiver is faced with too much information, concerns that are irrelevant to the job, or situations over which he or she has no control.
- Be specific rather than general. Provide observable, recent examples of behaviors. Avoid using general statements such as "You always" or "You never." Don't present perceptions as facts or present one person's opinion as everyone's opinion.
- Be descriptive rather than evaluative. If possible, present data graphically. Doing so provides "a readily understandable comparative benchmark" for future discussions.[31] For example, show monthly figures and say, "As the figures here show, 6 months ago the customer service department was among those with the lowest turnover in our division. Over the last 6 months, the customer service department has developed the highest turnover in the division and is above the industry norm as well." Avoid evaluative language such as "bad" or "worse" that can create defensiveness. For example, don't say, "The turnover rate in your department is awful."
- Provide positive feedback, not just criticism.[32] For example, say, "I've noticed that although employee turnover has increased by 15 percent, customer satisfaction has also increased by 10 percent. What do you think is going on?"
- Describe your feelings, if appropriate. For example, say, "I worry that the customer service department will get a reputation as a difficult place to work, and we won't be able to get top-caliber employees to work there."
- Check that the receiver has understood the feedback as intended. Ask the receiver to rephrase what he or she heard you say.
- Encourage a response. Ask open-ended questions such as, "What do you think is going on?" "What do you think needs to be done to curtail the turnover?" and "How can I help?"
- Give time to react. If a person gets defensive or emotional, let him or her react. You may even learn something new and be better able to help the person find effective solutions.
- Encourage the receiver to check the accuracy of the feedback with others. Is this just your impression, or is it shared by others?
- End on an encouraging note. Discuss how the organization will benefit from the recipient's efforts to change and show confidence in the recipient's abilities. Let the employee know that you are available to help and ask what resources he or she needs to succeed (including training, equipment, staff, information, or budget).
- Follow up on the feedback session. Remember to notice and acknowledge when the recipient's behavior has changed. Avoid holding onto previous perceptions of the recipient once he or she has changed the behaviors discussed.

Finally, if you are giving feedback—particularly negative feedback—to someone in a lower level of the organizational hierarchy, be aware that the employee may be particularly sensitive to the information. For example, you may think an employee is generally very effective, yet you may give the employee feedback on one area of his or her performance that you feel could be improved. The employee may overinterpret your feedback and assume that you are unhappy with his or her performance in general. Rather than focus on improving that one area, the employee may decide to look for a new job, and you may lose a valuable employee because of a misunderstanding. Therefore, it is important to help employees, particularly those over whom you have significant power, keep feedback in perspective.

Receiving Feedback

There are only two people who can tell you the truth about yourself— an enemy who has lost his temper and a friend who loves you dearly.
Antisthenes

Receiving helpful feedback is an important developmental opportunity, yet most of us do not actively pursue it. We may not ask for feedback because we are afraid that asking for feedback may draw attention to our weaknesses or make us look "insecure, uncertain, or incompetent."[33] Professors Susan Ashford and Greg Northcraft suggest that these concerns are not unfounded. In a study of middle managers, they found that when managers who were perceived as high performers asked for feedback (particularly negative feedback), their boss's and subordinates' positive impressions of them increased. But when managers who were perceived as average or below average performers asked for feedback (particularly negative feedback), the results were less positive. This suggests that although average or below average performers are more likely to benefit from the learning that comes from receiving negative feedback, they are also more likely to harm their reputations by asking for it.

So, should you ask for feedback? Absolutely. Receiving feedback is a critical developmental opportunity that you shouldn't forgo—but request feedback wisely. Remember that you are managing impressions as well as looking for information that can enhance your performance. There are many people who can give you useful feedback—your bosses, peers, subordinates, customers, friends, and professional coaches—so select your sources carefully and get feedback from multiple sources. You also can monitor your environment for insights into how you are doing. For example, you can pay attention to trends in customer or employee satisfaction surveys, note whether people are coming to you for help and advice more or less often, and so on.

Also remember to time your requests for feedback carefully. Ashford and Northcraft warn that it sometimes is wise to avoid asking for feedback, at least for a while, when you are trying a new or risky task that requires persistence. They say that a strategy of avoiding feedback may be useful "for maintaining a necessary level of self-efficacy to allow some level of persistence at [the] tasks."[34]

Once you decide to ask for feedback, the following guidelines can help you make the most of the feedback.[35]

- Request feedback from people whom you trust and who will be honest with you.
- If the feedback is too general ("You're doing a fine job" or "There's room for improvement"), ask for examples of specific, recent behavior.
- Don't be defensive, make excuses, or blame others when you hear criticism. Listen carefully, let the person finish speaking, and try to understand what the

person is trying to tell you. Even if you disagree with the feedback, you may learn something new. For example, you may learn that you need to better manage people's perceptions of you, be more clear about your needs or accomplishments, or use a different management style to be more effective.
- Do not overreact or underreact to feedback. Be aware that you may overreact to the feedback, particularly when the person giving you feedback is your boss or has power over you. Conversely, you may underreact to feedback if the person giving you feedback is in a lower hierarchical position than you are.
- Once the feedback is complete, summarize what the speaker said to make sure that you understand. Ask for (or develop together) clear performance measures so you both can evaluate future performance.
- Explain what you are going to do in response to the feedback, do it, evaluate the consequences on performance, and then let the feedback-giver know of the outcome, particularly if you can show that your performance has improved.
- Thank the person for his or her concern and advice.
- Follow up with the feedback provider to let him or her know how you are doing in the future.

The Effectiveness of Multirater Feedback

We often think about feedback as a personal one-on-one process. Yet almost all Fortune 500 companies use multirater feedback, often spending millions of dollars to implement multirater feedback programs.[36] The most commonly used form of multirater feedback is 360-degree feedback that involves anonymously surveying subordinates, peers, bosses, and others (e.g., customers and supplies) to gain information about a specific manager's performance across a standard set of competencies (e.g., communicating effectively, providing clear direction, setting clear performance measures, showing care and concern, and inspiring creativity). A survey of the Society of Human Resource Managers members found that 360-degree feedback is used almost exclusively for managers, and most often used for executives and middle- to upper-level managers.[37]

These surveys often include a self-assessment as well so that managers can compare their self-assessments with how they are perceived by others. Notably, researchers have found that the most effective managers tend to rate themselves more similarly to their raters, which suggests that having an accurate perception of your skills is associated with high performance. People who rate themselves significantly higher than others rated them tend to be poorer performers.[38] In one study, individuals whose feedback from raters was most different (lower) than their own were more likely to believe that the feedback they received was less accurate and less useful than did those with smaller gaps in self-other perception.[39] Some research suggests that the larger the gap between one's self-perception and raters' perceptions, the more likely the person being rated will believe that the feedback was not useful and become discouraged.

Organizational leaders are willing to spend a considerable amount of time, effort, and money on these programs because they expect these programs to help managers improve their on-the-job performance and by doing so enhance organizational results. This assumption is intuitively appealing and is based on several assumptions. First, obtaining feedback from a variety of sources who interact with the manager on a regular basis should provide a well-rounded and more accurate view of the manager's performance in specific areas. Second, because the feedback is typically anonymous and combined with other sources, there is reason to believe that raters will feel comfortable enough to provide more honest feedback. Third, once a manager knows how he or she is perceived by others, the manager will be motivated to improve his or her performance in ways that will enhance bottom-line results.

Despite these high hopes, researchers have found that multirater feedback enhances managerial performance in about one-third to one-half of the cases, and has no effect or a negative effect on performance in the rest of the cases (regardless of whether the manager received high or low ratings).[40] Although multi-rater feedback has the potential for enhancing performance, it is no guarantee, and the success of such interventions depends, in part, on the type of person who receives the feedback.

What kind of people are likely to respond well and poorly to 360-degree feedback? People who follow up with the raters after receiving feedback to discuss what they learn from the process tend to gain from the 360-degree feedback process.[41] Furthermore, people whose performance is rated as low to moderate tend to be more likely to change their performance in response to feedback than people who are evaluated more highly. Research suggests that people who are cynical with the organization or the feedback process or who were overly concerned about protecting their ego may be less likely to engage in feedback processes.[42] People who are cynical may not believe that acting on the feedback will result in positive outcomes. People who are focused on protecting their self-image or looking good in the eyes of others may become too emotional, more anxious about image management, and distracted from efforts to improve their performance.[43]

If you use 360-degree feedback in your organization, what can you do to increase the possibility that the feedback will lead to better performance and bottom-line results?

- Select assessments that evaluate performance on skills that are related to bottom-line results.
- Choose an appropriate time to conduct the 360-degree feedback so the process will be successful. For example, avoid collecting feedback when employees are cynical or when the organization is in the midst of a significant and possibly threatening transition.
- Prepare feedback providers to give feedback. Explain what the process entails, ask that they provide honest responses, ensure anonymity, let them know what the feedback will be used for, and answer any questions they have about the feedback process.
- Tell the person who completes a self-assessment that it doesn't pay to inflate their scores on their self-assessments. Gently warn them that people who do so may be out of touch with how others perceive them and, consequently, may not be performing at their best.
- Tell the person what the ratings will be used for. People are likely to react positively to feedback when they believe it is to be used for personal development rather than for promotion or salary decisions.
- Help the person interpret the feedback they receive. Keep explanations simple and focus on specific skills rather than personal characteristics. Present feedback in a way that doesn't threaten the person's self-concept.

- Help the person who receives feedback create a goal-setting plan that focuses on specific skill development. Focus the plan on areas that the person wants to develop. Again, keep it simple.
- Provide training and development opportunities (including coaching) in the relevant skill areas.
- Encourage the person who receives feedback to follow up with the feedback providers to explain what he or she has learned and to gain additional insights.
- Repeat the 360-degree feedback process again to determine if there has been any improvement.

Managerial Language That Motivates Employees

Language, as symbol, determines much of the nature and quality of our experience. **Sonia Johnson, The Ship that Sailed into The Living Room**

Considerable research has shown that a manager's communication style is related to employee loyalty, motivation, stress level, job satisfaction, and job performance.[44] Managerial communication that motivates falls into three categories:

Direction Giving and Uncertainty Reducing: Using language that minimizes employee role and task ambiguity. This includes clarifying goals, tasks, performance measures, and rewards.

Relationship Building: Using language that develops an emotional connection with employees (e.g., sharing feelings, showing care and concern, and expressing appreciation).

Meaning Making: Using language, stories, and personal examples that explain the organization's vision, values, culture, structure, challenges, and opportunities (what our organization does, how we do it, and why we do it) so that employees can make sense of the organization and their place in it. This is most useful during periods of organizational entry, change, or uncertainty.

Managers who use these three forms of communication in their everyday interactions with employees are more likely than others to create a work environment that motivates and enables employees to do their best work. The assessment in Box 4-3 lists a series of questions you can ask employees to determine whether you are communicating in a way that brings out the best in employees (or whether your manager is communicating in a way that motivates you).

Are You Getting Enough Bad News?

Undoubtedly, managers who are unable to see problems quickly and accurately face a "major liability in our increasingly complex and fast-paced world."[45] Effective managers find out that trouble is brewing through employees who are willing to give them frequent, honest information—including bad news. Unfortunately, employees are often reluctant to give their boss unfavorable information.

For example, early in President Bill Clinton's administration, political analysts concluded, "No one in the Clinton operation has the stature, guts, and willingness to rein in the president when his own judgment is faulty."[46] Says researcher Walter Scott, "All of us have had our share of bonehead ideas. Having someone tell you it's a bonehead idea before you do something about it is really a great blessing."[47] Walter Kiechel III of

BOX 4-3

Motivating Language Scale

The examples below show different ways that your boss might talk to you (or you might talk to employees). Please choose the answer that best matches your perceptions. Be sure to mark only one answer for each question.

Very Little	Little	Some	A Lot	A Whole Lot
VL	L	S	A	WL

DIRECTION-GIVING/UNCERTAINTY-REDUCING LANGUAGE

1. Gives me useful explanations of what needs to be done in my work.   VL L S A WL
2. Offers me helpful directions on how to do my job.   VL L S A WL
3. Provides me with easily understandable instructions about my work.   VL L S A WL
4. Offers me helpful advice on how to improve my work.   VL L S A WL
5. Gives me good definitions of what I must do in order to receive rewards.   VL L S A WL
6. Gives me clear instructions about solving job-related problems.   VL L S A WL
7. Offers me specific information on how I am evaluated.   VL L S A WL
8. Provides me with helpful information about forthcoming changes affecting my work.   VL L S A WL
9. Provides me with helpful information about past changes affecting my work.   VL L S A WL
10. Shares news with me about organizational achievements and financial status.   VL L S A WL

EMPATHETIC LANGUAGE

11. Gives me praise for my good work.   VL L S A WL
12. Shows me encouragement for my work efforts.   VL L S A WL
13. Shows concern about my job satisfaction.   VL L S A WL
14. Expresses his/her support for my professional development.   VL L S A WL
15. Asks me about my professional well-being.   VL L S A WL
16. Shows trust in me.   VL L S A WL

MEANING-MAKING LANGUAGE

17. Tells me stories about key events in the organization's past.   VL L S A WL
18. Gives me useful information that I couldn't get through official channels.   VL L S A WL

19. Tells me stories about people who are admired in my organization.	VL	L	S	A	WL
20. Tells me stories about people who have worked hard in this organization.	VL	L	S	A	WL
21. Offers me advice about how to behave at the organization's social gatherings.	VL	L	S	A	WL
22. Offers me advice about how to "fit in" with other members of this organization.	VL	L	S	A	WL
23. Tells me stories about people who have left this organization.	VL	L	S	A	WL
24. Tells me stories about people who have been rewarded by this organization.	VL	L	S	A	WL

SOURCE: Mayfield Rowley, Jacqueline, Milton Ray Mayfield, and Jerry Kopf. 1998. "The Effects of Leader Motivating Language on Subordinate Performance and Satisfaction." *Human Resource Management*, 37(3): 235–248. Used with permission.

The day soldiers stop bringing you their problems is the day you have stopped leading them. They have either lost confidence that you can help them or concluded that you do not care. Either case is a failure of leadership. *General Colin Powell*

Fortune magazine puts it more bluntly: "You can't afford to become isolated at the top, hearing only agreeable tidings borne by simpering yea-saying subordinates."[48]

There are several reasons that managers don't get bad news from their subordinates. Researcher Fernando Bartolome explains:

Candor depends on trust, and in hierarchical organizations, trust has strict natural limits. In a hierarchy, it is natural for people with less power to be extremely cautious about disclosing weaknesses, mistakes, and failings—especially when the more powerful party is also in a position to evaluate and punish. Trust flees authority and, above all, trust flees a judge.[49]

In organizational hierarchies, employees are likely to promote and exaggerate good news and hide or minimize bad news.[50] Even the most kind-hearted and well-intentioned boss may not get the bad news he or she needs. Why not? Employees may not want to bother a boss who seems too busy to listen. They may be trying to protect a boss who seems to prefer hearing good news and is overly sensitive to bad news. They may try to solve the problem themselves or hope that the problem will correct itself over time. They may be afraid that asking for help to solve a problem will make them look incompetent. Or there may be too many levels of the hierarchy that impede upward communication. Ultimately, however, small problems can grow into big ones, and bosses get blindsided when they should have seen the problems coming.

Much unhappiness has come into the world because of bewilderment and things left unsaid. *Dostoyevsky*

Because hierarchy has such a powerful effect on employee behavior, managers must take proactive steps to encourage the communication of bad news. The most important thing you can do is to build a reputation as someone who can be trusted with bad news. Building such a reputation takes time, but there are many steps you can take to speed up the process.[51]

- *Be accessible.* Don't surround yourself with gatekeepers. Take employees out to breakfast, lunch, or dinner. Visit employees' work areas and establish regular times when people can come to see you.
- *Be approachable.* Create an atmosphere in which subordinates feel comfortable speaking up. Avoid intimidating surroundings.
- *Surround yourself with independent minds.* In many organizations, people move ahead by adhering to the status quo and not making waves. Top performers who feel secure in their jobs are more likely to feel comfortable giving bad news, so ask them first.
- *Run meetings that encourage independent thinking and honest feedback.* Don't give your opinions first; develop processes that ensure that all views are heard; create a devil's advocate role; and regularly ask questions such as "What do you think of this?" "Has anyone seen or heard of any problems?" "Can this backfire in any way?" and "Is there any other way to look at this?" Publicly support employees who express contrary opinions or provide bad news.
- *Be discreet about sources.* Don't betray confidences. Provide ways for employees to give information anonymously, including suggestion boxes, questionnaires, open bulletin boards, and 360-degree feedback.
- *Never shoot the messenger.* Many employees have learned through experience that people who give bad news can get punished. When people come to you with bad news, you should spend most of your time listening, not speaking. Walter Kiechel wisely advises that managers should respond with three statements when they hear bad news: Can you tell me more about what happened? What do you think we should do? Thanks for letting me know. And then, of course, managers should do something about what they hear.

COMMUNICATING ACROSS CULTURES

Most of us have heard stories of humorous, embarrassing, and costly cross-national communication blunders. For example, when Coca-Cola introduced the soft drink to the Chinese market, "the bottles were marked with Chinese characters that presented the sounds of 'Coca-Cola' but that in fact meant 'Bite the wax tadpole.'"[52] When the Chevy Nova was introduced to Latin America, many people were reluctant to purchase a car whose name means "doesn't go" in Spanish.

> The sum of human wisdom is not contained in any one language, and no single language is capable of expressing all forms and degrees of human comprehension.
> *Ezra Pound, The ABC of Reading*

Even the same words can mean different things in different cultures. It's commonly said, "Even though the British and Americans speak English, this doesn't mean that they speak the same language." For example, when Americans say that they want to "table an idea," it means that they want to put it aside for the moment. When the British say that they want to "table an idea," it means that they want to attend to it immediately. The meaning of gestures and body language may differ from culture to culture as well. For example, Anglo Americans show that they are paying attention to another person by making eye contact and using fillers such as "uh huh" or "I see." But many cultures don't use eye contact or fillers routinely in conversation.[53] And hand motions used in one country (e.g., the hand signals commonly used to say "OK" or "come here" in the United States) may be considered obscene in another.

One manager described his perception of the difference between Japanese and North American communication styles this way: "The Japanese probably will never become gabby. We're a homogeneous people and don't have to speak as much as you do here. When we say one word, we understand 10, but here you have to say 10 to understand one."[54] Table 4-1 describes one of the most common communication differences across national cultures: low context versus high context communication.

Effective managers enhance communication across cultures not by stereotyping but by paying attention to potential cultural differences in communication. By doing so, they show respect, avoid misunderstandings, and build common ground. The following guidelines can help you enhance your cross-cultural communication when people speak different languages:

- Speak clearly, use commonly known words and short sentences, but don't be patronizing.
- Avoid slang, jargon, buzzwords, and abbreviations that may not be understood.
- Avoid humor and sarcasm. Never criticize nationalities or other cultures.
- Don't judge people or their message because of the way that they speak.
- Do your homework and learn preferred communication styles, including body language.
- Do not assume that "yes" and "no" are straightforward responses. "Yes" may mean "I understand" or "I'm saying yes to help you save face, but you should be able to tell from my body language that I really mean to say no."
- Learn to decipher silence.
- Be flexible, especially with time. Consider norms regarding pace and punctuality.
- Learn some words in the language of the country you are visiting.
- Learn appropriate greetings. For example, learn to pronounce people's names correctly; determine whether they prefer to be referred to by formal titles, first name, or last name; and determine whether they prefer to be met with a handshake, a bow, or other greeting.

TABLE 4-1 Differences between High Context and Low Context Communication	
Low Context	*High Context*
Message is carried primarily by words ("Read my lips.").	Message is carried in large part through nonverbal signals and situational cues (such as status).
Communication is direct ("Get to the point.").	Communication is indirect.
Primary purpose of communication is to exchange information.	Primary purpose of communication is to build relationships.
Conflicts are depersonalized. It is possible to separate the person from the issues.	Conflicts are personalized. Face-saving is important.
Business relationships start and end quickly and do not require trust.	Business relationships are developed slowly and are built on trust.

- If you are unsure of the appropriate degree of formality, err on the side of being too formal. Dress formally at first meetings. Be punctual. In some cultures, it is appropriate to address higher status and older people first. Do not ask personal questions.
- Be aware of important social rituals. For example, remember that in some cultures, people want to "get down to business" quickly, whereas in other cultures business discussions should be avoided until relationships are developed. In the United States, the front seat of the car is the seat of honor. In Japan, it's the back seat.
- When in doubt, follow the others' lead.

Differences in communication are not limited to national borders. Many researchers argue that men and women tend to have different communication styles.[55] For example, research suggests that:

- Men are more likely to express themselves directly, and women are more likely to express themselves indirectly. In other words, a man is more likely to say "Turn in the report by tomorrow," and a woman is more likely to say "Would it be possible to get the report to me by tomorrow?" Yet both men and women expect the report to be turned in tomorrow.
- Women are more likely to emphasize relationship building in communication, and men are more likely to emphasize information giving in communication. Communications researcher Deborah Tannen refers to this difference as "rapport talk" versus "report talk."[56]
- Women are more likely than men to give verbal and nonverbal signals that they are listening to others, such as making eye contact, nodding their heads, smiling, and saying "uh huh."[57]
- Both men and women don't interrupt men, but men are more likely than women to interrupt women. This pattern has been found both in children and adults. Researcher Holly Craig notes that "this pattern is not limited to conversations among peers. Boys interrupt women as well as girls who are closer to their own age."[58]

As always, when making generalizations about cultural patterns, an important caveat is in order. Our communication styles and preferences are the result of many factors, not only nationality, gender, or any other common cultural category. Personality, experience, training, and even family dynamics influence our communication styles. One woman, for example, explained, "At our house, we warn new friends to be careful because we treat conversation like a competitive sport. The first one to take a breath is considered the listener."[59]

Culture, Language, and Power

In the end, we will remember not the words of our enemies, but the silence of our friends. *The Reverend Martin Luther King Jr.*

The late anthropologist Edward Sapir once said, "All in all, it is not too much to say that one of the really important functions of language is to be constantly declaring to society the psychological place held by all of its members."[60] In other words, we signal and perpetuate our assumptions about status and power through our ways of communicating in our families, communities, and workplaces.

In organizations, we can see these assumptions in action by noting who speaks more often, who gets credit for ideas, who interrupts and who gets interrupted, who gets heard and who gets ignored, and which ways of speaking are assumed to signal confidence and competence and which are not.[61]

Changing how we communicate is a powerful way that we can influence assumptions about power and status. Change, of course, doesn't come easily. For example, in the 1970s, many women and men in the United States challenged the common practice of using male nouns and pronouns to refer to both men and women (e.g., "A manager should make sure that all employees communicate regularly with him.") and promoted gender-inclusive language (such as using "chairperson" rather than "chairman"). Researcher Wendy Martyna notes that efforts to promote the use of sex-unbiased language were met with significant resistance. Critics, she says, called these efforts "ardent Amazonian," and "sisspeak." *Time* magazine called these efforts "ms-guided," a syndicated columnist called them "linguistic lunacy," and linguistic faculty at Harvard called it "pronoun envy." Many argued that the use of male nouns and pronouns to refer to both men and women was simply a linguistic convention with no exclusion or offense intended; that using "he or she" rather than a simple "he" sounded awkward and "offends the traditional eye"; and that people who promoted gender-inclusive language were too sensitive, seeing injustice and inequality where none was intended.

The unnamed should not be taken for the nonexistent. *Catherine MacKinnon, Sexual Harassment of Working Women, 1979*

However, research suggests that using male nouns and pronouns to refer to both men and women may indeed reinforce cultural beliefs that promote inequality (e.g., the belief that men, more so than women, are expected to become managers and executives). For example, in a study of male and female responses to employment advertisements, researchers Sandra Bem and Daryl Bem found that when employment advertisements used male pronouns in their text (e.g., "The applicant should have a degree in business administration. In addition, he should have strong communication skills."), women were less likely to apply for stereotypically male jobs than they were when the advertisement used sex-unbiased pronouns.[62]

In addition to its potential for promoting inequality, sex-biased language can be confusing, particularly as more women and men enter professions that were previously dominated by one gender. For example, it is unclear whether the statement "Businessmen are retiring earlier today than in the past" refers to a pattern for businessmen only or for businesswomen as well. Sex-biased language can also sound silly. Martyna provides these clever examples:

> Startled laughter often greets such sentences as "Menstrual pain accounts for an enormous loss of manpower hours" or "Man, being a mammal, breast-feeds his young." We do a double take when hearing of the gynecologist who was awarded a medical award for "service to his fellowman."[63]

Increasingly, the business press, as well as the academic community, is moving away from sex-biased language. For example, most business communication textbooks in the United States, the *Harvard Business Review, Fast Company* magazine, and the *Academy of Management Journal* now use gender-inclusive language. What are the advantages of using nonsexist language at work? In a *Business Horizons* article, Bill Daily and Miriam Finch explain:[64]

> Nonsexist language puts the emphasis on roles and the work produced, not the gender. Dropping gender distinctions is one tangible method management can use to announce that these distinctions are unnecessary and, what is more important, inappropriate. Most employees, both male and female, will appreciate this overt gesture and follow the lead. Nonsexist language also helps employees reach their full potential . . . [because it] allows no false links between knowledge, skills, abilities, and gender. Nonsexist language helps create a supportive work climate. . . . When sexist language is the norm, management may falsely assume that everyone supports or at least accepts its use. Even though employees may not express their disapproval, however, they may vent it in some indirect manner, such as subtly withholding support or cooperation. This type of backlash can be avoided by using language that supports every employee, not just some. Nonsexist language unifies the workforce instead of dividing it.

Table 4-2 provides guidelines for using gender-inclusive language.[65] I realize that many readers are already using gender-inclusive language. However, there are still many people who are willing to do so but find it awkward and who would appreciate advice. And there are still many people (you've seen them on television or read their articles or books) who think that using gender-inclusive language is unnecessary. For those who fall into the latter category, Martyna notes that philosopher and psychologist William James once said that a new idea moves through three stages: "It is first attacked as absurd; then admitted to be true, but seen as obvious and insignificant; and finally, seen as so important that its adversaries claim they discovered it."[66]

COMMUNICATING TO MOBILIZE ACTION

Today's managers mobilize employees to go above and beyond the call of duty not by instilling fear but by creating meaning that inspires collective action. Says retired Allied Signal CEO Larry Bossidy, "The day when you could yell and scream and beat people into good performance is over. Today you have to appeal to them by helping them see how they can get from here to there, by establishing some credibility, and by giving them some reason and help to get there. Do all those things, and they'll knock down doors."[67]

As mentioned in chapter 2, organizational researchers Linda Smircich and Gareth Morgan explain that effective leaders influence others by:

> . . . framing experience in a way that provides a viable basis for action, e.g., by mobilizing meaning, articulating and defining what has previously remained implicit or unsaid, by inventing images and meanings that provide a focus for new attention, and by consolidating, confronting or changing prevailing wisdom. . . . The person that is most easily recognized as an organizational leader is one who rises above and beyond the specification of formal structure to provide members of the organization with a sense that they are organized, even amidst an everyday feeling that at a detailed level everything runs the danger of falling apart.[68]

TABLE 4-2   Guidelines for Using Gender-Inclusive Language

Don't	*Do*
Don't use the word "man" or "mankind" to refer to both men and women ("Let's get the best man for the job.").	Use words such as "person" or "humanity" that are gender inclusive ("Let's get the best person for the job.").
Don't use the generic terms "he" or "his" to refer to both sexes.	• Use "he or she" or "his or her" ("Every employee should check his or her electronic mail daily.").
	• Use plural pronouns ("Employees should check their electronic mail daily.").
	• Alternate the use of "he" and "she" (e.g., use "he" in one paragraph and "she" in the next).
	• Avoid pronoun use altogether ("Electronic mail should be checked daily.").[69]
Don't use gender-specific prefixes or suffixes such as "businessman", "chairman", "workman", "manpower", "man-made", and "man-hours."[70]	• Use gender-inclusive prefixes and suffixes such as "businessperson", "chairperson", "person-hours", or "work hours".
	• Use words such as "employees" (instead of "manpower") or "manufactured" (instead of "man-made").
	• If you need help changing sexist job titles, see the *O'Net Dictionary of Occupational Titles* compiled by J. Michael Farr, 1998.[71]
Don't use "man" as a verb ("Someone needs to man the office over the holiday.").	Use generic terms ("Someone needs to be at the office over the holiday.").
Don't use nonparallel language ("I'd like to introduce Mr. Kim and Susan" or "Let's get the men and girls from the mailroom to join us for lunch today.").[72]	Use parallel language ("I'd like to introduce Bob Kim and Susan Park," "I'd like to introduce Mr. Kim and Ms. Park," or "Let's invite the men and women from the mailroom to lunch today.").
Don't use occupational stereotyping ("When the doctor writes a prescription, he should make sure the handwriting is legible.").	Use gender-inclusive language ("When the doctor writes a prescription, he or she should make sure the handwriting is legible" or "When doctors write prescriptions, they should make sure their handwriting is legible.").
Don't use qualifiers that reinforce stereotypes ("male secretary" or "woman CEO").	Use the appropriate title such as "the secretary" or "CEO."
When you don't know the gender of the recipient, don't begin written correspondence or telephone messages with gender-biased salutations ("Dear Sir" or "I'd like to leave a message for Mr. Smith.").	Use gender-inclusive salutations ("Dear Customer," "Dear Reader," or "I'd like to leave a message for customer service representative Smith.").

Source: Adapted from: Lentz, Richard. 1984. "A Checklist of Nonsexist Writing." *Performance and Instruction Journal* August: 13; Munter, Mary. 1987. *Business Communication: Strategy and Skill.* New York: McGraw-Hill; Daily, Bill, and Miriam Finch. 1993. "Benefitting from Nonsexist Language in the Workplace." *Business Horizons.* March–April: 30–34; Murphy, Herta A., and Herbert Hildebrant. 1991. *Effective Business Communications*, 6th ed. New York: McGraw-Hill, 79–80.

Meaning making is particularly important when employees first enter an organization, during times of transition, and during crises.[73] How do effective leaders inspire others? They use inspiring language, images, and stories.

Using Inspiring Language

When researchers compared the speeches of charismatic versus noncharismatic international leaders, they concluded that the speeches of charismatic leaders contained more references to:[74]

- Collective history and to the continuity between the past and the present
- Collective identity and fewer references to individual self-interest
- Followers' worth and efficacy as individuals and as a collective
- The leader's similarity to followers and identification with the followers
- Values and moral justifications, and fewer references to tangible outcomes and instrumental justifications
- Distant goals and the distant future, and fewer references to short-term goals and the near future
- Hope and faith

In a study of presidential rhetoric, Purdue University researcher Cynthia Emrich and her colleagues found that U.S. presidents who used more image-based rhetoric in their most significant speeches were rated higher in both charisma and greatness. The researchers explain: ". . . leaders who use words that evoke pictures, sounds, smells, tastes, and other sensations tap more directly into followers' life experiences than do leader who use words that appeal solely to followers' intellects. By engaging followers' senses, not only their minds, leaders make their messages more immediate, real, and appealing to followers." Imagery-based rhetoric works because it engages people's attention, helps them understand and remember key points, and engages their emotions. People who use only "abstract, concept-based rhetoric run the risk of delivering a message that will, in effect, 'go in one ear and out the other'"[75] or send listeners into a "state of what can feel like total sensory deprivation."[76]

Consider the Reverend Martin Luther King's 1963 "I Have a Dream" speech that he delivered in front of the Lincoln Memorial in Washington, D.C., as the keynote address on the March on Washington for civil rights. He did not say, "Racism is very bad, and I want us to end racism within the next generation," nor did he use bullet points to summarize his message.[77] Instead, he said:

> I have a dream that my four little children will one day live in a nation where they will not be judged by the color of their skin but by the content of their character . . . I have a dream that one day, right here in Alabama, little black boys and black girls will be able to join hands with little white boys and white girls as sisters and brothers . . . I have a dream that one day every valley shall be exalted, every hill and mountain shall be made low, and rough places shall be made plain, and the crooked places shall be made straight and the glory of the Lord will be revealed and all flesh shall see it together. This is our hope.[78]

As Emrich explains, the Reverend King could have repeatedly proclaimed in his speech, "I have an idea," but it's doubtful that it would have had the same moving and

What kind of people we become depends crucially on the stories we are nurtured on.
Chinweizu, Voices from Twentieth Century Africa

historical impact as repeatedly using the word "dream."[79] In his speech, the Reverend King used compelling rhetoric including creating a visual picture of the future, referring to God, appealing to the listeners' shared rights and responsibilities as American citizens, and framing racial equality as a common hope. Note that he also used linguistic techniques such as rhythm, balance, and repetition, all of which can mesmerize an audience and increase retention.[80]

Telling Stories

Stories are not simply entertainment or escapism. We tell and listen to stories to make sense of our world and our place in it. Stories help us remember our past, make sense of our present, and create our futures. Some stories tell us who we are or who we can be. Other stories tell us what we should and shouldn't do. Some stories help us simplify an overwhelming and confusing world; other stories help us rise above the details of everyday life to remind us how truly awesome the world is. Chip Bell of *Training and Development* magazine explains:

> People love stories. They love to tell them and they love to hear them. A really good story makes a campfire worth lighting, a cocktail party worth attending, and a reunion worth holding. A story can evoke tears and laughter. A good story can touch something familiar in each of us, and yet show us something new about our lives, our world, and ourselves."[81]

People don't ask for facts when making up their minds. They would rather have one good soul-satisfying emotion than a dozen facts.
Robert Keith Leavitt

The most effective communicators know that most people are notoriously poor at remembering facts and statistics, yet quite adept at remembering and passing on interesting stories.[82] Yet too many managers and professionals assume the facts will speak for themselves and move people to take action. Indeed, Stanford researcher Chip Heath cautions organizational leaders to be wary of "insider knowledge that makes it hard to communicate to outsiders. The curse of knowledge can be particularly hard to overcome."

Ira M. Levin, principal in Ernst and Young's Business Change Implementation Practice in California, says that many companies' visions are stated as "en vogue phrases, buzzwords, and managementese that . . . resemble bumper sticker slogans . . . [and] can be readily interchanged across companies with minimal editing." He argues that visions are more compelling when they are stated as a "high lucid story of an organization's preferred future in action."[83] Some companies use stories to develop and promote products. Patagonia designs new products by listening to customers' stories about their outdoor adventures. Kimberly Clark invented Huggies Pull-Ups for toddlers and created a $500 million market by listening to parents' stories about what it was like to toilet train their toddlers.[84] The Body Shop uses stories to show customers that their products are worth using. Says Anita Roddick, founder and CEO of the Body Shop:

> We communicate with passion—and passion persuades. We preach and teach; we educate and inform. We do not, for example, train our staff to sell; I hate high-pressure sales techniques. The idea that everyone should walk out of

our shops having bought something is an anathema to me. We prefer to give staff information about the products, anecdotes about the history and derivation of the ingredients, and any funny stories about how they came on to Body Shop themselves. We want to spark conversations with our customers, not browbeat them to buy.[85]

There is no agony like bearing an untold story inside you. **Zora Neale Hurston, "Dust Tracks on a Road."** Why do stories work? Stories are natural "cognitive units" that human beings use to store, make sense of, and pass on information.[86] By giving us a clear beginning, middle, and ending, stories help us simplify a complex world and provide us with a sense of reason, order, and predictability among the chaos. They give us a way to express our fears, joys, and dreams that might otherwise be unspeakable or incomprehensible. They help us see through the eyes of others[87] and gain understandings we may not have had before.[88] And they help us preserve the wonder and mystery of the world by enabling us to believe in that which we cannot see. Stories work, in part, because they reach us at an emotional level, and emotions can influence our thinking and behavior more than logic can. That's why a scary movie frightens us even though we know "it's only a movie."[89]

Given the powerful way that stories shape our thinking and behavior, it's no surprise that they play an important role in employee socialization, organizational change, and public relations.[90] Stories are particularly useful for describing and explaining complex situations. Although stories are central to human understanding and motivation, our formal management education tends to "de-story" us.[91] Encouraged to depend on facts, theories, numbers, bullet points, and executive summaries, we tend to forget the power of stories in everyday work life. In the following sections, I hope to rekindle your desire and ability to tell stories at work.

Creating a Powerful Story

The most powerful organizational stories inform employees and inspire them to take action. A story doesn't have to be complex to be powerful. Indeed, some of the best stories are short and simple. Says David M. Armstrong, grandson of the founder of Armstrong International, "You don't need an MBA to tell stories—or to understand them."[92] Consider the following story that gets passed around Amazon.com.

> When an elderly woman e-mailed [Amazon.com] to say that she loved the service but had to wait for her nephew to come over and break through the packaging, Bezos had it redesigned in a way that was no less protective of the goods, but required much less violence to open.[93]

CEO Jeff Bezos uses this simple one-sentence story to emphasize the importance of "Amazon.com's inordinate responsiveness to customers" and his belief that Amazon.com is "the most customer-obsessed company to ever occupy planet Earth." IBM employees sometimes tell the following story about its former CEO, Tom Watson, Jr.:

> A young executive had made some bad decisions that cost the company several million dollars. He was summoned to Watson's office, fully expecting to be dismissed. As he entered the office, the young executive said, "I suppose after that set of mistakes you will be wanting to fire me." Watson was said to have

replied, "Not at all, young man, we have just spent a couple of million dollars educating you."[94]

The Watson story sends the message that IBM is committed to its employees and that employees can make mistakes as long as they learn from them. Are these stories true? No one knows for sure. Many powerful stories aren't necessarily based on verifiable facts. Organizations, like all communities, have myths. Over time, the details of the story may change, some points may get exaggerated, and other points may be forgotten. The story will survive if its message feels genuine and relevant to employees, customers, and other constituents. However, once the message is no longer seen as genuine or relevant, it loses its power. Powerful organizational stories have some or all of the following characteristics:

- *Simple.*   Listeners are not overwhelmed by details.
- *Relevant.*   They are told for a purpose that matters to organizational members. They reflect organizational beliefs, values, or goals, or they help organizational members gain an understanding of complex or ambiguous situations.
- *Inclusive.*   All organizational members can see themselves in the story. Everyone who hears it is able to say, "These are my people," "This is my story," and "I can delight customers too."
- *Concrete, temporal, and action oriented.*   They have a protagonist(s) who faces a hurdle to be overcome or a dilemma to be resolved; a sequence of causally related events that evolve over time; a climax and resolution; and a moral or a lesson that people find useful for their day-to-day work lives.
- *Emotional.*   They excite, delight, surprise with an unexpected twist, or otherwise move the listener at an emotional level. Powerful stories are not simply a series of facts strung together in a logical order. Researchers have found that stories that evoke the strongest emotions (positive or negative) spread farther and last longer.[95]
- *Friendly, not cynical.*   Even sad stories should leave the listener with feelings of hope, joy, or satisfaction.[96]
- *Shared by many people.*   They are interesting and important enough to be told and retold throughout the organization and passed on to newcomers as well as outsiders.
- *Appeal to uniqueness.*   They make the people in the organization feel that the organization and the people in it are different and special in some important way.

Organizational researcher Joanne Martin and her colleagues argue that even though many organizational stories are told to express members' belief in the uniqueness of the organization (e.g., we're the "best," the "fastest," the "most innovative," the "most customer-obsessed company on earth"), the most powerful organizational stories that get told and retold tend to fall into predictable archetypes.[97] In other words, although the details of the stories may differ across organizations, the basic messages are the same: We're better than others, anyone can be a hero, anyone can make a difference, the little person can win, even the big people make mistakes, you cannot trust the boss, and so on. In other words, the power of organizational stories is not that they are truly unique, but that they help organizational members *feel* unique ("I work in the most customer-driven company on earth.").

Telling a Powerful Story

Telling a good story requires thinking clearly about the message that you want to convey, anticipating the reactions of the audience, and using rhetorical techniques that keep the listener listening.[98] To tell a good story:

- ***Know why you're telling the story and the key beliefs or values that you want to express.***   The audience should not be asking themselves, "What's the point?" "Why are you telling me this story?" "Where does this fit in?"[99]
- ***Know how you want listeners to feel.***   Do you want them to be worried about the competition? Humble and/or proud of their accomplishments? Connected to people in other parts of the organization? Strong, competent, and resilient when facing danger? Adaptable when facing change?
- ***Know your audience.***   Lee Iacocca, former CEO of Chrysler, explains that "it's important to talk to people in their own language. If you do it well, they say, '. . . he [sic] said exactly what I was thinking.'"[100] Adapting the message or language to the audience says, "We're in this together."
- ***Be credible.***   People need to believe the story is plausible and reflects not only the perspectives of leaders or a small group but of followers and others as well.[101]
- ***Set the context.***   Be visual so that people can watch the story unfold in their minds. ("It was 5 minutes before I was scheduled to go to the podium and speak. Three hundred angry people were in the audience. My hands were already sweating from nervousness, and then I realized that I had left my notes for my speech in my briefcase on the airplane that was on its way back to Singapore.")
- ***Be dramatic.***   Integrate well-placed pauses, vary your gestures, and mimic the characters' voices or actions. Build slowly to the climax or punch line to create a sense of mystery, excitement, irony, humor, joy, or warmth. Comedian Bill Cosby, for example, keeps audiences spellbound by using these techniques, particularly the use of the pause (just listen to one of his one-man comedy performances).
- ***Don't fill in too many details.***   Give listeners the space to use their imagination. A good rule of thumb is to use more detail in the beginning of the story to set the stage and then give fewer details as the story unwinds. Consider which points should be exaggerated and embellished and which points should be played down or excluded.[102]
- ***Don't overexplain.***   The story should be clear enough to speak for itself. You shouldn't have to explain what it means or why it's relevant.
- ***Don't preach.***   Remember that the best stories "don't tell people what to think, but to create a space for them to think in."[103]

Are stories and storytelling in organizations really that straightforward? Well, yes and no. They do simplify a complex world, help us express organizational values, and play an important role in organizational socialization. But like most aspects of organizational life, we don't have as much control over our stories as we like to think.

Researchers have found that organizations have multiple stories being told around the organization at the same time; not all of these stories are initiated by managers and

History will be kind to me, for I intend to write it. *Sr. Winston Churchill*

executives; and not all of these stories support the organization's espoused beliefs, values, or goals. Furthermore, every story we tell, regardless of how carefully we choose our words, is open to multiple interpretations depending on the audience (e.g., hierarchical level or culture) and the particular context, and these interpretations can change over time.[104]

Researcher David Boje gives examples of competing stories at Disney World, the quintessential storytelling organization. Employees at Disney World tell as many stories about Walt Disney as they tell about princesses and princes, giants and elves. Some of the Walt Disney stories are the official stories started by Disney himself. In these stories, he frames himself as a pioneer in animation who brought happiness to millions of people. However, some of the Walt Disney stories were started by employees who frame him as an egotistical tyrant who took credit for the ideas of the underpaid animators who worked for him.

Power consists to a large extent in deciding what stories will be told. *Carolyn Heilbrun, Writing a Woman's Life*

Which stories are true? Was Walt Disney's organization a happy kingdom or oppressive workplace? Did Walt Disney really say, "I love Mickey Mouse more than any woman I have ever known?" and, if so, was this his real feeling or was he just trying to make a point? We may never know. But we do know that each of the stories has a message that is designed to frame experience; that each story may have exaggerated some elements and left some things out; and that multiple stories, taken together, show a more complex and comprehensive picture than any one story can do alone.

Be Wise When Listening to Stories

The previous section discussed how to tell a story so that people will support your ideas. In this section, I discuss the risks of being taken in by a good story. When you are listening to a well-crafted story that is designed to gain your support, how can you tell if the ideas illustrated by the story deserve your support? University of California researcher Kimberly Elsbach conducted a fascinating study of Hollywood executives who routinely received pitches from screenwriters who were trying to sell their ideas. Elsbach found that the way in which the ideas were presented were more influential than the quality of the ideas themselves (which, as she says, is probably one of the reasons why plenty of bad television shows get aired).

She explains, "We all like to think that people judge us carefully and objectively on our merits. But the fact is, they rush to place us into neat little categories—they stereotype us . . . People on the formal end of pitches have no formal, verifiable, or objective measures for assessing that elusive trait—creativity . . . therefore [they] apply a set of subjective and often inaccurate criteria very early in the encounter, and from that point on, the tone is set." In other words, Hollywood executives make judgments about whether a person is creative, dependable, and so on within seconds of meeting the person. Then, the executive listens to the pitch either with an open or closed mind based on these stereotypes. Elsbach warns that we "should beware of relying on stereotypes. It's all too easy to be dazzled by pitchers who ultimately can't get their projects off the ground, and it's just as easy to overlook the creative individuals who can make good on their ideas."

We are all busy and often must make quick decisions based on limited information. So, it's easy to get wooed by a good story—and stereotypes about the storyteller—and then be seduced into supporting ideas that have little merit or backing people who can come up with good ideas but cannot implement them. There are several things you can do to minimize this risk. Most importantly, you should recognize that you are easily seduced by stereotypes. Then, if you find yourself being swept away by a good story, a charming storyteller, or an engaging presentation, ask for data to support the idea. Ask the person to provide concrete evidence of experience in the area of interest, and ask if they can show completed projects to show that they have a track record of following through on their ideas. Ask them what kinds of failures and hurdles they have faced in the past and what they learned from these experiences. This will provide you with insights about how they will work when things don't go as planned. Ask to speak with people who have worked with them before. Get opinions from other people who may not share the same stereotypes that you do about what success, creativity, and professionalism look like.[105]

TALK AND TECHNOLOGY

The great baseball player Yogi Berra once said, "Prediction is hard, especially when it's about the future." In 1943, Thomas Watson, founder of IBM, declared, "I think there is a world market for maybe five computers." In 1977, Ken Olsen, founder of Digital Equipment Corporation, predicted that "there is no reason anyone would want a computer in their home."[106] In 1981, Bill Gates said, "640K ought to be enough for anybody." Their predictions about the impact of computer technology on everyday life were wrong. Researchers estimate that:

- In early 2004, 75 percent of Americans (204.3 million) had access to the Internet from home, up from 66 percent in February 2003.[107]
- Slightly more women than men surf the Internet; 82 percent of women between the ages of 35 and 54 surf the Internet, whereas 80 percent of men in that same age group surf the net. Seventy-seven percent of women between the ages of 25 and 34 surf the Internet, and 75.6 percent of men do. Although the percentages are quite similar, it's not surprising that women have the edge because women do most of the household purchasing and may be doing much of the research and purchasing online.[108]

BOX 4-4

Digital Storytelling

The technologically savvy reader may want to consider a new trend called "digital storytelling" in which organizational storytellers use movie editing software to create video stories. Daniel Pink of *Fast Company* magazine reports that digital storytelling is becoming "something of a movement among both artists and businesspeople."[109] Pink describes how Bill Dauphinais of PricewaterhouseCoopers LLP uses digital storytelling to tell stories about the company's founders, partners, and clients to describe and perpetuate the firm's values to employees and constituents around the world. You can learn more about digital storytelling by visiting www.storycenter.org, The Center for Digital Storytelling.

- In 1991, only 1 percent of the world's population had a mobile phone. In 2001, one of six people had a mobile phone. Cell phone users in the United States now spend more time talking on their cell phones than on their traditional phones.[110]
- Online shoppers spent $18.5 billion online (not including travel) during the 2003 holiday season, 35 percent more than the $13.7 billion spent during the holiday season a year earlier.[111]
- More than 20 million children between the ages of 2 and 17 used the Internet from home in 2003 in the United States; 13 million children in Europe under 18 used the Internet during the same year.[112]
- The number of senior citzens in the United States age 65 and older who go online grew from 7.6 million (5.9 percent) to 9.6 million (7 percent) between 2002 and 2003, making senior citizens the fastest growing group of Internet users; 11.5 million Europeans age 55 or older used the Internet in 2003, up 28 percent since 2002.[113]
- Half the United States' population has access to the Internet, 38 percent from home and 17 percent elsewhere. The people without access tend to be poorer and less educated.[114]
- In February 2002, 41.7 percent of employed persons age 25 or older used the Internet at work, up from 26.1 percent in August 2000.[115]
- Nine of 10 companies have systems for monitoring employee e-mail. Sales of monitoring technologies are estimated to be $140 million annually worldwide.[116]

We are drowning in information but starved for knowledge. *John Naisbitt, Futurist*

Computer technology is significantly changing the way we communicate and spend our time. Today, we communicate with a broader and more diverse audience through a wider range of communication channels than ever before. If we have something to say, we can say it face-to-face or through fax, voice mail, e-mail, overnight mail, or snail mail (that's the old-fashioned stamped letter). Just to be sure that the receiver gets our message, many of us e-mail the receiver and then send the person the same message by fax or overnight mail, and then phone to confirm receipt. Then we make hard copies of all the correspondence for our files. It is no surprise that shipments of office paper to U.S. companies has risen by 51 percent since 1983.[117] PricewaterhouseCoopers estimates that when electronic mail is introduced to an office, printing volume increases by 40 percent.[118]

A recent Stanford study concluded that "the more hours people use the Internet, the less time they spend in contact with real human beings." Approximately 25 percent of the 4,113 adults who participated in the study thought that their use of the Internet reduced the time they spent with family and friends. Another 25 percent of study participants said that the availability of the Internet increased the amount of time they spent working at home but did not decrease the amount of time they spent working at the office. The good news is that the people who reported using the Internet most often also reported spending less time in traffic, at shopping malls, and watching television. The people who reported the biggest impact of Internet usage on their lives spent at least 10 hours a week on the Internet.[119]

Although several technologies are transforming the way we communicate and spend our time, I focus on electronic mail in this section because it has become a taken-for-granted part of everyday work life in many organizations. Electronic mail is appealing because it is easy, accessible, relatively economical, and serves as a written record of organizational communication. We can send messages to many people simultaneously; overcome many barriers associated with time, distance, and physical disabilities; and work flexibly and productively from home (and from the beach, mountain, or airplane, for that matter).

Critics argue that e-mail can be too much of a good thing. Access to unlimited information can lead to information overload. Expectations of around-the-clock availability can lead to unrealistic demands on employees' time. And the speed at which the Internet operates may contribute to an unrealistic sense of time. Says Jerry Riftin:

> The computer introduces . . . a time frame in which the nanosecond is the primary temporal measurement. The nanosecond is a billionth of a second, and though it is possible to conceive theoretically of a nanosecond . . . it is not possible to experience it. Never before has time been organized at a speed beyond the realm of consciousness.[120]

Communication consultant David Ancel argues that the Internet may also give us an unrealistic sense of place. He explains:

> If you travel 18 hours and 10,000 miles to Asia and you step off the plane and are hit by the heat and humidity, you know that you're someplace different and you're going to have to make some adjustments. But if you send an e-mail from your desk or walk around the corner to a videoconference room, you haven't moved at all off of your cultural space.[121]

Other concerns about e-mail have been more highly publicized. Most of us are aware that the Internet has opened the doors to cyberthieves who abscond with company secrets, cyberhackers who bring organizations' information and communication systems to a standstill, cybermarketers whose unsolicited e-mail messages annoy people and clog computer networks, and cyberslackers who use company-provided computers and Internet services to shop, play games, download pornography, send personal messages, look for other jobs, or start their own business—all on company work time. The *Wall Street Journal* reported that "of 1,244 employees surveyed by Vault.com, a New York job-search Web site, 90.3 percent acknowledge surfing nonwork-related sites, a practice one respondent describes as 'the millennium cigarette break.'"[122] And as Bill Gates, Monica Lewinski, and investment banker Frank Quattrone (who earned $120 million in 2000) painfully learned, there's that pesky privacy issue when using e-mail. Indeed, the "smoking gun" in Quattrone's obstruction of justice case was an e-mail he sent in which he asked his group to "clean up" their files after he learned that Credit Suisse First Boston's initial public offering was being investigated by the Securities and Exchange Commission.[123]

Despite its annoyances and risks, most of us appreciate the convenience, speed, and ease of using e-mail. Electronic mail, like all communication tools, is most effective when used thoughtfully.

Rules for Effective E-Mail Communication

Rule 1: Use the right medium for the message. Electronic mail is not as effective as face-to-face communication if you are trying to build relationships, influence people, or deal with sensitive topics. The more important the message, the more important face-to-face communication becomes.

- Use electronic mail when you need to send simple messages to or retrieve simple messages from an individual, group, or large audience.
- Use electronic mail for instrumental purposes such as setting up meetings, sending agendas, or following up on action plans.
- Use electronic mail when you want to keep a record of the communication.
- Do not use electronic mail for sensitive topics, complex communications, urgent messages, or confidential information. There are some things people don't want to read on the computer.
- Consider sending a hard copy of a long document rather than attaching it to an e-mail message.

Rule 2: Think before you hit the "send" key. Before you send a message, ask yourself what would happen if your message was posted in a public place, sent to someone by mistake, or forwarded to someone by the receiver. If you have any concerns, use a more private communication method.

- Check all destination addresses.
- Don't forward any e-mails until you ask the sender for permission.
- Don't forward jokes and inspirational messages to everyone on your e-mail list.

Rule 3: Be professional. Because electronic mail is fast and easy to use, it can lead to overuse, sloppiness, or inappropriate informality. To counter these tendencies:

- ***Be sensible about distribution.***   Send only pertinent e-mail and do not overdistribute. Use electronic bulletin boards for general-interest messages.
- ***Be concise.***   Make the subject heading brief and meaningful. Cover only one topic per message. Keep messages short. Use short paragraphs, with headings if necessary, for quick reading.
- ***Be clear.***   Use common language. Define all acronyms and jargon if you must use them. Avoid abbreviations. Identify the e-mail to which you are responding. When making requests, be clear about what you need, what form you need it in, and when you need it.
- ***Be attentive to style.***   Use proper grammar, spelling, and punctuation. Proofread e-mail before sending it. Don't type in all caps: It's seen as shouting.
- ***Be respectful.***   When in doubt, err on the side of formality rather than informality. Think before responding emotionally. Don't send e-mail when you are angry. Be cautious when using humor, and don't be sarcastic. Never send or forward any e-mail that has any sexist, racist, political, or other comments that may be perceived by some people as inappropriate.
- ***Be sensitive to culture.***   When in doubt, use formal titles. Be aware of time differences, work hours, and holidays. Be considerate of nonnative speakers. Don't assume that the meaning of emoticons transfers across cultures. North Americans use the emoticon : -) to express a smile. The Japanese (who call emoticons *kao maaku,* which means "face marks") use ^-^ to express a smile.[124]

- ***Be accessible.*** Read your e-mail regularly. Let people know how often you check your e-mail. Respond to messages as soon as possible. Let people know when you are out of the office and whom they should contact if you are unavailable.
- ***Be sensitive to power.*** Remember that when you send e-mail messages to people with less power, they may read more into the messages than you intended. For example, if you send a message to a subordinate that says, "Please see me in my office at 2:00 tomorrow," the employee may worry about the purpose of the meeting, even though you intend to surprise the employee with a promotion or pay raise.
- Use a signature file that includes your name, title, address, and phone number (and fax number if appropriate).

Rule 4: Be organized.

- Create folders for any e-mails that you want to keep.
- Delete or file messages as soon as you are finished with them.

Rule 5: Be careful.

- Assume all e-mail is as public as a postcard.
- Never give your password to anyone.
- Get top-quality antivirus software and use it regularly. Update the software so that new viruses are covered.
- Don't open unsolicited attachments from anyone you don't know because they may contain viruses.
- Be wary of opening attachments from people that you know if the attachment did not originate with the sender (such as humorous attachments or chain letters) or if the subject or message is too general (i.e., "important information attached").
- Don't reply to unsolicited marketing e-mails (also known as "spam") because that lets the marketer know that they have reached an active address. Purchase antispam software or sign up for spam protection through your Internet service provider.[125]
- Be careful when posting your e-mail address or personal information on the Web. Personally, I have not had any problem with reputable on-line retailers; however, I always check their policies regarding privacy, and I let them know that I don't want my name or personal information given to anyone else, nor do I want to receive any unsolicited advertising. Nonetheless, giving personal information to a Web site carries some risk.
- If you are concerned about privacy, you may want to remove the "cookies" that are "small data files left on your hard drive by Web pages to track your surfing habits." Although they are mostly harmless, they can pose privacy concerns. Note that removing cookies can affect your ability to use some Web sites.[126]

Rule 6: Develop and distribute official organizational policies regarding e-mail.

- Be clear about what e-mail should and should not be used for; whether employees are allowed to send personal messages, jokes, and other nonwork-related messages over e-mail;[127] and what distribution policies (e.g., bulletin boards versus direct e-mails) are approved by the organization.

- Be clear about what Internet uses are approved and which are not (such as on-line shopping, games, or porn sites).
- Let employees know if the organization will be inspecting e-mail messages and monitoring Internet use. Make sure employees know of the Electronic Communications Privacy Act. At this writing, employers can monitor Internet use and retrieve and read saved and deleted messages that employees send without getting employees' permission.
- Let employees know of the consequences for noncompliance with organizational e-mail policies.

Rule 7: Stay informed of new technologies. Software is routinely developed to manage some of the problems associated with e-mail, including "remote paper shredders"; technologies that prevent people from copying, printing, or forwarding messages to others; and "fire walls" that prevent recipients from forwarding messages outside the organization's intranet or approved destinations.[128] See Box 4-5 for tips for managing voice mail.

BOX 4-5

Tips for Managing Voice Mail

1. Update your greeting daily.
   - Include the name, date, and when you'll get back to the caller.
   - Give instructions on how to reach a live person or send you an e-mail.
   - Ask the caller to leave a brief message.
   - Speak slowly and clearly, especially when giving out numbers or names.

2. Let callers know when you are out of the office, when you will return, and whom they can speak with in the meantime.

3. Redirect calls to another person when you're out of the office or on vacation. When you are not available, forward incoming calls directly to the phone mail system so that it will answer after only one ring.

4. Check messages when you are out of the office if possible.

5. Return calls promptly and keep paper by the phone to take notes when listening to voice mail.

6. Call yourself and listen to your own greeting. Is it clear and concise? Do you sound friendly and relaxed?

7. Don't overrely on voice mail to avoid human interaction.

8. When leaving a message on voice mail, prepare your message prior to making your call so that you can be thorough yet clear and concise and let the receiver know what you want him or her to do after hearing your voice mail. Remember that your voice mail message has an impact on how the receiver perceives you. People shouldn't have to call back for more information. State your name and organization's name; say why you're calling; tell the caller what you want her or him to do; say all names, numbers, and addresses (including electronic mail addresses) slowly, repeat them, and spell names, if necessary.

9. Never leave angry voice mails or voice mails that criticize others. Remember that voice mail messages can be forwarded to others, so be certain that you'd be comfortable having your message heard by others.

BOX 4-6

Employee Resistance through Communication

Employees have always found subtle and clever ways to resist organizational power and exert their own power. Here are a few examples.

BUZZWORD BINGO

To express their frustration at the escalating use of buzzwords in organizations, employees at several organizations are playing a new game called "Buzzword Bingo." To play the game, employees create a bingo-style sheet (say, a four-by-four matrix) and insert common buzzwords in each of the boxes. When they go to meetings, they bring their bingo sheets. When a buzzword is used during the meeting, employees check their bingo sheets to see if the word is in one of the boxes. If so, they check the box. When all the boxes in a horizontal row or vertical column are checked, the holder of the sheet shouts "Bingo!" Bill Ellet of *Training and Development* magazine explains that the game is a "lighthearted attempt to promote clear communication" and "have some fun." He also explains that employees use this game to react to what they may feel is an inappropriate use of power. He explains, "Buzzwords are often a tacit currency of power: 'I know what this means, and you

don't. Therefore, I'm more important than you are.' Buzzwords are deliberately exclusive . . . [and] can dress up vacuousness."[129]

"DIGITAL DECEPTION" OR IMPRESSION MANAGEMENT?

Some employees are using e-mail to convince their employers and colleagues that they are working late when they are snoozing or playing instead. These employees compose e-mail messages to their bosses, coworkers, subordinates, and clients and then program their computers to automatically send the messages when they will be postmarked after hours (say, 11:00 P.M. or 5:00 A.M.). It looks like the sender is working beyond normal work hours.[130]

PANIC BUTTONS AND OTHER DIVERSIONS

Some Web sites, including the Dilbert Web site, have what are called "panic buttons." Employees who are using the site can click on the panic button if their boss, coworkers, or customers come near. A screen will appear that includes a fake spreadsheet, fake news report, or other fake but responsible-looking material.

CONCLUSION

Undoubtedly, organizational communication is becoming increasingly complex. Today's manager must communicate with people who don't speak the same language or share the same culture, align diverse employees toward shared organizational goals, and create synergy among many different kinds of communication media.[131] Despite the new communication challenges that managers face today, the basic lessons of communication have not changed nor will they change in the future. Employees will continue to want to be heard, understood, and respected. They will want to know what they should be doing, for whom, and by when. They will want to know how they're doing and where they stand. And they will want to find meaning in their work so that they can feel that they are giving their time and energy toward something worth doing.

Box 4-7 describes best the practices of organizations that take organizational communication seriously and leverage it to achieve organizational goals.

BOX 4-7

Leadership Lessons in Communication

Based on a study of ten leading U.S. corporations known for exemplary employee communications practices, researchers Mary Young and James Post identified the leadership's best practices:[132]

1. *They champion communication.* They are committed to communicating frequently and personally with employees. Notably, their success as communicators isn't necessarily tied to their style. One executive was described as "a bit wooden in front of television cameras," but he was praised for his willingness to "communicate often, frequently in person, display a willingness to address challenging questions, listen carefully, and respond quickly to sensitive topics."

2. *They have a clear employee communication strategy.* They systematically incorporate many different ways of communicating: slide shows, television, in person, videos, newsletters, question-and-answer sessions, e-mail, Web sites, and so on.

3. *They emphasize face-to-face communication, particularly in times of uncertainty and change.* They communicate quickly and candidly, even when the news isn't expected or favorable. They explain not only what happened but also who, why, when, where, and how. They don't tell people how people should feel about news. Says one manager, "It is insulting to tell people how they should feel about

change."[133] Rather, they legitimate different perspectives.

4. *They manage the bad news/good news ratio.* They make sure that they hear about failures, mistakes, and customer complaints. Employees in these organizations know that bad news is as important to hear as good news.

5. *They are committed to two-way communication.* They set up meetings, informal lunches, and interactive television broadcasts, and regularly request and reward upward feedback—all designed to get important information, hear new ideas, and encourage bad news. In the best organizations, employees use these methods of communicating and take them seriously.

6. *They match their words and actions.* They know that when employees see a mismatch between what the leaders say and do, they stop listening.

7. *They know their audiences.* They are familiar with their various employee groups, customers, and other constituents. They know what kind of information their constituents want, when they want it, and in what form. They adapt their content and presentation to the needs and style of the audience.

8. *They share responsibility for employee communication.* They expect all managers to communicate personally and frequently with employees.

SOURCE: Adapted from Young, Mary, and James Post. 1993. "Managing to Communicate, Communicating to Manage: How Leading Companies Communicate with Employees." *Organizational Dynamics.* Summer: 31–43.

CHAPTER SUMMARY

Communication is the real work of managers. Effective managers spend much of their time in informal and unplanned communication. This communication enables them to obtain timely information, build relationships, and develop support for their ideas.

Active listening refers to listening to understand another person's point of view without evaluating or judging the other person or his or her views. Active listening involves listening with intensity, listening with empathy, demonstrating acceptance, taking responsibility for completeness, and being yourself. Remember that active listening is more a sincere attitude of openness and respect than a set of rigid techniques.

Employees want feedback so that they can know how they are doing. Feedback answers employees' questions, sets clear expectations, reduces uncertainty, encourages desired behaviors, helps employees learn new skills, enhances employee performance, and is a necessary part of coaching. Effective feedback is given in a way that the receiver understands the information, accepts the information, and is able to do something about it.

Managers need to see problems quickly and accurately so that they can respond before the situation gets worse. However, employees are often reluctant to give their managers bad news. To encourage employees to bring you bad news, be accessible, be approachable, surround yourself with independent minds, run meetings that encourage independent thinking and honest feedback, be discreet about sources, and "never shoot the messenger."

Effective managers know how to communicate effectively across cultures. They pay attention to differences in the meanings of words and phrases, body language (such as the appropriateness of eye contact), and communication styles (such as high context versus low context).

Many researchers have concluded that men and women tend to have different communication styles. Specifically, they say that men tend to be more direct than women, women are more likely to emphasize relationship building and men are more likely to emphasize information giving, women are more likely than men to give verbal and nonverbal signals that they are listening to others, and men and boys are more likely to interrupt women and girls.

Communication practices perpetuate assumptions about power differences. You can see these assumptions in action by noting who speaks more often, who gets credit for ideas and who doesn't, who interrupts and who gets interrupted, and who gets heard and who gets ignored. Changing how people communicate is an effective way to change assumptions about status and power. Using gender-inclusive language is one technique that many managers, organizations, and business publications are using to create an inclusive workplace.

Effective leaders know that creating meaning that mobilizes action is an important part of their job. They know that bullet points and executive summaries aren't enough. They use influential language and compelling stories to create a common vision, encourage a collective identity, and inspire coordinated action toward common goals. Stories are powerful because they are convincing and memorable. They are natural cognitive units that human beings use to store, make sense of, and pass on information. In addition, they help human beings simplify a complex world, manage ambiguities and contradictions, see order among the chaos, see through the eyes of others, and gain new understandings.

Computer technology, particularly the Internet, is significantly changing the way we communicate at work. Electronic mail is appealing because it is easy, accessible, relatively economical, less intrusive than meetings or telephone calls, and serves as a written record of organizational communication. Because e-mail can be abused, effective users of e-mail know its advantages and risks and follow practices that increase their e-mail effectiveness.

FOOD FOR THOUGHT

1. What is the most useful thing you learned in this chapter, and why?
2. Based on the personal strategies described in this chapter, what can you do to enhance your communication effectiveness? Practice this behavior and note any benefits and progress you make.
3. How does effective communication contribute to individual and organizational success?
4. Consciously use active listening when you have a conversation with someone. What did it feel like? What were the consequences? How did the other person react? What did you like about it? What didn't you like about it?
5. Think about a time when you felt that you weren't listened to. Describe the situation, as well as the consequences. Describe how you may have contributed to the situation. What did you learn from the situation that can make you a better manager today?
6. Imagine that you have an employee named Pat Buonafeste. Pat is a supervisor in the customer service department of an on-line book retailer. You have heard from two of Pat's subordinates that the workload in Pat's area has been escalating over the past 2 months and that Pat is becoming increasingly stressed and difficult to work for. They also told you that Pat has been taking long lunches several times a week and leaving early every Friday. They said that they resent having to work so hard while Pat is taking extra time off. They are very responsible employees, yet they are threatening to leave the company and go work for a competitor if you don't solve the problem. You feel that you need to give Pat feedback on the employees' concerns and find out what is going on. What will you say to Pat?
7. Observe a team meeting or classroom. Write down some of the conversation patterns that you observe. For example, who speaks most often, who interrupts most, who is most quiet, who gets taken most seriously, and how do people get themselves heard? Are any power dynamics being expressed through these communication patterns? What are the potential consequences of these patterns? If you were a communications consultant, what recommendations would you make to improve the performance of this team or class?
8. Meet with someone from another culture and discuss communication differences between your culture and this person's culture. What are the three most interesting communication differences? How might they lead to misunderstandings or hinder effectiveness?
9. Think about a story that gets told in your organization. What is the underlying message in the story? Are there other stories in the organization that support or contradict this message?
10. Think about one of the most inspiring speeches you've ever heard. Why was it so inspiring? Did it move you to take action? If so, what actions did you take?
11. Imagine that you are a manager named Fran. While you were reading your e-mail today, you received a copy of a message that was not intended for you to see. The employee sent the following e-mail to a peer and inadvertently copied you: "Can you believe it? No wonder Chris didn't want to work here anymore. Fran really doesn't seem to know what's going on and just cannot leave well enough alone." Would you tell the person who wrote and copied the e-mail that you received and read the message? Why or why not? If you did decide to speak with the person who wrote the email, what would you say? What else might you do to manage the situation?
12. MIT Nobel Prize winner Robert Solow once said, "We see computers everywhere but in the productivity statistics."[115] Think about your organization's use of e-mail. In what ways does

the use of e-mail add to your productivity? In what ways does it distract from your productivity? What can you do to make your own use of e-mail more productive?

13. Many employees are using the Internet at work to shop, browse favorite Web sites (e.g., on gardening or movie reviews), and send personal messages to their friends and family. Is this abusive "cyberslacking" or a legitimate "equivalent of the millennium coffee break?" Why? Is it appropriate for employees to use the organization's Internet access to look for new jobs or promote their own businesses? Why or why not?

ENDNOTES

1. Murhy, Herta, and Herbert Hildebrandt. 1991. *Effective Business Communications* 6th ed. New York: McGraw-Hill.
2. 1997. "Calling Mission Control." *Training and Development*. August: 9–10.
3. Mintzberg, Henry. 1990. "The Manager's Job: Folklore and Fact." *Harvard Business Review,* 68(2): 163–177.
4. Gayeski, Diane, and Jennifer Majka. 1996. "Untangling Communication Chaos: A Communicator's Conundrum for Coping with Change in the Coming Century." *Communication World*, 13(7): September 1.
5. Ibid.
6. "Perspectives." *Newsweek.* March 2001.
7. *Newsweek.* January 13, 2003.
8. Naughton, Keith with Joan Raymond, Ken Shulman, and Diane Struzzi. 1999. "Cyberslacking." *Newsweek.* November 29: 62–65.
9. Crossen, Cynthia. 1997. "Blah, Blah, Blah: The Crucial Question for These Noisy Times May Just Be 'Huh?'" *Wall Street Journal.* July 10: B1.
10. Ibid.
11. Lancaster Hal. 1997. "It's Time to Stop Promoting Yourself and Start Listening." *Wall Street Journal.* June 10: B1.
12. Yale Ditty on Benno Schmidt. *New York Times Magazine*, 1992.
13. Morgenson, Gretchen. 1999. "Barbie Guru Stumbles: Critics Say Chief's Flaws Weigh Heavily on Mattel." *New York Times* November 7.
14. 2003. "Ann Fudge. Gets Top Y&R Post as Dolan Quits." *Wall Street Journal*, B1 and B4.
15. Kiechel, Walter. 1990. "How to Escape the Echo Chamber." *Fortune* June 18: 12–13.

16. Freire, Paulo. 1994. *Pedagogy of the Oppressed.* (revised edition, first published in 1970). New York: Continuum Publishing, 71; cited in Dixon, Nancy. 1996 *Perspectives on Dialogue.* Greensboro, NC: Center for Creative Leadership, 6.
17. Rogers, Carl, and F. Roethlisberger. 1991. "Barriers and Gateways to Communication." *Harvard Business Review.* November–December.
18. Miller, Gerald R., and Mark Steinberg. 1975. *Between People.* NY Science Research Associates, Inc.
19. Covey, Steven 1991. *Thirty Methods of Influence.* FranklinCovey Press.
20. Stone, Douglas, Bruce Patton, and Sheila Heen. 1999. *Difficult Conversations: How to Discuss What Matters Most.* New York: Penguin Books.
21. Robbins, Stephen, and Phillip Hunsaker. 1989. *Training in Interpersonal Skills: Tips for Managing People at Work.* Upper Saddle River, NJ: Prentice Hall.
22. Meyer, Peter. 1998. "So You Want the President's Job." *Business Horizons.* January–February: 2–6.
23. Ibid.
24. Bell, Chip, and Ron Zemke. 1992. "On-Target Feedback." *Training.* June: 36–44.
25. Hequet, Marc. 1994. "Giving Good Feedback." *Training* September: 72–76.
26. Barnes, Louis. 1989. "Managing Interpersonal Feedback." *Harvard Business School Note 483027.*
27. Ashford, Susan, and Gregory Northcraft. 1992. "Conveying More (or Less) than We Realize: The Role of Impression-Management in Feedback Seeking." *Organizational Behavior and Human Decision Processes,* 53: 310–334.

28. Johnson, Spencer, and Kenneth Blanchard. 1993. *The One-Minute Manager.* Berkeley, CA: Berkeley Publishing Group.

29. Barnes, Louis B. 1982. "Managing Interpersonal Feedback." *Harvard Business Review*; September, Clawson, James. 1989. *Some Principles of Giving and Receiving Feedback.* Charlottesville, VA: Darden Graduate Business School Foundation.

30. Hequet, Marc. 1994. "Giving Good Feedback." *Training.* September: 72–76.

31. Bell, Chip, and Ron Zemke. 1992. "On-Target Feedback." *Training.* June: 36–44.

32. Ng, Michael. 1994. "Effective Feedback Skills for Trainers and Coaches." *HRFocus* July: 7.

33. Ashford, Susan, and Gregory Northcraft. 1992. "Conveying More (or Less) than We Realize: The Role of Impression-Management in Feedback Seeking." *Organizational Behavior and Human Decision Processes,* 53: 310–334.

34. Ibid.

35. Barnes, Louis B. 1982. "Managing Interpersonal Feedback." *Harvard Business Review;* Clawson, James. 1989. *Some Principles of Giving and Receiving Feedback.* Charlottesville, VA: Darden Graduate Business School Foundation.

36. Ghorpade, Jai. 2000. "Managing Five Paradoxes of 360-Degree Feedback." *Academy of Management Executive*, 14(1): 140–154.

37. Lepsinger, Richard, and Antoinette D. Lucia. 1997. *The Art and Science of 360-Degree Feedback.* San Francisco: Jossey-Bass.

38. Brett, Joan, and Leanne Atwater. 2001. "360-Degree Feedback: Accuracy, Reactions, and Perceptions of Usefulness." *Journal of Applied Psychology,* 86: 930–942; Church, Allan. 1997. "Do You See What I See? An Exploration of Congruence in Ratings with Multiple Perspectives." *Journal of Applied Social Psychology,* 27(1): 983–1020; Atwater, Leanne, Cheri Ostroff, Francis Yammarino, and John Fleenor. 1948. "Self-Other Agreement: Does It Really Matter?" *Personnel Psychology,* 51: 577–598; Van

Velsor, Ellen, Sylvester Taylor, and Jean Leslie. 1993. "An Examination of the Relationship Among Self-Perception Accuracy, Self-Awareness, Gender and Leader Effectiveness." *Human Resource Management,* 32(2–3): 249–264; Atwater, Leanne, David Waldman, and Joan Brett. 2002. "Understanding and Optimizing Multisource Feedback." *Human Resource Management,* 41(2): 193–208; Atwater, Leanne, and Francis Yammarino. 1992. Does Self-Other Agreement on Leadership Perceptions Moderate the Validity of Leadership and Performance Predictions? *Personnel Psychology,* 45: 141–164.

39. Brett Joan, and Atwater, Leanne. 2001. "360-Degree Feedback: Accuracy, Reactions and Perceptons of Usefulness." *Journal of Applied Psychology,* 86: 930–942.

40. Kluger, Avraham N, and Angelo DeNisi. 1996. "The Effects of Feedback Interventions on Performance: A Historical Review, A Meta-Analysis, and Preliminary Feedback Theory." *Psychological Bulletin,* 119: 254–284; Atwater, Leanne, A., Paul Rousch, and Allison Fischthal. 1995. "The Influence of Upward Feedback on Self- and Follower Ratings of Leadership." *Personnel Psychology,* 48: 35–60.

41. Goldsmith, Marshall, and B. Underhill. 2000. "Multisource Feedback for Executive Development." In David Bracken, Carol Timmreck, and Allan Church (eds.). *The Handbook of Multisource Feedback.* San Francisco: Jossey-Bass, 275–288.

42. Atwater, Leanne, Waldman, David, Atwater, David, and Cartier, Priscilla. 2000. "Upward Feedback Field Experiment. Supervisors' Cynicism, Follow-up and Commitment to Subordinates." *Personnel Psychology,* (a)53: 275–297; Tuckey, Michelle, Neil Brewer, and Paul Williamson. 2002. *Journal of Occupational and Organizational Psychology,* 75: 195–216.

43. DeNisi, Angelo, and Avraham Kluger, "Feedback Effectiveness: Can 360-Degree Appraisals be Improved?" *Academy of Management Executive*, 14(1): 129–139.

44. Mayfield Rowley, Jacqueline, Milton Ray Mayfield, and Jerry Kopf. 1998. "The Effects of Leader Motivating Language on Subordinate Performance and Satisfaction." *Human Resource Management,* 37(3): 235–248.

45. Larson, Erik, and Jonathan King. 1996. "The Systematic Distortion of Information: An Ongoing Challenge to Management." *Organizational Dynamics,* 22(3): 49–61.

46. Birnbaum, Jeffrey. 1993. "Ex-Chief of Staff Ponders Clinton Woes and Urges Advisors to Stand Up to Boss." *Wall Street Journal.* May 27.

47. Kiechel, Walter. 1990. "How to Escape the Echo Chamber." *Fortune.* June 18: 12–13.

48. Ibid.

49. Bartolome, Fernando. 1994. "How to Get Bad News, Too." *Executive Female.* May/June: 15–18.

50. Fulk, Jane, and Sirish Mani. 1974b. "Distortion of Communication in Hierarchical Relationships."

51. Kiechel, Walter. 1990. "How to Escape the Echo Chamber." *Fortune.* June 18: 12–13; Bartolome, Fernando. 1994. "How to Get Bad News, Too." *Executive Female.* May/June: 15–18; Fernandes Bartoleme 1989. "Nobody Trusts the Boss Completely, Now What?" *Harvard Business Review,* 67(2): 135–143.

52. The Working Communicator. Undated. New York: Japan Airlines.

53. Kennedy, Jim, and Anna Everest. 1991. "Put Diversity in Context." *Personnel Journal.* September: 50–54.

54. Ibid.

55. Tannen, Deborah. 1990. *You Just Don't Understand: Women and Men in Conversation.* New York: Ballentine Books.

56. Ibid.

57. Craig, Holly. 1991. *Gender Differences in Language.* Ann Arbor, MI: Communicative Disorders Clinic Publication.

58. Ibid.

59. Crossen, Cynthia. 1997. "Blah, Blah, Blah: The Crucial Question for These Noisy Times May Just Be 'Huh?'" *Wall Street Journal.* July 10: B1.

60. Sapir, Edward. 1963. *Selected Writings of Edward Sapir in Language, Culture, and Personality.* David Mandelbaum (ed.). Berkeley, CA: University of California Press; cited in Martyna, Wendy. 1980. "Beyond the He/Man Approach: The Case for Nonsexist Language." *Signs: Journal of Women in Culture and Society,* 5(3): 482–492.

61. Tannen, Deborah. 1995. "The Power of Talk: Who Gets Heard and Why." *Harvard Business Review.* September–October: 139–148.

62. Bem, Sandra, and Daryl Bem. 1973. "Does Sex-Biased Job Advertising Aid and Abet Sex Discrimination?" *Journal of Applied Social Psychology,* 3(1): 6–18.

63. Martyna, Wendy. 1980. "Beyond the He/Man Approach: The Case for Nonsexist Language." *Signs: Journal of Women in Culture and Society,* 5(3): 482–492.

64. Daily, Bill, and Miriam Finch. 1993. "Benefiting from Nonsexist Language in the Workplace." *Business Horizons.* March–April: 30–34.

65. The material for the figure was developed from a variety of sources including Daily, Bill, and Miriam Finch. 1993. "Benefiting from Nonsexist Language in the Workplace." *Business Horizons.* March–April: 30–34; Munter, Mary. 1986. *Business Communication: Strategy and Skill.* Upper Saddle River, NJ: Prentice Hall; Murphy, Herta, and Herbert W. 1991. Hildebrandt. *Effective Business Communications,* 6th ed. New York: McGraw-Hill. Lentz, Richard 1984. "Job Aids: A Checklist for Nonsexist Writing." *Performance and Instruction Journal* 13.

66. Martyna, Wendy. 1980. "Beyond the He/Man Approach: The Case for Nonsexist Language." *Signs: Journal of Women in Culture and Society,* 5(3): 482–492.

67. Conger, Jay. 1998. "The Necessary Art of Persuasion." *Harvard Business Review.* May–June: 85–95.

68. Smircich, Linda, and Gareth Morgan. "Leadership: The Management of Meaning." *The Journal of Applied Behavioral Science,* 18(3): 258.

69. Daily, Bill, and Miriam Finch. 1993. "Benefiting from Nonsexist Language in the Workplace." *Business Horizons.* March–April: 30–34.

70. Murphy, Herta A., and Herbert Hildebrandt. 1991. *Effective Business Communications*, 6th ed. New York: McGraw-Hill, 79–80.

71. Daily, Bill, and Miriam Finch. 1993. "Benefiting from Nonsexist Language in the Workplace." *Business Horizons.* March–April: 30–34.

72. Munter, Mary. 1987. *Business Communication: Strategy and Skill.* New York: McGraw-Hill.

73. Mayfield, Jacqueline Rowley, Milton Ray Mayfield, and Jerry Kopf. 1998. "The Effects of Leader Motivating Language on Subordinate Performance and Satisfaction." *Human Resource Management,* 37(3&4): 235–248.

74. Hartog, Den, Deanne N., and Robert M. Verburg. Winter 1997. "Charisma and Rhetoric: Communicative Techniques of International Business Leaders." *Leadership Quarterly,* 8(4): 355–391; citing Shamir, B., M. B. Arthur, and R. House. 1994. "The Rhetoric of Charismatic Leadership: A Theoretical Extension, a Case Study and Implications for Research." *Leadership Quarterly,* 5: 25–42.

75. Emrich, Cynthia, Holly Brower, Jack Feldman, and Howard Garland. 2001. "Images in Words: Presidential Rhetoric, Charisma, and Greatness." *Administrative Science Quarterly,* 46: 527–557.

76. Morgan, Nick. 2001. "The Kinesthetic Speaker: Putting Action into Words." *Harvard Business Review*, 113–120.

77. Conger, Jay. 1991. "Inspiring Others: The Language of Leadership." *The Academy of Management Executive.* February: 31–45.

78. Washington, James M. (ed.). 1986. *A Testimony of Hope: The Essential Writings and Speeches of Martin Luther King, Jr.* San Francisco, CA: Harper, 217–220.

79. Emrich, Cynthia, Holly Brower, Jack Feldman, and Howard Garland. 2001. "Images in Words: Presidential Rhetoric, Charisma, and Greatness." *Administrative Science Quarterly,* (46): 527–557.

80. Conger, Jay. 1991. "Inspiring Others: The Language of Leadership." *The Academy of Management Executive,* 5(1): 31–45.

81. Bell, Chip. 1992. "The Trainer as Storyteller." *Training and Development.* September: 53–56.

82. Heath, Chip, Chris Bell, and Emily Sternberg. 2001. "Emotional Selection in Mimes: The Case of Urban Legends." *Journal of Personality and Social Psychology*, 81; Kounios, John, and Philip J. Holcomb. 1994. "Concreteness Effects in Semantic Processing: ERP Evidence Supporting Dual-Coding Theory." *Journal of Experimental Psychology: Learning, Memory and Cognition,* 20: 804–823; Marsharck, Mark, Charles L. Richman, John C. Yuille, and R. Reed Hunt. 1987. "The Role of Imagery in Memory: On Shared and Distinctive Information." *Psychological Bulletin,* (102): 28–41.

83. Levin, Ira M. 2000. "Vision Revisited: Telling the Story of the Future." *Journal of Applied Behavioral Science,* 36(1): 92–93.

84. Lieber, Ronald. 1997. "Storytelling: A New Way to Get Close to Your Customer." *Fortune.* February 3: 102–108.

85. Roddick, Anita. 1991. *Body and Soul.* New York: Crown Trade Paperbacks, 25.

86. Schank, Roger, and Robert Abelson. 1995. "Knowledge and Memory: The Real Story." In R. J. Wyer, Jr. (ed.) *Advances in Social Cognition.* Vol. 8. Hillsdale, NJ: Erlbaum, 1–86.

87. Sander, Russell Scott. 1997. "The Most Human Art: Ten Reasons Why We'll Always Need a Good Story." *Utne Reader.* September–October: 54–56.

88. Hequet, Marc. 1992. "Poof! Myth and Fable Appear as Human Development Tools." *Training.* December: 46–50.

89. Decker, Bert with James Denney. 1992. *You've Got to Be Believed to Be Heard.* New York: St. Martin's Press.

90. Wilkins, Alan. 1989. "Corporate Culture: The Role of Stories." In Morgan, Gareth (ed.). *Creative Organizational Theory: A Resource Book.* Newbury Park, CA: Sage.

91. Zempke, Ron. 1990. "Storytelling: Back to a Basic." *Training.* March: 44–50; Conger, Jay. 1991. "Inspiring Others: The Language of Leadership." *Academy of Management Executive,* 5(1): 31–45.

92. Armstrong, David. 1992. "Management by Storytelling." *Executive Female.* May/June: 38–77.

93. De Jonge, Peter. 1999. "Riding the Wild, Perilous Waters of Amazon.com." *New York Times.* March 14: 36–81.

94. Schein, Edgar. 1997. *Organizational Culture and Leadership.* San Francisco, CA: Jossey-Bass, 13.

95. Heath, Chip, Chris Bell, and Emily Sternberg. 2001. "Emotional Selection in Mimes: The Case of Urban Legends." *Journal of Personality and Social Psychology*, 81.

96. Bell, Chip. 1992. "The Trainer as Storyteller." *Training and Development.* September: 53–56.

97. Martin, Joanne, Martha Feldman, Mary Jo Hatch, and Sim Sitkin. 1983. "The Uniqueness Paradox in Organizational Stories." *Administrative Science Quarterly,* 28: 438–453.

98. Many of the following ideas are from Bell, Chip. "The Trainer as Storyteller." *Training and Development.* September: 53–56.

99. Ibid.

100. Iacocca, Lee with William Novak. 1984. *Iacocca: An Autobiography*. Bantam Books.

101. Brown, Andrew and Michael Humphreys. 2003. "Epic Tales and Tragic Tales: Making Sense of Change." *The Journal of Applied Behavioral Science,* 39(2): 121–144.

102. McGregor, Ian, and John Holmes. 1999. "How Storytelling Shapes Memory and Impressions of Relationship Events Over Time." *Journal of Personality and Social Psychology,* 76(3): 403–419; citing Shank, Roger, and Robert Abelson. 1995. "Knowledge and Memory: The Real Story." In Robert J. Wyer, Jr. (ed.). *Advances in Social Cognition*. Vol. 8. Hillsdale, NJ: Erlbaum, 1–86.

103. Zempke, Ron. 1990. "Storytelling: Back to a Basic." *Training.* March: 44–50.

104. Boje, David. 1995. "Stories of the Storytelling Organization: A Postmodern Analysis of Disney as 'Tamara-Land'." *Academy of Management Journal,* 38(4): 997–1036; Brown, Andrew, and Michael Humphreys. 2003. "Epic Tales and Tragic

Tales: Making Sense of Change." *The Journal of Applied Behavioral Science,* 39(2): 121–144.

105. Elsbach, Kimbery. 2003. "How to Pitch a Brilliant Idea." *Harvard Business Review*, 117–122.

106. Ibid.

107. Pink, Daniel. 1999. "Report from the Future: What's Your Story." *Fast Company.* January: 32–34.

108. Borden, Mark. 1999. "Thinking about Tomorrow." *Fortune.* November 22: 170.

109. Three Out of Four Americans Have Access to the Internet, According to Nielsen// Netratings, www.nielsen-netratings.com, 2004.

110. International Telecommunications Report, Internet for a Mobile Generation; Cell Phone Usage Overtakes Landlines in the U.S. www.cellular-news.com/sory/8773.shtml.

111. Online Consumers Spent $18.5 Billion During 2003 Holdiay Season, According to Goldman Sachs, Harris Interactive, and Nielsen//Netratings Holiday Spending Report www.nielsen-netratings.com, 2004.

112. Kids Account for One out of Five Internet surfers in the U.S., www.nielsen-netratings.com, 2003; 13 Million Kids Using the Internet Across Europe, www.nielsen-netratings.com.

113. Senior Citizens Lead Internet Growth, According to Nielsen//Netratings, www.nielsen-netratings.com, 2003; Older Internet Audience Continues to Increase in Europe, www.nielsen-netratings.com, 2003.

114. Nie, Norman, and Lutz Erbring. "Study Offers Early Look at How Internet Is Changing Daily Life." Stanford Institute for the Quantitative Study of Society, www.stanford.edu/group.siqss/PressRelease/press_release.html.

115. Hoffman, W. Michael, Laura P. Hartman, and Mark Rowe. 2003. "You've Got Mail . . . and the Boss Knows." *Business and Society Review*, 108(3): 285–307.

116. Hoffman, W. Michael, Linda Hartman, and Mark Rowe. 2003. "You've Got Mail and the Boss Knows." *Business and Society Review,* 108(3): 285–308.

117. Veiga, John, and Kathleen Dechant. 1997. "Wired World Woes: www.help." *Academy of Management Executive,* 11(3): 73–86.

118. 1999. "Paperless Office?" *Training and Development*. November: 31.

119. Nie, Norman, and Lutz Erbring. "Study Offers Early Look at How Internet Is Changing Daily Life." *Stanford Institute for the Quantitative Study of Society*, www.stanford.edu/group.siqss/PressRelease/press_release.html.

120. Veiga, John, and Kathleen Dechant. 1997. "Wired World Woes: www.help." *Academy of Management Executive,* 11(3): 73–86; citing Juliet Schorr. 1992. *The Overworked American*. New York: Basic Books.

121. Gundling, Ernest. 1999. "How to Communicate Globally." *Training and Development.* June: 28–31.

122. 1999. "A Special News Report about Life on the Job—and Trends Taking Shape There." *Wall Street Journal.* December 21: A1.

123. Smith, Randal. 2004. "Quattrone Found Guilty on 3 Counts in Big U.S. Win." *Wall Street Journal.* May 4.

124. 1996. *Training and Development.* December: 7.

125. Abernathy, Donna. 1990. "Seven Ways to Work Smarter On-line." *Training and Development.* June: 20.

126. Ibid.

127. Stepanek, Marcia with Steve Hamm. 1998. "When the Devil Is in the E-Mails." *Business Week.* June 8: 72–74.

128. Gross, Neil. 1999. "Innovations." *Business Week* October 25: 95.

129. Ellet, Bill. 1999. "Can't Beat 'Em? Play with 'Em." *Training and Development* November: 84.

130. Schrage, Michael. 1999. "The Tangled Web of E-Deception." *Fortune.* September 27: 269.

131. Gayeski, Diane, and Jennifer Majka. 1996. "Untangling Communication Chaos: A Communitator's Conundrum for Coping with Change in the Coming Century." *Communication World,* 13(7): September 1.

132. Young, Mary, and James Post. 1993. "Managing to Communicate, Communicating to Manage: How Leading Companies Communicate with Employees." *Organizational Dynamics.* Summer: 31–43.

133. Ibid.

-------------------------V I D E O   C A S E-------------------------
Case 2   Communicating

Although many managers experience much of the day-to-day formal and information communication in their jobs as a distraction from their real work, effective managers understand that communication is the real work of managers. They know that planned and unplanned communication is critical to building all-important relationships, building trust, obtaining timely information, developing support for their ideas, and enhancing employee performance.

Active listening and giving effective feedback are two of the most critical communication skills that managers can have. Active listening requires that we listen carefully to others on their own terms and resist the tendency to quickly judge or evaluate them on what they are saying. It requires empathy, respect, concentration, and an open mind. It builds trust and reduces defensiveness. Giving effective feedback requires that we tell people information designed to enhance their performance. To be effective, feedback must be given in a way that the person can understand, accept, and use to improve performance.

The way that we give feedback can motivate or demotivate a person, gain sup-port or build resistance, enhance under-standing, or increase confusion. Choosing the right time and place, focusing on only one or two issues at a time, linking feedback to the person's and organization's goals, providing positive as well as negative feed-back, and adapting a communication style to that of the receiver are good ways to begin. It is also important to be specific by using examples and explaining concerns in terms that are descriptive, not judgmental ("Your department had the lowest results in the last quarter," not, "Your department results are terrible."). Finally, it is important to check that the receiver has understood your feedback as you intended; listen to what he or she has to say in response, let the receiver know that you have confidence in him or her, follow up to see if the receiver has made changes in response to the feed-back, and acknowledge positive changes when they occur.

In this video segment, we'll see how Mia handles a problem with allaboutself.com's receptionist, Sarah, whose mediocre perfor-mance and disappointing attitude call out for management intervention. What do you think of Mia's feedback session? ■

DISCUSSION QUESTIONS

1. In each of the feedback scenes por-trayed, is Mia doing an effective job of providing feedback to Sarah? Why or why not?
2. If she is, what is particularly effective about her communication style?
3. If she is not, what feedback strategies would help Mia improve the job she is doing?
4. What else could Mia do to help Sarah improve her performance?
5. What motivates Sarah? Has Mia tried hard enough to find this out?
6. How has Sarah been communicating her feelings about her job? Is this an effective strategy? Why or why not?

5

Gaining and Using Sustainable, Ethical Power and Influence

This chapter will help you:

■ Develop a working definition of sustainable, ethical power

■ Understand the characteristics of people with sustainable, ethical power

■ Learn how to read and adapt to the styles of other people so that you can become more influential with many different types of people

■ Learn how to use (and resist) six universal forms of influence

■ Learn how organizational politics can enhance organizational effectiveness and how you can engage in politics ethically

> *Power is America's last dirty word. It is easier to talk about money—and much easier to talk about sex—than it is to talk about power.*
> —ROSABETH MOSS KANTER

From our first cry until our last will and testament, we try to influence the world around us. As toddlers, we try to assert our power with the emphatic use of the word, "No." We soon learn that we can influence people more successfully by charming them with a smile and heartfelt compliment ("You're my best friend."). As we get older, we try to impress the people with whom we have romantic aspirations through the way that we dress and talk. When we become adults, we try to convince our children to do their homework, be polite, and go to college. We try to persuade the people we love to take good care of themselves. We try to negotiate a lower sales price when we want to buy the house of our dreams. And when we move into that dream house, we try to persuade our neighbors to stop mowing their lawn with a power mower at 7:00 A.M. on Saturdays.

In the working world, we try to prove to recruiters that we're exactly the kind of employee their organization needs. We try to persuade our boss that we deserve the training, mentoring, and high profile assignments that will help us gain valuable experience, as well as career advantages such as promotions and salary increases. We try to encourage the employees who work for us to do their best work and go above and beyond the call of duty when necessary. And we try to convince our colleagues and others over whom we have no formal control to pay attention to our ideas and help us when we need their support.

Power doesn't corrupt people; people corrupt power. *William Gaddis, Author and Journalist*
Although we all try to influence people throughout our lives, most of us don't take the time to learn the art and science of gaining power and influence. There are two reasons for this. First, some people are unaware that researchers have been studying the best practices for gaining and using power and influence for over four decades. Second, some people are ambivalent about power. This ambivalence is due, in part, to having a mistaken and narrow view of power. They believe that power naturally corrupts. But for every scandal about the abuse of power, there are multiple stories about the ethical use of power that has transformed organizations and the world for the better.

Undoubtedly, there will always be people who gain and use power in unscrupulous ways, but that shouldn't stop you from understanding and using power ethically. If you shy away from understanding and using power and influence, you leave the world in the hands of those who would abuse it. Indeed, Harvard Professor Linda Hill explains that powerlessness can corrupt. She explains that people with power can shape their environment, whereas the powerless are "destined to be molded and constrained by theirs. How often have we heard of people who believed they had 'no choice' but to engage in some unethical act because they did not have the 'power to change the way things are usually done?' "[1]

People who are skilled at influencing others reap significant rewards; those who are not can pay dearly for their lack of influence skills. In addition to inhibiting your job effectiveness, believing that you cannot influence your environment can have negative effects on your psychological and physical well-being. For example, researchers have found that people who feel that they have some control over the most important roles in their lives tend to live longer.[2] Researchers have also found that employees who feel that they lack control over their work and their workplace tend to have a higher incidence of heart disease, as well as job dissatisfaction.[3] A lack of influence skills can also negatively affect your income. For example, in a *Wall Street Journal* article, Carnegie Mellon management professor Linda Babcock explained that "skipping or bungling a single negotiation can inflict a huge penalty. A 22-year-old woman who fails to get her first job offer of $25,000 boosted by $5,000 stands to lose more than $568,000 by age 60."[4]

Some people seem to have a natural talent for getting people to buy into their ideas, gaining support from others, and being at the right place at the right time. Fortunately for the rest of us, there is a science to gaining and using power and influence. This chapter helps you learn techniques that will help you gain sustainable, ethical power and influence. By using these skills, you will be better able to achieve the goals that are important to you, your organizations, your communities, and the people who depend on you. You will be able to use these skills at work or at home, whether you are a manager, individual contributor, salaried employee, consultant, or hourly employee. At the end of this chapter I discuss how organizational politics can enhance organizational effectiveness and how you can ethically engage in politics to achieve the results that you desire.

FOUNDATIONS OF SUSTAINABLE, ETHICAL POWER AND INFLUENCE

Power refers to the willingness and ability of a person or group to influence the attitudes, beliefs, and behaviors of others so that they are willing to support the goals that the person or group believes are important.[5] In short, power enables people to influence their environment and get things done. Note that the use of power is necessary only when there is real or potential conflict over interests, goals, or the means by which to achieve those interests or goals.[6]

Although we often describe people or groups as "powerful," power is not a stable characteristic of a person or group. Rather:

- Power must be actively sought and continuously replenished.
- Power is negotiated in a relationship. You can only have power over another person if that person perceives you as having something that he or she wants or needs.[7]
- Power is situational. You may have power in one situation yet be powerless in another. For example, you may be in charge at your office, but the dentist is clearly in charge when performing a root canal.

Thus, to have sustainable power that transcends a particular time, position, and place, you must (1) have a variety of resources to offer that people believe they need or want, (2) know many different strategies for gaining the support of others, and (3) adapt your strategy based on the situation.

Power can be gained and used ethically or unscrupulously. You are gaining and using power ethically when:[8]

- You explicitly tell people what you want to achieve and why.
- You put the interests of others and the organization at least on par with your own interests and, when appropriate, are able to put others' interests ahead of your own.
- You treat everyone with respect, administer organizational policies and procedures fairly, and do not abuse anyone's rights or exploit people.[9]
- You leave yourself reasonably open to be influenced by others.
- You back your requests with honest supporting data.

Why We Need Power and Influence Skills

Many people believe that if everyone simply focused on their jobs and followed standard organizational procedures, the most competent people would be promoted, the best ideas would rise to the top, and everyone would cooperate with each other to implement the best decisions for the greater good. Many people also believe that organizational decisions are typically made from a careful analysis of all available information. But the organizational world doesn't—and will never—work this way for several reasons.[10]

People Are Boundedly Rational

Although we like to think of ourselves as rational and knowledgeable decision makers, all human beings are instead "boundedly rational"[11] and "lazy information processors."[12] In other words, our human minds are incapable of taking in all the information that comes our way, remembering everything that we learn, and interpreting information from every conceivable angle. Because of our cognitive limitations and inevitable lack of complete information, we often (1) "satisfice"—look for good enough answers—rather than the best possible answers and (2) use cognitive shortcuts to determine the course of action we believe we should take. In other words, instead of systematically seeking out and sifting through all available information, we make decisions based on questions such as "What have we done in the past?" "Who is the person with the most expertise?" "What are other people doing about this kind of problem?" and "Who can I trust to give me advice?" It is worth noting that our ability to process information is increasingly challenged. Persuasion researcher Robert Levine warns that "the burden [on our ability to process information] is greater today than ever before. A recent study estimated that one week of the *New York Times* carries more information than a person in the sixteenth century digested in a lifetime.'"[13]

Uncertainty

In an increasingly complex world, we cannot predict all the consequences of the different courses of action we could take, nor can we accurately predict the costs of lost opportunities. And even if we had all the information we needed to make the best decision today, we cannot predict how future events will shape the consequences of our decisions in the long term.

Mutual Interdependence

Most organizational decisions are made and implemented together with others.[14] However, the people who depend on each other to achieve important organizational goals often have different interests, perspectives, values, work styles, and objectives. Although these differences can lead to creativity, innovation, and higher quality decisions, these differences can also cause misunderstanding, conflict, and resistance.

Limited Resources

Only so many projects can be funded, only so many people can be promoted, and only so many issues considered by organizational leaders. Consequently, organizational members sometimes must compete with each other to achieve their organizational and career goals.[15]

In short, we need to understand how to influence others because we compete for limited resources in an uncertain world with people who have imperfect decision-making abilities and conflicting interests (and over whom we have limited, if any, formal authority).

Characteristics of People with Power

Power is not revealed by striking hard or often, but by striking true.
Honore De Balzac,
Journalist and Writer

People who have sustainable power—power that transcends a particular time, position, and place—behave in ways that enable them to convince people that they are worth listening to, that their ideas have merit, and that they deserve the support of others. Contrary to the battlefield or bully image of power, people with sustainable power realize that they don't gain power by hoarding it or beating people over the head with it. Instead, people with sustainable, ethical power gain and use their power subtly and respectfully. They pay attention to things that other people miss, see situations from multiple perspectives, adapt their behavior so that they can be successful in many different settings, spend a great deal of time trying to understand and support others, and make *other* people feel powerful.[16] One manager described his boss this way:

> Most of the people here would walk over hot coals in their bare feet if my boss asked them to. He has an incredible capacity to do little things that mean a lot to people. Today, for example, in his junk mail he came across an advertisement for something that one of my subordinates had in passing once mentioned that he was shopping for. So, my boss routed it to him. That probably took 15 seconds of his time, and yet my subordinate really appreciated it. To give you another example, two weeks ago he somehow learned that the purchasing manager's mother had died. On his way home that night, he stopped off at the funeral parlor. Our purchasing manager was, of course, there at the time. I bet he'll remember that brief visit for quite a while.[17]

The above example illustrates that sustainable power is accumulated through small but significant and sincere acts over time. Although people who develop sustainable, ethical power differ in many ways, they tend to share much in common:

- They focus on achieving the goals that they believe are important.
- They are action oriented and want to shape their environment.
- They are competent, dependable, and have the expertise required to do their job well. In the long run, people support those who can be counted on to get results and who follow through with their responsibilities and commitments.[18]
- They are planners. They do their homework and develop systematic strategies for gaining support.
- They are willing to use the informal organization that operates outside official policies, procedures, and chains of commands to achieve their goals.
- They are astute observers of human behavior and have solid social skills.[19] They try to understand the interests of other people, identify who is likely to support and resist their ideas, and build mutually supportive relationships with many different kinds of people and groups.
- They love information. They want to know the who, what, when, why, and where of everyday life.
- They are great listeners and have an open mind. They know that they cannot obtain information, learn new ideas, observe other people's reactions, and hear other people's perspectives unless they stop talking and start listening.
- They realize that managing perceptions is at least as important as managing reality. They do not change the facts or the merits of their case, but they frame their requests in ways that respect other people's point of view so that their ideas will be heard, understood, and supported.
- They think in shades of gray rather than black and white. Says Kathleen Reardon in her practical book *The Secret Handshake: Mastering the Politics of the Business Inner Circle*, "Their worlds are not a neat series of do's and don'ts, but rather avenues of extensive possibilities."[20]
- They are adaptable. Although they continuously focus on their objectives, they are willing to be flexible about how they achieve them.[21]

- They have integrity, a characteristic that builds trust and predicts job performance and leadership potential.[22]

Anyone who is committed to achieving their goals can adopt the mindset and learn the skills that will help them gain sustainable, ethical power. The rest of this chapter focuses on three types of influence skills: (1) being able to read other people and adapt your message in ways that will help you be understood and supported; (2) using six universal forms of influence; and (3) developing political savvy. Figure 5-1 summarizes these influence strategies. Before you read the following sections, consider at least three people whom you want to influence and identify what you would like them to do. Write their names and what you would like them to do in Table 5-1. Then, as you read the following sections, write down several strategies that you can use to gain their support.

FIGURE 5-1 Developing Ethical, Sustainable Power and Influence

different settings, spend a great deal of time trying to understand and support others, and make *other* people feel powerful.[16] One manager described his boss this way:

> Most of the people here would walk over hot coals in their bare feet if my boss asked them to. He has an incredible capacity to do little things that mean a lot to people. Today, for example, in his junk mail he came across an advertisement for something that one of my subordinates had in passing once mentioned that he was shopping for. So, my boss routed it to him. That probably took 15 seconds of his time, and yet my subordinate really appreciated it. To give you another example, two weeks ago he somehow learned that the purchasing manager's mother had died. On his way home that night, he stopped off at the funeral parlor. Our purchasing manager was, of course, there at the time. I bet he'll remember that brief visit for quite a while.[17]

The above example illustrates that sustainable power is accumulated through small but significant and sincere acts over time. Although people who develop sustainable, ethical power differ in many ways, they tend to share much in common:

- They focus on achieving the goals that they believe are important.
- They are action oriented and want to shape their environment.
- They are competent, dependable, and have the expertise required to do their job well. In the long run, people support those who can be counted on to get results and who follow through with their responsibilities and commitments.[18]
- They are planners. They do their homework and develop systematic strategies for gaining support.
- They are willing to use the informal organization that operates outside official policies, procedures, and chains of commands to achieve their goals.
- They are astute observers of human behavior and have solid social skills.[19] They try to understand the interests of other people, identify who is likely to support and resist their ideas, and build mutually supportive relationships with many different kinds of people and groups.
- They love information. They want to know the who, what, when, why, and where of everyday life.
- They are great listeners and have an open mind. They know that they cannot obtain information, learn new ideas, observe other people's reactions, and hear other people's perspectives unless they stop talking and start listening.
- They realize that managing perceptions is at least as important as managing reality. They do not change the facts or the merits of their case, but they frame their requests in ways that respect other people's point of view so that their ideas will be heard, understood, and supported.
- They think in shades of gray rather than black and white. Says Kathleen Reardon in her practical book *The Secret Handshake: Mastering the Politics of the Business Inner Circle*, "Their worlds are not a neat series of do's and don'ts, but rather avenues of extensive possibilities."[20]
- They are adaptable. Although they continuously focus on their objectives, they are willing to be flexible about how they achieve them.[21]

- They have integrity, a characteristic that builds trust and predicts job performance and leadership potential.[22]

Anyone who is committed to achieving their goals can adopt the mindset and learn the skills that will help them gain sustainable, ethical power. The rest of this chapter focuses on three types of influence skills: (1) being able to read other people and adapt your message in ways that will help you be understood and supported; (2) using six universal forms of influence; and (3) developing political savvy. Figure 5-1 summarizes these influence strategies. Before you read the following sections, consider at least three people whom you want to influence and identify what you would like them to do. Write their names and what you would like them to do in Table 5-1. Then, as you read the following sections, write down several strategies that you can use to gain their support.

FIGURE 5-1 Developing Ethical, Sustainable Power and Influence

Foundations of Ethical Influence

- You explicitly tell people what you want to achieve and why
- You put interests of others and organization on par and sometimes ahead of your own
- You treat everyone with respect, administer organizational policies and procedures fairly, and do not abuse anyone's rights or exploit people
- You leave yourself reasonably open to influence from others
- You back your requests with supporting honest data

Influence Skills

Developing Interpersonal Flexibility:

Adapting your communication style so that people with different styles are more likely to understand and support you.

Using Six Universal Forms of Influence:

- Reciprocation
- Commitment and consistency
- Authority
- Social proof
- Scarcity
- Liking

Developing Political Savvy:

- Using personal resources (expertise, track record of results)
- Using relational resources (strategically visiting people, communicating to build relationships)
- Using structural resources (position, autonomy, job criticality, network centrality, and coalitions)

Ethical, Sustainable Power, and Influence

Enhanced ability to achieve important goals for yourself (job effectiveness, career success and well-being), your organization, your community, and the people who depend on you.

TABLE 5-1 Implementing Influence Strategies		
Person You Want to Influence	*What You Want That Person to Do*	*Strategies You Can Use to Influence the Person*
Person #1		
Person #2		
Person #3		

DEVELOPING INTERPERSONAL POWER: READING AND ADAPTING TO OTHER PEOPLE'S INTERESTS AND STYLES

You can change the way people listen to you. Altering the direction of your communication can change your today, tomorrow, and potentially the direction of your career. Kathleen Kelley Reardon, Author of The Secret Handshake

Influential people have well-developed social skills. They enjoy watching people and figuring out why people do what they do. They understand that people who seem unreasonable may simply have different goals, perspectives, and ways of reasoning. They know that people are more likely to listen to, understand, and support someone they trust and who treats them well. They create positive interactions with others by building on similarities, respecting differences, aligning different interests toward common goals, and expressing their desires in ways that are understandable and palatable to others.

In this section, I describe a model that will help you understand and adapt to people with different styles so that you are more likely to achieve mutually supportive goals. Specifically you will:

- Learn the Social Styles model that identifies four different types of behavioral styles.
- Identify your preferred behavioral style, as well as the strengths and weaknesses associated with that style.
- Understand how your style may be perceived by others and how those perceptions may influence whether people support or resist you.
- Develop strategies for influencing people with different styles.

The Social Styles Model

The Social Styles model provides a useful framework for understanding your own behavioral preferences and the preferences of others.[23] This model assumes that (1) we all have predictable and taken-for-granted ways of behaving, including how we make decisions, interact with others, and resolve conflicts; (2) if we understand our preferred styles as well as the preferred styles of the others, we can avoid some of the problems that arise from the misunderstandings, conflicts, and frustrations that can occur when people with different styles interact; and (3) we are more likely to influence others if we build relationships based on mutual understanding and respect.

Note: Before you read any further, please take the Social Styles assessment in Box 5.1 at the end of this chapter.

The Social Styles model focuses on two dimensions:

- ***Assertive/probing:*** This refers to whether a person prefers to assertively push his or her ideas or patiently draw ideas out from other people.
- ***High responsiveness/low responsiveness:*** This refers to whether a person prefers to be rational, objective, and task-focused or emotionally expressive, intuitive, and relationship-focused.

Based on these two dimensions, a person's social style can usually be categorized into one of the four categories: driver (assertive/low responsiveness), expressive (assertive/high responsiveness), amiable (probing/high responsiveness), and analytic (probing/low responsiveness). Tables 5-2 through 5-6 describe the common characteristics of each style, the potential strengths and limitations of each style, how each style may be perceived by others, and how people with each style tend to react under stress. Table 5-7 describes influence strategies for each style. When using Social Styles to gain a better understanding of yourself and others, keep in mind:

- People are much more complex in their thinking and behaving than the Social Style model (or any model for that matter) can portray.
- Style descriptions should be used as guidelines for understanding behavior and building mutually supportive relationships rather than as templates for stereotyping or pigeon-holing people into simplistic categories.
- One style is not generally better or worse than the others. All styles bring important perspectives and skills, as well as blind spots and limitations.
- Everyone uses all four of these styles at different times, but we tend to prefer one style more than the others and use that style most often, especially under stress.
- One's Social Style may change over time.
- Some styles may be more appropriate than others in particular situations.
- Successful people respect and leverage the strengths of each of the four styles.
- Everyone can learn how to be more flexible and use all four styles.

You can use the following tables to learn the strengths and weaknesses of each style, how people with each style may be perceived by others, and what strategies you can use to influence people with each style. As you read through these tables, return to Table 5-1 on which you listed the three people whom you identified as people you want

TABLE 5-2 General Characteristics of Each Social Style	
Analytic	*Driver*
Emphasizes facts, data, and procedures	Emphasizes goals and bottom-line results
Well organized	Decisive and direct
Systematic, logical, objective	Encourages risk taking
Careful, detailed, disciplined	Competitive
Conservative	Impatient
Reserved	Uses report talk (facts and information)
Uses report talk (facts and information)	Fast-talking and may interrupt
Asks questions	Focuses on content not style
Chooses words carefully	Uses bold gestures and direct eye contact
Focuses on content not style	Leans forward and may be loud
Uses limited gestures and facial expressions	May not praise others
Uses deliberate and slow decision making	May be formal
May need to be right	May not want to be told what to do
Amiable	*Expressive*
Emphasizes collaboration	Emphasizes positive vision of the future
Good listener and agreeable	Enthusiastic, energetic, can-do attitude
Uses rapport talk (building relationships)	Uses rapport talk (building relationships)
Tries to see others' perspectives	Likes to think out loud
Empathetic	Optimistic, dramatic, and spontaneous
Asks questions	Encourages innovation and risk taking
Wants to include everyone	Social, playful, and comfortable with most people
Prefers consensus	
Likes routine	Leans forward, uses bold eye contact
Often quiet, slow, and steady	Uses animated gestures/facial expressions
Easygoing and modest	Fast-talking
Uses open, unhurried gestures	Expresses emotions and concern
May not give direct statements/opinions	Likes to be center of attention
May avoid making big decisions	May speak in generalities
	May not seek out data to back up intuition

to influence. What do you think each person's social style is? Based on what you've learned about the Social Styles model, write down the strategies that may be useful for each person. Remember that people give clues about how they can be influenced.[24] If you take the time to look for these clues, you will be much more successful in your influence attempts. For example, you can ask people questions (what do you think the most important issues are in this organization and how do you think we can solve them?), observe their reactions (including body language), and listen carefully to the

TABLE 5-3   Potential Strengths of Each Social Style

Analytic	Driver
Planning	Taking initiative
Analyzing	Getting things done fast
Organizing	Blocking out distractions
Ensuring accuracy	Focusing on results
Adhering to principles	Being decisive
Following procedures	

Amiable	Expressive
Getting along with others	Inspiring enthusiasm
Listening to others	Public speaking
Providing service	Building alliances
Being patient and dependable	Gaining support
Earning trust and cooperation	Generating ideas for
Keeping commitments	breakthrough solutions

TABLE 5-4   Potential Weaknesses of Each Social Style

Analytic	Driver
May miss the big picture	May be impatient
May assume data speaks for itself	May be too independent
May spend too much time on details	May assume they have best answer
May have inappropriate perfectionism	May underestimate need for building
May be slow to make decisions	relationships
May not share information	May be intimidating so people obey out of fear
May underestimate need for building relationships	or may not give necessary bad news

Amiable	Expressive
May be indecisive	May be disorganized
May not use time effectively	May be impulsive/unpredictable
May be slow to make decisions	May have short attention span
May be too dependent	May procrastinate
May have difficulty expressing opinions or disagreeing	May ignore data and details
May be taken advantage of by more assertive people	May make generalizations based on too little information
May overcommit	May underestimate reality of implementation
	May miss deadlines

TABLE 5-5 Potential Behavior under Stress for Each Social Style	
Analytic	*Driver*
Avoiding	Fighting
May be too critical	May be autocratic and controlling
May obsess and get lost in the details (paralysis by analysis)	May rant and rave but bark may be worse than bite
May have excessive perfectionism	May forget what made them angry in the first place
Amiable	*Expressive*
Avoiding	Fighting
May close down/get stuck	May attack when challenged
May passively wait for someone else to take charge	May be unpredictable
	May say too much to too many (loose lips sink ships)

TABLE 5-6 Weaknesses as They May Be Perceived by Others	
Analytic	*Driver*
Picky	Dominating
Indecisive	Pushy
Slow	Unpredictable
Moralistic	Bully
Stuffy	Scary and uncomfortable to be around
Too critical	Cold and insensitive
Amiable	*Expressive*
Too conforming	Undisciplined
Uncertain	Impulsive
No independent thinking	Egotistical
Too wishy-washy	Manipulative
	Superficial
	Too emotional

way that they speak. You can pay attention to what people say and how they interact at meetings. You can observe how people make presentations (do they emphasize the vision, results, data, or people?),[25] and you can ask someone who knows the people you want to influence to describe their styles and preferences.

When using Social Styles to influence others, keep the Platinum Rule in mind: Do unto others as they'd like done unto them.

TABLE 5-7 Influence Strategies for Different Social Styles

Analytic	*Driver*
Motivated by: Control and security through accuracy, precision, consistency, and attention to process	Motivated by: Power, control, competence, achievement, winning (being #1), independence, competition, change, being right, results, action, promotions, salary
Fears: Being out of control, criticism, sudden or uncontrolled change, embarrassment, mistakes	Fears: Not being on top, being seen as "soft," being taken advantage of, falling into routines, not meeting deadlines
What they don't like in others: Lack of predictability, unsubstantiated claims, disorganization, too much emotion	What they don't like in others: Lack of motivation, weaknesses, indecision, inaction
To influence: Be formal, systematic, detailed, direct, precise, and organized; Provide facts, data, and examples to back up claim; Explain how to do things; Show how plan fits with existing policies, practices, procedures; Ask for their advice; Focus on process; Schedule extra time for meetings; Support the person's principles; Give reasons for need for speed	To influence: Be decisive, directive, controlled, confident, and efficient; Emphasize immediate actions and results; Explain what needs to be done; Support person's priorities; Focus on future; Schedule short, direct meeting; Be viewed as someone who gets results
What they need from you: Provide deadlines; Break large projects into smaller steps; Refocus on big picture as appropriate; Refocus on importance of results as well as process	What they need from you to succeed: Provide candid feedback even if they don't ask for it; Don't take criticisms from drivers personally (they simply may not be tactful); Provide independence yet focus on working with others as appropriate; Refocus on importance of process as well as results

Amiable	*Expressive*
Motivated by: Belonging, acceptance, involvement, stability, security, attention to process	Motivated by: Meaning, dreaming, making a positive difference, change, popularity, recognition, prestige, compliments, applause, approval
Fears: Conflict, not being liked, sudden change, risk	Fears: Loss of prestige, not being where the action is, being isolated, not being liked, public humiliation, falling into routines
What they don't like in others: Insensitivity, people not keeping their commitments, pushy people, aggressiveness, conflict seekers	What they don't like in others: Lack of enthusiasm, inattention to values/people, lack of vision, naysayers and pessimism

Analytic	*Driver*
<u>To influence</u>: Be friendly, agreeable, and specific; Proceed gently; Explain why; Show concern for people and feelings; Support need for inclusion; Focus on process for making decisions	<u>To influence</u>: Be stimulating, enthusiastic, creative, inspiring, optimistic, flexible; Explain who needs to be brought on board; Support person's desires, accomplishments; Focus on results; Focus on feelings and the distant future
<u>What they need from you to succeed:</u> Provide opportunity to show initiative; Provide clear deliverables and deadlines; Offer assistance with time management; Refocus on results as well as process	<u>What they need from you to succeed:</u> Provide structure and discipline; Provide clear deliverables and deadlines; Refocus on process (attending to details and data gathering) as well as results

USING THE SIX UNIVERSAL FORMS OF INFLUENCE

Although human beings differ in many ways, we all share some fundamental human needs. People who understand these common needs and help people fulfill these needs are more likely to be successful in their attempts to influence others. After reviewing decades of research, social psychologist Robert Cialdini concluded that "persuasion works by appealing to a limited set of deeply rooted human drive and needs, and it does so in predictable ways."[26] In his thoughtful and practical book *Influence: Science and Practice*, Cialdini identifies six universal forms of influence that transcend personality and culture:[27]

- *Reciprocation:*   People feel obligated to pay back favors, gifts, and help that they receive from others. ("If you scratch my back, I'll scratch your back.").
- *Commitment/consistency:*   People are more likely to agree with a request if they feel it is consistent with a commitment they have made (especially a commitment that they make publicly or write down) or a behavior they have taken in the past.
- *Authority:*   People tend to obey people they perceive to be authorities and experts.
- *Social proof:*   People are more willing to support an idea if they know that other people support it, especially if they perceive the other people to be similar to them.
- *Scarcity:*   People tend to want what they believe is unique, rare, or in limited supply.
- *Liking:*   People want to support the people they like.

Cialdini explains that these forms of influence work because they act as cognitive shortcuts that help us bypass more complicated and costly decision-making processes. As mentioned earlier, we cannot gather all the data we need for every decision we make, nor can we interpret all the data we gather from every possible angle. So, we use cognitive shortcuts to help us make both the small and large decisions we face every day. We help someone out because he helped us out last week (reciprocity). We donate money every year to the same charities (commitment and consistency). We buy a particular brand of toothpaste because an advertisement says that 90 percent of dentists recommend this toothpaste (authority). We agree to a costly proposal at work because everyone else at the meeting seems to support it (social proof). We purchase an item in response to a "limited time offer" (scarcity). We select a physician because someone we trust recommends them (liking).

We are more likely to use cognitive shortcuts under particular conditions: when we are confused, uncertain, surprised, faced with too little or too much information, or feeling pressured, as well as when we trust the person requesting our support.[28] Cialdini warns that we are more likely to use cognitive shortcuts today than we were in the past. He explains:

> The evidence suggests that the ever-accelerating pace and informational crush of modern life will make this particular form of unthinking compliance even more and more prevalent in the future . . . The issues may be so complicated, the time so tight, the distractions so intrusive, the emotional arousal so strong, or the mental fatigue so deep that we are in no cognitive condition to operate mindfully.[29]

Cialdini adds, "All this leads to an unnerving insight: With the sophisticated mental apparatus we have used to build world eminence as a species, we have created an environment so complex, fast-paced, and information-laden that we must increasingly deal with it in the fashion of the animals we long ago transcended."[30]

"Triggers" tend to set these cognitive shortcuts in motion. Seeing someone in a white lab coat triggers us to believe that person is a scientist, so we assume that the person is a credible expert and we are more likely to comply with his or her request. Hearing that a book is on a "best seller" list or is recommended in a book review triggers us to purchase that book. It is not surprising that people who understand these triggers are more likely to be influential than are people who don't understand these triggers.

Note that something as simple as a well-placed word can trigger compliance. Psychologist Ellen Langer and her colleagues conducted an experiment in which they had people use different verbal strategies for cutting into a line of unsuspecting people waiting to make copies at a copy machine. Some people who tried to cut in line said, "Excuse me, I have five pages. May I use the Xerox machine *because I'm in a rush?*" Ninety-four percent of the people waiting in line complied. Other people who tried to cut in line said, "Excuse me, I have five pages. May I use the Xerox machine *because I have to make some copies?*" In this condition, 93 percent of the people in line complied with the request to cut in line, even though the person making the request did not offer any specific reason for cutting in line. The simple use of the word "*because*" not the actual reason given, seemed to act as a trigger for compliance.[31] Langer and her colleagues explain that we often respond mindlessly—without thinking and as if we are on automatic pilot—to certain triggers. In contrast, mindfulness means that we think before we act, and we think in complex ways.

Much of the time, responding automatically to cognitive shortcuts serve us well, but sometimes it doesn't. If you know these six universal forms of influence and are mindful of the triggers that set them in motion, not only will you be more influential than someone who is unaware of them but you will also be less likely to be on automatic pilot—and be an easy target—when someone tries to influence you.

"You should have an open mind, but not so open that your brain falls out." Philosopher Jacob Needleman cited by Robert Levine, The Power of Persuasion

Some readers of this book believe that they are quite resistant to persuasion attempts. If you are one of these people, you should keep in mind that researchers have found that people who feel invulnerable to influence attempts may be more susceptible to influence attempts than are others because they are less likely to take precautions. They may not take precautions because they often have the mistaken belief that people who try to influence others are obvious and pushy in their attempts. They don't realize that the most effective influencers are subtle and indirect in their approach. To make this point, advertising critic Jean Kilbourne says:

> Almost everyone holds the misguided belief that advertisements don't affect them, don't shape their attitudes, don't help define their dreams . . . What I hear more than anything else, as I lecture throughout the country, is 'I don't pay attention to ads . . . I just tune them out . . . They have no effect on me.' Of course, I hear this most often from young men wearing Budweiser caps.[32]

In the following sections, you will learn about each of six universal forms of influence in more detail. You will learn why they work, gain specific strategies for using each form of influence, and learn strategies for resisting mindless compliance to each of the influence strategies so that you can make more mindful and informed decisions. As you read these sections, you can return to Table 5-1 to write down additional strategies you can use to gain the support of the three people whom you would like to influence.

Be aware that each of these forms of influence can be used ethically or unethically. Ethical persuaders ask themselves, "How can I genuinely present the *honest* merits of my case in a way that is more likely to gain compliance?" They never provide false information or artificially inflate the merits of their case. They do not pretend to be authorities or experts if they are not. They do not engage in false flattery. They do not promise what they cannot deliver. Remember that using unethical influence attempts may get you what you want in the short term, but will harm your credibility and often the reputation of the organizations that you represent in the long term. In Cialdini's words, "Time wounds all heals."[33]

The Reciprocation Rule

If you don't go to other people's funerals, they won't come to yours. Yogi Berra, Hall of Fame baseball player and former manager of New York Mets

Simply stated, the reciprocition rule is this: If you give me something—help, favors, information, gifts, support, concessions—I will feel obligated to give you something in return.[34] If you pay for my lunch today, I will feel obligated to pay for your lunch in the future. If you give me a gift on my birthday, I will feel obligated to give you a gift on your birthday. If you send me a holiday card, I will feel obligated to send you a holiday card. If you invite my child to your house for a play date, I will feel obligated to invite your child to my house for a play date. If you support my ideas at today's meeting, I will feel obligated to support your ideas at a future meeting. If you give me information when I request it, I will feel obligated to give you information when you request it. If you come to an event that I am sponsoring, I will feel obligated to come to a future event that you are sponsoring. If you give me a concession in our negotiation, I will feel obligated to give you a concession, too.

Because the reciprocity rule is shared by all cultures, researchers believe it is based, in part, on a universal survival instinct. Individuals and societies can survive only if people cooperate with each other and help each other when help is needed. Therefore, we are willing to support others because, in the long run (consciously or unconsciously) we want to be able to count on others when we need something. The late philosopher Erich Fromm explained that all human beings believe and support the wisdom, "Inasmuch as we are all human, we're all in need of help. Today I, tomorrow you."[35] It is not surprising that people who do not participate in the social give and take of mutual obligation are less likely to receive support when they need it.

For several decades, researchers have illustrated the power of the reciprocity rule through experiments. The research design typically involves someone doing someone else a small, often unexpected favor, and then asking the recipient of the favor for some help to see if the act of giving would increase compliance. One often cited experiment by social psychologist Dennis Regan is described below:

> Regan had subjects work in pairs on a bogus task supposedly measuring art appreciation. One of the subjects, let's call him Andy, was actually a paid actor working as Regan's assistant. During a short rest period in the middle of the experiment, Andy left for a couple of minutes. For half the subjects (the gift group), Andy returned with two Cokes, handing one to the subject and keeping one for himself, explaining, "I asked him [the experimenter] if I could go get myself a Coke and he said it was ok, so I brought one for you, too." For the other half (the control group), Andy returned without a gift. In both conditions, Andy later asked the subject to do him a favor. Andy said that he was selling raffle tickets for his high school back home and that he'd get a prize if he sold the most tickets. Would the subject be willing to buy one or more tickets? In clear support of the reciprocity theory, Andy sold almost twice as many tickets to people he'd given a free Coke earlier.[36]

Most examples of the power of reciprocity are found outside the experimental lab. During the Civil War, nurse Clara Barton delivered medical supplies to the front line, cared for wounded soldiers, helped locate missing soldiers, and helped create the Red Cross. Later, Clara Barton became an active supporter of the suffrage movement and hoped to gain women's right to vote. As she campaigned for women's right to vote, she told men who had been soldiers during the Civil War, "When you were weak and I was strong, I toiled for you. Now you are strong and I am weak. Because of my work for you, I ask your aid. I ask the ballot for myself and my sex. As I stood by you, I pray you stand by me and mine."[37]

More recently, after the 2002 terrorist attack in Bali, the Australian government donated two medical centers to thank the Balinese for taking care of Australian citizens after the attack. A South China *Morning Post* newspaper article, "Repaying a Debt of Gratitude," described the gift this way:

> Australian Prime Minister John Howard yesterday inaugurated two medical centers to thank the Balinese who cared for so many Australians after the terrorist bombings one year ago. Mr. Howard officially opened an intensive care

and burn unit at the Sangla hospital, in Bali, which treated most of the victims. Australia has donated A$4.5 million (HK $24 million) toward the intensive care unit, which is still under construction. Another A$2.94 million is building and equipping the Bali Memorial Eye Centre, a small specialist hospital. "This is the most practical and tangible way to express our gratitude to the people of Bali," Mr. Howard said.[38]

Because the feeling of obligation is an extremely powerful source of influence, its power does not diminish over time. People will feel obligated to repay a favor decades and generations later, as illustrated in the following examples. The first example describes a parent's surprise at some unexpected help from a college administrator.

As the son of a college professor myself, I hoped my sons would go to college. But after our oldest found that the courses he wanted to take at the university were full, he got discouraged. I went to the registrar. I'd heard he was a stickler for rules, so I was floored when the man asked, "What classes would he like?" and took care of the problem on the computer. Seeing my surprise, he explained that years before, he was in the same situation as my son. He'd met a professor who took him to the enrollment office and got him into every class he wanted. "That man was your father. By any chance is he still alive? I nodded. He smiled. "Good," he said. "Tell him we're even."[39]

The second example describes how the pharmaceutical giant Merck became the first non-Japanese company to enter the highly protected Japanese pharmaceutical market in the early 1980s. Why was Merck granted access? Because immediately following World War II, Merck provided Japan with free medical support. In his book *The Leadership Moment*, leadership researcher and professor Michael Useem described Merck's entry into the Japanese market as follows:

Tuberculosis, for example, had surged in Japan in the years after World War II, and the war's devastation left few in a position to pay for a powerful Merck product that worked wonders against it: streptomycin. The company finally decided to donate a large supply to the Japanese public. Coming at a moment of great hardship, Merck's generosity has long been remembered. When the company sought access to Japan's domestic market in 1983, Japanese authorities took the rare step of approving Merck's $300 million purchase of 50.02 percent of Banyu Pharmaceutical, Japan's tenth largest drug maker. At the time it was the largest direct investment by a foreign company in a notoriously closed market. 'We received help from the Japanese government in making the first acquisition of this kind to be allowed,' remembers [former Merck CEO] Vagelos, and it should come as no surprise that Merck is the largest American pharmaceutical company in Japan today.[40]

Cialdini explains that even concessions can trigger the desire to reciprocate. For example, imagine that you go to a meeting with your boss and ask for a raise and the boss says, "No." Rather than leave the office immediately, this moment provides an opportunity to draw on the reciprocity rule.[41] Your gracious acceptance of your boss's refusal of a raise is likely to be seen by your boss as a concession. So, rather than simply leave the office immediately, you could use that moment to thoughtfully ask for a concession in return. If you can't have the raise, perhaps you can have something else of value to you: a new laptop computer, a high-profile assignment, or additional training in a new skill that will help you get the raise the next time (and boost your marketability should the raise not come through next year either). The *Wall Street Journal* gave this example of a young woman's smart negotiation when she accepted her job as a human resource manager. "In hiring the human resources manager, a suburban Boston biotech concern balked at giving her more than its promised 10% raise. But the company agreed to immediately pay all expenses so she could complete graduate school. Official policy partly covered tuition after six months of service. She also got time off to study. '[She said] it was a mutual gain for both of us.'"[42]

If you give me a cup of tea, I'll give you a glass of wine. *Chinese proverb*

The most important lesson to learn from the reciprocity rule is this: If you want to have sustainable influence over time, you must be willing to give often—and be the first to give. When you walk into a new setting—neighborhood, work organization, school—your immediate instinct should be to learn what other people need and then help them meet those needs.

Leveraging the Reciprocity Rule

- Give generously and sincerely to others, and give first.
- Remember that gifts, favors, assistance, and concessions are most influential when they are perceived as sincere and valuable by the receiver (not gratuitous, manipulative, or trivial).
- Remember that you'll get what you give. If you give kindnesses, favors, help, and concessions, you are more likely to get these in return. If you are unwilling to help others when requested to do so, others will be unwilling to help you when you need help.
- Do not negate the value of your help or concessions with statements such as "it was nothing" or "no problem." Such statements imply that you have given nothing and thus reciprocity is not warranted in return. Instead, when someone acknowledges having received something from you (such as favors or help), respond with a straightforward "Thank you" or, as Cialdini suggests, "I know you'd do the same for me."[43]
- Remember to enjoy the pleasures of giving freely with no intent of gaining something in return.

Resisting the Reciprocity Rule

- If you accept a favor, frame it as generosity freely given and do not assume obligation, particularly in advertising or marketing attempts.
- When you do feel obligated, remember that you can choose when and how you repay the favor. Just be sure to repay it.

The Scarcity Rule

People tend to value things that are unique, rare, or in limited supply. The scarcity rule works because the belief that something is scarce arouses our panic emotions and "now or never thinking" so we tend to pursue that which appears to be in short supply.[44] This is why advertisers regularly use statements such as "one time offers," "limited edition," "24-hour sale," "once-in-a-lifetime opportunity," and "only 15 items left in stock."

Guy Laliberté, founder of the Cirque Du Soleil, uses the scarcity rule to continue to build demand for his avant-garde circus featuring opulent sets, colorful costumes, and gifted performers. Born to a middle-class family in Quebec City, Canada, Laliberté left home at 18 years old to work in Europe as a street performer, often living hand-to-mouth to learn the basics of fire-breathing, stilt-walking, and other circus talents. Today, he is a billionaire and 95 percent owner of the Cirque Du Soleil that employs more than 25,000 employees worldwide. More than 7 million attended one of Cirque Du Soleil's performances in 2003, bringing in over $650 million in revenues that year from performances around the world. *Newsweek* reported that Laliberte, concerned about overexposure:

> ... insists that despite the Cirque boom, he is strictly following a business policy of slightly undersatisfying the public's appetite. Laliberte likens his strategy to that of Enzo Ferrari, explaining, "When Enzo Ferrari was putting out a new car model, he would ask how many cars he could sell ... If it came to, say, 250, he'd say, 'OK, we'll do 249.' At every performance, I want there to be at least one person who hits his nose on the closed door of the theatre because it's sold out."[45]

A clever business strategy perhaps, although the *Newsweek* reporter who reported the story lamented, "Who said running a circus was about keeping the kids smiling?"[46]

Clothing marketers also leverage the scarcity rule. One national clothing chain orchestrated its own shortage of a heavily advertised $198 jacket to enhance the chain's reputation as a merchandiser of hip and highly desirable clothing. The *Wall Street Journal* reported, "Hoping to make the item a 'fashion moment,' the company featured it heavily in its fall advertising campaign and promoted it with fashion glossies. Then it limited its shipments to just 5,000 jackets, no more than half the normal run for such a product. The result, a flurry of waitlists, which didn't move the company to reorder. 'When we sell out, we sell out,' said [one of the clothing chain's executive vice presidents]. 'It adds to the allure.'"[47]

The above examples illustrate how some businesses use the scarcity rule to increase customer demand. But these examples also illustrate a problem with this strategy. If people feel as though they've been manipulated, the strategy can backfire and the people who artificially create scarcity may lose the credibility and support they seek to gain for their organization.

Leveraging the Scarcity Rule

- Highlight real (not contrived) unique benefits, scarcity, and exclusive information.

Resisting the Scarcity Rule

- Don't rush to a decision because you feel pressured or respond to claims of scarcity with "panic emotions." Take time to get the facts, use a systematic decision-making process, determine alternative courses of action, and weigh the costs and benefits of rushing to a decision.

The Authority Rule

Most of us are taught in childhood to obey authority figures (e.g., parents, teachers, religious leaders, bosses, and social leaders) and heed the advice of experts (e.g., physicians, scientists, and researchers). Therefore, even as adults we're more likely to comply with a request if the person making the request is an authority figure or expert. We look for titles, style of dress (e.g., lab coats), claimed expertise, degrees posted on the wall, and initials following one's name for cues that signal that someone is an authority or expert. Because of our trust in authority and experts, we often want management gurus to tell us how we should manage our organizations, financial advisers to tell us how we should invest our money, and restaurant critics to tell us where we should dine.

Usually our reliance on experts and authority figures serves us well. But our willingness to obey authority figures and be impressed by experts can backfire. Authority figures and experts are fallible human beings. People may claim to be experts when they are not. An expert in one area (e.g., engineering) may not be an expert in another (e.g., understanding customer needs). We may disregard our own instincts when listening to authority figure and experts. In a classic study of obedience to authority, researcher Stanley Milgram designed an experiment in which naive subjects were asked by a "scientist" (who was actually an actor in a white lab coat) to deliver electric shocks to another human being (who, unknown to the subject, was another actor and not really receiving the shocks) under the pretense that the "scientist" was studying the effect of punishment on learning. Over half of the experiment's research subjects complied with the authority figure's request to deliver electric shocks even though the victim screamed for them to stop and said he was having heart problems during the experiment.[48] Milgram concluded that the subjects' desire to obey authority superseded their desire to stop delivering shocks to the suffering victim.

Another experiment illustrates that we may be more likely to believe that someone is an expert if that person uses incomprehensive jargon rather than language that is simple to understand. In this mock jury experiment:

> . . . subjects were asked to evaluate a plaintiff's claim that the company he'd worked for exposed him to a dangerous chemical that caused his cancer. Some jurors listened to the supposed expert witness, Dr. Thomas Fallon, a professor of biochemistry, explain in simple terms that the chemical in question causes the type of liver cancer the plaintiff had been stricken with. Fallon described, for example, how previous studies found that the chemical "caused not only liver disease but also cancer of the liver and . . . diseases of the immune system as well." Other subjects heard Dr. Fallon go off on the dangers of the chemical in complicated, often incomprehensible language. He explained how the chemical led to "tumor induction as well as hepatomegaly, hepatomegalocytosis, and lymphoid atrophy in both spleen and thymus." The results of the study found that when Dr. Fallon was presented as a man of outstanding credentials, the jury was almost twice as likely to be convinced if he spoke in obscure jargon than if he presented in simple and straightforward language. The researchers concluded that when the witness spoke simply the jurors could evaluate his argument on its merits. But when he was unintelligible, they had to resort to the mental shortcut of accepting his title and reputation in lieu of comprehensible facts. And so, another paradox: experts are sometimes most convincing when we don't understand what they're talking about.

The researchers also found that using cryptic language works only if one has the title and credentials to be seen as a credible expert. In the same mock jury experiment, when Dr. Fallon was introduced with "shakier credentials," jurors were less convinced by his jargon than when he spoke in straightforward terms.[49] The lesson is this: Although we often rely on other people's expertise to make decisions, we are not always the best judges of expertise.

Leveraging the Authority Rule

- Develop real expertise in something that people value, need, and want.
- Do not assume your authority or expertise is obvious to others. If you have a title, use it. If you have degrees or if you have won awards, post them. If you are an expert in an area, tell people. If there are people who can endorse your expertise, have them do so.[50]
- Show that high status people and known experts support your ideas.
- Present a professional image.

Resisting the Authority Rule

- Remember that trust in authority figures and experts is often useful, but should not be given uncritically.
- Be reasonably cautious with claims of expertise. Check credentials to determine if the person who claims to be an expert is truly an expert in the area in which you need advice.
- Be careful of the halo effect. Recognize that an expert in one area is not necessarily an expert in another area.

The Rule of Social Proof

Many of us remember our parents telling us when we were growing up: "If everyone jumped off a cliff, would you jump off a cliff, too?" Our parents were trying to warn us of the universal tendency to follow the crowd, even when it is against our best interest. They knew intuitively what researchers have spent years studying: For better and worse, we look to other people to make decisions about how to act, particularly when we are uncertain about what to do, when we are seeking the approval of others (e.g., when we want to fit in), and when we believe that the people moving in a particular direction are similar to us.[51]

Television show producers use this rule when they add laugh tracks to sitcoms, knowing that we are more likely to laugh if we hear other people laughing. Bartenders use this rule when they put a few dollars in the tip jar at the beginning of their shift to encourage customers to add new tips. Management team members use this rule when they go along with a decision at a meeting because they believe that everyone else in the meeting wants to go along with the decision. So, if you want to convince your boss, colleagues, employees, neighbors, parents, or children to accept one of your ideas, you are more likely to get their buy-in if you show them that other people they respect support the idea, especially if they see themselves as similar to the people who already support the idea.

Because we cannot (and sometimes do not want to) analyze every situation in depth, we watch others to get a sense of the best (or at least good enough) decision. This rule usually serves us well because most people we follow are not headed in a direction that would harm them. But, as with all cognitive shortcuts, following the crowd can also lead us down the wrong path.

Leveraging the Rule of Social Proof

- Show that other people already support your idea or request.
- Obtain testimonials from satisfied people, especially people who are experts or similar to the people you want to influence.

- Show how others have succeeded by complying with your request (or similar request).

Resisting the Rule of Social Proof

- Realize that you are more susceptible to following others when you perceive them to be similar to you, when you want to fit in, and in times of uncertainty.
- Remember that "When birds of a feather flock together, they can turn into sitting ducks."[52]

The Commitment and Consistency Rule

We all have a desire to maintain a positive and consistent self-concept. So, we all want to believe that our actions are consistent with our values, that people can count on us to live up to our commitments, and that once we choose a course of action we will follow through with it. This is especially true when we believe that the commitments we make are freely chosen rather than coerced. So, once we say we are committed to a belief, we are likely to act in ways that support that belief. And once we freely choose a course of action (e.g., voting for a particular political party, supporting a particular charity), we are likely to follow that course again and again.

The commitment and consistency rule is indeed powerful. Once we begin going in a certain direction, we are unlikely to stop or change course even if evidence suggests we are making a mistake. Researchers call this phenomenon "escalating commitment to a failing course of action."[53] For example, couples get married even though they do not love each other because they publicly announced their engagement, had an engagement party, purchased the wedding attire, reserved the reception hall, and hired the caterer. People stay in careers that no longer satisfy them because they have already invested a lot of money to obtain a degree in that profession or spent several years of their lives in that profession. People make business decisions that do not serve the organization well because they have already invested substantial company funds into the project.

The implications of this rule are clear: If you want someone to take a particular course of action, you will be more successful if you (1) link your request to a publicly made voluntary commitment or (2) ask for compliance with a small request and then build to a larger request (this is known as the "foot-in-the-door technique").[54] Restaurants advertise free appetizers because they know that once people are in the restaurant, they are more likely to order the full meal, including expensive drinks and desserts. The commitment and consistency rule is even more powerful if you can convince people to put their commitment in writing.[55] Cialdini gives this example:

> Writing in 1996 in the *Personality and Social Psychology Bulletin*, Delia Cioffi and Randy Gardner described an experiment in which college students in one group were asked to fill out a printed form saying they wished to volunteer for an AIDS education project in the public schools. Students in another group volunteered for the same project by leaving blank a form stating that they didn't want to participate. A few days later, when the volunteers reported for duty, 74% of those who showed up were students from the group that signaled their commitment by filling out the form.[56]

Cialdini explains that "people live up to what they have written down."[57] So, if you want a team to meet a deadline, have them put their agreement to meeting the due date in writing. If you want an employee to perform to a higher standard or develop a new skill, get his or her commitment in writing. If you want to achieve a goal (e.g., eat healthier, get a new job, be a kinder person), put your commitment in writing and post it where you will be reminded of your commitment—better yet, tell other people of your commitment as well. But remember that the power of this rule comes from people's beliefs that they made their commitment of free will. The rule is unlikely to work if people feel they were coerced into making a commitment.

Leveraging the Commitment and Consistency Rule

- Connect your request to *voluntary* commitments, publicly stated beliefs, and existing behaviors.
- Begin with small requests and build up to bigger requests.
- Have people put their commitments in writing.

Defense

- Be careful of what you promise, because you will hold yourself accountable.
- Do not feel obligated to commit to a large request just because you made a small commitment.
- Remember that you can disengage from a commitment at any time, no matter how far you've gone down a path. Learn to say "I changed my mind," "I have a different perspective now," and "I was wrong." Remember the sage advice of billionaire Warren Buffet: "When you find yourself in a hole, the best thing you can do is stop digging."[58]

The Liking Rule

If you could master one element of personal communication that is more powerful than anything ... it is the quality of being likable. I call it the magic bullet, because if your audience likes you, they'll forgive just about everything else you do wrong. If they don't like you, you can hit every rule right on target and it doesn't matter. **Roger Ailes, Public relations adviser to Presidents Reagan and Bush, Sr.**

The liking rule is based on the simple principle that we tend to be drawn to people we like and resist people we do not like. This rule is powerful because human beings are quick to judge people as good or bad, competent or incompetent, motivated or unmotivated, smart or stupid, strong or weak, trustworthy or dishonest, and so on. Indeed, most of the approximately 18,000 adjectives English speakers use to describe each other are either complimentary (e.g., "competent," "honest," or "motivated") or noncomplimentary (e.g., "incompetent," "dishonest," or "lazy").[59] Our tendency to evaluate people positively or negatively influences who we listen to and who we ignore, who we interact with and who we avoid, who we promote and who we pass over, and whose ideas we support and whose ideas we resist.[60]

We want to support the people we like for at least three reasons. First, we assume the people we like will be benevolent toward us, will cooperate with us, and will not harm us. Because we believe in their goodwill, we are more likely to seek out and follow their advice, support their interests, and agree to their requests. For example, researchers estimate that 70 percent of people in the United States ask for advice in choosing a physician, 53 percent of moviegoers ask for recommendations from people they know, and 91 percent of people who make a major purchase obtain recommendations from people they know.[61] The second reason that liking is such a powerful form of influence is that we want to please the people to whom we are attracted so that they will like us back. The third reason we support people we like is that we want to be associated with them. This is why teenagers spend so much money buying clothing advertised by well-known sports figures and pop idols.

What makes people likable? We are attracted to people who reward us in some way. We like people who raise our self-esteem, pay positive attention to us, and make us feel comfortable, happy, heard, competent, successful, proud, powerful, and safe. The late Mary Kay Ash, founder and CEO of Mary Kay cosmetics, put it simply: "Everyone has an invisible sign hanging from their neck saying: Make me feel important." We dislike people when we feel punished by our association with them. So, we avoid or resist people who make us feel uncomfortable, unhappy, unheard, incompetent, unsuccessful, insignificant, embarrassed, or afraid. Notably, some researchers have concluded that people from North America tend to be particularly drawn to three types of rewards: attention, approval, and success.[62]

Don't open a shop unless you like to smile.
Chinese proverb

The smallest acts can increase liking. Seeing another person smile, for example, makes us feel good. Successful waiters and waitresses who depend on tips from customers for much of their income are exceptionally skilled in the art of being likable. For example, they know that they are likely to earn larger tips simply by smiling. In one study, researchers "examined the effects of smiling on the tips earned by cocktail waitresses who served 48 male and 48 female customers. Although the number of drinks ordered was not affected by the smiling, the amount of tips was. A broad smile brought in $23.20, while a minimal smile earned only a total of $9.40."[63] Successful waiters and waitresses also engage in small acts such as acting as allies ("Let me see if I can get you an extra serving of rice at no extra charge."), repeating what the customer wants so the customer feels heard and understood ("Let me make sure I have your order right. You said that you want a large pizza with red, not green, peppers, is that correct?"), writing "thank you" on the check, and giving a piece of candy with the bill. All these small acts tell customers that they are liked and in return customers express their appreciation to their server with larger gratuities.[64]

Researchers have found that attractiveness, positive interactions, proximity, perceived similarity, and flattery predict whether we like someone, and thus how much influence this person has with us. Each of these predictors of likability is described below.

Attractive Physical Appearance   We tend to be drawn to people we perceive to be physically attractive. However, this form of influence can be short-lived. For example, what is considered attractive in one setting may be viewed as unattractive in another setting. A person wearing a sharp designer business suit may draw positive reviews on Wall Street but may be seen as pretentious, flashy, and untrustworthy in a more modest setting. Being thin is viewed as attractive in some cultures, but carrying more weight is viewed as a sign of wealth and health in other cultures.[65] Youth is valued in some cultures, but age is valued in others. Another limitation of attractiveness is that although people who are perceived as attractive are more likely to get their foot in the door more quickly, other characteristics such as expertise, helpfulness, and reciprocity will quickly override attractiveness as a form of influence.[66]

Positive Experiences   We tend to like people with whom we share positive experiences.[67] We like people who are accessible, who cooperate with us, who help us, who like us, who are considerate, and who are open, genuine, and spontaneous.[68] Likable people behave in ways that make others feel good. A nod of approval, a warm smile, a few words of agreement, and an accepting tone of voice all make other people feel as though they are seen, heard, and appreciated. We also are inclined to like people with whom we share an enjoyable experience.[69] For example, we tend to feel good when we are dining, so we tend to transfer those good feelings to the people with whom we share an enjoyable dining experience.[70] And we don't have to share the same positive experience with someone else simultaneously to feel a common bond. For example, alumni from the same university will often help each other out if they attended the university years, even decades, apart.

Proximity   The closer we are to each other physically, the more likely we will be attracted to each other. Proximity gives us the opportunity to gather information about and experience with someone. Because social norms dictate that people be polite and helpful, it is likely that we will have more positive than negative interactions with the people who are near us—and this will increase our liking of them. Furthermore, if we work near someone, live near someone, or attend the same social functions, it is likely that we share significant similarities (e.g., culture, income, educational level, attitudes), and similarity breeds attraction as well.[71]

Perceived Similarity   We tend to be attracted to people whom we perceive to be similar to us on characteristics such as attitudes, status, work style, personality characteristics, physical characteristics, dress, culture, and life experience.[72] We are attracted to people who are similar to us for many reasons. First, we want to protect and enhance our self-image, so we want to see people whom we believe are similar to us as having positive characteristics. Second, we want to invest in the success of people whom we believe are similar to us because we believe that doing so may enhance our own chances for success.[73] Third, we want to be around similar others because we believe we are more likely to be able to predict their behavior, expect goodwill, and interact easily.[74]

The power of perceived similarity was illustrated in an experiment in which researchers gave subjects a scenario in which a car was parked on a hill with the hand brake securely set. Unknown to the driver, the brake cable was in poor repair. The subjects were told that the car "rolled down the hill, crashed into a store window, slightly injured a small girl, and caused a merchant to be hospitalized for a year." When subjects were told to assume the driver's characteristics were either "very much like your own" (rather than "not at all like your own"), they believed that he was less responsible for the accident and assigned more lenient penalties to him.[75]

Understanding the liking rule is particularly important for people who are demographically different from the people they want to influence. In a recent study, researchers found that "demographically different people may have more control over the impressions others form of them than has been considered in previous research."[76] People who are in a demographic minority are more likely to be viewed through stereotypical assumptions. However, they can break down stereotypes and build opportunities to build connections if they "individuate" themselves from these stereotypes, interact often, communicate personal information, reveal in subtle and explicit ways who they are and who they are not, emphasize their commitment to common goals and a common fate, and build on the similarities they have with the people with whom they want to connect. The researchers found that people who were demographically different from others in their group and who took steps to individuate themselves from stereotypes were perceived more positively, connected more with their group, felt more satisfied, and performed better than those who didn't actively differentiate themselves from stereotypes.

Praise and Flattery Cialdini explains that praise "both charms and disarms."[77] Most of us respond positively to flattery because we all want to feel good about ourselves.[78] So, we tend to be attracted to and support people who confirm our positive impressions of ourselves. We are particularly susceptible to flattery when it focuses on characteristics that we care about (I am likely to be more impressed if you praise my presentation skills than if you say you like my socks.), when our self-esteem needs a boost (I am more likely to appreciate a compliment when I'm having a bad day.), and when we are uncertain of our skills (I am more likely to appreciate praise for my talent at building an innovative Web site if I am a novice rather than if I am an expert at building Web sites.).[79] We are also more susceptible to flattery when we believe it is sincere. In fact, if we are certain that we are not good at something, we are more likely to respect the person who gives us honest feedback rather than the person who gives us false feedback because we may believe that the latter person may be manipulative or lacking in judgment.[80]

The most important lessons from the liking rule are these: People are more likely to support you if they like you. They are more likely to like you if they perceive you to be attractive, if they have positive experiences with you, if you are near them, if they perceive you as similar to them, and if you genuinely compliment characteristics that are important to them.

There's an important caveat to the liking rule. Although liking is a powerful form of influence, reciprocity appears to be even more powerful. For example, in one experiment, researchers wanted to determine whether subjects would be more likely to support someone they liked or someone who had done them a favor. In the experiment, they manipulated liking by having the naïve subject overhear a confederate talking on the telephone either pleasantly or in an insulting and unattractive way. In one experimental condition, the confederate left the room but returned with two drinks and told the subject that he was given time to buy himself a drink so he brought one to the subject as well. In another experimental condition, the experimenter brought drinks to both the confederate and the subject. And in the third experimental condition, neither the confederate nor the experimenter brought any drinks to the subject. Toward the end of the experiment, the confederate asked the subject to help him gather data for a survey. In the experimental condition in which the subject received no drink from the experimenter or confederate, the subject was more likely to comply with the requests by the confederate who was pleasant (more likable), rather than unpleasant (less likable), during the alleged telephone conversation. However, in the experimental condition in which the subject received a drink from the confederate, he was more likely to comply with the confederate's request for help regardless of whether the confederate was pleasant (likable) or unpleasant (unlikable) during the telephone conversation. In other words, the sense of obligation to repay a favor (help with collecting data for a survey in return for a free drink) outweighed attraction as a form of influence.[81]

Leveraging the Liking Rule

- Be kind, genuine, and respectful to everyone.
- Use body language that shows approval and interest.
- Create opportunities to have positive cooperative interactions with others.
- Offer sincere compliments when you have the opportunity to do so.
- Individuate yourself from stereotypes and build on similarities with others, especially if you are in a minority.
- Repair damaged relationships by building on similarities, offering sincere compliments, creating opportunities for positive interactions, and using body language that shows goodwill.

Resisting the Liking Rule

- Separate your attraction to a person from the merits of the case that is being made.
- Broaden your perception of attractiveness as well as the diversity of your network so that you are not overly dependent on the knowledge, viewpoints, resources, or influence of a few people or groups. Notably, some research suggests that the more "psychologically secure" a person is, the more likely that person will want to go beyond associating with people who are similar and associate with a diverse group of people.[82]

Summarizing the Six Universal Forms of Influence

Goodwill is the one and only asset that competition cannot undersell or destroy.   **Marshall Field, American Merchant, 1834–1906**

If you know the six universal forms of influence, you are more likely to achieve the goals that you set out for yourself, your organizations, your communities, and the people who depend on you. Taking time to strategize how you will present your case to others can make the difference between gaining and losing the support you desire. Cialdini explains, "One more breath, a few more words, a carefully crafted request, and you can increase people's willingness to say yes."[83]

In addition, if you are aware of these forms of influence, you will be less likely to react mindlessly to other people's attempts to influence you. Remember that you are more likely to use cognitive shortcuts when you are under time pressure, during periods of uncertainty, when you lack critical information, and when you are feeling distracted, stressed, or tired. To avoid responding mindlessly to influence attempts, give yourself time before you make a decision so you can (1) reduce ambiguity by gathering more information from multiple and diverse sources, (2) identify the actual merits of the case as well as alternative choices, (3) consider the costs and benefits of compliance, (4) use a systematic process for gathering data and making decisions, and (5) remember that you have the right to say "no" gracefully. Persuasion researcher Robert Levine warns that you should be particularly cautious when "the intensity of your reaction exceeds the seeming importance of the situation."[84] Levine also warns, "Be careful when the same people who want to fill your expectations are also in the business of creating them," noting that the same corporation that owns Ben and Jerry's ice cream also owns Slimfast.[85]

Finally, remember that ethical influence is based on *honestly* telling people what you want to accomplish, presenting the real merits of your case in a genuine way, and

- *Reciprocation:* People feel obligated to pay back favors, gifts, and help that they receive from others. ("If you scratch my back, I'll scratch your back.").
- *Commitment/consistency:* People are more likely to agree with a request if they feel it is consistent with a commitment they have made (especially a commitment that they make publicly or write down) or a behavior they have taken in the past.
- *Authority:* People tend to obey people they perceive to be authorities and experts.
- *Social proof:* People are more willing to support an idea if they know that other people support it, especially if they perceive the other people to be similar to them.
- *Scarcity:* People tend to want what they believe is unique, rare, or in limited supply.
- *Liking:* People want to support the people they like and they tend to like people they perceive as attractive or similar to them, people who are near them, people with whom they've shared positive experiences, and people who compliment them.

FIGURE 5-2   The Six Universal Forms of Influence

following through on your promises.[86] Robert Cialdini and Noah Goldstein explain the importance of ethically implementing the six universal forms of influence:

> It is imperative to stress that knowledge of the fundamental principles of social influence does not carry with it the right to use this information unscrupulously. In trying to persuade others, one can ethically point to the genuine expertise, accurate social validation, real similarities, truly useful favors, legitimate scarcity and existing commitments. Those who do attempt to dupe or to trap others into compliance are setting themselves up for a double-barreled whammy—by breaking the code of ethics and by risking getting caught—that can produce the disagreeable consequences of diminished self-concept and diminished future profit.[87]

DEVELOPING POLITICAL SAVVY

In 1920, Winston Churchill said, "Politics are almost as exciting as war, and quite as dangerous. In war you can be killed only once, but in politics many times."[88] Churchill's statement reflects how many people feel about organizational politics. However, although some individuals and organizations follow the "kill or be killed" and "eat or be eaten" school of organizational politics, successful people engage in a more ethical and productive form of organizational politics that is based on mutual support and that promotes organizational effectiveness as well as personal success.[89]

Political behavior in organizations refers to activities that (1) people engage in to influence important personal or organizational outcomes; (2) are not part of one's official

Politically adept people recognize that they're at least 75 percent responsible for how others treat them. *Kathleen Kelly Reardon, Author, The Secret Handshake*

job description; and (3) are not carried out through official and explicitly stated organizational policies and procedures.[90] Political behavior is often called "knowing the ropes," "working the system," and "greasing the wheel." When not taken to extremes and when used ethically to serve organizational and personal goals, political behavior in organizations can enhance productivity. Many researchers argue that political behavior is an inevitable and desirable part of organizational life because it helps people get things done faster—and often better—than if they operated solely within the constraints of their official job descriptions and standard organizational procedures.[91] Furthermore, researchers have found that some forms of political behavior increase innovation in organizations.[92]

Job descriptions and standard procedures, while necessary and useful, share two limitations. First, they are rarely detailed or flexible enough to cover all the situations that employees must handle when navigating the complex and ambiguous realities of organizational life. Consequently, the most effective employees know that they sometimes must work outside official job descriptions and organizational procedures to get their job done to the best of their ability. Second, job descriptions and standard procedures are based on the assumptions that human beings always think and act rationally, that the environment will stay relatively stable over time, and that conflicts over goals and resources will be minimal. But people are not rational despite their best intentions, change is a constant in most organizations, and multiple agendas and limited resources guarantee that conflict will always be an organizational reality.

Therefore, it should come as no surprise that people who understand the informal and unwritten rules in their organizations—and who are competent at their work—tend to be more successful than those who don't understand these rules.[93] Says one astute political player, "There's a formal set of rules and an informal set. You need to learn the informal set or you're only playing on half the court."[94]

Unfortunately, in a recent *Business Week* article, MBA program graduates lamented that they received few, if any, lessons in business school about managing organizational politics and thus were caught unaware and unskilled when faced with the real world of organizations:

> Perhaps the loudest complaint was about just how ill-prepared alums felt when faced with the politics and challenges of managing in the middle. Many said they should have been forced to take more organizational behavior classes, though, "it's like trying to get someone to eat their spinach," concedes 40-year-old Charles W. Breer, . . . who has spent most of his post-MBA career working for Northwest Airlines Corp. Still, actual office politics—the tricky mix of sociology, personality, and corporate culture that exists in every workplace—can make a mockery of B-School theory. Breer says his hardest times were managing a 12-person staff. "At a minimum, I wish someone had told me this would be one of the biggest challenges, and then given me some tips," said Breer.[95]

Can you survive without understanding and engaging in organizational politics? Probably. Can you thrive without a general understanding and at least a limited engagement in organizational politics? Unlikely. As *Fortune* magazine says, "If you simply follow the rules, do your job well, and wait to be promoted, it could be a very long wait."[96] This view has been supported by substantial research.[97] If you choose to work only within the specific guidelines of your job and connect only with people who are directly related to your job, then you are most likely performing below your potential. If you are a manager, you also are inhibiting the performance of the people who work for you. Why? Because you may not have the influence you need to give the employees who work for you access to contacts, information, and resources that can help them do their job better and obtain the assignments, promotions, and salary increases they may desire.[98]

Because of the important role that political behavior plays in organizations, some organizations hire coaches to teach new high-potential employees how to use the informal organization to get their work done better and faster. Executive search and development firm Korn/Ferry International charges companies as much as $10,000 to teach new employees the ropes over an intensive six week period. The *Wall Street Journal* reported that one of Korn/Ferry's biggest challenges is helping new employees answer the following question: "How can you champion enough change to justify your hiring—without rocking the boat so much that you endanger your latest gig? Failure to strike the right balance often derails newcomers. 'They push too hard, too fast, and do it in an undiplomatic way,' says Ben Dattner, a New York industrial psychologist. Rather than jump in . . . full speed ahead, it makes more sense to understand the kind of organizational culture you're working in, and then strategize accordingly."[99]

The rest of this chapter will help you understand which political strategies work, why they work, and how to avoid dysfunctional organizational politics. In the following sections, I discuss the characteristics of politically savvy people, as well as techniques for gaining political influence. I also discuss what managers can do to minimize dysfunctional organizational politics.

Characteristics of Politically Savvy People

Robert Sternberg, IBM professor of psychology and education at Yale University, in his book *Why Smart People Do Stupid Things*, likes to tell this a story about Jack, a bully who delights in making others feel stupid, and Jack's target Irvin who subtly and cleverly achieves his own goals.[100]

> Jack, who considers himself smartest in his class, likes to make fun of Irvin, the boy he has identified as the stupidest in the class. Jack pulls aside his friend Tom and says, "You want to see what 'stupid' means, Tom? Watch this. Hey Irvin, here are two coins. Take whichever one you want. It's yours." Irvin looks at the two coins, a nickel and a dime, for a while and then selects the nickel. "Go ahead, Irv, take it, it's yours," Jack laughs. Irvin takes the larger coin and walks away. An adult who has been watching the transaction from a distance walks up to Irvin and gently points out that the dime is worth more than the nickel, even though it is smaller and that Irvin has just cost himself five cents. "Oh, I know that," replies Irvin. "But if I picked the dime, Jack would never ask me to choose between the two coins again. This way, he'll keep asking me again and again. I've already collected over a dollar from him, and all I have to do is keep choosing the nickel."

Jack thinks that he's clever and that he made a fool out of Irv. However, Irvin appears to be the wiser of the two—especially if his goal is to make money off of Jack's nasty desire to make Irvin look stupid. Irvin, more so than Jack, is a budding political player.

People who have finely tuned political skills know how to conduct themselves in different situations so that they are more likely to achieve their goals. They certainly don't make other people feel stupid. They take time to read situations before jumping in. They know what they want to achieve and, with their goals in mind, they decide which battles to fight, which battles to avoid, and when to give in. They decide when to confront directly, when to be subtle, and when to back off completely. They know that timing matters.[101] Irvin may eventually let Jack know that he understands that the dime is worth more than the nickel, but not yet. He still wants to earn more money off of Jack's foolish attempt to be a bully.

A hallmark characteristic of political savvy people is that they focus on understanding people (their styles, needs, and wants) and situations and then use this knowledge to devise strategies that will help them advance themselves, others, and the organization. In her practical and engaging book *The Secret Handshake: Mastering the Politics of the Business Inner Circle*, University of Southern California professor Kathleen Reardon explains: "The politically astute don't assume—they assess. They read each significant situation in terms of the benefits to those involved. They nurture a healthy skepticism regarding easy answers, and choose instead to study human nature. They are not casual observers; they are *professional* observers."[102]

A common misconception is that if you want to get ahead in your organization, you must sometimes engage in activities that are not consistent with your interests, talents, or values. Savvy political actors realize that there are many ways to find opportunities to interact with others, build relationships, find common ground, get information, and be visible. Consequently, they do not feel constrained if they choose not to participate in certain activities. They realize that they don't have to play golf or tennis if they do not play the game, go out drinking if they don't want to, miss all of their children's soccer games, or participate in activities that may not be consistent with their interests or values. Because they have developed a broad range of political strategies for achieving their goals, they are not tied to simplistic assumptions about what they must do to achieve their goals. And if they ever do feel pressured to do something that is against their values, savvy political players are often in better shape than others to leave the situation and find work environments in which they can thrive without compromising their fundamental values.

Politically savvy people draw on three sets of resources to achieve the goals they desire for themselves, others, and their organizations: personal, relational, and structural. Personal resources refer to characteristics that build one's reputation and credibility such as expertise, experience, education, job tenure, likability, and professional activity.[103] Relational resources refer to one's willingness and ability to create mutually supportive relationships with a broad and diverse group of people. Structural resources refer to one's formal position in the organizational hierarchy (e.g., hourly worker, manager, senior manager, and president) or informal position in important organizational networks.[104] Each of these resources is described in more detail in the following sections. As you read these sections, consider the many opportunities you have for enhancing your political influence in your organization.

Personal Power
The most savvy political players make sure that they have knowledge, skills, and experience that are valuable and visible to others. Harvard professor John Kotter advises, "The larger the achievement and the more visible it is, the more power the manager

tends to develop."[105] Therefore, you will have more power in your organization if you are an expert in something that people need and if you show how your expertise adds significant value to the organization.[106]

Most of us know a few people who spend so much time focusing on politicking and advancing their careers that they forget to focus on achieving measurable business results as well. Gerry Roche of the executive search and development firm Heidrick and Struggles International explains:[107]

> I have 400 recruiters working for me here, and they're all trying to "get ahead." This one fellow goes off to a five-day conference on career development, and while he's there he doesn't bother to check his voice mail back at the office. And all week long a very big, important client is trying and trying to reach him and getting more and more frustrated. Finally, this client calls me, furious, and he says, 'What's the deal with this guy?' So naturally when he gets back from his career-development conference, I call him into my office, and I explain it to him very carefully: "Stop worrying about your career, and return your damn phone calls."

The lesson is this: Don't focus so much on getting ahead that you forget to take care of the business at hand. If you are in a new position—whether it's a new job, a recent promotion, or a new assignment as a team or project leader—you'll want to build your reputation for having expertise that adds bottom-line value early. In his book *The First 90 Days: Critical Success Strategies for New Leaders at All Levels*, Harvard professor Michael Watkins advises readers to secure early wins with tangible and visible results. He says, "The best candidates [for early wins] are problems that you can tackle reasonably quickly with modest expenditure and that will yield visible organizational operational or financial gains . . . Identify two or three key areas, at most, where you will seek to achieve rapid improvement."[108]

Relational Power

If you're one of the few experts at something that everyone needs, you're in a very good position indeed. And if you are socially skilled and invested in the success of others as well, you will be nearly irreplaceable.[109] Politically sophisticated people develop mutually supportive relationships and draw on these relationships to achieve their goals. They develop these relationships by strategically identifying and interacting with people who can help them achieve their goals and by communicating in ways that draw people toward them and toward their ideas.

Strategically Visiting People   Savvy political players seem to have a "radar" that enables them to get themselves in the right place, at the right time, with the right people. But, as Reardon explains, "this radar comes from having done their homework. Before conferences and dinners, they find out who will be attending, and by the time the conference starts they know whom they'll try to arrange or 'strategically chance' to meet. A true mover and shaker works the room—any room—intelligently. While others are spinning their wheels, they're zeroing in on those they need to attract to their web of relationships."[110] Note, however, that Reardon warns that these relationships are effective "only to the extent that the people you're accessing consider you reliable, consistent, and professional."[111]

FIGURE 5-3	When Expertise Backfires

A word of warning: You want to be sure that your expertise and reputation don't back-fire. One of the biggest complaints I hear from very competent and results-oriented professionals is that their boss wants to keep them in their current position rather than promote them. Explicitly or implicitly, their boss is telling them, "I can't afford to lose you from your current position" or "You're a great individual contributor but I just don't see you as a leader." If you find yourself in this position, there are at least six ways to deal with your boss's resistance to promoting you.

- Help the boss find someone else who can perform your responsibilities so that you can be free to move ahead without leaving a gap in expertise in your current position.
- Ask your boss to tell you which specific steps you must take to get promoted to the next level. Ideally, you should get your boss to write down his or her advice, perhaps as part of your performance review, because your boss will want to behave consistently with what he or she commits to do in writing. For example, your boss may say that you need to demonstrate advanced technical skills, presentation skills, or leadership skills such as coaching and mentoring others, motivating others, leading teams, and navigating the political environment.
- Make sure that you let your boss and other influential people outside of your area know that you want to be promoted and that you want to take on new responsibilities.
- Be visible and create opportunities for interacting positively and cooperatively throughout the organization so that your name comes up when discussions of promotions are raised.
- Ensure that your boss and other influential people see you as someone with leadership potential rather than solely as an individual contributor. This means:
  - having relevant leadership (not only technical) skills; in other words, being able to create a context in which *others* can do their best work.
  - being seen as someone who possesses the characteristics that predict success, including conscientiousness (hard work and dependability), proactivity (a "can-do" attitude), interpersonal awareness, adaptability, social skills, and positive emotions such as hope, optimism, and resilience.
  - being someone that other leaders in the organization know, understand, and are comfortable with—and breaking down any stereotypes they may have of you that may interfere with their ability to see you as someone with leadership potential.
  - volunteering to lead projects, interact with customers and people outside of your unit, mentor newcomers in your area, and engage in other activities that demonstrate your leadership potential and enable you to increase your visibility throughout the organization.
- If you have done the above and you still cannot get promoted within your department or organization, you may have to leave your current job and get a new job through which you can build the reputation that you want from the start.

Says one successful employee, "I make myself get up from this desk a few times each day to visit with people. I always go in with something to ask or say of interest, and then I read the situation and decide how long to stay. I got ahead by doing this when other people wouldn't."[112] By visiting people outside her immediate work area, she learns about different parts of the organization, gains insight into other people's interests and skills, builds common ground, figures out how she can help others, gets visibility with key people, identifies who is likely to support and resist her, and gains support in case she may need it in the future.[113]

Communicating with Others Savvy political players communicate with others not only to give and get information, but to build relationships, make sense of situations, and promote their ideas in ways that increase the probability that their ideas will be understood and supported. They understand that each time they communicate with someone, they have an opportunity to build a relationship and deepen mutual commitment. Reardon explains, "Making valuable connections involves conveying to others a sense of having truly noticed them ... Politically adept people find something intriguing about each person they meet ... With the ones potentially helpful to them in the future, politically savvy are especially attentive. They ask questions of them, seek elaboration of their comments identify mutual interests about which they can comfortably converse, and express a good reason why they should share business cards to enable future interactions."[114]

Savvy political players also communicate in ways that help them make sense of situations. They listen to people with different points of view to get a well-rounded picture of a situation. They seek out opinions from senior executives, employees working on the front line, people from different departments, people outside of the organization with whom they interact on a regular basis, and customers who use the products or services they provide. By doing so, they not only get the information they need, but they build connections along the way. Michael Watkins suggests that when you get a new job or take on a new project, you visit people from many different areas inside and outside of the organization and ask them the same set of questions so that you can get a well-rounded view of the situation: "What are the biggest challenges this organization is facing (or will face) in the near future? Why is this organization facing (or going to face) these challenges? What are the most promising unexploited opportunities for growth? What would need to happen to exploit the potential of these opportunities? If you were me, what would you focus attention on?"[115]

Savvy political players also know that they must communicate their ideas in ways that other people will understand and support. Although they do not change the honest merits of their message, they do adapt the way they express these merits based on the interests of their audience. For example, they will emphasize a compelling vision of the future, bottom-line results, data-driven decisions, or concern for employees and customers depending on their audience's primary focus.

Structural Power

Location, location, location. Politically savvy people place themselves where they can have the greatest impact. They understand the complex web of relationships inside and outside of the organization, and they know that their ability to influence others is based, in part, on their location in this network of relationships. Some of this power comes from having a formal position in the organization (e.g., being a manager or director) that gives them control over information, decisions, and resources.[116] But much structural power comes not from where one sits in the organizational hierarchy, but rather where one places oneself in the informal social networks inside and outside of the organization.[117] Five avenues for gaining structural power are described below: position, autonomy, criticality, centrality, and coalitions.

Position   Power is associated with particular roles in organizations and thus is attributed to people hired into those roles. People at higher organizational levels have more official sources of power than people at lower levels because they can control resources that people value at lower levels of the hierarchy. For example, if you are a manager, then you can control important resources such as information and budgets, as well as important career benefits such as training opportunities, high profile assignments, promotions, and salary increases. Furthermore, people in most societies are socialized to view hierarchical power as legitimate, so people are likely to listen to you because of the position you hold. Position power has two notable limits. First, your position gives you power with the employees who work for you, but it does not necessarily give you power to control resources and outcomes outside your immediate chain of command. Second, when you leave a position in which power is invested, you lose the power associated with that position as well (although you may still be respected for having held that position, particularly if you were competent and developed goodwill).[118]

Autonomy   People who work in positions that allow discretion over how, when, and where their work is done are more likely to be able to create opportunities in which they can leverage and showcase their skills, develop new talents, and interact and build relationships with many different kinds of people who can offer them information, opportunities, and support. In contrast, people who work in a routine job that offers little autonomy, requires limited judgment, and offers few opportunities to develop new skills or interact with others are more easily replaced.[119]

Criticality   People who work on tasks that have a direct impact on organizational performance or that are critical links in the workflow are likely to have more influence than if they work on tasks that are perceived to be peripheral to organizational performance.[120]

Centrality   People who are central to important organizational networks have access to and control many organizational resources and are integral to the flow of information, funding, and other resources that other people need to achieve their goals. There are many ways in which you can increase your centrality. You can take a job that gives you control over resources that others need. You can place your office physically close to where things are happening so that you stay "in the know" and maintain visibility. You can get to know many people inside and outside of the organization and thus play an important role in linking people together, providing advice, offering support, and managing the information flow between people and places.[121]

Coalitions   A coalition is an informal group of people who work together to promote issues that are important to them.[122] People in coalitions support each other's goals and provide information, resources, and connections that can make things happen for each other. These "influence networks" are particularly powerful when you need the

Never doubt that a small group of thoughtful, committed citizens can change the world. Indeed, it is the only thing that ever has.
Margaret Mead, Anthropologist

support of people over whom you have no direct authority. Coalitions are also useful when the voice of one or a few people isn't enough to influence people who have the power to change the ways things are done. For example, if a few people in an organization say they want flex-time, they may get little response. But if hundreds of people say they want flex-time to be offered in the organization, they are more likely to get a response. A common mistake of new professionals and managers is that they spend too much time focusing up and down the organizational hierarchy and not enough time building coalitions with colleagues and other constituents who can help them achieve common goals over time.[123]

The main point to remember about developing personal, relational, and structural power is this: Your power is based, in large part, on your ability to control resources that are important to others. The more that people are dependent on your expertise, connections, and access to information and financial resources, the more power you have.[124] The less dependent you are on others to achieve your goals, the more choices and flexibility you have—and the more power you have.

Remember that you must create *multiple* bases of power if you want to achieve the goals that are important to you, your organizations, your communities, and the people who depend on you. It is a mistake to become dependent on only a few sources of power. For example, a job that is critical to the organization today may be obsolete tomorrow. Expertise that is in demand today may be old news 6 months from now. A mentor who supports you today may leave or be demoted. A reorganization in your workplace or industry can shift the configuration of your network and your place in it. Politically savvy people follow the sage and simple advice, "don't put all of your eggs in one basket."

Minimizing Dysfunctional Organizational Politics

Undoubtedly, some people are uncomfortable engaging in organizational politics—and sometimes for good reason. If taken too far, engaging in organizational politics can promote self-interest, distract people from their jobs, and become an end in itself. But engaging in organizational politics wisely and ethically can encourage innovation, increase flexibility, speed up decision making and implementation, build networks of mutually supportive relationships inside and outside of the organization, and help the organization adapt to an increasingly complex environment.

Although some political behavior is inevitable and desirable in organizations, excessive political behavior can result in dysfunctional behaviors that are unethical and disrupt effective organizational functioning. People who work in highly politicized organizations can spend too much time, energy, and resources engaging in self-protective political activity rather than focusing on serving customers, creating high-quality products, and enhancing shareholder value. Politically charged environments tend to be characterized by me-first thinking, lack of trust, divisiveness between people and groups, secretive decision-making processes, limited flow of information, fear of providing honest opinions and negative feedback, and unwillingness to help others. Consequently, highly politicized organizations tend to have less cooperation, flexibility, and innovation than organizations whose politics are kept in check.[125]

FIGURE 5-4   **Increasing Your Political Power**

<u>Goals</u>: Have you identified the goals you want to achieve for your unit, career, and life in general?

<u>Personal influence</u>:

- Do you have expertise that is valued by the organization?
- Do you have a track record of achieving results?
- What do you have that people want and need in order to achieve their goals?
- What can you do to increase your visibility? Consider volunteering for task forces and high profile assignments, engaging in organizationally sponsored community services, participating in professional meetings, publishing articles (including publishing on the Internet), speaking up appropriately at meetings, giving presentations, meeting people in person rather than sending e-mails, helping others achieve their goals, and sending thank you notes and congratulatory messages. Even seemingly insignificant things like wearing name tags or reintroducing yourself when you see someone you've met before ensures that people are more likely to remember your name.

<u>Relational influence</u>:

- *Strategic visits:* Have you identified whose support you need, as well as who is likely to support or resist you? Have you planned visits to these people to begin building mutually supportive relationships? Have you asked people how you can help them achieve their goals?
- *Strategic communication:* Have you identified people's styles, wants, and needs so that you can help them achieve their goals and describe the merits of your case in ways that are likely to gain their support?

<u>Structural influence</u>:

- *Position:* Do you have a hierarchical position that controls people's access to resources such as information, contacts, budgets, training and development opportunities, promotions, or salary increases?
- *Autonomy:* Can you build autonomy into your job so that you have more freedom in terms of where, when, and with whom you do your work?
- *Criticality:* Can you ensure that your job is perceived as critical to the workflow of the organization? Can you measure how your job contributes to important organizational outcomes? How many people are dependent on you to get their job done? Do you work in a unit that is central to organizational success? How specialized are the knowledge and skill required for your job? How easily would it be to replace you or others in your unit? If your organization was in a crisis, would you be able to help it get out of that crisis?
- *Centrality:* Do people come to you for advice, to gain access to other people, or to gain access to other resources that help them accomplish their tasks? Can you increase your centrality to organizational networks by gaining control of information, expertise, connections, and other resources that people need to achieve their goals? Can you join projects and teams that are central to the organization's goals?
- *Coalitions:* What coalitions can you join and create to promote common interests?

Also remember to know several influence techniques and be able to use the technique that is appropriate for the situation rather than your favored approached.

If you are a manager in a highly politicized organization (or if you want to prevent your organization from becoming dysfunctionally politicized), you can take steps to minimize dysfunctional political behaviors. Employees are more likely to engage in political behavior when organization goals and performance measures are uncertain, when organizational decision-making processes (including decisions about career advancement) are not transparent, when employees feel that they do not have input into decisions that affect them, and when trust in people and organizational processes is lacking.[126] You can minimize dysfunctional political behavior by:

- Providing clear goals, performance measures, and feedback so employees stay focused on the task and can link their behavior to important organizational results.[127]
- Rewarding individuals and groups for achieving not only personal and unit results, but overall organizational results.
- Providing clear guidelines for the attitudes and behaviors that can lead to promotions, salary increases, and other forms of career advancement.
- Providing training in how to demonstrate these attitudes and behaviors—and visibly promote people based on these characteristics.
- Using a systematic and transparent process for making important organizational decisions, including decisions about career advancement, and ensuring that employees understand how these decisions are made.
- Providing people with opportunities to participate in decision making, as well as with the information they need to make and implement effective decisions.
- Making it clear that dysfunctional political behavior—excessive self-promotion, turf building, and other behaviors that harm other employees, departments, customers, shareholders, or the organizational goals—will not be tolerated.
- Encouraging critical thinking and reporting bad news so that employees don't feel silenced by fear.

CONCLUSION

Some people are more adept at gaining and using power and influence than others. However, what looks like natural talent or street smarts is the result of thoughtful and systematic day-to-day efforts designed to gain the willing support of others. Successful people know that they must translate their intelligence, expertise, and experience into resources that are of value to others. They know that power is not something they have, but rather something that they must nurture and grow every day through small acts that build trust and support. People who develop ethical and sustainable power know that people listen to them not because they *have* to but because they *want* to.

I'm no longer afraid of storms, for I am learning how to sail my own ship.
Louisa May Alcott, Author

Regardless of your position in your organization, you have resources that you can draw on to gain the willing support of others so that you can be more effective and increase your career potential. Undoubtedly, some people are more inclined than others to seek out power and influence. But if you are in a managerial or leadership role, it is your responsibility—not a choice—to know how to influence others so that you can help the employees who depend on you achieve their goals.

Remember that both the politically naïve and the politically abusive can self-destruct, one with a whimper and the other with a bang. People who are politically naïve assume they don't have power and aren't aware of the many resources that they have to offer, so they don't try to influence others. Consequently, they are unlikely to achieve their potential because their skills, efforts, and contributions tend to go unnoticed and unappreciated. In addition, they are unable to fully support their staff who need their boss's influence and political sophistication to achieve their goals. People who are politically abusive treat people as adversaries rather than allies, focus on getting rather than giving, want to be right rather than effective, and try to force or trick people into compliance rather than earn support through honest means. More often than not, their influence is short-lived because they do not gain the sustained support they need to be successful in the long term. It's usually just a matter of time before their strategies backfire.

My hope is that by reading this chapter you can avoid falling into the trap of political naiveté or abuse. Instead, by using the strategies for gaining and using ethical, sustainable influence described in this chapter, you will be better able to gain and use power and influence ethically and wisely so that you can achieve the goals that are important to you, your organizations, your communities, and the people who depend on you.

CHAPTER SUMMARY

Power refers to the willingness and ability of a person or group to influence the attitudes, beliefs, and behaviors of others so that they are willing to support the goals that the person or group believes are important.[128]

Power is necessary only when there is real or potential conflict over interests, goals, or the means by which to achieve those interests or goals.[129]

Power is not a stable characteristic of a person or group. Rather, it must be actively sought and continuously replenished, is negotiated through relationships (to be powerful, you must have something the other person wants), and is situational because you may be powerful in one situation yet not in another.

We need power and influence skills because we often must try to gain support from people over whom we have no official power. People who have well-developed power and influence skills, as well as competence and a track record of results, are better able to achieve goals that are important to them, their organizations, their communities, and the people who depend on them.

To have sustainable power that transcends a particular time, position, and place, you must (1) have a variety of resources to offer that people believe they need or want,

(2) know many different strategies for gaining the support of others, and (3) adapt your strategy based on the situation.

You have many opportunities to influence others because human beings live in an uncertain world, are boundedly rational, and have imperfect decision-making abilities, inadequate and imperfect information on which to base decisions, and conflicting goals or ideas about the means by which goals should be achieved.

You are gaining and using power ethically when you explicitly tell people what you want to achieve and why; you put the interests of others and the organization at least on par with your own interests and, when appropriate, are able to put others' interests ahead of your own; you treat everyone with respect, administer organizational policies and procedures fairly, and do not abuse anyone's rights or exploit people; you leave yourself reasonably open to be influenced by others; and you back your requests with supporting data.

People who have sustainable power—power that transcends a particular time, position, and place—behave in ways that enable them to convince people that they are worth listening to, that their ideas have merit, and that they deserve the support of others.

Although people with sustainable power differ in many ways, they share much in common: they focus on achieving the goals that they believe are important; they are action oriented and want to shape their environment; they are competent, dependable, and have the expertise required to do their job well; they do their homework and develop systematic strategies for gaining support; they are willing to use the informal organization that operates outside official policies, procedures, and chains of commands to achieve their goals; they are astute observers of human behavior and have solid social skills; they love information, are great

listeners, and have an open mind; they realize that managing perceptions is at least as important as managing reality; they frame their requests in ways that don't change the merits of their case but that respect other people's point of view so that their ideas will be heard, understood, and supported; they are flexible in the ways that they think and act; although they continuously focus on their objectives, they are willing to be flexible about how they achieve them; and they have integrity.

Understanding and using the Social Styles model:

- The Social Styles model provides a useful framework for understanding your own behavioral preferences and the preferences of others. This model assumes that (1) we all have predictable and taken-for-granted ways of behaving, including how we make decisions, interact with others, and resolve conflicts; (2) if we understand our preferred styles as well as the preferred styles of the others, we can avoid some of the problems that arise from the misunderstandings, conflicts, and frustrations that can occur when people with different styles interact; and (3) we are more likely to influence others if we build relationships based on mutual understanding and respect. The Social Styles model focuses on two dimensions:

  - *Assertive/probing:* This refers to whether a person prefers to assertively push his or her ideas or quietly draw ideas out from other people.
  - *High responsiveness/low responsiveness:* This refers to whether a person prefers to be rational,

objective, and task-focused or emotionally expressive, intuitive, and relationship-focused. Based on these two dimensions, a person's social style can usually be categorized into one of the four categories: driver (assertive/low responsiveness), expressive (assertive/high responsiveness), amiable (probing/high responsiveness), and analytic (probing/low responsiveness). You can use this model to understand other people, how other people may perceive you, how you and others may act under stress, and how you can influence people with each of the different styles.

Although human beings differ in many ways, we all share some fundamental human needs. People who understand these common needs and help people fulfill these needs are more likely to be successful in their attempts to influence others. Social psychologist Robert Cialdini says, "persuasion works by appealing to a limited set of deeply rooted human needs, and it does so in predictable ways." According to Cialdini, there are six universal forms of influence:

- *Reciprocation:*   People feel obligated to pay back favors, gifts, and help that they receive from others. ("If you scratch my back, I'll scratch your back.").
- *Commitment/consistency:*   People are more likely to agree with a request if they feel it is consistent with a commitment they have made (especially a commitment that they make publicly or write down) or a behavior they have taken in the past.

- *Authority:*   People tend to obey people they perceive to be authorities and experts.
- *Social proof:*   People are more willing to support an idea if they know that other people support it, especially if they perceive the other people to be similar to them.
- *Scarcity:*   People tend to want what they believe is unique, rare, or in limited supply.
- *Liking:*   People want to support the people they like. People tend to like people they perceive to be attractive, people they believe to be similar to them in important ways, people with whom they have positive interactions, people they are near, and people who flatter them.

These forms of influence work because they act as cognitive shortcuts that help us bypass more complicated and costly decision-making processes. We are more likely to use cognitive shortcuts under particular conditions: when we are confused, uncertain, surprised, faced with too little or too much information, or feeling pressured, as well as when we trust the person requesting our support.[130] "Triggers" tend to set these cognitive shortcuts in motion.

Much of the time responding automatically to cognitive shortcuts serve us well, but sometimes it doesn't. If you know the six universal forms of influence and are mindful of the triggers that set them in motion, not only will you be more influential than someone who is unaware of them but you will also be less likely to be on automatic pilot—and be an easy target—when someone tries to influence you.

Each of these forms of influence can be used ethically or unethically. Ethical persuaders ask themselves, "How can I genuinely present the *honest* merits of my case in a way that is more likely to gain compliance?" They never provide false information or artificially inflate the merits of their case. They do not pretend to be authorities or experts if they are not. They do not engage in false flattery. They do not promise what they cannot deliver.

To avoid responding mindlessly to influence attempts, give yourself time before you make a decision so you can (1) reduce ambiguity by gathering more information from multiple and diverse sources, (2) identify the actual merits of the case as well as alternative choices, (3) consider the costs and benefits of compliance, (4) use a systematic process for gathering data and making decisions, and (5) remember that you have the right to say "no" gracefully.

Political behavior in organizations refers to activities that (1) people engage in to influence important personal or organizational outcomes, (2) are not part of one's official job description, and (3) are not carried out through official and explicitly stated organizational policies, and procedures.

When not taken to extremes and when used ethically to serve organizational, as well as personal, goals, political behavior in organizations can enhance productivity and innovation because it helps people get things done faster—and often better—than if they operated solely within the constraints of their official job descriptions and standard organizational procedures. Engaging in organizational politics wisely and ethically can encourage innovation, increase flexibility, speed up decision making and implementation, build networks of mutually supportive relationships inside and outside of the organization, and help the organization adapt to an increasingly complex environment. If taken too far, engaging in organizational politics can promote self-interest, distract people from their jobs, and become an end in itself.

If you choose to work only within the specific guidelines of your job and connect only with people who are directly related to your job, then you are most likely performing below your potential. If you are a manager, you also are inhibiting the performance of the people who work for you because you may not have the influence you need to give the employees who work for you access to contacts, information, and resources that can help them do their job better and obtain the assignments, promotions, and salary increases they may desire.

Politically savvy people draw on three sets of resources to achieve the goals they desire for themselves, others, and their organizations: personal, relational, and structural. Personal resources refer to characteristics that build one's reputation and credibility such as expertise, experience, education, job tenure, likeability, and professional activity. Relational resources refer to one's willingness and ability to communicate with and strategically create mutually supportive relationships with a broad and diverse group of people. Structural resources refer to one's position in the organizational hierarchy, job autonomy, job criticality, job centrality, and membership in coalitions.

The main point to remember about developing personal, relational, and structural power is this: Your power is based, in large part, on your ability to control resources that are important to others. The more that people are dependent on your expertise, connections, and access to information and financial resources, the more power you have. The less dependent you are on specific others to achieve your goals, the more choices and flexibility you have—and the more power you have.

Remember that you must create *multiple* bases of power if you want to achieve the goals that are important to you, the people who depend on you, and the organizations and societies to which you belong. It is a mistake to become dependent on only a few sources of power.

Although some political behavior is inevitable and desirable in organizations, excessive political behavior can result in dysfunctional behaviors that are unethical and disrupt effective organizational functioning. Politically charged environments tend to be characterized by me-first thinking, lack of trust, divisiveness between people and groups, secretive decision-making processes, limited flow of information, fear of providing honest opinions and negative feedback, and unwillingness to help others. Consequently, highly politicized organizations tend to have less cooperation, flexibility, and innovation than organizations whose politics are kept in check.

Employees are more likely to engage in political behavior when organizational goals and performance measures are uncertain, when organizational decision-making processes (including decisions about career advancement) are not transparent, when employees feel that they do not have input into decisions that affect them, and when trust in people and organizational processes is lacking. You can minimize dysfunctional political behavior by providing clear goals, performance measures, and feedback so employees stay focused on the task and can link their behavior to important organizational results as well; rewarding individuals and groups for achieving not only of personal and unit results, but overall organizational results; providing clear guidelines for the attitudes and behaviors that can lead to promotions, salary increases, and other forms of career advancement; providing training in how to demonstrate these attitudes and behaviors—and visibly promote people based on these characteristics; using a systematic and transparent process for making important organizational decisions, including decisions about career advancement, and ensuring that employees understand how these decisions are made; providing people with opportunities to participate in decision making, as well as with the information they need to make and implement effective decisions; making it clear that dysfunctional political behavior—self-promotion, turf building, and other behaviors that harm other employees, departments, customers, shareholders, or the organizational goals—will not be tolerated; and encouraging critical thinking and bad news so that employees don't feel silenced by fear.

Some people are more adept at gaining and using power and influence than others. However, what looks like natural talent or street smarts is the result of thoughtful and systematic day-to-day efforts designed to gain the willing support of others. Successful people know that they must translate their intelligence, expertise, and experience into resources that are of value to others. They know that power is not something they have, but rather something that they must nurture and grow every day through small acts that build trust and support. People who develop ethical and sustainable power understand that people listen to them not because they *have* to but because they *want* to.

BOX 5-1

Social Styles

Used with permission of *Leadership Development Associates*, Canton, GA, (800) 258-5987.

DIRECTIONS

Please respond to each statement in the survey on how well it describes the person you are assessing (or yourself). On a scale of "1" to "7" circle the number that best fits the person you are describing (This could be yourself or someone else). Try to use the ratings of "1" and "7" only in exceptional cases.

As a guide:

"1" means that I have never or rarely observed this behavior in this individual.
"4" means that I have observed this behavior to an average extent.
"7" means that I have observed this behavior very often or always.

Of course, you may use the other ratings:

"3" and "2" represent varying degrees between average and little.
"5" and "6" represent varying degrees between average and often.

To start, please check one of the following to indicate your work relationship with the person you are assessing.

☐ You are the person named   ☐ This person reports to you   ☐ Other
☐ You report to this person   ☐ This person is your peer

This person

1.	Tends to focus on immediate goals and objectives	1.	1	2	3	4	5	6	7
2.	Is detailed oriented	2.	1	2	3	4	5	6	7
3.	Sees the big picture	3.	1	2	3	4	5	6	7
4.	Comes across in a friendly manner	4.	1	2	3	4	5	6	7
5.	Is organized	5.	1	2	3	4	5	6	7
6.	Makes friends quickly	6.	1	2	3	4	5	6	7
7.	Is talkative	7.	1	2	3	4	5	6	7
8.	Usually makes quick decisions	8.	1	2	3	4	5	6	7
9.	Is spontaneous	9.	1	2	3	4	5	6	7
10.	Is trusting	10.	1	2	3	4	5	6	7
11.	Is methodical	11.	1	2	3	4	5	6	7
12.	Is conscious of time	12.	1	2	3	4	5	6	7
13.	Prefers facts and logic to opinion and instinct	13.	1	2	3	4	5	6	7
14.	Is very considerate of others	14.	1	2	3	4	5	6	7
15.	Has a lively imagination; thinks creatively	15.	1	2	3	4	5	6	7
16.	Prefers to make decisions without consulting others	16.	1	2	3	4	5	6	7
17.	Prefers to work alone	17.	1	2	3	4	5	6	7
18.	Is very cooperative and easy to work with	18.	1	2	3	4	5	6	7
19.	Likes being the center of attention	19.	1	2	3	4	5	6	7

20. Aggressively pursues goals	**20.**	1	2	3	4	5	6	7
21. Opinion and feeling enter into decision making process	**21.**	1	2	3	4	5	6	7
22. Is deliberate in making decisions.	**22.**	1	2	3	4	5	6	7
23. Expresses strong opinions	**23.**	1	2	3	4	5	6	7
24. Can be very impatient	**24.**	1	2	3	4	5	6	7
25. Is loyal to friends and organization	**25.**	1	2	3	4	5	6	7
26. Likes to have all the facts before making a decision	**26.**	1	2	3	4	5	6	7
27. At times makes snap decisions	**27.**	1	2	3	4	5	6	7
28. Likes to be in control	**28.**	1	2	3	4	5	6	7
29. Has a warm and pleasant personality	**29.**	1	2	3	4	5	6	7
30. Is persuasive	**30.**	1	2	3	4	5	6	7
31. Does not allow emotion to influence decisions	**31.**	1	2	3	4	5	6	7
32. Weighs ideas and suggestions carefully	**32.**	1	2	3	4	5	6	7
33. In pursuit of goals can come across as uncaring	**33.**	1	2	3	4	5	6	7
34. Takes a personal interest in people	**34.**	1	2	3	4	5	6	7
35. Is open to new ideas or change	**35.**	1	2	3	4	5	6	7
36. At times appears deep in thought	**36.**	1	2	3	4	5	6	7
37. Can be loud or even boisterous	**37.**	1	2	3	4	5	6	7
38. Likes facts and figures and bottom-line results	**38.**	1	2	3	4	5	6	7
39. Takes things seriously, does not "kid around"	**39.**	1	2	3	4	5	6	7
40. Is easy to get along with	**40.**	1	2	3	4	5	6	7
41. Is articulate; gets right to the point	**41.**	1	2	3	4	5	6	7
42. Tends to be quiet and reserved	**42.**	1	2	3	4	5	6	7
43. Thinks and expresses self in broad terms	**43.**	1	2	3	4	5	6	7
44. Is very tolerant and forgiving	**44.**	1	2	3	4	5	6	7
45. Conforms to change	**45.**	1	2	3	4	5	6	7
46. Is perceptive in "reading" a situation	**46.**	1	2	3	4	5	6	7
47. Takes a practical approach	**47.**	1	2	3	4	5	6	7
48. Can be stubborn	**48.**	1	2	3	4	5	6	7
49. Is competitive	**49.**	1	2	3	4	5	6	7
50. Seeks accommodation to resolve or avoid conflict	**50.**	1	2	3	4	5	6	7
51. Is business-like	**51.**	1	2	3	4	5	6	7
52. Finds it difficult to admit error	**52.**	1	2	3	4	5	6	7
53. Easily adapts to change	**53.**	1	2	3	4	5	6	7
54 Can be blunt at times	**54.**	1	2	3	4	5	6	7
55. Is insightful	**55.**	1	2	3	4	5	6	7
56. Easily voices opinions	**56.**	1	2	3	4	5	6	7
57. Is a reasonable person	**57.**	1	2	3	4	5	6	7
58. Likes to argue the point	**58.**	1	2	3	4	5	6	7
59. Is tactful	**59.**	1	2	3	4	5	6	7
60. Reacts defensively to negative feedback	**60.**	1	2	3	4	5	6	7
61. Respectful towards others	**61.**	1	2	3	4	5	6	7
62. Finds it difficult to concede to other person's views	**62.**	1	2	3	4	5	6	7
63. Tends to be critical of others	**63.**	1	2	3	4	5	6	7
64. Not quick to accept change	**64.**	1	2	3	4	5	6	7
65. Is very resourceful	**65.**	1	2	3	4	5	6	7
66. Usually sees things in black or white; right or wrong	**66.**	1	2	3	4	5	6	7
67. Tends to blame others for own shortcomings	**67.**	1	2	3	4	5	6	7
68. Looks for compromise to resolve issues	**68.**	1	2	3	4	5	6	7

(*continued*)

Box 5-1 (*cont.*)

SCORING – PART ONE

Enter the rating for each item 1 through 44 in the corresponding numbered spaces in the columns below

I	II	III	IV
1._____	3._____	2._____	4._____
8._____	7._____	5._____	6._____
12._____	9._____	11._____	10._____
16._____	15._____	13._____	14._____
20._____	19._____	17._____	18._____
24._____	23._____	22._____	21._____
28._____	27._____	26._____	25._____
31._____	30._____	32._____	29._____
33._____	35._____	36._____	34._____
38._____	37._____	39._____	40._____
41._____	43._____	42._____	44._____

TOTALS _____ _____ _____ _____

(Add or subtract   (−2)   (+1)   (+2)   (−6)
to total)

Net Total _____ _____ _____ _____

Place totals from each column in the appropriate quadrant.

INTERPRETING YOUR STYLE

The quadrant having the highest score is your dominant style. The quadrant with the lowest score is your least used style. A tie score in two or more quadrants indicates equal dominance in those styles.

III_____	I_____
ANALYTICAL	DRIVER
IV_____	II_____
AMIABLE	EXPRESSIVE

SCORING – PART TWO – VERSATILITY SCALE

Now enter the ratings for items 45 through 68 in the appropriate spaces in Columns A and B

	Column A	Column B
	45._____	48._____
	46._____	49._____
	47._____	52._____
	50._____	54._____
	51._____	56._____
	53._____	58._____
	55._____	60._____
	57._____	62._____
	59._____	63._____
	61._____	64._____
	65._____	66._____
	68._____	67._____
TOTALS	_____	_____

Total each column and enter the sum for each in the space provided. Calculate the net difference between the sums. If the sum of column A is greater than the sum of column B, plot the net difference in the left side of the scale. For example, if A is greater than B by 15 points, draw an arrow at the number 15 just below the word "High" on the left side of the scale. If column B is greater than column A by a net difference of 15, then place an arrow pointing at 15 on the right side of the scale. People with high versatility are move likely to be able to "read" and adapt to different social styles.

35 ___ 30 ___ 25 ___ 20 ___ 15 ___ 10 ___ 5 ___ 0 ___ 5 ___ 10 ___ 15 ___ 20 ___ 25 ___ 30 ___ 35

High	Moderate	Low

FOOD FOR THOUGHT

1. Identify someone whom you believe has sustainable, ethical influence. What does this person do to develop and maintain power and influence? If possible, interview this person and ask (1) how they've developed influence and (2) advice they can offer you for gaining sustainable, ethical influence.
2. Identify three sources of power that you have and when they are useful. Identify three sources of power that you need to develop to have an even greater positive impact on your environment.

3. Identify a person that you want to influence.

    a. Using the Social Styles model, identify that person's dominant style, identify three strategies that you will use to try to influence this person, and develop a plan of action for implementing these strategies. Review your progress after one week, then again at one month. Did you get the support you wanted? Why or why not?

    b. Based on the six universal forms of influence, identify three strategies that you will use to try to influence this person and develop a plan of action for implementing these strategies. Review your progress after one week, then again at one month. Did you get the support you wanted? Why or why not?

4. Over the next few days, watch television commercials and read print advertisements and identify as many of the six universal forms of influence that you can (reciprocity, authority, scarcity, social proof, commitment and consistency, and liking). Also identify which form of influence is used most often in advertisements.

5. Consider the last time you did something you didn't want to do. Why did you do it? Were you influenced by any of the six universal forms of influence? Could you have resisted the influence better if you had understood your susceptibility to these forms of influence? List at least four things you can do to protect yourself from being mindlessly influenced by others.

6. Think about someone with whom you have a difficult relationship, yet whose support you need now or may need in the future. Identify at least three strategies for building mutual trust and respect in the relationship and develop a plan of action for implementing these strategies. Review your progress after one week, then again at one month. Is the relationship better after implementing these strategies than it was in the past. What did you gain by taking steps to improve the relationship?

7. Likability is one of the most powerful forms of influence. List at least five ways you can make yourself more likable to others. Remember that people are drawn to people who make them feel good them and avoid people who make them feel bad about themselves. Consider that attractiveness, positive interactions, proximity, perceived similarity, and genuine compliments build attraction.

8. If you are currently working in an organization, identify at least six steps you can take within the next month to increase your political influence in the next six months.

9. Imagine that you and a colleague are both interested in obtaining a high-profile assignment. In general, you have the same set of skills, same educational background, and have been with the organization for the same amount of time. Based on what you've learned in this chapter, what can you do to increase the probability that you will get the assignment?

ENDNOTES

1. Hill, Linda. 1995. "Power Dynamics in Organizations." *Harvard Business School Case Note*, 9-494-083, March 22.

2. Fry, Prem S. 2004. "Protecting the Quality of Life of Older Adults." *Geriatric Times.* July/August, Vol. II, http://www.geriatrictimes.com/g010719.html; Krause, Neale, and Benjamin Shaw. 2000. "Role-Specific Feelings of Control and Mortality." *Psychology and Aging.* American Psychological Association, http://apa.org/journals/pag/pag 154617.html.

3. Sutton, R., and Kahn, R. L. 1984. "Prediction, Understanding, and Control as Antidotes to Organizational Stress. In J. Lorsch (ed.). *Handbook of Organizational Behavior.* Boston, MA: Harvard University Press, Boston; Sauter, S., J. Hurrell, and C. Cooper (eds.). 1989. *Job Control and Worker Health.* New York: Wiley.

4. Lublin, Joann. 2003. "Women Fall Behind When They Don't Hone Negotiation Skills." *Wall Street Journal.* November: B1.

5. Hill, Linda. 1995. "Power Dynamics in Organizations." *Harvard Business School Case Note*, 9-494-083, March 22; French, John R., and Bertram Raven. 1959. "The Bases of Social Power." In Dorwin Cartwright (ed.).

Studies in Social Power. Ann Arbor, MI: University of Michigan Institute for Social Research, 159–167; Tushman, Michael T. 1977. "A Political Approach to Organizations: A Review and Rationale." *Academy of Management Review,* 2: 206–216.

6. Pfeffer, Jeffrey. 1977. "Power and Resource Allocations in Organizations." In Barry Staw and Gerald Salancik (eds.). *New Directions in Organizational Behavior.* Chicago, IL: St. Clair Press, 235–266.

7. Fiol, C. Marlene, Edward J. O'Connor, and Herman Aguinis. 2001. "All for One and One for All? The Development and Transfer of Power Across Organizational Levels." *Academy of Management Review,* 26(2): 224–242.

8. Tedeschi, James. 1974. "Attributions, Liking, and Power." In Ted Huston (ed.). *Foundations of Interpersonal Attraction.* New York: Academic Press, 193–215; DeLuca, Joel R. 1999. *Political Savvy: Systematic Approaches to Leadership Behind-the-Scenes.* Berwyn, PA: Evergreen Business Group; Reardon, Kathleen Kelley. 2001. *The Secret Handshake: Mastering the Politics of the Business Inner Circle.* New York: Currency.

9. Cavanaugh, Gerald, Dennis J. Moberg, and Manuel Velasquez. 1981. "The Ethics of Organizational Politics." *Academy of Management Review,* 6(3): 363–373.

10. Kotter, John. 1985. *Power and Influence.* New York: Free Press; Pfeffer, Jeffrey. 1992. *Managing with Power: Politics and Influence in Organizations.* Boston: Harvard Business School Press; DeLuca, Joel R. 1999. *Political Savvy: Systematic Approaches to Leadership Behind-the-Scenes.* Berwyn, PA: Evergreen Business Group.

11. March, James, and Herbert Simon. 1993. *Organizations.* 2nd ed. Oxford: Blackwell; March, James. 1994. *A Primer on Decision Making: How Decisions Happen.* New York: Free Press.

12. Langer, Ellen. 1978. "Rethinking the Role of Thought in Social Interactions." In H. Harvey, W. Ickes, and R. Kidd (eds.). *New Directions in Attribution Research.* Vol 2. Hillsdale, NJ: Erlbaum, 35–50; Reardon, Kathleen Kelley. 2001. *The Secret Handshake: Mastering the Politics of the Business Inner Circle.* New York: Currency.

13. Levine, Robert. 2003. *The Power of Persuasion: How We're Bought and Sold.* Hoboken, NJ: John Wiley and Sons.

14. Kotter, John. 1977. "Power, Dependence and Effective Management." *Harvard Business Review.* July/August: 125–136; Pfeffer, Jeffrey. 1992. *Managing with Power: Politics and Influence in Organizations.* Boston, MA: Harvard Business School Press.

15. Pfeffer, Jeffrey. 1992. *Managing with Power: Politics and Influence in Organizations.* Boston, MA: Harvard Business School Press.

16. Bennis, Warren, and Burt Nanus. 1985. *Leaders.* New York: Harper and Row.

17. Kotter, John. 1977. "Power, Dependence and Effective Management." *Harvard Business Review.* July/August: 125–136.

18. Stapleton, R., P. L. Nacci, and J. T. Tedeschi. 1973. "Expertise Power Interpersonal Attraction and the Reciprocation of Benefits." *Journals of Personality and Social Psychology,* 27(2): 199–205; French, John R., and Bertram Raven. 1959. "The Bases of Social Power." In Dorwin Cartwright (ed.). *Studies in Social Power.* Ann Arbor, MI: University of Michigan Institute for Social Research, 150–167.

19. Reardon, Kathleen Kelley. 2001. *The Secret Handshake: Mastering the Politics of the Business Inner Circle.* New York: Currency.

20. Reardon, Kathleen Kelley. 2001. *The Secret Handshake: Mastering the Politics of the Business Inner Circle.* New York: Currency.

21. Kanter, Rosabeth. 1984. *The Change Masters: Innovation and Entrepreneurship in the American Corporation.* New York: Touchstone Books; cited in Reardon, Kathleen Kelley. 2001. *The Secret Handshake: Mastering the Politics of the Business Inner Circle.* New York: Currency, 204.

22. Becker, Thomas E. 1998. "Integrity in Organizations: Beyond Honesty and Conscientiousness." *Academy of Management Review,* 23(1): 154–161.

23. Alessandra, Tony, Michael O'Connor with Janice Van Dyke. 1994. *People Smarts: Bending the Golden Rule to Give Others What They Want.* San Francisco, CA: Jossey Bass; Alessandra, Tony, and Michael O'Connor. 1996. *The Platinum Rule:*

Discover the Four Basic Business Personalities and How They Can Lead You to Success. New York: Warner Books; Merrill, David, and Roger Reid. 1999. *Personal Styles and Effective Performance*. New York: CRC Press; Social Styles Survey. *Leadership Development Associates*. Canton, GA, (800) 258-5987; Caproni, Paula. 2003. *Enhancing Productivity Through Relationships: The Social Style Model*. Teaching Note.

24. Reardon, Kathleen Kelley. 2001. *The Secret Handshake: Mastering the Politics of the Business Inner Circle*. New York: Currency.

25. Douglas, Eric F. 2001. *Straight Talk: Turning Communication Upside Down for Strategic Results at Work*. 2nd ed. Sacramento, CA: LRI Publishing, 60–61.

26. Cialdini, Robert B. 2001. "Harnessing the Science of Persuasion." *Harvard Business Review*. October: 72–79; Cialdini, Robert B. 2001. *Influence: Science and Practice*. Needham Heights, MA: Allyn and Bacon, 47.

27. Cialdini, Robert B. 2001. *Influence: Science and Practice*. Needham Heights, MA: Allyn and Bacon.

28. Levine, Robert. 2003. The *Power of Persuasion: How We're Bought and Sold*. Hoboken, NJ: John Wiley and Sons; Cialdini, Robert B. 2001. *Influence: Science and Practice*. Needham Heights, MA: Allyn and Bacon; P. Worchel, and B. McCormic. 1963. "Self-concept and Dissonance Reduction." *Journal of Personality*, 31: 588–599.

29. Cialdini, Robert B. 2001. *Influence: Science and Practice*. Needham Heights, MA: Allyn and Bacon, x, 9.

30. Cialdini, Robert B. 2001. *Influence: Science and Practice*. Needham Heights, MA: Allyn and Bacon, 235.

31. Langer, Ellen, A. Blank, and B. Chanowitz. 1978. "The Mindlessness of Ostensibly Thoughtful Action: The Role of 'Placebic' Information in Interpersonal Interaction." *Journal of Personality and Social Psychology*, 36: 635–642; cited in Cialdini, Robert B. 2001. *Influence: Science and Practice*. Needham Heights, MA: Allyn and Bacon, 4.

32. Kilbourne, Jean. 1999. *Deadly Persuasion*. New York: Free Press, 127; cited in Levine,

Robert. 2003. The *Power of Persuasion: How We're Bought and Sold*. Hoboken NJ: John Wiley and Sons, 18.

33. Cialdini, Robert. 1999. "Of Tricks and Tumors: Some Little-Recognized Costs of Dishonest Use of Effective Social Influence." *Psychology and Marketing*, 16(2): 91–99.

34. Gouldner, Alvin. 1960. "The Norm of Reciprocity: A Preliminary Statement." *American Sociological Review*, 25: 161–178.

35. Fromm, Erich. 1956. *The Art of Loving*. New York: Harper, 48; cited in James T. Tedeschi. 1974. "Attributions, Liking, and Power." In Huston, Ted Huston (ed.). *Foundations of Interpersonal Attraction*. New York: Academic Press, 193–215.

36. Levine, Robert. 2003. The *Power of Persuasion: How We're Bought and Sold*. Hoboken, NJ: John Wiley and Sons, 66; citing Dennis Regan. 1971. "Effects of a Favor and Liking on Compliance." *Journal of Experimental Social Psychology*, 7: 627–639.

37. "Eminent Opinions on Woman Suffrage." *The Women's Suffrage Cookbook*. 1886. Published in Aid of the Festival and Bazaar, Boston, December 13–19: 146.

38. Agence France-Presse. 2003. "Repaying a Debt of Gratitude." *South China Morning Post*. October 13: A8.

39. Wade-Benzoni, Kimberly A. 2002. "A Golden Rule Over Time: Reciprocity In Intergenerational Allocation Decisions." *Academy of Management Journal*, 45(5): 1011–1028; citing Morgan. 2000.

40. Useem, Michael. 1998. *The Leadership Moment: Nine True Stories of Triumph and Disaster and Their Lessons for Us All*. New York: Random House.

41. Cialdini, Robert B. 2001. *Influence: Science and Practice*. Needham Heights, MA: Allyn and Bacon.

42. Lublin, Joann. 2003. "Women Fall Behind When They Don't Hone Negotiation Skills." *Wall Street Journal*. November: B1.

43. Cialdini, Robert. 2001. "The Power of Persuasion." *Executive Briefings: Strategies for the Competitive Edge*. Mill Valley, CA: Kantola Productions.

44. Cialdini, Robert. 2001. "Harnessing the Science of Persuasion." *Harvard Business Review*. October: 72–79.

45. "Cirque Dreams Big." 2003. *Newsweek.* July 14: 42–44.

46. "Cirque Dreams Big." 2003. *Newsweek.* July 14: 42–44.

47. Daspin, Eileen. 2003. "The T-Shirt You Can't Get." *Wall Street Journal.* October 10: W1 and W10.

48. Milgram, Stanley. 1969. *Obedience to Authority.* New York: Harper and Row.

49. Levine, Robert. 2003. The *Power of Persuasion: How We're Bought and Sold.* Hoboken, NJ: John Wiley and Sons; citing J. Cooper, E. Bennett, and H. Sukel 1996. "Complex Scientific Testimony: How Do Jurors Make Decisions?" *Law and Human Behavior,* 20: 379–394.

50. Cialdini, Robert B. 2001. *Influence: Science and Practice.* Needham Heights, MA: Allyn and Bacon, 77.

51. Festinger, Leon. 1957. "A Theory of Social Comparison Process." *Human Relations,* 7: 117–140.

52. Levine, Robert. 2003. The *Power of Persuasion: How We're Bought and Sold.* Hoboken, NJ: John Wiley and Sons.

53. Staw, Barry. 1976. "Knee-deep in the Big Muddy: A Study of Escalating Commitment to a Chosen Course of Action." *Organizational Behavior and Human Performance,* 16: 27–44.

54. Freedman, J. L., and S. C. Fraser. 1966. "Compliance without Pressure: The Foot in the Door Technique." *Journal of Personality and Social Psychology,* 4: 195–202.

55. Cialdini, Robert. 2001. "Harnessing the Science of Persuasion." *Harvard Business Review.* October: 72–79.

56. Cialdini, Robert. 2001. "Harnessing the Science of Persuasion." *Harvard Business Review* October: 72–79.

57. Cialdini, Robert. 2001. "Harnessing the Science of Persuasion." *Harvard Business Review* October: 72–79.

58. Levine, Robert. 2003. The *Power of Persuasion: How We're Bought and Sold.* Hoboken, NJ: John Wiley and Sons, 186.

59. Berscheid, Ellen, and Elaine Hatfield. 1978. *Interpersonal Attraction.* 2nd ed., New York: Random House, 22.

60. Berscheid, Ellen, and Elaine Walster. 1974. "A Little Bit About Love." In Ted Huston (ed.). *Foundations of Interpersonal Attraction.* New York: Academic Press, 355–381; Walster, Elaine, and G. W. Walster. 1976. "Interpersonal Attraction." In Bernard Seidenberg and Alvin Snadowsky (eds.). *Social Psychology: An Introduction.* New York: Free Press, 276–308.

61. Levine, Robert. 2003. *The Power of Persuasion: How We're Bought and Sold.* Hoboken, NJ: John Wiley and Sons, 54.

62. Lott, Albert, and Bernice Lott. 1974. "The Role of Reward in the Formation of Positive Interpersonal Attitudes." In Ted Huston (ed.). *Foundations of Interpersonal Attraction.* New York: Academic Press, 174–192.

63. Jidd, K. J., and J. S. Lockard. 1978. "Monetary Significance of the Affiliative Smile." *Bulletin of Psychonomic Society* 11: 344–346; cited in Pfeffer, Jeffrey. 1992. *Managing with Power: Politics and Influence in Organizations.* Boston. MA: Harvard Business School Press.

64. Lynn, M., and M. McCall. 1998. "Beyond Gratitude and Gratuity." Unpublished manuscript. Ithaca, NY: Cornell University, School of Hotel Administration; cited in Cialdini, Robert B. 2001. *Influence: Science and Practice.* Needham Heights, MA: Allyn and Bacon; Rind, Bruce, and Prashant Bordia. 1996. "Effect of Restaurant Tipping of Male and Female Servers Drawing a Happy, Smiling Face on the Backs of Customers' Checks." *Journal of Applied Social Psychology,* 26(3): 218–225; cited in Cialdini, Robert, and Noah Goldstein. 2002. "The Science and Practice of Persuasion." *Cornell Hotel and Restaurant Administration Quarterly,* 43(2): 40–50.

65. Rosenblatt, Paul. 1974. "Cross-Cultural Perspective on Attraction." In Ted L. Huston (ed.). *Foundations of Interpersonal Attraction.* New York: Academic Press, 79–95.

66. Tedeschi, James. 1974. "Attributions, Liking, and Power." In Ted L. Huston (ed.). *Foundations of Interpersonal Attraction.* New York: Academic Press, 193–212.

67. Tedeschi, James. 1974. "Attributions, Liking, and Power." In Ted L. Huston (ed.). *Foundations of Interpersonal Attraction.* New York: Academic Press, 193–212.

68. Le Gaipa, J. J. 1974. "Testing a Multidimensional Approach to Friendship." In Steve Duck (ed.). *Theory and Practice in Interpersonal Attraction*. London: Academic Press, 249–270.

69. Lott, Albert J., and Bernice B. Lott. 1974. "The Role of Reward in the Formation of Positive Interpersonal Attraction." In Ted L. Huston (ed.). *Foundations of Interpersonal Attraction*. New York: Academic Press, 171–189.

70. Razran, G. H. S. 1938. "Conditioning Away Social Bias by the Luncheon Technique." *Psychological Bulletin,* 35: 693; cited in Cialdini, Robert B. 2001. *Influence: Science and Practice*. Needham Heights, MA: Allyn and Bacon, 167.

71. Berscheid, Ellen, and Elaine Hatfield. 1978. *Interpersonal Attraction*. 2nd ed. New York: Random House, 34.

72. Byrne, Donn. 1971. *The Attraction Paradigm*. New York: Academic Press; Tim Emswiller, Kay Deaux, and Jerry E. Willits. 1971. "Similarity, Sex, and Requests for Small Favors." *Journal of Applied Social Psychology,* 1: 284–291.

73. Byrne, Donn, and Gerald L. Clore. 1967. "A Reinforcement Model of Evaluative Responses." *Personality: and International Journal,* 1: 103–128; Tajfel, H., and Turner J. "The Social Identity Theory of Intergroup Behavior." In Worchel, S., and W. G. Austin (eds.). 1986. *The Psychology of Intergroup Relations*. Chicago, IL: Nelson-Hall, 7–24; Tsui Ann, Terri Egan, and Charles O'Reilly. 1992. "Being Different: Relational Demography and Organizational Attachment." *Administrative Science Quarterly*, 37: 549–579.

74. Kelvin, Peter. 1977. "Predictability, Power and Vulnerability." In Steve Duck (ed.). *Theory and Practice in Interpersonal Attraction*. London: Academic Press, 355–378.

75. Tedeschi, James. 1997. "Attributions, Liking, and Power." In Ted L. Huston (ed.). *Foundations of Interpersonal Attraction*. New York: Academic Press, 193–212.

76. Flynn, Francis, Chatman, Jennifer, and Sandra Spataro. 2001. "Getting to Know You: The Influence of Personality on Impressions and Performance on Demographically Different People in Organizations." *Administrative Science Quarterly,* 46: 414–442.

77. Cialdini, Robert. 2001. "Harnessing the Science of Persuasion." *Harvard Business Review.* October: 72–79.

78. Brass, Daniel, and Marlene E. Burkhardt. 1993. "Potential Power and Power Use: An Investigation of Structure and Behavior." *Administrative Science Quarterly,* 36(3): 441–470.

79. Dutton, D. G. 1972. "Effect of Feedback parameters on Congruency versus Positivity Effects in Reactions to Personal Evaluations." *Journal of Personality and Social Psychology,* 24: 366–371.

80. Shrauger, J. S. 1972. "Response to Evaluation as a Function of Initial Self-Perception." *Psychological Bulletin,* 82: 581–596.

81. Regan, D. T. 1971. "Effects of a Favor and Liking on Compliance." *Journal of Experimental Social Psychology,* 7: 627–639; cited in Tedeschi, James. 1997. "Attributions, Liking, and Power." In Ted L. Huston (ed.). *Foundations of Interpersonal Attraction*. New York: Academic Press, 193–212.

82. Goldstein, J. W., and H. Rosenfeld. 1969. "Insecurity and Preference for Persons Similar to Oneself." *Journal of Personality,* 37: 253–268; Berscheid, Ellen, and Elaine Hatfield. 1978. *Interpersonal Attraction*. 2nd ed. New York: Random House, 89.

83. Cialdini, Robert, 2001. "The Power of Persuasion." *Executive Summaries: Strategies for the Competitive Edge*. Mill Valley, CA: Kantola Productions.

84. Levine, Robert. 2003. *The Power of Persuasion: How We're Bought and Sold*. Hoboken, NJ: John Wiley and Sons, 241.

85. Levine, Robert. 2003. *The Power of Persuasion: How We're Bought and Sold*. Hoboken, NJ: John Wiley and Sons, 238.

86. Cialdini, Robert. 2001. "Harnessing the Science of Persuasion." *Harvard Business Review* October: 72–79.

87. Cialdini, Robert, and Noah Goldstein. 2002. "The Science and Practice of Persuasion." *Cornell Hotel and Restaurant Administration Quarterly,* 43(2): 40–50.

88. Witt, L. Alan. 2003. "Influences of Supervisor Behaviors on the Levels and Effects of Workplace Politics." In Lyman Porter, Harold L. Angle, and Robert W. Allen (eds.).

Organizational Influence Processes.
Armonk, New York: M.E. Sharpe, 209–228.

89. Pfeffer, Jeffrey. 1992. *Managing with Power: Politics and Influence in Organizations.* Boston, MA: Harvard Business School Press; Kotter, John. 1977. "Power, Dependence and Effective Management." *Harvard Business Review.* July/August: 125–136; DeLuca, Joel R. 1999. *Political Savvy: Systematic Approaches to Leadership Behind-the-Scenes."* Berwyn, PA: Evergreen Business Group; Reardon, Kathleen Kelley. 2001. *The Secret Handshake: Mastering the Politics of the Business Inner Circle.* New York: Currency.

90. Pfeffer, Jeffrey. 1992. *Managing with Power: Politics and Influence in Organizations.* Boston, MA: Harvard Business School Press; Kotter, John. 1977. "Power, Dependence and Effective Management." *Harvard Business Review.* July/August: 125–136; DeLuca, Joel R. 1999. *Political Savvy: Systematic Approaches to Leadership Behind-the-Scenes."* Berwyn, PA: Evergreen Business Group; Reardon, Kathleen Kelley. 2001. *The Secret Handshake: Mastering the Politics of the Business Inner Circle.* New York: Currency.

91. Pfeffer, Jeffrey. 1981 "Management as Symbolic Action: The Creation and Maintenance of Organizational Paradigms." In Larry L. Cummings and Barry M. Staw (eds.). *Research in Organizational Behavior,* Greenwich, CT: JAI Press, 1–52; Schein, V. (ed.). 1977. "Individual Power and Political Behavior." *Academy of Management Review,* 2: 64–72.

92. Kanter, Rosabeth. 1983. The Change Masters: Innovations and Entrepreneurship in the American Corporation. New York: Simon and Schuster; Ibarra, Herminia. 1993. "Network Centrality, Power and Innovation Involvement: Determinants of Technical and Administrative Roles." *Academy of Management Journal,* 36: 471–501; Frost, Peter, and Carolyn Egri. 1991. "The Political Process of Innovation." In Lawrence L. Cummings and Barry M. Staw (eds.). 1991. *Research in Organizational Behavior.* 13: Greenwich, CT: JAI Press, 229–295.

93. Pfeffer, Jeffrey. 1992. *Managing with Power: Politics and Influence in Organizations.*
Boston, MA: Harvard Business School Press; Reardon, Kathleen Kelley. 2001. *The Secret Handshake: Mastering the Politics of the Business Inner Circle.* New York: Currency; Kanter, Rosabeth Moss. 1979. "Power Failure in Management Circuits." *Harvard Business Review.* July/August: 65.

94. Reardon, Kathleen Kelley. 2001. *The Secret Handshake: Mastering the Politics of the Business Inner Circle.* New York: Currency.

95. Merritt, Jennifer with Kate Hazelwood. 2003. "What's an MBA Really Worth?" *Business Week.* September 17: 90.

96. Stewart, Thomas. 1997. "Get with the New Power Game." *Fortune.* January 13: 58–59; Pfeffer, Jeffrey. 1992. *Managing with Power: Politics and Influence in Organizations.* Boston, MA: Harvard Business School Press.

97. Brass, Daniel, and Marlene Burkhardt. 1993. "Potential Power and Power Use: An Investigation of Structure and Behavior." *Academy of Management Journal,* 36(3): 441–471; Kipnis, David, Stewart Schmidt, and Ian Wilkinson. 1980. "Intraorganizational Influence Tactics: Explorations in Getting One's Way." *Journal of Applied Psychology,* 65: 440–452.

98. Kanter, Rosabeth. 1979. "Power Failures in Management Circuits." *Harvard Business Review,* 57: 65–75.

99. Lublin, Joann. 2003. "Women Fall Behind When They Don't Hone Negotiation Skills." *Wall Street Journal.* November: B1.

100. Sternberg, Robert. 2002. *Why Smart People Can Be So Stupid.* New Haven, CT: Yale University Press.

101. Pfeffer, Jeffrey. 1992. *Managing with Power: Politics and Influence in Organizations.* Boston, MA: Harvard Business School Press.

102. Reardon, Kathleen Kelley. 2001. *The Secret Handshake: Mastering the Politics of the Business Inner Circle.* New York: Currency, 95.

103. Ibarra, Herminia. 1993. "Network Centrality, Power and Innovation Involvement: Determinants of Technical and Administrative Roles." *Academy of Management Journal,* 36: 471–501.

104. Ibarra, Herminia. 1993. "Network Centrality, Power and Innovation

Involvement: Determinants of Technical and Administrative Roles." *Academy of Management Journal,* 36: 471–501.

105. Kotter, John. 1977. "Power, Dependence and Effective Management." *Harvard Business Review.* July/August: 125–136.

106. French, John R., and Bertram Raven. 1959. "The Bases of Social Power." In Dorwin Cartwright (ed.). *Studies in Social Power.* Ann Arbor, MI: University of Michigan Institute for Social Research, 150–167.

107. Stewart, Thomas. 1997. "Get with the New Power Game." *Fortune.* January 13: 58–59.

108. Watkins, Michael. 2003. *The First 90 Days: Critical Success Strategies for New Leaders at All Levels.* Boston, MA: Harvard Business School Press, 93.

109. Pfeffer, Jeffrey. 1992. *Managing with Power: Politics and Influence in Organizations.* Boston, MA: Harvard Business School Press.

110. Reardon, Kathleen Kelley. 2001. *The Secret Handshake: Mastering the Politics of the Business Inner Circle.* New York: Currency, 77.

111. Reardon, Kathleen Kelley. 2001. *The Secret Handshake: Mastering the Politics of the Business Inner Circle.* New York: Currency, 78.

112. Reardon, Kathleen Kelley. 2001. *The Secret Handshake: Mastering the Politics of the Business Inner Circle.* New York: Currency, 63.

113. Watkins, Michael. 2003. *The First 90 Days: Critical Success Strategies for New Leaders at All Levels.* Boston, MA: Harvard Business School Press; Reardon, Kathleen Kelley. 2001. *The Secret Handshake: Mastering the Politics of the Business Inner Circle.* New York: Currency.

114. Reardon, Kathleen Kelley. 2001. *The Secret Handshake: Mastering the Politics of the Business Inner Circle.* New York: Currency, 79.

115. Watkins, Michael. 2003. *The First 90 Days: Critical Success Strategies for New Leaders at All Levels.* Boston, MA: Harvard Business School Press, 46.

116. French, John R., and Bertram Raven. 1959. "The Bases of Social Power." In Dorwin Cartwright (ed.). *Studies in Social Power.* Ann Arbor, MI: University of Michigan Institute for Social Research, 150–167.

117. Ibarra, Herminia. 1993. "Network Centrality, Power and Innovation Involvement: Determinants of Technical and Administrative Roles." *Academy of Management Journal,* 36: 471–501.

118. Brass, Daniel. 1984. "Being in the Right Place: A Structural Analysis of Individual Influence in Organizations." *Administrative Science Quarterly,* 29: 518–553; French, John R., and Bertram Raven. 1959. "The Bases of Social Power." In Dorwin Cartwright (ed.). *Studies in Social Power.* Ann Arbor, MI: University of Michigan Institute for Social Research, 150–167.

119. Kanter, Rosabeth. 1979. "Power Failure in Management Circuits." *Harvard Business Review.* July/August 65–75; Reardon, Kathleen Kelley. 2001. *The Secret Handshake: Mastering the Politics of the Business Inner Circle.* New York: Currency.

120. Pfeffer, Jeffrey. 1992. *Managing with Power: Politics and Influence in Organizations.* Boston, MA: Harvard Business School Press; Freeman, L. C. 1979. "Centrality in Social Networks: Conceptual Clarification." *Social Networks,* 1: 215–239; Brass, Daniel, and Marlene Burkhardt. 1993. "Potential Power and Power Use: An Investigation of Structure and Behavior." *Academy of Management Journal,* 36(3): 441–471; Ibarra, Herminia. 1993. "Network Centrality, Power and Innovation Involvement: Determinants of Technical and Administrative Roles." *Academy of Management Journal,* 36: 471–501.

121. Freeman, L. C. 1979. "Centrality in Social Networks: Conceptual Clarification." *Social Networks,* 1: 215–239; Brass, Daniel, and Marlene Burkhardt. 1993. "Potential Power and Power Use: An Investigation of Structure and Behavior." *Academy of Management Journal,* 36(3): 441–471; Ibarra, Herminia. 1993. "Network Centrality, Power and Innovation Involvement: Determinants of Technical and Administrative Roles." *Academy of Management Journal,* 36: 471–501.

122. Robbins, Stephen. 2000. *Organizational Behavior.* 9th ed. Upper Saddle River, NJ:

Prentice Hall; citing W. B. Stevenson, J. L. Pearce, and L. W. Porter. 1985. "The Concept of Coalition in Organizational Theory and Research." *Academy of Management Review.* April 10(2): 261–263; Watkins, Michael. 2003. *The First 90 Days: Critical Success Strategies for New Leaders at All Levels.* Boston, MA: Harvard Business School Press.

123. Watkins, Michael. 2003. *The First 90 Days: Critical Success Strategies for New Leaders at All Levels.* Boston, MA: Harvard Business School Press.

124. Pfeffer, Jeffrey, and Alison Konrad. 1991. "The Effects of Individual Power on Earnings." *Work and Occupation,* 18: 385–414.

125. Eisenhardt, Kathleen, and L. J. Bourgeous III. 1998. "Politics of Strategic Decision Making in High Velocity Environments: Toward a Mid-Range Theory." *Academy of Management Journal,* 31: 737–770.

126. Tushman, Michael E. 1977. "A Political Approach to Organization: A Review and Rationale." *Academy of Management Review,* 2: 206–216; Cobb, A. T. 1986a. "Informal Influence in the Formal Organization." *Group and Organizational Studies,* 11: 229–253; March, James, and Herbert Simon. 1958. *Organizations.* New York: Wiley. Pfeffer, Jeffreys. 1978. *Organizational Design.* Arlington Heights, IL: AHM Publishing; Robbins, S. E. 1976. *The Administrative Process: Integrating Theory and Practice.* Englewood Cliffs, NJ: Prentice-Hall; Madison, D. L., Allen, R. W., Porter, L. W., Renwick, P. A., and Mayes, B. T. 1980. "Organizational Politics: An Exploration of Managers' Perceptions." *Human Relations,* 33: 79–100; Eisenhardt, Kathleen, and L. J. Bourgeous III. 1998. "Politics of Strategic Decision Making in High Velocity Environments: Toward a

Mid-Range Theory." *Academy of Management Journal,* 31: 737–770; Witt, L. Alan. 2003. "Influences of Supervisor Behaviors on the Levels and Effects of Workplace Politics." In Lyman Porter, Harold L. Angle, and Robert W. Allen (eds.). *Organizational Influence Processes.* Armonk, NY: M.E. Sharpe, 209–228.

127. Pfeffer, Jeffrey. 1978. *Organizational Design.* Arlington Heights, IL: AHM Publishing; cited in Witt, L. Alan. 2003. "Influences of Supervisor Behaviors on the Levels and Effects of Workplace Politics." In Lyman Porter, Harold L. Angle, and Robert W. Allen (eds.). *Organizational Influence Processes.* Armonk, NY: M.E. Sharpe, 209–228.

128. Hill, Linda. 1995. "Power Dynamics in Organizations." *Harvard Business School Case Note,* 9-494-083, March 22; French, John R., and Bertram Raven. 1959. "The Bases of Social Power." In Dorwin Cartwright (ed.). *Studies in Social Power.* Ann Arbor, MI: University of Michigan Institute for Social Research, 150–167; Tushman, Michael T. 1977. "A Political Approach to Organizations: A Review and Rationale." *Academy of Management Review,* 2: 206–216.

129. Pfeffer, Jeffrey. 1977. "Power and Resource Allocations in Organizations." In Barry Staw and Gerald Salancik (eds.). *New Directions in Organizational Behavior.* Chicago, IL: St. Clair Press, 235–266.

130. Levine, Robert. 2003. The *Power of Persuasion: How We're Bought and Sold.* Hoboken, NJ: John Wiley and Sons; Cialdini, Robert B. 2001. *Influence: Science and Practice.* Needham Heights, MA: Allyn and Bacon; P. Worchel, and B. McCormic. 1963. "Self-concept and Dissonance Reduction." *Journal of Personality,* 31: 588–599.

C H A P T E R

<table>
<tr><td>

6

</td></tr>
</table>

Managing Relationships with Your Bosses, Subordinates, and Peers

This chapter will help you:

- ■ Understand how managing your relationships with your subordinates, bosses, and peers influences your effectiveness as well as your effectiveness, career success, and well-being

- ■ Understand how authority dynamics influence your relationship with your boss and subordinates

- ■ Improve your relationship with your boss, including a bad boss

- ■ Create a context that brings out the best in employees

- ■ Enhance your mentoring and networking skills

- ■ Understand the role of impression management in everyday work life

> *Business, after all, is nothing more than a bunch of human relationships.*
> —LEE IACOCCA,
> *Former Chairman of Chrysler*
> *(now DaimlerChrysler)*

Decades of research on organizational effectiveness have led to the same conclusion: The quality of your relationships with bosses, subordinates, and peers has a significant impact on your work effectiveness, career success (in terms of number of promotions, salary increases, and job satisfaction), and personal well-being. For example, research suggests that:

- Social skills are a stronger predictor of executive success than are technical skills, and the need for social skills increases as one moves higher in the organizational hierarchy.[1]

 212 ■

- Employees' commitment to their supervisors is a stronger predictor of their productivity than is their commitment to their organization.[2]
- Employees in "high-quality, trusting relationships with managers" are likely to receive higher performance ratings than those who are not in such relationships.[3]
- People who are willing and able to understand other people's needs and adapt their behavior in response to other people's needs tend to get promoted more, receive higher salaries, and have more mentors than do those who don't do so.[4]
- People who have a strong network of relationships tend to live happier, healthier, and longer lives.[5]

Undoubtedly, investing in relationships with your subordinates, bosses, and peers is one of the most important things that you can do for yourself, others, and the organization. Indeed, if you are a manager, it's your job to manage your relationships consciously and systematically. After all, the manager's job is to get work done with and through others. But it's not only managers who benefit from building high-quality relationships. For example, research suggests that technical professionals who have strong networks tend to receive higher salaries than do technical employees who don't have strong networks.[6] This is not surprising because today's problems are too complex for even the smartest person to solve alone, and most jobs are designed to be interdependent with others. Unfortunately, many of us get so busy with the technical details of our day-to-day tasks that we don't invest enough time to build relationships with others who can help us become more effective.

In this chapter, we will focus on developing high-quality relationships with your subordinates, bosses, and peers. Regardless of whether you are managing up, down, or sideways, remember the following two assumptions about human relationships:

- High-quality relationships are built on trust, respect, and reciprocity.
- We are all fallible human beings who depend on each other for our professional effectiveness, career success, and personal well-being.[7]

At the end of the day you bet on people, not strategies. Larry Bossidy, former CEO of Allied Signal

With these assumptions in mind, we move onto the rest of this chapter. We first focus on how we develop our attitudes toward boss-subordinate relationships and the consequences of these attitudes on our effectiveness. We then focus on strategies for managing your relationships with your subordinates and bosses and then look at three skills that are useful regardless of whether we are managing up, down, or sideways: mentoring, networking, and impression management.

AUTHORITY RELATIONS AT WORK

Despite all the talk about flattened organizations, participative management, and empowerment, hierarchy is alive and well in most work organizations today. Indeed, one of the most important lessons that effective managers learn is that their everyday behaviors get interpreted "through the lens of authority relations."[8] In other words, our assumptions about boss-subordinate relationships influence what (and who) we pay attention to, how we interpret what we attend to, and how we behave toward others. We develop our attitudes toward authority in at least two ways: our place in the organizational structure (e.g., whether we are in a boss or subordinate role at work) and our personality (e.g., the attitudes about authority that we unconsciously develop early in our lives).

Organizational Structure and Authority Relations

Research suggests that subordinates tend to pay more attention to and develop more complex interpretations of the behavior of people who are higher than they are in the organizational hierarchy.[9] In contrast, bosses tend to pay less attention to individual subordinates, develop relatively simplistic interpretations of their behavior, think less about individual differences among subordinates, and often don't realize how their behaviors affect subordinates.[10] Subordinates' keen interest in their boss's attitudes, feelings, and behaviors is understandable because the boss has a significant impact on the subordinates' task effectiveness, career development, job satisfaction, and psychological well-being. Certainly, subordinates have an impact on the boss's effectiveness, career development, and well-being, as well. However, as psychologist Marty Grothe, coauthor of *Problem Bosses: Who They Are and How to Deal with Them*, explains, when things go wrong in a relationship, "the person who has the least power will hurt more."[11]

Harvard professor Linda Hill says that bosses tend to be particularly unaware of "how their everyday behaviors get scrutinized and amplified by subordinates" and how "seemingly insignificant actions can have broad consequences."[12] Picture the boss who calls an employee into his or her office without an explanation ("Smith, I'd like to see you in my office at 11:00 tomorrow morning."). Not knowing what to expect, Smith may imagine a variety of reasons for the meeting ("What did I do?" "Am I in trouble?" "Is there going to be a downsizing, and am I going to be laid off?"). The manager may have called Smith to the office to offer a promotion, challenging job assignment, or reward for a job well done. However, Smith may imagine at least some worst-case scenarios unless he or she is given information about the purpose of the meeting in advance. Although the manager probably won't give the meeting another thought until the next morning, Smith may lose a little sleep worrying about the purpose of the meeting.

Although subordinates tend to have less power than their boss, they also tend to underestimate how much the boss depends on them and how much power the subordinates have in the relationship. Researcher Kenwyn K. Smith explains that all groups in an organizational hierarchy have power, albeit different kinds.[13] People at upper levels have the power to define the organization's reality (by setting the organization's direction, rules, policies, procedures, and quality standards). People at lower levels have the power to support or resist that reality (by offering or withholding support, psychologically or physically withdrawing from the organization, joining unions, and engaging in public protest). People at middle levels have the power to either bring the people at the lower and upper levels together or keep them apart, often by acting as filters for information and resources. Notably, the people in the middle may be invested in keeping those at upper and lower levels apart, because if people at upper and lower levels could figure out how to work directly and effectively with each other, then the people at the middle level would lose a significant base of power. Indeed, the security of the

Nobody is as powerful as we make them out to be. *Alice Walker, In Search of Our Mother's Gardens*

people in the middle is often dependent on maintaining distance between people at upper and lower levels.

In short, organizational structure creates psychological and physical boundaries between hierarchical groups. Therefore, where we sit in the organizational hierarchy influences how we think and act within our group and toward others.

Personality and Authority Relations

We develop our attitudes toward authority long before we enter the world of work, and we bring these attitudes into every boss-subordinate relationship that we have.[14] Psychoanalysts argue that we develop our beliefs about authority through our experiences with our earliest authority figures—our parents and primary caretakers. These experiences influence our relationships toward authority figures throughout our lives primarily by unconsciously shaping our assumptions about the goodwill and dependability of authority figures. Boston University researchers William Kahn and Kathy Kram describe three orientations toward authority:[15]

- *Interdependent.* If our primary caretakers are responsive toward our needs in our earliest years, we are likely to develop the belief that we are worthy of their goodwill and can depend on them to take care of us. Consequently, our attitudes toward authority figures will be that authority figures are likely to be trustworthy and dependable unless proven otherwise. Whether we are in the boss or subordinate role, we are likely to view the authority relationship as being built on mutual respect and responsibility ("We're in this together." "How can we help each other?"). Kahn and Kram argue that interdependent attitudes are likely to lead to the most effective and satisfying boss-subordinate relationships.
- *Dependent.*   If our primary caretakers are inconsistent in their care of us (e.g., sometimes being accessible and caring, while at other times being distant and uncaring), we may develop the belief that we can sometimes count on authority figures and sometimes not. Because we see that our caretakers are able to care for us at least some of the time, we attribute their inconsistency not to their willingness or ability to take care of us but to our own worthiness. In other words, we believe it is our fault when the caretaker does not respond to us. Consequently, we spend much of our time and effort trying to win the caretaker's attention and affection. When we become adults, our attitude toward authority figures is likely to be one of dependence, and we will try to do whatever it takes to please authority figures to earn their goodwill and support. Whether we are in the boss or subordinate role, we will expect that the boss's job is to take care of the subordinate and the subordinate's job is to please the boss ("Whatever you say, boss." "The boss is always right.").
- *Counterdependent.* If our primary caretakers are psychologically or physically absent in our early years, we may develop the belief that we cannot depend on authority figures to take care of our needs and that we can only count on ourselves to get what we need in life. Consequently, as adults, we are

likely to view authority figures as irrelevant or hurdles to overcome. Whether we are in the boss or subordinate role, we are likely to resist authority by assuming that the role of the boss is irrelevant and that the boss should stay out of their subordinates' way ("You can't count on the boss to get anything done." "You don't need the boss to help you accomplish your goals.").

No one can make you feel inferior without your consent. **Eleanor Roosevelt**

Simply stated, we unknowingly bring our childhood attitudes toward authority into our roles as bosses and subordinates at work when we are adults. Because we see certain types of authority relations as "normal" (interdependent, dependent, or counterdependent), we are likely to act in ways that create the authority dynamics that we expect. For example, if we have a dependent attitude toward authority, then we are likely to expect our bosses to take care of us and act more helpless than we really are. When we are in the boss role, we are likely to encourage the people who work for us to be dependent on us, often by withholding important information, training, or material resources that would enable subordinates to become more independent.

If we have a counterdependent attitude toward authority, we are likely to reject the authority of our boss, which will further strain our relationship with the boss. When we are in the boss role, we are likely to dismiss our own authority and responsibility toward employees and not offer support and assistance even when subordinates want and need our help. If we have an interdependent attitude toward authority, we are likely to act in ways that bring out the best in the boss-subordinate relationship. These different orientations toward authority are illustrated in Figure 6-1.

In short, our personality and our place in the organizational hierarchy significantly shape what we notice, how we interpret what we notice, and how we behave

FIGURE 6-1   Authority Relations at Work

Source: Model based on Kahn, William and Kathy Kram. 1994. "Authority at Work: Internal Models and Their Organizational Consequences." *Academy of Management Review*, 19(1): 17–50. Reprinted by permission of Academy of Management Review.

toward our bosses and subordinates. To avoid falling into dysfunctional patterns of boss-subordinate relationships, remember the following:

- The boss-subordinate relationship is a partnership between two fallible human beings who are dependent on each other's expertise, support, and goodwill for their professional effectiveness, career success, and psychological well-being.[16]
- Our position in an organizational hierarchy (lower, middle, upper) and our childhood attitudes toward authority may pull us into unconscious and often misguided assumptions and behaviors that can undermine our effectiveness, as well as that of our bosses, our subordinates, and the organization.
- Both bosses and subordinates have power in the relationship. Indeed, the higher we go in the organizational hierarchy, the more dependent we are on others to get our work done.

The best steps you can take to develop effective relationships with your bosses and subordinates are to develop an understanding and appreciation for authority relations at work; be aware of your own attitudes toward authority and how they influence your ability to have an effective relationship with your boss; learn strategies that are likely to enhance the quality of your relationship with your bosses and subordinates; and systematically apply these techniques in your everyday work life.

MANAGING SUBORDINATES

You must genuinely like and respect those who are performing under your command, for neither the liking nor the respect can be successfully faked. *Benjamin Davis*

People tend to get promoted to managerial positions because they are excellent individual contributors. In other words, they are effective engineers, marketers, salespeople, teachers, nurses, social workers, and so on. They accomplish their day-to-day tasks thoughtfully, thoroughly, and quickly. But when they are rewarded with a promotion to a managerial position, they are often surprised that the skills that helped them succeed as individual contributors are insufficient for success in their managerial roles. They have to make the transition from getting jobs done themselves to getting the jobs done with and through others. They often find that their biggest challenges are forming effective work relationships with employees[17] and creating a work environment that enables the people who work for them to succeed.

When people are promoted to managerial positions, their immediate concern is "How do I motivate the people who work for me?" One of the most important lessons that you will learn in this chapter is that you cannot motivate anyone because people must motivate themselves. *Instead, your job is to create a work context in which people will be inspired and enabled to do their best work.* Be aware that creating a context for high performance doesn't necessarily mean spending more money. Rather, it means being aware of what drives people (e.g., meaning, belonging, competence, control, and consistency) and creating opportunities to enable them to fulfill these drives at work. Another critical lesson you will learn is that the direct manager or supervisor—not just top leadership or organizational culture—is one of the most important determinants of an employee's commitment and productivity.[18] In other words, if you are a manager, *you* can help your employees add value to the organization through your everyday actions even if you don't have the unbridled support of your manager.

Although some managers struggle in the managerial role, others thrive. Consider the case of General Motors supervisor Pat Kerrigan. The former public school psychologist and successful plant manager explains what being a manager means to her:

> I have to say I've never made a part in my life and I don't really have any plans to make one. That's not my job. My job is to create an environment where people who do make them can make them right, make them right the first time, can make them right at a competitive cost, and can do so with some sense of responsibility and pride in what they're doing. And I don't have to know how to make a part to do any of those things. . . . My role is supporting, enabling, and empowering.[19]

Paul Orfalea, founder and Chairperson Emeritus of Kinko's, echos Kerrigan's view. The son of Lebanese immigrants, Orfalea is severely dyslexic, was frequently expelled from school, graduated 8th from the bottom of his high school class of 1,200 students, and barely made it through college. He admits that even today he cannot read very well, is not mechanically inclined, and hasn't quite figured out how a computer works. He began his business in 1970 in 100 square feet of space near the University of Southern California with a $5,000 loan, naming his business Kinko's after his boyhood nickname that referred to his curly hair. Orfalea recently stepped down as CEO of Kinko's at age 52, with a personal worth of $225 million, more than 23,000 employees, and a stellar reputation for corporate responsibility. Kinko's has been listed in *Fortune* magazine's 100 best companies in America, *Forbes* magazine's 500 biggest private companies, and *Working Mother* magazine's best companies for working mothers. He attributes his success to his passionate commitment to taking care of employees and customers, his ability to make the complex simple, and his drive to hire good people, give them what they need to serve the customers well, and then let them do their work.

What do effective managers like Pat Kerrigan and Paul Orfalea do to to ensure that employees are both willing and able to perform at their best so that they can add value to the organization? Although they have different work styles, strengths, and weaknesses, they share the ability to create a work context that enables people to do their best work. They understand that all people everywhere are driven by fundamental needs for meaning, belonging, competence, control, and consistency, They also understand that each person has his or her unique interests, needs, life situations, and definitions of success—and these must be attended to in order for the employee to feel committed to and effective in the organization.

Successful leaders are cognitively and behaviorally complex.[20] Rather than using one-size-fits-all management styles, they analyze problems from a variety of perspectives, determine the most appropriate management style for each situation, and adapt their behaviors accordingly. They can be inspirational visionaries and detail-driven policy makers, hands-off delegators and hands-on technical advisors, participative managers and buck-stops-here decision makers—all depending on the needs of the situation.

In this section, I present two models of leadership that are based on the assumption that effective managers are able to diagnose the managerial style that is most appropriate for a given situation and adapt their management style to the needs of the situation so that they can bring out the best in others. The first model is Situational Leadership, created by Paul Hersey and Ken Blanchard. The second model is the Denison Leadership Development Model, created by Daniel Denison.

The Situational Leadership Model

Don't be irreplaceable.
If you can't be replaced,
you can't be promoted.
Anonymous

Situational leadership is one of the most widely known employee-centered models of leadership. It has been used in training programs in more than 400 of the *Fortune* 500 companies, and more than 1 million managers have been exposed to it.[21] According to the Situational Leadership model, the manager's goal is to develop employees so that the employees become increasingly competent and confident in their work and less dependent on the manager for technical and psychological support.[22] In short, Situational Leadership is about developing employees through appropriate degrees of delegation. To determine the appropriate delegation style to use, Hersey and Blanchard advise managers to focus on three criteria:

- *Leadership style.*   Effective managers develop employees by using both task-focused and relationship-focused behaviors. Task-focused behaviors reflect a "concern for production" (e.g., clearly stating task goals, procedures, policies, and performance measures). Relationship-focused behaviors reflect a "concern for people" (e.g., praising people and showing personal concern).[23] Both task- and relationship-focused behaviors are essential to getting work done effectively and efficiently, although one or the other may be more appropriate at any given time, depending on the developmental level of the employee.
- *Employee readiness.*   Employees must be both psychologically willing (be motivated and confident) and technically able (have the necessary skills, knowledge, and experience) to accomplish a task effectively and independently.[24] When an employee is doing a task for the first time, the employee may need to be told what to do, how to do it, and when to do it, and typically requires training, assistance, and follow-up. As the employee becomes more confident and competent to perform the task independently, the employee needs less technical assistance (task-focused behaviors) and more encouragement (relationship-focused behaviors) to build the employee's confidence and independence.
- *The characteristics of the task.*   Every task has its own demands. Each of us excels in some tasks, needs help in others, and resists some tasks altogether. For example, a professor may be very effective at research, but not very effective at teaching, or vice versa. An engineer may be very capable at writing technical reports but less able to convey his or her ideas in a compelling way when faced with a nontechnical audience. A salesperson may be excellent at getting orders from clients but less effective in filling the orders correctly and on time. Consequently, managers need to adapt their style based on employees' willingness and ability to do a particular task.

In short, each employee has different developmental needs, and these needs change with the situation. If an employee is able and willing to effectively handle a task, the manager should offer the employee significant independence to do that task. If an employee is unable and unwilling to effectively handle a task, the manager should reduce the employee's independence on that task. Hersey and Blanchard describe four managerial styles, each based on employees' willingness and ability to accomplish a particular task.[25] Each style is most effective when matched to the needs of the situation.

- *Telling or directing.* This style is low on relationship-focused behaviors and high on task-focused behaviors (e.g., telling the employee what to do, how to do it, and when to do it, as well as closely supervising and following up on the employee's performance). This style is best used when an employee is lacking in specific skills and lacks the confidence or motivation to complete the specific task independently. This does not mean that the manager should offer no relationship-focused behaviors but that these are secondary to task-focused behaviors. When an employee is unwilling and unable to do a task, the best way to boost that employee's motivation, confidence, and skill is to teach him or her how to do the job well. If a manager does not provide enough structure and direction, the employee is likely to flounder, perform substandard work, and lose confidence in his or her ability to perform the task.
- *Persuading or coaching.* This style is high on both task- and relationship-focused behaviors. This style is best used when an employee may have some relevant skills but still needs technical support and follow-up but is gaining in ability and motivation. At this point, the employee needs encouragement to maintain his or her confidence, particularly as the manager begins to encourage more independence.
- *Participating or supporting.* This style is low on task-focused behaviors and high on relationship-focused behaviors. This style is best used when an employee is experienced and capable with a particular task but lacks the confidence to complete the job successfully without help or psychological support from the manager. For example, an employee may be able to do an excellent job preparing and giving a presentation to senior managers, but he or she wants the manager to attend the presentation for backup and to provide feedback after the presentation.
- *Delegating.* This style is low on both task- and relationship-focused behaviors. This style is best used when an employee is both willing and able to perform a particular task independently with no input or follow-up needed or wanted from the manager. Indeed, the employee may be more proficient at the task than the leader is. A manager's attempts to intervene either by offering technical or psychological support may be viewed by the employee as micromanaging or meddling.

How can you tell if the employee is willing and able to successfully complete a particular task?[26] To assess *ability*, find out whether the person has the necessary job knowledge. Does the person know what needs to be done, why it needs to be done, where to get appropriate resources and support, who should be involved, level of quality standards, and appropriate performance measures? Does the person have the skills and experience to successfully complete the project without supervision? Does the person tend to seek out help when needed? Does the person consistently show high levels of performance with this type of task? Remember that high performance in one type of task does not necessarily predict high performance in another type of task. Does the person consistently meet deadlines? Based on your responses, would you rate the person as high or low on ability to take on this task?

To assess *willingness*, determine whether the person shows confidence and motivation to take on the responsibility for the task. Does the person proactively seek out accountability in terms of asking for deadlines, quality standards, and other performance standards? Based on your responses, would you rate the person as high or low on willingness and confidence to take on this task?

The simplicity and intuitive appeal of the Situational Leadership model have contributed significantly to its becoming one of the most well-known and appreciated models used in management training. Some researchers have concluded that the model is useful for managing recently hired employees[27] and employees at low to moderate readiness levels,[28] but less useful for managing employees at high readiness levels. Researchers generally agree that the Situational Leadership model is valuable because it reminds managers to avoid one-size-fits-all management styles, to adapt their styles to the needs of employees and the situation, to take advantage of opportunities to build subordinates' skills and confidence, and, most importantly, to take seriously their role as teachers and developers of others.

The Denison Leadership Development Model

Based on more than 20 years of research with over 1,000 organizations and 40,000 individuals, researcher Daniel Denison concluded that effective managers are able to analyze situations from a variety of perspectives and adapt their behavior accordingly. Furthermore, they focus their attention on creating an organizational culture that inspires and enables high performance.[29] He argues that managers create effective organizational cultures by focusing on four critical areas: communicating a clear and engaging mission; ensuring consistency through clear policies, procedures, and norms; encouraging employee involvement; and promoting adaptability. He found that attention to these four areas has significant bottom-line results in terms of productivity, quality, profitability, and growth.

As you can see in Figure 6-2, effective managers focus on both the internal organization (consistency and employee involvement) and the external environment (mission and adaptability). They also promote both stability (mission and consistency) and change (employee involvement and adaptability). Each of the four critical areas is divided into three skills.

Mission

You manage things; you lead people. *Admiral Grace Murray Hopper, U.S. Navy*

Managers who communicate a clear and engaging mission know that people want purpose and meaning in their day-to-day work lives. A clear and engaging mission provides direction and makes the work worth doing. Effective managers know that every employee needs to see how he or she contributes to the organizational mission.

The three skills associated with creating a clear and engaging mission are:

- Defining strategic direction and intent by communicating the organization's long-term strategies to all employees so that everyone can see where the organization is headed, why it is going in that direction, and how they can help the organization get there.

- Focusing on goals and objectives by articulating ambitious yet realistic goals, ensuring that employees know why these goals and objectives are important, and tracking progress against these goals so that employees can see the consequences of their efforts.

- Creating shared vision by promoting an engaging view of the organization's desired future state so that employees feel excited about the future and can see the link between short-term results and achieving the long-term vision.

FIGURE 6-2 Denison Model: Linking Culture and Leadership to Performance

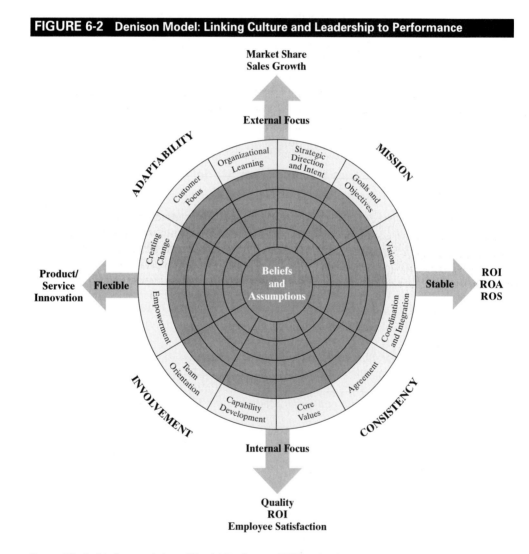

Source: Used with the permission of Daniel Denison and William Neale, creators of the Denison Leadership Development Survey. For a more in-depth look at the questions and to obtain an on-line analysis of your personal leadership style or organization culture, see www.denisonculture.com.

Consistency

Managers who promote consistency understand that employees need a sense of predictability and control in their day-to-day work lives. This is particularly important during times of change and when coordination across different parts of the organization is needed. Managers promote consistency by clearly communicating a set of values, methods for doing business, and a code of ethics that employees collectively use to support their day-to-day decisions and actions. By providing clear procedures, policies, values, and norms, effective managers promote a sense of predictability, control over the environment, a distinct way of doing business, and organization-wide coordination. The three skills associated with building consistency include:

- Defining core values by clearly communicating the organizational values and living by those values.
- Working to reach agreement among different people and parts of the organization by creating a cohesive culture, encouraging diverse opinions, supporting constructive conflict, and promoting win-win solutions.
- Managing coordination and integration by encouraging people from different parts of the organization to work together toward common organizational goals and providing a clear set of policies, procedures, and values to guide day-to-day decisions.

High Involvement

Remember that change is most successful when those who are affected are involved in the planning. *Warren Bennis, Why Leaders Can't Lead*

Managers who create high-involvement work cultures understand that employees will be more likely to invest their energy in organizations in which they feel like they have some control, opportunities for personal development, and opportunities to make an impact on the organization. These managers emphasize employee participation, autonomy, and growth, which in turn enhance employees' sense of ownership in the organization and responsibility for the organization's success. The three skills associated with creating a high-involvement work environment include:

- Empowering others by sharing information, encouraging participation in organizational decisions, and enhancing employees' belief that they personally can make a difference in the organization.
- Building a team orientation by encouraging teamwork (both within and across organizational units), cooperation toward common goals, and a sense of collective accountability for the achievement of goals.
- Developing organizational capability by investing in the ongoing development of employee knowledge and skills, delegating authority so that employees can use their skills to make and implement decisions, and viewing employees' capabilities as an important source of competitive advantage.

Adaptability

Managers who promote adaptability know that the organization's growth and survival depends on its ability to align its internal policies, practices, and norms with the external environment. Consequently, effective managers pay attention to customers, competitors, and other critical constituents—and adapt their internal policies, practices, and norms in response. The three skills associated with promoting adaptability are:

- Creating change by encouraging flexibility, responsiveness, continuous improvement, adaptability, and cooperation across organizational units.
- Emphasizing customer focus by enabling all employees to attend to customer needs, understand what customers want, and respond quickly to customer input.
- Promoting organizational learning by encouraging and rewarding innovation and risk, seeing failure as opportunity for learning, and sharing learning across organizational units.

Through his research, Denison concluded that managers who are skilled at creating mission, consistency, high-involvement, and adaptability are likely to create organizational cultures that positively influence the bottom line. All four areas are positively correlated with return on assets. Mission and consistency tend to have a positive impact on financial performance measures such as return on assets, return on investment, and return on sales. Consistency and involvement tend to have a positive impact on product and service quality (fewer defects, less rework, efficient use of resources), employee satisfaction, and return on investment. Involvement and adaptability tend to have a positive impact on creativity, innovation, product development, and adaptability. Adaptability and mission tend to have a positive impact on revenue, sales growth, and market share.

> **Routine is not organization, any more than paralysis is order.**
> *Sir Arthur Helps, English historian*

Denison's Leadership Development Model reinforces the assumption that effective managers are cognitively and behaviorally complex. That is, they are able to see the organization from a variety of perspectives, diagnose the needs of a particular situation, and adapt their behavior in response. Most importantly, the Leadership Development Model reminds managers that their effectiveness depends on their ability to create a work culture that inspires high performance. Box 6-1 provides a list of questions that you can answer to determine how well you are doing in each of the four critical areas (mission, consistency, involvement, and adaptability).

A Note on Empowerment: It's More than a Feeling

There is a lot of talk about empowerment these days, but few managers understand what it is and how they can create conditions that inspire it. When employees feel empowered, they believe that they can influence their work environment, and this belief motivates them to take actions to have an impact on their environment. Based on a review of several studies of empowerment, University of Michigan professor Gretchen Spreitzer concluded that employees who feel empowered share four beliefs:[30]

- *Meaning.* The employee believes that the job is aligned with his or her values and preferred ways of behaving.

- *Competence.*   The employee believes that he or she can effectively accomplish the tasks associated with the work role.
- *Self-determination.*   The employee believes that he or she has the freedom to make choices associated with the task and can regulate his or her own behavior.
- *Impact.*   The employee believes that he or she can influence the work environment, particularly the "strategic, administrative, or operating outcomes."[31]

Taken together, these beliefs help to create an active rather than passive orientation toward shaping their work role and organization in which the employee works.[32] Employees who feel empowered are self-motivated to perform their work to the best of their abilities and to go above and beyond the call of duty at work.

BOX 6-1

Denison's Leadership Development Model: How Effective Are You at Creating an Organizational Culture That Inspires High Performance?

This is a sample of the items that comprise the Denison Leadership Development Survey. The entire survey consists of 96 items.

MISSION TRAIT: CREATES SHARED VISION

1. I help create a shared vision of what this organization will be like in the future.
2. I translate the vision into reality in a way that helps guide individual action.
3. I encourage others in ways that ensure buy-in and commitment.

CONSISTENCY TRAIT: DEFINES CORE VALUES

1. I do the "right thing" even when it is not popular.
2. I practice what I preach.

3. I live up to my promises and commitments.

INVOLVEMENT TRAIT: EMPOWERS PEOPLE

1. I see that decisions are made at the lowest possible level.
2. I create an environment where everyone feels that his/her efforts can make a difference.
3. I delegate authority so that others can do their work more effectively.

ADAPTABILITY TRAIT: PROMOTES CUSTOMER FOCUS

1. I encourage direct contact with customers.
2. I actively seek feedback from customers.
3. I respond quickly and effectively to customer feedback.

SOURCE: Used with the permission of Daniel Denison and William Neale, creators of the Denison Leadership Development Survey. For a more in-depth look at the questions and to obtain an on-line analysis of your personal or organization's profile, see www.denisonculture.com. Reprinted with permission of Denison Consulting.

Can you empower employees? The answer is no. You can't force empowerment on anyone, but you can create conditions that increase the possibility that employees will feel empowered and behave accordingly. Spreitzer's research suggests that six conditions are likely to inspire employees' feelings of empowerment:[33]

1. ***Low role ambiguity.*** Clear boundaries, goals, and performance measures, as well as clearly defined tasks and lines of responsibility, are likely to increase employees' feelings of control over their work environment, and thus reduce feelings of insecurity and stress that can block action. Spreitzer found that this condition had the strongest relationship to feelings of empowerment.

2. ***Working for a boss who has a wide span of control.*** When a boss is responsible for managing several employees, he or she is likely to be too busy to micromanage subordinates. Consequently, employees are likely to have more freedom to make and implement decisions on their own.

3. ***Sociopolitical support.*** When employees feel like they are "integrated into the key political channels for getting work done in organizations," they feel as if they have more power to influence the organization.[34]

4. ***Access to information.*** When employees have access to information, they feel that they can make higher quality decisions and thus are more optimistic that they will succeed in their efforts to have an impact on their environment.

5. ***A participative unit climate.*** When employees believe that their opinions are sought after and valued, they feel that they can have a direct influence on their environment.

6. ***Education and training.*** When employees receive work-related training, they feel as though the organization is investing in them (and thus values them). They also are likely to feel (and be) more competent and more willing to take the risks involved in trying to influence their work environment.

Spreitzer and others have concluded that access to abundant resources is not significantly related to empowerment.[35] The stories of the humble beginnings of Apple Computer, Microsoft, and Kinko in garages and other sparse environments illustrate this point. Indeed, people who feel empowered may see lack of resources as a challenge to be overcome with ingenuity rather than a block to performance.

The ultimate test for a leader is not whether he or she makes smart decisions and takes decisive action, but whether he or she teaches others to be leaders and builds an organization that can sustain its success even when he or she is not around. Noel Tichy, "The Leadership Engine"

Who is responsible for creating conditions that inspire employees to do their best work? A Gallup Organization study of more than 100,000 employees and 2,500 business units in 24 countries found that the direct manager or supervisor, more so than the top leadership or organizational culture, influenced whether employees were committed to and added value to the organization. They also found that organizations whose employees could answer the following six questions positively were significantly more likely to have increased customer satisfaction, productivity, and profitability, as well as less turnover:[36]

"Do I know what is expected of me at work? Do I have the materials and equipment I need to do my work right? Do I have the opportunity to do what I do best every day? In the last seven days, have I received recognition

FIGURE 6-3   Dilbert Cartoon by Scott Adams

Source: Dilbert © Distributed by United Features Syndicate. Reprinted by permission.

or praise for good work? Does my supervisor, or someone at work, seem to care about me as a person? Is there someone at work who encourages my development?"

The most important point to remember from the above studies is that you cannot empower anyone. Rather, you can create conditions that are likely to help employees feel empowered, which will in turn influence their commitment to the organization and their willingness and ability to proactively try to add bottom-line value.

A CAUTIONARY NOTE: OBEDIENCE TO AUTHORITY

Most people in positions of authority (e.g., managers, teachers, and parents) spend time worrying about how they will get employees, students, and children to listen to them and obey them. Yet few people in positions of authority worry about an equally troubling problem: People are likely to obey those in positions of authority even when doing so is unethical and against their own conscience.

In the 1960s, Yale psychologist Stanley Milgram conducted one of the most well-known and disturbing experiments on human behavior. Born in 1933, Milgram grew up during World War II. Like many psychologists of his era, he wanted to understand why so many seemingly normal people were willing to follow Hitler's orders to systematically imprison and kill millions of European Jews and others who didn't fit into Hitler's vision of the ideal future. In search of an answer, Milgram conducted a series of experiments designed to understand the dynamics of obedience to authority. He described his experiment as follows:

> In order to take a close look at the act of obeying, I set up a simple experiment at Yale University. Eventually, the experiment was to involve over 1,000 participants and would be repeated at several universities, but at the beginning, the conception was simple. A person comes to a psychological laboratory and is told to carry out a series of acts that come increasingly into conflict with conscience. The main question is how far the participant will comply with the experimenter's instructions before refusing to carry out the actions required.[37]

Milgram recruited about 1,000 participants through newspaper advertisements and direct mail solicitation. Upon entering the laboratory, each recruit met an "experimenter" and another "recruit" who was waiting to participate in the experiment. The "experimenter" wore a professional-looking gray lab coat when he greeted the participants and told them that they would be participating in a study on memory and learning. What the recruit who responded to the advertisement or direct mail solicitation didn't know was that the other recruit and the experimenter were confederates of the experiment. The confederate recruit was a 47-year-old white male accountant of Irish American descent who was trained to act out his role in a mild-mannered and likable way. The experimenter was a 31-year-old high school teacher who was trained to act stern and impartial. The real purpose of the study was to determine how many of the actual recruits would obey the experimenter's requests to inflict harm on another human being against that person's will.

The experimenter told the naive recruit and the confederate recruit that one person would be the "teacher" in the experiment and the other would be the "learner." Unknown to the naive recruits, they were always given the role of the teacher, and the confederate recruit was always given the role of the learner. The experimenter then told the naive teacher and the learner that the teacher's goal was to test the learner's memorization of a series of word pairs (such as "blue box" and "nice day"). For example, the teacher was to say the world "blue," and the learner was supposed to respond with the word "box." If the learner gave the correct answer, the teacher would move on to the next word pair. If the learner gave the wrong answer (e.g., if the learner said "blue sky" when the correct answer was "blue box"), the teacher was supposed to punish the learner by subjecting him to increasingly intensive electrical shocks.

After describing the teacher's duties, the experimenter brought the teacher and learner to a small windowless room where the learner would stay during the experiment. He then showed the teacher and learner a "shock machine" that was designed to give the learner the electrical shocks. He seated the learner in a chair, strapped his arms to a machine to "prevent excessive movement," and attached an electrode to the learner's wrist. The experimenter then took the teacher to another room and showed him an impressive "shock generator" that had "a horizontal line of 30 switches, ranging from 15 volts to 450 volts, in 15-volt increments." Each switch was labeled with a verbal designation ranging from "slight shock" to "danger—severe shock." The experimenter then told the teacher to quickly move on to the next question whenever the learner gave a correct answer. When the learner made a mistake, the teacher was to give the learner a shock by pushing the appropriate switch on the shock generator, beginning with the lowest shock level and then increasing the shock level with each successive mistake. The experimenter then gave the teacher a sample shock so that the teacher could experience what the shocks would feel like to the learner.

Unknown to the teacher, the learner wasn't really going to receive electrical shocks. Instead, the learner (confederate of the experiment) was pretending to receive the shocks. The learner gave approximately three wrong answers for each correct answer and had the same programmed response for each level of shock for each experiment. For example, the learner grunted at 75 volts, complained that the shocks were getting painful at 120 volts, groaned in pain at 135 volts, demanded to be released from the experiment at 150 volts, said "I can't stand the pain" at 180 volts, screamed out in pain at 270 volts, stated he would no longer respond to questions at 300 volts, shouted

"Let me out of here, my heart's bothering me" at 330 volts, and gave no response at all after 330 volts.[38]

   When Milgram asked a group of psychiatrists to predict at what level of shock the teacher would refuse to continue with the experiment, the psychiatrists predicted that most teachers would stop at 150 volts (the point at which the learner began demanding to be released). They also predicted that less than one-tenth of a percent of the subjects would shock the learner up to the maximum 450 volts. However, approximately 65 percent of the teachers continued to shock the learner up to 450 volts. The mean maximum shock level was 350 volts, and the earliest break-off point was 135 volts. Why were so many of the teachers willing to subject the learner to painful and potentially dangerous shocks at the request of an experimenter? Milgram offered this explanation:

> A commonly offered explanation is that those who shocked the victim at the most severe level were monsters, the sadistic fringe of society. But if one considers that almost two-thirds of the participants fall into the category of "obedient" subjects, and that they represented "ordinary" people drawn from working, managerial, and professional classes, the argument becomes very shaky.... This is, perhaps, the most fundamental lesson of our study: Ordinary people, simply doing their jobs, and without any particular hostility on their part, can become agents in a terribly destructive process. Moreover, even when the destructive effects of their work become patently clear, and they are asked to carry out actions incompatible with fundamental standards of morality, relatively few people have the resources needed to resist authority."[39]

Courage is at bottom the capacity and process of maintaining one's identity and values in the face of psychic challenge. *Peter Vaill citing Paul Tillich*

Remember that the scientist used no coercive power (such as threats of punishment) to ensure the teacher's obedience. He simply explained the experiment and the participant roles and then urged the teacher to continue to perform the task with polite but firm and impassive statements such as "The experiment must go on," "Continue, teacher," "It is absolutely essential that you continue," and "You have no other choice, you must continue." He also provided assurances that "although the shocks may be painful, there is no permanent tissue damage."[40] Milgram and other researchers suggest that subtle but very powerful forces were at play:

- *Trappings of legitimacy.* The experiment looked legitimate. The language of "scientific experiment" was trustworthy. The "experimenter," always a Caucasian male in Milgram's experiments, wore a lab coat, and spoke with authority. The laboratory was clean and professional-looking.
- *Emphasis on technical rather than human aspects of the interaction.* The experimenter repeatedly emphasized the technical aspects of the "procedure" and encouraged the "teacher" to carry out the procedures as quickly as possible. The "experimenter" also depersonalized the learner by always referring to him as "learner" and never by his name. By assuming an unemotional demeanor and focusing on procedures, the experimenter reduced the interactions to a technique rather than a human interaction with consequences.
- *Abdication of personal responsibility.* One of the most poignant interactions in the series of experiments was when one of the "teachers" hesitated

before shocking the distraught learner and asked the "experimenter" who would take responsibility if anything happened to the learner. When the "experimenter" responded, "I will take responsibility," the teacher continued to shock the learner as instructed. Later analysis showed that teachers who administered the lowest shock levels were more likely to believe that they, not the "learner" or "experimenter," were more responsible for their actions. The teachers most likely to resist increasing the shocks felt that they had personal responsibility for their behavior.

- *Group dynamics.* In a variation of the study, Milgram found that "teachers" were more inclined to participate in shocking the learner if they were playing a subsidiary role in a group (e.g., if another "teacher" actually pushed the lever on the shock machine while the subject stood by). Milgram also found that teachers were more likely to refuse to obey if others in the group refused to obey.

- *Closeness to authority figure and victim.* In other variations of the study, Milgram found that the farther away the "experimenter" was from the "teachers," the less likely they were to obey him. For example, obedience declined substantially when the "experimenter" gave his orders from a different room. Milgram also found that the closer the "teacher" was to the "learner," the less likely the teacher was to comply with the experimenter's orders.

- *Cultural norms.* One study conducted with Australian citizens found a significantly lower rate of obedience (28 percent) than Milgram found with his U.S. subjects (62.5 percent). The researcher suggested that this difference may reflect "national differences in obedience ideology that contribute to a predisposition to obey or defy authority."[41]

- *Personality.* Some researchers argue that personality characteristics and "enduring beliefs" may play a role in obedience to authority.[42] These characteristics include social intelligence, tendencies toward hostility, attitudes toward authority figures, internal versus external locus of control, and degree of belief in scientific authority.

Researcher Thomas Blass suggests that self-awareness can lessen the risk that someone may blindly follow authority down a path that goes against their conscience. He explains:

> The conditions that prevail within the setting of a Milgram obedience experiment are typically conducive of an inhibition of self-awareness, rather than enhancement of it. The subject's attention is focused outward rather than inward, absorbed in the mechanical details of the procedure. In fact ... [t]he considerable amount of physical activity to work a shock machine might actually artificially depress the subject's self-awareness ... Also drawing attention away from the self is the subject's attunement to the experimenter's commands and to the learners' answers and complaints. .... Features of the typical Milgram-type obedience experiment are anything but promotive of self-awareness.[43]

Lessons for Everyday Work Life

The most important lesson of the Milgram experiments is that each of us may be more prone to obey the orders of a legitimate authority than we think we are. Situational pressures, such as the presence of authority figures, symbols of legitimacy, organizational routines, and the actions of our peers, can exert significant influence on our behavior. Fortunately, there are people who resist and do the right thing when faced with unethical and immoral situations. There are also leaders who ensure that their employees have the courage to question them on organization policies when they are headed down the wrong path. Undoubtedly, there are actions that you can take to minimize the risk of blind obedience to authority. For example, when you are in a position of authority, assume that people will take your authority and the authority of the organization seriously. In other words, be careful of what you ask people to do (or what followers may think you want them to do even if you haven't asked them to do so explicitly) because they may do it, even if it is unethical, illegal, or goes against their conscience. Indeed, researchers have found that "the behavior of one's superiors is among the strongest influences on ethical behavior, playing a larger role than the behavior of peers or even one's personal ethical frameworks."[44] In addition, you can:

- Keep the trappings of authority at a minimum.
- Regularly encourage employees to speak their mind and question the status quo.
- Reward employees when they challenge and resist what they perceive to be troublesome requests or behaviors. Reward small acts of courage so that employees will be more likely to engage in large acts of courage when necessary.
- Create a work context that promotes self-awareness.

When you are in a subordinate position:

- Be aware of your own attitudes toward authority and how they may influence your behavior. Remember that authority figures are fallible human beings and that you have more choices in any given situation than may immediately seem obvious.
- Recognize that when it comes to immoral acts, you—not anyone else (not a leader or organization)—are responsible for your behavior.
- Prime yourself to be ready to leave or expose a morally questionnable situation. Reading this section of this book, as well as reading "Bad Apples and Bad Barrels" in Box 6-2 will help you recognize situations that become slippery slopes into moral decline.
- When you find yourself in a morally questionable situation, try to get yourself a peer who will join you in resistence. People are more likely to resist when others are doing so as well.
- If possible, distance yourself from the situation to get perspective. Make sure that you have "walk money." A former MBA student once told me that she always had money in the bank so that she could walk away from any job if she felt it was necessary.
- Practice small acts of courage. Says Professor Peter Vaill, "Courage is at bottom the capacity and process of maintaining one's identity and values in the face of psychic challenge. . . . [I]f one has not made a habit of turning toward a situation courageously, no matter how small and mundane, one will not know how to turn toward the big situations courageously."[45]

Notably, Milgram has been widely praised for the profound insights his experiment offers into human behavior. He also has been widely criticized for conducting an

BOX 6-2

Bad Apples and Bad Barrels

When the images of the horrific abuse by U.S. military personnel at Abu Ghraib prison in the aftermath of the 2003 Iraq War emerged in 2004, people worldwide were appalled. Yet psychologists, though appalled, were not surprised. Experiments (and historical events) repeatedly have shown that, regardless of nationality, normal human beings, when placed in certain contexts, will engage in abusive behaviors that they would not otherwise do.

For example, in August 1971, Stanford psychologist Philip Zimbardo conducted the now-famous prison experiment in which he recruited male college students from various colleges to participate in a prison simulation for which the students would receive $15 per day. The recruits were given personality tests, and the experimenters selected twenty-one students who they considered to be normal and healthy. Through a random selection process, twelve students were chosen to act as guards and nine were chosen to act as prisoners. The guards were given mirrored sun glasses, khaki uniforms, a whistle, and sticks. The prisoners were picked up at their homes by Palo Alto police, handcuffed, deloused, forced to wear prison outfits and chains, and brought to the makeshift prison in a Stanford University basement.

Zimbardo's original purpose was to study the "prisoners," but his interest soon shifted to the "guards" as they quickly began abusing the prisoners. The guards began to use the prisoners as playthings for their amusement, especially as they became increasingly bored and at night when they thought they weren't being observed. They amused themselves in several ways, including stripping the prisoners, putting them in solitary confinement, putting bags over their heads, sexually humiliating them, waking them up repeatedly in the middle of the night, and degrading them in a variety of other ways. Although the experiment was scheduled to last for two weeks, Zimbardo cancelled it after six days because the guards' abuse and prisoners' distress escalated to unpredicted levels. Zimbardo explains that he stopped the experiment after Christina Maslach, a recently graduated Ph.D., visited the simulated prison and strongly protested against continuing the experiment. Zimbardo notes that she was the only visitor out of 50, including a priest, who had asked to stop the experiment. He also notes that he, too, found himself thoroughly engaged in his role as scientific researcher and thus didn't stop the experiment earlier.

experiment that may have had troubling consequences for the people who participated in the study, particularly those who learned that they were willing to inflict harm on another human being against his will. Some people have argued that Milgram's well-intended willingness to put the "teachers" through significant psychological trauma illustrated his own theory of obedience to authority. Simply stated, even scientists may engage in unethical behaviors in the service of science. In the 1970s, the American Psychological Association instituted national guidelines to protect research subjects from intended or unintended negative consequences of experiments. The Milgram experiment, as designed in the 1960s, does not meet those guidelines.

Zimbardo concluded that the demands of the situation in the prison experiment were more powerful than the personalities of the students involved. After the abuses at Abu Ghraib prison were exposed, Zimbardo argued that, even though we'd like to think more kindly of human nature, the abuses were practically inevitable because the situation was conducive to bringing out the worst in guards. Zimbardo identified the following precipitating conditions: Secrecy, dehumanization of the prisoners, lack of accountability from top down, vague or changing rules, lack of standard operating procedures or lack of enforcement of those that existed, ambiguous requests from authorities, a seemingly legitimizing ideology, lack of proper training of the guards, diffusion of responsibility, obedience to authority, few visits by senior leaders to the site, a "lack of supervision that conveys a sense of permissiveness," a few bad apples who act as role models to others, subtle social pressure to conform, bystanders who chose not to intervene, and significant power differentials. When these conditions are present, says Zimbardo, "hell becomes the ordinary situation"—so ordinary that prison guards felt comfortable taking photos of their abuse, often with the guards looking into the camera and smiling in the background.

This experiment, as well as historical events, teach us that we must recognize the power of the situation to bring out not only the best in us, but the worst in us as well—regardless of our gender, nationality, or religious orientation. If we changed the guards in the Zimbardo experiment or Abu Ghraib prison, it is likely that some of those who took their place would have acted abusive as well because the conditions created a context that was likely to bring out the worst in many people. This doesn't absolve individuals of personal responsibility for their actions, but Zimbardo warns that it is misleading to assume that the problem was caused by a few "rotten apples" rather than a "rotten barrel." Note also that there were some people who resisted and reported the abuses at Abu Ghraib prison, and these people illustrate that just as some individuals fall into abusive behaviors under certain conditions, others develop the courage to resist.

To see slides and text by Zimbardo describing the 1971 Stanford Prison experiment, go to http://www.prisonexp.org./links.htm.

SOURCE: Zimbardo, Philip. 2004. "Power Turns Good Soldiers Into Bad Apples." May 9. http://users.crocker.com/~afsc/statements/APPLES.HTML; "Stanford Prison Experiment Foretold Iraq Scandal." 2004. May 8. www.religionnewsblog.com; Stanford Prison Experiment. 2004. www.prisonexp.org/links.htm; "Why Did They Do It? Are Those Charged with Abuse a Few Bad Apples, or Are They Just Like the Rest of Us?" *Time.* May 17; O'Connor, Anahad. 2004. "Pressure to Go Along with the Abuse Is Strong, but Some Soldiers Find the Strength to Refuse." *New York Times.* May 14.

MANAGING YOUR BOSS

Your relationship with your boss plays a critical role in your task effectiveness, performance ratings, career progress, and psychological well-being.[46] Although most people take it for granted that it is the boss's job to manage employees, fewer people realize that it's equally important for employees to manage their boss. When they do realize the importance of managing their boss, their strategy is often one of "cautious adaptation."[47]

Why is managing up so important? It is not only important to you in terms of your effectiveness, promotions, salary, and well-being, but it's important to your boss and the people who work for you as well. Your boss *needs* you to give him or her information, advice, and support in order to make the right decisions and achieve organizational goals. Your employees *need* you to manage your boss so that they can get the information, support, and resources they need to do their best work, and so that they can get the visibility and credibility they need for their own career advancement. In short, by proactively managing your boss, you increase your ability, your boss's ability, and your employees' ability to achieve results.

In her book *The Secret Handshake: Mastering the Politics of the Business Inner Circle*, researcher Kathleen Kelly Reardon profiles Beth Klein, vice president and general manager of General Electric's nuclear medicine systems business:

> As a leader, you have to pick the best people and give them the tools to be successful and help them realize their dreams . . . so it's my responsibility to get visibility for my team at the senior management level. To ensure this, Ms. Klein, who overseas several hundred employees in the U.S., France, Sweden, and Israel, stays in close communication with her direct reports. Each Friday, her top managers e-mail her notes about competitive gains or improvements that they have achieved that week. She in turn consolidates their reports into a "global weekly highlights" e-mail, which she then shares with her superiors, as well as her far-flung employees. "It's a way for me to keep in touch and to let them know how we are doing." Every time she is assigned a new boss, she tries to determine exactly what method of communication he or she prefers—and she advises junior managers on her staff to do the same. "I tell them to sit down and have a discussion about how to best communicate and when," she says, "Some bosses prefer very regular communications while others prefer to be contacted only with specific problems."

Unfortunately, many employees believe that there is little that they can do to influence their boss directly, so they use indirect means. They try to guess what the boss wants, bend over backward to try to please the boss, or keep a low profile to avoid the boss. These self-protective strategies rarely bring out the best in the boss-subordinate relationship. Instead, these strategies are likely to detract from the task, inhibit honest communication, and hinder upward feedback.[48]

These self-protective strategies are not surprising. In an organizational hierarchy, it is easy for subordinates to forget the power that they have in the relationship. Bosses need employees' talent and support to accomplish their goals. After all, the boss, the subordinate, and the organization gain from high-quality boss-subordinate relationships that are based on high levels of trust, communication, and interaction between the manager and subordinate.[49] Thus, it makes sense to manage your relationship with your boss in a way that benefits you, your boss, and the organization.

The first step toward managing your boss is to understand your own attitudes toward authority and how these attitudes may help or hinder your relationship with your boss. For example, do you tend to have an interdependent, dependent, or counterdependent attitude toward authority, and what are the consequences on the effectiveness of the relationship? The next step toward managing your boss is to answer the questions in Box 6-3 to identify areas in your relationship with your boss that need improvement. The third step, of course, is to change your behaviors based on your assessment so that you and your boss can enjoy a more productive relationship.

BOX 6-3

How Effective Are You at Managing Your Boss?[50]

To see how well you are managing your boss, answer the following questions:

1. Do I know my boss's goals?

2. Do I give the boss what he or she needs to achieve these goals?

3. Do I know my boss's preferred styles of working, and do I adapt my behavior accordingly? For example, is my boss a reader (someone who prefers to receive information in writing) or a listener (someone who prefers to receive information face-to-face)?[51]

4. Do I know my boss's strengths and weaknesses so that I can build on the strengths and compensate for the weaknesses?

5. Does my boss trust me? In other words, have I built a reputation for being honest, loyal, and dependable?

6. Do I keep the boss informed of important information and events so that he or she is never taken by surprise?

7. Do I show appreciation to the boss when appropriate?

8. Do I use the boss's time and resources sensibly?

9. Do I help the boss look good in the eyes of others?

10. Do I tell the boss what my goals, wants, and needs are and what I need to be successful in my job and career?

SOURCE: Adapted from Drucker, Peter. 1986. "How to Manage the Boss." *The Wall Street Journal* August 1; Gabarro, John, and John Kotter. 1993. "Managing Your Boss." *Harvard Business Review*, 150–157; Randall, Iris. 1992. "How to Manage Your Boss." *Black Enterprise* September: 86–92.

Managing Abrasive Bosses

Although most of us have been blessed with one or more wonderful bosses during our career, most of us also have faced the agony of working with a boss who behaves badly. Indeed, in their study of the developmental experiences of successful executives, researchers Michael Lombardo, Morgan McCall, and Ann Morrison found that most of these executives had worked for a bad boss at one time or another, and these executives viewed their experience with a troublesome boss as important to their professional growth.[52]

In March 2001, for example, the president of Cerner Corporation, Kansas-based supplier of health care information technology, sent the following e-mail to 400 managers:

> We are getting less than 40 hours of work from a large number of EMPLOYEES. The parking lot is sparsely used at 8am; likewise at 5pm. As managers, you either do not know what your EMPLOYEES are doing or you do not CARE. You have created expectations of the work effort which allowed this to happen inside Cerner, creating a very unhealthy environment. In either case, you have a problem and you will fix it or I will replace you. NEVER in my career have I allowed a team which worked for me to think they had a 40-hour job. I have allowed YOU to create a culture which is permitting this. NO LONGER.

Says the Bully Online Web site (http://www.bullyonline.org/news/usnews.htm), "His tirade continued, adding that hell would freeze over before he increased employee benefits. He wanted to see the car park nearly full by 7:30 A.M. and half full at weekends. The missive concluded, 'You have two weeks. Tick Tock.' " Cerner's stock fell 22 percent after a manager who received the e-mail posted it on Yahoo. The company president promptly apologized, beginning his e-mail this way, "Please treat this memo with the utmost confidentiality. It is for internal dissemination only. Do not copy or e-mail to anyone else."

There are many ways in which bosses can behave badly, but I will focus on the highly authoritarian and abrasive boss. These bosses have been described as "psycho-bosses from hell,"[53] organizational vampires who "suck the life blood out of the organization,"[54] Dr. Jekyll and Mr. Hyde personalities whose erratic behavior can drive employees crazy,[55] "toxic bosses," and "petty tyrants" who micromanage and belittle employees.[56] Although these characterizations may seem extreme, they represent an intimidating managerial style built on the abuse of power. Whether loud and in-your-face forceful or low key and simmering with intensity, authoritarian and abrasive bosses share several characteristics. Researcher Blake Ashforth offers the following profile:

> Recurring elements appear to include close supervision, distrust and suspicion, cold and impersonal interactions, severe and public criticism of others' character and behavior, condescending and patronizing behavior, emotional outbursts, coercion, and boastful behavior; they suggest an individual who emphasizes authority and status differences, is rigid and inflexible, makes arbitrary decisions, takes credit for the efforts of others and blames them for mistakes, fails to consult with others or keep them informed, discourages informal interaction among subordinates, obstructs their development, and deters initiative and dissent. Pervasive themes in these descriptions are a tendency to overcontrol others and to treat them in an arbitrary, uncaring, and punitive manner.[57]

I have learned silence from the talkative, toleration from the intolerant; and kindness from the unkind; yet strange, I am grateful to these teachers.
Kahlil Gibran, Lebanese novelist

Their hallmark characteristic is that they tend to lack empathy and believe that employees cannot be trusted. This characteristic is illustrated by the story of a manager who "demanded that employees taking time off for funerals show a copy of the obituary to verify their relationship to the deceased."[58] Abrasive bosses usually believe that employees are not motivated or capable of doing their job well, and so must be carefully supervised, controlled, and forced into obedience. It is not surprising that their bad behavior tends to escalate during times of stress such as deadlines and crises.[59]

Psychiatrist Harry Levinson says that abrasive bosses often are technically very capable, action-oriented, and achievement-driven. Consequently, organizational leaders often tolerate their interpersonal shortcomings. But this tolerance is costly.[60] Employees who feel abused by their boss report greater dissatisfaction with their jobs and life, greater psychological distress, and greater intentions to leave their job. They are also less likely to engage in organizational citizenship behaviors—going above and beyond the call of duty—that organizations depend on to achieve their goals.[61] Feelings of fear can discourage employees' creativity and initiative, minimize risk taking, decrease information flow (especially to the petty tyrant who needs information to make effective decisions), suppress healthy conflict, hinder task performance, inhibit cooperation among employees and across departments, and increase employee absenteeism.[62] Furthermore, abusive bosses can be lawsuits waiting to happen.

The petty tyrant can make employees nervous and more prone to mistakes and accidents. For example, in a study of airline flight crew performance, researchers found that the crews made fewer mistakes when their captains were "warm, friendly, self confident, and able to stand up to pressure (i.e., agreeable and emotionally stable)" and made more mistakes when their captains were "arrogant, hostile, boastful, egotistical, passive aggressive, or dictatorial."[63]

Although authoritarian and abrasive bosses often see themselves as perfectionists who only want what's best for the organization, their behavior tends to cause many of the problems they claim they want to solve.

> **Seagull manager: A manager who flies in, makes a lot of noise, dumps over everything, and then leaves.**
> *From www.lc21.com/ humor10.html*

Why do abrasive bosses act the way that they do? Research suggests that abrasive bosses may have had childhood difficulties that resulted in problems with self-esteem and self-confidence, lack of trust in others, lack of impulse control, lack of empathy, and high needs for control.[64] Research also suggests that people with an authoritarian personality tend to be domineering, rigid, impersonal, focused on status, and prefer strict adherence to policies.[65] Some abrasive bosses act the way that they do because their behavior is consistent with that of the organizational culture. After all, it's hard to swim with the sharks over a long period of time without becoming one in the process.

> **Given a choice of being effective or being in control, most of us choose being in control.**
> *Robert Quinn, Change the World*

What can you do if you have a bad boss? You're not going to ask your boss if he or she grew up in a dysfunctional family. You're not a psychologist, and it's really none of your business. You're going to have to deal with the boss's current behaviors with the best tools you have—your self-awareness and social skills.

Before focusing on the boss, you need to think first about yourself. Have all your bosses been jerks? If you have never had a good boss, then it is likely that you are part of the problem. Perhaps your attitude or behavior brings out the worst in bosses. Maybe you have an unrealistic expectation of what your bosses can and should do for you, in which case they are guaranteed to disappoint you. Maybe you developed a counterdependent attitude toward authority early in life and carry that attitude of distrust of authority into your adult relationships with bosses at work. Maybe you're bashing the boss to relieve stress, but this can be a problem if it undermines your relationship with your boss.

Let's say that your boss is indeed abrasive, and you are not a significant cause of his or her behavior. Even if you're not part of the problem, you can be part of the solution. Remember that your relationship with your boss is built on mutual dependence, and you have some power to influence the situation.[66] Also remember that you can't change another person, but you can change yourself (which may inspire the other to change). Most importantly, remember to never let your boss "take away your dignity and self-respect."[67] To help improve your relationship with a troubling boss, first answer the questions in Box 6-3, and then consider the following strategies:

- *Analyze the situation.* Does the boss act badly primarily with you (in which case it's probably personal) or with all employees? Is the problem really the boss, or might it be that the boss is simply following organizational policies or procedures? Is it possible that your boss is socially inept but is well intentioned, technically competent, and has no ill will toward you or others?

What specifically makes the boss angry or stessed? Your analysis of the situation will influence your strategy to improve the relationship.

- *Get clear expectations.*   Together with your boss, identify goals, quality standards, and performance measures.
- *Keep careful records.*   Document the goals, quality standards, performance measures, and requests that your boss has made so that you both can refer to them to evaluate your performance. Also document any contributions you have made to the department or organization, including quantifiable data, employee and customer comments, and 360-degree feedback results. Keep records of any abusive behavior from your boss. Some of this behavior, such as sexual harassment or other discriminatory practices, may be illegal.
- *Look for something good in your boss.*   Inside a rough exterior, you may find a gem of a human being. Perhaps your boss has great technical skills, brings in a lot of business, or tenderly takes care of his or her elderly parents. Remember that most difficult bosses welcome any appreciation and kindness you show toward them because they probably don't get a lot of positive interpersonal feedback.
- *Determine your boss's goals, needs, wants, styles, and pressures, and adapt accordingly.*   What can you do to adapt to your boss's style? What do you have in common with your boss that you can build on? What can you offer the boss that is of value to him or her? What do you do that may annoy the boss?
- *Create and celebrate small wins.*   Look for small opportunities for you and your boss to succeed together—creating an outstanding report or presentation, getting a new client, or developing a new strategy. When you succeed together, take time to acknowledge your joint success. Doing so reminds your boss that you are loyal and capable, that he or she can count on you, and that the two of you make an effective team.
- *Ask friends and colleagues how to handle your relationship with your boss.* People who have developed a good relationship with the difficult boss can be particularly helpful. Learn what you can do to help the boss see you as a competent ally.
- *"Don't invest your ego in the relationship.*   Don't look for empathy, interest in your life, or praise. You won't get it," says Michael Maccoby, author of *The Productive Narcissist: The Promise and Peril of Visionary Leadership.*[68]
- *Confront your boss.*   If you decide to challenge your boss, do it professionally. When planning your strategy, be clear about what you want to accomplish from the meeting and what you need from the boss. Remember to consider the boss's goals and style, and have data available to support your concerns.
- *Learn a lesson.*   If you cannot improve your relationship with a difficult boss, then think of your experiences with this boss as an education in persistence, stress management, how to deal with conflict, and how not to treat people.[69]
- *If all else fails, leave.*   Always keep your resume updated, your network in place, and money in the bank so that you can leave your job. Before you accept a new job, pay attention to the potential new boss's character. *Wall Street Journal* columnist Susan Shellenbarger suggests that, when considering a new position, you should ask people what it's like to work for the boss. Does the boss have a reputation as a people developer? Do employees seem

intimidated? Is there a lot of turnover in that boss's area? How does this manager work in a crisis or under stress?[70]

- *Be creative.* There's a story about an employee who was very frustrated with her intolerable boss. When a headhunter called the employee to see if she was interested in a promotion in a new company, the employee said that she wasn't interested at the time, but that her boss might be. The headhunter called the boss, the boss took the job, and the employee was promoted to her boss's job.
- *Have empathy for the boss.* Psychologist Harry Levinson says that the sad truth is that, sooner or later, the problem may solve itself because bosses with abrasive personalities are "vulnerable to coronaries," and your boss's behavior—particularly hostility—may cause his or her own demise.[71]

You do not lead by hitting people over the head. That's assault, not leadership. *Dwight D. Eisenhower*

Finally, while you are thinking about your own bad boss, it's a good time to ask yourself if you are a difficult boss. Psychologist Marty Grothe explains that although most of us complain about our bad bosses, few of us think about how we may be a burden to our own subordinates.[72]

MANAGING MENTOR-PROTÉGÉ RELATIONSHIPS

Mentoring is the process by which a person with more experience (a mentor) consciously helps a person with less experience (a protégé) achieve his or her professional goals. Researchers Kathy Kram and Lynn Isabella explain that mentors help protégés by offering two kinds of support:[73]

> *Instrumental support.* This includes helping protégés develop their technical and political skills, providing opportunities for challenging and high-visibility assignments, providing feedback on performance, role-modeling appropriate attitudes and behaviors, connecting protégés to people who can help their careers, and protecting protégés from people and situations that can hurt their careers.
>
> *Psychosocial support.* This includes providing emotional support, giving career advice, inviting protégés to informal social activities (such as lunch, dinner, or tennis), and helping protégés manage the stresses of everyday work life. Psychosocial support is critical because it influences the protégés' self-esteem, self-confidence, and motivation, which in turn influences the protégés' effectiveness.[74]

I've had a lot of experience with people smarter than I am. *Gerald Ford, Former U.S. president*

Both mentors and protégés gain from mentoring relationships. Mentors benefit from the increasing effectiveness of the protégés, the organizational insights and information that protégés provide, and the protégés' increasing power and influence. Mentors also benefit from the personal satisfaction that comes from helping others and gaining a reputation for being effective people developers.[75] Research suggests that employees who have mentors are more likely to have greater self-confidence, more influence over organizational policies, more access to important people and organizational resources, higher salaries, more promotions, greater job mobility, and more satisfaction with their jobs and careers.[76]

This does not mean that people who don't have dedicated mentor relationships can't reap the same organizational advantages; however, mentors can make some advantages easier and faster to come by. Harvard professor Linda Hill argues that most employees do not have mentors, and those who do soon realize that their mentors cannot solve all of their career problems.[77] In her study of new managers' experiences during their first year on the job, Hill found that few of the new managers "relied on their current bosses as resources" during that time, perhaps because they wanted their boss to perceive them as competent, and they didn't want their bosses to know that they needed help.[78] Indeed, for most of these new managers, peers tended to be the greatest source of support.

Indeed, researchers are finding that the most successful people do not depend on one or two mentors, but instead develop a network of mentors, including peers, who provide different kinds of support. Today, many researchers are shifting their focus from the mentor-protégé relationship to how people develop and use a "developmental network" in which several people take "an active interest in and action to advance the protégé's career by providing developmental assistance." From this viewpoint, mentors are not only found in higher levels of the organization, but in friendship networks and advice networks that span all levels of the organization, as well as sources external to the organization. Researchers Monica Higgins and Kathy Kram point out that people who proactively develop a network of developmental relationships are likely to benefit in the areas of career change, personal learning (e.g., learning about oneself, one's professional identity, and what one needs to do to achieve one's goals), organizational commitment, and work satisfaction.[79]

Mentoring relationships, like all relationships, carry risks as well as benefits. Mentors may take unfair advantage of their protégés or feel threatened by their protégés' increasing skill and influence. They also may invest too much time in their protégés and ignore the needs of other employees who also need their help.[80] Protégés may become overdependent on their mentors and may be perceived by others as being unable to stand alone (known as the "sidekick" effect).[81] Protégés also may fail to develop other relationships that are important to their effectiveness and success. And their reputations may be harmed if their mentors get caught in political battles, fall out of favor, or leave the organization (known as the "guilt by association" effect).[82]

Recent research has found that "bad mentoring may be worse than no mentoring at all" and may negatively affect the protégé's self-esteem, reduce job satisfaction, increase stress, increase absenteeism, and inspire the protégé to quit. Understanding the consequences of poor mentoring is important because many organizations are instituting formal mentoring programs in which mentors and protégés are matched by the organization. In some of these cases, the mentor may not want the mentoring role, may not be trained in appropriate mentoring practices, may be out of touch with the issues faced by the employee, or may have dysfunctional behaviors (e.g., may be tyrannical, selfish, deceitful, manipulative, or sabotaging) that inhibit rather than support the protégé's development.[83–84]

It is not surprising that building a network of developmental relationships can minimize many of these risks.

Diversity and Mentoring

Mentoring relationships that cross cultural groups, such as gender, race, and nationality, are often more complex than mentoring relationships in which the mentor and protégé belong to similar cultural groups. The challenges that mentors and protégés with different cultural identities (e.g., race, gender, or nationality) face can make these relationships more enjoyable, result in greater learning for both the mentor and protégé, and inspire pride in overcoming any real or perceived challenges associated with such mentoring relationships. Furthermore, people who are in the minority at managerial levels can benefit from mentors from the dominant cultural group who help them overcome the emotional and structural barriers to advancement.[85] When mentors and protégés manage their relationship effectively, they enhance their reputations as effective managers of diversity and serve as role models for the rest of the organization.

Research suggests that cross-gender, cross-race, and cross-national mentoring relationships may be more difficult to develop. Human beings tend to feel more attracted to, more positively toward, and more comfortable with people whom they perceive to be similar to themselves (known as the similarity-attraction effect).[86] Researcher Stacy Blake-Beard, in her research on male mentors and female protégés, explains that perceived similarity "provides a foundation for identification to occur between mentor and protégé. Identification is the process by which the mentor is able to see something of himself in the protégé that he would like to nurture and support; the protégé also sees something in the mentor that she would like to role model and emulate." Blake-Beard advises mentors and protégés to look below surface differences and identify "deep-level" similarities such as values, attitudes, knowledge, and skills. Identifying similarities is important because, as Blake-Beard notes, "past studies have found that attitudinal similarity has been associated with higher group cohesiveness, satisfaction, performance ratings, and pay ratings," as well as a "catalyst for effective communication."[87] In addition, identifying and building on other surface-level similarities such as having grown up in the same part of the country, having attended the same college, having some common interests, or having some of the same acquaintences can build attraction.[88] And showing ability and a track record of success are important ways to attract a mentor.[89]

When similarities are not identified and built on, there can be several consequences. Potential mentors and protégés may find it difficult to identify with and trust each other because of real or perceived differences in values, life styles, and organizational experiences. Consequently, they may consciously or unconsciously avoid developing a mentoring relationship with each other.[90] When they do engage in a mentoring relationship, they may be less likely to initiate conversations with each other, confide in each other, spend time together, and have confidence in each other.[91] They also may be excessively cautious with each other. For example, the mentor may be overly concerned about being politically correct and fail to give the protégé critical feedback. The protégé, on the other hand, may attribute critical feedback to the mentor's stereotypes or attitudes toward the protégé's identity group rather than as a helpful critique of the protégé's work performance.

Furthermore, protégés may find it difficult to view mentors from a different gender, race, or nationality as role models. Mentors may find it difficult to give protégés the psychosocial support that can enhance the protégés' self-esteem, confidence, and motivation.[92] Consequently, protégés who are of different race, gender, or nationality than their mentor often must get their role-modeling and psychosocial needs met elsewhere.[93] Indeed, research suggests that cross-race and cross-gender developmental relationships are more likely to be "sponsor" relationships that provide primarily instrumental support rather than "mentor" relationships that provide both instrumental and psychosocial support.[94]

Cross-race and cross-gender mentoring relationships may also be subject to more intense public scrutiny, as well as rumors, sexual innuendo, and claims of reverse discrimination.[95] Finally, when there are relatively few women and people of color in higher organizational levels, the few who are in these positions may be expected to be mentors, sponsors, and role models to the other women and people of color coming up the ranks. This can create an additional burden of responsibility on women and people of color, distract them from their other responsibilities, create excessively high expectations of them, and reinforce stereotypes that they are helpful primarily to women and people of color rather than to all employees.[96] When asked if she feels an "obligation to be a role model for other women," Donna Dubinsky, former president and CEO of Palm Computing, who is credited with being "the marketing brain behind the Palm-Pilot," responded:

> I like being a role model to a certain extent. But what I try to do is to be very successful and [have] very high integrity and [be] a real contributor to my field. By doing so I believe that it sets an example for other women that they too can achieve that. That's what it means to be a role model, as opposed to the idea that I have an obligation to help every person who comes through the door who happens to be a woman. I'm going to help the high performers in my organization, men and women alike.[97]

How to Make the Most of Mentoring Relationships

Like all effective professional relationships, successful mentor-protégé relationships are built on trust and respect between two imperfect human beings who have multiple demands on their time. Furthermore, successful mentor-protégé relationships are based on reciprocity, change over time, and can take considerable planning, risk, and hard work on the part of the mentor and protégé.[98] The following advice can help you find and make the most of your mentoring relationships.

Advice for Protégés

- *Have realistic expectations.*   Mentors are not "guardian angels who dedicate their careers to the altruistic mission of nurturing protégés."[99] Remember that there are risks as well as rewards in any mentoring relationship and that a mentor is only one of many resources that you have to enhance your effectiveness, career development, and job satisfaction.
- *Develop a reputation as a high-potential protégé.*   Mentors want to invest their time and resources in protégés whom they believe will be successful. Indeed, research has shown that mentors are more likely to select a protégé based on his or her perceived ability rather the protégé's need for help.[100]

Therefore, show that you are committed to your professional development, develop a reputation as someone who works well with others, ask for help when you need it, and be open to feedback.

- *Be sensitive to the mentor's goals, needs, and style.*   Most mentors want help getting their work done and want to look good in the eyes of others. Therefore, you should do your best to make it pleasurable, not painful, for the mentor to work with you. At a minimum, this means understanding and adapting to the mentor's goals and preferred work styles. Notably, research suggests that high self-monitors (people who are able to read others' behaviors and adapt in response) are more likely to ask for and receive mentoring.[101]

- *Give to mentors.*   Remember that mentor-protégé relationships are "based on the principle of reciprocity."[102] Think about what you can offer the mentor and make sure that you take time to show appreciation.

- *Do your best to get out of dysfunctional mentoring relationships.*   These include those in which the mentor is tyrannical, selfish, deceiptful, manipulative, distancing, neglectful, trying to clone you into his or her self-image, clueless about the challenges that you face, sabatoging rather than supporting your success, inappropriate in other ways, or simply a bad fit.[103]

- *Develop a network of developmental relationships.*   Your mentor is only one source of instrumental and psychosocial support. Other high status contacts, as well as your peers, subordinates, customers, and people outside your organization can also play important roles in your professional development. Indeed, research suggests that the "effective use of multiple sequential mentors . . . [is] a key ingredient in career success."[104] Note that your peers are likely to be more accessible to you than are your bosses, and they can be useful sources of technical information, political advice, empathy, and emotional support, particularly if your peer relationships aren't overly competitive.[105] If you are unable to find mentoring opportunities in the organization, go outside of the organization for support or hire a professional career coach.

- *Realize that mentor-protégé relationships will—and should—change over time.*   Be ready to notice when the relationship is—or should be—transitioning to a new stage and move forward gracefully. Based on her observations of several mentoring relationships, researcher Kathy Kram concluded that mentoring relationships tend to go through four stages: initiation, in which the parties show an initial interest in each other and get to know each other; cultivation, in which the interactions between the mentor and protégé become more frequent and increasingly based on trust; separation, in which the mentor and protégé begin to go their own ways; and redefinition, in which the mentor and protégé redefine their relationship (e.g., the protégé and mentor may become peers, or the protégé may leave the organization and hire the former mentor as a consultant or employee).[106]

- *Be prepared to accept additional complexity and greater learning in mentor-protégé relationships that cross cultural identity groups (e.g., race, gender, and nationality).* If you are in the minority in an organization, remember that you may have to face more barriers in getting a mentor, work harder to demonstrate your competence, clearly articulate your desire for challenging and high-visibility assignments (e.g., international assignments), put more effort into making the mentor or protégé feel comfortable, manage external perceptions, and get more of your social and emotional needs filled outside the mentoring relationship.[107] In their research on the developmental experiences of successful minority executives, Harvard professors David Thomas and John Gabarro concluded that successful minority executives attributed much of their early success to their broad range of developmental relationships early in their careers, and they had "many more such relationships and with a broader range of people [than white executives in the study had], especially early in their careers."[108]

Advice for Mentors

What does it take to be an effective mentor? Research suggests that people who become effective mentors are likely to have reputations for being good "people developers" who enjoy helping others. They tend to be known as informal, even tempered, and good listeners who interact frequently with employees. They also tend to have high standards, hold employees accountable, are comfortable delegating, provide developmental experiences and useful feedback, give employees the room to make their own mistakes, and share political insights about their organization. In short, they are committed to the long-term development of employees.[109]

There are many reasons for you to be a mentor. Someone may have caught your eye as a particularly high-potential employee. You need good employees and believe that mentoring is one way to develop competent, loyal employees. Perhaps you are at a life stage where you want to invest in the next generation. Mentoring may be an official part of your job, so you do it because you have to mentor employees, not because you really want to. Regardless of the reasons you choose to become a mentor, there are several steps that you can take to make your relationships with protégés mutually rewarding. See Table 6-1 for mentoring dos and don'ts.[110]

NETWORKING

Many hardworking and high-achieving professionals think that interpersonal relationships often get in the way of their work performance, particularly when they are busy or when a relationship doesn't add immediate instrumental value. The thinking—and the potential consequences of this thinking—goes somewhat like this:

> I thought it was enough to know my job and to work hard. I stayed on top of the new developments in my field. I even won a few industry awards for my designs. I came in early and worked late. Heck, I rarely went out to lunch—I just kept working. Sometimes I worked so hard that I didn't even have enough time to return phone calls or e-mail messages, especially those messages from people who I didn't know very well or who were asking for favors that I didn't have time to do. Priorities, priorities, priorities, you know. Frankly, I don't have much in common with many of the people here anyway, nor do I ever expect to. I barely have enough time to get to know my own family. I have two children, one in the second grade and one in the fourth grade. Or is it the third and

TABLE 6-1 Mentoring Dos and Don'ts	
Do	*Don't*
Be yourself and share your knowledge and experience.	Don't expect the protégé to follow in your footsteps. He or she may not share your career goals.
Set realistic expectations and boundaries for the mentoring relationship. Explain your role as a mentor, how much time you can offer, the best times to meet, the best way to reach you, and your preferred working style.	Don't neglect the protégé. Respond quickly to requests, even if it's just to say that you can't meet right away. Let the protégé know where he or she can go for information and assistance if you can't help. Don't make promises you can't keep.
Plan what you intend to say, particularly at first meetings. What points do you want to cover and in what order? How do you want the protégé to feel?	Don't wing it, particularly at first meetings.
Ask good questions. What are your goals? What do you want to know? How can I know? How can I help? Listen carefully to the answers.	Don't dominate the conversation or spend too much time talking about yourself.
Encourage the protégé's long-term as well as as short-term growth.	Don't limit your discussion to the protégés current job.
Provide a "safe haven" where the protégé can be free from judgment and free to express his or her concerns and opinions. Give positive feedback. Remind the protégé that learning comes from overcoming hurdles and failures, as well as from successes.	Don't judge the protégé or breach a confidence.
Be sensitive to style and cultural differences. Differences influence the relationship most in the beginning. Over time, sharing common values and a common organizational identity can override real or perceived differences. Focus on commonalties as professionals and members of the organization.	Don't give in to stereotypes. Don't give up if the "chemistry" isn't right immediately. Remember that an effective mentoring relationship is built on trust, caring, and commitment rather than chemistry.
If you have a long-distance mentoring relationship, systematically plan telephone meetings, e-mail check-ins, and similar communication strategies to keep in touch. Schedule extra time to spend together when you happen to be at the same location.	Don't assume that distance should end the relationship.

fifth grade? And friends, who has time for friends? So, you ask me if I was surprised when my colleague was promoted and I wasn't? Definitely. I don't get it. Hasn't anyone noticed how hard I work and the contributions that I make to this company? Maybe it's true what they say: "It's not what you know, it's who you know."

The preceding passage reflects a common naivete about professional life. The assumption is that it's either what you know or who you know. But in reality, it's both. University of Michigan researcher Wayne Baker explains that "success depends on two factors: what a person knows (his or her human capital) and the network of relationships he or she has developed (the person's social capital). The world has changed in such a way that no one person can know enough about his or her profession anymore, so he or she has to draw on information, knowledge, and resources that other people offer. One of the biggest lessons people need to unlearn as they enter the world of business is that success is an individual matter."[111]

The following example, told by former Secretary of Labor Robert B. Reich illustrates the ironic power of connections.

A few years ago, a woman named Marcia Lewin used a political connection to help secure a job for her daughter. Lewin contacted her friend Walter Kaye, a retired insurance executive from New York who was a major donor to the democratic party, having enriched its coffers by between $300,000 and $350,000. Not incidentally, Kaye was a friend of Hillary Rodham Clinton, the First Lady. With the help of Kaye, Marcia's daughter Monica got a job as a White House intern, and the rest, sad to say, is history (p. 136).[112]

Networking is the deliberate, systematic process of building and maintaining relationships based on mutual benefit. Some of these relationships are with people inside the organization, and others are with people outside the organization. Some of these relationships provide immediate instrumental benefits, whereas others have no immediate or apparent work-related benefits. Some of these relationships are based on formal organizational ties such as those with direct bosses, subordinates, colleagues, and customers. Others are based on informal ties such as those with people from other departments and people you meet at professional conferences, social events, clubs, religious institutions, schools, child or elder care, and so on. Some are close relationships with people with whom you interact often and who provide emotional, as well as instrumental, support. Others are relationships that are based on little more than the exchange of a business card.

If the organization man defined the workplace of the 1950s, the individual networker will be the model of the 2000s.
Ann Reilly Dowd, Kiplinger Newsletter Online, Liberation Technology

All of these relationships can contribute to your professional effectiveness, career advancement, and psychological well-being. Research suggests that people with well-developed networks have access to more information and material resources, are more central to organizational innovations, are perceived as more powerful, are better able to influence others and implement ideas, have stronger and more far-reaching reputations, and hear about job leads more quickly and more often—all of which enhance their probability of success in terms of on-the-job effectiveness, as well career benefits such as more promotions, higher salaries, and greater job satisfaction.[113]

Research also suggests that people with strong networks have access to more social and emotional support that can enhance their psychological well-being, particularly in times of change or crisis.[114]

Unfortunately, many people associate networking with superficial schmoozing, taking advantage of people, or playing politics, so they find the idea of systematically building relationships for mutual benefit distasteful. Certainly, networking—like all good things—can be abused. Some people try to use their network as a substitute for personal competence, spend so much time networking that they pay little attention to their day-to-day tasks, overinvest in superficial relationships, or use people for their own ends without offering anything in return. Others see every social event as an opportunity to meet people who can help them instrumentally in their jobs or careers. Indeed, someone once suggested that I join a particular local church not because it could fulfill my spiritual needs but because it's a "great place to network."

Networking, when done responsibly, is ethical for many reasons. It is ethical because we all have the responsibility to make our organizations and ourselves more effective. Building and nurturing a broad range of high-quality work relationships enables us to do so. It is ethical because high-quality relationships are built on trust, respect, and reciprocity. Indeed, a fundamental assumption of effective networking is that networks are built not on what you get from the people in your network but from what you give to the people in your network. It is ethical because building our network inspires us to reach out and interact with people with whom we wouldn't normally interact, which broadens our worldview and experience. And it is ethical because people who have effective networks are likely to be competent, as well as connected.[115]

Characteristics of Effective Networks

There is no such thing as an ideal network. Your ideal network depends on what you want to accomplish.[116] Nonetheless, the most effective professional networks have several characteristics in common. They are broad, diverse, include high-status contacts, and include both strong ties (people you are close to and interact with often) and weak ties (people you don't know very well and interact with infrequently).

The diversity of your network matters because if your network is made up of people who are similar to you in identity (e.g., race, gender, nationality, religion, or class) or organizational (e.g., hierarchical level and departmental affiliation) group memberships, they are more likely to have similar experiences, perceptions, and networks as you have.[117] Consequently, if you have a diverse network, you are likely to have access to a greater range of resources that can provide task, career, and social support.[118] For example, someone who has a network that includes positive relationships with peers, bosses and bosses of bosses, subordinates, and people from many different departments is likely to be perceived as more powerful and is likely to have an easier time implementing a new idea than someone whose network is limited to peers or to people in his or her own department. As Baker explains, this is because "repeated interaction encourages cooperation."[119] Unfortunately, the comfort associated with similarity tends to get stronger in turbulent and uncertain times—ironically, just when new ways of thinking and interacting among different groups in the organization are needed most.[120]

The status of people in your network matters because people who are perceived to have high-status contacts in their network are viewed as more competent and powerful.[121] The key word here is "perceived." In an intriguing study, researchers Martin

Kilduff and David Krackhardt concluded that a person's "performance reputation" is based in part on that person's ability to do high-quality work and in part on people's perceptions that the person has a prominent friend. Kilduff and Krackhardt note that their study suggests that it is the perceptions of a person's relationship with an influential person, not the actual existence of the relationship, that matters.[122] They refer to this as the "basking-in-reflected-glory effect."[123] It is not surprising that we base our assumptions about a person's competence on whom we think they know. It is often difficult to assess a person's performance, so we look for other signals that they are competent. If we think that an influential person believes that someone is competent, then we are likely to use this information to make assumptions about that person's competence as well, given no evidence to the contrary.

Having both strong ties and weak ties in your network matters because both types of ties offer particular kinds of benefits. Tie strength refers to the degree of intimacy, interaction, emotional investment, and expectations of reciprocity in a relationship.[124] Strong ties offer more trust, closeness, and emotional support than do weak ties, and they tend to last longer.[125] Although strong ties provide deeper levels of ongoing instrumental and emotional support, weak ties provide broader exposure and a wider range of resources (e.g., a job lead from someone that you met briefly at a conference). You need the ongoing instrumental and emotional support that you get from strong ties, but you also need the broad exposure and access to resources that you get from weak ties. After all, you can't know everyone well, so your effectiveness and professional growth also depends on the cooperation and support of people that you don't know very well, if at all.

Diversity and Networks

In the last decade, researchers have become increasingly interested in how the networks of people from various cultural groups differ, why they differ, and whether these differences have consequences. As of this writing, most researchers who study networks agree that people from different organizational groups (e.g., department and hierarchical level) and identity groups (e.g., race, gender, and nationality) tend to have different kinds of networks and take different approaches to gaining instrumental, career, and emotional support.[126]

For example, research suggests that managers, in contrast to nonmanagers, tend to have more relationships outside of their immediate work group, belong to more clubs and societies (e.g., chambers of commerce), and have more coworkers in their informal networks.[127] This is not surprising because managers depend on a greater number and variety of people to get their work done. Indeed, a broad and diverse network should be seen as a basic requirement of a manager's job. In one study, researchers found that nonmanagers who had more contacts outside their work group were more likely to have higher salaries than the nonmanagers who did not, although this wasn't the case for managers. This may be because managers are expected to have strong networks, whereas nonmanagers who have strong networks are more likely to be able to exceed expectations.

A growing body of research suggests that successful women and people of color tend to have a more diverse network of relationships and more ties outside their departments and organizations than do their equally successful white peers and less successful women and people of color.[128] Why is this so? Researchers use two theories to explain this pattern: the similarity-attraction hypothesis and distinctiveness theory. Research on the similarity-attraction dynamic suggests that people in the majority are less likely to seek out, interact with, and feel comfortable with people who are in the minority. Consequently, when women and people of color are underrepresented at upper levels of the hierarchy, they often have to go outside their departments and organizations to find other women and people of color with whom to develop strong ties that offer both instrumental and psychosocial support.[129]

Researchers Ajay Mehra, Martin Kilduff, and Daniel Brass suggest another dynamic may be at work as well. Drawing on distinctiveness theory, they argue that "people in a social context tend to identify with others with whom they share characteristics that are relatively rare in that context."[130] In other words, if someone is in the minority in an organization, department, or hierarchical level, they will notice the similarity between themselves and other minorities and thus be more attracted to and seek out each other. Thus, two women in a crowd of men will tend to notice, identify with, and interact with each other on the basis of gender. However, the same two women will be less likely to notice and seek out each other in a predominantly female group. Distinctiveness theory assumes that the same would hold true for African Americans, Asians, religious minorities (e.g., Muslims in an organization that is predominantly Christian), or members of other underrepresented groups in the organization. It would also hold true for Caucasian males when they are in the minority.

> **We need leadership that thinks about the future and encourages us to invest in ourselves.**
> *Anita De Frantz,*
> *American Visions*

The similarity-attraction and distinctiveness dynamics have several implications for the networks of women and people of color. They suggest that if people in the minority tend to be located primarily at lower levels of the organizational hierarchy, then they are likely to have more relationships with people who also have lower organizational status and fewer relationships with people who have higher organizational status. They also are likely to be viewed as more marginal to the organization.[131] Consequently, they may have less access to important information and material resources, feel more alienated from the organization, and be less satisfied with their work.

To deal with the lack of information, resources, and power associated with marginality, many people who are in the minority in organizations form network groups. Researcher Raymond Friedman describes network groups as "groups that bring together female or minority employees for the purpose of meeting each other, helping each other succeed, and identifying issues within the organization that are a common concern."[132] One of the first and most well-known network groups is the Black Caucus Group at Xerox. Decades ago, this group was formed by older and experienced African American salespeople to socialize, promote, and provide support to younger and less experienced African American salespeople at Xerox. Raymond Friedman and Caitlin Deinard explain:

> The group provided blacks with a support network. Although the black sales representatives were Xerox employees and were part of the formal organization at Xerox Corporation, in the early 1970s this affiliation did not make them a part of the informal network that existed among the white employees. The black employees did not have access to relationships that come from having a beer together after work, living in the same neighborhood, or belonging to the same country club. Informal networks were a source of useful information

about corporate politics, policy changes, and career opportunities. A mentoring relationship was most likely to occur between people who interacted informally and felt comfortable together. The black support group compensated for this disadvantage. It provided black role models and mentors, as well as an informal network for information. It was an atmosphere in which black sales representatives felt comfortable asking questions they felt might make them look uninformed with white managers. Their goal was to be the best Xerox sales representatives possible, and by helping the company do well, they hoped they would achieve personal success.[133]

Friedman and colleagues have been studying minority network groups for more than a decade and conclude that well-managed network groups provide several benefits.[134] Minority managers who join network groups are more likely to stay with the organization, in part because network groups provide professional and psychological support, increase job satisfaction, and strengthen organizational commitment. Network groups, when well run, provide greater access to information about the company (e.g., new technologies, corporate strategy, and career systems), enable more opportunities for mentoring and presentations by senior people, promote social gatherings, offer seminars and workshops, provide contacts that may lead to other prospects, and provide opportunities to give back to one's community (e.g., through mentoring programs or fundraising for minority scholarships). Each of these benefits can increase the minority member's power base and enhance job effectiveness, career opportunities, and general well-being.

Ray Friedman and Brooks Holtom explain that network groups can be more effective than other efforts to promote diversity because "formal mentoring programs have met with little success and diversity training can be somewhat controversial." Notably, one study found that racial minorities [in U.S. companies that supported network groups] were more likely to have a white mentor, in part because effective network groups help members create more cross-race ties.[135]

Network groups tend to be initiated and managed by members of minority groups who reach out to the organizational leaders for support and legitimacy. Friedman and his colleagues recommend the following strategies for building an effective network group:

1. Be sure the group does not become "factionized" or too political. Focus on helping members achieve the success that they desire.
2. Create an effective means of selecting network group leaders and managing the transition between leaders.
3. Provide many different kinds of activities so that the network group meets the needs of members with different goals, life situations, and interests.
4. "Attract high potential minority employees" and make "membership in the group a symbol of success."
5. Regularly reach out to organizational members who are not members of the network group and maintain positive relationships with organizational leaders.
6. Include high-level and successful minority managers who can provide the network group with legitimacy, power, and connections with important organizational networks.

Note that when not well managed, network groups can run the risk of being perceived as promoting "symbolic separation," rather than greater integration into the organization.[136] In other words, people who join network groups may be perceived as taking a separatist strategy at work. Ironically, when people who are in the minority join effective network groups that separate them at times from the majority for the purpose of professional development and emotional support, they are also more likely to succeed in the organization, which promotes their integration into the majority. To take advantage of the benefits of network groups, while simultaneously managing perceptions of separatism, the most useful strategy for women, people of color, and others who are minorities in organizations is to maintain ties to network groups and simultaneously develop a broad network of relationships with members of the majority group both within and outside the organization.[137]

Networking Advice

Wayne Baker says that "there's virtually no correlation between personality type and social network. People can change their networks more easily than they can change their personality. Everyone can learn new skills." The most important things that you can do to build your network are to be systematic and proactive—and remember that "small steps can have a big payoff.[138] Remember that your network grows by what you *give* to people."

Also remember that your ideal network depends on what you want to gain from your network. At a minimum, determine what you want and need in three areas:

- *Task accomplishment.*　Who can help you get your work done? What experts do you need to know? What kinds of influential people can help your reputation, offer you support, and provide you with opportunity and visibility? Who can provide you with critical information, material resources, and support? Who can you talk with about organizational politics?
- *Career advancement.*　Who can help you with your career? Who would make a good mentor and role model? Who can you call on if your company is downsized and you lose your job? Who can give you leads about job opportunities?
- *Psychological and social support.*　What kinds of people do you enjoy being around? Do you know people who appreciate you primarily for who you are, not just for your professional accomplishments? Do you know people who will support you when you are down and not only when you are riding high? Do you know people who will provide help and emotional support if you have a medical emergency, need help caring for children or aging parents, need to discuss delicate organizational problems, or lose your job?

Once you have analyzed what you want from your network, identify who is in your current network and identify the strengths and weaknesses of your network. To what degree does your current network help you achieve your task, career, and psychosocial goals? How diverse is your network? Do you have high-status people in your network? Do you have both strong and weak ties? The assessment in Box 6-4 can help you identify your networking strengths and weaknesses.

Next, take steps to systematically develop your network. Remember that developing your network is an ongoing process, and your needs may change over time. Box 6-5 describes several small steps that you can take to develop and nurture your network.

BOX 6-4

How Skilled Are You at Networking?

Answer the following questions to identify your networking strengths and weaknesses.

	Not at All	Rarely	Some-times	Frequently	Always
I have a reputation for excelling at what I do.					
I have an expertise that I am known for.	____	____	____	____	____
I am reliable. I keep my word and don't promise more than I can deliver. I do my work on time, within budget, and I do it right the first time.	____	____	____	____	____
I'm the kind of person people want to be around.					
I show genuine respect for everyone.	____	____	____	____	____
I am optimistic and positive.	____	____	____	____	____
I am a good listener.	____	____	____	____	____
I invest in the success of others.	____	____	____	____	____
I give more than I receive from others.	____	____	____	____	____
I reach out to people outside my cultural or organizational groups.					
My network includes people from many different cultural and organizational groups.	____	____	____	____	____
I am able to help people from other cultures feel comfortable.	____	____	____	____	____
I am considerate of other people's cultures.	____	____	____	____	____
I seek out common ground between myself and others.	____	____	____	____	____
I'm aware of the impact of my culture on how others may perceive me and relate to me.	____	____	____	____	____
I am loyal and trustworthy.					
I am discrete and protect the confidentiality of others.	____	____	____	____	____
I support others when they are going through difficult as well as successful periods.	____	____	____	____	____
I return messages (telephone calls, mail, e-mail, faxes) quickly.	____	____	____	____	____

I am visible.

I know several high-status people who are aware of my strengths.   ____ ____ ____ ____ ____

I participate in committees and positions of responsibility.   ____ ____ ____ ____ ____

I attend professional meetings and conferences.   ____ ____ ____ ____ ____

I participate in community events (e.g., neighborhood events, religious institutions, political events).   ____ ____ ____ ____ ____

I systematically plan my network.

I know what I want to achieve from my network.   ____ ____ ____ ____ ____

I know what people I need in my network.   ____ ____ ____ ____ ____

I know what I can offer people in my network.   ____ ____ ____ ____ ____

I keep in touch with people in my network.   ____ ____ ____ ____ ____

I actively fill the gaps in my network.   ____ ____ ____ ____ ____

I use my network.

I request information and materials resources from people when I need them.   ____ ____ ____ ____ ____

I let people know when I need their support.   ____ ____ ____ ____ ____

I manage the downside of networking.   ____ ____ ____ ____ ____

I can say "no" to requests gracefully to avoid getting overcommitted.   ____ ____ ____ ____ ____

I set personal boundaries gracefully.   ____ ____ ____ ____ ____

I manage my time well.   ____ ____ ____ ____ ____

I make time to spend time with the people I love.   ____ ____ ____ ____ ____

1. Based on your assessment of your networking skills, what are your strengths?

2. What are your weaknesses?

3. What do you resist doing most? Why? What would you gain and lose if you did what you are resisting?

4. List three things that you will do in the next week to improve your network.

5. List three things that you will do in the next three months to improve your network.

6. List three things that you will do in the next year to improve your network.

BOX 6-5

Fifteen Steps Toward Developing and Nurturing Your Network

1. Always treat everyone with respect.

2. Always carry your business card. Know the norms for giving and receiving business cards in different cultures; for example, the Japanese consider it rude to write on a business card.

3. Invest in your social skills. Attend workshops that enhance your social skills. Practice these skills every day.

4. During conversations, ask people about themselves, their work, or their interests and listen carefully. Remember to thank people when the conversation is over.

5. Give sincere compliments. People like to be appreciated.

6. Follow up with people you have recently met or contacted. For example, send notes thanking people for their time or assistance. Pass on articles or information that may be of interest to them.

   One consultant sends three notes of appreciation each workday, which takes approximately 15 minutes a day. At the end of a workweek, she's nurtured at least 15 relationships, which add up to 750 relationships a year if she works 50 weeks a year.[139]

7. Take time to meet with people with whom you wouldn't normally interact. Get out of your office. Volunteer for committees and assignments that take you out of your immediate work area. Invite different people to breaks, breakfast, lunch, or dinner.

8. Participate in company events and functions.

9. Don't overrely on e-mail. Face-to-face interactions are still the best way to build relationships, particularly new relationships.

10. Find the time to help others. Offer unsolicited help.

11. Help people meet others outside their network who can help them.

12. Join professional groups such as alumni associations, network groups, and community groups.

13. Attend conferences, trade shows, and other professional gatherings. Choose your conferences carefully. Prior to attending a conference: (1) set objectives for what you want to achieve; (2) write out your agenda, including events you want to attend and people you want to meet; (3) attend social events; (4) sit with people you don't know during the event and with a different group at different times; (5) plan your conversations (e.g., plan on asking questions such as "What are the greatest challenges your organization—or profession—has today?" "How did you first get involved with your organization?" and (6) always wear a name tag and exchange business cards when appropriate.

14. Be organized. Start a network file that lists the names and contact information for people you want in your network.

15. Don't burn any bridges. Whenever possible, leave relationships on a positive note. If you ask someone for help and they say no, remember to thank them anyway.

IMPRESSION MANAGEMENT

No discussion of managing up, down, and sideways would be complete without a discussion of impression management. After all, says researcher Susan Ashford, organizations "are made up of people who observe and make judgments about each other."[140] The judgments people make about us influence our task effectiveness, career success,

255 ■

and self-esteem. Consequently, it is not surprising that we sometimes use impression management strategies to influence other people's judgments of us in order to achieve a desired goal.[141]

> If you ever do a survey, you'll find that people prefer illusion to reality, ten to one. *Judith Guest, Ordinary People*

Our goal may be to get something for ourselves—organizational resources, a high performance rating, or a job promotion. Or our goal may be to help someone else feel comfortable, save face ("No, I really don't think anyone on the board noticed that you were reading your mail during the meeting."), or feel joy ("What a beautiful baby!")—all of which help build the trust from which goodwill, cooperation, and coordination grow.

In short, impression management is both a self-preservation technique in hierarchical organizations and an important social ritual that helps make organizational relationships more satisfying and productive. Indeed, impression management is so taken for granted in everyday organizational life that we often don't notice when we or others are doing it. We consciously and unconsciously use a variety of impression management strategies.[142] For example:

- We use ingratiation to make others feel better in the hope that doing so will enhance their perceptions of us.[143] Ingratiation strategies include flattering, doing favors, conforming to other people's opinions, and smiling to show support, agreement, or friendliness. Although ingratiation is usually associated with someone who is trying to influence someone who is higher in the organizational hierarchy ("buttering up the boss"), we also use ingratiation with our peers, subordinates, clients, and others.

- We use self-enhancement to promote a positive image of ourselves to enhance other's impressions of us.[144] We may, for example, actively promote our strengths ("Did I ever tell you I was the valedictorian of my class?"), take credit for a job well done ("The team helped out so much after I got that million-dollar contract."), or "dress for success" ("Dress for the job you want, not the job you have.").

- We use a basking-in-reflected-glory strategy when we associate ourselves with someone or something that is viewed positively by others to enhance another person's impression of us. We often refer to this as "riding someone else's coattails" or "being seen in the right places with the right people." To illustrate, the story is told that a businessman once asked the wealthy financier Baron de Rothschild for a loan. De Rothschild is reported to have responded, "I won't give you a loan myself; but I will walk arm-in-arm with you across the floor of the stock exchange, and you soon shall have willing lenders to spare."[145]

- We use intimidation when we want to force someone to do something. Examples include threatening to quit, firing someone, or telling a boss about someone's undesirable action. We are more likely to use these strategies when we have power over someone, when the target is not in a position to retaliate, and when our goal isn't to be liked by the person we are intimidating.[146]

- We use self-deprecation and self-handicapping strategies when we want to make ourselves look bad to achieve a desired goal.[147] For example, we may say, "I'm sorry I acted discourteously at yesterday's meeting" to increase our chances of getting forgiveness from someone whom we offended. We may claim to have a bad back to get out of playing in the company's annual volley-ball tournament. We may use excuses to explain why we did a poor job ("I was just getting over the flu and I probably should have stayed home but I really wanted to finish the job on time."). We may pretend to be incompetent to get someone else to do something that we don't want to do ("Can you make the 50 copies of the report, please? I can never get that copier to work.").

Research suggests that "playing dumb" at work is quite common. Researchers conducted a telephone survey of 2,247 working adults from forty-eight states in the United States and asked them if they ever "pretended to be less intelligent or knowledgeable than they were" at work. More than 25 percent of the respondents admitted to doing so. Almost 15 percent of the male workers admitted to playing dumb with their bosses, and 7 percent of the women workers admitted to doing so. Seventeen percent of the men admitted to playing dumb with their coworkers, and 9 percent of the women admitted to doing so. Younger workers reported playing dumb more often than did older workers.[148]

It appears that many of our efforts at impression management work. Several studies suggest that subordinates who use ingratiation tend to be better liked by their bosses, have more positive communication with their supervisors, receive more favorable performance evaluations, and receive more feedback, resources, chal-lenges, pay raises, and promotions than their equally qualified coworkers who do not use ingratiation.[149]

Why does impression management work? In part, it's because we are social ani-mals and, as such, have a natural desire to be liked by others. Flattery, favors, and simi-lar behaviors make us feel noticed and appreciated. Impression management techniques also work because we often need to make judgments based on limited information, and sometimes the only information we have about someone is the image that they project. The more ambiguous the situation and the less objective data we have about a person, the more likely we are to "judge the book by its cover," even though doing so can lead us down the wrong path.

> The aim of flattery is to sooth and encourage us by assuring us of a truth of an opinion we have already formed about ourselves.
> *Edith Sitwell*

But impression management is risky business. People who invest too much time in impression management may not devote enough time to their job duties.[150] People who oversell themselves may have trouble living up to the expectations that they raise.[151] People who routinely engage in opinion conformity (i.e., going along with the opinions of others even when they privately disagree) may withhold important information, feedback, and bad news. People who use flattery too often may come across as smarmy or manipula-tive. Self-promotion can come across as conceited and tiresome.[152] Indeed, research suggests that ingratiation techniques such as flattery are more likely to be successful than self-enhancement techniques ("By the way, I really like your haircut."). What may be perceived as flattery in one culture may be insulting in another.

So, what can you do to avoid some of the risks associated with impression man-agement? To avoid falling for form over substance, set clear performance standards and performance measures, and routinely assess whether your impressions match the per-son's actual performance. If possible, use a 360-degree feedback system to hear how people at all levels of the hierarchy perceive this person. Remember, we tend to evalu-ate people whom we perceive to be similar to ourselves more positively, so try to keep this bias in check.

To avoid being seen as an empty suit (someone who makes all the right moves but does not perform well when it comes to completing assignments and contributing to the organization), make sure you are competent at your work and focus on completing tasks as well as developing relationships. Be respectful and sincere toward everyone and not only toward people that you feel can help you achieve your career goals. Perhaps most importantly, remember that although impression management is necessary for developing effective and rewarding work relationships, being overdependent on other people's judgments for your self-esteem and career success can be a stressful and fragile existence.

CONCLUSION

Regardless of whether we are subordinates, peers, or bosses (and we are often all three), we are all fallible human beings who depend on each other's help and goodwill for our professional effectiveness, career success, job satisfaction, and well-being. Undoubtedly, our individual knowledge and technical skills are important to our professional effectiveness. In today's complex organizational environment, however, these individual assets are underused unless they are leveraged through our relationships with others. The most important thing to remember from this chapter is that every interaction with our bosses, peers, and subordinates is an opportunity to build a stronger and more productive relationship.

CHAPTER SUMMARY

The quality of your relationships with your subordinates, bosses, and peers significantly influences your task effectiveness, career development (promotions and salary), job satisfaction, and personal well-being.

Regardless of whether you are managing up, down, or sideways, remember the following assumptions about human relationships: High-quality relationships are built on trust, respect, and reciprocity. We are all fallible human beings who depend on each other for our professional effectiveness, career success, and personal well-being.

Our relationships with bosses and subordinates are shaped by our attitudes toward authority relationships (i.e., our beliefs about whether authority figures are competent, trustworthy, and caring). Our attitudes toward authority are shaped by where we sit in the organizational hierarchy as well as our earliest experiences with authority figures—our parents and primary caretakers.

Effective managers are cognitively and behaviorally complex. They are able to perceive situations from a variety of perspectives, assess the appropriate action required for each situation, and adapt their behavior accordingly.

Managers who use the Situational Leadership model adapt their task and relationship-focused behaviors to the willingness and ability of subordinates to accomplish specific tasks.

Managers who use the Denison Leadership Development Model adapt their behavior to the needs of the situation as well. They base their behavior on their analysis of the internal and external organizational environment, as well as the employees' and organization's needs for stability and change. They respond to this analysis by focusing on four areas: creating a clear, engaging mission; ensuring consistency across organizational units (e.g., through policies, procedures, and norms); promoting teamwork within and across units; and empowering employees. Research suggests that managers who focus on these areas contribute to performance measures such as organizational growth, profitability, customer service, and employee satisfaction.

Empowerment refers to an employee's belief that he or she can have an impact on the organizational environment. Employees are likely to feel empowered when they believe that the work is meaningful; that they have the competence to do the work; that they have the freedom to choose the way to achieve goals; and that they can influence the organization's "strategic, administrative, or operating outcomes."[153]

Although you cannot ensure that employees will feel empowered, you can create a context that promotes empowerment by providing clear boundaries, goals, and performance measures, and provide sociopolitical support, information, education and training, and a participative work climate. Notably, abundant resources are not related to empowerment.

Research suggests that many employees are likely to obey the wishes of authority figures, even if doing so is unethical. Be careful of what you ask from employees, because you might get it.

The ability to manage your boss is a critical managerial skill. Managing your boss involves understanding your boss (goals, styles, strengths, and weaknesses), understanding yourself (goals, styles, strengths, and weaknesses), and adapting your behavior in ways that bring out the best in you, your boss, and your organization.

Mentor-protégé relationships provide the protégé with both instrumental and psychosocial support. To benefit most from mentoring relationships, remember that they are built on trust and respect between two imperfect human beings who have multiple demands on their time, are based on reciprocity, change over time, and take considerable planning, risk, and hard work on the part of the mentor and protégé.

Research suggests that mentors and protégés from different cultural groups may be less likely to interact with each other, confide less in each other, and have less confidence in each other. The protégé may find it difficult to see the mentor as a role model, and the mentor may find it difficult to provide appropriate psychosocial support. However, both mentors and protégés may benefit from overcoming the challenges together, developing a broader worldview, and being role models for managing diversity in the organization.

Networking is the deliberate, systematic process of building and maintaining relationships based on mutual benefit. The best kind of network depends on what you want to accomplish. However, a general rule is that your network should be broad and diverse, have high-status people in it, and include both strong and weak ties.

Research suggests that people who are in the minority in organizations are likely to benefit from maintaining ties to network groups (e.g., same-gender or same-race groups) while simultaneously developing a broad network of relationships with people who are in the majority in the organization.

We use impression management when we behave in ways designed to influence another person's feelings toward us to get a desired end. Impression management techniques include ingratiation, self-enhancement, basking-in-reflected-glory, intimidation, self-deprecation, and self-handicapping. Remember that although impression management is taken for granted, unavoidable, and often useful, in everyday organizational life, it also carries risks.

FOOD FOR THOUGHT

1. What is the most useful thing you learned in this chapter, and why?
2. Based on the strategies for managing up, down, and sideways described in this chapter, what can you do to increase your own effectiveness? Practice one of these behaviors over the next week and note any benefits and progress you make.
3. Think about the best and worst boss (or authority figure) you ever had. What were the characteristics of the best boss? Worst boss? How might you have contributed to the situation with your worst boss? What lessons did you learn from the best boss and worst boss that you can use to make yourself a better manager?
4. Think of a time when you felt empowered at work. What did it feel like? What did you accomplish? Did your boss, colleagues, or organizational leadership do anything that helped you feel this way?
5. Think of a time when you were courageous enough to resist what you believed was an unethical or immoral situation. What made you resist and what were the consequences? How can you ensure that you will have the courage to resist a slippery moral slope in the future?
6. As you read earlier in this chapter, Donna Dubinski, former president and CEO of Palm Computing, stated that although she likes being a role model, she downplays any general sense of obligation to developing women in her organization any more than she feels obligated to develop men in her organization. In contrast, the founders of the Black Caucus Group at Xerox felt a general sense of obligation to African American salespeople at Xerox. Do you agree with Dubinski? The founders of the Black Caucus Group? Why or why not?
7. Do you have a network of developmental relationships? If so, describe who is in it and what benefits the different relationships offer you. Also describe what benefits you provide in the different relationships. If you don't have a network of developmental relationships, what can you do to create one? Who should be in it and why?
8. What can you do to make yourself more attractive to mentors?
9. Complete the networking assessment in this chapter. What are your networking strengths and weaknesses? What steps can you take this week, this month, and this year to improve your network?
10. Think back over the past week. Identify three impression management techniques that you used at work or at home. What were you trying to accomplish? Do you think you were effective? Why or why not? Describe any benefits and risks associated with using these techniques.

ENDNOTES

1. Goleman, Daniel. 1998. "What Makes a Leader?" *Harvard Business Review*. November–December: 93–102; Rosenbaum, James E. 1984. *Career Mobility in a Corporate Hierarchy*. Orlando, FL: Academic Press.
2. Becker, Thomas, Robert Billlings, Daniel Eveleth, and Nicole Gilbert. 1996. "Foci and Bases of Employee Commitment: Implications for Job Performance." *Academy of Management Journal*, 39(2): 464–482.
3. Duarte, Neville, Jane R. Goodson, and Nancy Klich. 1994. "Effects of Dyadic Quality and Duration on Performance Appraisal." *Academy of Management Journal*, 37(3): 499–521.
4. Kilduff, Martin, and David Day. 1994. "Do Chameleons Get Ahead? The Effects of Self-Monitoring on Managerial Careers." *Academy of Management Journal*, 37(4): 1047–1060; Turban, Daniel, and Thomas W. Dougherty. 1994. "Role of Protégé Personality in Receipt of Mentoring and Career Success." *Academy of Management Journal*, 37: 688–702.
5. Baker, Wayne. 1994. *Networking Smart: How to Build Relationships for Personal and Organizational Success*. New York: McGraw-Hill, xv.

6. Carroll, Glenn, and Albert Teo. 1996. "On the Social Network of Managers." *Academy of Management Journal*, 39(2): 421–440.

7. Gabarro, John, and John Kotter. 1993. "Managing Your Boss." *Harvard Business Review*. May–June: 150–157.

8. Hill, Linda. 1992. "Why Won't They Do What I Ask?" *Executive Female.* September/October: 13–20.

9. Bartolome, Fernando, and Andre Laurent. 1988. "Managers: Torn between Two Roles." *Personnel Journal*, 6(10): 72–83; Hill, Linda. 1992. *Becoming a Manager: Mastery of a New Identity*. Boston, MA: Harvard Business School Press; Smith, Kenwyn K. 1982. *Groups in Conflict: Prisons in Disguise*. Dubuque, IA: Kendall Hunt Publishers.

10. Bartolome, Fernando, and Andre Laurent. 1988. "Managers: Torn between Two Roles." *Personnel Journal*, 6(10): 72–83; Smith, Kenwyn K. 1982. *Groups in Conflict: Prisons in Disguise*. Dubuque, IA: Kendall Hunt Publishers.

11. Kiechel, Walter. 1991. "Dealing with the Problem Boss." *Fortune.* August 12.

12. Hill, Linda. 1992. "Why Won't They Do What I Ask?" *Executive Female.* September/October: 13–20.

13. Smith, Kenwyn K. 1982. *Groups in Conflict: Prisons in Disguise*. Dubuque, IA: Kendall Hunt Publishers.

14. Bowlby, John. 1988. *A Secure Base: Parent-Child Attachment and Healthy Human Development*. London: Basic Books; Kahn, William, and Kathy Kram. 1994. "Authority at Work: Internal Models and Their Organizational Consequences." *Academy of Management Review*, 19(1): 17–50.

15. Kahn, William, and Kathy Kram. 1994. "Authority at Work: Internal Models and Their Organizational Consequences." *Academy of Management Review*, 19(1): 17–50.

16. Gabarro, John, and John Kotter. 1993. "Managing Your Boss." *Harvard Business Review.* May–June: 150–157.

17. Hill, Linda. "Why Won't They Do What I Ask?" *Executive Female.* September/October: 13–20.

18. Buckingham, Marcus, and Curt Coffman. 1999. *First, Break All the Rules: What the World's Greatest Managers Do Differently*. New York: Simon and Schuster.

19. Marx, Robert, Todd Jick, and Peter Frost. *Management Live: The Video Collection*. Upper Saddle River, NJ: Prentice Hall. Excerpts from the leadership alliance with Tom Peters.

20. Denison, Daniel R., Robert Hoojiberg, and Robert Quinn. 1995. "Paradoxes and Performance: Toward a Theory of Behavioral Complexity in Managerial Behavior." *Organization Science,* 6: 524–539.

21. Fernandez, Carmen, and Robert P. Vecchio. 1997. "Situational Leadership Theory Revisited: A Test of an Across-Jobs Perspective." *Leadership Quarterly,* 8(1): 67–84.

22. Hersey, Paul, and Kenneth Blanchard. 1993. *Management of Organizational Behavior: Utilizing Human Resources*. 6th ed. Upper Saddle River, NJ: Prentice Hall.

23. Blake, Robert, and Jane Mouton. 1981. *The Managerial Grid*. Houston, TX: Gulf Publishing.

24. Hersey, Paul, and Kenneth Blanchard. 1996. "Revisiting the Life-Cycle Theory of Leadership." *Training and Development,* 50(1); Blake, Robert, and Jane Mouton. 1981. *The Managerial Grid*. Houston, TX: Gulf Publishing.

25. Hersey, Paul, and Kenneth Blanchard. 1993. *Management of Organizational Behavior: Utilizing Human Resources*. Upper Saddle River, NJ: Prentice Hall.

26. Hersey, Paul. 1992. *Situational Leader*. Warner Books.

27. Vecchio, Robert. 1987. "Situational Leadership Theory: An Examination of a Prescriptive Theory." *Journal of Applied Psychology,* 72(3): 444–451.

28. Norris, William, and Robert Vecchio. 1992. "Situational Leadership Theory." *Group and Organization Management,* 7(3): 331–342.

29. Denison, Daniel. 1990. *Corporate Culture and Organizational Effectiveness*. New York: John Wiley & Sons; Denison, Daniel, and Aneil Mishra. 1995. "Toward a Theory of Organizational Culture and Effectiveness." *Organization Science*, 6(2): 204–223.

30. Spreitzer, Gretchen. 1996. "Social Structural Characteristics of Psychological Empowerment." *Academy of Management Journal*, 39(2): 483–504.

31. Ibid.
32. Spreitzer, Gretchen, Suzanne De Janasz, and Robert E. Quinn. 1999. "Empowered to Lead: The Role of Psychological Empowerment in Leadership." *Journal of Organizational Behavior,* 20: 511–526.
33. Spreitzer, Gretchen. "Social Structural Characteristics of Psychological Empowerment." *Academy of Management Journal,* 39(2): 483–504.
34. Ibid.
35. Spreitzer, Gretchen. 1996. "Social Structural Characteristics of Psychological Empowerment." *Academy of Management Journal,* 39(2): 483–504; Katzenbach, Jon, and Douglas Smith. 1993. *The Wisdom of Teams.* New York: Harper Row; Lipman-Blumen, Jean, and Harold J. Leavitt. 1999. *Hot Groups: Seeding Them, Feeding Them, and Using Them to Ignite Your Organization.* New York: Oxford; Biederman, Patricia, and Warren Bennis. 1998. *Organizing Genius: The Secrets of Creative Collaboration.* New York: Perseus Press.
36. Buckingham, Marcus, and Curt Coffman. 1999. *First, Break All the Rules: What the World's Greatest Managers Do Differently.* New York: Simon and Schuster.
37. Milgram, Stanley. 1969. *Obedience to Authority.* New York: Harper and Row.
38. Ibid.
39. Ibid.
40. Ibid.
41. Blass, Thomas. 1991. "Understanding Behavior in the Milgram Obedience Experiment: The Role of Personality, Situations, and Their Interactions." *Journal of Personality and Social Psychology,* 60(3): 398–413; citing Kilham, W., and L. Mann. 1974. "Level of Destructive Obedience as a Function of Transmitter and Executant Roles in the Milgram Obedience Paradigm." *Journal of Personality and Social Psychology,* 29: 697–702.
42. Blass, Thomas. 1991. "Understanding Behavior in the Milgram Obedience Experiment: The Role of Personality, Situations, and Their Interactions." *Journal of Personality and Social Psychology,* 60(3): 398–413; citing Adorno, Thomas, Elise Frenkel-Brunswick, and Daniel Levinson. 1950. *The Authoritarian Personality.* New York: Harper and Row.
43. Blass, Thomas. 1991. "Understanding Behavior in the Milgram Obedience Experiment: The Role of Personality, Situations, and Their Interactions." *Journal of Personality and Social Psychology,* 60(3): 398–413.
44. Schminke, Marshall, Deborah Wells, Joseph Peyrefitte, and Terrence Sebora. 2002. "Leadership and Ethics in Work Groups." *Group & Organization Management,* 27(2): 272–293; Arlow, P., and T. Ulrich. "A Longitudinal Study of Business School Graduates' Assessments of Business Ethics." *Journal of Business Ethics,* 7: 295–302.
45. Vaill, Peter. 1997. "A Note on the Idea of Courage." *Organizational Behavior Teaching Review.*
46. Duarte, Neville, Jane Goodson, and Nancy Klich. 1994. "Effects of Dyadic Quality and Duration on Performance Appraisal." *Academy of Management Journal,* 37(3): 499–521; Wayne, Sandy, Robert C. Liden, Maria L. Kraimer, and Isabel Graf. 1999. "The Role of Human Capital, Motivation, and Supervisor Sponsorship in Predicting Career Success." *Journal of Organizational Behavior,* 20: 577–595.
47. Bartolome, Fernando, and Andre Laurent. 1988. "Managers: Torn between Two Roles." *Personnel Journal,* 6(10): 72–83.
48. Tepper, Bennett. 1995. "Upward Maintenance Tactics in Supervisory Mentoring and Nonmentoring Relationships." *Academy of Management Journal,* 38(4): 1191–1205.
49. Dienesch, R. M., and R. C. Liden. 1986. "Leader-Member Exchange Model of Leadership: A Critique and Further Development." *Academy of Management Review,* 11: 618–634.
50. Drucker, Peter. 1986. "How to Manage the Boss." *Wall Street Journal.* August 1; Gabarro, John, and John Kotter. 1993. "Managing Your Boss." *Harvard Business Review.* May–June: 150–157; Randall, Iris. 1992. "How to Manage Your Boss." *Black Enterprise.* September: 86–92.
51. Drucker, Peter. 1986. "How to Manage the Boss." *Wall Street Journal.* August 1.

52. Lombardo, Michael, and Morgan McCall, Jr. 1984. "The Intolerable Boss." *Psychology Today.* January: 44–48.

53. Dumaine, Brian. 1993. "America's Toughest Bosses." *Fortune.* October 18: 44.

54. Jardin, Andrew. 1992. "Frankenstein and Other Monsters We Love to Hate." *Supervision.* October: 8–26.

55. Lee, Tony. 1996. "Are You More of a Street Fighter or a Jeckle and Hyde?" *Wall Street Journal.* June 11:B1.

56. Ashforth, Blake. 1994. "Petty Tyranny in Organizations." *Human Relations*, 47(7): 755–778.

57. Ibid.

58. 1993. "Psychobosses from Hell." *Fortune.* October 18:44.

59. Ashforth, Blake. 1994 "Petty Tyranny in Organizations." *Human Relations*, 47(7): 755–778.

60. Levinson, Harry. 1978. "The Abrasive Personality at the Office." *Psychology Today.* May: 78–84.

61. Zellas, Kelly, Bennett Tepper, and Michelle Duffy. 2002. "Abusive Supervision and Subordinate's Organizational Citizenship Behavior." *Journal of Applied Psychology*, 87(6); 1068–1076.

62. Hall, Francine. 1991. "Dysfunctional Managers: The Next Human Resource Challenge." *Organizational Dynamics.* Autumn: 48–57; Tepper, Bennett. 2000. "Consequences of Abusive Supervision." *Academy of Management Journal,* 43(2): 178–190.

63. Chidester, T. R., R. L. Helmreich, S. E. Gregorich, and C. E. Geis. 1991. "Pilot Personality and Crew Coordination." *International Journal of Aviation Psychology*, 25–44.

64. Ashforth, Blake. 1994. "Petty Tyranny in Organizations." *Human Relations,* 47(7): 755–778; Levinson, Harry. 1978. "The Abrasive Personality at the Office." *Psychology Today.* May: 78–84.

65. Ashforth, Blake. 1994. "Petty Tyranny in Organizations." *Human Relations,* 47(7): 755–778.

66. Gabarro, John, and John Kotter. 1993. "Managing Your Boss." *Harvard Business Review.* May–June 150–157.

67. Miller, James R. 1996. *Best Boss/Worst Boss.* Arlington, TX: The Summit Publishing Group, 30.

68. Maccoby, Michael. 2003. *The Productive Narcissist: The Promise and Peril of Visionary Leadership.* Broadway Books.

69. Lombardo, Michael, and Morgan McCall, Jr. 1984. "The Intolerable Boss." *Psychology Today.* January: 44–48.

70. Shellenbarger, Susan. 1999. "Spotting Bad Bosses before You Get Stuck Working for Them." *Wall Street Journal.* September 29:B1.

71. Levinson, Harry. 1978. "The Abrasive Personality at the Office." *Psychology Today.* May: 78–84.

72. Kiechel, Walter. 1991. "Dealing with the Problem Boss." *Fortune.* August 12.

73. Kram, Katherine. 1985. *Mentoring at Work.* Glenville, IL: Scott, Foresman.

74. Scandura, T., and R. Viator. 1994. "Mentoring in Public Accounting Firms: An Analysis of Mentor-Protégé Relationships, Mentorship Functions, and Protégé Turnover Intentions." *Accounting Organizations and Society,* 19(8): 717–734; cited in Blake, Stacy Denise. 1996. *The Changing Face of Mentoring in Diverse Organizations.* Unpublished Doctoral Dissertation, University of Michigan.

75. Erikson, Eric. 1963. *Childhood and Society.* New York: W. W. Norton; Levinson, Dan. 1978. *Seasons of a Man's Life.* New York: Alfred Knopf.

76. Wayne, Sandy, Robert C. Liden, Maria L. Kraimer, and Isabel K. Graf. 1999. "The Role of Human Capital, Motivation, and Supervisor Sponsorship in Predicting Career Success." *Journal of Organizational Behavior,* 20: 577–595; Fagenson, Ellen A. 1988. "The Power of a Mentor: Protégés and Non-protégés' Perceptions of Their Own Power in Organizations." *Group and Organization Studies,* 13(2): 182–194; Whitely, William, and Pol Coetsier. 1993. "The Relationship of Career Mentoring, Early Career Outcomes." *Organization Studies,* 14(3): 419–441; Cox, Taylor, and Stacy Blake. 1991. "Managing Cultural Diversity: Implications for Organizations." *Academy of Management Executive,* 5(3):

45–52. Burlew, L. D. 1991. "Multiple Mentor Model: A Conceptual Framework." *Journal of Career Development,* 17: 213–221.

77. Hill, Linda, and Nancy Kamprath. 1998. "Beyond the Myth of the Perfect Mentor." Boston, MA: Harvard Business School Note 9-491-096; McCall, Morgan, Michael Lombardo, and Ann Morrison. 1989. *Lessons of Experience: How Successful Executives Develop on the Job.* New York: The Free Press.

78. Hill, Linda. 1992. *Becoming a Manager: Mastery of a New Identity.* Boston, MA: Harvard Business School Press.

79. Higgins, Monica, and Kathy Kram. 2001 "Reconceptualizing Mentoring at Work: A Developmental Network Perspective." *Academy of Management Review,* 26(2): 264–288.

80. Howell, Baum. 1992. "Mentoring: Narcissistic Fantasies and Oedipal Realities." *Human Relations,* 45(3): 223–318.

81. Baum, Howell. 1992. "Mentoring: Narcissistic Fantasies and Oedipal Realities." *Human Relations,* 45(3): 223–318; Higgins, Monica, and Nitin Nohria, in press; cited by David Thomas and John Gabarro. 1999. *Breaking Through: The Making of Minority Executives in Corporate America.* Boston, MA: Harvard Business School Press.

82. Lancaster, Hal. 1996. "You Might Need a Guide to Lead You around Career Pitfalls." *The Wall Street Journal.* July 30: B1.

83. Ragins, Belle Rose, John L. Cotton, and Janice S. Miller. 2000. "Marginal Mentoring: The Effects of Type of Mentor, Quality of Relationship, and Program Design on Work and Career Attitudes." *Academy of Management Journal,* 43(6): 1177–1194; Scandura, Terri A., "Dysfunctional Mentoring Relationships and Outcomes." *Journal of Management,* 24: 449–467; Eby, Lillian; and Tammy Allen. 2002. "Further Investigation of Protégés' Negative Mentoring Experiences." *Group & Organization Management,* 27(4): 456–479; Blake-Beard, Stacy. 2001. "Taking a Hard Look at Formal Mentoring Programs: A Consideration of Potential

Challenges Facing Women." *The Journal of Management Development,* 20(4): 331–345; Scandura, Terri. 1998. "Dysfunctional Mentoring Relationships and Outcomes." *Journal of Management,* 24(3): 449–67; Eby, Lillian, and Tammy Allen. 2002. "Further Investigation of Protégés' Negative Mentoring Experiences." *Group & Organizational Studies,* 27(4): 456–479.

84. Scandura, Terri. 1998. "Dysfunctional Mentoring Relationships and Outcomes." *Journal of Management,* 24(3): 449–67; Eby, Lillian, and Tammy Allen. 2002. "Further Investigation of Protégés' Negative Mentoring Experiences." *Group & Organizational Studies,* 27(4): 456–479.

85. Kanter, Rosabeth Moss. 1977. *Men and Women of the Corporation.* New York: Basic Books; Ragins, Belle Rose. 1997 "Barriers to Mentoring: The Female Manager's Dilemma." *Human Relations,* 42: 1–22; Blake, Stacy Denise. 1996. "The Changing Face of Mentoring in Diverse Organizations." Unpublished Doctoral Dissertation, University of Michigan.

86. Isen, Alice M., and Robert A. Baron. 1991. "Positive Affect as a Factor in Organizational Behavior." In Cummings, Larry, and Barry Staw (eds.). *Research in Organizational Behavior.* Vol. 13. Greenwich, CT: JAI Press, 1–53; Pfeffer, Jeffrey. 1984. "Organizational Demography." In Cummings, Larry, and Barry Staw (eds.). *Research in Organizational Behavior.* Vol. 5. Greenwich, CT: JAI Press.

87. Blake-Beard, Stacy. 2001. "Taking a Hard Look at Formal Mentoring Programs: A Consideration of Potential Challenges Facing Women." *The Journal of Management Development,* 20(4): 331–345; Harrison, D. A., K. H. Price, and M. P. Bell. 1998. "Beyond Relational Demography: Time and the Effects of Surface- and Deep-Level Diversity on Work Group Cohesion." *Academy of Management Journal,* 41(1): 96–107; Tsui, Ann, and Charles O'Reilly. 1989. "Beyond Simple Demographic Effects: The Importance of Relational Demography in Superior-Subordinate Dyads." *Academy of Management Journal,* 32(2): 402–23.

88. Cialdini, Robert. 2001. *Influence: Science and Practice*. Needham Heights: Allyn and Bacon.

89. Allen, Tammy, Mark Poteet, and Joyce E. Russell. 2000. "Protégé Selection by Mentors: What Makes the Difference?" *Journal of Organizational Behavior,* 21: 271–282.

90. Feldman, Daniel, William R. Folks, and William H. Turnley. 1999. "Mentor-Protégé Diversity and Its Impact on International Internship Experiences." *Journal of Organizational Behavior,* 20: 597–611.

91. Jackson, Susan, V. Stone, and E. Alverez. "Socialization amidst Diversity: The Impact of Demographics on Work Teams, Old-Timers, and Newcomers." In Staw, Barry, and Larry Cummings (eds.). *Research in Organizational Behavior.* Vol. 15. Greenwich, CT: JAI Press; Kram, Kathy. 1985. *Mentoring at Work*. Glenview, IL: Scott Foresman.

92. Ragins, Belle Rose, and D. McFarlin. 1990. "Perceptions of Mentor Roles in Cross-Gender Mentoring Relationships." *Journal of Vocational Behavior,* 37: 321–339; Blake, Stacy Denise. 1996. "The Changing Face of Mentoring in Diverse Organizations." Unpublished Doctoral Dissertation, University of Michigan. Thomas, David, and John Gabarro. 1999. *Breaking Through: The Making of Minority Executives in Corporate America*. Boston, MA: Harvard Business School Press.

93. Ragins, Belle Rose. 1997. "Diversified Mentoring Relationships in Organizations: A Power Perspective." *Academy of Management Review,* 22(2): 482–521; Clawson, James, and Kathy Kram. 1984. "Managing Cross-Gender Mentoring." *Business Horizons.* May–June: 222–232.

94. Kram, Kathy. 1988. *Mentoring at Work: Developmental Relationships in Organizational Life*. New York: University Press of America.

95. Hill, Linda, and Nancy Kamprath. 1998. "Beyond the Myth of the Perfect Mentor: Building a Network of Developmental Relationships." Boston, MA: Harvard Business School Press, Note 9-491-096.

96. Ragins, Belle Rose, and D. McFarlin, 1990. "Perceptions of Mentor Roles in Cross-Gender Mentoring Relationships." *Journal of Vocational Behavior,* 37: 321–339; Ragins, Belle Rose, and John Cotton. 1991. "Easier Said than Done: Gender Differences in Perceived Barriers to Gaining a Mentor." *Academy of Management Journal,* 34(4): 939–951; Thomas, David. "The Impact of Race on Managers' Experiences of Developmental Relationships (Mentoring and Sponsorship): An Intraorganizational Study." *Journal of Organizational Behavior,* 11: 479–492.

97. Interview with Donna Dubinsky, co-founder and CEO, Handspring. 2000. *Careers and the MBA*. Cambridge, MA: Crimson and Brown Associates 32(1).

98. Hill, Linda, and Nancy Kamprath. 1998. "Beyond the Myth of the Perfect Mentor: Building a Network of Developmental Relationships." Boston, MA: Harvard Business School Press, Note 9-491-096.

99. Ibid.

100. Allen, Tammy, Mark Poteet, and Joyce E. Russell. 2000. "Protégé Selection by Mentors: What Makes the Difference?" *Journal of Organizational Behavior,* 21: 271–282.

101. Turban, Daniel B., and Thomas W. Dougherty. 1994. "Role of Protégé Personality in Receipt of Mentoring and Career Success." *Academy of Management Journal,* 37: 688–702.

102. Hill, Linda, and Nancy Kamprath. 1998. "Beyond the Myth of the Perfect Mentor: Building a Network of Developmental Relationships." Boston, MA: Harvard Business School Press, Note 9-491-096.

103. Scandura, Terri. 1998. "Dysfunctional Mentoring Relationships and Outcomes." *Journal of Management,* 24(3): 449–67; Eby, Lillian, and Tammy Allen. 2002. "Further Investigation of Protégés' Negative Mentoring Experiences." *Group & Organizational Studies,* 27(4): 456–479.

104. Burlew, L. D. 1991. "Multiple Mentor Model: A Conceptual Framework." *Journal of Career Development,* 17: 213–221; Kram, Kathy, and Lynn Isabella. 1985. "Mentoring Alternatives: The Role of Peer Relationships in Career Development." *Academy of Management Journal (1985),* 28(1): 110–133; Higgins, Monica, and Kathy Kram. 2001. "Reconceptualizing Mentoring

at Work: A Developmental Network Perspective." *Academy of Management Review,* 26(2): 264–288.

105. Hill, Linda, and Nancy Kamprath. 1998. "Beyond the Myth of the Perfect Mentor: Building a Network of Developmental Relationships." Boston, MA: Harvard Business School Press, Note 9-491-096; Baker, Wayne. 1994. *Networking Smart: How to Build Relationships for Personal and Organizational Success.* New York: McGraw Hill.

106. Kram, Kathy. 1985. *Mentoring at Work.* Glenview, IL: Scott, Foresman.

107. Ragins, Belle Rose. 1989. "Barriers to Mentoring: The Female Manager's Dilemma." *Human Relations,* 42: 1–22; Hill, Linda, and Nancy Kamprath. 1998. "Beyond the Myth of the Perfect Mentor: Building a Network of Developmental Relationships." Boston, MA: Harvard Business School Press, Note 9-491-096; Thomas, David. 1990. "The Impact of Race on Managers' Experiences of Developmental Relationships (Mentoring and Sponsorship): An Intraorganizational Study." *Journal of Organizational Behavior,* 11: 479–492; Blake, Stacy Denise. 1996. *The Changing Face of Mentoring in Diverse Organizations.* Unpublished Doctoral Dissertation, University of Michigan, 1996.

108. Thomas, David, and John Gabarro. 1999. *Breaking Through: The Making of Minority Executives in Corporate America.* Boston, MA: Harvard Business School Press.

109. Hill, Linda, and Nancy, Kamprath. 1998. Boston, MA: Harvard Business School Press, Note, 9-491-096; Clawson, James, and Kathy Kram. 1984. "Managing Cross-Gender Mentoring." *Business Horizons.* May–June: 22–32.

110. Lindenberg, Judith, and Lois Zachary. 1999. "Play 20 Questions to Develop a Successful Mentoring Program." *Training and Development.* February: 13–14.

111. Baker, Wayne. 1999. "How Rich are You? Wayne Baker on the Value of Social Capital." *Dividend.* Fall: 21–26.

112. Reich, Robert B. 2002. *The Future of Success: Working and Living in the New Economy.* New York: Vintage Books, 136.

113. Ibarra, Herminia. 1993. "Network Centrality, Power, and Innovation Involvement: Determinants of Technical and Administrative Roles." *Academy of Management Journal,* 36(3): 471–501; Kanter, Rosabeth. 1983. *The Changemasters.* New York: Simon and Schuster; Krackhardt, David. 1990. "Assessing the Political Landscape: Structure, Cognition, and Power in Organization." *Administrative Science Quarterly,* 35: 342–369; Kotter, John. 1985. *Power and Influence: Beyond Formal Authority.* New York: Free Press; Seibert, Scott, Maria Kraimer, and Robert Liden. 2001. "A Social Capital Theory of Career Success." *Academy of Management Journal,* 44(2): 219–238; Seidel, Marc-David, Jeffrey Polzer, and Katherine Stewart. 2000. "Friends in High Places: The Effects of Networks on Discrimination in Salary Negotiations." *Administrative Science Quarterly,* 45: 1–24.

114. Wellman, B., P. J. Cartington, and A. Hall. 1988. "Networks as Personal Communities." In B. Wellman, and S. D. Berkowitz (eds.). *Social Structures: A Network Approach.* New York: Cambridge University Press.

115. De Souza, Gita. 2002. "The Influence of Inclusion in Influential Networks: Perceptions of Ability and Personality Traits on Promotions within Management." *Journal of Behavioral and Applied Management,* 4(1).

116. Baker, Wayne. 1999. "How Rich Are You? Wayne Baker on the Value of Social Capital." *Dividend.* Fall: 21–26.

117. Ibarra, Herminia. 1993. "Personal Networks of Women and Minorities in Management: A Conceptual Framework." *Academy of Management Review,* 18(1): 56–87.

118. Ibarra, Herminia. 1995. "Race, Opportunity, and Diversity of Social Circles in Managerial Networks." *Academy of Management Journal,* 38(3): 673–703; Baker, Wayne. 1999. "How Rich Are You? Wayne Baker on the Value of Social Capital." *Dividend.* Fall: 21–26.

119. Baker, Wayne. 1994. *Networking Smart: How to Build Relationships for Personal and Organizational Success.* New York: McGraw-Hill.

120. Baker, Wayne. 1999. "How Rich Are You? Wayne Baker on the Value of Social Capital." *Dividend.* Fall: 21–26.

121. Ibarra, Herminia. 1995. "Race, Opportunity, and Diversity of Social Circles in Managerial Networks." *Academy of Management Journal,* 38(3): 673–703.

122. Kilduff, Martin, and David Krackhardt. 1994. "Bringing the Individual Back In: A Structural Analysis of the Interaction Market for Reputation in Organizations." *Academy of Management Journal,* 37(1): 87–106.

123. Cialdini, Robert B., R. J. Borden, A. Thorne, M. Walker, R. Freeman, and L. R. Sloan. "Basking in Reflected Glory: Three (Football) Field Studies." *Journal of Personality and Social Psychology,* 34: 366–375.

124. Granovetter, Mark. 1982. "The Strength of Weak Ties: A Network Theory Revisited." In P. V. Masden and N. Lin (eds.). *Social Structure and Network Analysis.* Beverly Hills, CA: Sage.

125. Ibarra, Herminia. 1993. "Personal Networks of Women and Minorities in Management: A Conceptual Framework." *Academy of Management Review,* 18(1): 56–87.

126. Ibarra, Herminia. 1995. "Race, Opportunity, and Diversity of Social Circles in Managerial Networks." *Academy of Management Journal,* 38(3): 673–703.

127. Carroll, Glenn, and Albert Teo. 1996. "On the Social Network of Managers." *Academy of Management Journal,* 39(2): 421–440.

128. Thomas, David, and John Kotter. 1999. *Breaking Through: The Making of Minority Executives in Corporate America.* Boston, MA: Harvard Business School Press; Ibarra, Herminia. 1993. "Personal Networks of Women and Minorities in Management: A Conceptual Framework." *Academy of Management Review,* 18(1): 56–87; Ibarra, Herminia. "Paving an Alternative Route: Gender Differences in Managerial Networks for Career Development." *Social Psychological Quarterly,* 60(1): 91–102.

129. Thomas, David, and John Kotter. 1999. *Breaking Through: The Making of Minority Executives in Corporate America.* Boston, MA: Harvard Business School Press; Ibarra, Herminia. 1993. "Personal Networks of Women and Minorities in Management: A Conceptual Framework." *Academy of Management Review,* 18(1): 56–87.

130. Mehra, Ajay, Martin Kilduff, and Daniel Brass. 1998. "At the Margins: A Distinctiveness Approach to the Social Identity and Social Networks of Underrepresented Groups." *Academy of Management Journal,* 41(4): 441–452.

131. Ibid.

132. Friedman, Raymond A. 1996. "Defining the Scope and Logic of Minority and Female Network Groups." *Research in Personnel and Human Resources Management,* 14: 307–349.

133. Friedman, Raymond A., and Caitlin Deinard. 1994. *Black Caucus Groups at Xerox Corporation.* Boston, MA: Harvard Business Review, Harvard Business School Publishing Division.

134. Friedman, Raymond, and Brooks Holtom. 2002. "The Effects of Network Groups on Minority Employee Turnover Intentions." *Human Resource Management,* 41(4): 405–421.

135. Friedman, Raymond, Melinda Kane, and David Cornfield. 1998. "Social Support and Career Optimism: Examining the Effect of Network Groups on Black Manager." *Human Relations,* 51(9): 1155–1178.

136. Friedman, Raymond A. 1996. "Defining the Scope and Logic of Minority and Female Network Groups." *Research in Personnel and Human Resources Management,* 14: 307–349.

137. Friedman, Raymond A. 1996. "Defining the Scope and Logic of Minority and Female Network Groups." *Research in Personnel and Human Resources Management,* 14: 307–349; Thomas, David, and John Kotter. 1999. *Breaking Through: The Making of Minority Executives in Corporate America.* Boston, MA: Harvard Business School Press; Ibarra, Herminia. 1993. "Personal

Networks of Women and Minorities in Management: A Conceptual Framework." *Academy of Management Review,* 18(1): 56–87; Cox, Taylor, and Stella Nkomo. 1990b. "Factors Affecting the Upward Mobility of Black Managers in Private Sector Organizations." *Review of Black Political Economy,* 13(3): 39–48; Ibarra, Herminia. 1995. "Race, Opportunity, and Diversity of Social Circles in Managerial Networks." *Academy of Management Journal,* 38(3): 673–703.

138. Baker, Wayne. 1999. "How Rich Are You? Wayne Baker on the Value of Social Capital." *Dividend.* Fall: 21–26.

139. Nierenberg, Andrea. 1999. "Masterful Networking." *Training and Development,* February: 51–53.

140. Ashford, Susan, and Gregory Northcraft. 1992. "Conveying More (or Less) than We Realize: The Role of Impression Management in Feedback-Seeking." *Organizational Behavior and Human Decision Processes,* 53: 310–334.

141. Wayne, Sandy J., and Robert Liden. 1995. "Effects of Impression Management on Performance Ratings: A Longitudinal Study." *Academy of Management Journal,* 38(1): 232–260.

142. Gardner, William. 1992. "Lessons in Organizational Dramaturgy: The Art of Impression Management." *Organizational Dynamics.* Summer: 33–46.

143. Liden, Robert, and Terence Mitchell. 1988. "Ingratiatory Behaviors in Organizational Settings." *Academy of Management Review,* 13(4): 572–587; Wortman, C. B., and Linsenmeier, J. A. 1977. "Interpersonal Attraction and Techniques of Ingratiation in Organizational Settings." In Barry Staw and Gerry Salancik (eds.). *New Directions in Organizational Behavior.* Chicago, IL: St. Clair Press.

144. Gardner, William. 1992. "Lessons in Organizational Dramaturgy: The Art of Impression Management." *Organizational Dynamics.* Summer: 33–46.

145. Kilduff, Martin, and David Krackhardt. 1994. "Bringing the Individual Back In: A Structural Analysis of the Internal Market for Reputation in Organizations." *Academy of Management Journal,* 37(1): 87–108; citing Cialdini, R. B. 1989. "Indirect Tactics of Image Management: Beyond Basking." In Robert A. Giacolone and Paul Rosenfeld (eds.). *Impression Management in the Organization.* Hillsdale, NJ: Erlbaum.

146. Gardner, William. 1992. "Lessons in Organizational Dramaturgy: The Art of Impression Management." *Organizational Dynamics.* Summer: 33–46.

147. Liden, Robert, and Terrence Mitchell. 1988. "Ingratiatory Behavior in Organizational Settings." *Academy of Management Review,* 13(4): 572–587.

148. Becker, Thomas, and Scott L. Martin. 1995. "Trying to Look Bad at Work: Methods and Motives for Managing Poor Impressions in Organizations." *Academy of Management Journal,* 38(1): 174–199.

149. Gardner, William. 1992. "Lessons in Organizational Dramaturgy: The Art of Impression Management." *Organizational Dynamics.* Summer: 33–46; Wayne, Sandy, and Robert Liden. 1995. "Effects of Impression Management on Performance Ratings." *Academy of Management Journal,* 38(1): 232–261.

150. Baumeister, Roy F. 1989. "Motive and Costs of Self-Presentation in Organizations." in Robert A. Giacalone, and Paul Rosenfeld (eds.). *Impression Management in the Organization.* Hillsdale, NJ: Erlbaum, 57–71.

151. Ibid.

152. Leary, Mark R., Patricia A. Rogers, Robert Canfield, and Celine Coe. 1986. "Boredom in Interpersonal Encounters: Antecedents and Social Implications." *Journal of Personality and Social Psychology,* 51(5): 968–975.

153. Spreitzer, Gretchen. 1996. "Social Structural Characteristics of Psychological Empowerment." *Academy of Management Journal,* 39(2): 483–504.

-------------------------------V I D E O   C A S E------------------------

Case 3 Relationships: Gaining Power and Motivating

Whether you are the boss or subordinate, the ability to effectively manage the boss-subordinate relationship is a management skill that is critical to your productivity, career success, and well-being. It is not surprising that bosses and subordinates often tend to see the world differently. For example, bosses tend to underestimate the power they have to affect their employees' everyday work lives. They are often unaware that a simple request such as "see me at the office in 5 minutes" can raise a subordinate's anxiety level to unreasonable levels. On the other hand, subordinates tend to assume that their boss has all the power in the relationship, when in fact, subordinates have quite a bit of power in the relationship as well. The most effective boss-subordinate relationships are built on mutual support and goodwill.

To make the best of a boss-subordinate relationship, effective managers adapt their behavior to the needs of the employee and the situation. Effective managers know when to use a direct, task-focused, hands-on style; when to use a supportive, coaching style; and when to stay out of the subordinate's way altogether. They also know that employees have five basic needs: meaning, belonging, competence, control, and consistency. They help employees meet these needs by providing a clear and engaging mission, promoting teamwork, empowering employees to make the most of their abilities, and providing consistent policies and procedures that give employees a sense of control, even during times of radical change. Effective managers also know that one of the most important roles that they have is to be mentors to their employees.

In this segment, Mia responds to Sarah's innovative marketing idea by asking Sarah to take responsibility for developing the idea and analyzing its costs and benefits for allaboutself.com. The way in which she turns this responsibility over, and the type of boss-subordinate relationship she tries to develop with Sarah, will very likely have a strong impact on the final result of the project, and on Sarah's future with the company as well.

DISCUSSION QUESTIONS

1. Do you think Mia handled this meeting with Sarah appropriately? Why or why not?
2. What do you think Sarah needs from Mia to successfully complete this assignment?
3. Did Sarah handle the meeting well? Why or why not?
4. If you were Sarah's career coach, how would you have recommended that she handle this meeting as well as develop a productive relationship with Mia, her boss?
5. What should be Sarah's next steps? Outline a plan of action for her, including resources that she will need to be successful.

7

Managing Cultural Diversity

This chapter will help you:

■ Understand why effectively managing diversity is a competitive advantage

■ Learn a definition of culture that goes beyond simplistic demographic categories

■ Identify important cultural differences that affect work behavior

■ Understand why some well-intentioned diversity efforts fail

■ Improve your multicultural competence

■ Create a workplace that leverages diversity

> *Diversity calls for managing people who aren't like you and who don't aspire to be like you. It's taking differences into account while developing a cohesive whole.*
>
> —R. ROOSEVELT THOMAS, JR., AUTHOR
> *Beyond Race and Gender*

A s we enter the twenty-first century, we live and work in a social and organizational world that is increasingly diverse and offers more "opportunities for interaction among people who do not share a common history or culture."[1] It is not surprising that top companies agree that managing diversity within and across nations is a critical managerial skill. Recently, more than 70 percent of the *Fortune* 50 companies had formal diversity management programs in place, and another 8 percent were developing such programs.[2] Many management schools, however, are lagging behind practice. According to recent research conducted by the International Association of Colleges and Schools of Business, business leaders say they are concerned "that business school graduates are not leaving school with the cultural competence they need to work effectively in a diverse and global business environment."[3]

This chapter is designed to answer business leaders' call to improve managers' multicultural competence. It is divided into two parts. Part I answers the following questions: (1) What is culture? and (2) How does culture influence what we see, how we act, and—most importantly for the purposes of this book—our managerial effectiveness? Part II discusses why organizations that effectively manage diversity tend to have a competitive advantage over those that do not. It also identifies some of the risks associated with diversity in organizations and offers strategies that you can use to increase your effectiveness as a manager of a diverse workforce.

PART I
WHAT IS CULTURE?

Most of us tend to see culture through the lens of demographic categorizations such as nationality, race, gender, and so on. In addition, many of us tend to view demographic categories such as race and gender as having been created by nature, clearly bounded, stable over time, and objectively observable. However, most categories used by societies to classify people are in large part created by human beings rather than Mother Nature. Lawrence A. Hirschfield, professor of anthropology and sociology at the University of Michigan, explains that our use of demographic categories helps us make sense of our social world, but these categories don't necessarily represent an objective reality. Using racial categorizations as an example, he explains that:

> **We didn't all come over on the same ship, but we're all in the same boat.** *Bernard Baruch, American financier and statesman*

> It is important to begin by talking about what race is not. Regardless of what our senses seem to tell us, race is not a biologically coherent story about human variation simply because the races we recognize and name are not biologically coherent populations. There is as much genetic variation within racial groups as there is between them. Now, this does not mean that race is not real psychologically or sociologically. It is obvious that race is real in both these senses. People believe in races, and they use this belief to organize important dimensions of social, economic, and political life. But this does not make race a real thing biologically. . . . In view of this, it makes more sense to think of race as an idea, not as a thing.[4]

Viewing demographic categories as ideas created by human beings rather than natural categories makes these categories no less potent. Indeed, it explains why demographic categorizations such as gender, race, nationality, sexual orientation, and class are often extremely important to individuals and societies. They are important because they carry historic, economic, and political meanings that have significant implications for people's sense of identity, relationships with others, and quality of life. Thus, although our categorizations are not objectively real, our emotional reactions to our categorizations are genuine. In the workplace, these demographic categorizations influence people's task effectiveness, career advancement, and job satisfaction.

What about gender or age? Aren't those real? Yes, of course, babies are born with either male or female parts, and people certainly do get older. Some human functions and abilities are biologically determined (e.g., giving birth to babies, although science is gaining some control over of how that happens). But culture refers to the meanings that people attribute to physiological parts and natural life processes such as birth, aging, and death. For example, societies perpetuate norms about how boys and girls should dress, communicate, and behave, as well as what paths they should choose in life and how much they should get paid for their work. Societies also develop and perpetuate norms about when childhood ends and old age begins, how people of different ages should relate to each other, what people of different ages should feel like, and what they are—and are not—capable of accomplishing.

Some researchers argue that it is useful to think of demographic categorizations such as gender, race, and age, in large part, as something that we do as a consequence of our socialization rather than something that we naturally are as a consequence of biological givens. Researchers Candace West and Don Zimmerman illustrate this distinction by using the word "sex" to refer to biological parts and functions (we have male/female parts) and using the word "gender" to refer to the roles men and women take as a consequence of social expectations (we do gender).[5]

The crucial differences which distinguish human societies and human beings are not biological. They are cultural. *Ruth Benedict, in Margaret Mead, An Anthropologist at Work*

There are several problems with dividing human beings into "natural" demographic categories. When we do so, we tend to see people within a demographic category as more similar than they are ("That's just like a man.") and see people from different cultural categories as more different than they really are ("Men are from Mars; women are from Venus."). However, there is much diversity among people within demographic groups, and there is much similarity among people between demographic groups. Researcher Deborah Litvin gives this example: "Black and white employees who were watching the same television programs at home the previous night, and perhaps eating the same junk food at the mall during lunchtime, are taught to think of each other as exotic creatures from different worlds."[6]

Another limitation of overemphasizing demographic categories is that we can lose sight of many other "factors that make up the essence of who we are as human beings."[7] Novelist Gish Jen explains:

From all of this, we may learn that there are two races of men [sic] in this world, but only these two—the "race" of the decent man and the "race" of the indecent man [sic]. Both are found everywhere; they penetrate into all groups of society. No group exists entirely of decent or indecent people. *Viktor Frankl, Psychologist and Holocaust survivor*

The way I am defined from the outside . . . is as Asian-American. To most people, that's who I "obviously" and "naturally" am, even though in my daily life, it's not always the most obvious thing about my identity. In fact, probably more of me is shaped by my temperament and rebelliousness. And my talkativeness. And my being a mother. And being a woman is a big, big, big shaping thing, probably more than my race . . . I resent all efforts to pigeonhole and ghettoize you.[8]

Gish Jen is not alone in her concerns about being categorized. The U.S. Census Bureau is finding that more and more people, particularly young adults, see the Census Bureau's demographic categories as "arbitrary or offensive." In a recent census, nearly 10 million people surveyed by the Bureau "refused to describe themselves as white, black, Asian, or American Indian."[9]

So, how should we view culture? Rather than thinking of culture as being based on natural, stable, clearly bounded, and objectively identifiable categories, we may best be served by thinking of culture as a form of social identity that carries certain meanings and social expectations. A cultural-identity group (e.g., race, gender, nationality, religion, age, or sexual orientation) is a categorization that has meaning to a society; that people identify themselves as members of; that shapes how people within that group make sense of the world and relate to others; and that shapes how people outside the group perceive and relate to members of that group. Note that even if you don't identify yourself as a member of a particular cultural-identity group, people inside or outside the cultural-identity group may do so and then relate to you based on their stereotypes about people in that cultural-identity group. In some sense, our cultural-identity groups are inescapable and have consequences on our relationships with others whether we intend them to or not. The differences between defining demographic categories as natural versus socially constructed ideas are summarized in Table 7-1.

When we assume that demographic categories are based on cultural meaning systems, we assume the following:

- All human beings have the desire and ability to learn about their culture and their place in it.
- As a result of socialization, human beings develop cultural identities that they view as meaningful and distinctive (e.g., race, gender, nationality, religion, and class) and to which they are emotionally attached. They develop these cultural identities through teachings and expectations from cultural group members, through teachings and expectations from people outside the cultural group, and by sharing a common history and social context.[10]
- Cultural identities influence one's self-concept, relationships with people within and outside one's cultural groups, and relationships between cultural groups.[11]
- Cultural meaning systems are often so taken for granted that members of dominant cultural-identity groups typically don't think about them. Although these meaning systems are culture specific, group members tend to be ethnocentric (i.e., they tend to see their meaning systems as universal standards for what is normal, moral, and effective behavior).
- Cultural-identity group members tend to interpret—and often misinterpret—the worldview and behaviors of others through their own cultural lenses, a process known as transubstantiative error.[12] In short, we tend to see the world not as it is but as we are.[13]
- The most important cultural knowledge is that which the cultural group believes will help members solve two fundamental problems of survival: internal integration (How do we stay together as a group?) and external adaptation (How do we respond to our environment?).[14] This knowledge helps people cope with everyday problems and dilemmas of everyday life such as: Who am I? How should I relate to others? How do I communicate with others? How do I deal with time? What is truth? How do I relate to my environment? What is the relationship between work and life?
- Cultures are "dynamically stable."[15] To survive, all cultures must change over time. However, deep cultural change happens slowly. Change happens when members of the culture view change as necessary for survival or when a critical mass of cultural group members are repeatedly exposed to alternative ways of thinking and acting that they find appealing.
- There is significant diversity within cultures. Each person's worldview, values, and behavior are significantly influenced by factors other than culture. These factors include (but are not limited to) genetics, family history, and experience.

TABLE 7-1 Differences between Defining Demographic Categories as Natural versus Socially Constructed	
Demographic Categories (e.g., race and gender) as Natural	*Demographic Categories (e.g., race and gender) as Socially Constructed*
Belief that demographic categories are natural, stable, clearly bounded, and objectively observable.	Belief that demographic categories are, in large part, socially created and reinforced by social institutions.
Rooted in biology.	Rooted in ideology (social beliefs, history, economic conditions, politics).
Demographic categories are something we *are* ("I *am* a woman" or "*I am* a man").	Demographic categories are, in large part, something we *do* (we *do* gender).
Focus on physical attributes, traits, and behaviors.	Focus on the meanings of cultural group membership and the consequences of these meanings on identity, worldview, status, and behavior.

In short, cultural meaning systems are simplified models of the world that help us make sense of the world and provide guidelines for our behavior. These meaning systems and behavioral norms are valuable because they give us a sense of identity and feelings of belonging, and they make coordinated social action possible. However, cultural meaning systems can cause problems when they create blinders that prevent us from seeing alternative points of view or when they create dysfunctional dynamics within or across cultural-identity groups. As managers, it is important to understand our cultural meaning systems as well as the cultural meaning systems of others. These meaning systems influence the ways that we think, our expectations of others, how we do our work, and our definitions of effectiveness and success.

DIMENSIONS OF CULTURE

It has been said that people are 95 percent the same and 5 percent different, but that the 5 percent makes a big difference. Consequently, managers not only must understand and manage the similarities human beings from all cultures share, but the relevant cultural differences as well.

This lesson is put into practice by Orin Smith, CEO of Starbucks, the well-known upscale coffee bar chain. The *Wall Street Journal* states that it is now "among the fastest growing global consumer brands and, for better or worse, one of the most visible emblems of U.S. commercial culture overseas." In the article, Smith explains:[16]

> The biggest lesson is not to assume that the market or the customers are just like Americans, even if they speak English or otherwise behave as if they were. They're not. This happened in the U.K. [and] it has been happening in Canada . . . [We] took to some of these English-speaking countries the same operating concerns and practices [as in the U.S.] and they just don't work the same way in all markets. For example, in the U.S. our real estate strategy was to find the best corners in the bests markets and open the stores. It worked very well. If you go to the U.K. and find the best corner . . . you'll do a great business

but you can't afford the real estate. If you locate there as we did in a number of places, it's a big mistake . . .

We have green tea frapuccino in Taiwan and Japan. It's the largest-selling frapuccino in these countries . . . We don't offer it anywhere else . . . The vanilla frapuccino was popularized in Asia [and is now in the U.S.]. We will be introducing strawberries and creme [frapuccino] out of the U.K. next year. That one will be extremely popular here . . . Frapuccino type products are popular everywhere . . . you have a little bit less drip coffee in some markets because there are more espresso drinkers. In other countries, we don't sell as much whole-bean coffee. They're not into as much home brewing as we are here. We are trying to change that.

This section summarizes several cultural differences that are relevant to managing in a multicultural context. I discuss several dimensions on which cultures differ (e.g., preferences for independence or interdependence). This list of dimensions is not exhaustive. Rather, it focuses on cultural dimensions that have been particularly well researched, that have implications for behavior at work, and that are likely to influence your work performance in multicultural organizations if not understood and managed. I have categorized the dimensions based on the following issues that people in all cultures and work organizations must address: Who am I? How do I relate to others? How do I communicate with others? How do I deal with time? What is truth? How do I relate to my environment? What is the relationship of work to life?

When you read about the various dimensions of culture, it will be useful to think about the differences mentioned (e.g., independence versus interdependence, formality versus informality) as extreme ends of a continuum rather than discrete categorizations. Cultures and the individuals within them fall somewhere between these extremes. For example, all human beings need and express both independence and interdependence in their day-to-day life. However, people tend to emphasize one over the other, in part, because of the influence of their culture. After you have read this section, you may want to complete Box 7-1, "Work-Related Cultural Preferences," to identify some of your own preferences and compare them with those of your significant others.

Who Am I?

One of our most basic human drives is to make sense of ourself, the world, and our place in it. Through socialization in our cultures, we learn whether we should view ourselves as primarily independent from or dependent on others, whether we should emphasize our quality of life (being) or our achievements (doing), and how we attain status in our culture.

Independence and Interdependence

One of the most fundamental differences between cultures is the degree to which they emphasize independence (individualism) or interdependence (collectivism). Independence emphasizes taking care of oneself, separating from others, making one's own decisions, rewarding personal accomplishments, and putting one's own interests and well-being above those of the group. In contrast, interdependence emphasizes connecting with others, taking care of others, making collective decisions, rewarding group accomplishments, and putting the group's interests and well-being above one's own. An MBA student from Japan noted this difference, saying: "When I was learning

BOX 7-1

Work-Related Cultural Preferences

After reading the description of these dimensions in this chapter, circle the number that represents where you feel you are on each dimension.

Who am I?

Independent	1	2	3	4	5	Interdependent
Doing	1	2	3	4	5	Being
Status through achievement	1	2	3	4	5	Status through ascription

How do I manage relationships?

Low-power distance	1	2	3	4	5	High-power distance
Universalistic	1	2	3	4	5	Particularistic
Informal	1	2	3	4	5	Formal

How do I communicate?

Low context	1	2	3	4	5	High context
Report talk	1	2	3	4	5	Rapport talk
Neutral	1	2	3	4	5	Emotional

How do I relate to time?

Fixed	1	2	3	4	5	Fluid
Monochronic	1	2	3	4	5	Polychronic
Linear orientation	1	2	3	4	5	Cyclical orientation
Future focus	1	2	3	4	5	Past focus
			Present			

Standards for truth

Inductive	1	2	3	4	5	Deductive
Seek consistency	1	2	3	4	5	Maintain contradictions

How do I relate to my environment?

Control environment	1	2	3	4	5	Adapt to environment
		Harmonize				
Change	1	2	3	4	5	Stability
Make my own choices	1	2	3	4	5	Have choices made for me

What is the relationship of work to life?

Live to work	1	2	3	4	5	Work to live
Work unlimited work hours	1	2	3	4	5	Work limited work hours
Business open around the clock	1	2	3	4	5	Business hours limited

English at 'my' junior high school, one of the things I couldn't understand was that Americans refer to 'our school' as 'my school,' 'our teacher' as 'my teacher,' and so on. It seemed selfish to me."

Research suggests that, compared with employees from interdependent cultures, employees from independent cultures are more likely to be more competitive with their colleagues, appreciate being singled out for praise, and are more comfortable with open conflict. In cultures that emphasize interdependence, employees are more likely to emphasize cooperation with their colleagues, be embarrassed by being singled out for individual praise, and be uncomfortable with open conflict.

Research suggests that North American, Northern European, and Western European cultures tend to emphasize independence. Southern European, Central and South American, African (with the exception of South Africa), Middle Eastern, and Asian cultures tend to emphasize interdependence. Some research suggests that, in the United States, women and people of color tend to emphasize interdependence more so than do Anglo American men.[17]

Doing and Being

In action-oriented cultures that emphasize "doing," people tend to focus on personal achievements, task accomplishments, and improving their standards of living. In cultures that emphasize "being," people tend to focus on personal qualities, relationships, and the quality of life (that may not be measured in the acquisition of material goods or financial gains).[18] In their book *Doing Business Internationally*, Terence Brake, Danielle Walker, and Thomas Walker give the following example:

> In cross-cultural training seminars, we will often ask the participants, "Who are you?" not just once, but several times. Invariably, Americans will answer with their job titles, and only later with family information or personal interests. Latin Americans, Africans, and those from the Middle East will tend to answer with an affiliation-type answer, such as family, clan, or tribe name. Europeans, in their first three answers, will often answer with a brief description of their humanistic or philosophical outlook.[19]

Status: Achievement and Ascription

All cultures have different ways in which people earn status. In achievement-based cultures, people earn status primarily through personal achievements such as educational attainment, technical skills, and personal talents. In ascription-based cultures, people earn status primarily through their age, family, social connections, and the class into which they were born. Researcher Fons Trompenaars explains that "In an achievement culture, the first question is likely to be 'What did you study' while in a more ascriptive culture the question will more likely be 'Where did you study?'"[20] Achievement-based cultures are likely to encourage more individualistic, less formal, and more competitive behaviors and often value youth over age. Ascription-based cultures are likely to encourage the use of formal titles, respect social and organizational hierarchies, and value age over youth.

In his research, Trompenaars concludes that North America is primarily an achievement-based culture, although he finds less consistency with the other continents. However, he notes that "there is a correlation between Protestantism and achievement orientation, with Catholic, Buddhist, and Hindu cultures scoring considerably more ascriptively."[21]

How Do I Relate to Others?

All cultures have norms regarding appropriate ways of relating to others, including how people should relate to authority, how strictly people should interpret and enforce rules of social conduct (e.g., policies or laws), and the degree of formality that people should use in various social contexts.

High- and Low-Power Distance

Different cultures have different norms for managing authority relations. Culture researcher Geert Hofstede distinguishes between high- and low-power distance cultures.[22] In cultures that are high in power distance, people are likely to expect social inequality and expect managers to know the right answers, make decisions for employees, and tell employees what to do. In addition, relationships across levels of the hierarchy tend to be more formal. Managers are likely to be called by their formal titles; hierarchies tend to be highly developed; and following the chain of command is likely to be important protocol. In cultures that are low on power distance, inequalities (although they exist) tend to be minimized, denied, and resisted. Managers are expected to draw on the expertise of subordinates, empower employees to make their own decisions, and encourage employees to take independent action. Relationships with managers tend to be less formal and organizational hierarchies flatter. Employees are more likely to bypass the formal hierarchy if they feel it is necessary to get things done.

In cultures with high-power distance, managers who overzealously try to empower employees may make employees uncomfortable, get the answers that the employees think the managers want, and lose the respect of subordinates who believe that managers should be able to solve organizational problems on their own. In cultures with low-power distance, managers who do not involve workers may be seen as dictatorial, power-hungry micromanagers and may face employee resistance and loss of employee support. Research suggests that Asian, Arab, Central and South American (with the exception of Argentina and Costa Rica), and Southern European cultures tend to have higher power distance orientations compared to Israel, Northern European, and North American cultures.

Universalism and Particularism

Organized action depends on shared rules for social behavior. Not only do all cultures have rules about right and wrong behavior but they also have norms about how strictly those rules should be interpreted and enforced. In cultures with a universalistic orientation, "a rule is a rule," and it holds for all people and circumstances. In cultures with a particularistic orientation, rules are meant to be symbolic or general guidelines to be adapted to a particular person or situation. In such cultures, people are likely to be more flexible when applying rules to friends, relatives, or people inside their cultural groups than they are with others. People with a universalistic perspective fear that the system will collapse if they make exceptions to the rules. People with a particularist perspective fear that the system will collapse if they don't make exceptions to the rules.[23] North American, Northern European, and Western European cultures tend to be more universalistic relative to Asian, Central and South American, and Southern and Eastern European cultures. Some research suggests that in the United States, women and people of color tend to be more particularistic than are Anglo American men.[24] Table 7-2 summarizes the differences between universalist and particularist cultures.

TABLE 7-2 Differences between Universalism and Particularism	
Universalist Perspective	*Particularist Perspective*
Focuses on rules.	Focuses on relationships and circumstances.
Believes in one right way: Morality based on universal principles and consistent standards that are independent of the person and context.	Believes in relativity: Morality is situational and standards depend on the person and context.
Assumes all people should be treated the same.	Assumes some people (e.g., family and friends) should be treated differently from others.
Emphasizes legal contracts: A trustworthy person is someone who honors his or her contract.	Emphasizes personal promises: A trustworthy person is someone whom you can depend on to look out for you.
"A deal is a deal."	"Things change" and "It depends."

Source: Adapted from Trompenaars, Fons. 1994. *Riding the Waves of Culture.* New York: Irwin, 49.

Formality and Informality

In some cultures, people show respect for others by adhering to decorum—dressing appropriately for occasions, choosing words carefully, and attending to protocol. In other cultures, people are more casual in how they dress, speak, and act. For example, Central and South American, Arab, Asian, and European cultures are more formal relative to Australia and North America.

The following is one of my favorite stories about U.S. tendencies toward informality. The first time I taught in Helsinki, a colleague gave me a tour of the city. Coming from a North American city, I told my colleague that I was surprised that I didn't see any homeless people. My colleague replied that few people lived on the street because of Finland's extensive social services. She then pointed to a man with a scraggly beard, patched corduroy jacket, baggy pants, and scuffed shoes and said, quite seriously, "Well, he could be a homeless person or an American professor."

How Do I Communicate with Others?

Communicating effectively across cultures means paying attention to the meaning of the words, the intent of the speaker, and the social context in which communication takes place. Cultures differ in the degree to which they emphasize the spoken word or reading between the lines; whether the primary purpose of communication is to convey facts, assert status, or develop relationships; and whether expressing emotions supports or undermines the credibility of the speaker and the message.

High- and Low-Context Communication Styles

People with low-context communication styles emphasize the spoken word. They tend to focus on the facts, get right down to business, and directly express their views and wants. Because they value facts and directness, communication is likely to move along quickly, and conflicts tend to be depersonalized. In contrast, people with high-context communication styles emphasize the intent behind the words and pay careful attention to the context in which the communication takes place. They emphasize the credibility and trustworthiness of the speaker and the relationship as much as the facts and the spoken word. They take time to get to know a person before getting down to business and look for cues that help them determine whether they should trust the person and invest in the relationship. Consequently, communication takes more time, and conflicts are likely to be personalized. In cultures in which face-saving is important, direct criticism can seriously damage a relationship.

In low-context cultures, the surrounding social context is seen as noise or static that gets in the way of clear communication. In high-context cultures, the surrounding social context is seen as sending important signals that enhance communication. Furthermore, in low-context cultures, harmony is sometimes sacrificed for directness. In high-context cultures, directness is sometimes sacrificed for harmony. The use of the word "yes" is commonly used to illustrate the difference between high- and low-context cultures. In high-context cultures, the word "yes" doesn't always mean agreement or affirmation. In fact, there is no word for "no" in Thailand.[25] Therefore, when working with people from high-context cultures, you may want to phrase your questions so that you avoid yes or no answers.

A personal example may be helpful here. A few years ago, I taught in an executive education program for a group of South Korean executives who, like many people from Asian cultures, tend to emphasize high-context communication. I developed a respectful relationship with the leader of the group who, consistent with cultural norms, was also the oldest person in the group. One day, I asked him if he thought the program was going well. Rather than answering "yes" or "no," he tactfully answered, "It is all going as planned." I understood from his ambiguous response that he might not have been completely pleased with the program and that he was reluctant to tell me so directly. By reading possible dissatisfaction into his response, I was able to look into the matter further, make appropriate changes, and develop a successful program that better met the participants' needs. Researcher Jeffrey Sanchez-Burks provides another example:[26]

> Imagine an exchange between two people working together on a project. One person explains to a colleague an idea for how to present the results of the report in an upcoming departmental meeting. The colleague strongly dislikes the idea. However, in an effort to save face for the person, the colleague responds that "it's an interesting idea" and relies on relational cues such as vocal intonation and body language to convey the actual unfavorable opinion. If the person who proposed the idea is not attentive to these relational cues, the person will infer a positive response . . . [As] the person moves toward implementing the idea, the colleague may withdraw from the project, offended that the person ignored the negative feedback. The person may then resent what appears to be an unannounced change in support for the idea . . ."

North American and Northern European cultures emphasize low-context communication. Southern European, Central and South American, African, and Asian cultures emphasize high-context communication. Notably, understanding and adapting to the differences between low- and high-context cultures is particularly important in the United States today because an increasing number of immigrants and people entering the United States workforce come from high-context cultures, whereas executives are predominantly from low-context cultures.[27]

Notably, Sanchez-Burks and his colleagues have found that people who have "a Protestant Relational Ideology"—the belief that one should maintain a polite but work-focused style at work—are more likely than others (including Catholics with Caucasian European backgrounds) to minimize high-context communication, as well as emotional expression, at work. Outside of the workplace, however, the researchers found little difference between people with Protestant Relational Ideologies and others in their ability to read contextual cues, as well as in their willingness to express emotions. This suggests that some differences may be more pronounced—and more inclined to produce misunderstandings—at work.[28]

Report and Rapport Talk

In her best-selling book *You Just Don't Understand: Women and Men in Conversation*, communications researcher Deborah Tannen refers to two different styles of communicating: report talk and rapport talk.[29] Similar to low-context communication style, the goal of report talk is to state the facts. However, report talk is also associated with a desire to stand out, to exhibit knowledge and expertise, to reinforce or maintain status, and to win. In contrast, the goal of rapport talk is to establish connection with another person by looking for "similarities and matching experiences" or deferring to others to establish connection. Tannen's research suggests that North American men are more likely to use report talk and North American women are more likely to use rapport talk. She attributes this difference in communication styles to socialization practices that begin in childhood. She notes that boys are encouraged to emphasize status and winning in their games and interpersonal relationships, and girls are encouraged to emphasize connection.

Neutral and Expressive Emotional Displays

In some cultures, displays of emotion are used to emphasize a point, display interest, and show commitment. In such cultures, acting neutral can be seen as disinterest, a lack of understanding, or a lack of motivation. In other cultures, people are expected to show restraint and moderation during communication, particularly in business settings. Japan and many Northern European cultures tend to be less demonstrative of emotions than are Southern European cultures and the United States. In such cultures, displays of extreme emotions—happiness, disappointment, anger—are seen as immature and inappropriate. In their book *Managing Diversity*, Lee Gardenswartz and Anita Rowe tell a story about a North American employee of a Japanese organization. During a business meeting, she expressed her satisfaction with the company's success in achieving its goals with the enthusiastic exclamation, "Yeah!" Her boss later told her that her zealous expression of emotion was unprofessional in a business meeting.[30]

How Do I Deal with Time?

Regardless of their culture, all human beings must deal with the passing of time. However, different cultures emphasize different ways of understanding and managing time, including whether time is viewed as a scarce resource to be saved and spent wisely or a series of moments to be savored; whether people should manage their time by doing one thing at a time or many things at once; whether people should focus primarily on the past, present, or future; and whether time progresses in a linear or circular fashion. For managers, these assumptions have implications for day-to-day time management and coordinations, as well as for strategic planning.

Fixed and Fluid Time Orientation

People from cultures with a fixed orientation toward time tend to manage time with the clock and calendar in mind. They manage their time carefully, adhere to schedules, and expect punctuality. In addition, cultures with a fixed orientation tend to view time as a scarce resource to be managed. North Americans and Northern Europeans tend to prefer a fixed orientation. North Americans, for example, speak of saving time, borrowing time, wasting time, spending time, and running out of time. Businesspeople are warned, "The early bird gets the worm," "If you snooze, you lose," "Invest time wisely," and "Time is money." To better control their time, people invest in time management courses, buy time-saving devices, and eat fast food. Many North Americans schedule social lunches with friends weeks in advance and schedule "quality time" with their children.

Japan and other industrialized Asian cultures also tend to have a fixed orientation toward time, although the proper use of time, rather than speed, is likely to be the main concern. In Japan, it often takes a long time to make a decision because it is important to follow protocol. However, once the decision is made, implementation happens quite quickly.[31] In Japan, it is also important to pay attention to "properness, courtesy, and tradition" when managing time. Many Japanese business and social gatherings unfold carefully and ritually from one phase to another. Successful time management in such an environment means doing the "right thing at the right time."[32]

In Central and South America, the Middle East, Africa, and some Asian cultures, time tends to be experienced as more fluid. A focus on relationships is more likely to drive people's use of time more so than do clocks and calendars. The clock and calendar matter little if someone is engaged in a relationship or an important event. Serendipity and savoring the moment take precedent over schedules. Time should adapt to the vagaries of people's lives.

It is not surprising that conflict may result between people who expect strict adherence to punctuality, agendas, schedules, and deadlines and people who see punctuality, agendas, schedules, and deadlines as loose guidelines for behavior. Someone with a fixed orientation toward time may see being late for a meeting as rude and irresponsible. In contrast, someone with a fluid orientation toward time may see cutting off a good conversation or leaving a meeting that is in progress to rush off to another meeting as rude and irresponsible.

Monochronic or Polychronic Time Orientation

All managers have multiple demands on their time, but they differ in the way that they manage these time demands. Researcher Allen Bluedorn and his colleagues explain that people with monochronic time orientations prefer to do one thing at a time, focus on the immediate task, and adhere to schedules. People with a polychronic time orientation prefer to do many things simultaneously, focus on relationships and process, and are likely to change plans often.[33] Northern European, North American, and industrialized Asian cultures tend to be monochronic. Southern European, Central and South American, Middle Eastern, and nonindustrialized Asian cultures tend to be polychronic. Take the assessment in Box 10.4 in chapter 10 to assess whether you have a polychronic or monochronic orientation toward time.

Past, Present, and Future Focus

All people must learn from the past, live in the present, and plan for the future. However, managers from different cultures differ in the degree to which they emphasize the past, present, and future. Cultures that focus on the past pay significant attention to tradition, with the hope that they can repeat the successes and avoid the mistakes of the past. Cultures that focus on the present tend to "seize the day" and focus on short-term thinking and quick results. Many European businesspeople, for example, complain that "Americans always live by their quarterly results."[34] Cultures that focus on the future tend to emphasize long-term planning and results and are willing to sacrifice short-term gains for long-term success.

The following story from *U.S. News and World Report* illustrates different orientations toward time, as well as lessons in diplomacy. In the late 1990s, United States Secretary of State Madeleine Albright visited the foreign ministers from the Gulf States. Although she dressed conservatively in keeping with the local traditions for women, she couldn't resist asking the men, "How many women do you have in your cabinet?" Startled, the men, trying to be polite, stumbled for answers. After a while, Saudi Arabia's foreign minister replied, "In the Middle East, where we define time differently, you must be patient."[35]

Linear versus Cyclical Time

Some cultures experience time passing in a linear, sequential fashion, one event taking place after another. The manager's goal is to move systematically from one point in time to another toward the future. Other cultures experience time as more cyclical. Every hour, day, week, season, and year follows a predictable cycle. The manager's goal is to understand the cycle and harmonize with the particular rhythms of the cycle. North American cultures tend to experience time as linear, whereas many Asian cultures tend to experience time as cyclical.

When planning, managers who emphasize linear thinking tend to focus primarily on the end result. For example, business author Steven Covey advises managers to "begin with the end in mind." The assumption is that focusing on the end result will lead to an effective process for meeting that goal. Cyclical thinking tends to emphasize the process and finding ways to harmonize with current conditions (which most likely have been seen before because of the cyclical nature of time). From this perspective, the assumption is that focusing on developing an appropriate process will lead to an effective end result.

What Is Truth?

Researcher Mary Belenky and her colleagues explain, "Our basic assumptions about the nature of truth and reality and the origins of knowledge shape the way we see the world and ourselves as participants in it. They affect our definition of ourselves, the way we act with others, our public and private personae, our sense of control over life events, our views of teaching and learning, and our conceptions of morality."[36] Different cultures tend to emphasize different ways of creating and using knowledge.

Inductive and Deductive Reasoning

Cultures that value inductive reasoning emphasize data, facts, objectivity, proof, direct observation, cause and effect, breaking things down into small parts, and understanding the separate parts. People who emphasize inductive reasoning tend to prefer using measurements and scientific methods for investigating problems and justifying conclusions. In contrast, people who emphasize deductive reasoning take a more holistic approach, with many elements and perspectives being held at one time in an attempt to get the "gestalt of the parts."[37] They tend to stress abstract thinking, symbolism, understanding the whole rather than individual parts, and often rely on analogies, metaphors, and stories for explanations.[38] For people who prefer inductive processes, the credibility of an explanation depends on claims of objectivity and the credibility of the facts and methodology—the data must speak for themselves. For people who prefer deductive reasoning, the credibility of an explanation often depends on the credibility of the speaker and the ability of the speaker to engage the imagination and emotional commitment of the audience. For example, North American cultures tend to emphasize inductive reasoning, whereas French and Central and South American cultures tend to emphasize deductive reasoning.[39]

Seeking Consistency and Maintaining Contradictions

In some cultures, people tend to categorize the world and their experience in it into clear dichotomies. They believe something is either one way or another—true or false, right or wrong, real or unreal. Contradictions must be resolved for the situation to make sense. In other cultures, something can be simultaneously true and false, right and wrong, real and unreal. Contradictions must be maintained to see the complexity of the situation more clearly. This difference in perspective is nicely illustrated in the following statement: "In the West, we consider consistency a virtue. In the East, consistency is an attribute of small minds and children. For example, in the West a person who acts inconsistently with their attitudes are called hypocrites; in the East they are thought to be sophisticated, i.e., they do what they must rather than what they like to do."[40]

How Do I Relate to the Environment?

Regardless of their culture, all human beings and organizations must manage their relationship with the environment to survive. Managing this relationship involves assumptions about the degree to which the environment can be controlled; whether change and uncertainty are welcome or threatening; and the importance of having choice.

Controlling, Harmonizing with, and Being Constrained by the Environment

To survive, people must control and change the environment to better meet changing human needs. However, as many environmentalists warn, people must also adapt to their environment or they will deplete critical resources and create unintended consequences that can risk human survival. Cultures tend to differ in the degree to which they prefer to control, harmonize with, or adapt to their environment. In his book *Riding the Waves of Culture*, Fons Trompenaars gives the following example of the difference between preferences for controlling versus harmonizing with the environment.

> The [late] chairman of Sony, Mr. Morita, explained how he came to conceive of the Walkman. He love[d] classical music and wanted to have a way of listening to it on his way to work without bothering any fellow commuters. The Walkman was a way of not imposing on the outside world, but of being in harmony with it. Contrast this to the way most Westerners think about using the device. "I can listen to music without being disturbed by other people. . . ." Another obvious example is the use of face masks that are worn over the nose and mouth. In Tokyo, you see many people wearing them, especially in winter. When you inquire why, you are told that when people have colds or a virus,

they wear them so they will not pollute or infect other people by breathing on them. In New York they are worn by bikers and other athletes who do not want to be polluted by the environment.[41]

Change: High and Low Uncertainty Avoidance

Organizational success requires integrating both change and stability. Uncertainty avoidance refers to the degree to which people feel that change is to be promoted or minimized.[42] Some cultures encourage people to see personal and organizational change as productive and stimulating. Such cultures warn that organizations must "change or die." In this view, stability breeds complacency. Other cultures encourage people to promote stability over change. Tradition, routines, predictability, and staying the course are the foundations of long-term survival. In this view, change and uncertainty create anxiety that can be damaging to important traditions and can inhibit steady progress.

Choice

In the United States, choice is taken for granted. This is most obvious when one looks at supermarket shelves and finds no less than ten different brands of toothpaste, with each brand offering several options (e.g., "tartar control," "whitening," or "sensitive teeth"). American psychologists who study North Americans traditionally tend to assume that choice is a universal human need, results in a greater sense of personal control, increases intrinsic motivation, and leads to positive outcomes such as greater satisfaction and higher performance.

Recently, however, Stanford researchers Sheena Sethi and Mark Lepper conducted a fascinating series of studies in which they contrasted the performance of Asian American and Anglo American children in high-choice and low-choice task situations. They found that the Asian American children were likely to perform better when the choices were made for them, particularly when the choices were made within a trusted situation (clear rules of the game) or by a trusted person (the child's mother). In contrast, the Anglo American children performed best when they were able to make their own choices.[43]

Sethi and Lepper suggest that the desire for choice may not be universal, nor does having choices always lead to the best performance. Instead, a desire for choice may be related to whether a person has an independent or interdependent sense of self. People from cultures that promote an independent self-concept (e.g., the United States) may prefer choice because it enables them to assert their independence and show their uniqueness. In contrast, people from cultures that promote an interdependent sense of self (e.g., many Asian cultures) may prefer to defer to a trusted other or institution to make choices on their behalf. Doing so enables them to show respect for protocol and authority, learn from the experience of others, and enhance their sense of belonging to a group.

What Is the Relationship of Work to Life?

It has been said that some people work to live, whereas others live to work. In some cultures, work is often viewed as a calling, passion, even spiritual quest. In other places, work is often viewed as a necessary evil or a means to an end such as survival or a comfortable life. Although these descriptions are extreme views, trends regarding vacation time, work hours, and business hours suggest that there's some truth to them.

Harvard economist Juliet Schor, in her book *The Overworked American*, notes that although the average number of paid days off in the United States declined in the 1980s, "European workers have been gaining vacation time."[44] Most European nations have laws and labor agreements that guarantee employees between 4 and 5 weeks of paid days off a year, regardless of the employees' tenure in the organization. Indeed, the French companies Alcatel, Thomson-CSF, Carchain, and Credit Local de France have been raided by job inspectors whose role is to stop salaried executives and professionals, known as cadres, from working beyond the official 39-hour workweek without claiming overtime.

A Note on Cultural Differences

When we discuss cultural differences, it is wise to keep in mind several caveats. First, all descriptions of differences across cultures are, of course, oversimplified. Cultural meaning systems are much more complex than the human mind can understand and the written word can express. Second, cultures change. Globalization, increased diversity within nations, and transportation and communication technologies are exposing us all to more cultures more often than ever before. Consequently, cultural norms that were prevalent 10 years ago may be less prevalent today, particularly among people from younger generations. Third, several scholars and practitioners worry that focusing on cultural differences can be divisive. Certainly this is the case when descriptions of cultural differences lead to stereotyping.

The minority of one generation is usually the majority of the next. *Gertrude Atherton, The Aristocrats*

Researcher Taylor Cox describes the differences between stereotyping and valuing diversity.[45] Stereotyping often implies negative value judgments and "involves the assumption that characteristics thought to be common in a cultural group apply to every member" (e.g., assuming that all Japanese are collectivists or all North Americans are individualists). Furthermore, stereotyping tends to be one-dimensional. That is, when we stereotype, we tend to overemphasize a person's membership in one cultural-identity group and underemphasize other factors, including other cultural-group memberships, which also shape that person's worldview and behavior. For example, we may overemphasize someone's race and underestimate the influence of gender, class, religion, education, and nationality.

In contrast to stereotyping, valuing diversity "views cultural differences as positive or neutral," attends to people's multiple cultural-identity group memberships, and "is based on the concept of greater probability" that a person from a particular culture may share the worldview, values, and behavioral norms of their cultural-identity groups.[46] Stereotyping narrows our perspective and constrains our behavior; valuing diversity broadens our perspective, gives us multiple ways to interpret people's behaviors, expands our ability to make sense of complex situations, and enables us to build a broad and diverse network of relationships built on mutual trust and respect.

Fear of difference is fear of life itself. *Mary Parker Follett, Creative Experience*

No matter how much we learn about the nuances of different cultures, managing across cultures is a constant process of interpretation, trial, and adjustment. People are influenced by many factors other than their cultures, so there is no surefire way to predict another person's worldview, preferences, and behavior. The best guiding principle in cross-cultural interactions is what is called the platinum rule: Do unto others as they'd like done unto them. And remember that when managing across cultures, ignorance is not bliss.

PART II
WHY MANAGING DIVERSITY EFFECTIVELY
IS A COMPETITIVE ADVANTAGE

Research suggests that recruiting and *effectively* managing a diverse workforce is a competitive advantage in the domestic and global marketplace. In an often-cited study, researchers contrasted the stock market performance of companies that received awards for exemplary affirmative action programs with the performance of companies that had recently settled discrimination suits.[47] They found that the stock price of companies that received awards for their affirmative action programs increased after the awards were announced. Conversely, the stock price of companies that were charged with discrimination lawsuits decreased after the settlements were announced. The researchers viewed "high-quality affirmative action programs as a proxy for the effective management of diverse human resources" and concluded that these programs "contribute to sustaining a competitive advantage and are valued in the marketplace."[48] Effectively managing diverse human resources may contribute to sustained competitive advantage in several ways.

Positive Publicity
Certainly, positive publicity can help and negative publicity can hurt an organization's image. Positive publicity about diversity management may send a signal to the market that the organization is using its human resources effectively and is likely to be progressive with other important and complex organizational initiatives as well.

Recruitment, Development, and Retention of the Best Talent
Global competition and world-class quality standards make it necessary to recruit, develop, and retain the most talented people. Organizations with high-quality diversity programs and policies may be more willing and able to draw from a wider pool of potential recruits and, thus, may be able to obtain and train the best and the brightest employees. Eastman Kodak's former CEO George Fisher explains, "We can no longer afford to discount the talents, skills, and contributions of any employee. We must instead create an environment where every person matters and every person is fully enabled to contribute to his or her maximum potential."[49]

Better Problem Solving and Decision Making
Diversity researchers David Thomas and Robin Ely explain that groups that are traditionally "outside the mainstream ... bring different, important, and competitively relevant knowledge and perspectives about how to actually do work—how to design processes, reach goals, frame tasks, create effective teams, communicate ideas, and lead. When allowed to, members of these groups can help companies grow and improve by challenging basic assumptions about an organization's functions, strategies, operations, practices, and procedures."[50]

Enhanced Team Performance
Diverse groups, when well managed, tend to make better decisions than homogeneous groups, particularly when dealing with nonroutine, complex problems. In one U.S. study, researchers Taylor Cox, Sharon Lobel, and Poppy McLeod contrasted the performance

of homogeneous groups of all Anglos versus groups made up of Asians, Blacks, Anglos, and Hispanics on a creative task that required that they generate multiple ideas. Although there was no significant difference in the quantity of ideas, a group of judges rated the ethnically diverse groups' ideas "an average of 11 percent higher than those of the homogeneous groups on both feasibility of implementation and overall effectiveness."[51]

In another study, researchers contrasted the decision-making quality of homogeneous groups made up of all Japanese nationals versus diverse groups made up of members from different nations. They found that the cross-national groups tended to outperform the homogeneous teams. The researchers concluded that "exposure to different points of view may have triggered alternative cognitive processes in group members, which in turn improved performance."[52] They also found that "the performance of heterogeneous groups showed a more consistent pattern of improvement over time than did the performance of homogeneous groups."[53] Despite their better performance, the heterogeneous groups did not rate themselves as high on cohesiveness and group process as the homogenous groups did, although their opinions did increase over time.

Lower Legal Costs

In 1994, Denny's Restaurants was charged with discriminatory service toward African American customers and settled to pay more than $54.4 million to 300,000 customers.[54] Notably, things can change. Advantica, the owner of Denny's Restaurants, was rated #1 in *Fortune* magazine's list of "America's 50 Best Companies for Minorities" in July 2000 and has continued to earn a place on *Fortune* magazine's list of Best Companies for Minorities. In 1997, both Salomon Smith Barney and Merrill Lynch settled class-action sexual discrimination suits. Salomon Smith Barney paid between $20,000 and $150,000 to each of 2,500 plaintiffs and spent another $5 million in legal bills. Merrill Lynch paid between $60,000 and $85,000 to each of 22,500 plaintiffs and spent another $9.5 million in legal bills.[55] Also in 1997, Mitsubishi Motor Manufacturing of America settled a class-action sexual harassment suit with the Equal Employment Opportunity Commission (EEOC) for $150 million. Although the Mitsubishi case is one of the most notorious sexual harassment suits in recent history, it is not alone. In 2004, Morgan Stanley settled a sex bias suit for $54 million.[56] In 2004, a San Francisco judge certified a Wal-Mart sex discrimination class-action lawsuit in which up to 1.6 million women could be part of the class. The suit filed in June 2001 claimed that women's salaries were lower than those of their male peers doing comparable work and that men had a disproportionate share of managerial jobs even though women constitute the majority of the Wal-Mart workforce. While awaiting the development of the case and the potential of a bitter public trial, Wal-Mart began to take steps to adjust hiring and promotion practices, created a Director of Diversity and compliance group, and tied executive bonuses to their ability to meet employment-diversity standards.[57]

Lower Operating Costs

Effectively managing diversity can reduce costs associated with turnover. Organizations that effectively manage diversity may have lower operating costs because women and people of color tend to be more satisfied with the organization, are better able to use their abilities at work, and are less likely to leave the organization to look for better opportunities elsewhere. For example, in the 1980s, Corning found that women were resigning at twice the rate of white men, and people of color were resigning at two and a half times the rate of white men.[58] Corning estimated that the cost of this turnover was $2 to $4 million a year, a reasonable figure given that researchers estimate that the cost to replace an hourly worker is between $5,000 and $10,000, and the cost to replace an executive at the $100,000 salary level is between $75,000 and $211,000.[59] The high cost of turnover is an increasingly important concern in a global economy. Researchers estimate that up to 50 percent of U.S. managers leave their foreign assignments before expected,[60] costing organizations between $50,000 and $200,000 for each early return.[61]

Success in Serving Diverse Markets

Shifting demographics within nations, emerging global markets, and increased consumer affluence within these markets offer substantial opportunities for organizations that have the capacity to understand and respond to the multicultural marketplace and shifting demographics. Wisse Dekker, founding member of the Roundtable of European Industrials, notes that the European Union represents a single European market of approximately "320 million people compared with 220 million in the United States and 120 million in Japan."[62] In 1996, the consulting firm Towers Perrin reported that Asian Pacific Rim countries buy 60 percent of U.S. exports.[63] Towers Perrin also reported that people of color in the United States buy more than any country that trades with the United States; women spend 85 percent of the consumer dollar; and older Americans control more than 50 percent of all discretionary income. In the United States, Asians, African Americans, and Hispanics together represent more than $650 billion annually in consumer spending.[64] The number of Americans over 65 years of age is expected to increase from approximately 3.8 million in 1997 to 4.3 million in 2005.[65] Organizations that understand and promote cultural diversity may be better able to capitalize on these trends.

Effective Response to Advocacy Groups

Women and people of color are harnessing their growing economic power, asking organizations "What have you done for me lately?" and holding organizations accountable for the answers. *Black Enterprise* magazine publishes the "Best Places for Blacks to Work." *Working Woman* magazine publishes the "100 Best Organizations for Working Women," the "Best Organizations for Women Executives," and the "Best Business Schools for Women." In 1998, *Fortune* magazine published its first yearly ranking of the "Diversity Elite," which they define as "companies that are truly inclusive in hiring, promoting, and retaining People of Color."[66] Many organizations take these rankings seriously. Organizations that earn a place on these rankings use this status to build their reputations among employees, customers, potential recruits, and other constituencies. Organizations that do not earn a place in these rankings use the ranked organizations to benchmark effective diversity management practices in the hope that they, too, will be among the best in subsequent years.

There are also rankings that organizations prefer to avoid. In 1997, as part of its Fair Share Program, the National Association for the Advancement of Colored People (NAACP) began to grade hotel chains on their responsiveness to the African American community and published their findings in popular business publications such as the *Wall Street Journal* and *Black Enterprise*. The assessment criteria included five categories: the percentage of African Americans in managerial and professional positions; marketing and advertising to African Americans; the number of relationships with African American vendors; investment opportunities and franchise ownership; and philanthropic giving that benefited African Americans. By 2004, The NAACP had expanded its rankings to include automotive, banking, merchandizing and telecom industries. The methodology and rankings are published at http://www.naacp.org/work/economic.shtml.

IF DIVERSITY IS SO GOOD FOR ORGANIZATIONS, WHY DOES PROGRESS SEEM TO LAG BEHIND THE PROMISE?

Based on the logic in the previous sections, organizations that have strong diversity programs should be better able to recruit, retain, and leverage the talent of the best and the brightest employees, lower costs by increasing productivity and avoiding expensive legal suits, tap into diverse markets both nationally and globally, and enhance their reputations among their constituents. But if diversity is so good for organizations, why do many diversity programs fail to have the positive impact that organizations desire? A recent study designed to assess the success of diversity programs found that having a diverse workforce, in itself, did not predict positive organizational outcomes. Rather, how the organization managed the diverse workforce determined whether the organization reaped the potential rewards and minimized the potential risks of a diverse workforce.[67]

The most important reason may be a lack of systematic planning and patience. As with all organizational resources, a diverse workforce is a competitive advantage only if it is understood, carefully managed, and viewed as a long-term investment. Consultant Ann Morrison of the Center for Creative Leadership explains: "Usually with high hopes and little expertise, organizations . . . are spending millions of dollars trying to solve a complex problem that is always misunderstood and always controversial."[68] She notes that many organizations are "moving in 500 directions all at once," rather than developing comprehensive and systematic programs.[69] Furthermore, the benefits of diversity programs often emerge slowly over time. Consequently, many organizational leaders lose interest when the rewards are not immediately apparent. Without long-term commitment, diversity programs often get the reputation as being "flavor of the month" or "showcase programs" with much fanfare but little change.[70]

People are easier to control when they are all alike. *Lynn Maria Laitala, In the Aftermath of Empire*

Another problem is that many organizations focus their diversity efforts primarily on reaching numerical goals. Researchers David Thomas and Robin Ely explain that such organizations measure progress by "how well the company achieves its recruitment and retention goals rather than by the degree to which conditions in the company allow employees to draw on their personal assets and perspectives to do their work more effectively. The staff, one might say, gets diversified, but the work does not."[71] Although these organizations may have good intentions, their narrow focus on increasing numbers without changing their fundamental assumptions about how work gets done (e.g., how decisions should be made, how work hours should be arranged, what work can be done off-site and what must be done on-site) can backfire. Without a change in the organizational culture, employees who are outside the cultural norm in these organizations often feel marginalized, are unable to identify with the organization, and become frustrated at their inability to use their perspectives and talents that can help make their organizations more successful.[72]

In their research, Ely and Thomas found that organizations that promoted an "integration and learning" perspective were more likely to benefit from the sustained benefits of workplace diversity than were the organizations that had an "access and legitimacy" or "discrimination and fairness" perspective.[73] They describe the three perspectives as follows:

Integration and learning: According to this perspective on diversity, "the insights, skills, and experiences employees have developed as members of various cultural identity groups are potentially valuable resources that the work group can use to rethink its primary tasks and redefine its markets, products, strategies, and business practices in ways that will advance its mission. This perspective links diversity to work processes—the way that people do and experience work—in a manner that makes diversity a resource for learning and adaptive change."[74]

Access and legitimacy: According to this perspective, an organization's diversity efforts are guided by the "recognition that the organization's markets and constituencies are culturally diverse. It therefore behooves the organization to match that diversity in parts of its own workforce as a way of gaining access and legitimacy to those markets and constituent groups. Work groups in which this perspective prevails use their diversity only at the margins, to connect with a more diverse market; they do not incorporate the cultural competencies of their diverse workforces into their core functions."[75]

Discrimination and fairness: According to this perspective, a culturally diverse workforce is "a moral imperative to ensure justice and the fair treatment of all members of society. It focuses diversification efforts on providing equal access opportunities in hiring and promotion, suppressing prejudicial attitudes, and eliminating discrimination."[76]

Ely and Thomas argue that the integration and learning perspective adds value to the organization because it focuses on integrating the different experiences, skills, and knowledge a diverse workplace brings to the workplace in such a way that the organization's members broaden their perspectives and behaviors. This integration and broadening of mindsets and behaviors enables organizational members to be more innovative and adaptive in ways that better meet customer needs and add to bottom line results. Simply stated, they don't just have a diverse workforce, they proactively use it to obtain results.

Efforts to manage diversity are often emotional journeys steeped in a nation's turbulent history of inequality and animosity among various groups. Consequently, efforts to promote diversity are met with both passionate support and equally passionate resistance. When *Fortune* magazine ran a cover story about the fifty most powerful women in the United States, managing editor John Huey lamented: "I have learned that no matter how good our intentions are on this subject, the truth is, we are damned if we do and damned if we don't."[77] On the one hand, he argued, the article would be applauded as timely, relevant, and representing women's progress into the executive ranks. On the other hand, the article would be seen as marginalizing successful women, treating them as special cases, and misrepresenting the progress (or lack of progress) that women have made into the executive ranks.

What worried me about coming out was that I would be marginalized, I'd be a one-issue person. *Allan Gilmore, vice chairman of the board at Ford Motor Company, cited in Fortune Magazine, 1997*

Researcher Rae Andre argues that increased diversity in organizations can lead to "diversity stress," which she describes as "the discomfort [people] feel when they face a situation in which, because of the presence of multicultural factors, their usual modes of coping are insufficient."[78] Some employees, for example, may be uncomfortable in cross-cultural interactions because they are concerned that they will say or do something inappropriate or that they may be misunderstood. Thus, they may avoid cross-cultural interactions in an effort to minimize the possibility of discomfort, embarrassment, and conflict. Others may hide parts of their identity, such as their religious affiliation or sexual orientation, because they fear that they would be discriminated against if they revealed these identities. It's not surprising, then, that some research suggests that diverse groups can perform worse and have higher turnover than relatively homogeneous groups unless they are well trained and well managed.[79]

Indeed, research suggests that training is critical to the success of diversity programs.[80] Diverse groups that are trained in managing their differences tend to outperform homogeneous groups. Furthermore, the benefits of training tend to increase over time.[81] In one study, researcher Joycelyn Finley found that African Americans and Anglo Americans who were trained in skills designed to help them discuss emotionally hot topics felt that they were able to have more productive discussions about affirmative action than were those who did not have the training. Furthermore, the people who received the training also experienced the discussions as less stressful than did those who did not receive the training.[82]

Although training is important to an organization's diversity efforts, well-intentioned training programs can be undermined by poor facilitation. Although many employees welcome diversity training programs, others consider such programs to be "white male-bashing or a pointless waste of time," "punishment for the insensitive," "PC's [political correctness's] final frontier," and "sensitivity overload."[83] Diversity training programs are likely to backfire when facilitators make sweeping statements about cultural differences, suppress divergent opinions, assume one group alone is the cause of all the problems, and do not state the business case for diversity in a language that employees and executives can understand.[84]

GIVEN THESE HURDLES, WHAT'S A MANAGER TO DO?

Having good intentions is a necessary but insufficient step toward gaining the competitive advantages of a diverse workforce. To achieve the benefits of diversity in the workplace, managers must create a work climate that leverages the potential advantages of diversity while minimizing potential disadvantages.[85]

Managing diversity is not rocket science, but it is not common sense either. Historically, the common organizational wisdom was to manage diversity through assimilation. In other words, organizational leaders, consultants, and researchers created a model of the ideal manager. The manager was someone who was expected to look, think, and act a lot like the leaders, consultants, and researchers themselves. Organizations then recruited, developed, and promoted people who conformed to fit that model. In 1956, business journalist William Whyte referred to people who fit this managerial ideal as "organization men," people for whom conformity is central to their professional identity.[86]

Two decades later, when women and people of color increasingly began to enter the managerial ranks in many countries, assimilation was still the norm. In 1977, Betty Leehan Harragan wrote the popular book *Games Mother Never Taught You* to teach women how to think, talk, dress, and act more like organizational men to succeed in the organization. At the time, the book was applauded by the president of the National Organization for Women and the *Wall Street Journal* as a breakthrough in women's career development. Harragan told women that "to get a chance to play [the business game with men], you must look and act like the rest of the team and the recognized experts."[87] She argued, for example, that the language of business is based on sex, sports, and war analogies, and she advised women to learn this language and to use this language strategically. She also advised women that children "present a special problem" and to resist the temptation to bring children to work, presumably because colleagues might have a difficult time understanding that the woman could be a manager and a mother as well.

> Diversity without unity makes about as much sense as dishing up flour, sugar, water, eggs, shortening, and baking powder on a plate and calling it a cake.
> C. William Pollard, The Soul of the Firm

Today, most organizational leaders, consultants, and researchers agree that the personal and organizational costs of excessive assimilation are high and that the manager's goal is to create a work environment that aligns employees toward common goals while leveraging diversity. How can you achieve these dual goals? First, you can enhance your personal multicultural competence (i.e., your ability to be effective and feel comfortable in cross-cultural situations).[88] Second, you can create a work environment that promotes cultural synergy rather than excessive assimilation. In the following section, I describe skills that can enhance your personal multicultural competence and your ability to create an effective multicultural work environment. These skills are also summarized in Figure 7-1.

ENHANCING YOUR PERSONAL MULTICULTURAL COMPETENCE

Successful multicultural managers have particular attitudes and skills that travel well across cultures. In a *Business Horizons* article, Thomas Fitzgerald describes an effective cross-cultural manager as someone "who can move in and out of social, cultural, and mixed-gender encounters with relative ease; one who is able to handle diversities of many sorts and to be flexible in the face of rapid social changes—in short, a psychologically secure person who believes in the common unity of humankind."[89] Hal Lancaster, columnist for the *Wall Street Journal*, interviewed executives about the qualities of effective global leaders. He concluded that an effective global leader "is someone who can handle more complexity and uncertainty than domestic managers are typically accustomed to, who relates well with diverse groups of people, who listens more than talks, who craves adventure over the status quo, and who accepts that there is more than one way to skin a business problem. As one executive put it, good global leaders like getting up in the morning and saying, 'I have no idea what's going to happen today.'"[90]

**Developing Personal
Multicultural Competence**

Culture-Specific Skills: Learn the language, work norms, *do*s and taboos, and cultural history of a particular culture.

Culture-General Skills: Develop skills that enable you to be effective across multiple cultures, including self-awareness, empathy, perspective skills, boundary-spanning relationship skills, flexibility, personal grounding, emotional resilience, and courage. (Colleen Kelly and Judith Meyers)

**Effective Management of
Diversity**

Creating a "climate in which the potential advantages of diversity for organizational or group performance are maximized while the potential disadvantages are minimized." (Taylor Cox)

**Creating Cultural Synergy
(creating a context for
high performance)**

- Ensure top-level commitment.
- Role-model desired behavior.
- Obtain information.
- Know the law.
- Break the glass ceiling.
- Endorse support groups.
- Change the way work gets done.
- Pay attention to language, stories, rites and rituals, and other symbolic mechanisms that transfer cultural norms.
- Create a common identity.
- Increase interaction across diverse groups.
- Develop external relationships with diverse groups.
- Measure results and reward progress.

FIGURE 7-1   Skills for Multicultural Competence

The curious are always in some danger. If you are curious you might never come home.
*Jeanette Winterson,
Oranges Are Not the
Only Fruit*

It is not surprising that characteristics that inhibit the ability to effectively manage across cultures include rigidity, perfectionism, narrow-mindedness, self-centeredness, emotional immaturity, overemphasizing task and technical skills, underemphasizing relationships, lack of cross-cultural skills, and lack of interest in working across cultures.[91] Colleen Kelly and Judith Meyers, creators of the Cross Cultural Adaptability Inventory, argue that effective multicultural managers have both culture-specific knowledge and culture-general skills.[92] Culture-specific knowledge helps a manager be effective in a specific culture. This includes knowledge such as how to manage a meeting with Brazilians, negotiate a deal with Japanese, or conduct a presentation for Germans. Culture-general skills, rather than focusing on the norms of a particular culture, refer to a frame of mind and set of competencies that enable you to be effective and at ease anywhere, with any culture, and with multiple cultures simultaneously.

Culture-Specific Skills

To be an effective multicultural manager, you should make an effort to understand the particular cultures with which you are working. These efforts include the following:

- *Learn at least some of the language.* This shows respect for the culture, makes communication easier, and indicates to others that you have a willingness and ability to go outside your comfort zone. Pay attention to nonverbal communication such as body language, norms about who speaks first, and acceptable levels of formality or informality. For example, North Americans move their heads up and down to say yes. Bulgarians and Indians move theirs from side to side to say yes. The common sign for "OK" in the United States is considered vulgar in many countries (including Brazil, Greece, Ghana, and Turkey) and means "worthless" in France and Belgium.

- *Learn the work norms.* Learn which business practices tend to work best, how success is defined, and what people expect from a manager. Culture researcher Andre Laurent explains that "there is no such thing as Management with a capital M. The art of managing and organizing has no homeland. Every culture has developed through its history some specific and unique insight into the managing of organizations and of their human resources."[93] Remember that you need credibility, trust, and respect to be effective, and these are earned in different ways in different cultures. For example, in some nations managers are expected to be good "people managers" and coaches, whereas in others they are expected to be technical experts who can help subordinates solve technical problems.[94]

- *Learn the dos and taboos.* Effective multicultural managers learn appropriate business and social conventions that show respect for others in a culture. These include norms about how to dress for different functions, how to greet people, what kinds of conversations are appropriate, and what types of gifts are welcome. For example, in Japan, business cards are taken very seriously. Many Japanese businesspeople use business cards to determine the status of the person with whom they are dealing. Therefore, it is a good idea to list your degrees and honors on your business card and translate it into Japanese. In addition, it can be offensive to take a business card and put it away without reading it carefully. It also may be offensive to write on a person's business card—it would be like writing across the person's photograph.[95]

- *Understand the social context.* Try to understand how particular norms and customs reflect deeper assumptions and values of a culture. Specifically, take time to learn the history, politics, laws, religions, labor issues, and economic conditions of the cultures with which people work. To illustrate this point, cross-cultural consultant Fons Trompenaars describes a situation in which he and another Dutch consultant were conducting a change management seminar with Ethiopian managers. Initially, the seminar was going quite poorly. The seminar became successful only when the consultants took time to learn the history of Ethiopia. They learned that many Ethiopians' identity is tied to a wealthy and regal past. They integrated this treasured past into the seminar by asking participants, "What had Ethiopia done right in that period to make its cities and trade flourish?" For the participants, "the future was now seen as a way of recreating some of the greatest glories of the past; suddenly, the management of change seminar had captured the enthusiastic support of everyone."[96]

Understanding history, however, is not as simple as it may seem. When I told this story to an Ethiopian friend of mine, she noted that many Ethiopians, because of the history of intergroup conflicts in Ethiopia, would have been offended by the consultants' reference to Ethiopia's wealthy past. Discussing Ethiopia's wealthy past easily could have undermined the seminar, depending on which Ethiopians were in attendance.

Culture-General Skills

Culture-specific knowledge is necessary but insufficient for long-term managerial success because it is limited to specific cultural contexts. As cross-cultural interactions become the norm rather than the exception, you cannot always prepare for cross-cultural interactions in advance, nor can you learn all the nuances of every culture. Furthermore, you must know how to work with people from many different cultures simultaneously. For example, you may find yourself at a meeting with one Italian, one German, two Finns, one North American, one Japanese, and two Mexicans, all in the same room at the same time—with only 2-hour notice. In short, you must be able to cross multiple cultural boundaries anytime and any place. Therefore, you need cultural-general skills that do not depend on in-depth culture-specific knowledge. At a minimum, these include a desire to work with people from diverse cultures.[97] In addition, you should:

- *Invest in self-awareness.*   Take time to learn how your own culture affects how you see the world, why you do the things you do, and how your behavior affects others. Also take time to learn how you or your culture may be perceived by people whose cultures differ from your own.
- *Develop boundary-spanning relationship skills.*   Remember that every interaction is an opportunity to build a relationship. Try to make every cross-cultural interaction a positive one. Keep in mind the platinum rule: Treat others as they would like to be treated. By following the platinum rule, you will be better able to make others feel comfortable, develop mutual trust and respect with a wide variety of people, and get the support of people from many cultures.
- *Perception skills.*   Pay attention to the social context in which you are working. Look for cues that can help you understand important business norms regarding how people want to be treated at work, how they expect managers and professionals (including you) to act, and how decisions get made and implemented.[98]
- *Flexibility.*   Develop what is called cognitive flexibility. This refers to the ability to think in broad and complex ways, consider multiple goals and perspectives simultaneously, integrate divergent information, maintain rather than resolve contradictions, make sense out of ambiguity, and see uncertainty as an opportunity.[99] Also develop behavioral flexibility, which refers to the ability to be adaptable in your management styles and quick on your feet.[100]

- *Personal grounding.* Remember that effective multicultural managers are not so flexible that they give up their personal values or standards and adapt indiscriminately to every situation.[101] Rather, they balance adaptability with a healthy respect for their own culture, personal beliefs, and treasured values. Mahatma Gandhi eloquently described the art of balancing adaptability with personal grounding when he said: "Let all my windows be open. Let all cultures blow in. But let not culture blow me off my feet."

- *Emotional resilience.* Cross-cultural encounters can be rewarding and invigorating, but they can also create feelings of anxiety, confusion, and embarrassment, especially when things don't go as planned and when people don't react in ways that you are used to.[102] Effective multicultural managers rebound quickly from stressful experiences, persist when faced with obstacles (often by trying different strategies or adjusting their goals), and maintain an optimistic attitude and sense of humor.

- *Courage and attention to inequities.* Most organizations and societies are stratified into hierarchies in which people from some cultural groups have more power than do people from other cultural groups. Of course, this does not mean that people from some cultural groups are innately better or worse than are people from others.[103] To understand these inequities, pay attention to subtle and not-so-subtle patterns of inequities in everyday work life, such as who does and doesn't get taken seriously at meetings, who speaks and who doesn't, and which cultural groups tend to be over or underrepresented in various professions or at different levels of the hierarchy. Understanding and managing inequities is a particularly thorny issue when outside one's own country where sincere but naive interventions in the spirit of equality can do more harm than good. Understanding the religion, laws, and history of inter-group relations is particularly critical for managers who want to transport their cultural or personal ideologies abroad.

Only equals can be friends. *Ethiopia*   Note that many of the culture-general skills also are important to success in relatively homogeneous settings. However, although managers may get by without some of these skills and attitudes in homogeneous settings, they are critical to success in multicultural settings. Remember that multicultural competence is more an attitude of humility, empathy, and respect than it is a set of techniques.

Developing Multicultural Competence

How can you develop culture-specific and culture-general skills? As always, experience is a good teacher. Meena Wilson and Maxine Dalton, researchers for the Center for Creative Leadership, found that successful expatriates often learned "lessons of difference and lessons of accommodation" at an early age. Many were exposed to diversity at a young age through "an immigrant parent, a foreign-born spouse, an international schooling experience, or childhood in a border town or ethnically diverse community. These individuals seemed to have learned early the lessons of difference—that there is more than one way to living one's life."[104] They also found that successful expatriates tend to have succeeded in handling disruptions earlier in their lives, such as moving several times as children. These experiences taught them how to take care of themselves, how to get along with new people, and how to survey the environment for cues that help them make sense of and succeed in new situations.

What if you haven't had some of these early experiences? It helps to remember that having these experiences doesn't guarantee that a person necessarily learns lessons of value from them. Nor does it mean that people who don't have these early experiences lacked opportunities to develop attitudes and skills that help them become effective in cross-cultural situations. I know many people who have traveled the world over and failed to develop the emotional, cognitive, or behavioral flexibility that are the foundations of effective cross-cultural relationships. And I've known people who grew up in small, homogeneous communities who developed the qualities of curiosity, openness, empathy, and respect toward others—characteristics that are critical for cross-cultural effectiveness.

Structured activities, such as organized training programs and reading books about effective cross-cultural management, can help. In addition, you can learn a great deal by reading novels and watching movies about other cultures, particularly when they are created by the people from those cultures. Put yourself in a variety of cross-cultural situations that challenge your worldview and take you out of your comfort zone. Most importantly, you can develop relationships with people from different cultures. The more opportunities you have to be with people from other cultures, the more you can learn about yourself, others, and the world; the more practice you can get at enhancing your cross-cultural skills; the more humble and resilient you can become; and the more likely you will develop a reputation as someone who enjoys and succeeds in multicultural situations.

CREATING CULTURAL SYNERGY

In the article "Managing Globally Competent People," culture researchers Nancy Adler and Susan Bartholomew note that effective multicultural managers not only pay attention to developing their own cultural competence but they create an organizational culture in which all employees are "capable of working with and learning from colleagues from several cultures and who are capable of creating cultural synergy."[105] There are several steps that you can take to create cultural synergy in your organization.

Ensure Top-Level Commitment

Equality cannot be seized any more than it can be given. It must be a shared experience.
James Farmer, All About Core

Leaders who are committed to cultural diversity take a public stand on their commitment, provide the strategic direction for creating an effective multicultural organization, and allocate the resources required to achieve their goals.[106]

Role-Model the Behavior You Want to See

Although you may not be able to ensure commitment from all top-level executives, you can be a role model and look for opportunities to exhibit your commitment to diversity through your day-to-day interactions. Researcher Catherine Herr Van Norstrand explains that being a role model is particularly important when we are in a leadership role because others "may unquestioningly buy into our words and actions because they believe in us—we have more expertise and are expected to know what we are doing. They assume that we have gotten a grip on our own hang-ups and are ready to provide them with uncontaminated guidance. However, when our self-awareness is lacking, or even when we detect personal bias but neglect to stop it, the results of our collusion can be far-reaching."[107]

Obtain Information about How Well Your Company Is Managing Diversity

It is in the little actions of day-to-day work that employees will be testing to see if their leaders are respectful of the concerns and traditions of a particular gender or ethnic group. **Jay Conger,** *Leadership researcher and consultant*

Take steps to understand how the current organizational culture helps and hinders diversity efforts. You can get this information in several ways, including written surveys, in-depth interviews, focus groups, and analysis of company data related to hiring, staffing, promotion, turnover, and employee and customer satisfaction. You can also look to other organizations for best practices. Although most of the "best" companies admit that they still have a long way to go, they provide useful measures and data against which other organizations can judge their own efforts. For example, when *Fortune* magazine analyzed the companies that made their 2004 "Diversity Elite" list, they found that "at the 'typical' best company, minorities account for 21 percent of boardrooms, compared to 11 percent in 2001."[108]

You can also get information by establishing a diversity committee or task force. Many organizations create an internal advisory group consisting of a diverse group of employees who meet regularly, have access to top leadership, identify problems and opportunities, recommend interventions, and monitor progress toward diversity goals. The findings of these task forces can identify several opportunities for change that may otherwise go unnoticed. For example, when Avon developed a diversity task force in the 1990s, they identified several areas of concern. They found that Asian Americans were clustered in staff departments, women were becoming more satisfied with their advancement possibilities but were also becoming increasingly concerned about caretaker benefits, and gay employees wanted benefits for significant others.[109]

Know the Law

I can't change my sex. But you can change your policy. **Helen Kirkpatrick,** *Women of the World*

Make sure that all employees understand the legal environment at home and abroad.[110] Note that laws and interpretations of laws change often, so you should regularly check the status of discrimination laws in your own countries and in the countries in which you conduct business.

Break the Glass Ceiling

People, given the choice, will want to work in environments where they feel comfortable, have the opportunity to do their best work, and will be fairly rewarded for their efforts. Organizations that lack a diverse workforce or have a high rate of turnover send signals that these conditions may not be met. If you don't already have a diverse workforce, you need to determine how to make your organization an employer of choice for diverse populations. One way to become an employer of choice is to break the glass ceiling. If your organization doesn't have diversity at all levels, including top management, executive, and director levels, it sends the message that opportunities to contribute and advance may not be available to people from all cultural groups.

Consequently, some of the most high-potential people in those cultural groups will look to other organizations (e.g., your competition) to find these opportunities.

To break the glass ceiling, make sure all employees have equal access to important developmental experiences that are stepping-stones to professional development, promotions, and higher salaries. These opportunities include early experiences such as supportive relationships and challenging assignments that are important to a manager's later career success.[111] Challenging assignments include important projects or task forces, foreign assignments, line positions with direct profit and loss responsibility, and high-risk, high-visibility projects such as turning around a business or starting up a new division.[112] Such assignments enable employees to increase their visibility, take a strategic view of the organization, learn new technical and relationship management skills, prove themselves under difficult conditions, and develop the self-confidence and political savvy they will need at higher levels of the organization.

> Sometimes, I feel discriminated against, but it does not make me angry. It merely astonishes me. How can any deny themselves the pleasure of my company? It's beyond me. *Zora Neale Hurston, How It Feels to Be Colored Me*

Avoid Reindeer Games

Law professor Theresa Beiner coined the term "reindeer games" to describe social activities that are not obviously work related, that provide work-related advantages, and that are made available to some employees but not others on the basis of their cultural-identity group membership.[113] These include activities such as lunches, dinners, and certain sport activities. Such activities can provide access to important executives, colleagues, customers, and other business contacts who can provide work-related information, support, and professional contacts. Participating in these social events may contribute to promotions and other career advantages as a consequence of the visibility, informal mentoring, and the other benefits they offer. Beiner uses the term "reindeer games" to refer to such activities because, as many people remember from childhood storybooks and songs, Santa Claus's reindeer excluded "poor Rudolf" from their reindeer games. She notes that "reindeer games" may be illegal in the United States under Title VII of the Civil Rights Act of 1964, which prohibits employment discrimination on the basis of sex, race, and religion because such "games" can result in "disparate treatment, exclusion, or psychological harm" to members of certain groups.[114]

> The more a leader represents the interests and goals of a single group or faction, the greater the resistance from the other groups. Thus, the challenge facing the next generation of leaders will be to create plans and goals that incorporate the needs of diverse groups, and to do so in a way that all feel a sense of ownership. *Jay Conger, Leadership researcher*

Endorse Support Groups

Research suggests that women and people of color in the United States benefit (in terms of effectiveness and promotions) when they belong to support groups, also known as network groups (e.g., groups that specifically support women, African Americans, or Latinos in the organization).[115] As people who traditionally have been outside the managerial ranks move into higher levels of the organization, they often find themselves increasingly in the minority at those levels. Consequently, they often want and need support from others who share similar life and work experiences. Several organizations, including A. T. Kearney, the British Civil Service, General Electric, JP Morgan-Chase, and Daimler Chrysler, promote "identity-based support groups" to provide support to their members and offer advice to the organization on how to make the organization more supportive and best use the talents of all employees.[116]

Provide Training

Diversity training falls into two categories: awareness training and skill-based training.[117] Awareness training is often the starting point for diversity training programs and is designed to increase employees' awareness of and sensitivity toward diversity issues.[118] Such training focuses on helping employees understand the organization's commitment to developing a multicultural organization, the competitive advantages of multicultural organizations, the legal climate (e.g., affirmative action, equal employment opportunity, and sexual harassment laws), and the potential impact of cultural differences on individual behavior, interpersonal relationships, and group dynamics. One of the most important learnings of awareness training is that although people "share the same work environment," people from different cultural-identity groups often "experience that environment in very different ways."[119] Skill-based training provides employees with specific skills that help them manage diversity at work. Topics include understanding and managing one's own cultural biases, understanding different cultural norms, communicating and negotiating across cultures, and facilitating multicultural team meetings.

Encourage Formal Education

Encourage people of all races and genders to pursue advanced education. In a study designed to find out why enrollment of women in MBA programs is substantially less than enrollment of women in law and medical schools (36 percent of MBA students were women versus 47 percent and 49 percent of medical school and law school students in 2002), researchers found that 42 percent of the women felt they didn't receive the encouragement of employers to pursue the MBA, in contrast to 25 percent of men who felt this way. Furthermore, African American women were more likely to feel that they weren't encouraged to get an MBA degree than were Caucasian American women.[120] It is notable that ACT, a college entrance exam used in the United States, recently revised the exam questions and decided to "toss out essay questions in which one gender or ethnic group scored especially high or low."[121]

Change the Way Work Gets Done

> Unity, not uniformity, must be our aim. We attain unity only through variety. Differences must be integrated, not annihilated, nor absorbed.
> *Mary Parker Follett, The New State*

Many organizational policies and routines were created for a bygone era. New perspectives can bring fresh ideas about how to improve quality, increase efficiency, decrease costs, inspire innovations, identify new markets, and meet customers' needs. Therefore, effective multicultural managers encourage employees to challenge current assumptions about when, where, and how work should be accomplished. They explore whether current organizational policies and norms are truly necessary for organizational effectiveness or whether they are rooted in taken-for-granted assumptions and routines that may add little value or even hinder progress.

For example, when I was pregnant with my second child, I was scheduled to teach an evening MBA course. For 20 years, evening MBA courses had been taught for 3 hours each week over 13 weeks. This schedule would have brought the last class precariously close to the date my daughter Leah was due to be born. So, I suggested to my department chairperson that I redesign the course to meet for 4 full days instead of 13 3-hour weekly sessions. The course would cover the same amount of material over the same number of classroom hours, but in a more compressed format. When the 4-day course format was approved, over 200 students signed up for only 50 seats (students said that they appreciated the reduced travel and reduced transition costs involved) and received top ratings from the students (students said that they appreciated the content, organization, and flow of the course material). Today, the business school where I teach has added several other courses in a compressed format because these courses are so well received by students and faculty.

Pay Attention to Language and Other Forms of Organizational Symbolism

Organizational assumptions about diversity are passed on through subtle, yet powerful symbolic mechanisms such as the taken-for-granted languages, stories, and rituals that are used in everyday organizational life. Consequently, be careful about what you communicate, intentionally or unintentionally, by the words that you use and the stories that you choose to tell. When you have people from many cultures in your organizational stories, for example, you show that you view people from all cultures as being able to succeed, fail, and make a difference in the organization. When you use inclusive language (e.g., using both "he" and "she" to refer to managers and secretaries), you send the message that you assume that both men and women can be effective in a variety of organizational roles.[122] When you avoid using "us versus them" language ("those Americans" or "those Germans"), you remind employees that "we are all in this together."

Some taken-for-granted organizational rites and rituals may exclude or abuse members of particular cultural groups. These rites and rituals may be so embedded in an organization's culture that they are not viewed as problematic. For example, until 1991, the U.S. Navy regularly sent officers to the annual Tailhook conference for military officers and contractors. For several years, many conference attendees participated in a ritual in which officers and civilians (mostly women) were forced down a gauntlet of naval and Marine aviators (mostly male) who assaulted them, often sexually. Many naval leaders knew of this yearly ritual but did not consider it to be abusive until naval officer Paula Coughlin was forced down the gauntlet. When she complained to her supervisor, he told her, "That's what you get when you go to a hotel party with a bunch of drunk aviators." Unable to get his support, she contacted the press, which covered her story in the international media. As a consequence, the Pentagon investigated her claims and concluded that the gauntlet, as well as other taken-for-granted activities and rituals that occurred at the conference, were indeed abusive to women.

Prejudice saves a lot of time, because you can form an opinion without the facts. *Anonymous*

More than 39 U.S. Navy officers were punished for their actions. Several high-ranking officers were relieved of duty, demoted, or received early retirement for knowing such abuses occurred and making no effort to stop them. A year after the Tailhook scandal, a top-ranking officer said, "I need to emphasize a very, very important message. We get it. We know that the larger issue is a cultural problem which has allowed demeaning behavior and attitudes toward women in uniform to exist within the Navy."[123]

Create a Common Identity

Research consistently shows that people who feel that they share a common identity see people in their group as more similar to themselves, see and remember more positive things about others in their group, see members of their group as more competent and, feel more comfortable with members of their group.[124] To develop a common identity among diverse employees, Ted Childs, IBM's vice president of global workforce diversity, regularly reminds employees that "the ties that bind us are stronger than the issues that divide us.... There is only one "ism" on which we need to focus—consumerism."[125]

Increase Interaction among Members of Different Groups

Research suggests that people may overly focus on differences early in their relationships but often recognize and develop shared values when they spend more time together, particularly when they view each other as equals and as bringing different kinds of expertise to the organization. Therefore, create opportunities for members of different cultural groups to get to know each other personally, to see their common bonds as well as differences, view each other as equals and colleagues,[126] and appreciate the diverse talents and resources they bring to the organization.

Develop External Relations with Diverse Groups

Develop relationships with customers and vendors from a variety of cultures. Also support the various cultures in the community through organizational goodwill efforts and philanthropy. Many organizations develop alliances with advocacy groups (e.g., catalyst and the NAACP, which focus on the advancement of women and people of color, respectively) that are committed to promoting diversity in organizations. Doing so shows your commitment to creating a diverse organization. It also helps you get information, ideas, support, and other resources that can help your organization achieve its goals.

Measure Results and Reward Progress

People tend to pay attention to what gets measured. Therefore, identify specific diversity areas that need improvement, set clear and measurable goals, adjust these goals as appropriate over time, develop ways to measure progress, hold employees accountable for meeting these goals, show employees how they personally contribute to achieving diversity goals, and reward small as well as big efforts and accomplishments.

SUMMARY

One of the most important things you can do to create a work context that enhances the potential advantages of diversity while minimizing the potential disadvantages is to remember that developing an effective multicultural organization is an ongoing process. It doesn't happen overnight—or in one to two years. Like all major organizational interventions, it will include setbacks as well as advances. And small wins can have a big impact. Say researchers Debra Meyerson and Joyce Fletcher, "...small wins have a way of snowballing. One small change begets another, and eventually these small changes add up to a whole new system."[127] Thinking strategically, focusing on both the short and long term, and modeling the behaviors that you want to see, will go a long way toward creating an organization that can recruit and retain the most talented people available, regardless of the cultural groups to which they belong.

CHAPTER SUMMARY

As societies and organizations become more multicultural, managers must view managing cultural diversity as a skill they will use every working day throughout their careers.

Demographic categories, such as race, gender, nationality, religion, and age, are socially constructed categorizations that have meaning to a society, that people identify themselves as members of, that may shape how people within that group make sense of the world and relate to people outside the group, and that shape how people outside the group make sense of and relate to people inside that group. This does not mean that categories such as age or sex don't have physiological roots, but that societies and organizations give these categories meanings that go beyond their physiological functions and characteristics.

Cultures promote different worldviews and behavioral norms that help people solve everyday problems and dilemmas of life such as: Who am I? How do I relate to others? How do I communicate with others? How do I deal with time? What is truth? How do I relate to my environment? What is the relationship of work to life?

Effective multicultural managers understand the ways that cultural differences can influence people's preferences, expectations, and behaviors at work and adapt their managerial style accordingly. Doing so enables managers to grow personally and professionally, develop the trust and respect that is the foundation of effective work relationships, and leverage the diversity in the organization.

Effective diversity programs can contribute to an organization's sustained competitive advantage in several ways, including increased probability of positive publicity, access to the best talent, better problem solving and decision making, enhanced team performance, lower costs, success in ethnic and global markets, adherence to global standards that provide access to new markets, and effective relationships with advocacy and "watchdog" groups that monitor and publicize organizations' commitment to diversity.

Although diversity can be a competitive advantage, not all organizations succeed in their efforts. There are many reasons that diversity programs fail to have the impact that organizations hope for, including lack of systematic planning and patience, overemphasizing numerical goals, not changing the way work gets done, emotional tensions from a history of conflictual relations across groups that carry over from society into the workplace, cultural ignorance that can make people uncomfortable working with each other and reduce personal commitment to a multicultural workplace, lack of training or poor quality training, and parochialism of management theories.

There are at least three perspectives that organizations that promote diversity have: integration and learning (leveraging the different perspectives and behaviors the diverse workforce offers to increase innovation and adaptability with a focus on enhancing bottom-line results), access and legitimacy (believing that the workforce should reflect the demographics of the community, customers, and other constituencies, but not changing the way work gets done), and discrimination and fairness (believing that a culturally diverse workforce is a moral and social imperative to ensure justice). Organizations that promote the integration and learning perspective are more likely to reap the rewards of diversity in ways that add bottom-line value.

The job of the multicultural manager is to promote both the cultural diversity that broadens the organization's capabilities and the interdependence that aligns this diversity toward common organizational goals.

Effective multicultural managers continuously develop their own multicultural competence (their ability to be comfortable and effective in cross-cultural situations) and a work environment that promotes cultural synergy.

Personal multicultural competence requires both culture-specific knowledge and culture-general skills. Culture-specific knowledge enables managers to be effective in specific cultural contexts (e.g., doing business in Spain). Cultural-general skills enable managers to be effective with any culture and with multiple cultures simultaneously.

An effective multicultural work environment is one in which employees view people from different cultures as equals, believe that diversity contributes to the organization's effectiveness, and believe that all employees should have the opportunity to contribute to the organization's success and be rewarded for their contributions.

FOOD FOR THOUGHT

1. What is the most useful thing you learned in this chapter, and why?
2. Based on the strategies for managing diversity in ways that contribute to your own success and organizational success for managing diversity described in this chapter, what can you do to increase your own effectiveness? Practice at least one of these behaviors and note any benefits and progress you make.
3. Fill in the circles in Figure 7-2, "Identifying Cultural Influences." Which of these cultural identities are most important to you, and why? Which have the most impact on your everyday work life, and why? Do you ever "manage" these identity groups in any way and, if so, how? Compare your answers with someone else who has also completed Figure 7-2. How might your similarities and differences enhance and/or influence your ability to work effectively with each other?
4. If you could clone the ideal manager, what would that manager be like? Discuss your answer with someone else. How similar and different are your answers?
5. Interview someone who has lived, studied, or worked in another country. Ask them about the obstacles they faced, the skills they needed to be successful abroad, how their experience abroad affected their worldview and behavior, and the most important advice they have for others who want to live, study, or work abroad.
6. Select a country. Do some research on it and identify work-related norms, dos and taboos, and how the social context (e.g., history, laws, religion, economic context, and intergroup relations) shapes assumptions and behavior at work.
7. Complete the assessment shown in Box 7-1, "Work-Related Cultural Preferences." Have another person complete the assessment as well. Given your cultural profiles, what might the strengths be in your work relationship? What might the problems be in your work relationship? What can you do to ensure you leverage the strengths and minimize potential weaknesses?
8. Think of a time when you observed a situation involving a cultural bias or inequity in which you intervened. Discuss what motivated you to intervene. What did you do, and how did you feel? What were the consequences of your intervention? Now think of a time when you observed a situation involving a cultural bias or inequity but you did not intervene. Why didn't you intervene? How did you feel? What were the consequences?
9. Which perspective does your organization have toward diversity: integration and learning, access and legitimacy, discrimination and fairness, or "we don't think about it at all"? What are the consequences of your organization's perspective for you, others, and the organization? Given that research has shown that the integration and learning perspective is most likely to add bottom-line value to the organization, what can you do to promote this perspective in your part of your organization?

FIGURE 7-2   Identifying Cultural Influences

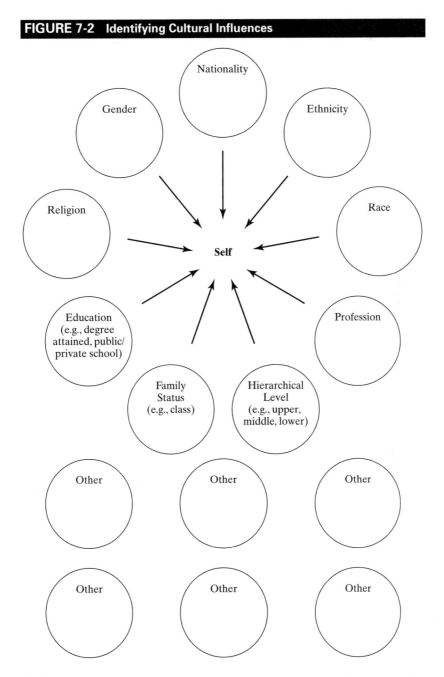

Fill in the information in each circle. How do your cultural identities influence your world view and behavior? How do they influence how others perceive you and act toward you? Do you ever actively "manage" any of your identities at work? If so, which ones and how?

ENDNOTES

1. Di'Tomaso, Nancy, Daria Kirby, Frances Milliken, and Harry Triandis. 1998. "Effective and Inclusive Learning Environments." A Report Commissioned by the International Association for Management Education (AACSB). St. Louis, MO: AACSB, 16.

2. 1995. "Survey Shows Many Companies Have Diversity Programs, Changes in Affirmative Action Perspectives." *Mosaics: Society of Human Resources Focus on Workplace Diversity,* 1(1): 1, 5.

3. Di'Tomaso, Nancy, Daria Kirby, Frances Milliken, and Harry Triandis. 1998. "Effective and Inclusive Learning Environments." A Report Commissioned by the International Association for Management Education (AACSB). St. Louis, MO: AACSB, 17.

4. Woodford, John. 1996. "Seeing Race: A New Look at an Old Notion." *Michigan Today.* June: 2.

5. West, Candace, and Don H. Zimmerman. 1987. "Doing Gender." *Gender & Society,* 1(2): 125–151.

6. Sowell, Thomas. 1993. "Effontery and Gall, Inc." *Forbes* 27: 52; cited in Litvin, Deborah R. 1997. "The Discourse of Diversity: From Biology to Management." *Organization,* 4(2): 187–209.

7. Litvin, Deborah R. 1997. "The Discourse of Diversity: From Biology to Management." *Organization,* 4(2): 187–209.

8. Gilbert, Matthew. 1996. "Gish Jen, All-American." *The Boston Globe,* 4: 53, 58; quoted in Litvin, Deborah R. 1997. "The Discourse of Diversity: From Biology to Management." *Organization,* 4(2): 187–209.

9. 1995. "Increasing Diversity Creates Definition Issues." *Mosaics Society of Human Resources Focuses on Workplace Diversity,* 1(1): 3, 7.

10. Alderfer, Clayton. 1983. "Intergroup Relations and Organizations." In Hackman, Richard J., Ed Lawler, and Lyman Porter (eds.). *Perspectives on Behavior in Organizations.* New York: McGraw-Hill.

11. Ibid.

12. Wells, Leroy Jr. 1985. "Misunderstandings of and among Cultures: The Effects of Transubstantiative Error." In D. Vails-Weber, and J. Potts (eds.). *Sunrise Seminars,* 2: 51–57. Arlington, VA: NTL Institute.

13. Earley, Christopher, and Miriam Erez. 1997. *The Transplanted Executive: Why You Need to Understand How Workers in Other Countries See the World Differently.* New York: Oxford.

14. Schein, Edgar. 1992. *Organizational Culture and Leadership.* 2d ed. San Francisco; CA: Jossey-Bass.

15. Brake, Terrance, and Danielle Walker. 1995. *Doing Business Internationally: A Workbook to Cross-Cultural Success.* New Jersey: Princeton Training Press.

16. 2003. "It's a Grand Latte World." *Wall Street Journal.* December 15: b1 and b4.

17. Gilligan, Carol. 1993. *In a Different Voice: Psychological Theory and Women's Development.* Cambridge, MA: Harvard University Press.

18. Brake, Terence, Danielle Medina Walker, and Thomas Walker. 1995. *Doing Business Internationally: The Guide to Cross-Cultural Success.* Princeton, NJ: McGraw-Hill.

19. Ibid.

20. Trompenaars, Fons. 1994. *Riding the Waves of Culture: Understanding Diversity in Global Business.* New York: Irwin.

21. Ibid.

22. Hofstede, Geert. 1984. *Culture's Consequences: International Differences in Work-Related Values.* Newbury Park, CA: Sage; Geert Hofstede. 1993. "Cultural Constraints in Management Theories." *Academy of Management Executive,* 7(1): 81–94.

23. Trompenaars, Fons. 1994. *Riding the Waves of Culture: Understanding Diversity in Global Business.* New York: Irwin.

24. Gilligan, Carol. 1993. *In a Different Voice: Psychological Theory and Women's Development.* Cambridge, MA: Harvard University Press.

25. Copeland, Lennie, and Lewis Griggs. 1985. *Going International, How to Make Friends and Deal Effectively in the Global Marketplace.* New York: Plume Books.

26. Sanchez-Burks, Jeffrey. 2002. "Protestant Relational Ideology and (In)attention to Relational Cues in Work Settings." *Journal of Personality and Social Psychology,* 83(4): 919–929.

27. Kennedy, Jim, and Anna Everest. 1991. "Put Diversity in Context." *Personnel Journal.* September: 50–54.

28. Sanchez-Burks, Jeffrey. 2002. "Protestant Relational Ideology and (In)attention to Relational Cues in Work Settings." *Journal of Personality and Social Psychology,* 83(4): 919–929; Sanchez-Burks, Jeffrey, Fiona Lee, Incheol Choi, Richard Nisbett, Shuming Zhao, and Jasook Koo. 2004. "Conversing Across Cultures: East-West Communication Styles in Work and Non-Work Contexts." Unpublished paper.

29. Tannen, Deborah. 1990. *You Just Don't Understand: Women and Men in Conversation.* New York: Ballentine Books.

30. Gardenswartz, Lee, and Anita Rowe. 1993. *Managing Diversity: A Complete Desk Reference and Planning Guide.* San Diego, CA: Pfeiffer and Company.

31. Copeland, Lennie, and Lewis Griggs. 1985. *Going International, How to Make Friends and Deal Effectively in the Global Marketplace.* New York: Plume Books.

32. Lewis, Richard. 1996. *When Cultures Collide.* London: Nicholas Brealey Publishing.

33. Bluedorn, Allen C., Carol Felker Kaufman, and Paul M. Lane. 1992. "How Many Things Do You Like to Do at Once? An Introduction to Monochronic and Polychronic Time." *Academy of Management Executive,* 6(4): 17–26.

34. Stone, Nan. 1989. "The Globalization of Europe: An Interview with Wisse Dekker." *Harvard Business Review.* May–June 67(3): 90–96.

35. 1997. *U.S. News and World Report.* December 1: 6.

36. Belenky, Mary Field, Blythe McVicker Clinchy, Nancy Rule Godberger, and Jill Mattuck Tarule. 1986. *Women's Ways of Knowing.* New York: Basic Books.

37. Kim, Heejung. 2002. "We Talk, Therefore We Think? A Cultural Analysis of the Effect of Talking on Thinking." *Journal of Personality and Social Psychology,* 83(4): 828–842.

38. Brake, Terrance, and Danielle Walker. 1995. *Doing Business Internationally: A Workbook to Cross-Cultural Success.* New Jersey: Princeton Training Press.

39. Brake, Terance, Danielle Walker, and Thomas Walker. *Doing Business Internationally: The Guide to Cross-Cultural Success.* Princeton, NJ: McGraw-Hill.

40. Di'Tomaso, Nancy, Daria Kirby, Frances Milliken, and Harry Triandis. 1998. "Effective and Inclusive Learning Environments." St. Louis, MO: The International Association for Management Education (AACSB), 57; citing Triandis, Harry. 1994. *Culture and Social Behavior.* New York: McGraw-Hill.

41. Trompenaars, Fons. 1994. *Riding the Waves of Culture: Understanding Diversity in Global Business.* New York: Irwin.

42. Hofstede, Geert. 1984. *Culture's Consequences: International Differences in Work-Related Values* Newbury Park, CA: Sage; Geert Hofstede. 1993. "Cultural Constraints in Management Theories." *Academy of Management Executive,* 7(1): 81–94.

43. Sethi, Sheena, and Mark Lepper. 1999. "Rethinking the Role of Choice in Intrinsic Motivation: A Cultural Perspective on Intrinsic Motivation." *Journal of Personality and Social Psychology,* 76(3): 349–366.

44. Schor, Juliet. 1991. *The Overworked American.* New York: Basic Books.

45. Cox, Taylor, Jr. 1997. "Distinguishing Valuing Diversity from Stereotyping." In Taylor Cox, Jr., and Ruby L. Beale (eds.). *Developing Competency to Manage Diversity: Readings, Cases, Activities.* San Francisco, CA: Berrett-Koehler Publishers.

46. Ibid.

47. Wright, Peter, Stephen Ferris, Janine S. Hiller, and Mark Kroll. 1995. "Competitiveness through the Management of Diversity: Effects on Stock Price Valuation." *Academy of Management Journal,* 38:(2): 272–287.

48. Ibid.

49. Fisher, George. 1996. "Foreword." In Morrison, Ann. *The New Leaders: Leadership Diversity in America.* San Francisco, CA: Jossey-Bass.

50. Thomas, David, and Robin Ely. 1997. "Making Differences Matter: A New Paradigm for Managing Diversity." *Harvard Business Review*, 74(5): 79–90.

51. Cox, Taylor, Sharon Lobel, and Poppy McLeod. 1991. "Effects of Ethnic Group Cultural Difference on Cooperative versus Competitive Behavior on a Group Task." *Academy of Management Journal*, 34(4): 827–847.

52. Thomas, David C., Elizabeth C. Ravlin, and Alan W. Wallace. 1996. "Effect of Cultural Diversity in Work Groups." *Research in the Sociology of Organizations*, 14: 1–33.

53. Ibid., p. 26.

54. Faircloth, Anne. 1998. "Guess Who's Coming to Denny's." *Fortune*. August 3: 108–110.

55. Cohen-Van Pelt, Elizabeth. 1998. "Lawyer Loot." *Working Woman*. November: 20.

56. Kelly, Kate, and De Baise, Colleen. 2004. "Morgan Stanley Settles Bias Suit for $54 Million." *Wall Street Journal.* July 13: A1–2.

57. Zimmerman, Ann. 2004. "Judge Certifies Wal-Mart Suit as Class Action." *Wall Street Journal.* June 23: A1–6.

58. Cox, Taylor H., and Stacy Blake. 1991. "Managing Cultural Diversity: Implications for Organizational Competitiveness." *Academy of Management Executive*, 5(3): 45–56.

59. Morrison, Ann. 1996. *The New Leaders.* Jossey-Bass. CA: San Francisco.

60. Thomas, Kecia M. 1996. "Psychological Privilege and Ethnocentrism as Barriers to Cross-Cultural Adjustment and Effective Intercultural Interactions." *Leadership Quarterly*, 7(2): 215–228.

61. Black, Stewart J., and Hal B. Gregersen. 1991. "Antecedents to Cross-Cultural Adjustment for Expatriates in Pacific Rim Assignments." *Human Relations*, 44(5): 497–515.

62. Stone, Nan. 1989 "The Globalization of Europe: An Interview with Wisse Dekker." *Harvard Business Review*, 91–96: 92.

63. Jones, Del. 1996. "Setting Diversity's Foundation in the Bottom Line." *USA Today*. October 15: 4B.

64. Copeland, Lennie. 1988. "Valuing Workplace Diversity: Ten Reasons Employers Recognize the Benefits of a Mixed Work Force." *Personnel Administrator*. November: 38–40.

65. 1998. "Can America's Workforce Grow Old Gainfully?" *The Economist*. July 25: 59–60.

66. Urresta, Lixandra, and Jonathan Hickman. 1998. "The Diversity Elite." *Fortune*. August 3: 114–122.

67. Kochan, Thomas, Katrina Bezrukova, Robin Ely, Susan Jackson, Aparna Joshi, Karen Jen, Jonathan Leonard, David Levine, and David Thomas. 2003. "The Effects of Diversity on Business Performance: Report of the Diversity Research Network." *Human Resource Management.* Spring 42(1): 3–21.

68. Morrison, Ann. 1996. *The New Leaders.* San Francisco, CA: Jossey-Bass.

69. Ibid.

70. Watson, W. E., K. Kumar, and L. K. Michaelson. 1993. "Cultural Diversity's Impact on Interaction Process and Performance: Comparing Homogeneous and Diverse Task Groups." *Academy of Management Journal*, 36: 590–602.

71. Thomas, David, and Robin Ely. 1996. "Making Differences Matter: A New Paradigm for Managing Diversity." *Harvard Business Review*, 74(5): 79–90.

72. Ibid., p. 82.

73. Ely, Robin, and David A. Thomas. 2001. "Cultural Diversity at Work: The Effects of Diversity Perspectives on Work Group Processes and Outcomes." *Administrative Science Quarterly*, 46: 229–273.

74. Ibid., p. 240.

75. Ibid., p. 243.

76. Ibid., p. 245–246.

77. Huey, John. 1998. "Here We Go Again." *Fortune*. October 12: 26.

78. Andre, Rae. 1995. "Diversity Stress as Moral Stress." *Journal of Business Ethics*, 14: 489–496.

79. Jackson, Susan, Joan Brett, Valerie Sessa, Dawn Cooper, Johan Julin, and Karl Peyronnin. 1991. "Some Differences Make a Difference: Individual Dissimilarity and Group Heterogeneity as Correlates of Recruitment, Promotion, and Turnover." *Journal of Applied Psychology*, 76(5): 675–689; O'Reilly, Charles, David Caldwell, and William Barnett. 1989. "Work Group Demography, Social Integration, and Turnover." *Administrative Science Quarterly*, 34: 21–37; Jackson, Susan E. 1991. "Team

Composition in Organizational Settings: Issues in Managing an Increasingly Diverse Work Force." In S. Worchel, W. Wood, and J. Simpson (eds.). *Group Process and Productivity*. Beverly Hills, CA: Sage.

80. Jackson, Susan E. 1991. "Team Composition in Organizational Settings: Issues in Managing an Increasingly Diverse Workforce." In S. Worchel, W. Wood, and J. Simpson (eds.). *Group Process and Productivity*. Beverly Hills, CA: Sage.

81. Triandis, Harry, Ed R. Hall, and R. B. Ewen. 1965. "Member Heterogeneity and Dyadic Creativity." *Human Relations*, 18: 33–35; Adler, Nancy. 1986. *International Dimensions of Organizational Behavior*. Boston, MA: Kent.

82. Finley, Joycelyn. 1996. "Communication Double Binds: The Catch-22 of Conversations about Racial Issues in Work Groups." Dissertation Submitted to the University of Michigan.

83. Nemetz, Patricia, and Sandra Christensen. 1996. "The Challenge of Cultural Diversity: Harnessing a Diversity of Views to Understand Multiculturalism." *Academy of Management Review*, 21(2): 434–462.

84. Mulvaney, Tim. "Why Diversity Becomes Irrelevant." *Managing Diversity*, 7(6): 6.

85. Cox, Taylor. 1993. *Cultural Diversity in Organizations: Theory, Research, and Practice*. San Francisco, CA: Berrett-Koehler; Cox, Taylor, and Ruby Beale. 1997. *Developing Competency to Manage Diversity: Readings, Cases, and Activities*. San Francisco, CA: Berrett-Koehler.

86. William Whyte. 1956. *The Organization Man*. New York: Doubleday.

87. Harragan, Betty Lehan. 1977. *Games Mother Never Taught You*. New York: Warner Books.

88. Kelly, Colleen, and Judith Meyers. 1995. *Cross-Cultural Adaptability Inventory*. Minneapolis, MN: National Computer Systems.

89. Fitzgerald, Thomas. 1997. "Understanding Diversity in the Workplace: Cultural Metaphors or Metaphors of Identity?" *Business Horizons*, 40(4): 66–70.

90. Lancaster, Hal. 1998. "Learning to Manage in a Global Workplace (You're on Your Own)." *Wall Street Journal*. June 2: B1.

91. Tung, Rosalie. 1987. "Expatriate Assignments: Enhancing Success and Minimizing Failure." *Academy of Management Executive*, 1(2): 117–126; Kelly, Colleen, and Judith Meyers. *Cross-Cultural Adaptability Inventory*. Minneapolis, MN: National Computer Systems.

92. Kelly, Colleen, and Judith Meyers. 1995. *Cross-Cultural Adaptability Inventory*. Minneapolis, MN: National Computer Systems.

93. Laurent, Andre. 1986. "The Cross-Cultural Puzzle of International Human Resource Management." *Human Resource Management*, 25(1): 91–102.

94. Stewart, Rosemary. 1996. "German Management: A Challenge to Anglo-American Managerial Assumptions. *Business Horizons*. May–June: 52–54.

95. Kennedy, Jim, and Anna Everest. 1991. "Put Diversity in Context." *Personnel Journal*. September: 50–54.

96. Trompenaars, Fons. 1994. *Riding the Waves of Culture: Understanding Diversity in Global Business*. New York: Irwin.

97. Kelly, Colleen, and Judith Meyers. 1995. *Cross-Cultural Adaptability Inventory*. Minneapolis, MN: National Computer Systems.

98. Ibid.

99. McGill, Andrew, Michael Johnson, and Karen Bantel. 1994. "Cognitive Complexity and Conformity: Effects on Performance in a Turbulent Environment." *Psychological Reports*, 75: 1451–1472.

100. Kelly, Colleen, and Judith Meyers. 1995. *Cross-Cultural Adaptability Inventory*. Minneapolis, MN: National Computer Systems.

101. Hodgetts, Richard. 1993. "A Conversation with Geert Hofstede." *Organizational Dynamics*, 57: 53–61.

102. Kelly, Colleen, and Judith Meyers. 1995. *Cross-Cultural Adaptability Inventory*. Minneapolis, MN: National Computer Systems.

103. Adler, Nancy J., and Susan Bartholomew. 1992. "Managing Globally Competent People." *Academy of Management Executive*, 6(3): 52–66.

104. Wilson, Meena S., and Maxine A. Dalton. 1997. "Understanding the Demands of Leading in a Global Environment: A First Step." *Issues and Observations*, 17(1, 2): 12–14.

105. Adler, Nancy, and Susan Bartholomew. 1992. "Managing Globally Competent People." *Academy of Management Executive,* 6(3): 52–65.

106. Cox, Taylor, and Stacy Blake. 1991. "Managing Cultural Diversity: Implications for Organizational Competitiveness." *Academy of Management Executive,* 5(3): 45–56.

107. Herr Van Norstrand, Catherine. 1993. "Leaders in Collusion: How Leaders Perpetuate Male Privilege." In *Gender Responsible Leadership.* Newbury Park, CA: Sage, 3–29.

108. Daniels, Cora. 2004. "50 Best Companies for Minorities." *Fortune.* June 28, 149(13): 136–142.

109. Thomas, Roosevelt, Jr. 1992. *Beyond Race and Gender.* New York: Amacom.

110. Feltes, Patricia, Robert K. Robinson, and Ross L. Fink. 1993. "American Female Expatriates and the Civil Rights Act of 1991: Balancing Legal and Business Interests." *Business Horizons.* March–April: 82–86.

111. Kirchmeyer, Catherine. 1995. "Demographic Similarity to the Work Group: A Longitudinal Study of Managers at the Early Career Stage." *Journal of Organizational Behavior,* 16: 76–83.

112. Van Velsor, Ellen, and Martha W. Hughes. 1990. *Gender Differences in the Development of Managers: How Women Managers Learn from Experience.* Greensboro, NC: Center for Creative Leadership.

113. Beirman, Leonard. 1997. "Regulating Reindeer Games." *Academy of Management Executive,* 11(4): 92–93; citing Beiner, Theresa A. 1996. "Do Reindeer Games Count as Terms, Conditions, or Privileges of Employment under Title VII?" *Boston College Law Review,* 37: 643–690.

114. Ibid.

115. Friedman, Raymond A. 1996. "Defining the Scope and Logic of Minority and Female Network Groups." *Research in Personnel and Human Resources Management,* 14: 307–349.

116. Cox, Taylor. 1994. *Cultural Diversity in Organizations: Theory, Research, and Practice.* San Francisco, CA: Berrett-Koehler Publishers.

117. Cox, Taylor, and Stacy Blake. 1991. "Managing Cultural Diversity: Implications for Organizational Competitiveness." *Academy of Management Executive,* 5(3): 45–56.

118. Carnevale, Anthony P., and Susan C. Stone. 1994. "Diversity: Beyond the Golden Rule." *Training and Development.* October: 22–39.

119. Fine, Marlene, Fern L. Johnson, and M. Sallyanne Ryan. 1990. "Cultural Diversity in the Workplace." *Public Personnel Management,* 19(3): 305–319.

120. 2000. "Women and the MBA: Gateway to Opportunity." University of Michigan Business School, Center for the Education of Women, and Catalyst; Sellers, Patricia. 2003. "Power: Do Women Really Want It." *Fortune.* Oct 13: 80–100.

121. Kronholz, June. 2004. "Graders Learn Fine Points of Scoring College-Exam Essays." *Wall Street Journal.* August 2: B1 and B4.

122. Martyna, Wendy. 1980. "Beyond the He-Man Approach: The Case for Nonsexist Language." *Signs: Journal of Women in Culture and Society,* 5(3): 482–493.

123. Caproni, Paula, and Joycelyn Finley. 1997. "When Organizations Do Harm: Two Cautionary Tales." In Prasad, Pushkala, Albert J. Mills, Michael Elms, and Anshuman Prasad (eds.). *Managing the Organizational Melting Pot: Dilemmas of Workplace Diversity.* Thousand Oaks, CA: Sage, 255–284; citing J. Lancaster. 1992. "The Sex Life of the Navy: After the Tailhook Scandal, an Attempt to Reform." *Washington Post.* May 17: 31.

124. John Dovidio, Ana Validzic, and Samuel Gaertner. 1998. "Intergroup Bias: Status, Differentiation, and a Common Ingroup Identity." *Journal of Personality and Social Psychology,* 75(1): 109–120.

125. Childs, Ted, Jr. 1998. "Work Force Diversity in the United States: Diversity at IBM." http://www.empl.ibm.com/diverse/ ltrchild.htm. September 9.

126. Dovidio, John, Ana Validzic, and Samuel Gaertner. 1998. "Intergroup Bias: Status, Differentiation, and a Common Ingroup Identity." *Journal of Personality and Social Psychology,* 75: 109–120.

127. Meyerson, Debra, and Joyce Fletcher. 2000. "A Modest Manifesto for Shattering the Glass Ceiling." *Harvard Business Review.* January–February: 126–136.

8

Creating
High-Performing Teams

This chapter will help you:

■ Identify the characteristics of high-performing teams

■ Understand when teams are and are not useful

■ Understand predictable stages of a team's life cycle

■ Learn how to avoid (or at least minimize) dysfuntional team processes

■ Become a more effective team member and team leader

> *When I started this business of teams, I was anxious to get it done and*
> *get back to my real job. Then I realized that, hey, this is my real job.*[1]
> —TEAM LEADER CITED IN FORTUNE

Teams are a fact of life for most organizations. We love them and we loathe them. Regardless of how we feel about teams, we know that most organizations cannot survive without them. People working in teams have the capacity to solve complex problems that cannot be solved by individuals working alone. People working in teams bring more resources to a task, including a variety of perspectives, knowledge, skills, and experience. When well managed, teams can turn these resources into greater productivity gains than any individual can accomplish working alone. When poorly managed, teams can feel like a nightmare.

Every day, we put great faith in teams. Each time we drive a car, fly in an airplane, have surgery, or leave our children at school, we place our lives and the futures of our families in products and services created and delivered by teams. We put our faith not only in the talent of individuals but also in their ability to work together cohesively and competently as a team. Often the teams in which we place our fate have never worked together before, as in the case of emergency medical teams and airplane cockpit crews.

Why do we put such faith in teams? In part, we just don't think much about it. When we fly in an airplane, for example, we sit down in our seat, buckle our seat belt, and we're off the ground. We take for granted the sophisticated interplay of intelligence and emotions, individual expertise and team coordination, technological sophistication and human insight that enable the flight crew and air traffic controllers to respond to both the routine and unexpected events in our journey miles above the earth and safely back.

Do you want a collection of brilliant minds or a brilliant collection of minds? **R. Meredith Belbin**

But we also put our faith in teams because we instinctively understand that group life is necessary for human survival. We know that in many situations "two heads (or more) are better than one." This is as true today as it was in the nomadic ages when human beings depended on groups to forage for food, protect themselves from predators, and move from place to place to find new resources to ensure their survival. Undoubtedly, we have different challenges in the twenty-first century. Increasingly, our individual, organizational, and societal survival requires that we regularly solve complex problems that we have never faced before, that have no right answers, and for which the consequences of our decisions are uncertain. Furthermore, for our organizations to survive, we must work faster and better than the competition, meet the rising expectations of a customer base that is increasingly more culturally diverse and globally dispersed, and deal with the onslaught of new technologies that seem to outpace our ability to learn how to use them.

Given this complex and fast-paced environment, it's no surprise that more and more organizations are using teams to achieve their goals. But high-performing teams don't just happen. They are created from talented individuals who are committed to doing something that they believe is important, who have ways of working together that help them reach their collective goals, and who have leaders that create a work context that enhances rather than hinders the team's efforts. In this chapter, I discuss the specific characteristics of high-performing teams and how you—as a team member and leader—can help create these characteristics. But first, I want to offer a reality check about teams.

BEYOND THE TEAM HYPE

Although teams are increasingly necessary for organizational success, it is a mistake to view them as the solution to all problems. As *Fortune* magazine journalist Kenneth Labich laments, "Weird fact of life: For every problem we face, someone has come up with a solution way too slick to be true. . . . In the corporate world, there's that supposed miracle cure for ailing organizations—team-based management."[2]

Like Labich, critical theorist Amanda Sinclair warns us against being seduced by the "tyranny of a team ideology."[3] She agrees that teams are not the solution to all organizational problems. However, she goes one step further and argues that an overzealous and naive use of teams can reinforce some of the problems that teams are intended to solve. She explains:

> Teams can contribute to getting work of all kinds done, but not when their application is informed by a narrow framework that nurtures inappropriate expectations. Further, and more critically, the team ideology . . . tyrannizes because, under the banner of benefits to all, teams are frequently used to camouflage coercion under the pretense of maintaining cohesion; conceal conflict under the guise of consensus; convert conformity into a semblance of creativity;

give unilateral decisions a co-determinist seal of approval; delay action in the supposed interests of consultation; legitimize lack of leadership; and disguise expedient arguments and personal agendas.[4]

In short, both Sinclair and Labich agree that teamwork can raise the level of individual, group, and organizational performance. But they also remind us that teamwork can lead to dysfunctional dynamics such as collective tunnel vision, inefficiencies, employee discontent, and moral lapses.[5]

Our team is well balanced. We have problems everywhere. *Tommy Prothro, American football coach*

The current team hype carries another risk. It may lead us to believe that teams are a basic building block of all organizations and that most employees participate in teams. Research suggests otherwise. A recent study of *Fortune*, 1,000 companies conducted by the Center for Effective Organizations at the University of Southern California concluded that 68 percent of the organizations in the study "use self-managed or high-performing teams ... but the study also shows that only 10 percent of workers are in such teams, hardly a number betokening a managerial revolution."[6]

The point I want you to take away from these warnings is not that our optimism about teams is unwarranted. On the contrary, the effective use of teams can be a competitive advantage and can enrich our lives. However, our optimism is more likely to lead to successful results if we use teams for the appropriate tasks, take the time to learn about human behavior in teams, and develop a set of techniques that can help guide our teams toward success. In this chapter, we look at the characteristics of high-performing teams and what you can do to help teams develop these characteristics. Let us begin by answering the question: What is a team?

WHAT IS A TEAM?

Teams come in many forms. They may be permanent, temporary, planned, or ad hoc. They may create products, provide services, or process people (as do human service agencies).[7] They may be formally chartered by organizational leaders or may emerge informally through employees' mutual interests and goals. They may be leader-led or self-managed. Team members may routinely meet face-to-face at the same time and in the same place (currently called "co-located" teams), or they may rarely see each other in person and instead use computer-mediated communication technologies to interact with each other (currently called "distributed" or "virtual" teams). Regardless of their purpose and form, all teams are made up of "individuals interacting interdependently" to achieve common organizational goals.[8] Furthermore, all teams share the following characteristics[9]:

- *Clear boundaries.*   Team members can identify who is and who isn't a member of the team. In addition, outsiders recognize the team as a legitimate organizational unit.
- *Common tasks.*   Team members have common tasks to perform and share collective responsibility for team outcomes.
- *Differentiated member roles.*   That is, each team member is expected to offer something distinctive and valuable to the team.
- *Autonomy.*   Team members have some discretion over how they do their work.

- *Dependence on external people and resources.* Team members must depend on other individuals and groups in the organization for information, resources, and support to accomplish their goals.
- *Collective responsibility.* Feedback and rewards are given, at least in part, to the team as a whole.

How do teams differ from work groups? Some researchers and practitioners see the difference as merely semantic and use the terms "group" and "team" interchangeably. Others, like myself, argue that although both work groups and teams are made up of individuals working interdependently toward common organizational goals, teams have several characteristics that go beyond those of work groups, particularly if they are high-performing teams.

Members of high-performing teams tend to develop a collective purpose that goes beyond that which the organization has established for them.[10] Often, team members develop a purpose that gives them an opportunity to showcase and leverage their particular talents. For example, the organization may ask the team to develop a new product, yet team members may decide to go beyond the organization's request and create a product that is the most technologically sophisticated product on the market. Because they have personalized the team's goal, team members feel greater ownership of their work and believe that they are working for each other as well as for the team leader and the organization. In addition, people working in teams tend to have more say over how they do their work and expect a greater degree of personal learning and fulfillment from the team than do people working in groups. And, members of teams are not likely to see themselves as interchangeable or easily replaceable.[11] When someone leaves a team, the remaining team members feel a greater sense of loss (unless, of course, the person who leaves has been unproductive or disruptive, in which case the remaining team members find ways to celebrate the person's departure).

Successful collaborations are dreams with deadlines. Warren Bennis and Patricia Biederman, Organizing Genius

Finally, leaders of high-performing teams spend less time in direct contact with the team and more time managing the context in which the team works. Rather than doing the team's work, they champion the team, provide direction and structure, supply resources and remove obstacles, and help the team manage the boundaries between the team and external people and groups.

No two teams follow the exact same path to success. Every successful team develops its own team culture and leadership norms. However, research suggests that high-performing teams tend to share several characteristics. These are summarized in Figure 8-1 and discussed in detail in the following sections.

CRITERIA FOR JUDGING TEAM EFFECTIVENESS

How can you distinguish a mediocre team from a high-performing team? According to Harvard researcher Richard Hackman, who has been studying teams for more than 20 years, high-performing teams meet three effectiveness criteria:[12]

- *The team must consistently produce high-quality output.* The team's products and services must consistently meet its customers' "standards of quantity, quality, and timeliness." A high-performing team may not succeed in its efforts all of the time, but it does succeed most of the time.

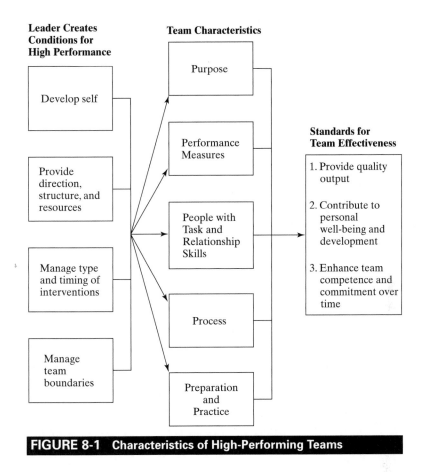

Leader Creates Conditions for High Performance
- Develop self
- Provide direction, structure, and resources
- Manage type and timing of interventions
- Manage team boundaries

Team Characteristics
- Purpose
- Performance Measures
- People with Task and Relationship Skills
- Process
- Preparation and Practice

Standards for Team Effectiveness
1. Provide quality output
2. Contribute to personal well-being and development
3. Enhance team competence and commitment over time

FIGURE 8-1 Characteristics of High-Performing Teams

- ***The team must promote the personal growth needs and well-being of team members.***   In high-performing teams, all team members feel as though they are better off because they are part of the team. Although some work groups frustrate members and block their ability to contribute and learn, high-performing teams motivate team members and offer ample opportunities for each member to contribute and learn.
- ***The team must grow and learn as a unit.***   High-performing teams become "increasingly capable over time" as performing units. They take the time to reflect on their collective experience and learn from their successes and failures so that they continuously improve the team's performance.

Note that a team can succeed in the short term without meeting all three of these effectiveness factors. For example, a team can initially produce high-quality products or services without enabling all team members to grow or contribute to its success. However, if some team members don't feel as though they are learning or contributing to the team's work, they may become detached, relationships may become strained, and the team's ability to create high-quality products may deteriorate over time.

How large can an effective team be? The appropriate size of the team depends on how many people it takes to ensure that the team has the necessary knowledge and skills it needs to successfully accomplish its goals. For example, physicians Paula Mahone and Karen Drake led the sixty-six-person team that made medical history by successfully delivering the McCaughey septuplets at the Iowa Methodist Medical Center in 1997. Each member of the team brought a specific expertise to the delicate task of bringing the seven babies into the world alive.

FOUNDATIONS OF HIGH-PERFORMING TEAMS: PURPOSE, PERFORMANCE MEASURES, PEOPLE, PROCESS, AND PRACTICE

Most of us have been part of work groups that felt like a waste of time. We didn't know why we were included, our energy was sapped by attention to petty details and personal agendas, we accomplished little, and we lost valuable time that we could have spent on other important tasks. Most of us also have been part of work groups that energized us. We knew why we were called together, we felt we were contributing to a greater purpose, we looked forward to working with the people on the team, we could see the concrete results of our labor, and we grew from the experience.

Why do some work groups drain us and others uplift us? Work groups are more likely to turn into high-performing teams when they are used for the right reason: to solve complex problems in which no one person has all the knowledge, skills, experiences, and other resources necessary to solve the problems and implement the solutions. If one person has all the resources to successfully solve a problem and implement the solution alone, then it is a waste of time, effort, and money to use a work group.[13]

If you see a snake, just kill it. Don't appoint a committee on snakes.
H. Ross Perot, Former presidential candidate

Effective work groups also are likely to turn into high-performing teams when they develop ways of working together that create synergy. Synergy occurs when the group's collective performance exceeds the potential of the most capable individual in the group. In short, the whole is greater than the sum of its parts. This increase is also referred to as process gains. In less effective work groups, the collective efforts of individuals often don't result in improved quality, productivity gains, or team member growth.[14] Indeed, some work groups misuse individual resources so badly that group performance is less than that which individuals could have achieved working alone on the problem. This decrease in performance is called process losses.

High-performing teams that achieve synergy are built on five foundations: an engaging purpose that mobilizes action; clear performance goals and measures that encourage high standards; highly skilled people who add value; carefully developed work processes that enable team members to work together productively; and ample opportunities for team members to practice working together so that they continuously build their team's competence as a performing unit. Each of these foundations is discussed in the following sections.

Foundation 1: Clear, Engaging Purpose

High-performing teams develop their sense of direction, inspiration, and momentum from a powerful sense of purpose. A clear, engaging purpose aligns the minds, hearts, and actions of team members toward a common goal. It also motivates team members to persist when they face obstacles and hurdles. Without a clear, engaging purpose, team members may pull apart, stray from the organization's expectations, or give up when the going gets tough.

As mentioned earlier, high-performing teams tend to create their own purpose that is at least as important to team members as is the organization's purpose. Although the team's purpose is aligned with and supports that of the organization, the purpose that the team members create for themselves has a deeper meaning to them, enables them to better leverage team members' special interests and talents, and reinforces their collective identity as a unique and important entity. Furthermore, a powerful purpose:

- Is consistent with organizational values and mission
- Creates a sense of urgency
- Is positive and inspiring
- Is easily understood and remembered
- Has a long-term focus
- Is performance based
- Is broad enough to be flexible
- Stretches team members' abilities yet seems attainable
- Can be personalized by each team member. Each team member can see how his or her efforts help the organization achieve its goals.

Potential Problems with the Team's Purpose

Although a powerful team purpose is an important foundation for team success, it also can cause problems. Team members may become so committed to achieving their team's purpose that they lose sight of the larger organizational purpose and pursue their team's objectives at the expense of the organization's objectives. Team members may become so enamored with their well-intentioned purpose that they become willing to use any means necessary to achieve their goals, even if these means are unethical.

Their well-intentioned purpose may mutate into winning at all costs, beating the competition, or proving their technical expertise and providing technical sophistication beyond that which the customer wants, needs, or can understand. They may fail to notice that the environment has changed and their purpose is outdated. In addition, team members may become so cohesive and committed to their team's goals that they see people and groups from other parts of the organization as distractions, obstacles, or enemies rather than as partners. To avoid these risks, members of high-performing teams regularly review the appropriateness of their purpose and the means by which they go about achieving their purpose.

Foundation 2: Performance Goals and Measures

High-performing teams develop specific and measurable performance goals by which they evaluate their progress. Effective performance goals are simultaneously challenging and achievable. For example, a team's performance goals may be to reduce cycle time by 20 percent, achieve a zero defect rate, get all patients admitted within 1 hour, or return all customer calls within 3 hours. Specific and measurable performance goals such as these focus the team's efforts on getting results; enable each team member to see how he or she contributes to achieving these goals; stretch team members' abilities; and enable the team to experience small wins that are invaluable to building team members' confidence, commitment, and competence.[15]

BOX 8-1

Disney Team's Joke Backfires

Entertainment Weekly magazine reported that "video editions of 1988's *Who Framed Roger Rabbit* contained what looked to be a brief flash of Jessica Rabbit sans underwear (corrected in later versions). And the original prints of *The Little Mermaid* apparently contained a passing glimpse of Mickey Mouse and a menacing knife. Such scenes are sometimes inserted by animators as inside jokes." Such insider jokes, often intended to promote camaraderie among team members and release tension, can be costly. Disney recalled 3.4 million copies of *The Rescuers* in 1999 when Disney found an almost imperceptible image of a naked woman in the background of one scene. The media attention certainly cast shadows on Disney's reputation as a family-friendly operation. On the other hand, original video versions that contain the recalled insider jokes have turned into collectors' items.

SOURCE: Lee, Will. 1999. "Mouse Droppings." *Entertainment Weekly*. January 22: 9.

Foundation 3: People

> In crowds we have unison, in groups harmony. We want the single voice but not the single note.
> *Mary Parker Follett, The New State, 1918*

Members of high-performing teams aren't perfect. Rarely do they have all the technical, problem-solving, and relationship skills that their team needs for long-term success. However, members of high-performing teams take time to identify the skills that they need to help the team accomplish its goals, determine whether team members have those skills, and then find ways to fill the gaps, either by investing in the development of team members or importing the skills from people outside the team. In addition, members of high-performing teams tend to have the following characteristics:

- They are committed to the team's purpose.
- They have a specific expertise to offer the team, such as functional knowledge, technical abilities, or facilitation skills.
- They are not advocates of a particular method or function, even though they may be experts in a particular area.[16]
- They have general problem-solving, decision-making, and implementation skills.
- They have relationship skills, including the willingness and ability to develop mutual trust and respect, communicate effectively, manage conflict, and respect diversity. As one Disney executive puts it, effective team members are able to "play in the sandbox with others."[17]
- They are adaptive. Maryfran Hughes, who manages 55 to 60 nurses in Massachusetts General Hospital's emergency area, says that "an adaptive personality can be as important as technical competence, particularly when 'people have to deal with situations where they have no control.'"[18]
- They are aware of their own strengths and weaknesses, understand how these affect team performance, and are willing to invest in ongoing personal development.

Must team members sacrifice themselves to the team and forego individual objectives? No, because high-performing teams find ways to enable the individual, as well as the team, to grow and develop. As Texas Instruments manager Shaunna Sowell found, a successful team experience can lead to individual learning, recognition, and promotions. Her experience was described in the *Wall Street Journal* as follows:

> Ms. Sowell was leading a plant design team ... when she was tapped for a product-quality steering committee that was loaded with bosses. She was intimidated at first, but her confidence grew with her experience. "I left one meeting thinking, my God, I've ruined my career," she recalls. "I'd just told a guy four levels above me he was wrong." Actually, she impressed an executive on the team who was casting about for a vice president of corporate environmental safety. ... "You have to be a great individual contributor," she says. "That's how you get picked for the next team."[19]

Foundation 4: Results-Driven Processes

Leadership is at its best when the vision is strategic, the voice persuasive, the results tangible.
Michael Useem, The Leadership Moment

Teamwork involves managing more complex tasks and managing a more complex set of relationships than does individual work. Team members must develop a shared understanding of their goals and their environment, identify multiple problems and opportunities, generate solutions, make trade-offs, agree on decisions, implement solutions, and evaluate the consequences of their decisions—all while managing the social dynamics that are inevitably part of everyday group life.

To manage these complex group tasks and relationships, effective teams develop systematic task and relationship processes for working together. A process is an agreed-upon sequence of steps and behaviors designed to help the team achieve their collective goals.[20] Task processes refer to the systematic methods team members use to solve problems, make decisions, implement solutions, maintain accountability, coordinate their efforts, and evaluate results. Relationship processes refer to the social skills that team members use to create a productive work climate that promotes a foundation of trust, openness, and psychological safety that leads to cohesiveness, commitment, creativity, critical thinking, and constructive conflict—all of which are necessary for effective group learning and decision making.[21] Note that although effective task processes may enable a group with poor relationship skills to produce a high-quality product in the short run, effective relationship processes must be in place if group members are to remain committed to the team and produce high-quality results in the long run. The importance of creating high-quality relationships to the long-term success of teams is supported by considerable research that is finding that team members who feel positively toward their leader, each other, and the task are more likely to cooperate with each other, less likely to have dysfunctional conflict, less likely to be overly focused on the self over the team, more likely to manage the delicate balance between advocating and challenging each other's ideas, and more likely to have higher perceptions of the team's effectiveness.[22]

Norms

Effective teams create clear norms that ensure that team member resources are well utilized, time isn't wasted, and team goals are achieved. Simply stated, norms refer to team members' implicit and explicit agreements about "how we do things around here." Team norms express the team's central values, increase the predictability of team members' behaviors, and help team members coordinate their efforts. For example, a team may promote norms that team members are supposed to check their electronic mail every morning and afternoon, carry cellular phones when they are not at the office, and return telephone calls from team members immediately. One Finnish executive development program that I work with has the norm that if a cellular phone rings during a training session, the carrier of the phone must buy all participants in the group a cognac that evening. In addition, participants who come late to sessions must sing a song for the group later in the day. Norms may be implicit or explicit. Some teams have members who break an important norm donate a small amount of money (e.g., $1.00 US). After a period of time, the team uses the money collected to go to dinner or to make a charitable donation.

Implicit Norms

Blamestorming: The practice of sitting around in a group discussing why a deadline was missed or a project failed and who was responsible. *New Management Words, www.lc21.com/ humor9.html*

Many team norms are not explicitly planned or articulated. Rather, they evolve informally over time, are not written down, are rarely discussed, are often unconscious, and are reinforced through subtle and often unspoken means such as peer pressure. Implicit norms are unavoidable. No team can—or would want to—explicitly articulate all their norms. Doing so would waste precious time and would undoubtedly feel oppressive. However, implicit norms can be problematic because, even when dysfunctional, they are usually not discussed. Consequently, team members cannot assess the impact of these norms on the team's effectiveness. Therefore, although team members cannot and should not regulate all team behaviors, they should develop explicit norms about behaviors that are important to the team's effectiveness.

Explicit Norms

Explicit norms refer to behavioral guidelines that team members openly discuss, clearly understand, and explicitly communicate to new team members. Effective team norms:

- Are consistent with the team's and organization's goals
- Address only those behaviors that affect team performance (such as quality standards, availability, accountability, communication, problem-solving approaches, desired levels of effort, meeting management, and ways of showing respect for each other)
- Address only those behaviors that each team member can control
- Are viewed as appropriate and achievable by all team members
- Are revisited over time to make sure that they continue to help the team achieve its goals

All team members should be involved in establishing team norms for two reasons. First, each team member brings a particular set of values, personal goals, pressures, cultural norms, talents, perspectives, and work styles to the team. If these are not considered, the norms may undermine rather than enhance each team member's willingness and ability to perform well. Second, team members are more likely to be committed to norms that they help develop because they understand why each norm was created (e.g., how it helps the team achieve its goals) and how each norm will be enforced.

Explicitly developing team norms takes time and effort, but the payoffs are significant. Effective norms help a team get started quickly, keep behavior directed toward the team's purpose, provide clear standards against which members can judge their performance and be held accountable, increase predictability and coordination, enhance efficiency by helping team members use their collective resources (e.g., time, materials, knowledge, skills, and experience) wisely and get the team back on track if it gets stuck or derailed. Box 8-2 provides a checklist of guiding questions that you can use in developing your team's norms. Box 8-4 helps you assess the direct financial costs of meetings. Box 8-5 provides guidelines for structuring effective team meetings.

BOX 8-2

Guidelines for Creating Team Norms

The following questions are designed to guide the development of your team's norms.

Evaluating Team Effectiveness
_____ We have clear standards for quality.
_____ We have ways to help individual team members grow and develop.
_____ We have ways to ensure that the team as a whole engages in continuous learning.

Purpose
_____ We have a clear and engaging team purpose that is aligned with the organization's purpose.
_____ Team members believe that the purpose is important.
_____ Each team member can see how he or she contributes to that purpose.

Performance Measures
_____ Team members have clear and measurable performance criteria for individuals and for the team as a whole.
_____ Team members know who is responsible for each task.
_____ Team members have clear milestones and guidelines for each task.
_____ Team members know the consequences of submitting substandard or late products.

People
_____ Team members have the task skills they need to do their work (e.g., technical skills, project management skills).
_____ Team members have the relationship skills they need to do their work.

(continued)

Box 8-2 (*cont.*)

Process

_____ Team members have predictable ways of coordinating with each other.

_____ Team members have predictable ways of communicating with each other.

_____ Team members know how often they should be available to the team.

_____ Team members have a systematic process for communicating with external people and teams (How often? For what reason? In what form?).

_____ Team members know how formal reports, presentations, and other written and verbal communication should be and what level of detail is important.

_____ Team members have norms for encouraging differences of opinion while maintaining team cohesiveness.

Meetings

_____ Team members know how often they will meet and for what purposes.

_____ Team members know how meetings will be structured to maximize productivity.

Practice

_____ Team members have systems in place for evaluating performance and learning from the team's successes and failures.

_____ Team members have systems in place for identifying and filling skill gaps.

Leadership

_____ Team members know how leaders will be selected and whether leadership will be rotated.

_____ If leadership is rotated, team members know how leadership transitions will be made.

_____ Team members know the team leader's role—what he or she will and will not do for the team.

_____ Team members know how to communicate with the leader, including feedback and bad news.

TEAM TRANSITIONS

_____ Team members have a systematic way of integrating new members into the team.

QUESTIONS TO ASK ABOUT THE TEAM NORMS

1. Are team norms consistent with the organization mission, values, and goals?
2. How will the team monitor team member compliance and uphold adherence to these norms?
3. How will we introduce new members to team norms?
4. How often will we reevaluate our norms to determine whether they are still appropriate and what our process will be?
5. How will we be sure that our norms are helping rather than hindering our process?

Foundation 5: Preparation and Practice

Researchers and practitioners often use sports teams as analogies for work teams. However, they often neglect one of the most critical factors for a sports team's success: preparation and frequent disciplined practice. High-performing teams routinely reflect on their performance. They systematically identify the skills they need to succeed, identify gaps between the skills that they have and those that they need, and then make the effort to learn and practice those skills. Coaching legend Bill Walsh, former head coach of the San Francisco 49ers and Stanford University's football team, explains:

> It's all in the way you prepare. Preparation allows us to overcome the fact that we might not be the most physically talented team. . . . Being prepared starts with identifying the essential skills our team needs to compete effectively. The next step is to create a format to teach those skills. . . . The way I coach, I know ahead of time how I am going to run the whole season's worth of practices. I have established the priorities for what we need to accomplish and allocated the time in which to teach the necessary skills. . . . Making judgments under severe stress is the most difficult thing there is. The more preparation you have prior to the conflict . . . the better off you will be. For that reason, in practice I want to make certain that we have accounted for every critical situation. . . . You need to have a plan even for the worst scenario. It doesn't mean that it will always work; it doesn't mean that you will always be successful. But you will always be prepared and at your best.[23]

Box 8-3 lists several questions that team members can discuss as part of a team review at critical stages of a team's life, particularly when a team completes a project.

In short, disciplined preparation and practice helps team members acquire a broad repertoire of skills that they can use in a variety of situations, learn to anticipate

---

BOX 8-3

Guidelines for Team Review

1. In what ways did we succeed? In what ways did we fail?

2. What did we do well that we should remember to do next time?

3. What could we have done better, faster, with higher quality, with fewer resources, and in less time?

4. Which team norms served us well?

5. Which team norms should we change?

6. Did anyone dominate our discussions, and why? Did anyone not speak up as much as the others, and why?

7. Did we have any sloppy hand-offs?

8. Did we listen to advice from anyone outside of the team who could have added value? If not, why not?

9. Did we miss any opportunities to build relationships or get support from people outside of our group? Who blocked our efforts? Whose support should we now build for the long-term?

10. Who outside of our team helped us and how should we thank them or reciprocate in some way?

BOX 8-4

Calculate the Cost of Your Meeting

HOW MUCH DOES YOUR MEETING COST?

Calculate the hourly salary and cost of benefits per attendee.

Attendee 1 　　　　　　 ———

Attendee 2 　　　　　　 ———

Attendee 3 　　　　　　 ———

Attendee 4 　　　　　　 ———

Attendee 5 　　　　　　 ———

Total hourly salaries and benefits: ———

Total hourly salaries and benefits multiplied by meeting length in hours equals the human cost of meetings. For example, if you have five people attending a meeting, each with salary and benefits worth $50 an hour, and the meeting lasts 2 hours, the human cost of the meeting would be ($50 × 5) × 2 = $500.

Effective meetings have the right people in the right place discussing the right issues in the right order.

BOX 8-5

Managing Meetings

To make sure you make the best use of participants' time, consider the following questions:

✓ How will we notify team members and others of meetings?

✓ Will we expect all team members to attend all meetings?

✓ Will we expect all team members to be on time and attend the entire meeting?

✓ How will we deal with team members who miss meetings, don't meet performance standards in terms of quality and timeliness, or who are repeatedly late or leave early?

✓ How long will our meetings be?

✓ How will we structure meetings to best use team members' expertise, time, and resources? For example:

   • What materials, if any, will be made available in advance?

   • Will agendas be used and who will make and distribute them?

• How will we manage time so that it is not wasted?

• Who will facilitate meetings and will the facilitator role be fixed or rotated?

• How will we manage task processes at meetings (gathering information, making presentations, making decisions, and evaluating results)?

• How will we manage relationship processes at meetings (encouraging participation, openness, constructive conflict, creativity; resolving disputes; managing status dynamics—higher-status people tend to speak more and are taken more seriously than lower-status people; making sure all team members have influence in the group)?

• Will team members have explicit roles to ensure that task and relationship processes are attended to? How will these roles be assigned? Will roles be rotated?

• How formal/informal will meetings be?

- How will we make sure the meetings stay on track?
- What will we do when we get stuck?
- How will we discourage dysfunctional individual and group behaviors (under- or overparticipation; problematic status effects; marginalization of some team members; substandard performance)?

- How will we identify action items and assign responsibilities?
- Will we take time to reflect on our process and improve team performance?
- Will we have minutes of the meetings taken and distributed? Who will take them and who will receive them?

each other's actions and contributions so that they can better coordinate their efforts in novel situations, and develop the confidence and ability to work under pressure without panicking or falling into dysfunctional behaviors.

TEAM LEADERSHIP: CREATING A CONTEXT FOR HIGH-PERFORMING TEAMS

High-performing teams do not develop the five foundations—clear, engaging purpose; performance measures; skilled people with task and relationship skills; results-driven processes; and disciplined preparation and practice—without capable leadership. Effective leadership depends on instinct and improvisation as much as it depends on knowledge and careful planning. To be effective, team leaders must know when to intervene and when to stay out of the team's way, when to reward individuals and when to reward the team, and when to connect the team to external individuals and groups and when to protect the team from external influences. For team leaders, knowing what not to do is as important as knowing what to do.

People who seem to have natural leadership talent do not become effective team leaders overnight. Says David Nadler, chairman of Mercer Delta Organizational Consulting Group in New York City, "Corporations underestimate the shift in mindset and behavioral skills that team leaders need."[24] Team leaders must learn to do more than facilitate effective team meetings. They must learn how to proactively build trust with team members because they realize that team members' trust in the leader significantly contributes to the team's performance.[25] They also must learn to delegate tasks that they used to do themselves (and may still want to do); give out information that used to be confidential; turn over spending authority; share power, control, and credit; earn credibility with team members who have more customer or technical knowledge than the team leader has; enable team members who have different goals, personalities, and quirks to work together cohesively; encourage team members to coordinate their efforts with external individuals and groups; and develop rewards that motivate the team without demotivating the individual. Yet most organizations prepare team leaders with "little more than a handshake and a pat on the back."[26]

The most important lesson effective team leaders learn is that their most important job is managing the context in which the team works rather than directly intervening in the team's work. Harvard professor Richard Hackman explains:

> Rather than attempting to manage group behavior in real time, leaders might better spend their energies creating contexts that increase the likelihood (but cannot guarantee) that teams will prosper—taking care to leave ample room for groups to develop their own unique behavioral styles and performance strategies.[27]

Hackman's advice is echoed in a newspaper clipping that former Xerox chief scientist Jack Goldman kept in his office: "There are two ways of being creative. One can sing and dance. Or one can create an environment in which singers and dancers flourish."[28] To create a context for high performance, team leaders should focus their efforts on four key areas:

- Invest in ongoing personal development
- Provide team members with the direction, structure, and resources that they need to accomplish their collective work
- Make the right interventions at the right time
- Help the team manage the boundaries between the team and external individuals and groups

Each of these leadership areas is discussed in more detail in the sections that follow. As you read, remember that there are many kinds of team leader roles. Team leaders can be officially designated or they can emerge informally in a team. The team leader role may be fixed or it may rotate among different team members. Some teams are explicitly leader-led, whereas others are self-managing. But even self-managing teams depend on organizational leaders to provide them with a work context that inspires high performance.

Team Leadership Skill 1: Invest in Ongoing Personal Development

The problem is not shall groups exist or not, but shall groups be planned or not? **Theodore Leavitt**

A leader has a responsibility not just for his or her own sake, but for everyone else in the organization. Unless the leader has a degree of self-knowledge and self-understanding, there is a risk that he or she will use the organization to address his or her own neuroses. **Peter Senge citing Alain Gauthier**

Effective team leaders know that team members pay particular attention to the attitudes, words, and behaviors of people in authority positions. Therefore, effective team leaders (1) take time to understand how their attitudes, words, and behaviors enhance and inhibit team performance and (2) develop strategies to improve their leadership perspectives and skills. Specifically, they invest in three kinds of personal development:

- *Self-awareness.* Effective leaders know that one of the most effective ways to change an individual's or team's behavior is to change their own behavior. Individuals and teams will adapt in response to the changes in their leaders. For example, if a team leader wants an individual or team to be more independent, then the team leader has to change his or her behavior in ways that encourage, rather than discourage, independence. If a team leader wants an individual or team to be more forthcoming with bad news, then the team leader has to exhibit behaviors that welcome rather than inhibit bad news. Therefore, effective team leaders regularly think about how their everyday taken-for-granted assumptions, language, behavioral styles, strengths, and weaknesses influence the team's behavior—and they change themselves as necessary so that the team can be more effective.

- *Understanding group dynamics.*   Effective team leaders understand how social dynamics in teams affect team members' ability to use their collective resources effectively and achieve the team's goals. They understand that team members' emotional lives—their hopes and fears—can powerfully influence the effectiveness of the team's process and thus the quality of their decisions. Therefore, effective team leaders invest in understanding these social dynamics so that they can be better able to anticipate problems, prevent or minimize damage, and channel the team's emotional energy toward productive ends.

- *Learning effective leadership techniques.*   Effective team leaders tend to have good instincts. However, they also take time to learn effective leadership techniques, systematically implement these techniques, and evaluate the impact of these techniques on the team's performance. In short, effective team leaders don't just "wing it."

Team Leadership Skill 2: Provide Team Direction, Structure, and Resources

To perform well, team members must be motivated to do their collective work, have the knowledge and skills that help them to do it well, and develop ways of working together that enhance rather than inhibit their ability to reach their goals.[29] Hackman advises team leaders to help team members develop these characteristics by providing a clear, engaging direction, structure, and resources that inspire and enable high performance.

Clear, Engaging Direction

Effective team leaders clearly and enthusiastically articulate the organization's vision and their commitment to that vision. For example, Steve Jobs, founder of Apple Computer, told employees that Apple would "put a dent in the universe" and create something "insanely great." Effective team leaders also help team members understand how the team's efforts help the organization achieve this vision. Leaders then give team members the freedom to work autonomously within the boundaries of that vision to turn it into reality.[30] Furthermore, effective leaders encourage the team to create a collective vision that is aligned with the organization's vision yet reflects team members' goals and talents.

Structure

Effective team leaders focus on three structural issues: staffing, task design, and reward systems.

- *Appropriate staffing.*   Effective team leaders put the right number of people on the team. It is of interest that some researchers argue that teams may operate best when they are slightly understaffed rather than overstaffed, what is referred to as "N-1 staffing" or "optimal understaffing." Slightly understaffing a team may inspire creativity, encourage the team to use their resources efficiently, and result in greater team pride about achieving their goals. Effective team leaders also ensure that team members—through activities such as training, coaching, and role modeling—develop the attitudes and skills that enhance team performance. In addition, effective team leaders bring enough diversity into the team so that team members can offer different perspectives and approaches to the work, yet not so many differences that they undermine the team's ability to work together.

- *Well-designed task.* A well-designed task provides clear boundaries, meaningfulness, autonomy, feedback, and opportunities for small wins.

  - *Clear boundaries.* Team members need clear boundaries. They need to know what their responsibilities are and are not, as well as which decisions are made by the leader and which decisions they make themselves. When boundaries are clear, team members can focus their efforts and use their collective energy to work effectively within those boundaries. When boundaries are unclear or constantly shifting, team members experience "chronic uncertainty," which can unfocus the team and sap the team's energy.[31]

  - *Meaningfulness.* Team members will experience their tasks as meaningful if they believe that the tasks are significant, if they can personally identify with the tasks, and if they can apply a variety of skills to the tasks.[32] Toni Morrison, winner of the 1993 Nobel Prize in Literature, illustrates the importance of identification with a task with this story about her father who worked at U.S. Steel when she was a child: "I remember my Daddy taking me aside—this was when he worked as a welder—and telling me that he welded a perfect seam that day, and that after welding the perfect seam he put his initials on it. I said, 'Daddy, no one will ever see that. Sheets and sheets of siding would go over that, you know?' And he said, 'Yes, but I'll know it's there.'"[33]

  - *Autonomy.* Team members who understand their task, have the skills required to accomplish their task, and have significant control over how they do their work are more likely to feel more ownership of their work and make appropriate decisions quickly.[34]

  - *Feedback.* Team members are more likely to maintain direction and momentum if they have regular feedback that tells them how well they're doing and whether they need to adjust individual and team strategies.

  - *Small wins.* Team members are more likely to persist when faced with obstacles if they are able to experience small wins along their way to achieving their goal. Small wins help team members see progress toward their goals, experience psychological success, provide opportunities to celebrate, and maintain enthusiasm for and commitment to achieving their goals.

Resources the Team Needs to Accomplish Their Goals

Research has found that high-performing teams do not always have the luxury of extra people or fine offices in which to do their work.[35] Indeed, researchers Patricia Ward-Biederman and Warren Bennis note:

> Great groups have some odd things in common. For example, they tend to do their brilliant work in spartan, even shabby surroundings. Someday someone will write a book explaining why so many pioneering enterprises, including

Walt Disney Company, Hewlett-Packard, and Apple, were born in garages. . . . We can speculate on why great things are often accomplished in dull or tacky surroundings. Perhaps a bland or unattractive environment spurs creativity, functions as an aesthetic blank slate that frees the mind to dream about what might be. . . . But the truth is that most people in great groups spend very little time thinking about their surroundings. They have wonderful tunnel vision.[36]

Although high-performing teams tend not to have fancy surroundings, they do have ample support such as information, training, and access to people who can help them achieve their goals.

Rewards

Rewards should encourage interdependence, be contingent on performance, and be given to individual team members as well as to the team as a whole. Rewards can be financial (e.g., raises and bonuses), small but meaningful gifts of appreciation (e.g., trophies), professional development opportunities (e.g., education or attendance at conferences), enhanced team resources (e.g., increased team budgets for team use), or psychological (e.g., recognition).

Team Leadership Skill 3: Help the Team Manage Boundaries

Teams don't operate in a vacuum. Rather, they depend on information, resources, cooperation, and goodwill from people and groups external to the team to progress in their work and achieve their goals. However, getting team members (the in-group) to work with external people and groups is often easier said than done.[37] A *Wall Street Journal* article about Richard Parsons who became CEO of Time Warner in 2002 explained that one of his primary objectives was to turn "business units that feuded for more than a decade" into a cooperative whole so that he could give shareholders a superior return on their investment.

> The most striking change at the company may be a cultural shift, ending the divisional feuding that characterized Time Warner since it was formed in 1989. Under Mr. Levin, sharp-elbowed divisional chiefs were freed to focus on their own businesses, without regard for the broader company, an approach that resulted in unresolved disputes between divisions like Warner Bros. and HBO . . . Mr. Parsons leaves divisional chiefs to concentrate on their own businesses but expects them to cooperate when it makes sense . . . Mr. Parsons doesn't let disputes fester . . . 'We are trying to run the company to maximize the value of the whole company,' says Mr. Parsons. 'You don't get credit [just] because you get good numbers . . . you get credit for being a member of the team.'[38]

The costs of intergroup conflict and lack of coordination became painfully apparent to Steve Case, former chairman of AOL Time Warner, when his brother died of brain cancer. Says Case, "I was very surprised to learn that no one knows what causes brain cancer or how to cure it, despite decades of work." Although his brother Daniel died of brain cancer, he cofounded the Accelerate Brain Cancer Foundation together with Steve, to promote collaboration among previously disconnected researchers and coordination of resources. As he told a Senate committee a few weeks before his brother died, "the only way we can find a cure is by working together."[39] Why is it often so difficult for different groups to work toward common goals? The roots of the difficulty in managing in-group/out-group relationships stem from our basic human needs to find meaning, to control our environments, to belong, and to feel competent.

Meaning

As human beings, we have a fundamental need to make sense of ourselves, the world, and our place in it. Our tendency to categorize our environment in terms of group memberships is a consequence of our need to make sense of the world. For example, we divide our work organizations into socially constructed professional groups such as engineers and accountants, hierarchical groups such as line workers and management, and functional groups such as production and marketing. Furthermore, we tend to see the world through the conceptual lenses provided by our groups, pay more attention to information that is relevant to our group, and see our own group's goals as more important and positive than those of other groups.[40]

Control

Categorizing our social world into groups gives us a sense of control, stability, and predictability in a complex and ambiguous environment. Without conceptual categories, we could not make sense of ourselves or others, nor could we take coordinated action with others. After all, Coca-Cola knows it's Cola-Cola because it's not Pepsi. Try to describe someone without using any categorizations (even eye color, height, parental status, and personality characteristics are based on categorizations). Imagine trying to organize and implement a project at work without using categorizations. Without our social categorizations, we would feel overwhelmed, confused, and paralyzed.

Belonging

Because of our basic need to belong to a social group, we tend to identify strongly with the groups to which we belong and develop an emotional attachment to our group and our membership in it.[41] We are likely to see ourselves as more similar to people from our groups than to people from other groups,[42] are more likely to remember positive information and forget negative information about our in-groups,[43] and see members of out-groups in more homogeneous ("They're all alike."), stereotypical ("They all do this or that."), and negative ways ("They're less trustworthy or cooperative."[44]) than we see members of our own groups.[45]

Competence

Because we develop our identity in part from the groups to which we belong, we tend to define our personal success and failure partly in terms of our groups' successes and failures. Consequently, we tend to want our groups to succeed and be viewed as competent by others. Furthermore, we develop a sense of responsibility for the status and success of our groups and thus are more likely to promote the interests of our groups[46] and help people from our groups.[47]

In short, our categorization of the world into social groups and our identification with our groups is positive because it helps us make sense of our social world and our place in it, gives us a sense of belonging, enables us to feel special and distinctive, and helps us take coordinated social action—all of which can increase our energy and involvement in tasks that we believe are relevant to our group. However, this categorization and identification becomes negative when it creates dysfunctional in-group dynamics and psychological barriers between groups that should be working together toward common organizational goals.[48]

For example, excessive in-group identification and cohesion can lead to isolation, conformity, overestimation of the in-group's competence (and underestimation of the out-group's competence), self-serving decisions, negative stereotyping and mistrust of outsiders, blindness to interdependencies with external individuals and groups, decreased communications with out-groups, and increased distortions of the communications that do take place.[49] These dynamics can lead to tunnel vision, moral lapses, groupthink, and other consequences that undermine individual, group, and organizational effectiveness. Box 8-6 describes Groupthink, one of the most well-known dysfunctional group processes.

BOX 8-6

Groupthink: Symptoms and Solutions

Why is it that intelligent and competent individuals, when put in a group, can make terrible decisions? Researcher Irving Janis coined the term "groupthink" to refer to "the mode of thinking that persons engage in when concurrence seeking becomes so dominant in a cohesive in-group that it tends to override realistic appraisal of alternative courses of action."[51] In other words, individuals want so much to belong to a group and to maintain the cohesiveness of the group that they engage in behaviors designed to maintain cohesiveness rather than the critical thinking that can lead to high-quality decisions. Groups engaging in groupthink tend to:

- *Reinforce conformity.* They pressure group members who express disagreement to "get with the program."
- *Censor themselves.* Although group members may have concerns about the group's analysis or decisions, they don't express their concerns.
- *Create mindguards.* They shield the group or the group leaders from information or people who challenge the assumptions of the group.
- *Develop illusions of unanimity.* Because group members silence themselves and others in the group, they begin to share an illusion that everyone

in the group agrees with the group's decisions.

- *Rationalize their decisions.* Because the group is invested in believing in the "rightness" of their decisions, they focus on data and arguments that support their position, and they minimize negative feedback or warnings from others.
- *Stereotype outsiders.* They develop negative stereotypes of outsiders so that they don't have to take the concerns of outsiders seriously.
- *Develop an unquestioned belief in the team's morality.* The group never questions the morality of their decisions. Indeed, they may justify their decisions on moral grounds.
- *Develop an illusion of invulnerability.* The group becomes overly optimistic about their capabilities and may take unreasonable risks.

These "concurrence-seeking" behaviors tend to increase when group members are under pressure to perform, such as when they are approaching deadlines or when they feel that a great deal is riding on their success. Some researchers argue that groupthink may have led to the decision to launch the Challenger space shuttle that failed less than 2 minutes after liftoff and killed all seven crew members

(continued)

Box 8-6 (*cont.*)

in 1986.[52] Sadly, an investigation concluded that similar dynamics played a part in the Columbia disaster 17 years later in which all crew members died in 2003 as a consequence of damage from detached insulation foam. The 248-page investigative report asserted that "NASA's organizational culture had as much to do with this accident as the foam did." The report stated that NASA mission managers began to accept flaws in the shuttle system as normal and tended to ignore the fact that these flaws could result in a catastrophe. The report also blamed "reliance on past success as a substitute for sound engineering practice; organizational barriers that prevented effective communication of critical safety information and stifled differences of opinion, lack of integrated management across program elements; and the evolution of an informal chain of command and decision-making processes that operated outside the organization's rules." The report added "little by little, NASA was accepting more and more risk in order to stay on schedule."[53]

As a first step toward preventing groupthink, group members and leaders can learn to identify its symptoms: Group members may limit discussion to a few courses of action, fail to reexamine the desired course of action, fail to reexamine rejected alternatives, fail to consult experts or reject expert opinion that does not support the group's decision, filter out new information that is perceived as negative or threatening, and not develop contingency plans.[54]

Team leaders can take other steps to prevent groupthink. Team leaders can be aware of the intended and unintended consequences of their authority in the group. If they want honest opinions from team members, they may want to remove themselves from at least some of the meetings. When team leaders are at meetings, they should watch their body language and not state their preferences first. When they are not at meetings, they should keep personal staff who might filter information to a minimum. They should encourage team members to give them bad news by never "shooting the messenger." Instead, they should use three basic statements when hearing bad news: Can you tell me more? What do you think we should do? Thank you for bringing this to my attention.[55]

Alfred Sloan, Jr., who became president of General Motors in 1993 and continued on as Honorary Chairman of the Board until his death in 1966, was credited with saying the following when his senior team came to conclusions too quickly: "Gentleman, I take it that we are all in complete agreement with the decision here . . . Then I propose we postpone further discussion of this matter until our next meeting to give ourselves time to develop disagreement and perhaps gain some understanding of what the decision is all about."[56]

In addition, team leaders should teach team members about groupthink and have team members assess their own potential for groupthink. They also should encourage team members to assign everyone the role of "critical evaluator," take warning signals seriously, seek outside opinions, consider worst case scenarios and develop contingency plans, and hold second-chance meetings to revisit decisions at a later date, if possible. They may also consider using outside consultants to facilitate meetings.

RESOURCE TIP: The "Groupthink Index: Can We Manage Our Agreements?" is a useful instrument for assessing your team's potential for groupthink. As of this writing, it is published by the HRD Quarterly, http://www.hrdq.com.

What Can a Leader Do to Promote Cooperation across Teams?

If a house be divided against itself, that house cannot stand.
Mark 3:25

The team leader's task is to help the team balance its need for internal cohesion and external integration. Team leaders must make sure that the team is both connected to and protected from external influences. For example, too little external communication can result in narrow-mindedness. Too much external communication can result in information overload. Too few external relationships can result in lack of support. Too many external relationships can interfere with a team's ability to complete its work in a timely manner. Team leaders can help team members achieve the delicate balance between internal cohesion and external integration in several ways.

Start with Yourself

Are you modeling behavior that promotes cooperation among various groups? Do you work cooperatively with leaders and members of other groups? Do you use language that says, "We're all in this together?" Notably, research has found that the use of words that suggest in-group or out-group status (such as "us" and "them") may perpetuate inter-group bias and conflict.[50]

Articulate a Common Vision That Inspires Interdependence

Sharing a common vision helps team members understand that, although their team's goals may be specific to the team, their goals overlap with those of other individuals and teams, and other individuals and teams can help the team achieve their goals.

Set Clear Expectations

Clearly articulate your expectation that the groups will work together. Have each group clarify what it needs from other groups to do its work and what it can give other groups so that they can do their work. Be clear about what is expected from whom and when, as well as what degree of quality is required.

Manage Communication

Effective teams have strategies for communicating with people and groups external to the team so that they can obtain timely and useful strategic and political information, coordinate resources and activities, and build goodwill with people and groups whose support is needed. Research suggests that successful teams do not necessarily communicate more often with outsiders than do less effective teams, but they do have a clearer strategy regarding what they are trying to accomplish with their communication. In short, it's the quality, not the quantity, of communication across team boundaries that enhances a team's performance.[57]

Promote Flexibility

Coordinating resources, activities, and schedules with external people and groups requires flexibility. Leaders can promote flexibility by encouraging team members to change their taken-for-granted routines, modify normal division of labor, and break down traditional boundaries between the team and outsiders.[58]

Reward Cooperation

Encourage groups to invest in each other's success by rewarding cooperation. Profit sharing or tying a percentage of bonuses to customer satisfaction or organizational performance (revenue and profit) can motivate different groups to work together.[59]

Have Teams Spend Time Together

Having members of different groups spend time together can reduce bias and misunderstandings, increase positive feelings, and enhance cooperation if managed carefully. Note, however, that research suggests that having teams spend time together can backfire if groups already have animosity toward each other. In such cases, getting the groups together can fuel rather than reduce existing ignorance and hostility.[60] To encourage mutual respect and cooperation rather than fuel conflict, team leaders should be sure that common events are designed to promote feelings of equality among groups and emphasize the different—but equally valuable—expertise and resources that each group brings to the common tasks.[61] Shared positive experiences that can enhance cooperation include common training, common meetings that are structured to maximize cooperation, and common celebrations of efforts and victories.

Change Physical Layout

The layout of a work site can either promote or inhibit a sense of collective responsibility. One study found that organizations that had physical layouts that enabled production employees from different areas "to see each other's work had cycle times 4.4 times faster than those with layouts that didn't. . . . This kind of layout . . . allows workers to share tasks easily, to observe when others are in trouble, and to offer assistance without letting their own performance deteriorate. . . . [It also enables employees from different areas] to analyze problems together, build prototypes, and discuss their individual and group-inspired ideas."[62]

Redefine Boundaries

Effective team leaders create new categorizations that integrate, rather than isolate or divide, groups that should be working together.[63] There are several ways to do this. Encourage employees to identify with the organization as a whole rather than with a function or department. Creating a common enemy or external threat can help groups feel that they must combine their efforts to overcome this enemy or threat. Be forewarned, however, that creating a common enemy can backfire if the groups begin to overreact to the perceived enemy and focus their energy on beating the enemy rather than achieving their goals (e.g., meeting customers' needs).

Create Gatekeeping Roles in the Team

Teams that have gatekeepers tend to perform better than those that don't.[64] Gatekeepers play an important role in managing the boundaries between the group and its external environment. Researchers Deborah Ancona and David Caldwell define gatekeepers as high-performing team members who "communicate more often overall and with people outside their specialty."[65] Effective gatekeepers engage in several boundary-spanning activities, including gathering information and resources, controlling the flow of information and resources that goes out of the team, connecting the team to relevant individuals and groups, and buffering the team from unwanted interruptions, premature judgment, and other influences that could slow the team down or take it off track.[66] These roles are summarized in more detail in Figure 8-2.

Scout	Ambassador
• Scans external environment for information. • Gathers information and resources for the team. • Seeks feedback from outside the team.	• Opens communication channels between the team and others. • Informs external people of team's progress. • Coordinates and negotiates. • Engages in team impression management.

Sentry	Guard
• Allows entry to team. • Filters information for relevance to the team. • Translates external information to make it useful to the team.	• Determines appropriateness and impact of external requests. • Delivers appropriate information to outside. • Protects team by denying inappropriate requests from outside.

Resource Tip: The "Intergroup Diagnostic Survey and Facilitator Guide" by John E. Jones and William E. Bearley is a useful instrument that teams can use for assessing how well they manage their relationship with other groups. The assessment is based, in part, on the research of Ancona and Caldwell. At this writing, the instrument is published by The HRD Quarterly, 2002 Renaissance Boulevard, Suite 100, King of Prussia, PA, 19406. Telephone (800) 633–4533

FIGURE 8-2   Boundary-Spanning Behaviors that Manage Information, Resources, and Relationships

Source: Adapted from Ancona, Deborah and David Caldwell. 1992. "Bridging the Boundary: External Process and Performance in Organizational Teams." *Administrative Science Quarterly*, 37(4): 634–666; and the Intergroup Diagnostic Survey.

Team Leadership Skill 4: Manage the Type and Timing of Interventions

One of the most critical challenges team leaders have is to know when to intervene in the team's work and when to stay out of the team's way. Effective leaders know that the wrong interventions or badly timed interventions can wreak havoc on a team's performance. Such interventions can demotivate the team, inhibit team learning, undermine team members' confidence in themselves and the team, and increase the team's dependence on the leader—all of which can throw the team off track or slow it down. In contrast, appropriate and well-timed interventions can propel the team forward, promote team learning, increase the team's confidence in itself, and enhance the team's long-term as well as short-term effectiveness.[67]

In most cases, the best types of interventions are those that support the team in doing its work rather than those that directly intervene in the day-to-day life of the team. Supportive interventions include providing direction, providing resources (information, training, materials and equipment, access to relevant people, and rewards), removing obstacles, and helping the team coordinate its work with external people and groups. To the degree possible, the team should manage its own internal team dynamics, design its own task processes, and carry out its own work.[68] As team researchers Patricia Ward Biederman and Warren Bennis say, "No great group was ever micromanaged."[69]

Interventions also must be well timed. Knowing when to give help and when to stay out of the team's way is a "balancing act between action and patience."[70] The best times to make interventions are at the beginning of the team's life together, at "natural breaks" (e.g., the midpoint, transitions, when newcomers enter the team, whenever the team needs additional resources, and when the team must make handoffs to others such as those who must implement their decisions), and at the end of a team's life.[71]

You will be better able to manage the type and timing of interventions if you understand the team life cycle. This is discussed in the next section.

THE TEAM LIFE CYCLE

Failing organizations are usually over-managed and under-led.
Warren Bennis

Teams, regardless of their task, duration, or member characteristics, tend to go through predictable stages of development.[72] Researchers Jessica Lipnack and Jeffrey Stamps explain: "A team is first and foremost a process: It has a beginning, a middle, and an end. No team springs to life full-blown and none lives forever. Words such as conception, gestation, birth, childhood, adolescence, adulthood, midlife crisis, and old age all apply to a team's life."[73]

Each stage presents team members with particular challenges to be overcome and opportunities to grow. Some teams move slowly and tediously through the various stages, struggling to surmount obstacles and take advantage of opportunities. Other teams move relatively easily through the various stages, although struggling and getting stuck is common even in the best teams. Team leaders can help move the team successfully through each stage if they understand the emotions and behaviors associated with each stage, the impact of these emotions and behaviors on team effectiveness, and how and when to intervene so that they help rather than hinder team progress.

The most well-known theory of group development is based on the assumption that teams tend to go through five stages: forming, storming, norming, performing, and adjourning.[74] This theory, like many others, assumes that the passing of time significantly affects the way team members react emotionally and behaviorally toward the task, each other, and the leader. These stages are summarized in Figure 8-3.

Forming

Forming occurs when people first come together as a group. During this stage, team members must get to know each other, understand the tasks before them, figure out how to work together, and make sense of the leader's role. Because the dynamics that occur during this stage often set the tone for later stages, team members and leaders must pay careful attention to what early decisions are made and the processes by which they are made. Researchers have found that teams that develop *early* the positive belief they will be successful working together tend to be more effective later in the team's life. Specifically, when team leaders take time early in the team's life to build

FIGURE 8-3 Stages of Team Development

Forming	Storming	Norming	Performing	Adjourning
Defining Characteristic: Pseudoteam	**Defining Characteristic:** Resistance	**Defining Characteristic:** Realistic appraisal of task, each other, and leader	**Defining Characteristic:** Task focus and productivity	**Defining Characteristic:** Closure and transition
Emotions: Ambivalence and anxiety	**Emotions:** Disillusionment, anger, and conflict	**Emotions:** Increased optimism and energy	**Emotions:** High energy, increased pride in their work, and confidence in each other	**Emotions:** Sadness and relief
Team Goal: Sense-making, dependence on leader	**Team Goal:** Resist task, each other, and leader	**Team Goal:** Create norms that enhance performance	**Team Goal:** Productivity and feedback on their efforts	**Team Goal:** Transfer learnings
Leader's Goals: • Get the team off to a good start. • Move team from dependence on leader to interdependence with each other.	**Leader's Goals:** • Channel team's emotional energy toward productive ends. • Help team members develop a realistic understanding of the task, each other, and the leader. • Make sure team members have the skills and resources they need to accomplish their task. • Continue to encourage interdependence among team members.	**Leader's Goals:** • Encourage team to focus on team goals and norms. • Provide resources team needs to do its work. • Stay out of team's way as much as possible.	**Leader's Goals:** • Keep team focused on goals. • Provide resources team needs to do its work. • Remind team of hazards of too much cohesiveness. • Connect the team to and protect the team from external individuals and groups. • Stay out of the team's way as much as possible.	**Leader's Goals:** • Help team get closure. • Transfer learning to new settings. Transfer relationships to new setting.

trust in the leader, effective communication processes, cooperative behavior among team members, and early successes, they are likely to create an upward spiral that propels the team toward continued success.[75]

At this stage, team members tend to be anxious and ambivalent. They are often unclear about the task, unsure of what obstacles lay ahead, and uncertain of their individual and collective abilities to achieve the team goals. Consequently, they tend to look to the leader to tell them what to do and how to do it. As team members will soon realize, this is a false hope because it is they and not the team leader who must figure out how to accomplish the tasks before them. One of the leader's main challenges at this stage is to help team members understand that the leader's job is to give team members the direction and resources they need to manage their own team process and solve their own problems.

Furthermore, team members usually don't know each other very well at this stage. Consequently, they are unable to accurately assess each other's potential contributions, understand each other's intentions, or predict each other's behaviors. Team members' influence in the team tends to be based on stereotypes or outside roles (e.g., engineer or sales representative) rather than the variety of talents they bring to the team. They scrutinize the words and behaviors of team members and leaders carefully to look for cues that will help them make sense of the situation, although they often misinterpret those cues because of their lack of experience with each other. Misunderstandings are common, and discussions tend to be superficial, polite, and guarded. Furthermore, team members tend to ignore or minimize problems to promote team harmony, a decision that is likely to backfire later in the team's life if not addressed early on. Although the team may appear cohesive, it is a fragile cohesion based on what consultants Jon Katzenbach and Douglas Smith characterize as "pseudo relationships."[76]

Team members try to figure out whether they can trust the leader (Does the leader care about us? Is the leader competent?) and team members (Can I depend on other team members?), as well as the role they will play in the group (Will I belong? Will I have influence in this group?). They also are concerned about practical matters (How much time is this going to take? How hard am I going to have to work? What are the standards for performance? How will our work be measured?). However, they may not make these concerns explicit. Simply stated, team members try to figure out whether this is a team to which they want to belong.

The team leader's role at this stage is to get the team off to a good start by providing direction, structure, and resources and move the team from dependence on the leader to interdependence with each other. To this end, team leaders should:

- Provide a clear, meaningful, and engaging direction with a sense of urgency
- Encourage the group to develop their own purpose that is consistent with those of the organization
- Provide clear task boundaries, emphasizing task significance, autonomy, and feedback mechanisms
- Set an expectation of high performance standards and develop performance measures
- Set clear milestones and deadlines because teams encounter problems when these are missing or constantly changing[77]

- Encourage team members to develop norms that will help them manage their task and relationship processes
- Provide necessary resources (materials and equipment, information, education, and access to external people and groups who can help the team)
- Give team members a chance to get to know each other
- Make sure everyone feels included (e.g., make sure each person feels he or she has something of value to offer the team)
- Help team members realize that any ambivalence or anxiety that they feel is normal and that they have the direction, talent, and resources they need to succeed
- Explain the team leader's role so that team members know what they can and cannot expect from the team leader

Storming

No one ever said that becoming a team would be easy, and the storming stage proves it. This stage tends to be characterized by avoidance of the task, conflict among team members, and disillusionment with the leader. As team members become overwhelmed with the workload and upcoming deadlines, they tend to question the validity of the task. As team members get to know each other better, personality conflicts tend to surface. As team members begin to realize that the leader cannot solve their problems for them, they become increasingly critical of the leader.

Team members express their resistance to the task, each other, and the leader both overtly and covently. They may psychologically withdraw from the group (come to meetings late or miss meetings), question each other's and the leader's qualifications, become defensive, and form subgroup alliances. Although it seems as though little is being accomplished, working through this conflict and developing a realistic (rather than overly optimistic or pessimistic) understanding of the task, each other, and the leader is the primary work of the team at this time.

The team leader's goal is not to eliminate the storming stage but to channel the emotional energy toward moving the team forward; help the team develop a realistic and appreciative understanding of the task, each other, and the leader; make sure team members have the skills and resources they need to accomplish their task; and continue to move the team from dependence on the leader to dependence on each other. There are several ways that team leaders can help the team move through this stage:

- Encourage team members to focus on the team's purpose
- Remind team members that, although the leader can't do the team's task for them, he or she can give the team the resources—training, information, and materials—that they need to accomplish the task
- Encourage team members to use their emotional energy toward refining the task, creating norms, and developing open and candid communication
- Encourage team members to break the task into small steps so that they don't feel overwhelmed
- Set up small wins so that team members feel a sense of accomplishment and movement toward completing the task

Norming

Teams that successfully enter the norming stage realize the validity of the statement "What doesn't kill you can make you stronger." This stage tends to be characterized by increasing positive emotions, realistic optimism, and increasing group cohesion, particularly if team members have overcome a few hurdles and experienced some small wins together. Team members now have a more realistic view of the team task, each other, and the team leader. As team members begin to feel more familiar with each other and competent as a team, they focus less on assessing each other and more on accomplishing the task. They now have explicit norms for working together, disagreements are less likely to feel personal, and interactions become easier and more predictable. Team members may also develop a sense of humor and a unique vocabulary. Rather than seeing each other as threats, they begin to feel more cohesive and see threats as external to the group (such as competitors).

At this stage, the team leader can help the team most by making sure the team stays focused on its goals, providing the resources the team needs to do its work, removing obstacles, and staying out of its way as much as possible. Specifically, team leaders should:

- Show faith in the team's abilities
- Foster commitment and interdependence by having team members spend formal and informal time together
- Encourage the team to form norms that foster creativity, critical thinking, and risk taking now that team members are increasingly secure
- Encourage the team to develop a process for incorporating new people into the team (getting new team members up to speed with the task and relationships)
- Intervene directly in the team's work only if it is clear that team members cannot handle the problem themselves
- Provide feedback and recognize important milestones so that team members see their progress
- Provide opportunities for the team to reflect on their performance and learn from their successes and failures
- Confront inadequate performance

Performing

This is a high-energy and productive stage when the team begins to see significant payoffs from their shared history and the work norms that they developed. Team members know what they can and can't expect from each other, are better able to anticipate each other's behaviors, and are able to coordinate with each other more easily and with less discussion. It is a time of increased creativity and confidence in the team's abilities. Team members take increasing pride in their work and become increasingly focused on getting results. They want to be able to measure the results of their efforts so that they can take necessary corrective actions quickly and effectively. Team members are likely to feel challenged rather than threatened by hurdles, and solutions come more quickly.

Some research suggests that a significant increase in performance tends to come around the midpoint of the team's life. Researcher Connie Gersick studied different project teams over several years. She concluded that, regardless of whether the project team lasted 3 months or 3 years, the teams tended to experience periods of inertia and struggle early in their lives followed by a "shift into high gear" and a "major jump in progress" around the midpoint of the team's life.[78] This midpoint was followed by a relatively smooth work period in which the teams felt the "consequences of its own past choices about how members would work together, about the amount of effort they had invested, and about how well they had attended to external requirements."

At this stage, the leader should continue to stay out of the team's way as much as possible; provide the resources it needs to do its work; focus on helping the team manage the boundaries between the team and external people and groups; and remind team members that their increased cohesion and confidence can lead to a decline in performance, particularly if team members begin to become insular and overconfident, suppress critical thinking, or make decisions that serve the team needs more than the needs of the organization.[79] Specifically, the team leader should:

- Continue to provide feedback on performance
- Acknowledge when the team reaches important milestones
- Remind the team of the potential negative consequences of excessive group cohesiveness
- Revitalize the team by reminding team members of the greater purpose, providing "fresh facts and information," and connecting the team to people who can offer new perspectives and useful support[80]
- Protect the team from too many external influences and distractions that could take them away from their team task
- Give the team credit and visibility for their collective efforts
- Help the team celebrate successes

Adjourning

Sooner or later, most teams break up. Endings, like beginnings, must be carefully managed. When endings are well managed, team members feel a sense of accomplishment, reflect on the benefits of teamwork, transfer their team learning to future work settings, and solidify relationships with each other for future mutual benefit. When endings are poorly managed, the team experience may quickly fade into the background, disappointments may be remembered more than accomplishments, important learnings may be lost, and potential future relationships may be lost. The team leader's goal at this stage is to help team members manage the psychological transition as they leave the team and help team members transfer learnings to new settings. To help team members manage endings, the team leader should:

- Clearly identify the team's accomplishments and what will happen with their work products
- Relate these accomplishments to the greater organizational purpose
- Provide opportunities to reflect on what lessons were learned from successes and failures that are applicable to other settings
- Provide opportunities for team members to see each other as future resources
- Celebrate

Making Sense of Team Life Cycle Theories

Remember that theories of the team life cycle are just that—theories. The boundaries between one stage and another are, of course, not as clear as the theories make them appear. Not all teams will experience the emotions and behaviors described in these theories or pass through all stages as described.[81] Furthermore, members of short-term project teams and ongoing teams may react differently to the task, each other, and the leader over time. But team life cycle theories are useful because they encourage us to view team life as a process, identify important psychological needs and milestones in a team's life, anticipate some of the emotions and behaviors that may affect a team's productivity, and design interventions that are appropriate for the team's changing needs.

CREATING AND MANAGING HIGH-PERFORMING TEAMS: THE BOTTOM LINE

Creating and managing high-performing teams is as much an art as it is a science. There is no magic formula that will guarantee team success, nor is there one best way to lead a team. Richard Hackman explains:

> There is no one best way to accomplish [team effectiveness], nor, despite volumes of research on the topics, is there any one leadership style that is optimal for coaching and helping work teams. . . . Coaching a group, like teaching a class, is done best when the leader exploits his or her own personality and style to get the lessons across. An active, energetic leader is likely to behave actively and energetically with his or her team, whereas a person who is generally soft-spoken and relaxed will tend to use that style. We would not have it any other way: When a leader tries to adopt a coaching style that is at variance with his or her personal style, leadership effectiveness inevitably suffers.[82]

In addition to leveraging your own style, there are several things that you can do to increase the probability that teams will succeed. You can remember that teams are not appropriate for all tasks, nor are they the cure-all for an organization's woes. However, teams are the best way to solve complex tasks that no one person can solve alone. You also can remember that high-performing teams are not blessed with flawless team members and leaders, nor do high-performing teams have perfect conditions in which to do their work. Rather, high-performing teams are able to rise to the challenges they face, have the persistence and skills to overcome obstacles, and leave the organization better off than it was before.

They are able to do so because they have an engaging purpose that focuses team members' efforts and mobilizes action; clear performance goals and measures that enable team members to judge their performance; highly skilled people; carefully developed task and relationship processes that help team members accomplish their collective work; and ongoing practice that builds the team's competence as a performing unit.

Most importantly, keep in mind that managing teams is an ongoing process, not a one-shot deal. Recognize that the best things that you can do for the team are to help it get off to a good start; provide direction, structure, and resources; help the team manage relationships with external people and groups; carefully plan the type and timing of interventions; and then stay out of the team's way as much as possible. In spirit, effective team leaders live by the words of the Chinese philosopher Lao-tse: "Leaders are best when people barely know that they lead. Good leaders talk little but, when the work is done, the aim fulfilled, all others will say, 'We did this ourselves'."

CHAPTER SUMMARY

A team is made up of individuals interacting independently to achieve common organizational goals. Furthermore, all teams share the following: clear boundaries, common tasks, differentiated member roles, autonomy, dependence on others, and collective responsibility.

The differences between a work group and a work team are these: Team members develop a purpose that is consistent with the organization's purpose but specific to the team members' interests and skills; team members have a greater sense of ownership of their work, develop a sense of mutual responsibility, and believe they are working for each other as well as for the team leader and organization; team members have more say over how they do their work and expect a greater degree of personal learning and fulfillment from the team; team members don't see each other as interchangeable or easily replaceable; team leaders spend less time directing the team's work and more time creating a context that enables team members to do their work.

Effective teams meet three criteria: The team must consistently produce high-quality results; the team must promote the personal growth needs and well-being of team members; the team must grow and learn as a performing unit.

Team synergy occurs when the collective efforts of team members create output that exceeds the potential of the most capable team member. This increase in productivity of the team over the individual is called process gains. Process losses occur when teams misuse individual resources such that the team's output is less than that which individuals could have achieved on their own.

High-performing teams that achieve synergy are built on five foundations: a clear, engaging purpose that mobilizes action; clear performance goals and measures that encourage high standards; highly skilled people who add value; carefully developed work processes that enable team members to work together productively; and ample opportunities for team members to practice working together and learn from their successes and failures.

The most important task of the team leader is to create a work context that inspires and enables the team to do its work rather than directly intervening in the team's day-to-day work.

To create a context for high performance, team leaders should focus on four key areas: investing in personal development; providing team members with the direction, structure, and resources they need to accomplish their collective work; helping the team manage boundaries between the team and external individuals and groups; and making the right interventions at the right time.

A well-designed team task has the following five characteristics: clear boundaries, meaningfulness, autonomy, feedback, and small wins.

Groupthink occurs when team members' desire for belonging and cohesiveness leads to excessive concurrence seeking that overrides their ability to think critically and make effective decisions.

The team leader's task is to help the team balance its need for internal cohesion and external integration. Team leaders must make sure the team is both connected to and protected from external influences. To manage cooperation across groups, team leaders should understand how their own attitudes and behaviors inspire or inhibit effective relationships across groups; articulate a common vision that inspires interdependence across groups; set clear expectations that the groups will work together; help the team develop strategies for communicating with external individuals and groups; reward team members' efforts to work with other groups; have teams spend time together, but be sure to emphasize equality and the expertise that each team brings to the task (otherwise, the time teams spend together can make relationships worse); change the physical layout in ways that promote interaction across teams; redefine boundaries by using language that integrates, rather than divides or isolates, teams; and create gatekeeping roles in the team.

Gatekeepers are high-performing individuals who communicate extensively with people and groups outside the team. Effective gatekeepers engage in several boundary-spanning activities, including gathering information and resources, controlling the flow of information and resources that go out of the team, connecting the team to relevant individuals and groups, and buffering the team from unwanted interruptions, premature judgment, and other influences that could slow the team down or take it off track.

Research suggests that teams tend to go through five stages of development: forming, storming, norming, performing, and adjourning. Each of these stages presents opportunities and hurdles for the team that the team leader can help the team manage. In particular, each stage has implications for team members' attitudes and behaviors toward the task, each other, and the team leader.

Effective leaders carefully manage the type and timing of interventions. They know when to intervene in the day-to-day activities of the team and when to stay out of the team's way. Team leaders can best manage the type and timing of interventions when they understand the team life cycle. Effective team leaders realize that creating high-performing teams is an ongoing process, not a one-shot deal.

FOOD FOR THOUGHT

1. What is the most useful thing you learned in this chapter, and why?
2. Based on the strategies for managing teams described in this chapter, what can you do to increase your own effectiveness as a team member or team leader and the effectiveness of your teams? Practice this behavior and note any benefits and progress you make.
3. Think about a team that you belonged to that you felt was particularly successful. What characteristics made it successful? How did you feel? What did you accomplish? What lessons can you take from this experience to become a better team member or leader?
4. Think about a team that you belonged to and felt was unsuccessful or a waste of time. What characteristics made it unsuccessful? How did you feel? What did you accomplish? What lessons can you take from this experience to become a better team member or leader?
5. Think about your most effective team leader. What are the five most important things he or she did that led to his or her effectiveness? Was he or she perfect? If not, how did the leader and team manage these imperfections?
6. Think about your least effective team leader. What are the five most troublesome things he or she did that led to his or her ineffectiveness?
7. Have you ever been involved in a team that engaged in groupthink? Describe the situation, the symptoms, and the consequences. What could the team leader and team members have done to intervene?

ENDNOTES

1. Dumaine, Brian. 1990. "Who Needs a Boss?" *Fortune*. May 7: 52–56.
2. Labich, Kenneth. 1996. "Elite Teams." *Fortune*. February 19: 90–99.
3. Sinclair, Amanda. 1992. "The Tyranny of a Team Ideology." *Organizational Studies*, 13: 611–626.
4. Ibid.
5. Robinson, Sandra, and Anne M. O'Leary-Kelly. 1998. "Monkey See, Monkey Do: The Influence of Work Groups on the Antisocial Behavior of Employees." *Academy of Management Journal*, 41(6): 658–672.
6. Dumaine, Brian. 1994. "The Trouble with Teams." *Fortune*. September 5: 86–92.
7. Hackman, J. Richard. 1990. *Groups that Work (and Those that Don't): Creating Conditions for Effective Teamwork*. San Francisco, CA: Jossey-Bass Publishers.
8. Lipnack, Jessica, and Jeffrey Stamps. 1997. *Virtual Teams: Reaching across Space, Time, and Organizations with Technology*. New York: John Wiley.
9. Alderfer, Clatyon. 1983. "Intergroup Relations and Organizations." In Hackman, J. Richard, Edward Lawler, and Lyman Porter (eds.). *Perspectives on Behavior in Organizations*. New York: McGraw-Hill; Hackman, J. Richard. 1990. *Groups that Work (and Those that Don't): Creating Conditions for Effective Teamwork*. San Francisco, CA: Jossey-Bass; Hackman, J. Richard. 1987. "The Design of Work Teams." In Jay W. Lorsche (ed.). *Handbook of Organizational Behavior*. Upper Saddle River, NJ: Prentice Hall. 1987.
10. Katzenback, Jon, and Douglas K. Smith. 1993. *The Wisdom of Teams: Creating the High-Performance Organization*. New York: HarperBusiness.
11. Leavitt, Harold, and Jean Lipman-Bluman. 1995. "Hot Groups." *Harvard Business Review*. July–August: 109–116.
12. Hackman, J. Richard. 1990. *Groups that Work (and Those that Don't): Creating Conditions for Effective Teamwork*. San Francisco: Jossey-Bass.
13. Vroom, Victor. 1976. "Can Leaders Learn to Lead?" *Organizational Dynamics*. Winter: 17–28.
14. Senge, Peter. 1990. *The Fifth Discipline: The Art and Practice of the Learning Organization*. New York: Doubleday.
15. Katzenback, Jon, and Douglas K. Smith. 1993. *The Wisdom of Teams: Creating the High-Performance Organization*. New York: HarperBusiness.
16. Lancaster, Hal. 1997. "That Team Spirit Can Lead Your Career to New Victories." *Wall Street Journal*. January 14: B1.
17. Bennis, Warren, and Patricia Ward Biederman. 1997. *Organizing Genius: The Secrets of Creative Collaboration*. Reading, MA: Addison-Wesley Publishing Company.
18. Labich, Kenneth. 1996. "Elite Teams." *Fortune*. February 19: 90–99.
19. Lancaster, Hal. 1997. "That Team Spirit Can Lead Your Career to New Victories." *Wall Street Journal*. January 14: B1.
20. Haywood, Martha. *Managing Virtual Teams: Practical Techniques for High-Technology Managers*. Boston, MA: Artech House.
21. Edmonson, Amy. 1999. "Psychological Safety and Learning Behavior in Work Teams." *Administrative Science Quarterly*, 44(2): 350–383.
22. Barsade, Sigel. 2002. "The Ripple Effect: Emotional Contagion and Its Influence on Group Behavior. *Administrative Science Quarterly*, 47: 644–675; Losada, Marcial, and Emily Heaphy. 2004. "The Role of Positivity and Connectivity in the Performance of Business Teams." *American Behavioral Scientist,* 47(6): 740–765.
23. Rapaport, Richard. 1993. "To Build a Winning Team: An Interview with Head Coach Bill Walsh." *Harvard Business Review*. January/February: 110–120.
24. Caminiti, Susan. 1995. "What Team Leaders Need to Know." *Fortune*. February 20: 93–100.
25. Dirks, Kurt. 2002. "Trust in Leadership: Meta-Analytic Findings and Implications for Research and Practice." *Journal of Applied Psycyohology*, 87(4): 611–628.

26. Ibid.

27. Hackman, J. Richard. 1990. *Groups that Work (and Those that Don't): Creating Conditions for Effective Teamwork*. San Francisco, CA: Jossey-Bass.

28. Bennis, Warren, and Patricia Ward Biederman. 1997. *Organizing Genius: The Secrets of Creative Collaboration*. New York: Addison-Wesley.

29. Ibid.

30. Imai, K., N. Ikujiro, and H. Takeuchi. 1985. "Managing the New Product Development Process: How Japanese Companies Learn and Unlearn." In R. H. Hayes, K. Clark, and Ed Lornez. (eds.). *The Uneasy Alliance: Managing the Productivity-Technology Dilemma*. Boston, MA: Harvard Business Review Press.

31. Eisenstat, Russell, and Susan Cohen. 1990. "Summary: Top Management Groups." In Hackman, J. Richard (ed.). *Groups that Work (and Those that Don't): Creating Conditions for Effective Teamwork*. San Francisco, CA: Jossey-Bass.

32. Hackman, J. Richard, and Gary Oldham. 1980. *Work Redesign*. Reading, MA: Addison-Wesley.

33. 2003. "Ghosts in the House." *New Yorker Magazine*. October 27: 54–69.

34. Ibid.

35. Hackman, J. Richard. 1990. *Groups that Work (and Those that Don't): Creating Conditions for Effective Teamwork*. San Francisco, CA: Jossey-Bass; Katzenback, Jon, and Douglas K. Smith. 1993. *The Wisdom of Teams: Creating the High-Performance Organization*. New York: HarperBusiness; Leavitt, Harold, and Jean Lipman-Bluman. 1995. "Hot Groups." *Harvard Business Review*. July–August: 109–116; Bennis, Warren, and Patricia Ward Biederman. 1997. *Organizing Genius: The Secrets of Creative Collaboration*. Reading, MA: Addison-Wesley Publishing Company.

36. Biederman, Patricia Ward, and Warren Bennis. 1997. *Organizing Genius: Secrets of Creative Collaboration*. New York: Addison-Wesley.

37. Alderfer, Clayton. 1983. "Intergroup Relations and Organizations." In Hackman, J. Richard, Edward Lawler and Lyman Porter (eds.). *Perspectives on Behavior in Organizations*. New York: McGraw-Hill; Stewart, Greg, Charles Manz, and Henry Sims. 1999. *Team Work and Group Dynamics*. New York: John Wiley and Sons; Brown, David. 1984. "Managing Conflict among Groups." In D. A. Kolb, I. M. Rubin, and I. N. McIntyre (eds.). *Organizational Psychology: Readings on Human Behavior in Organizations*. Upper Saddle River, NJ: Prentice Hall; Perdue, Charles, Michael Gurtman, John Dovidio, and Richard Tyler. 1990. "Us and Them: Social Categorization and the Process of Intergroup Bias." *Journal of Personality and Social Psychology*, 59(3): 475–486; Tajfel, Henri, and Turner, C. 1986. "The Social Identity Theory of Intergroup Behavior." In Stephen Worchel and William G. Austin (eds.). *Psychology of Intergroup Relations*. 2nd ed. Chicago, IL: Nelson-Hall.

38. Peers, Martin. 2003. "Tuning Up Time Warner." *Wall Street Journal*. December 11: B1 and B7.

39. Arnst, Catherine, John Carey, Arlene Weintraub, and Kerry Capell. 2002. "Cancer: The Hope. The Hype. The Reality." *Business Week* November 25.

40. Stewart, Greg, Charles Manz, and Henry Sims. 1999. *Team Work and Group Dynamics*. New York: John Wiley and Sons; Crocker, Jennifer, and Riia Luhtanen. 1990. "Collective Self-Esteem and In-Group Bias." *Journal of Personality and Social Psychology*, 58: 60–67; Turner J. C., M. A. Hogg, P. J. Oakes, S. D. Reicher, and M. S. Wetherell. 1987. *Rediscovering the Social Group: A Self-Categorization Theory*. Oxford, England: Basil Blackwell; Gaertner, Samuel L., Jeffrey Mann, Audrey Murrell, and John F. Dovidio. 1989. "Reducing Intergroup Bias: The Benefits of Recategorization." *Journal of Personality and Social Psychology*, 57: 239–249; Mullen, B., R. Brown, and C. Smith. 1987. "In-Group Bias as a Function of Salience, Relevance, and Status: An Integration." *European Journal of Social*

Psychology, 22: 103–122; Maass, A., and M. Schaller. 1991. "Intergroup Biases and the Cognitive Dynamics of Stereotype Formation." In W. Stroebe and M. Hewstone (eds.). *European Review of Social Psychology*. Vol. 2. New York: Wiley.

41. Tajfel, H. 1978. *Differential between Social Groups: Studies in the Social Psychology of Intergroup Relations*. London: Academic Press; Tajfel, Henri, and J. Turner. 1986. "The Social Identity of Intergroup Behavior." In S. Worchel and W. Austin (eds.). *Psychology and Intergroup Relations*. Chicago, IL: Nelson-Hall.

42. Allen, V. L., and D. A. Wilder. 1975. "Categorization, Belief Similarity, and Intergroup Discrimination." *Journal of Personality and Social Psychology*, 32: 971–977.

43. Howard, J. W., and M. Rothbart. 1980. "Social Categorization and Memory for In-Group and Out-Group Behavior." *Journal of Personality and Social Psychology*, 38: 301–310.

44. Williams, Katherine, and Charles O'Reilly. 1998. "Demography and Diversity in Organizations: A Review of 40 Years of Research." *Research in Organizational Behavior*, 20: 77–140; citing Brewer, M. 1979. "In-Group Bias in the Minimal Intergroup Situation: A Cognitive-Motivational Analysis." *Psychological Bulletin*, 86: 307–324; Tajfel, Henri. 1982. *Social Identity and Intergroup Relations*. Cambridge: Cambridge University Press.

45. Judd, Charles M., and B. Park. 1988. "Out-Group Homogeneity: Judgments of Variability at the Individual and Group Levels." *Journal of Personality and Social Psychology*, 54: 778–788.

46. Harquail, Celia. 1996. "When One Speaks for Many: The Influence of Social Identification on Group Advocacy in Organizations." Unpublished Dissertation, University of Michigan.

47. Piliavin, Jane A., John F. Dovidio, Samuel L. Gaertner, and R. D. Clark. 1981. *Emergency Intervention*. San Diego, CA: Academic Press.

48. Brown, L. David. 1984. "Managing Conflict among Groups." In D. A. Kolb, I. M. Rubin, and I. N. McIntyre (eds.). *Organizational Psychology: Readings on Human Behavior in Organizations*. Upper Saddle River, NJ: Prentice Hall.

49. Ibid.

50. Perdue, Charles, Michael Gurtman, John Dovidio, and Richard Tyler. 1990. "Us and Them: Social Categorization and the Process of Intergroup Bias." *Journal of Personality and Social Psychology*, 59(3): 475–486.

51. Janis, Irving. 1971. "Groupthink." *Psychology Today*. November: 43–44, 46, 74–76.

52. Marx, Robert, Charles Stubbart, V. Traub, and Michael Cavanaugh. 1987. "The NASA Space Shuttle Disaster: A Case Study." *Journal of Management Case Studies*. Winter: 300–318.

53. 2003. "Report on Columbia Disaster Faults NASA Management." *Wall Street Journal* August 27.

54. Ibid.

55. Kiechel, Walter. 1990. "How to Escape the Echo Chamber." *Fortune*. June 18: 129–130.

56. Janis, Irving. 1982. *Groupthink*. 2nd ed. Boston: Houghton Mifflin.

57. Ancona, Deborah, and David Caldwell. 1992. "Bridging the Boundary: External Process and Performance in Organizational Teams." *Administrative Science Quarterly*, 37(4): 634–666.

58. Dougherty, Deborah. 1992. "Interpretive Barriers to Successful Product Innovation in Large Firms." *Organization Science*, 3(2): 179–202.

59. Majchrzak, Ann, and Qianwei Wang. 1996. "Breaking the Functional Mindset in Process Organizations." *Harvard Business Review*, 74(5): 92–99.

60. Stewart, Greg, Charles Manz, and Henry Sims. 1999. *Team Work and Group Dynamics*. New York: John Wiley and Sons.

61. Dovidio, John, Ana Validzic, and Samuel Gaertner. 1998. "Intergroup Bias: Status, Differentiation, and a Common In-Group Identity." *Journal of Personality and Social Psychology*, 75(1): 109–120.

62. Majchrzak, Ann, and Qianwei Wang. 1996. "Breaking the Functional Mindset in Process Organizations." *Harvard Business Review*, 74(5): 92–99.

63. Dovidio, John, Ana Validzic, and Samuel Gaertner. 1998. "Intergroup Bias: Status, Differentiation and a Common In-Group Identity." *Journal of Personality and Social Psychology*, 75(1): 109–120.

64. Katz, R., and Tushman, M. L. 1981. "An Investigation into the Managerial Roles and Career Paths of Gatekeepers and Project Supervisors in a Major R&D Facility." *R&D Management*, 11: 103–110.

65. Brown, Shona, and Kathleen M. Eisenhardt. 1995. "Product Development: Past Research, Present Findings, and Future Directions." *Academy of Management Review,* 20(2): 343–378.

66. Ancona, Deborah, and David Caldwell. 1992. "Bridging the Boundary: External Process and Performance in Organizational Teams." *Administrative Science Quarterly*, 35: 634–665.

67. Hackman, J. Richard. 1990. *Groups that Work (and Those that Don't): Creating Conditions for Effective Teamwork*. San Francisco, CA: Jossey-Bass.

68. Ibid.

69. Biederman, Patricia Ward, and Warren Bennis. 1997. *Organizing Genius: Secrets of Creative Collaboration*. New York: Addison-Wesley.

70. Katzenback, Jon, and Douglas K. Smith. 1993. The Wisdom of Teams: Creating the High-Performance Organization. New York: HarperBusiness.

71. Ibid., p. 12.

72. Gersick, Connie, and Mary Lou Davis. 1990. "Summary: Task Forces." In Hackman, J. Richard (ed.). *Groups that Work (and Those that Don't): Creating Conditions for Effective Teamwork*. San Francisco, CA: Jossey-Bass; Bennis, Warren, and Herbert Shepard. 1956. "A Theory of Group Development." *Human Relations*, 9(4): 415–457; Tuckman, Barry W., and Mary Ann Jensen. 1975. "Stages of Small Group Development Revisited." *Group and Organizational Studies*, 2(4): 419–427.

73. Lipnack, Jessica, and Jeffrey Stamps. 1997. *Virtual Teams: Reaching across Space, Time, and Organizations with Technology*. New York: John Wiley.

74. Tuckman, Barry W., and Mary Ann Jensen. 1975. "Stages of Small Group Development Revisited." *Group and Organizational Studies*, 2(4): 419–427.

75. Lester, Scott, Bruce Meglino, and M. Audrey Koorsgaard. 2002. "The Antecedents and Consequences of Group Potency: A Longitudinal Investigation of Newly Formed Work Groups." *Academy of Management Journal*, 45(2): 352–368.

76. Katzenback, Jon, and Douglas K. Smith. 1993. *The Wisdom of Teams: Creating the High-Performance Organization*. New York: HarperBusiness.

77. Hackman, J. Richard. 1990. *Groups that Work (and Those that Don't): Creating Conditions for Effective Teamwork*. San Francisco, CA: Jossey-Bass.

78. Gersick, Connie, and Mary Lou Davis. 1990. "Summary: Task Forces." In Hackman, J. Richard (ed.). *Groups that Work (and Those that Don't): Creating Conditions for Effective Teamwork*. San Francisco, CA: Jossey-Bass.

79. Janis, Irving. 1993. *Groupthink in Small Groups and Social Interaction*. Vol. 2. New York: John Wiley & Sons.

80. Katzenback, Jon, and Douglas K. Smith. 1993. *The Wisdom of Teams: Creating the High-Performance Organization*. New York: HarperBusiness.

81. Gersick, Connie. 1988. "Time and Transition in Work Teams: Toward a New Model of Group Development." *Academy of Management Journal*, 31: 9–41.

82. Hackman, J. Richard. *Groups that Work (and Those that Don't): Creating Conditions for Effective Teamwork*. San Francisco, CA: Jossey-Bass.

9

Diverse Teams and Virtual Teams: Managing Differences and Distances

This chapter will help you:

■ Understand the advantages and risks of diverse and distributed teams

■ Learn techniques for effectively managing diverse and distributed teams

■ Understand why managing the relationship dynamics is as important as managing the task and technical aspects of diverse and distributed teams

■ Become a better leader and member of diverse and virtual teams

> *What do you do on the day after the merger when you wake up and find out half your team is on the other side of the country (or worse yet, on the other side of the world)?*
>
> —MARTHA HAYWOOD, AUTHOR
> *Managing Virtual Teams*

Imagine a typical management team in the 1960s in Dallas. The marketing manager is meeting with his new product development team that convenes weekly in the second floor conference room of his company's new high-rise building. The team's task is to develop a strategy to introduce a new product to the U.S. market within the next year. The team is made up of four North American college-educated white males of Western European descent, ranging from 32 to 38 years of age. They enjoy their jobs and expect to stay with the company until they retire at age 65. They are all married fathers and sole breadwinners for their families. When they arrive at their homes tonight, each man's wife and children will be waiting for him. Dinner will be on the table.

Fast-forward into the twenty-first century in the United States and imagine yourself on the following team. You live in New York and are a marketing manager who is in the middle of a conference call with your transnational team members. Your team's task is to develop a strategy to coordinate the introduction of a new product to five countries simultaneously within the next 3 months. In addition to yourself, your team is made up of a 48-year-old Korean man stationed in New York, a 29-year-old white American woman stationed in Tokyo, a 32-year-old Brazilian woman stationed in Mexico City, a 35-year-old African American man stationed in Chicago, a 25-year-old Italian woman stationed in Milan, and a 40-year-old Finnish man stationed in Stockholm.

Team members' educational backgrounds include a 2-year community college degree, an undergraduate degree in art history, an undergraduate degree in marketing, two masters degrees in business administration, and two Ph.D.s in engineering. Their tenure with the company ranges from 8 months to 20 years. You began working as a team 5 months ago, shortly after your company merged with a former competitor.

The conference call has been timed carefully so that all team members can be at the meeting. It's approximately 10:30 A.M. in Chicago and Mexico City, 11:30 A.M. in New York, 5:30 P.M. in Milan and Stockholm, and 12:30 A.M. in Tokyo. You have never met two of the team members in person. All your interactions with them have been through the telephone, e-mail, and videoconferences.

You enjoy your job, work 2 days a week out of your home, and spend about 6 days each month traveling on business. You are in a dual-career relationship and have two young children. Before you leave work tonight, you will check your telephone messages to see if the headhunter who asked you to consider a position as marketing director for a new line of low-carb products returned your call. You will then log onto the Internet to see how well your retirement portfolio has performed today. You plan to retire at age 55, so you are choosing your stocks carefully. When you arrive home tonight after picking your children up from day care, you'll realize that both you and your significant other forgot to order dinner.

These two scenarios reflect how shifts in demographics, social norms, work expectations, and new technologies are dramatically transforming the nature of teamwork. Team members are becoming more culturally diverse and geographically dispersed. Work tasks are becoming increasingly complex, and the processes by which team members do their work are being significantly altered by technological advancements, globalization, and increased competition.

> As a result of the changes brought about by technology, a typical executive today has to deal with thousands of interdependent relationships. . . . And the diversity of goals, opinions, and beliefs among these players is typically enormous. *John Kotter, Leadership Scholar*

Certainly, relatively homogeneous teams in which team members primarily meet face-to-face in the same place are still common in many organizations. But diverse teams and virtual teams are becoming increasingly commonplace, providing new opportunities for team members to enhance their personal growth, team productivity, and organizational competitiveness.

Many of the skills that we learned for managing relatively homogeneous, co-located teams are insufficient for effectively managing diverse and distributed teams. However, most organizations have not done enough to prepare employees to understand and manage these new team forms. Therefore, in this chapter I discuss the characteristics of diverse teams and virtual teams. I focus particularly on the ways in which they differ from relatively homogeneous teams that primarily meet face-to-face. I also suggest how team members and leaders can leverage the opportunities and minimize the risks that diverse and virtual teams offer.

PART 1
DIVERSE TEAMS

In their *Training and Development* magazine article, "Diverse Teams: Breakdown or Breakthrough?" Lewis Griggs and Lente-Louise Louw point out:

> Forming a cohesive team from relatively similar individuals is hard enough. The difficulties are multiplied when team members come from different ethnic or national cultures. They not only come to the group with their own individual ways of being, but they also bring cultural or national dictates about the proper ways to do things. As a consequence, diverse teams require more skill facilitation than homogeneous groups, especially in the early stages.[1]

Team diversity, of course, goes beyond ethnic and national culture. Today's team members are likely to differ from each other on relatively observable characteristics such as race, gender, nationality, and age, as well as job-related characteristics such as professional affiliation, functional department, hierarchical level, organizational membership, and tenure in the organization. Team members are also likely to differ significantly from each other on less visible characteristics such as cognitive styles, values, experience, education, and skills, as well as more private and often invisible characteristics such as religion, sexual orientation, and health challenges.[2]

After more than 40 years of research on diversity, most researchers agree that differences among team members matter. Specifically, diversity among team members affects:

- The variety of cognitive resources and behavioral styles team members bring to the team
- The interaction processes by which team members work together, including both task and relationship processes
- The team's ability to be a high-performing team; in particular, the team's ability to make effective decisions, promote the development and well-being of all team members, and enhance the team's performance over time

The Diversity Dilemma

Researchers also agree that diversity in teams is a "double-edged sword."[3] Members of diverse teams, when contrasted to relatively homogeneous teams, tend to bring a greater variety of perspectives, information, skills, relationship networks, and behavioral styles to their teams. This greater variety of resources can enhance a team's decision-making processes through increased creativity, critical thinking, and constructive task-related conflict, which in turn can result in higher quality decisions and enhanced performance.[4] These advantages are more likely to emerge when the team's resources are relevant to the team's task (e.g., when breadth of ideas or information about particular markets is important), when the different resources are integrated into the group, when differences among team members are well managed, and when team members have time to learn how to work together productively.[5]

Diversity in teams can also lead to dysfunctional dynamics that compromise the team's ability to leverage team members' resources. These dynamics include cultural ignorance and bias, marginalization of team members, and an inability of team members to identify with the team. These dynamics can lead to greater psychological detachment, less cohesion among team members, more communication problems, unproductive social conflict, and increased absenteeism and turnover.[6]

Researchers explain the roots of these potential problems in diverse groups through two theories: the similarity-attraction hypothesis and structural barriers. The similarity-attraction hypothesis assumes that people categorize themselves and others into social categories that they believe are relevant (e.g., race, gender, hierarchical level, and functional area); people who share the same social categories tend to see each other as more similar and indeed may be more similar in many ways because they are more likely to share similar life experiences; consequently, they may find interacting with each other "easier, positively reinforcing, and more desirable"[7] and may find interactions with people that they perceive as different from themselves as less predictable, more confusing, more stressful, and less desirable.

Structural barriers refer to social barriers that prevent the full participation of all team members. The structural perspective assumes that the dynamics in diverse teams reflect those of the larger society in which the team and organization are embedded. Consequently, if there is bias, misunderstanding, marginalization, and lack of cohesion among diverse groups in the larger society, then these social dynamics are likely to be replicated to some degree in the team.

For example, most societies and organizations promote beliefs about who has the "right stuff" to succeed in particular roles (e.g., manager and team leader) and may create explicit policies that exclude members of some cultural groups from equal participation in these roles regardless of their competence. Furthermore, even when equal opportunity is promoted, organizational values and norms often reflect those of the dominant cultural group(s). Consequently, team members who are in the minority and do not hold some of the same critical values and norms as the dominant cultural group may find it more difficult to adhere to the policies, fit the norms, and have their contributions recognized as valuable.[8]

In short, the diversity dilemma is this: Although diverse team members tend to bring a broader range of resources to the team, they also may tend to engage in dysfunctional dynamics that can hinder the team's ability to use those resources. Consequently, we should not focus on whether diverse teams are inherently better or worse than relatively homogeneous teams. Rather, we should focus on how organizational leaders and managers create a work context and culture that leverages the benefits and minimizes the risks.[9] The causes and consequences of the diversity dilemma in teams are discussed in more detail in the following sections and are summarized in Figure 9-1.

Potential Advantages and Disadvantages of Diverse Teams

The research on diverse teams provides useful insights into how diversity in teams may affect team process and performance in both positive and negative ways. On the positive side, compared with homogeneous teams, diverse teams (when well managed) tend to have the following advantages:

Enhanced Effectiveness on Intellective Tasks

Intellective tasks are defined as those that have objectively correct answers.[10] Some research suggests that diverse teams may be more likely to "hit" upon the right answers, particularly if the team has a greater variety of task-relevant knowledge and skill among team members.[11]

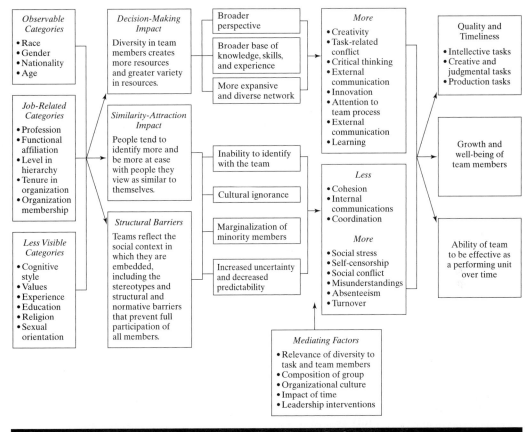

FIGURE 9-1   Effects of Diversity on Team Process and Performance

Enhanced Effectiveness on Creative and Judgmental Decision-Making Tasks

Many problems require using creativity and judgment to interpret a complex environment and come to a consensus on the "best" solution. Substantial research suggests that diverse teams tend to have a wider range of information, skills, and experiences that can increase the breadth of ideas available to the group. In contrast, relatively homogeneous teams may miss or misinterpret important data and trends, as illustrated in the following story about Avon's former CEO Jim Preston's top management team:

> Avon was your grandmother's beauty company.... [T]he thing that really gave [Preston] religion on women's issues was watching Avon practically destroy itself because the men at the top made a big miscalculation about women. They refused to believe the company's own market research, which even in the early 1970s pointed out that women were entering the labor force and would likely stay there. It was getting harder to recruit Avon Ladies because women had other job options. And sales were beginning to slow, since fewer women were home to answer the door. Avon's top executives first denied the trend.... Instead of pursing women into the workplace, capitalizing on their higher

incomes and lack of time, they went careening off on a disastrous acquisition binge. . . . Preston believes that if women executives had been in charge, they would have acknowledged that women were headed to work, embraced the trend, and said, "You're damned right this will continue. We'd better change."[12]

More Attention to Team Process

Because members of diverse teams are more likely to notice differences among each other and be concerned about their ability to work together, they may also pay more attention to the group process.[13] Consequently, they may be particularly thoughtful and systematic about setting explicit norms that enhance the decision-making processes (e.g., "Make sure no one is left out of the discussion" and "Make sure everyone's opinion is given a fair hearing"). Although explicit norms are beneficial to relatively homogeneous teams as well, members of homogeneous teams may take their relationships for granted, pay less attention to the quality of their interactions, and thus may miss opportunities to enhance their teams' process and productivity.

Broader and More Diverse External Networks

Technology can help put us in contact with each other—over oceans and over cultures—but it cannot make us understand one another. For that we must still depend on the oldest systems of all: human imagination, tolerance, determination, and the will to learn continuously. Mary O'Hara-Devereaux and Robert Johansen

Members of diverse teams tend to have access to a more diverse network outside the team. Access to these external networks can increase the information, resources, and support available to the team, which can enhance the team's performance if it is relevant to the team task and made accessible to the team.[14]

Enhanced Learning

In some cases, teams that have members with different levels of ability (e.g., some members are more proficient than others) may outperform groups whose members have similar ability levels. This suggests that both high- and low-ability members learn from interacting with each other. Certainly, members with lower ability levels can learn from those with higher ability levels. But, says researcher Susan Jackson, higher ability members also may

. . . learn during their interactions with others of lower ability because they take on the role of teacher. Playing the teacher role may lead high-ability members to sharpen their own thinking. Another possibility is that the questions and inputs of more naive members encourage the more expert members to unbundle the assumptions and rules they automatically use when dealing with issues and problems in which they are experts (Simon 1979). This unbundling may increase the probability of discovering assumptions that warrant scrutiny and decisions rules for which exceptions may be needed.[15]

Continuous Improvement

Some studies suggest that diverse teams tend to show a "more consistent pattern of improvement over time" than do homogeneous teams.[16] And when diverse teams outperform homogeneous teams, their advantage seems to increase over time.[17] These advantages, however, are more likely to occur when a diverse team is well managed.

Now the Hurdles

Compared with homogeneous teams, diverse teams are more likely to face the following risks:

More Stress

Members of diverse teams are more likely to find the team experience stressful for several reasons. Some team members may engage in negative stereotyping and biases that can result in more negative emotions in the people who exhibit these attitudes as well as in those who are their targets. Furthermore, diversity increases uncertainty and decreases predictability in social relations.[18] Consequently, team members are more likely to misinterpret each other's intentions and may be unsure about how to interact with each other, which can increase confusion and anxiety. For example, researchers Judith Claire, Joy Beattie, and Tammy MacLean note that there can be considerable stress associated with invisible identities such as sexual orientation or health challenges, regardless of whether one chooses to hide one's identity or reveal it. If one tries to "pass," then one must conceal parts of oneself that are important and live with the constant concern that someone might find out. If one decides to reveal one's identity, especially if it carries a social stigma, one must explain one's identity over and over again (which people who do not have this identity do not need to do—e.g., one doesn't have to explain that one is heterosexual or that one doesn't have a particular chronic illness).[19]

Reduced Group Cohesion

If I can't dance, I don't want to be part of your revolution. **Emma Goldman**

Social cohesion refers to the degree to which team members feel psychologically connected to each other. Cohesive groups tend to outperform noncohesive groups (as long as they aren't excessively isolated and self-absorbed), and "members of cohesive groups tend to be more satisfied, absent less, and more likely to remain in the group rather than leave it."[20] Members of diverse teams are more likely to have difficulty finding common ground, have problems communicating with each other, experience more stress, and engage in more social conflict, all of which can decrease group cohesiveness.

More Psychological and Physical Detachment from the Team

Diverse teams tend to have greater absenteeism and turnover than homogeneous teams.[21] Some studies conducted in the United States suggest that women and people of color are more likely to psychologically and physically withdraw from groups in which they are in a minority. However, other studies suggest that as diversity increases in a group, white men are more likely to feel less committed to the group and are more likely to leave.[22]

Decreased and More Distorted Internal Communication

People who view themselves as similar to each other are more likely to feel more comfortable with each other, which increases their desire to communicate with each other.[23] Conversely, people who view themselves as different from each other tend to communicate less often with each other. Furthermore, people who do not share common social and organizational categories (e.g., race, gender, nationality, profession, department, and hierarchical level) are less likely to share the same values, cultural knowledge, and behaviors. It is well known that the same words can mean different things in different cultures. Sylvia Odenwald, author of *Global Solutions for Teams*, explains, "Even the translation of silence is important to intercultural understanding."[24] Consequently, members of diverse groups are more likely to misinterpret each other's words, behaviors, and intent.[25]

The assessment in Box 9-1 can help you identify your own communication style, as well as the communication style of your team members.

More Difficulty Coordinating

Team member similarity may make it easier for team members to communicate with each other, trust each other, and anticipate each other's intentions and behaviors that can make coordination easier and faster. Some research suggests that tasks that have objective standards for performance based on proficiency and productivity (e.g., production tasks) may benefit from team member homogeneity.[26] For example, a study of underground mining crews investigated the impact of homogeneous tenure (i.e., all

---

BOX 9-1

Assess Team Members' Style Preferences

Please circle the number that best reflects your style in work groups. Remember that no one style is better or worse than the others. Then compare your responses with those of other team members.

Continuous Communication Style: When in a conversation, I tend to begin speaking before other people finish their sentences.	1	2	3	4	5	Discrete Communication Style: When in a conversation, I tend to wait for the other person to finish before I begin speaking.
Talker: I tend to be more of a talker than a listener.	1	2	3	4	5	Listener: I tend to be more of a listener than a talker.
Report Talk: I believe that the main purpose of communication is to share information.	1	2	3	4	5	Rapport Talk: I believe that the main purpose of communication is to build relationships.
Self-Enhancing: I like to promote my contributions and stand out from the group.	1	2	3	4	5	Group-Enhancing: I do not like to promote my personal contributions or stand out from the group.
Equality: I am comfortable challenging authority figures, even in public.	1	2	3	4	5	Hierarchy: I am not comfortable challenging authority figures, particularly in public.

people started working at the company around the same time) on the crew's performance. The researchers concluded, "Familiarity, which included an assessment of how long the crew had worked together, was positively related to higher levels of productivity and lower accident rates."[27]

More Perceptual Biases of Leaders

Several research studies have concluded that leaders tend to feel more positively toward people they perceive as similar to themselves and rate the performance of people who they perceive as similar to themselves higher than they rate the performance of people who they perceive as different.[28] Furthermore, research has also found that subordinates expect different styles from leaders based on stereotypes about the leader's sociocultural group membership (e.g., race and gender). These expectations can, in turn, influence the team leader's credibility, confidence, and ability to manage the team effectively.[29]

Team Members' Misperceptions about Team Performance

Some research suggests that even when diverse teams are performing well, team members may underestimate their team's effectiveness, perhaps because social stress in the team may cloud their ability to see their team's task-related strengths.[30]

Additional Factors to Consider

Certainly, all diverse teams do not display the preceding characteristics. Furthermore, even relatively homogeneous teams may have many of the advantages (creativity and attention to team process) and disadvantages (member detachment, communication problems, and lack of cohesion) listed earlier. However, these advantages and disadvantages tend to be more pronounced in diverse teams. Several factors influence whether these advantages and disadvantages will emerge in a diverse team.

- *Relevance of diversity to the task.* One of the advantages of diverse teams is that they are likely to have access to a greater variety of resources such as knowledge, skills, experience, and networks. However, if these resources are not relevant to the task, they are of little benefit to the team.[31] Diversity appears to be an advantage for complex, nonroutine problems that require creativity, judgment, and a broad range of information.[32]
- *Relevance of diversity to team members.* Some kinds of diversity tend to be more relevant to team members and have a greater impact than do other kinds of diversity.[33] For example, more visible differences tend to have more of an impact on team process than do less visible differences, particularly early in the team's life.
- *Differential impact of diversity on team members.* Diversity in teams does not affect all members the same way. For example, the less diverse a team is, the more likely a member who is different from the group will stand out.[34] Some research concluded that men in predominantly women's jobs tend to be integrated into the group and experience little, if any, hostility.[35] However, women in predominantly male jobs are less likely to be integrated into the group and are more likely to experience hostility.[36] However, research also suggests that when men are in the minority in mixed-gender groups, they tend to be less satisfied and experience "more negative psychological outcomes,"

absenteeism, and turnover than women do when they are in the gender-minority in such groups.[37] Indeed, some studies have shown that women's satisfaction is higher in male-dominated settings.[38] For men, their perceived losses seem to outweigh their perceived gains in mixed-gender teams; for women, their perceived gains seem to outweigh their perceived losses in such teams.

- *Impact of organizational culture.*   Recent research suggests that organizations that promote a collectivist (people look out more for each other and organizational goals) rather than individualistic (people look out more for themselves and their own goals) culture are more likely to benefit from team diversity because team members are more likely to focus on their common goals and shared fate rather than on team member differences.[39]

- *Impact of time.*   Although members of homogeneous teams tend to feel more comfortable with each other initially, some research suggests that this advantage of homogeneous teams over diverse teams tends to fade over time.[40] For example, in a study of 43 senior managers enrolled in an executive training program, researchers found that "similarity in demographic characteristics and in behavioral style preferences contributed significantly to the prediction of liking and coworkers preference" early on.[41] However, "Three weeks after initial interaction, demographic similarity ceased to contribute significantly to social liking and coworker preference. Only similarity in personal values predicted both liking and preference."[42]

Although diversity among team members has both advantages and risks, teams can benefit significantly from diversity, particularly under certain conditions. Diverse teams may have an advantage over relatively homogeneous teams when:

- The diversity among team members is relevant to the team's task (e.g., when tasks require creativity and judgment, when breadth of ideas is important, or when information about particular markets is important)
- When team members have time to learn how to work together productively
- When diversity among team members is well managed

Leading Diverse Teams

Resolving conflicts in a productive way that pulls people together, instead of driving them farther apart, and which produces creative decisions, instead of destructive power struggles, is a high level leadership skill.   John Kotter

Given the increasing use of diverse teams, as well as diversity's impact on team performance, team leaders cannot afford to ignore or mismanage diverse teams. As with all teams, effective leaders of diverse teams create conditions that help diverse teams leverage rather than squander their collective resources.

Certainly, members of effective diverse teams and homogeneous teams share many of the same qualities. They are committed to the team's purpose; they have a specific expertise to offer the team; they are not advocates of a particular method or function; they have general problem-solving, decision-making, and implementation skills; they have strong relationship skills; they know their own strengths and weaknesses and how these affect team performance; and they are adaptive.

However, members of diverse teams must be even more adept at understanding cultural and style differences, attending to group process, anticipating the consequences of their behavior on others, and dealing with new and unfamiliar situations. When diverse teams are also global teams, team members must be able to adapt to a variety of organizational structures, policies, and norms and be able to shift their mindset and behavior depending on the needs of the situation.[43]

To help members of diverse teams develop these characteristics, team leaders can do the following:

Create an "Integration-and-Learning" Perspective in the Work Team

The integration-and-learning perspective discussed in Chapter 7 will enable the team members (and you) to discuss, integrate, and leverage the different perspectives, skills, experience, and behaviors that a diverse team brings. Encourage the team to use differences among team members in ways that help it rethink how it does its work, how it defines its markets, how it solves problems, and how it conducts business on a day-to-day basis.[44]

Pay Particular Attention to First Meetings

As with all teams, what happens at the beginning of a team's life sets the tone for future interactions among team members. At early stages, team members learn about each other and negotiate their relationships. However, members of diverse groups tend to have more hurdles to overcome than do relatively homogeneous teams, including more stereotyping, bias, and social conflict. Some research suggests that training team members in each other's point of view may improve the team's ability to work together productively.[45] Team leaders can have team members discuss questions such as the following at first meetings:

- What are my preferred ways of relating to other people (communication, level of formality, addressing conflict/avoiding conflict, and dealing with authority)?
- What are my work-related values (time management, problem-solving methods, and definitions of effectiveness)?
- What do I expect from the team leader?

Based on team members' individual responses to the preceding questions, the team can consider the following questions collectively:

- In what ways are we similar to and different from each other?
- Which of our differences are relevant to team performance and which are not?
- What are our collective strengths that can help team performance?
- What are some potential dysfunctional dynamics that may hinder our ability to work together?
- How can we work together in ways that leverage our differences?

Cultural beliefs separate, through superficial differences, groups that reasonably should be united. Jennifer James, Thinking in the Future Tense

Create a Common Identity and Collectivist Culture

Because people tend to be attracted to and be more comfortable with people that they perceive as similar to themselves, it is important for team members to develop a collective identity that overrides other identities (at least while team members are working in the team). As mentioned previously, research suggests that organizations that promote a collectivist culture (one that promotes organizational goals, interdependence, cooperation, and a view of employees as more similar to than different from each other) rather than an individualistic culture (one that promotes the view that employees are unique and encourages employees to differentiate themselves from others) are more likely to develop a common identity among employees and benefit from diversity. Specifically, researcher Jennifer Chatman and her colleagues say:

> Feelings of similarity and a common fate among members cultivated in collectivist cultures lead members to consider more of their coworkers to be part of their in-group. Because in-group members seek out and prefer to interact with one another, members of organizations emphasizing collectivist values should interact with one another and participate in joint efforts to solve organizational problems more frequently than would members of individualistic cultures.[46]

Indeed, in their study of organizations with collectivist versus individualistic cultures, they concluded, "Dissimilar people in collective cultures had the highest creative output, both in terms of their own perceptions of creativity and the ratings of their creativity by experts."[47]

Pay Extra Attention to Norms

Explicit norms are particularly important in diverse teams because team members may have more difficulty with cohesion, communication, and coordination. Norms increase predictability, decrease misunderstandings, and reduce stress. Norms related to communication are particular important in diverse teams. For example, team members should be sure to actively request information from all team members and make sure it is taken seriously. If team members speak different languages, they should speak slowly and clearly, confirm mutual understanding, and avoid using language and mannerisms that may be considered offensive to other cultures. People from different cultural groups tend to have different networks outside the team, so team members should encourage communication with external people and groups who can offer information and support to the team.

Provide Early Opportunities to Succeed, Clear Performance Measures, and Ongoing Positive Feedback

It may be more important for diverse teams to experience small wins early in their team's life because they may be less optimistic about the team's ability to work together productively. Early visible success can increase team members' confidence in each other and the team, reduce concerns about the team's ability to work together, and increase team members' attractiveness to each other. Furthermore, because members of diverse teams may underestimate their team's effectiveness relative to homogeneous teams (even when they are outperforming homogeneous teams), it is particularly important for team leaders to provide clear and measurable performance measures so that team members can see their progress. It is also important for leaders of diverse teams to provide more positive feedback to diverse teams because members of diverse teams may be less likely to recognize the extent of their collective successes.

Role-Model the Behavior That You Want to See in Team Members

As always, the leader's behavior sends clear signals to team members about what behaviors are appropriate. Effective leaders of diverse teams manage their own stereotypes and biases, actively seek out diversity on the team, and show through their everyday interactions that they respect diversity and believe it benefits the team and organization. Simple things make a difference. For example, one leader of a cross-national management team made several interventions.

> His company badge listed his name in Latin, Cantonese, and Japanese characters. He coached his managers to watch for and address possible culturally based misunderstandings during their meetings. He would interrupt staff that were discussing an issue to see if one was not fully understanding the other. He encouraged his managers to do the same. He would also meet with his managers privately, like a diplomat, to bring up more sensitive issues, such as the possibility that one manager's style might be offensive to another.[48]

Conclusion

Undoubtedly, diverse teams will continue to enrich and challenge the organizations in which we work, and they will have an increasingly powerful impact on our daily lives. They will design and manufacture the products that we use, find cures for the diseases that plague us, perform complex surgeries on our bodies, and take care of our precious children at school. The quality of our lives depends not only on the individual competence of team members but also on their ability to leverage their diversity and work together as a cohesive team.

PART II
VIRTUAL TEAMS: WORKING TOGETHER APART[49]

Until recently, when you said that you worked with someone, you meant by implication that you worked in the same place for the same organization. Suddenly, in the blink of an evolutionary eye, people no longer must be in the same place—co-located—in order to work together. Now many people work in virtual teams that transcend distance, time zones, and organizational boundaries.[50]
Jessica Lipnack and Jeffrey Stamps, Virtual Teams: Reaching Across Time, Space, and Technology

Increasingly, virtual teams (also called "distributed" teams) are becoming commonplace in organizations. Indeed, many researchers and practitioners argue, "a key component of successful, twenty-first century organizations will be the effective use of virtual teams."[51] Similar to co-located teams, virtual teams are made up of individuals interacting interdependently on collective tasks to achieve common organizational goals. However, in contrast to co-located teams, virtual teams tend to be geographically dispersed, rarely meet face-to-face, and primarily depend on electronic and computer-based information and communication technologies to work together.

These technologies include, but are not limited to, voice mail, conference calls, fax machines, e-mail, Web pages, videoconferencing, electronic discussion environments, computer-supported group decision-making systems, and other collaborative technologies that enable team members to communicate in real or asynchronous time. Through these technologies, team members make decisions, manage projects, coauthor reports, hold meetings, serve customers, and conduct their other collective tasks.[52]

Why Virtual Teams?

Several technical, social, and economic trends make virtual teams not only possible but often preferable to co-located teams.

- Electronic and computer-based information and communication technologies are becoming increasingly affordable and available. Sophisticated desktop videoconferencing systems are now available for under $1,000 per station.[53]
- Global expansion, mergers, alliances, and acquisitions are creating organizational relationships that cross regional and national boundaries, making it more difficult for organizational members to meet face-to-face.
- A shift from production to knowledge work makes it unnecessary for team members to be in the same place in order to work together.
- Many teams depend on external consultants and experts who may not be able to attend face-to-face meetings on a regular basis. The high-technology research and consulting firm Gartner Group says that "more than 80 percent of large enterprises will routinely use consultants at the beginning of the twenty-first century."[54]
- E-commerce is creating organizational-customer relationships that are conducted primarily, sometimes solely, through computer-mediated information and communication technologies. With e-commerce, customer service can be available 24 hours a day, offer immediate service, and always be, at least in spirit, close to the customer.
- Organizations that want to recruit and retain the most talented employees are offering alternative work arrangements supported by information and communication technologies. The U.S. Bureau of Labor Statistics estimates that one in ten workers in the United States is in an alternative work arrangement.[55] Telecommuters were estimated to number between 7 and 13 million people in the late 1990s and continue to be one of the fastest growing segments of workers.[56]
- Organizations that want to make the best use of limited office space are increasingly using "hot desks" to reduce the number of private office spaces required. Hot desks are office spaces that include desks, computers, telephones, and storage areas that are shared by many people who spend little time in the office (e.g., part-time consultants and employees who spend much of their time working out of the office).[57] Notably, in a study of major U.S. corporations, Cornell University researchers concluded that "on an average day, 40 percent of desks are unoccupied."[58]
- Because of their ability to free team members from some of the constraints of time and place, information and communication technologies can help teams be faster and more flexible—distinct advantages in today's competitive economic environment.

Even team members who have the opportunity to meet face-to-face are increasingly using information and communication technologies to work together more effectively and efficiently. For example, employees who work on different shifts can use these technologies to be on the same team without altering their work schedules. It is of interest that most e-mail messages are sent to people who are at the same work location rather than far away.[59]

Certainly, the availability of communication and information technologies will not guarantee that a team will be faster, more flexible, or more effective. To be effective, all teams—whether they meet virtually or face-to-face—must have a clear and engaging purpose, clear performance measures, highly skilled people on the team who

We're only at the start of the dot.com learning curve. As the road gets steeper and you don't drive at Internet speed, you'd better keep an eye out for the tire marks on your back. Sun Microsystems CEO Scott McNealy

focus on both the task and relationships, and opportunities to practice and learn from their collective successes and failures. Members of virtual teams must also develop skills that will enable them to leverage the advantages of information and communication technologies.

The Secret to Successful High-Performing Virtual Teams

If there's a secret to the success of high-performing virtual teams, it's that their team members and leaders realize that managing the relationships in virtual teams is as important as managing the technology. Bernie DeKoven, director of the Institute for Better Meetings in California, describes effective virtual teams this way:

> When I think of virtual teams in the best light, I think of teams of people who are as comfortable with each other as they are with a wide variety of communication and computing technologies. When they meet "virtually," they take advantage of all their technical know-how to continue their work; and, when they meet face-to-face, they use the same technology to develop, organize, and refine their understanding. They have an emotional bandwidth that is as broad as their communication bandwidth, so that no matter how or where they meet they relate to each other with humor, understanding, and respect.[60]

DIFFERENCES BETWEEN CO-LOCATED AND DISTRIBUTED TEAMS

If I could live anywhere, it would be in cyberia. Gabe Doppelt, Editor of Mademoiselle

Research on distributed teams suggests that they differ in many ways from their face-to-face counterparts.[61] Teams as large as 300 members scattered around the world can collaborate effectively and efficiently using various information and communication technologies.[62] Distributed teams are more likely to bridge traditional organizational boundaries such as functions, departments, and organizations. Furthermore, members of distributed teams are more likely to be more diverse than are those in co-located teams because virtual teams are more likely to include people from different regions, nations, and organizations, as well as customers, temporary workers, consultants, and other constituents.[63] Distributed teams may be more flexible because schedules can be set "by due dates and milestones, not by the availability of team members."[64]

Furthermore, many researchers argue that electronic and computer-mediated meetings differ in significant ways from face-to-face meetings. For example, Lee Sproull and Sara Kiesler describe face-to-face meetings this way:

> Most meetings follow a predictable course. Participation is unequal; one person or a minority clique dominates the floor. Member status predicts who will dominate. Managers speak more than subordinates; men speak more than women; the person at the front of the room speaks more than those at the back. People are polite and considerate, and they avoid controversy. If a decision is necessary, the group converges on a decision over time by narrowing and discarding options through discussion. People prefer options that have obvious popularity. Often we can predict the decision by knowing who dominates the discussion.[65]

Research suggests that when compared with their face-to-face counterparts, teams that meet through electronic and computer-mediated technologies tend to:

- Be somewhat less influenced by the comments of people who have higher status or better social and communication skills
- Consult more people, which can increase the number of alternatives considered
- Have more task-related conflict, perhaps because status effects and politeness norms (e.g., taking turns or appearing to listen attentively) are more relaxed than in face-to-face meetings[66]
- Take longer to make complex decisions,[67] perhaps because members of distributed teams tend to consult more people, feel less pressure to defer to the opinions of high-status members, have more task-related conflict, and experience more delays in communication, particularly when team members communicate asynchronously (i.e., when there is a delay between the time that the sender sends the message and when the receiver receives it)
- Make "more extreme, unconventional, or risky decisions"[68]

Furthermore, members of teams that use electronic and computer-based information and communication technologies can have immediate access to more information and can communicate with more people more quickly than can members of co-located teams.[69] However, coordination can be more complex. Consider the following description of the problems one virtual team experienced:

> Communications were often fragmented, with gaps and misunderstanding among distant group members. There was confusion in telephone conferences, with people on different pages of documents. Group members failed to return telephone calls or respond to inquiries from distant members. Key group members at remote sites were left off e-mail distribution lists. Distant members were not informed of key decisions or information. Misunderstandings developed on the basis of different assumptions about the tasks and assignments. Messages were interpreted differently in different places, sometimes fueling ongoing conflicts among office sites.[70]

The preceding scenario illustrates how members of distributed teams, like their face-to-face counterparts, must develop work processes that promote a shared understanding of the task, create trust and respect among team members, and develop work processes that enable team members to coordinate their efforts. When virtual teams lack these processes, "confusion, insecurities, and resentment" can result.[71] The preceding scenario also illustrates how many of the problems in virtual teams result from the mismanagement of social dynamics, which is the topic of the next section.

SOCIAL DYNAMICS IN DISTRIBUTED TEAMS

Researchers have focused on four social processes that influence the effectiveness of virtual teams. These include team members' ability to:

- Communicate effectively with each other
- Develop feelings of belonging and cohesion

- Encourage team members to express minority opinions (that is, opinions that conflict with the dominant thinking in the team)
- Manage status effects

Science and technology multiply around us. To an increasing extent they dictate the languages in which we speak and think. Either we use those languages, or we remain mute.
J. G. Ballard, English novelist

Communication

Effective communication is central to team productivity. It is the means by which "all speakers and hearers attempt to construct a shared communication context in which their messages can be produced and understood. . . . [P]articipants in a conversation strive for a shared understanding of the situation, of the task, and of one another's background knowledge, expectations, beliefs, and attitudes."[72] However, constructing a shared reality through electronic and computer-mediated technologies can be challenging.

Researchers agree that one of the most important differences between face-to-face and electronic and computer-mediated communication is that the latter removes or minimizes many (though not all) of the taken-for-granted social cues that we use to interpret the spoken word.[73] There are three types of social cues:

Static cues refer to fixed markers such as titles (doctor or nurse, manager or secretary), appearance (style of dress or demographic group membership such as race, ethnicity, and gender), and seating arrangements (who is sitting at the head of the table). Based on these cues, we make assumptions about the status, expertise, and trustworthiness of the persons with whom we interact, which in turn influence how we interpret the content and value of their comments. Static cues also refer to visual aids such as reports, diagrams, and charts that help us to "get on the same page" during a conversation.

Dynamic cues refer to changing physical signals such as facial expressions (smiling or frowning), body language (nodding or hand gestures such as "thumbs up" and "thumbs down"), pace (interrupting or hesitating before replying), and tone of voice (soft-spoken or loud). Based on these cues, we make assumptions about people's self-confidence, interest, enthusiasm, understanding, and support of our comments.[74]

Situational cues refer to our understanding of the social context in which communication occurs.[75] This social context includes knowledge of people, relationships, issues, and events in the organization (e.g., political agendas and alliances, pending layoffs, and recent or potential lawsuits). Based on this understanding of the broader—often unspoken—organizational context, we often "read between the lines" of comments that are made. When making decisions, this reading of the situation helps us understand what alternatives can be realistically considered, as well as the potential intended and unintended consequences that might arise from any decision.

In short, social cues help us make assumptions about the person who is speaking—their status, credibility, and trustworthiness; how others react to us and our ideas; and the larger context in which our communication takes place. Although social cues often help us better understand the spoken word, they also can distort rather than enhance understanding. For example, we may perceive someone who avoids eye contact as lacking in confidence when, in fact, it is a way of showing respect in that person's culture. We may perceive a person who speaks loudly as rude rather than enthusiastic. We may perceive a high-status person to be more knowledgeable than a low-status person even when that is not the case, and our taken-for-granted assumptions about "the way things are around here" may restrict our ability to consider ideas that challenge the prevailing social wisdom.

Sending e-mail to co-workers instead of walking to deliver messages can contribute to a weight gain over time … Over 10 years, that could increase a person's weight by 11 pounds. **Haidee Allerton, citing a study in Training and Development**

A study by researchers Ray Friedman and Steven Currall illustrates the potential problems with distance communication. They found that conflict is more likely to occur when using e-mail than when using face-to-face communication. They also found that using e-mail to resolve existing conflicts can actually escalate the conflicts. They argue that in face-to-face situations, including conflicts, people are better able to develop a shared understanding of the situation—what is often called "common ground"; can read body language and hear vocal tones to make assumptions about how the other person is responding to one's message; and are more likely to engage in shorter and more frequent communication, including turn-taking, which leaves less time for misunderstandings to occur and escalate.

In contrast, when communicating through e-mail, people can't read body language or hear vocal tones to help them interpret comments—even well-intended comments can be easily misinterpreted; have more time between responses, which leaves time for misunderstandings and resentment to escalate; tend to write longer responses and bundle ideas together, so they may not get responses to all of their concerns and thus feel resentful; and may spend more time crafting the written response, which may lead the writer to become more committed to his or her position.[76]

The lesson for team members and leaders, whether they meet virtually or face-to-face, is not that social cues enhance or inhibit understanding (they do both). Rather, the lessons are:

- Clear communication is central to team effectiveness because it helps team members clarify expectations about the task and each other, avoid misunderstandings, make effective decisions, and coordinate their efforts.
- All teams—whether they meet virtually or face-to-face—must create norms for communication that enhance understanding.

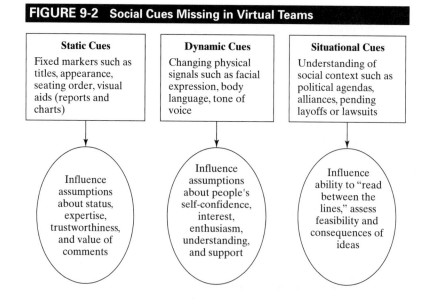

FIGURE 9-2 Social Cues Missing in Virtual Teams

Static Cues	**Dynamic Cues**	**Situational Cues**
Fixed markers such as titles, appearance, seating order, visual aids (reports and charts)	Changing physical signals such as facial expression, body language, tone of voice	Understanding of social context such as political agendas, alliances, pending layoffs or lawsuits
Influence assumptions about status, expertise, trustworthiness, and value of comments	Influence assumptions about people's self-confidence, interest, enthusiasm, understanding, and support	Influence ability to "read between the lines," assess feasibility and consequences of ideas

Belonging and Cohesion

Human beings are social animals. We have a basic need to belong to a community and interact with others. Our relationships give us a sense of identity, provide us with predictable rules for behaving, and enhance our psychological and physical health.[77] When we are at work, the quality of our relationships influence individual, team, and organizational effectiveness. Consider the following:

- We treat people with whom we have relationships differently than we treat people we don't know very well. Says Martha Haywood, author of the practical book *Managing Virtual Teams*: "It's a lot harder to ignore someone who has personified themselves to us, somebody who has thoughts, needs, feelings and a boss that might get mad at them if they don't get their work done. I know I'm more likely to respond to an e-mail I receive from my friend John than I am to respond to an e-mail from stranger@obscure.com."[78]
- Team members who feel more attached to their team are more likely to be committed to each other, team goals, and collective tasks.
- Organizations that develop their social capital, that is, the organization's internal and external networks of relationships, have a competitive advantage over those that don't develop these networks.[79]

However, many researchers and practitioners are concerned that high-quality relationships may be particularly difficult to achieve in teams in which team members are geographically dispersed. Co-located employees are more likely to participate in impromptu conversations in the hallway, take breaks together, share meals, see photos of colleagues' families on their desks, and participate in company-sponsored social events. Such face-to-face interactions "contribute to organizational socialization and commitment even though they perform no overt organizational task."[80] They humanize us to each other, help us develop a shared understanding of the organization and its goals and values, and increase our mutual trust, respect, commitment, and goodwill.[81] Some of our best ideas and opportunities are the result of chance face-to-face encounters and informal discussions.

Psychoanalyst Edward Hallowell refers to these face-to-face encounters as "the human moment." He describes the human moment as "an authentic psychological encounter that can happen only when two people share the same physical space." He explains:

> I have given the human moment a name because I believe that it has started to disappear from modern life. . . . The human moment has two prerequisites: people's physical presence and their emotional and intellectual attention.[82]

Technology . . . the knack of so arranging the world that we don't have to deal with it.
Max Frisch, Swiss author 1957

John Lock, author of *The De-Voicing of Society: Why We Don't Talk to Each Other Anymore*, poignantly echoes Hallowell's concerns about the impact of technology on human relationships: "Now when the [answering] machine kicks in, we can do something that previously would have been unthinkable as well as socially suicidal: decide whether to respond to the voice of our closest friends."[83]

Some researchers are more optimistic about technology's impact on human relationships and argue that psychological closeness is as important as physical closeness.

Researchers David Armstrong and Paul Cole conclude that psychological closeness is the result of several conditions, including "the degree of identification with group membership; the similarity of work goals, norms, role and procedure expectations (task cohesion); the accuracy of mutual comprehension; the degree of motivation toward shared goals; the amount of interdependency and mutual trust; and the frequency of communication among members."[84] All of these characteristics can be achieved virtually as well as face-to-face.

Indeed, electronic and computer-mediated technologies can help us overcome hurdles to psychological closeness. For example, we may find it easier to see ourselves as similar to each other when we don't have visual cues that highlight our differences. We may find it easier to cross traditional professional, functional, and hierarchical barriers in a virtual environment because we remove some of the visual physical reminders of these barriers. Many of us find electronic communication to be easier, more enjoyable, and more effective than face-to-face communication because we can take time to carefully organize and articulate our thoughts, avoid stage fright associated with speaking publicly, and possibly minimize some of the status effects in groups that affect our ability to speak candidly or be taken seriously.

Remember that not everyone wants intimacy at work. Martha Haywood quotes one manager as saying, "I don't care about this guy's inner feelings. I want to know when he's going to call me back."[85] Researcher Lee Sproull, who has been studying trust and relationships in on-line environments for many years, explains, "If I see this person is going to do a first-rate job with the information I provide, that he [sic] won't undercut it, won't embarrass me, then I'm more likely to trust [that person]."[86]

The U.S. Bill of Rights is just a local ordinance in cyberspace. *Mary O'Hara-Devereaux and Robert Johansen citing John Perry Barlow*

Indeed, trust is more important than intimacy in virtual work relationships. What creates trust? Researchers Sirkka Jarvenpaa and Dorothy Leidner explain that trust in global virtual teams is most likely to be created or lost during initial team interactions. Therefore, the time and planning that virtual team leaders invest up front is likely to pay off in the long run. Early behaviors that are most likely to create trust include articulating a clear task, showing optimism and enthusiasm about the task, creating shared experiences, encouraging repeated social and task-focused interactions, ensuring prompt and predictable communication to all team members (in other words, not excluding people), developing norms for interaction, and developing a well-managed technical environment (in other words, everyone has the right technology, the technology works, and everyone knows how to use it).[87]

The lessons for team members and team leaders, whether they meet virtually or face-to-face, are these:

- The quality of the relationships among team members significantly influences team effectiveness.
- Psychological closeness may be as important as physical closeness.
- Trust, the foundation of psychological closeness, is based on goodwill, competence, responsiveness, and predictability—all of which can be developed through electronic and computer-mediated communication technologies.

Social Influence

Regardless of whether we meet face-to-face or communicate through electronic and computer-based media, we must be able to influence others to get people to pay attention to us, take our comments seriously, and give us the time, information, and support that we need to get our work done. Case Western researcher Poppy McLeod and her colleagues provide some insights into how computer-mediated group decision-support technologies (e.g., groupware) may affect social influence, particularly in the area of expression of minority opinion in teams that use these technologies.[88]

Minority opinions are those that conflict with the opinions expressed by most team members. It is not surprising that research suggests that teams that encourage members to express minority opinions and take such opinions seriously tend to make better quality decisions than teams that suppress or ignore minority opinions. The expression of minority opinions in teams can enhance creativity and critical thinking, prevent dysfunctional dynamics such as groupthink, increase team member commitment to implementation, improve individual and team learning, and promote team cohesion.

However, team members are often reluctant to express minority opinions because doing so is often perceived as "socially risky" and may result in "social disapproval."[89] Specifically, team members often fear that expressing a minority opinion may hurt their credibility, result in psychological or physical exclusion from the team, increase team conflict, or slow the team down.

McLeod and her colleagues conducted a study designed to explore how computer-mediated group decision-making technologies affected team members' willingness to express minority opinions and the team's acceptance of the minority opinion once expressed.[90] They found that "group decision-support systems may increase the quantity of minority opinions but reduce the influence of those opinions," particularly when team members' identities remain anonymous during the decision-making session.

Why would team members be more willing to express minority opinions but be less willing to take such opinions seriously? McLeod and her colleagues suggest that anonymity tends to increase team members' willingness to express their opinions, perhaps because it removes some of the evaluation anxiety, social stigma, and other risks associated with stating opinions that counter those of the group. Anonymity may also

---

BOX 9-2

Managing Global Distributed Teams

To promote strong group cohesion among site managers around the globe, the leader of a newly designated organization committed his management staff to meeting face-to-face every 6 to 8 weeks. They rotated the location of each meeting around the globe so that they visited each other's country several times. Telephone conferences were held every 3 weeks between face-to-face meetings. During their first round of visits to each other's sites, the assembled management team also met face-to-face with each site's staff in discussions facilitated by a consultant. The group even developed shared humor and jokes, such as requiring each site manager to sing a song in his or her native tongue to the assembled management team at his or her first meeting. This became an entry ritual for new managers as membership turned over.

SOURCE: From Armstrong, David, and Paul Cole. 1994. *Culture and Social Behavior*. New York: McGraw-Hill.

reduce the impact of the minority opinions that are expressed, perhaps because team members who express minority opinions anonymously may not appear to be as committed to their ideas as do team members who are willing to take public social risks by identifying themselves with their ideas. Furthermore, politeness norms that exist in face-to-face meetings—such as taking turns and appearing to listen to each other—may increase the probability that team members actually will take the time to hear minority opinions rather than ignore them.

The lessons for team members and leaders, whether they meet virtually or face-to-face, are these:

- Effective team decision making depends on team members' willingness to express minority opinions and take them seriously.
- Effective teams must create norms that increase the probability that minority opinions will be expressed, heard, and integrated into the decision-making process.

Status and Power

Status and power dynamics are a taken-for-granted part of everyday life in organizations. A consistent finding in group research is that "in mixed-status groups, high-status people talk more, speak more frankly, have more control over the agenda, and through their dominance have more influence."[91] One of the most interesting debates among researchers of distributed teams is whether electronic and computer-mediated communication reduces status effects. Many researchers argue that the use of electronic and computer-mediated communication technologies can reduce some status effects that are common in face-to-face groups. Researchers Lee Sproull and Sarah Kiesler explain:

> Because it is harder to read status cues in electronic messages than it is in other forms of communication, high-status people do not dominate the discussion in electronic groups as much as they do in face-to-face groups. For instance, when groups of executives met face-to-face, the men in the groups were five times as likely as the women to make the first decision proposal. When those same groups met via computer, the women made the first proposal as often as the men did (McGuire, Kiesler, and Siegel 1987). When pairs of graduate students and undergraduates met face-to-face to decide their joint project, the pairs were likely to choose the topic preferred by the graduate student. When equivalent pairs of students discussed and decided electronically, they were equally likely to choose the topic initially preferred by the undergraduate (Huff and King 1988).[92]

In addition, there is some evidence that e-mail may increase communication across hierarchical boundaries, and employees may be more likely to send bad news to their bosses through e-mail.[93]

However, some researchers argue, quite convincingly, that the "equalization phenomenon" (the reduction of status effects) associated with computer-mediated communication (CMC) is overstated.[94] Researcher Guiseppe Montovani, for example, argues that "CMC is effective in overcoming physical barriers, but not, or at least not necessarily, social barriers."[95] He argues further: "Electronic links primarily enhance existing interaction patterns rather than creating new ones. . . . CMC usually operates by supplementing established preferences, respecting status barriers and already-developed communication clusters."[96] In other words, if a person is not taken seriously at face-to-face meetings, there is no reason that his or her e-mail will be taken seriously either.

If there is technological advance without social advance, there is, almost automatically, an increase in human misery, in impoverishment.
Michael Harrington, U.S. social scientist

Furthermore, electronic and computer-mediated communication technologies increase the ways that employers can monitor and control employee behavior. Using these technologies, employers can monitor employees' telephone calls, e-mail messages, and Internet use; count keystrokes that record the speed at which employees work; exclude people from information and on-line discussions; and increase the expectation that people will check their electronic and voice mail regularly, even on evenings, weekends, and vacations. Notably, an American Management Association's study concluded that "twenty-seven percent of major U.S. firms now store or review employee e-mail messages. That's up from 15 percent in 1997."[97]

Harvard researcher Jane Fountain argues that "women are the predominant users of information technology in the workplace." However, she argues that "women are poorly represented in the sector that constitutes the growth engine of the U.S. economy and that bears primary responsibility for the scientific and technological development of an Information society." Indeed, women represent "less than 30 percent of computer professionals."[98]

Says Montovani:

> [Technological] tools per se are unable to soothe or solve basic social problems like that of inequality. . . . Barriers in communication and status differences in organizations are clearly more a social than a technological issue, and the search for a technological remedy to social inequality seems somehow naive . . . and may result in misconceptions and disappointment.[99]

The lessons for team members and leaders, whether they meet virtually or face-to-face, are these:

- As long as there are social and organizational hierarchies, status and power dynamics will be a fact of everyday work life.
- Explicitly attending to status and power dynamics is important because they influence employees' feelings of inclusion and exclusion, willingness to express themselves honestly, sense of personal security and control, and feelings of commitment to their team and organization—all of which can enhance or inhibit team performance.
- These dynamics can be enhanced or minimized through the use of electronic and computer-mediated technologies, depending on how the technologies are used.

MANAGING DISTRIBUTED TEAMS

Information Technology is no longer a business resource. It is the business environment.
John Browning, The Economist

Undoubtedly, distributed teams that effectively use electronic and computer-based information and communication technologies are often able to work faster and more flexibly than their face-to-face counterparts, create productive relationships that span organizational and geographic boundaries, and develop new and improved ways of working together and serving their customers. But, as Dartmouth researcher Mary Munter puts it, "the latest technological changes are only as effective as the people using them."[100]

This section provides general guidelines for using electronic and computer-based information and communication technologies in teams. These guidelines are based on three broad recommendations:

- Determine the appropriate level of technology for the team task.
- Manage the technological environment.
- Develop work processes that enhance team performance.

Determine the Appropriate Level of Technology for the Team Task

Technology is not a "means-unto-itself but must remain a means-to-an-end with a critical appraisal of costs and benefits," say Graham Mercer and Matthew Barritt of the Global Learning Center at the University of Michigan.[101] When misused, electronic and computer-based information and communication technologies can lead to misunderstandings, slow a team down, result in lower-quality decisions, waste opportunities to build high-quality relationships, and squander organizational resources. When used appropriately, these technologies can help team members make and implement decisions faster, overcome the hurdles of time and distance, and use their resources more effectively. Therefore, effective team members and leaders know when it is best to meet face-to-face and when it is best to meet virtually.

Face-to-Face Meetings

Everybody gets so much information all day long that they lose their common sense. *Gertrude Stein*

When possible, face-to-face meetings are preferable in situations in which human contact is particularly important,[102] when visual cues enhance communication, or when the purpose of the meeting is highly symbolic. These situations include:

- First meetings when team members must create a common identity, define problems, develop shared work processes, and gain commitment to the goals, tasks, and each other
- When the team has significant turnover and must re-create a common identity
- When there are "higher levels of complexity and ambiguity in the messages"[103]
- When the goal of the meeting is to persuade team members to commit to a particular belief or course of action[104]
- When the team must deal with sensitive issues (e.g., hiring, promotion, discipline, and termination decisions)[105]
- During complex and delicate negotiations[106]
- When conflicts must be resolved[107]
- When acknowledging important milestones and celebrating successes
- When privacy and confidentiality must be maintained—electronic communications are more accessible and less private than face-to-face conversations or hard copy[108]

Electronic and Computer-Mediated Meetings

Electronic and computer-mediated communication technologies are most useful for "routine tasks done by a defined group with established roles and motives"[109] and situations in which human contact isn't critical. These situations include:

- "Fact-finding problems" or "problems that have one right answer"[110]
- Gathering preliminary information and opinions prior to a face-to-face meeting
- Keeping team members informed between meetings
- Working together on tasks that were assigned during face-to-face meetings
- Reducing some dysfunctional dynamics such as status effects or one person dominating conversations. (Remember, however, that "technology use will not resolve basic problems in group process.")[111]
- Experimenting with new technologies or new ways of working together that may increase productivity, learning, flexibility, or speed
- When team members cannot meet face-to-face
- When saving money in travel expenses outweighs the benefits of a face-to-face meeting
- When productivity can be increased by managing communication and workflow across time zones, particularly when teams direct their workflow from east to west. Martha Haywood explains: "Consider a hypothetical team where the software-engineering department is in Boston and the testing engineer department is in San Jose. If the software-engineering department arrives in the morning and creates a release for testing, they will be ready to transfer it to the test department in San Jose at about noon, Boston time. For the engineers in California, it's only 9:00 A.M. The team has gained 3 working hours."

I'm skeptical of these devices that find each other and then start doing things among themselves.
Handspring cofounder Jeff Hawkins, eweek

In addition to considering the task requirements, teams should consider the organizational culture when determining the degree of technology to use in their interactions with each other. Some organizational cultures are more likely than others to promote and support the use of electronic and computer-based technologies. For example, some organizations might view using new technology as too flashy or impersonal. Other organizations might view not using these technologies as old-fashioned.[112]

Manage the Technological Environment

Members of effective virtual teams are flexible enough to adapt to changing technologies, savvy enough to avoid computer viruses that can wreak havoc on a team's information and communication base, and resilient enough to handle hardware or software crashes that can bring a less savvy team's work to a standstill. Team members are likely to resist using electronic and computer-based information and communication technologies when they don't trust them; (i.e., when they don't believe that these technologies will make a difference, don't understand how to use them, or are suspicious of them. They wonder, often with good reason: Will the technology break down in the middle of an important discussion or presentation? Will data be safe? Will the technology be used to monitor, control, or evaluate my work behavior? Will the availability of communication technologies mean that I must always be available to the team—anywhere and any time of the day?

There are several things that team leaders can do to manage the technological environment.

- Make sure all team members have compatible information and communication technologies.
- Model and support the use of technology in words and deeds.
- Give team members a realistic picture of what technology can and cannot do for the team. Give specific examples of how it can improve team performance, such as ways that it can help the team manage information better, communicate more quickly, increase flexibility, complete projects faster, and save money.
- Train team members in how to use the various technologies.
- Provide ongoing organizational support for troubleshooting.
- Provide trained facilitators for meetings that use sophisticated technologies such as videoconferencing and groupware.
- Set up early small wins. Team members who experience early successes with technology will be motivated to continue using the technology.
- Develop and adhere to clear policies regarding privacy, access to information, monitoring of electronic communications, and expectations regarding availability both on and off work time.[113]
- Have contingency plans in place to deal with hardware and software crashes so that the team isn't completely dependent on the technologies and can rebound quickly from technical failures.
- Make sure all team members have the training and software that helps them avoid computer viruses.

Develop Work Processes That Enhance Team Performance

All teams, regardless of whether they meet virtually or face-to-face, must develop work processes that help team members form relationships built on trust and respect, create a shared reality about the team goals and tasks, and coordinate their efforts. When team members don't attend to these processes, discontent, confusion, and poor-quality decisions can result. Therefore, members and leaders of effective virtual teams must pay particular attention to processes that enhance team cohesion, communication, and coordination.

Cohesion

One of the challenges of distributed teams is developing a cohesive group with team members who rarely, if ever, meet each other face-to-face. Jessica Lipnack and Jeffrey Stamps explain, "To work with people you rarely or never meet, you need some basis to believe in their expertise and trustworthiness."[114] As mentioned earlier in this chapter, cohesiveness is built on trust. Trust is built on goodwill, competence, responsiveness, and predictability—all of which can be developed and reinforced by using electronic and computer-mediated communication technologies. To build team cohesiveness:

- Give the team a name to help create a common identity.
- Have team members create personal Web pages about themselves. One team leader created a Web site that encouraged team members to take time to get

to learn about each other. Each time a member of the team "logged onto the department Web page, the image of a different remote team member appears behind the picture of a reception desk." When team members clicked on the person's image, they could read information about that team member.[115]

- Remind team members that every interaction—whether virtual or face-to-face—is an opportunity to enhance a relationship.
- Encourage teams to develop shared language, stories, symbols (e.g., logos or coffee cups), and rituals. One team had a surprise pizza dinner delivered to their distant colleagues during a videoconference so that they could share a meal together.[116]
- Encourage team members to acknowledge and respect cultural traditions and business practices. Distributed teams are more likely to have team members from different cultures.
- Develop norms for integrating new members into the team.
- Create work policies and norms that enhance predictability because trust is based, in part, on having predictable routines and being able to anticipate another's behavior. Price Waterhouse, for example, has 45,000 employees in 120 countries. Sheldon Laube, formerly the national director of information and technology for Price Waterhouse, says "it would be unrealistic to put everyone on a plane for a get-together when all the necessary information can be coalesced quickly on networked computers." The company rarely gets people together in person before they begin working together as a team. Instead, the "company's set methodology and common language for conducting audits eases collaboration."[117]

Communication

Psychiatrist Edward Hallowell argues that today's communication problems derive "not from lack of communication but from a surplus of the wrong kind."[118] Although one of the key benefits of electronic and computer-based information and communication technologies is the ability to retrieve, store, and analyze large amounts of information quickly, more information is not necessarily better. A survey of more than 1,000 British e-mail users found that "over 90 percent wasted up to an hour per day reading, responding to, and deleting irrelevant messages."[119] Says Martha Haywood, "poorly trained distributed teams live in a state of unprioritized broadcast information overload."[120]

It's been said that "you can lead a group to information, but you can't make it think."[121] Effective communication and information management occurs when information is well managed (the right information gets to the right people in the right format); the receiver of the message understands what the sender means; and relationships are enhanced, rather than harmed, by the communication. To achieve these ends, effective team members and leaders:

- Plan knowledge repositories—content, organization, and access—carefully.[122]
- Create norms regarding which communication methods should be used for what purposes (face-to-face, telephone, e-mail, electronic bulletin boards, Web pages).
- Create norms for signaling priority messages and information.

- Create norms regarding which messages should be sent to all members and which can be sent to individuals or subgroups.
- Create common formats for organizing messages.
- Take care to speak and write clearly and concisely.
- Confirm that messages are understood as intended.
- Take time to discuss and learn cultural and location differences such as availability and quality of technology and key issues currently facing the organization or society.[123]
- Refer to page numbers, paragraph numbers, and designators for diagrams when referring to documents (e.g., "Turn to Figure 1 on page 10 of the document titled 'New Products.'"). One study found that teams with poorly annotated documents take up to three times longer to complete a given exercise.[124]
- Pay attention to the angle of cameras when using video so that facial expressions and bodily mannerisms can be easily seen and interpreted.

Coordination

Members of effective distributed teams develop norms for coordinating their efforts through electronic and computer-mediated information technologies. These norms include:

- ***Team member availability.*** How often should team members check their telephone messages, e-mail, and interoffice mail; whether they should acknowledge receiving messages; how quickly they should return messages and respond to requests; and whether team members should let each other know when they will be out of the office and, if so, how they should do so[125]
- ***Storing and using information.*** What information should be stored where and for what purposes, as well as how information should be maintained (updated and purged)
- ***Organizing and prioritizing work demands.*** Who should do what tasks by when, and how they should keep team members informed of their progress
- ***Meeting through these technologies.*** Who should attend and facilitate meetings, how group dynamics—including issues of belonging, trust, status, and influence—will be managed, what kinds of supporting documents should be given to the team before, during, and after meetings, and how quickly they should be made available[126]

Box 9-3 provides tips for creating successful teleconference and videoconference meetings.

Virtual Teams: The Bottom Line

Effective members and leaders of distributed teams know that electronic and computer-based information and communication technologies can improve a team's productivity and increase the team's problems if not carefully managed. They have a realistic view of what technology can and can't do for the team; have a systematic plan for managing the technology, decision-making process, and social relations in the team; and recognize that "cybermania is as dangerous as cyberphobia."[127] They know that more sophisticated technologies require more sophisticated understandings of human relationships as well.

Electronic and computer-mediated technologies will continue to challenge our assumptions about how, when, and where we work. But some things will never change. Although technology increases the ways in which people work together, intelligence and creativity will always be "between the ears of the people,"[128] and team performance will depend, in large part, on the quality of team members' relationships.

BOX 9-3

Tips for Successful Teleconference and Videoconference Meetings

PLAN IN ADVANCE

✓ Determine the date, starting and ending times, and number of participants. Be aware of time differences.

✓ Determine equipment needs and familiarize yourself with the equipment before the meeting.

✓ Prepare the participants:

- Notify them of the meeting date, how to access the conference, the moderator's name, and start and end times.

- If the participants have not met, send out an attendance list, as well as a short background of each attendee. Don't just list the names and titles. Where are they from? What do they do? Why are they invited to the meeting? Remember that you're trying to build relationships.

- Provide an agenda, limited to three to five topics, and let participants know how much time you intend to spend on each topic.

- Send out supporting documents. Remember to number pages (and paragraphs, if possible) and label diagrams. Let participants know whether they need to have the documents with them at the meeting.

- Let participants know if they must prepare anything in advance.

- Let participants know how absences will be handled (how they should

notify the appropriate parties, whether someone will take their place, how they should follow up).

✓ Develop an outline or script that includes opening comments, important announcements, agenda items (including the order and amount of time for each item), questions to stimulate discussion, and closing remarks.

✓ Be sure you can pronounce all participants' names prior to the meeting so that you can call them by name. Write the phonetic pronunciation of their names and plan to keep this list in front of you during the meeting.

✓ Have a fax machine at each site in case documents need to be sent to participants during the meeting.

✓ Particularly for videoconferences, consider scheduling a trained facilitator who can manage the technological environment and facilitate the meeting.

✓ Plan to have technical support available in case there are problems with the technology.

✓ If you are leasing equipment, room, and time, make sure that you lease for more time than you need so that you don't get cut off in the middle of a meeting.

✓ Have a contingency plan in place, as well as a way of notifying participants of changes, in case there are problems with technology. Notify participants in advance of this contingency plan.

(continued)

Box 9-3 (*cont.*)

MANAGE THE MEETING

✓ Make sure the area is quiet and free of distractions. Ask not to be disturbed during the conference.

✓ Start on time and stick to the schedule.

✓ Project your enthusiasm and interest from the moment you begin the teleconference.

✓ Welcome participants to the conference by:

- Summarizing key events that led up to the meeting.

- Taking a roll call. If people have not met, ask them to say something as a warm-up to get to know each other better.

- Reviewing the agenda and asking whether anyone needs clarification or wants to add or change anything.

- Identifying the objectives you'd like to achieve by the end of the meeting.

✓ Remind participants of the ground rules for the meeting:

- State name before speaking.

- Speak clearly and concisely and keep comments focused on the topic.

- Be specific when referring to documents (e.g., "Please turn to Figure 4 on page 3 of the document titled 'New Products' that was sent to you prior to the meeting.").

- Use the mute button when not speaking.

- Keep background noise to a minimum. For videoconferences, discourage the use of cordless or cellular phones because they may cause static or other interference. Also minimize fidgeting and hand gestures because they may cause enough static to disrupt the transmission.

✓ Restate participants' comments to confirm understanding.

✓ Call on people by name and location (e.g., "Let's hear from Maria at Fidelity in Boston.").

✓ Make sure that you have a process for managing turn-taking. To manage turn-taking, Martha Haywood recommends that participants use the "direct and self-identify" technique. Whenever someone makes a comment to a specific individual rather than the group, they should say, "Chris, this is Lee." Don't assume that people can recognize voices in teleconferences.

✓ Rotate the order in which you call on participants.

✓ Keep track of the people and sites that participate, as well as those you haven't heard from. Check in on those who haven't participated to get their input and maintain a balanced discussion.

✓ Ask questions to encourage participation and pause long enough for answers.

✓ Record key comments and decisions for each agenda item. Share your written summary with participants to check for agreement before moving to the next item.

✓ Be aware of cultural differences. These will influence participants' language, turn-taking, and responses to other participants and authority figures.

✓ For videoconferences:

- Be aware that there is often a slight delay in the transfer of images. Even the laughter that follows a joke may be delayed (which can be discomforting if you are not prepared for the delay).

- Be aware of the location of the camera(s). If you want to have eye contact, look into the camera rather than the screen when you are speaking.

- Be yourself; speak naturally (yet slowly) as if you were all in a room together.

- Tell people when you will be using a graphic and use simple, large-print graphics.

- Wear appropriate clothing. Solid colors (particularly blue and warm gray) are best. White, red, plaids, and prints (particularly bold patterns) may distort the picture. These rules also apply to the backgrounds at each site.

✓ Pay attention to the visual field and camera angle. The optimal visual field is from the top of the head to the bottom of the elbow to capture expressions, hand signals, and so forth. It's best to maintain a horizontal and vertical angle of less than 8 degrees. Otherwise, it will be difficult to "read" people's expressions. For example, if the camera angle isn't right, people may look disinterested or resistant when, in fact, they are not.

CLOSE THE MEETING

✓ Ask participants for summary statements.

✓ Summarize decisions and action items, as well as who is responsible for each action and how completion will be communicated to the group.

✓ Thank everyone for participating.

✓ Set a time for the next conference.

✓ End with a process check of meeting effectiveness and determine whether anything should be done to make the next meeting more effective.

✓ Send communication such as written minutes as soon after a meeting as possible, preferably within 1 day. Use all team members' names and locations in the communication.

✓ When there have been technical problems at the meeting, send a follow-up message to explain the technical details.

Note: Many of these tips came from

- Haywood, Martha. 1998. *Managing Virtual Teams: Practical Techniques for High-Technology Managers*. Boston, MA: Artech House.

- Henry, Jane E., and Meg Hartzler. 1998. *Tools for Virtual Teams: A Team Fitness Companion*. Milwaukee, WI: ASQ Press.

CHAPTER SUMMARY

Shifts in demographics, social norms, work expectations, and new technologies are dramatically transforming the nature of teamwork. Team members are becoming more culturally diverse and geographically dispersed. Work tasks are becoming more complex. The processes by which team members work are being significantly altered by technological advancements. Many of the skills we learned for managing relatively homogeneous, co-located teams are insufficient for effectively managing diverse and distributed teams.

Diverse Teams

Team diversity refers to differences among team members in their "observable" groups (race, gender, ethnicity, and so forth), organizational groups (function and level in hierarchy), and less visible categories such as religion and sexual orientation.

These differences among team members influence:

- The variety of cognitive resources and behavioral styles team members bring to the team
- The interaction processes by which team members work together, including both task and relationship processes
- The team's ability to become a high-performing team; in particular, the team's ability to make effective decisions, promote the well-being of team members, and enhance the team's ability to perform as an effective unit over time

Teams can benefit significantly from diversity, particularly under certain conditions. Diverse teams may have an advantage over relatively homogeneous teams when:

- The diversity among team members is relevant to the team's task (e.g., when tasks require creativity and judgment, when breadth of ideas is important, or when information about particular markets is important)
- When team members have time to learn how to work together productively
- When diversity among team members is well managed

Diverse team members are more likely to have a greater variety of resources to bring to the team's task that can enhance team performance, but they also are more likely to engage particular dysfunctional dynamics that can undermine the team's ability to use these resources wisely.

Two theories are used to explain dysfunctional dynamics in teams:

- The similarity-attraction theory assumes that people tend to prefer to be with and understand people they perceive as like themselves. Therefore, they are more likely to find it easier to interact with and understand team members who they see as like themselves.
- The structural barriers theory assumes that dynamics in diverse teams reflect those in the larger society in which the organization and team is embedded. Therefore, if there is bias, misunderstanding, and lack of cohesion among diverse groups in the society, the team is at risk for having the same problems.

Team leaders can make sure they create a context for high-performing diverse teams by paying extra attention to first meetings; training team members in understanding each other's differences and the impact of these on team process and performance; creating a common identity and collectivist culture; paying extra attention to team norms; providing early opportunities to succeed, clear performance measures, and ongoing positive feedback because diverse teams may underestimate their own performance; and role-modeling the behavior they want in team members.

Virtual Teams

A virtual team, also called a distributed team, is made up of individuals interacting interdependently on collective tasks to achieve shared organizational goals. However, in contrast to co-located teams, virtual teams tend to be geographically dispersed, rarely meet face-to-face, and primarily depend on electronic and computer-based information and communication technologies (e.g., voice mail, conference calls, videoconferences, e-mail, Web pages, and so forth) to work together.

In contrast to co-located teams, distributed teams can be larger and more fluid; are more likely to bridge organizational and geographical boundaries; are likely to have more diverse team members; can be more flexible because team members aren't limited by availability of team members; and may have different social dynamics.

The social dynamics in distributed teams may differ from those in co-located teams. For example, members of distributed teams may be somewhat less influenced by status effects, although some researchers argue that technology can increase status effects by enabling higher status employees to exert even more control over employees; may consult more people before making decisions; may have more task-related conflict; may take longer to make complex decisions; may make more extreme and unconventional decisions; may have more difficulty developing feelings of belonging and cohesion; may be more willing to express minority opinions if the opinions are anonymous, but may be less likely to take such opinions seriously; may have more problems coordinating; and may have problems communicating clearly.

We use social cues to help us interpret the meaning of the spoken word. There are three kinds of social cues: static cues, dynamic cues, and situational cues. These cues enable us to make assumptions about the person who is speaking—their status, credibility, and trustworthiness; how others react to us and our ideas; and the larger context in which the communication takes place.

Leaders can increase the success of virtual teams by:

- ***Determining the appropriate level of technology for the task:*** Face-to-face meetings are preferable in situations in which human contact is particularly important, when visual cues enhance understanding, or when the purpose of the meeting is highly symbolic. Virtual meetings are most useful for routine tasks, when human contact isn't critical, and when meeting face-to-face isn't possible.
- ***Managing the technological environment:*** Team members must have access to compatible technologies, be willing and able to use them, and have ongoing training and technical support.
- ***Managing the task and relationships:*** Develop work processes that enhance cohesion, communication, and coordination.

FOOD FOR THOUGHT

1. What is the most useful thing you learned in this chapter and why?
2. Based on the strategies for managing diverse virtual teams described in this chapter, what can you do to increase your effectiveness as a lead member of diverse and virtual teams? Practice this behavior and note any benefits and progress you make.
3. Think of a time when you felt like a minority in a work group or team. What did it feel like to be a member of that work group or team? How do you feel you were treated? What were the advantages? What were the disadvantages? Were you able to contribute to your fullest potential? Why or why not?
4. Observe a diverse team at a meeting. What are the different kinds of diversity represented on the team? What are some of the advantages this team may have (if managed well)? What are some of the dysfunctional dynamics that may occur (if not managed well)? What dynamics, both positive and negative, do you see? If you were a consultant to this group, what advice would you give team members to enhance team performance?
5. Answer the questions in Box 9-1, "Assess Team Members' Style Preferences." Then, work with at least one other person and compare your answers. In what ways are you similar? In what ways are you different? If you were part of a work team, how might these similarities and differences influence your team process and performance?
6. Attend a meeting or a class and pay attention to the social cues during the meeting. Describe the static, dynamic, and situational cues. How does each of the cues that you describe enhance understanding? How might each of the cues lead to misunderstandings? If these cues were missing in a virtual team, what might the consequences be?
7. Imagine you were the team leader of the following virtual team. What are the key problems? What steps would you take to improve the team's process and performance? What steps could you take with future virtual teams to prevent these dynamics from happening in the first place?

> Communications were often fragmented, with gaps and misunderstanding among distant group members. There was confusion in telephone conferences, with people on different pages of documents. Group members failed to return telephone calls

or respond to inquiries from distant members. Key group members at remote sites were left off e-mail distribution lists. Distant members were not informed of key decisions or information. Misunderstandings developed on the basis of different assumptions about the tasks and assignments. Messages were interpreted differently in different places, sometimes fueling ongoing conflicts among office sites.[129]

8. Imagine you are the team leader of the global, distributed team described at the beginning of this chapter. Describe how you would develop cohesiveness and enable coordination in this team. What problems might you anticipate, and how would you deal with them?

ENDNOTES

1. Griggs, Lewis Brown, and Lente-Louise Louw. 1995. "Diverse Teams: Breakdown or Breakthrough." *Training and Development.* October: 22–29.

2. Clair, Judith, Joy Beatty, and Tammy MacLean. 2003. "Out of Sight but Not Out of Mind, Managing Invisible Social Identities in the Workplace." *Academy of Management Review.* August. 2003.

3. Milliken, Francis, and Luis Martins. 1996 "Searching for Common Threads: Understanding the Multiple Effects of Diversity in Organizational Groups." *Academy of Management Review,* 21: 402–433.

4. Cox, Taylor, Sharon Lobel, and Poppy McLeod. 1991. "Effects of Ethnic Group Cultural Differences on Cooperative and Competitive Behavior on a Group Task." *Academy of Management Journal,* 34: 827–847; Jackson, Susan. 1991. "Team Composition in Organizational Settings: Issues in Managing an Increasingly Diverse Workforce." In S. Worchel, W. Wood, and J. Simpson (eds.). *Group Process and Productivity.* Beverly Hills, CA: Sage; Watson, Warren, Kamalesh Kumar, and Larry Michaelsen. 1993. "Cultural Diversity's Impact on Interaction Process and Performance: Comparing Homogeneous and Diverse Task Groups." *Academy of Management Journal,* 36: 590–602; Williams, Kathleen, and Charles O'Reilly. 1998. "Forty Years of Diversity Research: A Review." In Barry Staw and Larry Cummings (eds.). *Research in Organizational Behavior,* 20: 77–140.

5. Williams, Kathleen, and Charles O'Reilly. 1998. "Forty Years of Diversity Research: A Review." In Barry Staw and Larry Cummings (eds.). *Research in Organizational Behavior,* 20: 77–140.

6. Ibid.

7. Williams, Katherine, and Charles O'Reilly. 1998. "Demography and Diversity in Organizations: A Review of 40 Years of Research." In Barry Staw and Larry Cummings (eds.). *Research in Organizational Behavior,* 20: 77–140; citing Byrne, D. 1971. *The Attraction Paradigm.* New York: Academic Press; Byrne, D., G. Clore, and P. Worchel. 1996. "The Effect of Economic Similarity-Dissimilarity as Determinants of Attraction." *Journal of Personality and Social Psychology,* 4: 220–224.

8. Gutek, Barbara. 1985. *Sex and the Workplace.* San Francisco, CA: Jossey-Bass; Kanter, Rosabeth Moss. 1977b. *Men and Women of the Corporation.* New York: Basic Books; Pettigrew, Thomas, and Joanne Martin. 1987. "Shaping the Organizational Context for Black American Inclusion." *Journal of Social Issues,* 43: 41–78; cited in Elsass, Priscilla, and Laura Graves. 1997. "Demographic Diversity in Decision-Making Groups: The Experiences of Women and People of Color." *Academy of Management Review,* 22(4): 946–973.

9. Ely, Robin, and David A. Thomas. 2001. "Cultural Diversity at Work: The Effects of Diversity Perspectives on Work Group Processes and Outcomes." *Administrative Science Quarterly,* 46: 229–273; Kochan, Thomas, Katerina Bezrukova, Roby Ely, Susan Jackson, Aparna Joshi, Karen Jehn, Jonathan Leonard, David Levine, and David Thomas. 2003. "The Effects of Diversity on Business Performance:

Report of the Diversity Research Network." *Human Resource Management.* Spring: 3-21.

10. Jackson, Susan 1991. "Team Composition in Organizational Settings: Issues in Managing an Increasingly Diverse Workforce." In S. Worchel, W. Wood, and J. Simpson (eds.). *Group Process and Productivity*. Beverly Hills, CA: Sage.

11. Triandis, Harry, Eleanor Hall, and Robert Ewen. 1965. "Member Heterogeneity and Dyadic Creativity." *Human Relations,* 18: 33–55; Thomas, David, Elizabeth Ravlin, and Alan Wallace. 1991. "Effect of Cultural Diversity in Work Groups." *Research in the Sociology of Organizations,* 14: 1–33.

12. Morris, Betsy. 1997. "If Women Ran the World It Would Look a Lot like Avon." *Fortune.* July 21: 74–79.

13. Nemeth, C., and J. Kwan. 1992. "Minority Dissent as a Stimulant to Group Performance." In S. Worchel, W. Wood, and J. A. Simpson (eds.). *Group Process and Productivity*. Newbury Park, CA: Sage; cited in Thomas, David, Elizabeth Ravlin, and Alan Wallace. "Effect of Cultural Diversity in Work Groups." *Research in the Sociology of Organizations,* 14: 1–33.

14. Ancona, Deborah, and David Caldwell. "Beyond Boundary Spanning: Managing External Dependence in Product Development Teams." *Journal of High-Technology Management Research,* 1: 119–135.

15. Jackson, Susan. 1991. "Team Composition in Organizational Settings: Issues in Managing an Increasingly Diverse Workforce." In Stephen Worchel, Wendy Wood, and Jeffrey Simpson (eds.). *Group Process and Productivity*. Beverly Hills, CA: Sage; citing Simon Herbert. 1979. *The Science of the Artificial.* 2nd ed. Cambridge, MA: MIT Press.

16. Thomas, David, Elizabeth Ravlin, and Alan Wallace. 1996. "Effect of Cultural Diversity in Work Groups." *Research in the Sociology of Organizations,* 14: 1–33.

17. Watson, Warren E., Kamalesh Kumar, and Larry Michaelsen. 1993. "Cultural Diversity's Impact on Interaction Process and Performance: Comparing Homogeneous and Diverse Task Groups." *Academy of Management Journal,* 36: 590–602.

18. Andre, Rae. 1995. "Diversity Stress as Moral Stress." *Journal of Business Ethics* 14: 489–496.

19. Clair, Judith, Joy Beatty, and Tammy MacLean, 2003. "Out of Sight but Not Out of Mind, Managing Invisible Social Identities in the Workplace." *Academy of Management Review.* Accepted for Publication. August.

20. Jackson, Susan E. 1991. "Team Composition in Organizational Settings: Issues in Managing an Increasingly Diverse Workforce." In Stephen Worchel, Wendy Wood, and Jeffrey Simpson (eds.). *Group Process and Productivity*. Beverly Hills, CA: Sage.

21. McCain, B., C. O'Reilly, and Jeffrey Pfeffer. 1983. "The Effects of Departmental Demography on Turnover." *Academy of Management Journal,* 26: 626–641; O'Reilly, Charles, David Caldwell, and William Barnett. 1989. "Work Group Demography, Social Integration, and Turnover." *Administrative Science Quarterly,* 34: 21–37.

22. Hood, Jacqueline N., and Christine S. Koberg. 1994. "Patterns of Differential Assimilation and Acculturation for Women in Business Organizations." *Human Relations,* 47: 159–181; Elsass, Priscilla, and Laura M. Graves. 1997. "Demographic Diversity in Decision-Making Groups: The Experiences of Women and People of Color." *Academy of Management Review,* 22(4): 946–973.

23. Zenger, Todd R., and Barbara Lawrence. 1989. "Organizational Demography: The Differential Effects of Age and Tenure on Technical Communication." *Academy of Management Journal,* 32: 353–376.

24. Odenwald, Sylvia. *Global Solutions for Teams*. Chicago: Irwin.

25. Barnlund, D., and C. Harland. 1963. "Propinquity and Prestige as Determinants of Communications Networks." *Sociometry,* 26: 467–479; Triandis, Harry. 1960. "Cognitive Similarity and Communication in a Dyad." *Human Relations,* 13: 279–287.

26. Jackson, Susan E. 1991. "Team Composition in Organizational Settings: Issues in Managing an Increasingly Diverse Workforce." In S. Worchel, W. Wood, and J. Simpson (eds.). *Group Process and Productivity*. Beverly Hills, CA: Sage.

27. Goodman, P., E. Ravlin, and M. Schminke. 1987. "Understanding Groups in Organizations." In Larry Cummings and Barry Staw (eds.). *Research in Organizational Behavior*. Vol. 9. Greenwich, CT: JAI Press.

28. Cummings, A., J. Zhou, and Gary Oldham. 1993. "Demographic Differences and Employee Work Outcomes: Effects of Multiple Comparison Groups." Paper Presented at the Annual Meeting of the Academy of Management, Atlanta, GA; Judge, Timothy, and Gerald Ferris. 1993. "Social Context of Performance Evaluation Decisions." *Academy of Management Journal*, 36: 80–105; cited in Williams, Katherine, and Charles O'Reilly. 1998. "Demography and Diversity in Organizations: A Review of 40 Years of Research." *Research in Organizational Behavior*, 20: 77–140.

29. Chemers, Martin, and Susan Jackson. 1995. "Leadership and Diversity in Groups and Organizations." In Chemers, Mark, Stuart Oskamp, and Mark Constanzo (eds.). *Diversity in Organizations: New Perspectives for a Changing Workplace*. Thousand Oaks, CA: Sage.

30. Thomas, David, Elizabeth Ravlin, and Alan Wallace. 1996. "Effect of Cultural Diversity in Work Groups." *Research in the Sociology of Organizations*, 14: 1–33.

31. Jackson, Susan E. 1992. "Team Composition in Organizational Settings: Issues in Managing an Increasingly Diverse Workforce." In Stephen Worchel, Wendy Wood, and Jeffrey A. Simpson (eds.). *Group Process and Productivity*. Newbury Park, CA: Sage; Thomas, David, Elizabeth Ravlin, and Alan Wallace. 1996. "Effect of Cultural Diversity in Work Groups." *Research in the Sociology of Organizations*, 14: 1–33.

32. Shaw, M. E. 1976. *Group Dynamics: The Psychology of Small Group Behavior*. New York: McGraw-Hill; cited in Jackson, Susan E. 1992. "Team Composition in Organizational Settings: Issues in Managing an Increasingly Diverse Workforce." In Stephen Worchel, Wendy Wood, and Jeffrey A. Simpson (eds.). *Group Process and Productivity*. Newbury Park, CA: Sage.

33. Cummings, A., J. Zhou, and Gary Oldham. 1993. "Demographic Differences and Employee Work Outcomes: Effects of Multiple Comparison Groups." Paper Presented at the Annual Academy Meeting of the Academy of Management, Atlanta, GA; Stangor, Charles, Laure Lynch, and B. Glass. 1992. "Categorization of Individuals on the Basis of Multiple Social Features." *Journal of Personality and Social Psychology*, 62: 207–218.

34. Kanter, Rosabeth Moss. 1977. *Men and Women of the Corporation*. New York: Basic Books.

35. Schrieber, C. 1979. *Changing Places: Men and Women in Traditional Occupations*. Cambridge, MA: MIT Press; Fairhurst, Gail, and B. Kay Snavely. 1983. "A Test of the Social Isolation of Male Tokens." *Academy of Management Journal*, 26: 353–361; cited in Williams, Katherine, and Charles O'Reilly. 1998. "Demography and Diversity in Organizations: A Review of 40 Years of Research." In Barry Staw and Larry Cummings (eds.). *Research in Organizational Behavior*, 20: 77–140.

36. O'Farrell, B., and S. Harlan. 1982. "Craftworkers and Clerks: The Effect of Male Coworker Hostility on Women's Satisfaction with Nontraditional Jobs." *Social Problems*, 29: 252–264; Brass, Daniel. 1985. "Men and Women's Networks: A Study of Interaction Patterns and Influence in an Organization." *Academy of Management Journal*, 28: 327–343; Ibarra, Herminia. 1992. "Homophily and Differential Returns: Sex Differences in Network Structure and Access in an Advertising Firm." *Administrative Science Quarterly*, 37: 422–447.

37. Wharton, Amy, and James Baron. 1987. "So Happy Together? The Impact of Gender Segregation on Men at Work." *American Sociological Review*, 52: 574–587; Tsui,

Anne, Terri Egan, and Charles O'Reilly. 1992. "Being Different: Relational Demography and Organizational Attachment." *Administrative Science Quarterly,* 37: 549–579.

38. Wharton, Amy, and James Baron. 1987. "So Happy Together? The Impact of Gender Segregation on Men at Work." *American Sociological Review,* 52: 574–587.

39. Chatman, Jennifer, Jeffrey Polzer, and Margaret Neale. 1998. "Being Different Yet Feeling Similar: The Influence of Demographic Composition and Organizational Culture on Work Processes and Outcomes." *Administrative Science Quarterly,* 43: 749–780.

40. Stewart, Greg, Charles Manz, and Henry Sims. 1999. *Teamwork and Group Dynamics.* New York: John Wiley and Sons; citing W. E. Watson, K. Kumar, and L. K. Michaelsen. 1993. "Cultural Diversity's Impact on Interaction Process and Performance: Comparing Homogeneous and Diverse Task Groups." *Academy of Management Journal,* 36: 590–602.

41. Glaman, Joan, Allan P. Jones, and Richard M. Rozelle. 1996. "The Effects of Coworker Similarity on the Emergence of Affect in Work Teams." *Group and Organizational Management,* 21(2): 192–215.

42. Ibid.

43. Harris, Philip, and Robert Moran. 1996. *Managing Cultural Differences: Leadership Strategies for a New World of* Business. 4th ed. Houston, TX: Gulf Publishing.

44. Ely, Robin, and David A. Thomas, 2001. "Cultural Diversity at Work: The Effects of Diversity Perspectives on Work Group Processes and Outcomes." *Administrative Science Quarterly*, 46: 229–273.

45. Triandis, Harry, Eleanor Hall, and Robert Ewen. 1965. "Member Heterogeneity and Dyadic Creativity." *Human Relations,* 18: 33–55; Finley, Joycelyn. 1996. "Communication Double Binds: The Catch-22 of Conversations about Racial Issues in Work Groups." Dissertation Submitted to the University of Michigan.

46. Chatman, Jennifer, Jeffrey Polzer, and Margaret Neale. 1998. "Being Different Yet Feeling Similar: The Influence of Demographic Composition and Organizational Culture on Work Processes and Outcomes." *Administrative Science Quarterly,* 43: 749–780.

47. Ibid.

48. Armstrong, Robert, and Paul Cole. 1994. *Culture and Social Behavior.* New York: McGraw-Hill.

49. Lipnack, Jessica, and Jeffrey Stamps. 1997. *Virtual Teams: Reaching across Time, Space, and Technology.* New York: John Wiley.

50. Ibid.

51. Townsend, Anthony, Samuel DeMarie, and Anthony Hendrickson. 1998. "Virtual Teams: Technology and the Workplace of the Future." *Academy of Management Executive,* 12(3): 17–29.

52. Mercer, Graham, and Matthew Barritt. 1998. "An Integrated Approach to Business Education Summary." *Michigan Business School, Global Learning Center Publication.* November: 3.

53. Townsend, Anthony, Samuel DeMarie, and Anthony Hendrickson. 1998. "Virtual Teams: Technology and the Workplace of the Future." *Academy of Management Executive,* 12(3): 17–29.

54. Haywood, Martha. 1998. *Managing Virtual Teams: Practical Techniques for High-Technology Managers.* Boston, MA: Artech House.

55. Price Pridget. 1999. *New Work Habits for the Next Millennium: 10 Ground Rules for Job Success*; citing Bureau of Labor Statistics.

56. Townsend, Anthony, Samuel DeMarie, and Anthony Hendrickson. 1996. "Are You Ready for Virtual Teams?" *HR Magazine.* September: 122–226.

57. Norton, Bob, and Cathy Smith. 1997. *Understanding the Virtual Organization.* Hauppauge, NY: Barrons.

58. Haywood, Martha. 1998. *Managing Virtual Teams: Practical Techniques for High-Technology Managers.* Boston, MA: Artech House; citing Gray, Hodson, and Gopdon. 1993. *Teleworking Explained.* New York: John Wiley and Sons.

59. Smith, N., E. Bizot, and T. Hill. 1988. *Use of E-Mail in a Research and Development Organization.* Tulsa, OK: University of

Tulsa; Bikson, T. K. 1987. "Understanding the Implementation of Office Technology." In R. Kraut (eds.). *Technology and the Transformation of White Collar Work*. Hillsdale, NJ: Erlbaum.

60. Lipnack, Jessica, and Jeffrey Stamps. 1997. *Virtual Teams: Reaching across Time, Space, and Technology*. New York: John Wiley; citing Bernie DeKoven. 1990. *Connected Executives: A Strategic Communications Plan*. Palo Alto, CA: Institute for Better Meetings.

61. Sproull, Lee, and Sara Kiesler. 1991. *Connections: New Ways of Working in the Networked Organization*. Cambridge, MA: MIT Press.

62. Finholt, Tom, and Lee Sproull. 1990. "Electronic Groups at Work." *Organizational Science*, 1(1): 41–64.

63. Townsend, Anthony, Samuel DeMarie, and Anthony Hendrickson. 1998. "Virtual Teams: Technology and the Workplace of the Future." *Academy of Management Executive*, 12(3): 17–29.

64. Mankin, Don, Susan Cohen, and Tora Bikson. 1997. "Teams and Technology: Tensions in Participatory Design." *Organization Dynamics.* Summer: 63–75.

65. Sproull, Lee, and Sara Kiesler. 1993. *Connections: New Ways of Working in the Networked Organization*. Cambridge, MA: MIT Press.

66. McLeod, Poppy, Robert Baron, Mollie Marti, and Kuh Yoon. 1997. "The Eyes Have It: Minority Influence in Face-to-Face and Computer-Mediated Group Discussion." *Journal of Applied Psychology,* 82(5): 706–718.

67. Kiesler, Sara, and Lee Sproull. 1992. "Group Decision-Making and Communication Technology." *Organizational Behavior and Human Decision Processes,* 52(1): 96–123.

68. Ibid.

69. Finholt, Tom, and Lee Sproull. 1990. "Electronic Groups at Work." *Organizational Science,* (1): 41–64.

70. Ibid.

71. Hallowell, Edward M. 1999. "The Human Moment at Work." *Harvard Business Review.* January/February: 58–66.

72. Fussell and Benimoff. 1995. "Social and Cognitive Processes in Interpersonal Communication: Implications for Advanced Telecommunications Technologies." *Journal of Human Factors and Ergonomics.* June: 229; cited in Haywood, Martha. 1998. *Managing Virtual Teams: Practical Techniques for High-Technology Managers.* Boston, MA: Artech House.

73. Dubrovsky, Vitaly, Sara Kiesler, and Beheruz Sethna. 1991. "The Equalization Phenomenon: Status Effects in Computer-Mediated and Face-to-Face Decision-Making Groups." *Human-Computer Interaction,* 6: 119–146.

74. Ibid.

75. Haywood, Martha. 1998. *Managing Virtual Teams: Practical Techniques for High-Technology Managers.* Boston, MA: Artech House.

76. Friedman, Raymond, and Steven Currall. 2002. "E-Mail Escalation: Dispute Exacerbating Elements of Electronic Communication." *Sloan Management Review,* 44(1): 14–15.

77. Hallowell, Edward M. 1999. "The Human Moment at Work." *Harvard Business Review.* January/February: 58–66.

78. Haywood, Martha. 1998. *Managing Virtual Teams: Practical Techniques for High-Technology Managers.* Boston, MA: Artech House.

79. Baker, Wayne. 1994. *Networking Smart: How to Build Relationships for Personal and Organizational Success*. New York: McGraw-Hill.

80. Finholt, Tom, and Lee Sproull. 1990. "Electronic Groups at Work." *Organizational Science,* 1(1): 41–64; citing James Lincoln and Arne Kalleberg. 1985. "Work Organization and Workforce Commitment: A Study of Plants and Employees in the United States and Japan." *American Sociological Review,* 50: 738–760.

81. Ibid.

82. Hallowell, Edward M. 1999. "The Human Moment at Work." *Harvard Business Review.* January/February: 58–66.

83. Locke, John L. 1998. *The De-Voicing of Society: Why We Don't Talk to Each Other*

Anymore. New York: Simon & Schuster; cited in 1999. "The Decline of Conversation." *The Futurist.* February: 18–19.

84. Armstrong, David, and Paul Cole. 1995. "Managing Distances and Differences in Geographically Distributed Work Groups." In Susan Jackson and Marian Ruderman (eds.). *Diversity in Work Teams.* Washington, DC: American Psychological Association.

85. Haywood, Martha. 1998. *Managing Virtual Teams: Practical Techniques for High-Technology Managers.* Boston, MA: Artech House.

86. Geber, Beverly. 1995. "Virtual Teams." *Training.* April: 36–40.

87. Jarvenpaa, Sirkka, and Dorothy Leidner. 1999. "Communication and Trust in Global Virtual Teams." *Organization Science,* 10(6): 791–815.

88. McLeod, Poppy, and Robert Baron, Mollie Marti, and Kuh Yoon. 1997. "The Eyes Have It: Minority Influence in Face-to-Face and Computer-Mediated Group Discussion." *Journal of Applied Psychology,* 82(5): 706–718.

89. Ibid.

90. Ibid.

91. Dubrovsky, Vitaly, Sara Kiesler, and Beheruz Sethna. 1991. "The Equalization Phenomenon: Status Effects in Computer-Mediated and Face-to-Face Decision-Making Groups." *Human-Computer Interaction,* 6: 119–146.

92. Sproull, Lee, and Sara Kiesler. 1993. *Connections: New Ways of Working in the Networked Organizations.* Cambridge, MA: MIT Press.

93. Munter, Mary. 1998. "Meeting Technology: From Low-Tech to High-Tech." *Business Communication Quarterly,* 61(2): 80–87.

94. Mantovani, Giuseppe. 1994. "Is Computer-Mediated Communication Intrinsically Apt to Enhance Democracy in Organizations?" *Human Relations,* 47(1): 45–62.

95. Ibid.

96. Ibid.

97. 1999. "UpData." *Training and Development.* July: 20.

98. Fountain, Jane. 2000. "Constructing the Information Society: Women, Information Technology, and Design." *Technology in Society,* 22: 45–62.

99. Ibid.

100. Munter, Mary. 1998. "Meeting Technology: From Low-Tech to High-Tech." *Business Communication Quarterly,* 61(2): 80–87.

101. Mercer, Graham, and Matthew Barritt. 1998. "An Integrated Approach to Business Education." Working Paper. November; 1999. University of Michigan Business School, Global Learning Center Working Paper, p. 1.

102. McLeod, Poppy, Robert Baron, Mollie Marti, and Kuh Yoon. 1997. "The Eyes Have It: Minority Influence in Face-to-Face and Computer-Mediated Group Discussion." *Journal of Applied Psychology,* 82(5): 706–718; Munter, Mary. 1998. "Meeting Technology: From Low-Tech to High-Tech." *Business Communication Quarterly,* 61(2): 80–87.

103. "Face-to-Face: Making Networking Organizations Work." In N. Nohria, and R. Eccles (eds.). *Networks and Organizations: Structure, Form, and Action.* Boston, MA: Harvard Business School Press.

104. Munter, Mary. 1998. "Meeting Technology: From Low-Tech to High-Tech." *Business Communication Quarterly,* 61(2): 80–87.

105. Ibid.

106. Haywood, Martha. 1998. *Managing Virtual Teams: Practical Techniques for High-Technology Managers.* Boston, MA: Artech House.

107. Sproull, Lee, and Sara Kiesler. 1993. *Connections: New Ways of Working in the Networked Organization.* Cambridge, MA: MIT Press.

108. Munter, Mary. 1998. "Meeting Technology: From Low-Tech to High-Tech." *Business Communication Quarterly,* 61(2): 80–87.

109. Mcgrath, J., and A. Hollinshead. 1994. Groups Interacting with Technology. Newbury Park, CA: Sage.

110. McLeod, Poppy. 1999. "A Literary Examination of Electronic Meeting System Use in Everyday Organizational Life." *Journal of Applied Behavioral Science,* 34(2): 188–206.

111. Ibid.

112. Munter, Mary. 1998. "Meeting Technology: From Low-Tech to High-Tech." *Business Communication Quarterly,* 61(2): 80–87.

113. Townsend, Anthony, Samuel DeMarie, and Anthony Hendrickson. 1998. "Virtual Teams: Technology and the Workplace of the Future." *Academy of Management Executive,* 12(3): 17–29.

114. Lipnack, Jessica, and Jeffrey Stamps. 1997. *Virtual Teams: Reaching across Time, Space, and Technology.* New York: John Wiley; citing Bernie DeKoven. 1990. *Connected Executives: A Strategic Communications Plan.* Palo Alto, CA: Institute for Better Meetings.

115. Haywood, Martha. 1998. *Managing Virtual Teams: Practical Techniques for High-Technology Managers.* Boston, MA: Artech House.

116. Ibid.

117. Geber, Beverly. 1995. "Virtual Teams." *Training.* April: 36–40.

118. Hallowell, Edward M. 1999. "The Human Moment at Work." *Harvard Business Review.* January/February: 58–66.

119. Gladstone, Bryan. 1998. "The Medium is the Message: When Old Paradigms Meet New Technology." *Journal of General Management,* 24(2): 51–68; citing Lewis, David. 1997. *Shaming, Blaming, and Flaming: Corporate Miscommunication in the Information Age.* Bracknell, England: Novell.

120. Haywood, Martha. 1998. *Managing Virtual Teams: Practical Techniques for High-Technology Managers.* Boston, MA: Artech House.

121. Dennis, Alan R. 1996b. "Information Processing in Group Decision-Making: You Can Lead a Group to Information but You Can't Make It Think." *MIS Quarterly,* 20: 433–455.

122. Christina Gibson, and Susan Cohen (eds.). 2003. *Virtual Teams that Work: Creating Conditions for Virtual Team Effectiveness.* San Francisco, CA: Jossey Bass.

123. Ibid.

124. Haywood, Martha. 1998. *Managing Virtual Teams: Practical Techniques for High-Technology Managers.* Boston, MA: Artech House.

125. Ibid.

126. Ibid.

127. Norton, Bob, and Cathy Smith. 1997. *Understanding the Virtual Organization.* Hauppage, NY: Barrons.

128. Lipnack, Jessica, and Jeffrey Stamps. 1997. *Virtual Teams: Reaching across Time, Space, and Technology.* New York: John Wiley; citing Bernie DeKoven. 1990. *Connected Executives: A Strategic Communications Plan.* Palo Alto, CA: Institute for Better Meetings.

129. Ibid.

---------------------------V I D E O C A S E---------------------------

Case 4 Building Teams

Group life is necessary for human survival. Although we don't think about it often, we are highly dependent on teams of people who work together—face to face or virtually—to provide us with food, clothing, and shelter, not to mention transportation, communication, medical miracles, entertainment, education, and all the other underpinnings that we take for granted in our everyday lives.

It is becoming increasingly difficult to solve problems independently in today's complex, global, fast-changing, and technology-driven world. When well managed, teams have the potential to do great things because people working in teams bring a wide variety of perspectives, knowledge, skills, and experience to the task at hand. Although all teams differ in their task and team composition, all teams share some characteristics: clear boundaries that define who is and is not a member, a common task or tasks, distinct member roles, some degree of autonomy in how they do their work, dependence on fellow team members and on those outside the group to accomplish the task, and collective responsibility for achieving the team goals.

The most effective teams tend to have the following characteristics: They consistently produce high-quality products and services, they enable each team member to thrive in the team, and they grow in their capabilities as performing units. To achieve these goals, effective teams have a clear purpose, clear performance processes, the right people on the team, performance measures against which to judge their performance, and opportunities to practice and enhance team members' abilities to work together.

Effective leaders promote team success; ineffective leaders can seriously handicap the efforts of the group and its members. Leaders of high-performing teams provide direction and structure, supply resources and remove obstacles, manage the boundaries between the team and the external environment, and champion the team.

In this segment, Mia takes the advice of her consultant and forms an ad hoc or temporary team to look into ways to cut costs by eliminating some of the expensive extras that allaboutself.com has provided its staff. For a team leader she can select either the Webmaster Mike, who is very knowledgeable but something of a loner, or Anita, who is more outgoing and seems well organized. Each option shows a different result. As you watch the segment, try to assess the team leader's performance in particular. ∎

DISCUSSION QUESTIONS

1. Is this team off to a good start? Why or why not?
2. Evaluate the way the team leader has run the committee so far. List effective and ineffective ways in which the leader manages the meeting.
3. What could the leader do to help the team accomplish its goal?
4. What could Mia do to help support the team at this point?
5. How are the team members contributing to the team's mission? What could they do differently to ensure the success of the team?

CHAPTER

10

Crafting a Life

This chapter will help you:

- Learn what predicts well-being

- Understand how optimism, perfectionism, and Type A behaviors may influence productivity, health, and psychological well-being

- Learn why "flow" is important at work and how to create it

- See how the U.S. workforce is changing and the implications of these changes on individuals and organizations

- Understand how your job can affect your health

- Learn what many working parents want to know: How does day care affect children's well-being?

> *I have realized life is definitely not a straight line getting from point A to B but a series of detours; what you make of these detours defines your destiny.*
> —RAMKUMAR KRISHNAN
> *Acts of Faith*

I began this book by discussing the risks of professional derailment. Equally troubling are people who succeed in their professional lives in terms of their effectiveness, career progression, and salary, but who derail in their personal lives in terms of their non-work relationships, happiness, and health. My goal in this chapter is to provide you with insights from research that can help you craft a life that is personally and professionally rewarding.

How we spend our days is, of course, how we spend our lives. *Ann Dillard, The Writing Life*

Note that I don't say that this chapter will help you achieve "work-life balance." This is because I don't believe that work-life balance is a possible or even desirable goal. The search for balance will only frustrate you because it is elusive. After all, life's choices don't come in neat and perfectly timed packages. And having "work-life balance" is no guarantee of happiness. But take heart, for as the old saying goes, "the situation [in this case, finding balance] is hopeless but not serious." Although we are unlikely to achieve work-life balance, we can craft thoughtful, if not balanced, lives that are fulfilling to ourselves and to the people who count on us.

I begin this chapter by describing what researchers say leads to a happy life. I then describe why "flow" is important at work and how we can create it for ourselves and others. I then look at how personality characteristics, such as optimism, perfectionism, and Type A behavior, can affect your productivity, health, and psychological well-being.

Next, I present data on the changing U.S. workforce, particularly as the data relate to working parents and family caretakers (people who take care of ill or aging adults) and discuss the implications of these changes for individuals, families, and organizations. Because the data suggest that working parents make up a significant part of the workforce and because you are a working parent, will become a working parent, or will manage working parents now or in the future, I discuss how having children influences career success and the impact of day care on children's well-being. This information can help you make wise choices that will enable you to craft a life that is fulfilling for you, your family, and your organization.

HAPPINESS

What is happiness? Researchers dryly call happiness "subjective well-being" or, even more dryly, "SWB."[1] David Myers and Ed Diener explain that "high subjective well-being reflects a preponderance of positive thoughts and feelings about one's life." In other words, people who experience high subjective well-being (or happiness) are generally and genuinely pleased with themselves, their work, personal relationships, and other parts of their lives. They also tend to "feel primarily pleasant emotions." In contrast, people with low SWB see their lives as generally undesirable and feel more negative emotions such as "anxiety, depression, and anger."[2] Notably, nine of ten North Americans describe themselves as at least "pretty happy,"[3] and one of three say they are "very happy."[4]

What makes people happy? Let's begin by looking at what doesn't predict happiness. Research suggests that age, gender, and race make little, if any, difference in one's happiness level. Despite stereotypes about moody teenagers sulking in their bedrooms, middle-aged adults panicking through midlife crises and empty nests, and elderly men and women struggling through old age, none of these life stages appears to be generally happier or sadder than others.[5] Although women tend to feel higher emotional highs and lower emotional lows than men do, neither men nor women are more likely to report higher levels of overall happiness than the other. As for race, Myers and Diener explain, "African-Americans report nearly as much happiness as European Americans and are actually slightly less vulnerable to depression . . . and score similarly on tests of self-esteem."[6] Notably, major events, such as winning a lot of money in the lottery or having a handicapping accident, tend to have only a short-term effect on happiness.

May your every wish be granted. *Ancient Chinese Curse*

Does money buy happiness? In general, researchers who study subjective well-being conclude that income buys between 2 and 5 percent of one's happiness.[7] It is not surprising that money is likely to increase happiness more for the very poor because it can significantly enhance the quality of life. But once someone has enough money to buy the basic necessities of life, income is a poor predictor of happiness. People who make a lot of money are slightly more likely to be happy than people with moderate incomes, perhaps because they can pay others to do routine chores such as housecleaning, laundry, and cooking. This leaves them with more time to do things that may give them more pleasure. Keep in mind that expensive leisure activities typically don't tend to make people happy. Indeed, one study concluded, "People engaged in expensive leisure activities were significantly less happy than people engaged in inexpensive activities."[8]

You can't have everything. Where would you put it? *Stephen Wright*

Materialism (a focus on having more money and things) tends to decrease happiness, particularly for people who believe that having more money will make them happier. Researchers Aaron Ahuvia and Douglas Friedman explain, "Having more money doesn't necessarily lead to lower SWB, but wanting more money is likely to. Satisfaction with one's income is more important than the level of income itself."[9] Research by Abhishek Srivastava and colleagues found that "it's not the money, it's the motives" that predict whether money will have a positive or negative impact on a person's happiness. In their study of MBAs and entrepreneurs, they found that people whose drive for money was motivated by "social comparison, seeking power, showing off, and overcoming self-doubt" tended to have lower subjective well-being.[10] Myers and Diener illustrate the impact of material goods on happiness with this example:

> Compared with 1957, Americans have twice as many cars per person—plus microwave ovens, color TVs, VCRs, air conditioners, answering machines, and $12 billion worth of new brand-name athletic shoes a year. So, are Americans happier than they were in 1957? They are not. In 1957, 35 percent told the National Opinion Research Center that they were "very happy." In 1993, with doubled affluence, 32 percent said the same thing.[11]

It has long been my conviction that we learn far more about the conditions, and values, of a society by contemplating how it chooses to play, to use its free time, to take its leisure, than by examining how it goes about its work. *A. Bartlett Giamatti, Scholar, Former President of Yale University and Former Commissioner of Baseball*

So, what makes people happy? Summarizing several research studies, Ahuvia and Friedman conclude, "Achieving one's intrinsic goals for personal growth, close personal relationships, making a social contribution, and maintaining one's health were generally associated with higher levels of SWB. By contrast, achieving one's extrinsic goals for financial success, social recognition, and having an appealing appearance did not produce similar positive results."[12] Research also suggests that the following predicts subjective were-being:[13]

- *Temperament.* Some people tend to be consistently happy more so than others, either as a result of wired-in temperament or because they've developed a way of thinking about the world that keeps them happier. For example, they may be more likely to "attend to and recall the pleasant aspects of life more than others." Diener and his colleagues explain: "It's not just who we are that matters to happiness, but how we think about our lives."[14]
- *Self-esteem.* Say Myers and Diener, "Happy people like themselves." Indeed, happy people tend to have a self-enhancing bias and overestimate their capabilities (such as intelligence and taste).[15] Note, however, that this self-enhancing bias, like the pursuit of individual happiness, is more typical of people from individualist cultures than collectivist cultures.

- *Being a "satisficer" rather than "maximizer."*   A satisficer is someone who is happy with decisions that "cross the threshold of acceptability—something that is good enough." A maximizer is someone who wants to make the best possible decision. The problem for maximizers is that as options increase, the maximizers' chances for making the best decision among increasing options becomes more difficult so they are likely to get frustrated with the process of maximizing as well as with their final decision (for it will rarely seem good enough). Researcher Barry Schwartz and colleagues explain: ". . . although maximizers may in general achieve better objective outcomes than satisficers (as a result of their high standards and exhaustive search and decision procedures), they are likely to experience these outcomes as worse subjectively." Because there is often no perfect decision, maximizers experience more feelings of regret, depression, and dissatisfaction with what they have and these feelings can reduce subjective well-being.[16]
- *Having goals that one enjoys and that are congruent with each other.* Happiness researcher Ed Diener explains this simply: "If you want to be a lawyer but you hate conflict, you're going to be messed up."[17]
- *Having a sense of control.*   People who feel that they have a sense of control over domains of their life that are important to them tend to be more satisfied with their life.[18] The importance of having a sense of control over parts of one's life that one believes are important is one of the most significant predictors of well-being in old age.[19]
- *Relationships.*   People with close relationships tend to be happier, healthier, and longer-lived than people without these relationships.
- *Faith.*   Actively religious people tend to be happier, healthier, and longer-lived than people who are not and tend to report lower levels of depression.[20] Actively participating in a religious community can provide a network of supportive social relationships that enhance well-being, particularly during difficult times. Faith can contribute to happiness because it helps us find meaning and hope in our lives. Television personality and billionaire Oprah Winfrey illustrates the importance of faith in her life with this example:

The first time I got a huge check, I closed my office door, lit a candle, and sat there with it. I prayed to the force that I call God, all that is goodness and light, that my life might be an extension of the energy represented in that piece of paper, that it bring that kind of value to myself and others. I think about the wealth that I have acquired and the responsibility I now have to share it in the world in a way that brings honor to people, a greater sense of self-value.[21]

> Happiness is not something you get, but something you do.
> *Marcelene Cox*

- *Optimism.*   People who are optimistic tend to think that life, in general, will turn out well for them. Myers and Diener illustrate happy people's bias toward optimism with Sigmund Freud's joke about the man who told his wife, "If one of us should die, I think I would go live in Paris."[22] Notably, it's the optimists' belief in themselves and their ability to control their environment, not the objective truth of these beliefs, that leads to optimism. Says psychologist Mihaly Csikszentmihalyi, happiness "does not reside in outside events, but, rather, on how we interpret them."[23]

A Little Advice About Wealth

The media promotes the image of the wealthy person as having high status and abundant of material possessions. Yet many people who focus on status and collect material possessions aren't wealthy. Simply stated, if a person spends all of his or her high salary and bonuses on things that are not financial investments (e.g., expensive cars, dinners out, electronic toys, vacations, etc.), then he or she may not be as wealthy as the person who earns much less money yet saves a significant portion of his or her salary.

In studies of people who become wealthy through their own efforts (not through their parents' substantial financial gifts or inheritances), a few patterns stand out. Many people who are millionaires in the United States don't look like millionaires (and those who do look like millionaires aren't necessarily wealthy). Instead, the millionaires are the people who save, rather than spend, a large percentage of their income. Rather than accumulating material goods or worrying about status, they get pleasure out of watching their investments grow. They tend to live below their means, invest their money wisely, are skilled at finding good opportunities, and regularly spend their time doing financial planning. They tend to be at least moderate risk takers and are less drawn to immediate gratification. They do not dole out a lot of money to their children, except through their support of high-quality education.

In short, your attention to savings, investments, and finding good opportunities—not your salary or attention to appearances—determine your wealth.

SOURCE: Stanley, Thomas, and William Danko. 1996. *The Millionaire Next Door: The Surprising Secrets of America's Wealthy*. New York: Pocketbooks; Kiyosaki, Richard, and Sharon Lechter. 1997. *Rich Dad, Poor Dad*. New York: Warner Books.

HAPPINESS, WORK, AND FLOW

Work, it seems, makes most of us happy. When professor Robert Weiss surveyed people about whether they'd continue to work "if they had inherited enough to live comfortably, roughly 8 out of 10 people said yes."[24] In 1999, Steve Jobs had this to say about his work: "If I didn't enjoy it, I'd be on a beach somewhere. . . . Why bother, when running Apple and Pixar is so much fun?"[25] And Time Warner's former vice chairman, Ted Turner, had this to say about his feelings when he signed a $165 billion deal with America Online: "I did it with as much excitement as I felt the first time I made love some 42 years ago."[26]

Find something that you love to do and you will never work another day in your life. **George Fraser, Author, Success Runs in Our Race**

Without dwelling on the comparative pleasures of relaxing on a beach, making love, or working, the important point to be made here is this: When we are engaged in work that we enjoy—whether paid or unpaid, climbing the corporate ladder or caring for a home and family—we feel happy. What is it about work that so powerfully influences our sense of well-being?

Our work helps us define who we are and our place in the world ("I am a good manager," "I am a loving parent," "I am a creative artist," "I am the best deal-maker in the universe."). When our work involves being with others on a regular basis, it helps us fulfill our needs for belonging and social interaction. When our work challenges us, it helps us fulfill our needs for competence and growth. When our work involves familiar routines (e.g., getting children off to school, going to the office, or checking our e-mail in the morning), it helps us fulfill our needs for control and consistency in our everyday life. And, says Brian Dumaine of *Fortune* magazine, "In a time of uncertainty and upheaval, whether in the family or society, work also provides perhaps your best chance to create a world exactly as you want it to be."[27] To make this point, Dumaine quotes Debra Sandler, former marketing director at Pepsi's $8 billion soft drink division and now worldwide group vice president of marketing and strategic ingredient technology at McNeil Nutritional:

> I see myself as an agent of change. There are not many women of color in corporate America, and I place a heavy burden on myself to show that we can do it. And that we do it pretty darn well. And that I'm not here simply because someone said, "Let's pad the affirmative action numbers."[28]

To deprive a person of work is to negate a portion of his/her humanity. *John Convers, The Politics of Unemployment*

Certainly, not all work contributes to our well-being. Most readers of this book can think of work situations that are boring, unfulfilling, and unhealthy. For work to enhance our feelings of well-being—not just to put money on the table—it must be both meaningful and well designed.[29] Psychologist Mihaly Csikszentmihalyi explains that such work provides us with an opportunity to feel "flow," also known as "peak experience" or "optimal experience." We feel flow when we are fully immersed in an activity that is important to us—teaching, gardening, writing, creating a new product, or reading to a child. Csikszentmihalyi explains that we are most likely to feel flow in situations that have the following characteristics:[30]

- *Worthwhile goals.*   We are more likely to be committed to and excited by a task if we believe that the work is worth doing.
- *Challenge.*   We are more likely to feel engaged in a task if it requires skills that stretch our abilities yet are still within our reach.
- *Clear goals, rules, and feedback.*   We are more likely to feel flow if we have clear boundaries, such as goals, rules, and deadlines, which help us focus our attention without being sidetracked by irrelevant concerns. Csikszentmihalyi explains, "It is easy to enter flow in games such as chess, tennis, or poker because they have goals and rules that make it possible for the player to act without questioning what should be done and how."[31]
- *Periods of concentrated attention.*   We are more likely to feel flow when we are able to concentrate without distractions for extended periods of time. When we emerge from a concentrated period of flow, we realize that hours have gone

by in what seems like minutes. A study of engineers by organizational researcher Leslie Perlow supports Csikszentmihalyi's conclusions. When she began her study, she found that "on average, only 36 percent of the engineers' time occurs in uninterrupted blocks over one hour long. . . . Moreover, engineers have little control over the fragmentation of their schedules."[32] After Perlow helped the engineers design their jobs so that they would have "uninterrupted blocks of 'quiet time' during the day . . . no one found that the imposed structure hurt their productivity, and 65 percent felt that it had enhanced their productivity."[33]

- *Feelings of control.*   We are more likely to feel flow if we feel as though we have some control over how to do the task. Notably, we're unlikely to feel flow if the outcome is too easy to achieve. Says Csikszentmihalyi, "What people enjoy is not the sense of being in control, but the sense of exercising control in difficult situations. It is not possible to experience a sense of control unless one is willing to give up the safety of protective routines. Only when a doubtful outcome is at stake, and one is able to influence that outcome, can a person really know whether she [or he] is in control."[34]

In short, Csikszentmihalyi explains, "The best moments usually occur when a person's body or mind is stretched to its limits in a voluntary effort to accomplish something difficult and worthwhile. Optimal experience is something that we make happen."[35] It is not surprising that we're unlikely to feel flow when we're engaging in passive leisure activities such as watching television (although we may have other good feelings such as relaxation and rejuvenation). Activities that inspire flow may not always feel pleasant. Indeed, developing a new product, writing a book, or climbing a mountain can be painful, particularly during those periods in which the challenge of the activity temporarily exceeds our ability. But if we believe that the task is worthwhile, are able to focus on the task without distractions for extended periods of time, and have (or can learn) the required skills to accomplish the task, we are likely to persevere and experience flow.

Don't aim at success—the more you aim at it and make it a target, the more you are going to miss it. For success, like happiness, cannot be pursued; it must ensue, and it only does so as the unintended side effect of one's personal dedication to a cause greater than oneself or as the by-product of one's surrender to a person other than oneself.
Viktor Frankl, Man's Search for Meaning

The human need for challenge begins early in life. Recently, I went on vacation to the oceanside with my children, a friend, and my friend's children. I was fascinated with the fact that every time we went to the beach, the children's immediate reaction was to pick up their shovels and buckets and get to work digging deep holes that would become their temporary houses and building elaborate sand castles with water-filled moats. The children worked creatively and strenuously for hours. They didn't speak much to each other, except to coordinate their efforts and argue over a shovel now and then. Their bodies and minds were fully engaged in creating and working. It didn't matter to the children that their houses, castles, and moats would be washed away later that day. The children would simply return to the beach the next day to start building again, this time with lessons learned and ideas gained from the day before. This experience, more than any I've recently seen, seemed to most purely reflect our very human need to experience flow.

When we feel flow, we reap many rewards. The process of doing the work often feels good. When we finish the task, we feel a strong sense of accomplishment from a job well done. We gain new skills in the process that make us feel more competent and ready to take on more challenging tasks. And feeling flow is highly motivating. Says Csikszentmihalyi, "Once we have tasted this joy, we will redouble our efforts to taste it again."[36] Another important benefit, says Csikszentmihalyi, is that, "The self becomes more differentiated as a result of flow because overcoming a challenge inevitably leaves a person feeling more capable, more skilled. . . . Our identity becomes more complex. . . . [While we are engaged in flow] our concern for self disappears, yet paradoxically, the sense of self emerges stronger after the flow experience is over."[37]

If I could build one building in my life, I want to build a building that people feel in the stomach—you can call it comfort, beauty, excitement, guts, tears. . . . There are many ways to describe the reaction to architecture, but tears are as good as any.   Philip Johnson, age 92, Architect, Interviewed by John H. Richardson for Esquire, February 1999

Although most of us tend to enjoy working, it seems that many of us don't feel very positively about the organizations in which we do our work. In a study of 30,000 U.S. workers, the consulting firm Opinion Research "found that though most people generally feel positive about working, 47 percent now say they either dislike or are ambivalent about the company they work for."[38] The research on flow suggests why some people don't have strong positive feelings toward their organizations: meaningless work, excessive ambiguity, not having the skills to accomplish the task, not having the opportunity to learn new skills, not feeling in control of one's work, lack of trust, self-consciousness, and excessive distractions.

To see if your job is likely to foster feelings of flow, complete the assessment in Box 10-2. The higher the score, the more likely the job is to inspire flow. If you are curious about whether you are creating conditions that inspire flow for the people who work for you, have them complete the assessment as well.

OPTIMISM AND SUCCESS

After decades of studies, researchers are concluding that optimism—in most cases—provides many benefits, including greater achievement, psychological well-being, and better health. Indeed, research by Becca Levy and colleagues found that "older individuals with more positive self-perceptions of aging, measured up to 23 years earlier, lived 7.5 years longer than those with less positive perceptions of aging. This advantage remained after age, gender, socioeconomic status, loneliness, and functional health were included as covariates."[39]

There are two ways to live your life. One is as though nothing is a miracle. The other is as though everything is a miracle.   Albert Einstein

What are the characteristics of optimists? Research by social psychologist Shelly Taylor and others provides ample evidence that happy and effective people tend to be somewhat out of touch with reality. Specifically, they tend to interpret themselves and the world around them with a positive bias. They see themselves as more talented than they are, the environment as more controllable than it is, and the world as a considerably more positive place than watching

---

BOX 10-2

Rate Your Work's Potential for Flow

Task or Job Being Assessed: _____

1 Never
2 Rarely
3 Sometimes
4 Often
5 Always

1. Does the work feel worthwhile to me?	1	2	3	4	5
2. Are the goals clear?	1	2	3	4	5
3. Are the goals achievable?	1	2	3	4	5
4. Are there clear rules for accomplishing the work?	1	2	3	4	5
5. Does the work provide regular feedback so that I know how I'm doing?	1	2	3	4	5
6. Do I have the skills I need to do my work?	1	2	3	4	5
7. Is the work challenging (does it stretch my skills?)?	1	2	3	4	5
8. Am I able to concentrate on my work without distractions?	1	2	3	4	5
9. Does the work enable me to rise above worries and self-consciousness?	1	2	3	4	5
10. Do I feel like I have some control over the work?	1	2	3	4	5

SOURCE: Adapted from Csikszenmihalyi, Mihaly. 1990. *Flow: The Psychology of Optimal Experience.* New York: HarperPerennial.

---

the nightly news would suggest. They also see the future as holding "an unrealistically bountiful set of opportunities." Taylor calls these generous interpretations of reality "creative self-deceptions" or "positive illusions," and makes a strong case that they are foundations of personal effectiveness and well-being.[40]

> **Dreams, if they are any good, are always a little crazy.** *Ray Charles, Musician*

Taylor notes that although most optimists tend to have unrealistic interpretations of themselves and the world around them, they are not unreasonably optimistic. In other words, they don't deny bad news. Rather, they incorporate it into their lives with a positive bias. For example, an optimistic manager who receives negative feedback may say, "It's a good thing that I got the news now rather than later in my career so that I have time to develop the skills I need." Furthermore, realistic optimists focus their optimism on events over which they have some control. Taylor explains, "These qualities distinguish illusion from delusion. Delusions are false beliefs that persist despite the facts. Illusions accommodate them, though perhaps reluctantly."[41]

Taylor suggests that optimism can enhance productivity, health, and psychological well-being because it is likely to lead to self-fulfilling prophecies. Optimists are more likely than others to:[42]

- **Set high goals and standards.**   People who tend to judge themselves as more competent than average are likely to set high goals and standards.
- **Be highly motivated.**   People who attribute success to themselves rather than to external factors tend to be self-motivated.
- **Work hard and persevere.**   People who have positive feelings toward themselves tend to work hard and long on tasks because they believe they can accomplish them. They tend to persevere to overcome hurdles. This perseverance increases the likelihood that they will reach their goals.
- **Seek out feedback.**   Optimists tend to look for feedback so that they can assess whether they are on the right track toward achieving their goals.
- **Increase problem-solving capacity and speed.**   A good mood increases the likelihood that a person will use rapid and efficient problem-solving strategies.
- **Take risks.**   Optimists tend to take risks perhaps because they don't dwell on what can go wrong or because they assume that they can control the outcome.
- **Postpone gratification.**   People who believe that they will succeed tend to stick with their goals even when achieving these goals may take a long time because they can envision a positive outcome.
- **Reward themselves.**   People who feel good about themselves tend to reward themselves for their efforts.
- **Gain social support.**   People who focus on the positive things in life are typically pleasant to be around and are more likely to get help from others.
- **Effectively manage stress.**   Optimists tend to cope well with stress because they believe things will eventually get better, are able to draw on social support to help them deal with stressful situations, are proactive in taking actions to alleviate the stress, and see the advantages of difficult periods ("I learned a lot from it." or "What doesn't kill me makes me stronger.").

See Figure 10-1 for a summary of the impact of optimism on health, happiness, and effectiveness.

Optimism may be particularly important for leaders. James Kouzes and Barry Posner, authors of the book *Credibility*, explain:

Constituents look for leaders who demonstrate an enthusiastic and genuine belief in the capacity of others, who strengthen people's will, who supply the means to achieve, and who express optimism for the future. Constituents want leaders who remain passionate despite obstacles and setbacks. In today's uncertain times, leaders with a positive, confident, can-do approach to life and business are desperately needed. . . . Credible leaders sustain hope by painting positive images of the future. They arouse optimistic feelings and enable their constituents to hold positive thoughts about the possibilities of success.[43]

> A fundamental shortcoming in much of business today is that the leadership lacks vision and passion—the two most important ingredients to inspire and motivate. In the Body Shop we have both in abundance and we possess, in addition, a further secret ingredient: an extraordinary level of optimism, almost amounting to euphoria, that permeates the whole company. We are incurable optimists— and incurable optimists believe they can do anything. *Anita Roddick, Founder of the Body Shop International*

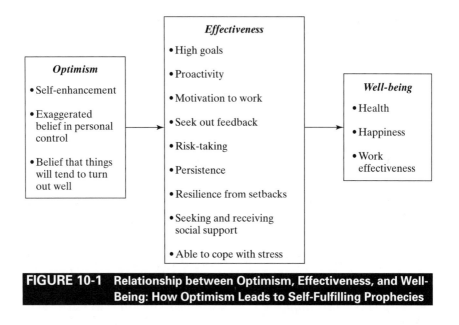

FIGURE 10-1 Relationship between Optimism, Effectiveness, and Well-Being: How Optimism Leads to Self-Fulfilling Prophecies

In short, optimism enhances success and well-being because, as Taylor says, a moderate detachment from reality—"an ability to see things not for what they are but what you wish they could be—is an effective offense mechanism, particularly when not taken to extremes and when tempered with the ability to incorporate negative information."[44]

The Role of Explanations in Optimism

Psychologist Martin Seligman argues that the difference between an optimistic and pessimistic view of the world is rooted in the explanations we use to explain the good and bad events in our lives.[45] He says that we use three types of explanatory styles:

- *Permanence (Do you see the cause of good and bad events as permanent or temporary?).* Optimists tend to see the causes of good events as permanent and the causes of bad events as temporary. In contrast, pessimists tend to see the causes of good events as temporary and the causes of bad events as permanent. For example, when an optimist receives a poor performance review, he or she is likely to believe that the poor performance was a temporary setback, whereas a pessimist is likely to believe that the review may reflect his or her future ability to perform well.

- *Pervasiveness (Do you see the causes of good and bad events as specific or global?).* Optimists tend to see the causes of good events as carrying over to several aspects of their lives and the causes of bad events as specific to only one aspect of their lives. In contrast, pessimists tend to see the causes of good events as specific to one aspect of their lives and the causes of bad events as carrying over to several aspects of their lives. For example, when an optimist gives a presentation that receives positive reactions, he or she is likely to think, "I'm good, period," whereas the pessimist is likely to think, "I'm good at giving presentations."

- *Personalization (Do you attribute the causes of good and bad events to yourself or to external causes?).* Optimists tend to give credit to themselves for good events and blame others or external causes for bad events. In contrast, pessimists tend to give credit to others or external causes for good events and blame themselves for bad events. For example, when an optimist does well on an exam, he or she is likely to think, "I studied hard" or "I'm smart," whereas the pessimist is likely to think, "It was an easy exam" or "The professor did a good job teaching the material."

> Our ability to delude ourselves may be an important survival tool.
> *Jane Wagner, The Search for Signs of Intelligent Life in the Universe*

Note that the relationship between self-enhancing biases and optimism may be more likely to exist for people from individualistic cultures (self-focused) than for people from collectivist cultures (relationship-focused). This pattern arises because individualistic cultures tend to promote a self-enhancing bias, whereas collectivist cultures tend to promote a self-critical bias.[46] Note also that self-enhancing biases can have negative consequences. For example, people who attribute problems to external causes alone and don't take responsibility for their actions may be overconfident, deny personal responsibility for failure, and avoid self-development.

> I am happy and content because I think I am.
> *Alain-Rene Lesage*

Seligman argues that we can learn to be more optimistic by changing the way that we interpret the causes of good and bad events in our lives. He trains people to become optimists by using what he calls the ABC method.[47] This method involves keeping a record of adverse events and how you react to them. "A" refers to the adversity that occurs ("I forgot to mail the Federal Express package and the package arrived late."). "B" refers to the belief that you have about the causes of that adversity ("I was busy yesterday." or "I'm stupid."). "C" refers to the consequences of your beliefs ("I'll write a list of what I need to accomplish each day and keep it on my desk to refer to throughout the day." or "I can't do much to improve my memory because I'm incompetent." or "There's always too much work to do around here and I'll never be able to get it all done correctly, so I'll just do what I can."). By recording the ways that you interpret adverse situations, you can identify the kinds of explanations that you use, determine how they affect your attitudes and behaviors (e.g., are they likely to make you proactive or reactive), and then reframe negative interpretations into positive ones.

When Optimism Is Overrated

It's wise to keep in mind that optimism isn't right for all people and all situations. For example, for decades many researchers and other well-intentioned people have been advising people who are ill with serious diseases to be optimistic and to think positively because doing so would enhance quality of life and perhaps even promote longevity. However, recent research suggests that such claims may be doing some people a disservice (e.g., the "tyranny of positive thinking."). For some people with serious diseases, being asked to be optimistic may be perceived as an additional burden to carry (e.g., "I'm really sick and now you want me to see the bright side?"). Instead of recommending positive thinking, it is often more helpful to encourage the person who is sick to cope in familiar ways that have worked for the person in the past. To make this point, the *Wall Street Journal* quotes Dr. Jimmie Holland, chair of Psychiatric

Oncology at Memorial Sloan-Kettering Hospital in New York: "You can be as curmudgeonly or angry or whiny as you want and still survive cancer, as long as it doesn't cause your doctor to throw you out of the office." Note, however, that having a positive attitude does seem to motivate people who are ill to seek out help, eat the right foods, exercise, and follow their doctors' orders. In addition, certain kinds of stress can weaken immune responses, which can lead to an earlier death, so stressful coping methods are likely to be less effective than less stressful coping methods.[48]

Furthermore, researcher Julie Norem found that some people—particularly people who have an anxious temperament—tend to perform better when they are pessimistic rather than optimistic.[49] Describing her early research, Norem says:

> I found myself surrounded by people who were notably successful, by virtually any definition, and not notably optimistic. According to the research on optimism, this shouldn't be. Pessimism should produce negative results. When we set low expectations, we initiate a self-fulfilling prophecy. . . . There was plenty of research that indicated that people like them should be depressed, sickly, unmotivated, helpless, and hopeless—yet they certainly didn't seem that way to me . . . I asked how these people were able to do so well *despite* their pessimism—and that's when things got really interesting.[50]

Norem found that many people who would be described as pessimists often do well *because* of their pessimism. They assume that anything that can go wrong will go wrong, they overprepare, and they recheck their work over and over again. This turns out to be an effective coping mechanism that helps them harness their anxiety in ways that help them achieve the results they desire. Norem notes that telling defensive pessimists to relax and not worry can actually decrease their performance. She also notes that defensive pessimists whose anxiety moves them to take results-oriented action are not the same as pessimists whose attitudes paralyze them into inaction. Defensive pessimists should keep in mind that although their anxious behaviors (e.g., worrying, overplanning, and "sweating the small stuff") often helps them perform at their best, the same behaviors may be perceived as signs of incompetence or lack of confidence by others (even if this is not true). Therefore, the defensive pessimist needs to manage these perceptions, perhaps by fretting in private rather than in public. Furthermore, the defensive pessimist, particularly if he or she is a manager, needs to be sure that this behavior doesn't cross the line into micromanagement that can inhibit employees from doing their work effectively. Complete the assessment in Box 10-3 to determine whether you're a defensive pessimist.

WORK AND HEALTH

Your job can be helpful or hazardous to your psychological and physical health.[51] For example, in a study that focused on employees' relationships with their supervisors, researchers concluded that "individuals who perceived supervisory support as being low reported significantly higher physiological and social dysfunction symptoms."[52]

Not everybody's life is what they make it. Some people's life is what other people make it.
Alice Walker, Author

The amount of control and autonomy you have in your job can influence your psychological and physical well-being. For example, you are likely to experience more stress when the demands of your job are high, but you have little control over how you meet those demands. However, when your job demands are

BOX 10-3

Defensive Pessimism Questionnaire

Think of a situation where you want to do your best. It may be related to work, to your social life, or to any of your goals. When you answer the following questions, please think about how you prepare for that kind of situation. Rate how true each statement is for you.

Not at all true of me 1   2   3   4   5   6   7 Very true of me

_____   I often start out expecting the worst, even though I will probably do OK.

_____   I worry about how things will turn out.

_____   I carefully consider all possible outcomes.

_____   I often worry that I won't be able to carry through my intentions.

_____   I spend lots of time imagining what could go wrong.

_____   I imagine how I would feel if things went badly.

_____   I try to picture how I could fix things if something went wrong.

_____   I'm careful not to become overconfident in these situations.

_____   I spend a lot of time planning when one of these situations is coming up.

_____   I imagine how I would feel if things went well.

_____   In these situations, sometimes I worry more about looking like a fool than doing really well.

_____   Considering what can go wrong helps me to prepare.

To figure out where you stand, add your scores for all the questions. Possible scores range from 12 to 84, and higher scores indicate a stronger tendency to use defensive pessimism. If you score above 50, you would qualify as a defensive pessimist in Norem's studies. If you score below 30, you would qualify as a strategic optimist. If you score between 30 and 50, you may use both strategies. How you score will be influenced by the kind of situation you were thinking about when you answered the questions because you may use different strategies in different situations.

SOURCE: *Julie Norem. The Positive Power of Negative Thinking.*
Used with permission.

high and you have control over how you address those demands, you are likely to experience increased motivation.[53] Studies also conclude that "employees with little control over their working environment face a significantly higher risk of heart disease than those with authority to influence their job conditions."[54] Michael G. Marmot, the lead researcher in one study and director of the International Center for Health and Society at University College in London, says that the research suggests that the way that jobs are designed—in particular, the amount of autonomy they provide—"appears to make an important contribution" to employees' health risks.

However, your relationship with your supervisor and the design of your job aren't the only health risks you face at work. Your attitude toward your work—particularly your tendencies toward perfectionism and Type A behavior—can influence your psychological and physical health, as well as your job effectiveness.

Perfectionism

Up to a point, perfectionism can be an admirable personal quality.[55] Indeed, when not taken to the extreme, some characteristics associated with perfectionism, such as orderliness, setting high standards, and the pursuit of excellence, can contribute to high performance and career success.[56] However, research suggests that excessive perfectionism can interfere with your judgment, damage your interpersonal relationships, decrease your productivity, and harm your health.[57]

Researcher Robert Slaney and his colleagues explain that people who are excessively perfectionistic "have extremely high, perhaps unattainable, standards for their own performance" and "tend to see anything short of perfection as unacceptable."[58] Although effective perfectionists enjoy what they do and are able to turn their perfectionism on and off as appropriate, extreme perfectionists are prisoners of their perfection. Psychologist Asher Pacht describes the self-defeating bind perfectionists put themselves in:

> Their goals are so unrealistically high that they cannot possibly succeed. They are constantly frustrated by their need to achieve and their failure to do so. . . . For them, being perfect is the magic formula for success. Even when perfectionists do something successfully, they are seldom able to savor the fruits of their accomplishments. . . . The real tragedy lies in the fact that, for the perfectionist, achieving 95 percent or even 99 percent of the goal is usually seen as a failure because it is not perfect.[59]

Effective perfectionists know that perfectionism is critical when designing airbags for automobiles, yet less important when choosing the font for a PowerPoint presentation, and even less important when choosing the dessert for an informal dinner party. Extreme perfectionists, however, see most situations as needing the same level of effort because the perfectionism is tied to their self-worth rather than to the demands of the situation. In short, extreme perfectionists have a distorted view of what is the possible and desirable. Specifically, perfectionism becomes a problem when:

- It is excessive and uncontrollable.[60]
- It is rooted in an obsessive desire to be perfect to fulfill one's own needs (self-worth or fear of failure) rather than the demands of the situation.[61]
- It involves excessive rumination about failures to meet personal or social standards (perfectionists can't stop thinking about their performance because they feel it is never good enough).[62]
- It results in "all or none" thinking (perfectionists tend to see performance as "perfect" or "bad" with nothing in between).[63]

True perfection exists only in obituaries and eulogies. **Psychologist Asher Pacht, American Psychologist, April 1984**

Extreme perfectionism creates several problems. It can result in anxiety, depression, and life dissatisfaction.[64] It can harm relationships because extreme perfectionists tend to set unrealistically high standards for others and can be excessively critical when others don't meet their relentless and impossible standards. It can harm work performance because perfectionists may be more likely to micromanage their employees, less likely to delegate, and have a difficult time finishing projects because they are unable to complete assignments to their own satisfaction.[65] Perfectionists may be less likely to admit failure and take risks because their self-worth is tied to their desire to be perfect.[66] Notably, extreme perfectionists tend to become even more perfectionistic in ambiguous situations in which performance is hard to measure because they have difficulty judging when good is good enough.[67] Unfortunately, the perfectionists' unrealistic standards for themselves and others can undermine the success that they hope to achieve.[68]

Always remember: If you're alone in the kitchen and you drop the lamb, you can always just pick it up. Who's going to know? *Chef Julia Child, Esquire, June 2000*

Regardless of where the tendencies toward perfectionism come from, these tendencies can be tempered. Indeed, psychologist Pacht argues that "the very nature of the problem makes perfectionists good patients once the intellectual defenses are breached." Furthermore, Pacht argues, "For the vast majority of patients, 20 to 30 degrees of change is far more than enough."[69] To temper tendencies toward perfectionism, Pacht offers the following advice:[70]

- Do not attach all of your self-worth to your performance.
- Give yourself permission to be imperfect.
- Set reasonable, achievable goals.
- Be more discriminating about when orderliness and high standards are critical and when they are not.
- Choose some activities that you can do without aiming for perfection.

Finally, remember that our imperfections make us human. Says Pacht, "To be perfect would require an individual to be an automaton without charm. . . . The human quality in each of us comes from our imperfections, from all those 'defects' that give us our unique personalities and makes us real people."[71]

Type A Behavior

Type A behavior refers to a tendency toward extreme ambitiousness, achievement-striving, high-performance standards, competitiveness, impatience/irritability, anger/hostility, speed in speech and behavior, and desire to do multiple tasks simultaneously.[72] Researchers have concluded that some of these characteristics—ambitiousness, high achievement-striving, and high performance standards—are associated with higher performance in a variety of settings: college students' grades in schools as well as their tendency to finish college; insurance agents' number of policies sold; academics' research productivity in terms of quality and quantity of publications; and employees' job performance, career success, and job satisfaction.

Although Type A behavior can be problematic, many people with Type A characteristics are happy peak performers. Says psychology professor Charles Garfield:

> Although peak performers may work very long hours, they experience their work as replenishing and nourishing rather than toxic; . . . They know how to use time wisely and, unlike workaholics, they tolerate chaos and ambiguity and aren't paralyzed by perfectionism. . . . [Poor performers] often end up managing

details and are powerfully addicted to busyness. . . . Although peak performers are motivated by a commitment to their work, workaholics are motivated by a fear of failure.[73]

For workaholics, all the eggs of self-esteem are in the basket of work.
Judith M. Bard Wick, In Praise of Good Business

Researcher Cynthia Lee and her colleagues studied the relationship between achievement orientation and optimism. They concluded that when achievement-oriented people are also optimistic (i.e., they believe that they can make things go their way and that things will turn out well), they are likely to be more productive than others because they will continue to "strive, work hard, persist when faced with obstacles, and cope actively with problems they encounter, whereas pessimists would give up and turn away."[74]

Lee and her colleagues also found that the optimistic achievement-oriented people in their study reported less anxiety and fewer health problems, perhaps because they tend to deal with "stressful encounters by using problem-focused strategies such as formulating action plans, keeping their minds on the task at hand, and not thinking about the negative emotions with which the stress was associated. Pessimism was associated with emotion-focused coping strategies of denial and distancing, focusing on stressful feelings, and avoidance or disengaging from the goal with which the stressor was interfering."[75]

Some Type A characteristics—particularly impatience/irritability and hostility—do not predict productivity and are associated with health problems such as loss of appetite, depression, headaches, and heart disease.[76] Research suggests that anger and hostility are the "most toxic" and are most closely associated with coronary heart disease.[77] In a recent study of 13,000 people published in the British journal *Lancet*, the researchers concluded that anger-prone people are three times as likely to have heart attacks than those who are not.[78] And it appears that the link between anger and heart attacks exists for both men and women.

It's true that hard work never killed anybody, but I figure, why take the chance.   *Ronald Reagan, former U.S. president*

The bottom line on Type A behavior is this: When focused on achievement-striving, not taken to extremes, and coupled with optimism, Type A behavior can be good for the individual and the organization. But if the Type A behavior is driven by hostility, fear of failure, or an excessive need for control, it can be hazardous to your health and of little benefit, if any, to your productivity.

What Are the Organizational Consequences of Perfectionism and Type A Behavior?

On the surface, it may seem that people who are obsessed with perfection or achievement may be an asset to their organizations because of the extreme focus, energy, and time they are willing to commit to their work. Certainly, many organizations reward such behaviors even when they come at the expense of employees' health and personal commitments. However, Center for Creative Leadership researcher Joan Kofodimos makes a compelling case that such managers may in fact be detrimental to their organizations.[79]

Kofodimos cautions that these managers are often unconscious of what drives them to invest primarily in their work—which is often a desire to avoid intimacy—and thus are "likely to make decisions, take actions, and approach problems in ways intended to serve [their] inner needs." For example, rather than focus on the needs of the organization, colleagues, subordinates, and customers, they may make decisions and take actions designed to fulfill their ego needs, prove themselves, gain recognition, and avoid failure. They may also be "insensitive to the emotional life of coworkers—their needs, their feelings, and the things that motivate them" because they are insensitive to their own emotional needs. Unable to provide empathy, support, and compassion, such managers are unlikely to receive "wholehearted support and commitment" from their employees.[80] Notably, perfectionism and Type A behaviors tend to escalate in stressful and ambiguous situations, precisely when clear thinking, strong relationships, and organizational focus are critical.

The assessment in Box 10-3 can help you determine whether your work behaviors might be undermining your effectiveness, as well as your psychological and physical health.

INTEGRATING WORK AND FAMILY

For many managers today, one of their most pressing challenges is combining their responsibilities toward work and family in ways that enable them to contribute responsibly and wholeheartedly to both.[83–84] As most readers of this book know, this can be tricky to achieve. The difficulty is fueled by scary headlines such as "The Workaholic Generation,"[85] "Why Grade 'A' Executives Get an 'F' As Parents,"[86] "Can Your Career Hurt Your Kids?"[87] "Is Your Family Wrecking Your Career (and vice versa)?"[88] and "Why on Earth Should I Promote a Pregnant Woman?"[89] Although these headlines sell magazines and newspapers, they also contribute to many myths about working parents and make it difficult for parents to make thoughtful choices about how to live their lives. My goal in this section is to provide you with data and insights from research that can help you make thoughtful choices.

BOX 10-4

Ten Signs That Your Work Behaviors May Be Having a Negative Impact on Your Effectiveness as well as Psychological and Physical Health

1. Do you enjoy your work more than time with your family, friends, and loved ones?

2. Do you take your work with you on every vacation?

3. Do you check your e-mail every day, including weekends and vacations?

4. Are you able to distinguish between critical tasks that demand perfection and those for which perfection isn't important?

5. Do you worry about the future, even when everything seems to be going well?

6. Do you think about your work when others are talking to you about nonwork topics?

7. Do you assume that people who have other commitments besides work are less effective than those who don't?

8. Do you judge your own and other's work performance by face-time rather than results?

9. Is your commitment to your work hurting your personal relationships?

10. Do you often feel irritable and hostile at work or at home?

Ever since mothers began to join the paid workforce in droves, the academic and popular press have framed working parents (particularly working mothers) as an organizational and social problem: Can employees with responsibilities at home also fulfill their responsibilities at work? If both men and women are working, who is looking after children, aging parents, and the community? How do working parents manage the stress of combining work and family?

From the organizational perspective, supporting employee's family responsibilities is likely to be a good thing. Researchers are finding that organizations that implement and announce work-family initiatives reap rewards in terms of shareholder returns. In one study of *Fortune* 500 firms, "the share price reaction to the announcement of a work-family initiative over a three-day window [was] .39 percent. The average share price reaction occurring after legitimation of work-family initiatives was slightly higher at .48 percent. ... The average dollar value of the change in share price associated with a work-family initiative is approximately 60 million dollars per firm." The results were particularly strong in high-tech industries and industries that employ a high proportion of women.[90] Another study found that the average increase in share price for firms named "The Best Companies for Working Mothers" was .69 percent.[91] Yet another study of 527 U.S. firms found that organizations with extensive work-family policies "have higher levels of organizational performance, market performance, and profit-sales growth," especially in older firms and those that employ larger proportions of women.[92]

A growing number of researchers are finding that integrating work and family has positive outcomes for many employees as well.[93] Say researchers Samuel Aryee and Vivienne Luk, "The expanded meaning of a successful life ... suggests that the work-family interaction be conceptualized not as a social problem but instead as a source of meaning and identity to which adults balance commitment."[94] As many working parents have learned, both work and family can be a "major source of gratification."[95]

In the midst of a turbulent week, I enjoy nothing more than spending a few private moments with my family, especially my three grandkids. They are the perfect reminder of why I take my work so seriously.
Paul Wellstone, U.S. Senator, Utne Reader, March-April 1997

Indeed, having multiple roles—parent, caregiver, and employee—can be an effective coping mechanism.[96] For example, after a bad day at work, it can be a relief to come home to your family. After a frenetic morning getting children off to school, it can be relaxing to quietly read your e-mail at the office. If you stumble in one part of your life, there is another in which to find comfort. For example, a few years ago I told my daughter Julia, then 5 years old, that I had been fired as a waitress when I was a teenager. She sweetly replied, "You may not be a good waitress, but you're a really good mother."

Many questions come to mind regarding working parents. Who is happier, working mothers or stay-at-home mothers? Research suggests that it's not whether a woman stays at home or goes to work that determines her satisfaction, but whether the choice to stay home or work outside the home was her own.[97] What about the consequences of day care on children's well-being? As you will read later in this section, research suggests that high-quality day care can benefit parents and children, but poor-quality day care can adversely affect children's cognitive and social development. Barring abuse or neglect at day care, the most important influence on young children is their parents.[98]

In the rest of this chapter, I provide insights from research that can help you make informed choices about integrating your own work-family responsibilities—now or in the future—and help you enable your employees do the same. I provide a profile of the changing U.S. workforce. I then discuss the impact of working parents on organizations, particularly how work-family benefits such as flextime, condensed work weeks, and on-site day care centers influence organizations and how having children affects parents' career advancement. Finally, I present conclusions from the National Institute of Child Health and Development's study of more than 1,300 children on the impact of day care on children's development.

Who Works?

No matter how long you've gone on a wrong road, turn back.
Turkish Proverb

The following statistics from the U.S. government and other sources provide a useful picture of today's working American and their families.

- Work hours tend to be related to educational level. For both men and women, work hours tend to increase with education levels.[99] Note, however, that research suggests that people may overestimate the hours that they spend working, and the higher their education, the greater is their tendency to exaggerate work hours.[100]
- Working women significantly contribute to family income. Approximately 80 percent of families depend partly or completely on mothers' income.[101] In dual-earner married couples, wives earn approximately 35 percent of combined spousal income. In those couples in which both husbands and wives work full-time all year, wives earn approximately 41 percent of combined spousal income. More than 25 percent of working wives earn more than their husbands today, compared to 16 percent in 1981.[102]
- Fewer families follow the breadwinner dad and stay-at-home mom model; 51 percent of families with children have both spouses working. Indeed, the two-job family is now the majority.[103]
- More children are growing up with two full-time working parents. In 1970, approximately 13 percent of the families with children had both a full-time working mother and father. By the early 1990s, approximately 25 percent of families with children included both a full-time working mother and father.[104]
- 70 percent of married mothers and more than 75 percent of single mothers with children under 18 participates in the labor force.[105]
- For the first time in more than two decades, the percentage of new mothers returning to work is declining; 55 percent of women who gave birth between July 1999 and June 2000 returned to their jobs within a year, down from 59 percent in 1998.[106]
- 91 percent of people looking for jobs say they will look for positions that will make it easier for them to balance work and home.[107]
- 26 percent of men with children under 13 say they would take flexible work arrangements over advancement.[108]

- In one study, 59 percent of the women and 38 percent of the men reported that they have "no flexibility in determining the start and end times of their workday"; 52 percent of women and 39 percent of men reported they "don't have any say about decisions about their work."[109]
- Use of day care is increasing. Approximately 50 percent of all preschoolers "spend at least part of the day in the care of adults other than their parents."[110] Employment in private day care increased by more than 250 percent during the last 2 decades, adding approximately 400,000 new jobs to the economy.[111]
- High-quality day care is difficult to find. An estimated 1.1 million mothers 21 to 29 years old reported that the lack of affordable, quality child care was the reason that they "did not seek or hold a job in 1986."[112] A recent study conducted by the National Institute of Child Health and Development concluded that day care in the United States is "at best fair." In 1992, the American Public Health Association and the American Academy of Pediatrics developed standards for child-adult ratios, safety precautions, caregiver education, and intellectual stimulation. Most childcare settings in the United States still do not meet these standards.[113]
- There were 35 million people 65 years of age or older in the United States in 2000, a 12 percent increase since 1990 when there were 31.2 million people in this age category. Currently, the oldest old, those 85 years and older and who need the most care, make up the fastest growing portion of those 65 and older, increasing 38 percent from 3.1 million in 1990 to 4.2 million in 2000.[114]
- More than one-third of the world's oldest people (80 and above) live in three countries: China (11.5 million), the United States (9.2 million), and India (6.2 million). Women in this category outnumber men in most of the world's countries, with the exception of India, Iran, and Bangladesh.[115]
- A study of more than 6,000 adults in the United States found that 21 percent of adults are unpaid caregivers of adults over age 18. Of these caregivers, 69 percent take care of one person, 22 percent take care of two people, and 8 percent take care of three or more people; 6 percent take care of a spouse, 28 percent take care of a mother, 85 percent take care of a father, 7 percent take care of a mother-in-law, 2 percent take care of a father-in-law, and 6 percent take care of adult children. Thirty-one percent of the caretakers did so for 1 to 5 years, 15 percent for 5 to 9 years, and 14 percent for 10 years or more; 59 percent of the caretakers work while providing care. Nearly four in ten caregivers are men, and male caretakers are more likely than female caretakers to be working full or part time.[116]
- In approximately 22.4 million households, someone is caring for an elderly person, and almost 2.5 million of those caretakers are elderly themselves.[117]
- 4.5 percent of those 65 and older live in nursing homes. The percentages rise with age, with 18.2 percent of people 85 and older living in nursing homes.

The preceding data tell a compelling story of work and family at the beginning of the twenty-first century. Dual-earner and single-parent families are increasing, whereas the dad-at-work-and-mom-at-home families are decreasing.[118] The 2000 census showed that families with two parents and their children living in the same home are making a slight comeback, and there's a slight increase in the women who are choosing to stay home for at least a year after childbirth. Women at all income levels increasingly are a significant part of the workforce and contributors to family income. As the population around the world ages, both men and women are spending more time taking care of ill and aging relatives. Furthermore, women in the United States are bearing fewer children and having them at older ages, so families are smaller than in the past.[119] Many of these trends are being noted worldwide.[120] In Japan, for example, the percentage of married-couple households has increased since 1960, but "family patterns are changing: Sharp drops in fertility have led to much smaller families, and the 3-generation household, once the mainstay of Japanese family life, is in decline."[121]

Because of these changes in the family, employment, and income patterns of both men and women, the husband's career is less likely to take precedent over the wife's career today than in the past.[122] Consequently, power dynamics in families are shifting, as are purchasing patterns (particularly those related to clothing, food away from home, and day care) and the career and social expectations of boys and girls.[123] Research suggests that women still spend more time on family care such as child care, housework, and shopping. However, men are spending more time on these activities today than men did in the past, and women are spending less time on these activities today than women did in the past.[124]

We find delight in the beauty and happiness of children that makes the heart too big for the body. *Emerson*

Notably, some high-profile fathers have made headlines regarding their choices to take—or not take—paternity leaves after their children's birth. In March 2000, the *Wall Street Journal Europe* speculated whether U.K. Prime Minister Tony Blair would take a paternity leave after his wife gave birth to their fourth child. *The Mirror*, a newspaper that supports labor, wrote, "Show new dads the way, Tony." Cherie Booth, Blair's wife, publicly praised Finnish prime minister Paavo Lipponen's decision to take a 6-day parental leave after the birth of his second daughter in 2000 (he had taken time off after the birth of his first daughter in 1998, as well). Britain's top-selling newspaper, the *Sun*, suggested that Prime Minister Blair work from home after the birth of his child.[125] In the end, Blair decided not to take the time off, but the speculation prior to his decision suggests that the model of a "good father" is changing.

Legislation in the United States suggests that the model of a "good mother" may be changing as well. Researchers Phillip Cohen and Suzanne Bianchi explain:

> Originally, mothers who had lost the wage support of the father of their young children because of his early death (or who were indigent because the child's father deserted the family or was unwilling or unable to financially support his children) were supported, at least at some minimal level, so that they could remain out of the labor force to nurture and raise their children. The Personal Responsibility and Work Opportunity Reconciliation Act is based on a quite different model of motherhood: A "good mother" locates child care for her young children and finds a job, perhaps after some additional job training, by means of which she can financially support herself and her children.[126]

Unfortunately, high-quality day care is in short supply, and poor-quality day care can have a negative influence on children's intellectual and social development.

What Is the Impact of Working Parents on Organizations?

In response to these trends, many organizations are offering employees options such as flextime, condensed workweeks, telecommuting, and on-site day-care centers. Some companies, such as Baxter International, base managers' pay, in part, on how well they "provide a supportive work-life environment."[127] Approximately 17 percent of Baxter's employees work alternative work schedules. As mentioned earlier, firms that promote supportive work-life programs believe that doing so helps them recruit and retain high-quality employees, encourage more efficient ways of working, and enhance their public image as family-friendly social citizens. Supportive work-life benefits may be particularly important to organizations wanting to recruit and retain high-potential employees in tight labor markets.

Researcher Ellen Kossek and her colleagues, in their extensive reviews of the research on corporate work-life programs, conclude that supportive work-life programs indeed tend to enhance employee recruitment, retention, and job satisfaction. This is illustrated in the following story from *Fortune* magazine:

> Wilfredo Tejada, a 34-year-old former marketing vice president at Cupertino, California-based Net-Manage, calls it "psychological warfare." One day every other week he got to work at 10:00 A.M. because he sat in on his daughter's first-grade class. "The whole time I was there I was thinking I just can't wait to be done because I need to be back at the office," he says. And why was that? Because the boss arrived at 6:30 A.M. and sat in a glass office where he could monitor everyone's comings and goings. Tejada left 3 years ago to co-found an Internet company, Aeneid Corp., where he vows to let his employees come and go as they please, as long as they get their work done.[128]

Tejada, like many managers today, believes productivity is best measured through bottom-line results, not through face-time at the office. His view appears to be shared by others. Say James Levine, director of the Fatherhood Project at the Families and Work Institute, and Todd Pittinsky, "When IBM asked a group of employees to assess the factors that influenced their decision to stay with the company, work-family benefits ranked five overall, and second among the company's top performers. According to NationsBank chairman Hugh McColl, the bank's turnover rate is 50 percent less among the 35,000 employees who have taken advantage of programs designed to help balance work and family."[129]

Notably, unlike the studies cited earlier, Kossek and her colleagues found no consistent pattern of relationship between work-life benefits and employee productivity. This suggests that although these benefits are increasingly important for recruitment and retention, other factors such as job design and managerial support that enable work-life integration may be more likely to influence employee productivity.

What Is the Impact of Children on Working Parents' Careers?

Because working parents manage dual roles, it's reasonable to wonder whether they are at a disadvantage in terms of career progression. The research suggests a few trends worth paying attention to, whether you are a working parent or not. Based on a study of managers and professionals in the public sector, researcher Phyllis Tharenou concluded:

Married men and women, childless or not, with spouses employed or not, advance more than childless singles. This is not because of greater productivity in terms of human capital and despite married women's greater employment disruption. The reasons for the reduced advancement of childless singles are not clear, however. The reasons could be a perceived lack of financial need, not conforming to social expectations, or a lack of spousal support.[130]

> Our society has become schizophrenic. We praise people who want balance in their lives, but reward those who work themselves to death.
> *Roy Neel, President Clinton's former Deputy Chief of Staff, who had to carry a beeper 24 hours a day, quoted in Newsweek, March 6, 1995*

In addition, the fathers in the study with nonworking wives advanced more and were paid more than were the fathers with working wives, a conclusion that is supported by earlier studies as well.[131] Working mothers in dual-earner families advanced almost as much as other married women and more than childless single women. Furthermore, although being a single father seemed to negatively affect advancement, being a single mother didn't. Both men and women with nonemployed spouses tended to "benefit in terms of increased advancement," which suggests that stay-at-home spouses may provide valuable support to working spouses.

As mentioned earlier, Tharneou's study was based on managers and professionals in the public sector. Although we don't know whether the results would be similar in the private sector, they certainly provide food for thought.

What Is the Impact of Working Parents on Children?

Single mother Allison Anders, director of the films *Gas Food Lodging* and *Mi Vida Loca*, wanted to add the names of the nannies who took care of Ruben, her 7-year-old son, to the credits of her film *Grace of My Heart*. Initially, Universal Pictures resisted, saying "there was no precedent for it." But Anders convinced them by explaining, "I was flying back and forth between Los Angeles and New York; I couldn't have made the film without them." The studio finally agreed, and "Ruben's nannies got on-screen credit for their indispensable—if invisible—roles."[132]

Anders' story illustrates the gratefulness that many working parents feel toward the people who help them care for their loved ones. For many men and women, deciding the best way to integrate work and family—indeed, whether to attempt to do so at all—is a difficult and often gut-wrenching decision. Access to thoughtful information can make that decision a bit easier. As *Wall Street Journal* columnist and parent Sue Shellenbarger says, this is "high time for an era of empowered child-care consumerism."[133]

> In the small matters, trust the mind; in the large ones, the heart.
> *Sigmund Freud, father of Psychoanalysis*

The information presented in this section is primarily based on conclusions from the National Institute of Child Health and Human Development's (NICHD) study of a diverse group of more than 1,300 children. Begun in 1991, this project is headed by Dr. Sarah L. Friedman and represents the largest and most comprehensive study done on the impact of child care on children in the United States. The children, who were less than 1 month old at the beginning of the research, come from all across the nation and from different income levels.

Researchers from fourteen universities are participating in the study. They are focusing on the impact of child care on the children's cognitive development (ability to perform at appropriate levels of intellectual development), social development (ability to get along with others), and attachment to their mothers. Researchers believe that children's early attachment to their mothers is important because it is "considered the cornerstone of children's subsequent development. . . . Infants with secure attachments to their mothers are found to be better able to solve problems, to explore, and to be independent in toddler years. In the preschool years, securely attached children tend to be more constructively involved at school, to play better with other children, and to be cooperative and compliant with adults."[134] The results of the study are summarized here.

Cognitive Development

Children in high-quality day care tended to score higher on tests of school readiness and language comprehension than did those in low-quality day care. Indeed, on average, children in day care settings that met all the standards developed in 1992 by the American Public Health Association and the American Academy of Pediatrics performed at above-average levels. On average, the children in day care settings that did not meet those standards performed at below-average levels. The acceptable standards include "child/staff ratios (3:1 for infants, 4:1 for 2-year-olds, 7:1 for 3-year-olds); group sizes (6 infants, or 8 2-year-olds, or 14 3-year-olds); and teacher training (some post-secondary training in child development and early childhood education or a related field)."[135]

Social Behavior

"Children's social behavior is influenced by the quality of the day care, the number of children in the day care, the consistency of the day care, and the mother's psychological well-being and behavior toward the child."[136] Specifically, children who were in high-quality day care (those that met the guidelines described earlier) and in day care with at least three other children were more socially competent and had fewer behavioral problems at ages 2 and 3 than those who weren't. "At age 2, children who had been in a number of different day care arrangements showed more problem behavior than did children who had been in fewer day care arrangements." The mothers' attitudes and behaviors toward their children appear to have a greater influence on children's social competence than does the children's day care arrangement.

Attachment

"Child-care experience has no discernible influence on the security of children's attachments to their mothers by age 3. Earlier reported findings from the study indicated that more experience with child care and lower quality child care in infancy were only related to secure infants' attachments to their mothers when mothers were relatively insensitive to their infants. In general, the education of the mothers was more strongly related to positive qualities of maternal care than was the amount or quality of child care. However, mothers were slightly more positive and supportive with their children when less child care was used or when child-care quality was higher."[137]

In the 1999–2000 school year, the children were in the third grade, and the researchers were studying the longer term consequences of day care, although the results are not yet available as of this writing.[138] If you want to stay abreast of their findings, go to the NICHD Web site at www.nichd.nih.gov/new/releases/news.cfm for updates on the research.

Some researchers remain skeptical of the positive effects of day care on children, particularly when it is used when children are less than 1 year old and when it is used extensively (more than 30 hours a week). Researcher Jay Belsky, who has conducted many studies on the impact of day care on children, argues that the less time a mother spends with her child in the first year of life, the less time she has to "learn the baby's signaling patterns and rhythms" and the less able she is to respond to the child appropriately and with sensitivity.[139]

Nobody has ever before asked the nuclear family to live all by itself in a box the way we do. With no relatives, no support, we've put it in an impossible situation.
Margaret Mead, 1978

Belsky cites studies, including his own, that suggest that children who were in early and extensive child care tended to be slightly more aggressive and disobedient than those who did not. However, he notes that these effects are small, that these studies typically did not consider the quality of the day care arrangements, and that most of these studies had fewer and less diverse families involved in the study than did the NICHD research (although the NICHD found a small but significant relationship between hours in day care and aggressiveness). Although Belsky remains reasonably cautious about the use of early and extensive day care, he concludes:

> At the same time, however, my reading of the evidence does not lead me to conclude that day care, even when provided to our youngest citizens, is inherently bad. Too much evidence indicates just the opposite when children experience good-quality care. Day care works when children receive care from individuals who will remain with them for a relatively long period of time (low staff turnover), who are knowledgeable about child development, and who provide care that is sensitive and responsive to their individualized needs.[140]

In general, researchers agree that day care can have a positive or negative effect on children's well-being and that the decision to use day care should be made thoughtfully. Furthermore, they believe that many factors influence the well-being of children of working parents, including the following:

Quality of Day Care

If our American way of life fails the child, it fails us all. *Pearl S. Buck*

One of the most important conclusions of the NICHD study is that high-quality day care can provide benefits to children, and low-quality day care can harm children's cognitive and social development. Say the researchers, "when child-care providers talk to children, encourage them to ask questions, respond to children's questions, read to them, challenge them to attend to others' feelings, and to develop different ways of thinking—children's language abilities and thinking skills are better than under conditions that are less enriched."[141]

Unfortunately, the researchers in the NICHD study concluded that only about 10 percent of the infant day care settings of children in the study met standards set by the American Public Health Association and the American Academy of Pediatrics, and 34 percent of the day care settings for 3-year-olds met these standards. Furthermore, only three of the fifty states have child care regulations that meet the APHA/AAP standards for child/staff ratios for toddlers, and only nine states have regulations that meet the recommended standards for teaching training for infants.[142]

In general, researchers who study the impact of child care on children's well-being argue for increasing the quality of day care available to parents in the United States (by promoting high wages for day care employees, setting and enforcing high standards for day care, and providing family leave for mothers and fathers so that they have more choices in how they manage the early months of a child's life). Says Ellen Galinsky, president of the Families and Work Institute in New York, "We know how to provide quality child care. We fail not because of a lack of knowledge but because of a lack of will."[143]

Parents' Personality, Self-Esteem, Education, and Income

Parents have a critical influence on their children's development, regardless of the quality of day care or the amount of hours the children spend in day care. For example, research suggests that working parents' self-esteem, education, and income influence the quality of care that they provide for their children. Education and income may be important because they enable parents to find and afford higher quality day care.

Marital/Relationship Quality

Parents who are supportive toward each other and who work well together as co-parents are more likely to provide high-quality care for their children.[144]

Choice

Try this bracelet: If it fits you, wear it; but if it hurts you, throw it away no matter how shiny.
Kenyan Proverb, 73

Research suggests that whether a mother *chooses* to work outside the home or stay at home to care for the children influences her emotional well-being, which in turn influences her child-rearing practices and the children's well-being.[145] In other words, it's not whether mothers work that makes them happy, but whether the choice to work or stay home was their own.

Parents' Work Experiences

For fathers and mothers, the quality of their work—such as supervisor sensitivity, interesting work, job autonomy, and schedule flexibility—affects their ability to be responsive and nurturing toward their children. This, in turn, can affect their children's cognitive skills and social behavior.[146] For example, in a study on the effects of fathers' employment on child development, researchers Wendy Stewart and Julian Barling concluded that a father's job decision latitude (e.g., "On my job, I am given a lot of freedom to decide how I do my work."), job demands (e.g., "My job requires working very fast."), job insecurity (e.g., "I can be sure of my present job as long as I do good work."), and interrole conflict (e.g., "My job takes up time I'd like to spend with my family.") can influence child outcomes such as "school-related competence" and social behavior.[147]

Ohio State University researchers Toby Parcel and Elizabeth Menaghan concluded that children with mothers "with more complex, responsible jobs have better home environments and in turn behave better and perform better over time on verbal, math and reading tests, after controlling for mothers' own education and mental skills."[148] University of California Irvine researcher Ellen Greenberger and others have concluded, "Parents with more stimulating, challenging jobs are warmer, less harsh and more responsive in their parenting."[149] Researcher Stewart Friedman and his colleagues concluded that children whose mothers have more control over their day-to-day work tend to have fewer behavior problems.[150]

As you probably noticed in the previous section, researchers have paid more attention to the impact of working mothers on their children than to the impact of working fathers on their children. This is a problem because fathers increasingly are participating in the day-to-day care of their children and feel the pleasures and stresses of managing their dual roles as fathers and employees, and it encourages organizations to focus on working mothers' needs more so than those of working fathers.[151]

What Do Children Say About Their Working Parents?

In a landmark study published in 1999, Ellen Galinsky, president of the Families and Work Institute, asked more than 1,000 children between the third and twelfth grade what they think about their working parents. The results: "Having a working mother is never once predictive of how children assess their mother's parenting skills on a series of 12 items that are strongly linked to children's healthy development, school readiness, and school success."[152] Galinsky also noted, "Children with employed mothers and those with mothers at home do not differ on whether they feel they have too little time with Mom."[153] This is supported by research by Sandra Hofferth at the University of Michigan Institute for Social Research, who concludes that working parents spend approximately 19 hours a week engaged with their children compared to 22 hours a week for families with stay-at-home mothers.[154]

Although 56 percent of the parents thought that their children would benefit from spending more time together, 67 percent of the children said that they spent enough time with their mothers, and 60 percent said they spent enough time with their fathers. The number of hours that parents spend with their children (within reason— remember that 33 percent of the children didn't feel they spent enough time with their mothers, and 40 percent felt the same about their time with their fathers) seems less important to children than the parents' attitudes and behavior during that time. For example, more than 44.5 percent of the children felt that their time with their mother is rushed, and 37 percent felt the same about the time with their father.[155]

> It doesn't matter who my father was; it matters who I remember he was.
> *Anne Sexton*

Galsinky concluded, "Although the amount of time children and parents spend together is very important, most children don't want more time with their parents. Instead, they give their mothers and fathers higher grades if the time they do spend together is not rushed but focused and rich in shared activities."[156] And, it's the simple things—not expensive vacations or elaborate hobbies—that seem to matter most. The children's responses suggest that eating meals together is particularly important, as are activities such as playing games or sports, doing homework, and watching television with parents. Children whose parents participate in these activities with them are more likely to see their parents as "putting families first" and being able to effectively manage both work and family.

> There is always one moment in childhood when the door opens and lets the future in.
> *Graham Greene, Novelist*

Less than 43 percent of the children in Galinsky's study "think their parents like their work a lot, compared with 62.5 percent of parents who say they do."[157] It is not surprising that the children who hear good things about work from their parents are more likely to want to manage work and family like their parents do. In addition, the children said that they learn more about their mothers' work than their fathers' work. Many parents, it seems, are less than inspiring when it comes to setting positive examples for the next generation of workers. When parents don't talk about their work, complain about their work, or say things like "I wish I didn't have to go to work today" (perhaps because they feel guilty about leaving the children), they may be intentionally or unintentionally giving children a negative impression of work.

The next generation of workers will be an interesting one, and their choices will be based, in part, on our choices and the way that we talk about our choices. Galinsky notes, "Few children want to work harder than their employed mothers and fathers. Only 11 percent of children want to work more than their fathers do. Children whose fathers work the longest and hardest are the most likely to want to work less than their fathers. Only 25 percent of children want to work more than their mothers do now."[158]

> Each child is an adventure into a better life—an opportunity to change the old pattern and make it new. *Hubert H. Humphrey, Former U.S. vice president*

Boys are more likely than girls to favor the father-as-breadwinner and mother-at-home lifestyle. Says Galinsky, "Almost twice as many boys as girls strongly agree with the idea that men should earn the money, and women should take care of the home and children. Forty-two percent of girls in the seventh through twelfth grades agree that children do just as well if mothers have the primary responsibility for earning the money, and fathers have the primary responsibility for caring for the children. Only 25 percent of boys agreed with that statement."[159] These are going to be very interesting relationships when these children grow up.

In short, it seems that the issue isn't whether parents work, but how parents feel about their work, how they talk with their children about their work, and how they use the time that they have with their children. Parenting skills seem to matter most of all. Galinsky identified eight critical parenting skills from her research:[160]

- *Make the child feel important and loved.* To reinforce this point, Galinsky quotes developmental psychologist Urie Bronfenner, "In order to thrive, every child needs someone who is crazy about him or her."[161]
- *Respond to the child's cues.* This means being emotionally and intellectually responsive to the child. Children who feel listened and responded to are better able to cope with stress.
- *Accept the child for who he or she is, but expect success.* Children see themselves as others see them, so the more you believe in a child, the more that child will believe in himself or herself.
- *Promote strong values.* This means talking and living the values that are important to the family.
- *Use constructive discipline.* Such discipline is designed to "teach children to internalize limits rather than to humiliate, hurt, or demean them."
- *Provide routines and rituals.* Routines associated with daily activities such as waking up, eating, playing, and bedtimes help children feel that their world is orderly, consistent, and predictable. Engaging in family rituals such as

singing special songs, reading favorite books, watching television shows together, and participating in birthday and holiday traditions help children develop memories and a family identity.
- ***Be involved in the child's education.***   Children's academic achievement is higher when parents participate in their education, both at the school and at home.
- ***Be there for the child.***   Children want to know that they can count on their parents to be there for them when they need them, particularly when they are sick or for important events.

My conclusion from the research on working parents is this: Sure, your career can hurt your kids if you place them in low-quality child care or if you have a nasty job that makes you tired, cranky, or distant from your children when you come home. Your career can also hurt your kids if you're a high-achieving perfectionist that treats your home like an office and your children like underachieving mini-employees. But if you are a loving and well-meaning parent who understands what children need to be happy and develop into loving and responsible adults, are emotionally and physically accessible to your children, have a job that you willingly chose and enjoy, have a supportive partner, and have high-quality day care for your children, research suggests that you can relax, knowing that you can make a contribution to your work and be a loving and competent parent as well. For a summary of the research on the impact of working parents on children's well-being, see Figure 10-2.

If you want to make integrating work and family easier for all working parents, be a supportive boss and coworker and support policies that promote high-quality day care (e.g., higher wages for day care employees and enforced standards for teacher/child ratios, group size, and teacher training). The next generation (who will take care of you in your old age and shape future policies on elder care) will thank you for it.

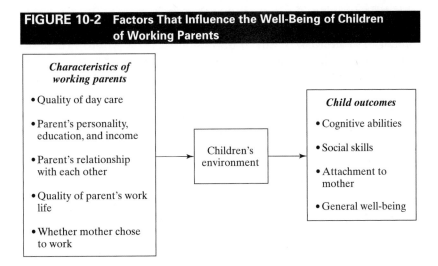

FIGURE 10-2   Factors That Influence the Well-Being of Children of Working Parents

CONCLUSION

Today, the materials and skills from which a life is composed are no longer clear. It is no longer possible to follow the paths of previous generations. ... Many of the most basic concepts we use to construct a sense of self or the design of a life have changed their meanings. *Mary Catherine Bateson, Composing a Life*

Crafting a life at the beginning of the twenty-first century requires that we let go of many old assumptions about success (e.g., the belief that money will make us happy), productivity (e.g., the belief that face-time at the office equals bottom-line results), happy families (the dad-at-work and mom-at-home model), and work-life balance (the belief that work-life balance is a desirable and achievable goal).

Our organizational and social worlds are not the same as those of our parents' generation. For that matter, our organizational and social worlds have changed considerably in just the last decade and no doubt will change considerably in the next. Consequently, many of the rules and tools that people used to craft a life in the past are less useful today.

Furthermore, we have more choices today in terms of the kinds of lives we can live. We can work from the office, the home, or the beach. We can meet with colleagues and customers face-to-face or conduct our business through the Internet. We can be full-fledged employees or offer our services as contractors, working on our own time and terms. We can be working parents or stay-at-home parents (or working-stay-at-home parents). And because we're more likely to live longer than our counterparts in the past, we will have many opportunities to change our minds and make new choices. At least one thing won't change: No matter how long we live, life will still be short enough to inspire us to make thoughtful choices.

There is no one formula for a good life. What works for one person may not work for another, and what works at one stage of one's life may not work at another stage. The late psychologist Viktor Frankl explained:

> What matters, therefore, is not the meaning of life in general but rather the specific meaning of a person's life at a given moment. To put the question in general terms would be comparable to the question posed to a chess champion, "Tell me, Master, what is the best move in the world?" There simply is no such thing as the best or even a good move apart from a particular situation in a game and the particular personality of one's opponent.[162]

More recently, researcher Julie Norem explains, "We can't casually adopt another person's strategy and expect it to work for us, any more than we can put their shoes on and expect to be comfortable . . . Indeed, we may find blisters instead of bliss if we aren't careful to equip ourselves properly."[163]

All growth is a leap in the dark, a spontaneous unpremeditated act without benefit of experience. *Henry Miller, U.S. author*

As I noted in the first chapter of this book, successful careers are built on characteristics that make us more open to our experiences and more flexible in response: self-awareness, conscientiousness, a fluid rather than concrete view of intelligence, proactivity, a learning orientation, creativity (a willingness to improvise), social skills, practical skills, and positive emotions. These characteristics are even more important when crafting a life because life—even more so than work—is ambiguous. Furthermore, our life goals are often less clear than our day-to-day work goals, and we often don't get feedback from our life decisions until years after we make them. For example, we don't know if the choices we make about our careers or raising our children are the right ones until years after we make our initial choices. All we can do is try to be thoughtful, consider the consequences of our decisions, and be willing to adapt as we learn from our experience and as we face the inevitable and unpredictable twists and turns of our life.

I'd like to end this book with one final piece of advice. Several years ago, I was helping out in my spunky daughter Leah's kindergarten classroom, and I heard a little girl ask the teacher, "Mrs. Weinmann, do dreams come true?" Without skipping a beat, the teacher replied, "Well, a dream can become a wish, and a wish can become a plan, and a plan can come true." The teacher responded so quickly and with such caring certainty that I felt as though she had heard and answered this question for kindergartners many times. And I thought her words would be a fine way to end this book, because I hope this book has given you many ideas that can help you make your dreams come true.

CHAPTER SUMMARY

People who are happy are generally and genuinely pleased with their lives. Research suggests that money predicts only about 2 to 5 percent of one's happiness. Gender, race, and age are also poor predictors of happiness, as are significant life events such as winning the lottery and handicapping accidents. What does predict happiness? Self-esteem, temperament, relationships, faith, optimism, a satisficing rather than maximizing orientation to decisions, having a sense of control over the parts of life that are important to us, and having goals that are congruent with each other.

Most people enjoy working because it fulfills basic human needs for identity ("I am a manager"), belonging (we tend to work with others), competence (we tend to learn and stretch our skills when we work), consistency and control (we tend to have routines at work), and making a difference (sometimes we can use our work to make an impact on the world).

We feel flow (optimal experience or peak performance) when we are fully engaged in doing something that we believe is important, when we have clear goals, rules, and feedback, when we can concentrate on the task without distraction, when

we have the skills to do the job yet feel challenged to learn new skills, and when we have control over how we do the task.

People who are optimistic have a positive bias toward themselves and the world. They see themselves as more competent than they are and the world as a more positive place than data would suggest. Research suggests that optimists tend to be happier, healthier, and more effective because they are likely to set higher goals for themselves, be persistent, take risks, reward themselves, and cope better with stress. Optimism can be learned by paying attention to the ways that we interpret the positive and negative events in our lives. However, optimism can sometimes be overrated. Recent research has shown that some people—defensive pessimists—tend to assume the worst and then plan to avoid the worst outcome, and thus enhance their performance through their excessive planning. Furthermore, it's unclear whether encouraging people to "think positive" when they are ill is always helpful, especially if they tend to have a history of success with other types of coping mechanisms.

Your job can affect your health. A bad relationship with a supervisor can increase your stress. A lack of control over your work not only increases stress, but research suggests that it can increase your risk of heart attacks.

Both perfectionism and Type A behavior can positively influence your effectiveness and career when they are not extreme. However, extreme perfectionism and Type A behavior (particularly the hostility component of Type A behavior) can negatively influence your effectiveness, psychological well-being, and physical health. Notably, perfectionism and Type A behavior can become more extreme in ambiguous and high-pressured situations, precisely when they can be most damaging.

Data from the U.S. Department of Labor suggest that the work patterns of the U.S. workforce have changed dramatically in the past 40 years. Women at all income levels are working more than in the past. The father-at-work and mother-at-home family is on the decline. There are more dual-career couples, single-parent families, women as primary breadwinners in families, and women working full-time who have young children. More than one-quarter of working women earn more than their husbands. An increasing number of women and men are taking care of ill and aging adults.

In a study of managers and professionals in the public sector, the researcher found that married men with children tend to earn more than married men without children, single men, and single fathers (who tend to earn less than the others). Married women with children tend to earn almost as much as married women without children, and more than unmarried women. Although being a single father seemed to negatively affect advancement, being a single mother didn't. Both married men and women with spouses at home advanced more than others. This suggests that a spouse at home provides valuable resources to the working spouse.

Many working parents must rely on day care to help take care of their children's needs while they are working. Research suggests that high-quality day care can benefit children's intellectual and behavioral development and interferes little, if at all, with children's feelings of attachment to their mothers. However, poor-quality day care can harm children's intellectual and behavioral development. Unfortunately, day care in the United States is considered by many to be "fair," at best.

Working parents' attitudes and behaviors influence their children's development more than day care does (unless day care is of very poor quality). Several factors influence parents' ability to positively influence their children: parents' self-esteem, income, and education; job quality; marital relationship quality; and whether the mother made her own decision about whether to work or not.

FOOD FOR THOUGHT

1. What is the most useful thing you learned in this chapter, and why?
2. Based on the personal strategies described in this chapter, what can you do to enhance the quality of your life (e.g., happiness, health, and longevity)? Make at least one of these changes and note any benefits and progress you make.
3. Using the assessment in Box 10-2, assess your day-to-day work (your job, classes, family care-taking). Is your day-to-day work high, medium, or low on flow? What parts of your work did you rate highest and lowest? Why? What can you do to increase flow in your day-to-day life? If you are responsible for others, what can you do to increase flow in their day-to-day life?
4. Tom and Kate Chappell founded Tom's of Maine, which produces organic toothpaste and other personal care products because they wanted to give people organic personal care options. John Scully left his job as president of Pepsi-Cola to become CEO of Apple Computer because he felt that "personal computers could change the way we live and

learn."[164] What makes your day-to-day work—at the workplace, at school, or at home— meaningful?

5. If you could hire a perfectionist or someone with Type A personality characteristics, would you want to? Why or why not? Would you want to work for a perfectionist? Why or why not? What professions do you think would benefit from having a perfectionist, which would have no impact, and which would be harmed? Why?

6. Take the assessment in Box 10-3 to identify whether you tend to be more like a strategic optimist or defensive pessimist. Under what conditions does your general strategy work for you? Under what conditions is it a problem?

7. Take the assessment in Box 10-7, "The Polychronicity Scale: How Many Things Do You Like to Do at Once?" Are you more monochronic (lower scores) or polychronic (higher scores) in your use of time? In what situations is your style helpful in managing your life? Not helpful?

8. Assume you are managing a high-performing working parent. The employee missed a key deadline recently and seemed unprepared for a presentation yesterday. Otherwise, the employee's work continues to be among the best in the department. You've heard that the employee recently started caring for an elderly and ailing parent at home. You are about to meet with the employee for a performance review. What will you say? Why? What kind of support can you offer the employee if needed?

9. If you want to increase your chances of living a long and healthy life, what changes do you need to make in your everyday life? What one change will you make immediately and why? How will you ensure that you maintain this change? Take either the www.realage.com or www.livingto100.com assessment to identify key areas that you can attend to that are likely to enhance your health and longevity.

BOX 10-5

A Note on Sleep Deprivation

Many people work long hours because of the demands of the job. Others do so because organizations reward face-time at the office. And others do so because of professional norms, as is the case with physicians and pilots. Regardless of the reason people end up working with too little sleep, research suggests that sleep deprivation can result in decreased alertness, slowed thinking, lapses in attention, and decreased motivation. Researcher Gregory Belenky and his colleagues who study performance of military personnel during combat operations concluded, "Sleep deprivation impairs alertness, cognitive performance, and mood. The ability to do useful mental work declines 25 percent for every successive 24 hours that an individual is awake. . . . Sleep deprivation degrades the most complex useful functions, including the ability to understand, adapt, and plan under rapidly changing situations."[81]

Sleep deprivation and disruption can result in what researchers call the "speed-accuracy trade-off."[82] This means that in tasks involving attention, reasoning abilities, and reaction time, a tired person is likely to be accurate or fast, but is unlikely to be both. The risks of sleep deprivation increase in nonroutine situations.

SOURCE: Belenky, Gregory et al. 1994. "The Effects of Sleep Deprivation on Performance during Continuous Combat Operations." In Bernadette M. Marriott (ed.). *Food Components to Enhance Performance*. Washington, DC: National Academy Press.

BOX 10-6

Steps to a Long Life: Lessons from Centenarian Studies

Thomas Perls, MD, and lead researcher on the New England Centenarian Studies, says that extreme longevity—living for a century or more—is rare and that most people who live this long probably have "genetic rocket boosters" that enable them to avoid age-related diseases such as diabetes, Alzheimer's, and cardiovascular disease. About 85 percent of the centenarians are women and 15 percent are men, but the men who reach extreme old age tend to function better than the women do. But Perls believes that most of us have the genetic makeup that would enable us to live to approximately 85 years old in good health. Whether we reach or exceed this age depends, in large part, on how we spend our everyday lives. The following advice is based in large part on what researchers have learned in the New England Centenarian Studies, the Georgia Centenarian Study, and the Okinawa Centenarian Study.

- *Have good eating habits. Eat lots of colorful fruits and vegetables.* Cut down on fatty and salty foods. Eat lean meats, poultry, and fish. Eat whole grains. And eat less. In the study of Okinawan centenarians, the centenarians tended to eat about 500 fewer calories less than most people.
- *Have good health care habits.* See your physician regularly to identify and treat any problems that may exist. Be sure you get your vaccinations. Although it may seem trite, evidence is growing that flossing your teeth may increase your longevity because flossing may be related to better cardiovascular health.
- *Stay physically active and engaged.* People's bodies age in part because of lack of exercise.

- *Cope well with stress.* Although the centenarians studied didn't have fewer stressful events in life (some had very traumatic experiences), they did cope well with these events. They faced their problems, grieved, accepted their losses, forgave themselves and others, made adjustments, moved on, and didn't dwell on the past.
- *Stay intellectually engaged.* Everything from doing crossword puzzles to writing helps.
- *Have an optimistic attitude, especially toward aging.* In one study, people who had an optimistic attitude toward aging lived 7.1 years longer than those who did not.
- *Socialize with a supportive network of family and friends.* Social connections help fight depression and may enhance the body's immune system.

Which parts of the world have the longest and healthiest average life expectancy? The World Health Organization now ranks countries not by life expectancy only but by healthy life expectancy. The new ratings reflect "the expected number of years to be lived in what might be termed the equivalent of full health. The top countries are Japan (74.5), Australia (73.2), France (73.1), Sweden (73.0), Spain (72.8), Italy (72.7), Greece (72.5), Switzerland (72.5), Monaco (72.4), and Andorra (72.3). The United States ranks 24, which is low among wealthy nations due to several factors: many people living in conditions that are equivalent to those "more characteristic of a poor developing country rather than a rich industrialized one," the HIV epidemic, cancers related to tobacco, a high coronary disease rate, and fairly high levels of violence. You can find the full rankings at www.photius.com/rankings/health_life_table2.html.

Two useful Web sites that have free on-line assessments that will help you identify whether your everyday attitudes and behaviors are increasing or decreasing your chances of living a long and healthy life are: www.realage.com and www.livingto100.com.

BOX 10-7

The Polychronicity Scale: How Many Things Do You Like to Do at Once?

Please use the following scale to indicate the extent to which you agree or disagree with each of the 10 statements by circling the appropriate number for each statement.

I like to juggle several activities at the same time.

Strongly Disagree	Somewhat Disagree	Slightly Disagree	Neutral	Slightly Agree	Somewhat Agree	Strongly Agree
1 pt	2 pts	3 pts	4 pts	5 pts	6 pts	7 pts

I would rather complete an entire project every day than complete parts of several projects.

Strongly Disagree	Somewhat Disagree	Slightly Disagree	Neutral	Slightly Agree	Somewhat Agree	Strongly Agree
7 pts	6 pts	5 pts	4 pts	3 pts	2 pts	1 pt

I believe people should try to do many things at once.

Strongly Disagree	Somewhat Disagree	Slightly Disagree	Neutral	Slightly Agree	Somewhat Agree	Strongly Agree
1 pt	2 pts	3 pts	4 pts	5 pts	6 pts	7 pts

When I work by myself, I usually work on one project at a time.

Strongly Disagree	Somewhat Disagree	Slightly Disagree	Neutral	Slightly Agree	Somewhat Agree	Strongly Agree
7 pts	6 pts	5 pts	4 pts	3 pts	2 pts	1 pt

I prefer to do one thing at a time.

Strongly Disagree	Somewhat Disagree	Slightly Disagree	Neutral	Slightly Agree	Somewhat Agree	Strongly Agree
7 pts	6 pts	5 pts	4 pts	3 pts	2 pts	1 pt

(continued)

Box 10-7 (*cont.*)

I believe people do their best work when they have many tasks to complete.

Strongly Disagree	Somewhat Disagree	Slightly Disagree	Neutral	Slightly Agree	Somewhat Agree	Strongly Agree
1 pt	2 pts	3 pts	4 pts	5 pts	6 pts	7 pts

I believe it is best to complete one task before beginning another.

Strongly Disagree	Somewhat Disagree	Slightly Disagree	Neutral	Slightly Agree	Somewhat Agree	Strongly Agree
7 pts	6 pts	5 pts	4 pts	3 pts	2 pts	1 pt

I believe it is best for people to be given several tasks and assignments to perform.

Strongly Disagree	Somewhat Disagree	Slightly Disagree	Neutral	Slightly Agree	Somewhat Agree	Strongly Agree
1 pt	2 pts	3 pts	4 pts	5 pts	6 pts	7 pts

I seldom like to work on more than a single task or assignment at the same time.

Strongly Disagree	Somewhat Disagree	Slightly Disagree	Neutral	Slightly Agree	Somewhat Agree	Strongly Agree
7 pts	6 pts	5 pts	4 pts	3 pts	2 pts	1 pt

I would rather complete parts of several projects every day than complete an entire project.

Strongly Disagree	Somewhat Disagree	Slightly Disagree	Neutral	Slightly Agree	Somewhat Agree	Strongly Agree
1 pt	2 pts	3 pts	4 pts	5 pts	6 pts	7 pts

Now add your points and divide the total by 10. Then plot your score on the scale below.

1.0	2.0	3.0	4.0	5.0	6.0	7.0

You can compare your score with the mean score of 3.720, marked on the scale with an H (standard deviation = 1.06) from 1,190 respondents in a study of a St. Louis area hospital system.

SOURCE: Allen C. Bluedorn, Thomas J. Kallath, Michael J. Strube, and Gregg D. Martin. 1998. "Polychronicity and the Inventory of Polychronic Values (IPV). The Development of an Instrument to Measure a Fundamental Dimension of Organizational Culture." *Journal of Managerial Psychology*, 14(3): 205–230. Reprinted with permission of MCB University Press.

ENDNOTES

1. Diener, Ed, Richard Lucas, and Shigehiro Oishi. 2002. "Subjective Well-Being." In C. R. Snyder and Shane Lopez (eds.). *Handbook of Positive Psychology*. Oxford: Oxford University Press, 63–73.

2. Myers, David, and Ed Diener. 1995. "Who Is Happy?" *Psychological Science*, 6(1): 10–19.

3. Ibid.

4. Myers, David. 1992. *The Pursuit of Happiness*. New York: Hearst Corporation.

5. Myers, David, and Ed Diener. 1995. "Who Is Happy?" *Psychological Science*, 6(1): 10–19.

6. Ibid.

7. Ahuvia, Aaron C., and Douglas Friedman. 1998. "Income, Consumption, and Subjective Well-Being: Toward a Composite Macromarketing Model." *Journal of Macromarketing*. Fall: 153–168.

8. Graef, R., Gianinno McManama, and Mihaly Csikszentmihalyi. 1981. "Energy Consumption in Leisure and Perceived Happiness." In J. D. Clayton and others (eds.). *Consumers and Energy Conservation*. New York: Praeger; cited in Ahuvia, Aaron, and Douglas Friedman. 1998. "Income, Consumption, and Subjective Well-Being: Toward a Composite Macromarketing Model." *Journal of Macromarketing*. Fall: 153–168.

9. Ahuvia, Aaron C., and Douglas Friedman. 1998. Income, Consumption, and Subjective Well-Being: Toward a Composite Macromarketing Model. *Journal of Macromarketing*. Fall: 153–168.

10. Srivastava, Abhishek, Edwin Locke, and Kathryn Bartol. 2001. "Money and Subjective Well-Being: It's Not the Money, It's the Motives." *Journal of Personality and Social Psychology*, 80(6): 959–971.

11. Myers, David, and Ed Diener. 1995. "Who Is Happy?" *Psychological Science*, 6(1): 10–19.

12. Ahuvia, Aaron C., and Douglas Friedman. 1998. Income, Consumption, and Subjective Well-Being: Toward a Composite Macromarketing Model. *Journal of Macromarketing*. Fall: 153–168; citing Kasser, T., and R. Ryan. "Be Careful of What You Wish for: Optimal Functioning and the Relative Attainment of Intrinsic and Extrinsic Goals." In P. Schmuck, and K. M. Sheldon (Eds.). *Life Goals and Well-Being*. Lengerich, Germany: Pabst Science Publishers.

13. Myers, David. 1992. *The Pursuit of Happiness*. New York: Hearst Corporation.

14. Diener, Ed, Richard Lucas, and Shigehiro Oishi. 2002. "Subjective Well-Being." In C. R. Snyder and Shane Lopez (eds.). *Handbook of Positive Psychology*. Oxford: Oxford University Press, 63–73.

15. Myers, David, and Ed Diener. 1995. "Who Is Happy?" *Psychological Science*, 6(1): 10–19.

16. Schwartz, Barry, Andrew Ward, Sonja Lyubomirsky, John Monterosso, Katherine White, and Darrin Lehman. 2002. "Maximizing Versus Satisficing: Happiness Is a Matter of Choice." *Journal of Personality and Social Psychology*, 83(5): 1178–1197.

17. Richardson, John. 2002. "Wheee!: A Special Report from the Happiness Project." *Esquire*. June: 83–130.

18. Staudinger, Ursula, William Fleeson, and Paul Baltes. 1999. "Predictors of Subjective Physical Health and Global Well Being: Similarities and Differences Between the United States and Germany." *Journal of Personality and Social Psychology*, 76(2): 305–319.

19. Diener, Ed, Richard Lucas, and Shigehiro Oishi. 2002. "Subjective Well-Being." In C. R. Snyder, and Shane Lopez (eds.). *Handbook of Positive Psychology*. Oxford: Oxford University Press, 63–73.

20. Myers, David, and Ed Diener. 1995. "Who Is Happy?" *Psychological Science*, 6(1): 10–19.

21. 2000. "When Fortune Smiles." *Utne Reader* 56: May-June, citing the Web site www.zukav.com.

22. Myers, David, and Ed Diener. 1995. "Who Is Happy?" *Psychological Science*, 6(1): 10–19, p. 14.

23. Csikszentmihalyi, Mihaly. 1990. *Flow: The Psychology of Optimal Experience*. New York: HarperPerennial.

24. Dumaine, Brian. 1994. "Why Do We Work?" *Fortune*. December 26: 196–204.

25. 2000. "Job's Juggling Act." *Business Week*. January 10: 69.

26. 2000. "Perspectives." *Newsweek*. January 24: 17.

27. Dumaine, Brian. 1994. "Why Do We Work?" *Fortune*. December 26: 196–204.

28. Dumaine, Brian. 1994. "Why Do We Work?" *Fortune*. December 26: 196–204.

29. Csikszentmihalyi, Mihaly. 1990. *Flow: The Psychology of Optimal Experience*. New York: HarperPerennial.

30. Csikszentmihalyi, Mihaly. 1990. *Flow: The Psychology of Optimal Experience*. New York: HarperPerennial.

31. Csikszentmihalyi, Mihaly. 1997. "Finding Flow." *Psychology Today*, 30(4): 47–71.

32. Perlow, Leslie. 1997. *Finding Time: How Corporations, Individuals, and Families can Benefit from New Work Practices*. Ithaca: Cornell University Press, 77.

33. Perlow, Leslie. 1997. *Finding Time: How Corporations, Individuals, and Families can Benefit from New Work Practices*. Ithaca: Cornell University Press, 116–122

34. Csikszentmihalyi, Mihaly. 1990. *Flow: The Psychology of Optimal Experience*. New York: HarperPerennial, 61.

35. Ibid., p. 3.

36. Ibid., p. 42.

37. Ibid., pp. 41–49.

38. Dumaine, Brian. 1994. "Why do we work?" *Fortune*. December 26: 196–204.

39. Levy, Becca, Martin Slade, Suzanne Kunkel, and Stanislav Kasi. 2002. "Longevity Increased by Positive Self-Perceptions of Aging." *Journal of Personality and Social Psychology*, 83(2): 261–270.

40. Taylor, Shelley. 1989. *Positive Illusions: Creative Self-Deception and the Healthy Mind*. New York: Basic Books.

41. Ibid.

42. Ibid.

43. Kouzes, James, and Barry Posner. 1995. *Credibility: How People Gain and Lose It, Why People Demand It*. San Francisco, CA: Jossey-Bass.

44. Taylor, Shelley. 1989. *Positive Illusions: Creative Self-Deception and the Healthy Mind*. New York: Basic Books.

45. Seligman, Martin. 1978. *Learned Optimism: How to Change Your Mind and Your Life*. New York: Pocket Books.

46. Shinobu Kitayama, Hisaya Matsumoto, Hazel Rose Markus, and Vinai Norasakkunkit. 1997. "Individual and Collective Processes in the Construction of the Self: Self-Enhancement in the United States and Self-Criticism in Japan." *Journal of Personality and Social Psychology*, 72(6): 1245–1267.

47. Seligman, Martin. 1990. *Learned Optimism: How to Change Your Mind and Your Life*. New York: Pocket Books.

48. Dockster Marcus, Amy. 2004. "Fighting Cancer With a Frown." *Wall Street Journal*. April 6: D1 and D5.

49. Norem, Julie. 2001. *The Positive Power of Negative Thinking: Using Defensive Pessimism to Harness Anxiety and Perform at Your Best*. New York: Perseus Books.

50. Ibid., pp. 4–5.

51. Barnett, Rosalind, Nancy Marshall, Stephen Raudenbush, and Robert Brennan. 1993. "Gender and the Relationship between Job Experiences and Psychological Distress: A Study of Dual-Earner Couples." *Journal of Personality and Social Psychology*, 6(5): 794–806.

52. Joplin, Janice R., Debra Nelson, and James Quick. 1999. "Attachment Behavior and Health: Relationships at Work and Home." *Journal of Organizational Behavior*, 20: 783–796; Nelson, Debra, and James Quick. 1991. "Social Support and Newcomer Adjustment in Organizations: Attachment Theory at Work?" *Journal of Organizational Behavior*, 12(6): 543–555.

53. Daniels, Kevin, and Andrew Guppy. 1994. "Occupational Stress, Social Support, Job Control and Psychological Well-Being." *Human Relations*, 47(12): 1433–1592.

54. Winslow, Ron. 1997. "Lack of Control over Job Is Seen as Heart Risk." *Wall Street Journal*. July 25: B1.

55. Frost, R., P. Marten, C. Hart, and R. Rosenblate. 1990. "The Dimensions of Perfectionism." *Cognitive Therapy and Research*, 14: 449–468.

56. Slaney, Robert, and Jeffrey Ashby. 1996. "Perfectionists: A Study of a Criterion Group." *Journal of Counseling and Development*, 74 (March/April): 393–398.

57. Burns, D. D. 1980. "The Perfectionist's Script for Self-Defeat." *Psychology Today*. November: 34–52.

58. Slaney, Robert, Jeffrey Ashby, and Joseph Trippi. 1995. "Perfectionism: Its Measurement and Career Relevance." *Journal of Career Advancement*, 3(3): 279–297.

59. Pacht, Asher. 1984. "Reflections on Perfection." *American Psychologist*. April: 386–390.

60. Flett, Gordon, Paul Hewitt, Kirk Blank-stein, and Lisa Gray. 1988. "Psychological Distress and the Frequency of Perfectionistic Thinking." *Journal of Personality and Social Psychology*, 75: 1363–1381.

61. Pacht, Asher. 1984. "Reflections on Perfection." *American Psychologist*. April: 386–390.

62. Flett, Gordon, Paul Hewitt, Kirk Blank-stein, and Lisa Gray. 1998. "Psychological Distress and the Frequency of Perfectionistic Thinking." *Journal of Personality and Social Psychology*, 75: 1363–1381.

63. Slaney, Robert, and Ashby Jeffrey. 1996. "Perfectionists: A Study of a Criterion Group." *Journal of Counseling and Development*, 74 (March /April): 393–398.

64. Ibid.

65. Slaney, Robert, Jeffrey Ashby, and Joseph Trippi. 1995. "Perfectionism: Its Measure-ment and Career Relevance." *Journal of Career Advancement*, 3(3): 279–297.

66. Kofodimos, Joan. 1990. "Why Executives Lose Their Balance." *Organization Science* 58–73.

67. Slaney, Robert, and Jeffrey Ashby. 1996. "Perfectionists: A Study of a Criterion Group." *Journal of Counseling and Development*, 74 March/April.

68. Kofodimos, Joan. 1990. "Why Executives Lose Their Balance." *Organization Science* 58–73.

69. Pacht, Asher. 1984. "Reflections on Perfection." *American Psychologist*. April: 386–390.

70. Ibid.

71. Ibid.

72. Fleet, Gordon, Paul Hewitt, Kirk Blank-stein, and Cyrill Dyninl. 1994. "Dimensions of Perfectionism and Type A Behavior." *Personality and Individual Differences*, 16(3): 447–485; Friedman, M., and R. H. Rosenman. 1974. *Type A Behavior and Your Heart*. New York: Knopf; Glass, D. C. *Behavior Patterns, Stress, and Coronary Disease*. Hillsdale, NJ: Erlbaum; Scherwitz, K., K. Bertonk, and H. Levanthal. 1978. "Type A Behavior, Self-Involvement, and Cardiovascular Response." *Psychosomatic Medicine* 1978. 593–609; Lee, Cynthia, Susan Ashford, and Linda Jameson. 1993. "The Effects of Type A Behavior Dimensions and Optimism on Coping Strategy, Health, and Performance." *Journal of Organizational Behavior*, 14: 143–157.

73. Glicken, Morley. 1997. "When It's OK to Be a Workaholic." http://public.wsj.com/careers/resources/documents/19971231glicken.html.

74. Lee, Cynthia, Susan J. Ashford, and Linda F. Jameson 1993. "The Effects of Type A Behavior Dimensions and Optimism on Coping Strategy, Health, and Performance." *Journal of Organizational Behavior*, 14: 143–157.

75. Scheier, Michael, F. Weintraub, Jagdish Kumari, and Charles S. Carver. 1986. "Coping with Stress: Divergent Strategies of Optimists and Pessimists." *Journal of Personality and Social Psychology*, 51(6); cited in Lee, Cynthia, Susan J. Ashford, and Linda F. Jamieson. 1993. "The Effects of Type A Behavior Dimensions and Optimism on Coping Strategy, Health, and Performance." *Journal of Organizational Behavior*, 14: 143–157.

76. Iribarren, Carlos, Stephen Sidney, Diane Bild, and Kiang Liu. 2000. "Association of Hostility with Coronary Artery Calcification in Young Adults: The CAR-DIA Study." *Journal of the American Medical Association*, 283(19): 246–2551; Barling, Julian, and Danielle Charbonneau.

1992. "Disentangling the Relationship between the Achievement-Striving and Impatience-Irritability Dimensions of Type A Behavior, Performance and Health." *Journal of Organizational Behavior*, 13: 369–377; Spence, Janet T., Robert Helmreich, and Robert Pred. 1987. "Impatience versus Achievement Strivings in the Type A Pattern." *Journal of Applied Psychology*, 72(4): 522–529.

77. Barefoot, J. C., G. Dallstrom, and R. B. Williams. 1983. "Hostility, CHD Incidence, and Total Mortality: A 25-Year Follow-Up Study of 255 Physicians." *Psychosomatic Medicine*, 45: 59–63; Booth-Kewley, Stephanie, and Howard Friedman. 1987. "Psychological Predictors of Heart Disease: A Quantitative Review." *Psychological Bulletin*, 101: 343–362; Williams, R. B., J. C. Barefoot, and R. B. Shekelle. 1985. "The Health Consequences of Hostility." In Chesney, M. A., and R. G. H. Rosenman (eds.). *Anger, Hostility, and Behavioral Medicine*. New York: Hemisphere/McGraw-Hill.

78. Williams, Stephen. 2000. "That Gnawing Anger." *Newsweek*. May 22: 81.

79. Kofodimos, Joan. 1990. "Why Executives Lose Their Balance." *Organization Science*. Summer: 58–73.

80. Ibid.

81. Belenky, Gregory, David Penetar, David Thorne, Katheryn Popp, John Leu, Maria Thomas, Helen Sing, Thomas Balkin, Nancy Wesensten, and Daniel Redmond. 1994. "The Effects of Sleep Deprivation on Performance during Continuous Combat Operations." In Bernadette M. Marriott (ed.). *Food Components to Enhance Performance*. Washington, DC: National Academy Press.

82. Penetar, David, Una McCann, David Thorne, Aline Schelling, Cynthia Galinski, Helen Sing, Maria Thomas, and Gregory Belenky. 1994. "The Effects of Caffeine on Cognitive Performance, Mood, and Alertness in Sleep-Deprived Human Beings." In Bernadette M. Marriott (ed.). *Food Components to Enhance Performance*. Washington, DC: National Academy Press.

83. Glicken, Morley. 1997. "When It's OK to Be a Workaholic." http://public.wsj.com/careers/resources/documents/19971231glicken.html.

84. Ibid.

85. Kiechel, Walter. 1989. "The Workaholic Generation." *Fortune*. April 10: 50–62.

86. Labich, Kenneth. 1991. "Why Grade A Executives Get an F as Parents." *Fortune*. May 20: 38–56.

87. O'Reilly, Brian. 1990. "Can Your Career Hurt Your Kids?" *Fortune*. January 1: 36–46.

88. Morris, Betsy. 1997. "Is Your Family Wrecking Your Career (and vice versa)?" *Fortune*. March 17: 70–73.

89. Schwartz, Felice. 1992. "Why on Earth Should I Promote a Pregnant Woman?" *Executive Female*. July/August: 38–41.

90. Arthur, Michelle. 2003. "Share Price Reactions to Work-Family Initiatives: An Institutional Perspective." *Academy of Management Journal*, 46(4): 497–505.

91. Hannon, John and George Milkovich. 1996. "The Effect of Human Resource Reputation Signals on Share Prices: An Event Study." *Human Resource Management*, 35(3): 405–424.

92. Perry-Smith, Jill, and Terry Blum. 2000. "Work-Family Human Resource Bundles and Perceived Organizational Performance." *Academy of Management Journal*, 23(6): 1107–1117.

93. Beyer, Janice, and David R. Hannah. 2002. "Building on the Past: Enacting Established Personal Identities in a New Work Setting." *Organization Science*, 13(6): 636–652; Ruderman, Marian, Patricia Ohlott, Kate Panzer, Sara King. 2002. "Benefits of Multiple Roles for Managerial Women." *Academy of Management Journal*, 45(2): 369–386; Settles, Iris, Robert Sellers, and Alphonse Damas, Jr. 2002. "One Role or Two? The Function of Psychological Separation in Role Conflict." *Journal of Applied Psychology*, 87(3) 574–582; Rothbard, Nancy. 2001. "Enriching or Depleting? The Dynamics of Engagement in Work and Family Roles." *Administrative Science Quarterly*, 46(4): 655–685; Ibarra, Herminia. 2003. *Working*

Identity: Unconventional Strategies for Reinventing Your Career. Boston, MA: Harvard Business School Press, 33; Moen, Phyllis, Donna Dempster-McClain, and Robin M. Williams Jr., 1992. "Successful Aging: A Life Course Perspective on Women's Multiple Roles and Health." *American Journal of Sociology*, 97(6): 1612–1638.

94. Aryee, Samuel, and Vivienne Luk. 1996. "Balancing Two Major Parts of Adult Life Experience: Work and Family Identity among Dual-Earner Couples." *Human Relations*, 49(4): 465–479.

95. Higgens, Christopher, and Linda Duxbury. 1992. "Work-Family Conflict: A Comparison of Dual-Career and Traditional Career Men." *Journal of Organizational Behavior*, 13: 389–411.

96. Ibid.

97. Gilligan, Carol. 1993. *A Different Voice: Psychological Theory and Women's Development*. Cambridge, MA: Harvard University Press.

98. 1999. "Only Small Link Found between Hours in Child Care and Mother-Child Interaction." *NIH News Alert*. http://www. nichd.nih.gov/new/releases/timeinchild care.html, November 7.

99. Hyerman, Alexis. 1999. Washington, DC: U.S. Department of Labor.

100. Jacobs, Jerry. "Measuring Time at Work: Are Self-Reports Accurate?" *Monthly Labor Bureau*, 121(12): 42–53.

101. Hyerman, Alexis. 1999. *Report on the American Workforce*. Washington, DC: U.S. Department of Labor.

102. Winkler, Anne. 1998. "Earnings of Husbands and Wives in Dual-Earner Families." *Monthly Labor Review*, 121(4): 42–48.

103. U.S. Census. 2000.

104. Hayghe, Howard, and Suzanne Bianchi. 1994. "Married Mothers' Work Patterns: The Job-Family Compromise." *Monthly Labor Review*, 117(6), pp. 24-30.

105. Bureau of Labor Statistics. 2002.

106. www.census.gov/Press-Release/www/2003/ cb03ff03.html

107. www.diversitybestpractices, com; citing *Working Mother* magazine.

108. www.employee.org/article daddy.html. "Daddies: A Side of Work/life Balance We Don't Hear Much About." Citing a Families and Work Institute study.

109. Heymann, S. J. 2000. "The Widening Gap: Why American Working Families Are in Jeopardy and What Can be Done About It.

110. Cattan, Peter. 1991. "Child-Care Problems: An Obstacle to Work." *Monthly Labor Review*, 114(10): 3–9.

111. Goodman, William. 1995. "Boom in Day-Care Industry the Result of Many Social Changes." *Monthly Labor Review*. August: 3–12; William Goodman, Howard Hayghe, and Suzanne Bianchi. 1994. "Married Mothers' Work Patterns: The Job-Family Compromise." *Monthly Labor Review*, 117(6): 24–30.

112. Cattan, Peter. 1991. "Child-Care Problems: An Obstacle to Work." *Monthly Labor Review*, 114(10): 3–9.

113. 1999. NICHD Child-Care Study Investigators' Report on Child-Care Quality: Higher Quality Care Related to Less Problem Behavior." *NIH News Alert*. http://www.nichd.nih.gov/new/releases/DA YCAR99.htm. January 26.

114. "The 65 Years and Over Population." Census 2000 Debrief.

115. World's Older Population Growing by Unprecedented 800,000 a Month. http://www.census.gov/Press-Release/www/2001/cb01-198.html, December 13, 2001.

116. National Alliance for Caregiving. 2004 Report of Caregiving in the United States.

117. Windham, Christopher. 2003. "Elderly Caregivers Face Stress Toll." National Alliance for Caregiving cited in the *Wall Street Journal*. July: D4).

118. Winkler, Anne E. 1998. "Earnings of Husbands and Wives in Dual-Earner Families." *Monthly Labor Review*, 121(4): 42–48.

119. Wetzel, James. 1990. "American Families: 75 Years of Change." *Monthly Labor Review*, 113(3): pp 4–13.

120. Sorrentino, Constance. 1990. "The Changing Family in International Perspective." *Monthly Labor Review*, 113(3): pp 4–13.

121. Ibid.
122. Winkler, Anne E. 1998. "Earnings of Husbands and Wives in Dual-Earner Families." *Monthly Labor Review*, 121(4): 42–48.
123. Jacobs, Eva, Stephanie Shipp, and Gregory Brown. 1989. "Families of Working Wives Spending More on Services and Nondurables." *Monthly Labor Review*, 112(2): 15–23.
124. Robinson, John P., and Geoffrey Godbey. 1997. *Time for Life: The Surprising Ways Americans Use Their Time*. University Park, PA: The Pennsylvania State University Press.
125. 2000. "A Pregnant Moment: Blair Weighs Duties as Premier and Father." *Wall Street Journal Europe* March 30: 25.
126. Cohen, Phillip, and Suzanne Bianchi. 1999. "Marriage, Children, and Women's Employment: What Do We Know?" *Monthly Labor Review*. December: 22–31.
127. Lublin, Joan. 2000. "Working Dads Find Family Involvement Can Help Out Careers." *Wall Street Journal*. May 30: B1.
128. Grover, Mary Beth. 1999. "Daddy Stress." *Forbes*. September 6: 203.
129. Levine, James, and Todd Pittinsky. 1997. *Working Fathers: New Strategies for Balancing Work and Family*. Reading, MA: Addison-Wesley.
130. Tharenou, Phyllis. 1999. "Is There a Link between Family Structure and Women's and Men's Managerial Career Advancement?" *Journal of Organizational Behavior*, 20: 837–863; Gray, Jeffrey. 1997. "The Fall in Men's Return to Marriage." *Journal of Human Resources*, 32: 481–504.
131. Schneer, Joy A., and Frieda Reitman. 1993. "Effects of Alternative Family Structures on Managerial Career Paths." *Academy of Management Journal*, 36(4): 830–843; Scheer, Joy, and Freida Reitman. 2002. "Managerial Life without a Wife: Family Structure and Managerial Career Success." *Journal of Business Ethics*. April, 37(1): 25–39.
132. 1997. *Family Circle*. May 13: 15.
133. Shellenbarger, Sue. 1997. "Good, Early Day Care Has a Huge Impact on Kids, Studies Say." *Wall Street Journal*. April 9: B1.
134. www.nichd.nih.gov/new/releases/DAYCAR99.htm, January 26, 1999.
135. Children Score Higher on Tests When Childcare Meets Professional Standards. *NIH News Alert*. www.nichd.nih.gov/new/releases/DAYCR992.htm, July 1, 1999.
136. Children Score Higher on Tests When Childcare Meets Professional Standards. *NIH News Alert* www.nichd.nih.gov/new/releases.DAYCR999.htm, July 1, 1999.
137. Children Score Higher on Tests When Childcare Meets Professional Standards. *NIH News Alert*, www.nichd.nih.gov/new/releases.DAYCR999.htm, July 1, 1999.
138. Only Small Link Found between Hours in Child Care and Mother-Child Interaction. *NIH News Alert*. http://www.nichd.nih.gov/new/releases/timeinchildcare.html; this research is also supported by Volling, Brenda, and Jay Belsky. 1993. "Parent, Infant, and Contextual Characteristics Related to Maternal Employment Decisions in the First Year of Infancy." *Family Relations*, 42: 4–12.
139. Belsky, Jay. 1999. "Quantity of Nonmaternal Care and Boys' Problem Behavior/ Adjustment at Ages 3 and 5: Exploring the Mediating Role of Parenting." *Psychiatry*, 62(1): 1–20.
140. Belsky, Jay. 1995. "A Nation (Still) at Risk?" *National Forum*, 75(3): 36.
141. Only Small Link Found between Hours in Childcare and Mother-Child Interaction. *NIH News Alert*. http://www.nichd.nih.gov/new/releases/timeinchildcare.htm.
142. Children Score Higher on Tests When Child Care Meets Professional Standards. 1999. *NIH News Alert*. www.nichd.nih.gov/new/releases/DAYCAR99.htm, July 1.
143. Galinsky, Ellen. 1993. "Infant Morality." *People Weekly*, 39(6): February 15: 103.
144. Gable, Sara, Jay Belsky, and Keith Crnic. 1995. "Co-Parenting During the Child's 2nd Year: A Descriptive Account." *Journal of Marriage and the Family,* 57(3): 609.
145. DeMeis, D. K., E. Hock, and S. L. McBride. 1986. "The Balance of Employment and Motherhood: Longitudinal Study of Mothers' Feelings about Separation from their First-Born Infant." *Developmental Psychology*, 22: 627–632; Hock, E., 1978. "Working and Nonworking Mothers with

Infants: Perceptions of Their Careers, Their Infants' Needs, and Satisfaction with Mothering." *Developmental Psychology*, 14: 37–43; Volling, Brenda, and Jay Belsky. 1993. "Parent, Infant, and Contextual Characteristics Related to Maternal Employment Decisions in the First Year of Infancy. *Family Relations*, 42: 4–12; Volling, Brenda, and Jay Belsky. 1991. "Multiple Determinants of Father Involvement during Infancy in Dual-Earner and Single-Earner Families." *Journal of Marriage and the Family*, May: 461–474.

146. Piotrkowski, C. S., and Crits-Christoph, P. 1982. "Women's Jobs and Family Adjustment." In J. Aldous (ed.). *Two Paychecks: Life in Dual-Earner Families*. Beverly Hills, CA: Sage, 105–127; MacEwen, K., and Julian Barling. 1982. "Effects of Maternal Employment Experiences on Children's Behavior via Mood, Cognitive Difficulties and Parenting Behavior." *Journal of Marriage and the Family*, 53: 635–644; Stewart, Wendy, and Julian Barling. 1996. "Fathers' Work Experiences Affect Children's Behaviors via Job-Related Affect and Parenting Behaviors." *Journal of Organizational Behavior*, 17: 221–232.

147. Stewart, Wendy, and Julian Barling, 1996. "Fathers' Work Experiences Affect Children's Behaviors via Job-Related Affect and Parenting Behaviors." *Journal of Organizational Behavior*, 17: 221–232.

148. Shellenbarger, Sue. 1996. "Work and Family: It's the Type of Job You Have that Affects the Kids, Studies Say." *Wall Street Journal*. July 31: B1.

149. Shellenbarger, Sue. 1996. "Work and Family: It's the Type of Job You Have that Affects the Kids, Studies Say." *Wall Street Journal*. July 31: B1.

150. Shellenbarger, Sue. 1996. "Work and Family: It's the Type of Job You Have that Affects the Kids, Studies Say." *Wall Street Journal*. July 31: B1.

151. Levine, James, and Todd Pettinsky. 1997. *Working Fathers: New Strategies for Balancing Work and Family*. Reading, MA: Addison-Wesley.

152. Galinsky, Ellen. 1999. *Ask the Children: What America's Children Really Think About Working Parents*. New York: William Morrow and Company.

153. Galinsky, Ellen. 1999. "Do Working Parents Make the Grade?" *Newsweek*. August 30: 52–55.

154. 1999. "Less Guilt for Working Mothers." *Good Housekeeping*. April: 83; citing Sandra Hofferth, Sr. research scientist, University of Michigan's Institute for Social Research.

155. Galinsky, Ellen. 1999. "Do Working Parents Make the Grade?" *Newsweek*. August 30: 52–55.

156. Ibid.

157. Gallinsky, Ellen. 1999. "Today's Kids, Tomorrow's Employees: What Children Are Learning about Work." *HR Magazine*, 44(11): 74–84.

158. Ibid.

159. Ibid.

160. Galinsky, Ellen. 1999. *Ask the Children: What America's Children Really Think about Working Parents*. New York: William Morrow and Company.

161. Ibid.

162. Frankl, Viktor. 1984. *Man's Search for Meaning*. Revised edition. New York: Simon & Schuster; originally published in 1959.

163. Norem, Julie. 2001. *The Positive Power of Negative Thinking: Using Defensive Pessimism to Harness Anxiety and Perform at Your Best*, New York: Perseus Books.

164. Dumaine, Brian. 1994. "Why Do We Work?" *Fortune*. December 26: 196–204.

Case 5 Managing Stress

Researchers believe that fulfilling work make most people happy. However, what about stressful work? Too much work? Work done under seemingly impossible deadlines? Although most of us can and do cope with occasional stressors, and some people may even be stimulated by certain kinds of pressure (particularly when they can control how they respond to that pressure), a constant diet of stress can take a toll on our productivity and our health.

Many managers have experienced the stress of realizing that a trusted subordinate is performing poorly. Sometimes a manager may decide that the best solution is to do the subordinate's work himself or herself, which only increases the manager's stress and does nothing to enhance the subordinate's competence or career development.

How do we avoid negative stress? Self-awareness is one way to minimize stress. Perfectionism, procrastination, and micromanagement can all lead to stress. Knowing whether we have these tendencies can help us try to minimize them and develop better coping skills. Planning and organization go a long way toward eliminating crisis situations.

Problems that we spot in the distance can be headed off; those that blindside us cause stress. Good communication skills can help eliminate misunderstandings that lead to stress. Time management skills also are essential for avoiding the backlog of work that plays havoc with priorities and damages our sense of control. A system for monitoring work, establishing schedule checkpoints, and communicating consistent expectations of high-quality results lets others know what we need from them. Some stress, however, may be inevitable. How should we deal with it?

In this video, Mia is caught off guard by a poorly done assignment she had delegated to Joan. Under deadline pressure, she is feeling severely stressed because she does not believe that Joan's article is good enough to post on the Web site as written, and she feels it cannot be postponed because it has already been promoted to customers and must be available when promised. Mia considers two options: She can take the evening off to be with a friend with whom she had promised to spend the evening, or she can work late rewriting the article and confront Joan the next day.

DISCUSSION QUESTIONS

1. Why do you think Mia is in the position of redoing someone else's work the night before the deadline? How could she have avoided being in this situation?
2. Do you think time management and organization are Mia's only problem?

Does she have any characteristics that fuel her need to stay late at the office?
3. What kind of message is Mia sending Joan by trying to redo her work?

ADDITIONAL TEXT QUESTIONS FOR OPTION 1

4. Do you think Chris offers Mia good advice? Why or why not? Did Mia make the right decision about how to spend the evening? Does Mia have options other than redoing the work tonight?

5. What do you think Mia should try to achieve when she talks to Joan in the morning? How should she approach the conversation?

ADDITIONAL TEXT QUESTIONS FOR OPTION 2

6. Did Mia make the right decision about how to spend the evening?
7. How well do you think she handled her conversation with Joan the next morning? If so, why? If not, why not and what do you think she should have done differently?

Index

Page numbers followed by *f* indicate figures; page numbers followed by *t* indicate tables; page numbers followed by *b* indicate boxes.

A

Abbot, Shirly, 54
ABC method, optimism, 401
Abilities, overestimation of, 4
Abrasive boss, management of, 235–239
Abu Ghraib prison, abuse in, 232–233*b*
Acceptance, demonstrating, 118
Accessibility, 128, 290
Acculturation stress, 62
Achievement-ascription dimension, 275
Achievement-based cultures, 275
Action orientation, 196, 275
Active listening, 114, 115–118, 148
  blocking, 116
  in communication, 156
Adams, Scott, 227*f*
Adaptability, 225*b*
  in powerful people, 161
  promoting, 223–224
Adaptation, cautious, 233
Adler, Nancy, 297
Advertisement, influence of, 171
Advocacy groups, effective response to, 288–289
Affirmative action, 300
Affluence, independent self-concept and, 40
African Americans
  advocacy groups for, 288–289
  support networks of, 249–250
Age, culture and, 270–271
Agreeableness, 10*b*
Ailes, Roger, 179
Albright, Madeleine, 57, 282
Alcott, Louisa May, 195

Alienation, biculturality and, 62
Allerton, Haidee, 366
Ally, acting as, 180
Amazon.com, story of, 136
Ambassador role, 335*f*
Ambiguity, 114
American culture, work orientation in, 285
American Express, 9/11 organizational crisis of, 103
American Public Health Association data, 411
Amiable style, 164
  characteristics of, 165*t*
  influence strategies for, 168–169*t*
  potential behavior under stress for, 167*t*
  potential strengths and weaknesses of, 166*t*
  weaknesses perceived by others, 167*t*
Analytic style, 164
  characteristics of, 165*t*
  influence strategies for, 168*t*
  potential behavior under stress for, 167*t*
  potential strengths and weaknesses of, 166*t*
  weaknesses perceived by others, 167*t*
Ancel, David, 142
Ancona, Deborah, 334
Anderson, Sparky, 2
Anderson, Walter Truett, 60
Andre, Rae, 291
Andres, Allison, 414
Angelou, Maya, 114
Anglo American culture, independence in, 39
Anniss, Michael, 38
Antisthenes, 122
Anxiety
  performance and, 402
  Type A behavior and, 404–406

Apology, 105
  art of, 96–97
Appetite, unbridled, 8
Apple Computer, 327
Approachability, 128
Approval, need for, 177–178
Armstrong, David M., 136, 367–368, 369b
Armstrong International, 136
Aryee, Samuel, 409
Ascription-based cultures, 275
Ash, Mary Kay, 180
Ashford, Susan, 122, 254–255
Ashforth, Blake, 236
Asian American culture
  independence in, 39
  individual performance in, 40
Asian cultures, time orientation of, 281
Assertive/probing dimension, 164, 196
Atherton, Gertrude, 285
Attachment, 415–416
  working parents and, 423
Attachment figures, 91, 105
  early experience with, 92–93
Attention
  in feeling of flow, 396
  self-concept and, 47
  speed of, 47
Attractive physical appearance, 180–181
Authoritarian bosses, 237
Authority, 169, 170
  obedience to, 227–233, 258
  predispositions toward, 230
Authority figure, closeness to, 230
Authority relationships, 257
  organizational structure and, 214–215
  personality and, 215–217
  in workplace, 213–217
Authority rule, 175–176, 184f, 197
  leveraging, 177
  resisting, 177
Autonomy, 191, 193f
  of team members, 313, 328
Avoidance goal orientation, 12
Avon, diverse teams of, 353–354

B

Babcock, Linda, 158
Bad news
  avoidance of, 8–9
  encouraging, 194, 199
  managing, 147b
  receiving, 125–128
Baker, Wayne, 246, 247
Ballard, J. G., 365
Balzac, Honore de, 160
Barad, Jill, 116, 118
Barlow, John Perry, 368
Barnes, Lou, 119
Barritt, Matthew, 372
Barshefsky, Charlene, 103
Bartholomew, Susan, 297
Bartoleme, Fernando, 99, 127
Barton, Clara, 172
Baruch, Bernard, 270
Basking-in-reflected-glory strategy, 248, 255, 258
Bates, Keirsey, 74b
Bateson, Mary Catherine, 21, 421, 422
Battner, Ben, 186
Baumeister, Roy, 36
Bearley, William E., 335f
Beattie, Joy, 355
Becoming a Manager (Hill), 20
Behaviors
  predicting success, 14f
  steps in changing, 25
  that no longer serve us, 15–17
Beiner, Theresa, 299
Belbin, R. Meredith, 312
Belenky, Gregory, 407b
Belenky, Mary, 282
Bell, Chip, 135
Bell, Ella, 62
Belonging need, 40, 49, 330
  in virtual teams, 367–368
Belsky, Jay, 416
Bem, Sandra, 131
Bemn, Daryl, 131
Benedict, Ruth, 271
Bennis, Warren, 18, 223, 314, 328–329, 336
Berra, Yogi, 140, 172
Beyer, Janice, 64
Bezos, Jeff, 95, 136
Bianchi, Suzanne, 412
Bias, in diverse teams, 357
Biculturality, 62
Biederman, Patricia, 314
Birth order, 45–46
Blair, Jayson, 9
Blair, Tony, 412
Blake-Beard, Stacy, 241
Blamestorming, 320

Blanchard, Ken, 95, 120, 219–221
Blass, Thomas, 230
Bluedorn, Allen C., 281, 425–426*b*
Body language
    cross-cultural meaning of, 128–129
    culture-specific, 294
    in social style, 165–167
Body Shop, The, 399
    stories of, 135–136
Boje, David, 139
"Book smarts," 4–6
Boss
    abrasive, 235–239
    management of, 233–239
    with wide span of control, 226
Boss-subordinate relationships, 257
    assumptions about, 213–214
    dysfunctional, 217
    organizational structure and, 214–215
    personality and, 215–217
Bossidy, Larry, 132, 213
Boundaries
    clear, 328
    redefining, 334
    team management of, 329–335
Boundary-spanning behaviors, 335*f*, 344
Boundary-spanning relationship skills, 295
Boundaryless organization, 17
Bowes, Pitney, 114
Bowlby, John, 49
Brake, Terence, 275
Branding, 34–35
Brannen, Mary Yoko, 62
Brass, Daniel, 249
Breer, Charles W., 185
Bricolage, 54–55
Bricoleurs, 60, 69
Brower, Charles, 118
Buck, Pearl S., 416
Buddha, 39
Buffet, Warren, 179
Bully Online Web site, 235–236
Bunker, Barbara Benedict, 96
Burr, Don, 7
Bush, George, communication skills of, 115*b*
Buzzwords, 135, 146*b*

C

Caldwell, David, 334, 335*f*
Cameron, Kim, 102

Campbell, David, 32
Candor, 127
Cappetta, Rossella, 94
Career
    impact of children on, 413–414
    networking in advancing, 251
Caregivers, unpaid, 411
Caring, in trustworthiness, 93
Case, Steve, 329–330
Categorizations, 330
Celebrities, identity and, 56–58
Census Bureau, demographic categories of, 271
Centenarians, lessons from, 406–407*b*
Centrality, 191, 193*f*
Cerner Corporation, organizational culture of,
    235–236
Challenge, 395
    feeling of flow and, 397
Change
    adaptability to, 224
    cultural attitudes toward, 284
    fast-paced, 68
    in management trends, 19–20*t*
    steps toward, 16–17
    willingness to engage in, 3
Characteristics, predicting success, 14*f*
Charismatic leaders, 9, 134–135
Charles, Ray, 399
Chatman, Jennifer, 4, 360
Chenault, Kenneth, 103
Chevy Nova, marketed in Latin America, 128
Child, Julia, 404
Child care, quality of, 416–417
Children
    impact of working parents on, 414–418
    impact on parents' careers of, 413–414
    of working parents, 423
    working parents and well-being of, 418–420
Childs, Ted, 302
Choice, 284
    for working parents, 417
Churchill, Sir Winston, 139, 184
Cialdini, Robert, six universal forms of
    influence theory of, 169–184
Cioffi, Delia, 178
Cipirano, Mia, 85
Cirque Du Soliel, 175
Civil Rights Act of 1964, Title VII, 299
Claire, Judith, 355

Clarity, 113–114
  in communications, 115*b*
Cleanliness, 50*b*
Clinton, Bill, 125–127
Clinton, Hillary Rodham, 246
Coaching, 220, 268
Coalitions, 191–192, 193*f*
Coca-Cola, introduced into China, 128
Cognitive development, 415
Cognitive flexibility, 295
Cognitive limitations, 160
Cognitive shortcuts, 170, 197
Cohen, Phillip, 412
Cohesion
  creating, 223
  of distributed teams, 374–375
  in diverse teams, 355
  in virtual teams, 367–368
Cole, Paul, 367–368, 369*b*
Collaborative capital, 88
Collective identity, developing, 98
Collective responsibility, 314
Collective self-concept, 76*b*
Collective tunnel vision, 313
Collectivism, 21, 274–275
Collectivist cultures, 41
  of diverse team, 359–360
  empowerment in, 42
Co-located teams, 363–364, 380
  cohesion in, 367
Commitment
  to supervisors, 213
  top-level, 297
Commitment and consistency rule, 178–179,
    184*f*, 197
  leveraging, 179
  resisting, 179
Commitment/consistency, 169
Common identity, creating, 301–302
Common sense, intelligence versus, 7
Communication. *See also* Body language;
    Language
  clear and concise, 113–114
  cross-cultural, 128–132
  distorted, 355–356
  effective, 113–150
  employee resistance through, 146*b*
  face-to-face versus electronic and computer-
    mediate, 365–366
  gateway of, 54
  great moments in, 115*b*

  high- versus low-contex, 129*t*
  Internet and, 54–56
  leadership lessons in, 147*b*
  management of in distributed teams, 375–376
  to mobilize action, 132–140
  politically savvy, 190
  strategic, 193*f*
  strategies for ineffective teams, 331
  technology in, 140–145
  trust in, 88
  via electronic mail, 142–145
  video case of, 156
  in virtual teams, 364
Communication skills, 3
  in trustworthiness, 93
Communication styles
  cultural differences in, 127–130
  gender differences in, 130
  high- and low-context, 278–280
  neutral and expressive, 279
  report and rapport talk, 279
Competence
  backfiring, 189*f*
  employee empowerment and, 225
  need for, 49
  positive emotions and, 102
  in power, 161
  in team leadership, 330–331
  in trustworthiness, 93
Competitiveness, diversity in, 286–289, 303
Complete information, taking responsibility for,
    118
Compliance, triggers for, 170
Computer-based information
  management of, 375–376
  virtual teams and, 361–363
Computer-mediated meetings, 373
Computer technology, 140–141, 148–149
  in team performance, 370–371
  in virtual teams, 364, 381
Conciseness, 113–114
Concurrence-seeking, 332–333*b*
Conference calls, in team management, 349–350
Confidentiality, communication, 115*b*
Conformity, 331
  reinforcing, 332*b*
Conger, Jay, 22, 298, 300
Connectedness, 38
Connections, power of, 246
Conscientiousness, 9–10
  backfiring, 10*b*

Consequences, belief in, 16*b*
Consistency, 169, 178–179, 225*b*
 cultural orientation toward, 283
 need for, 49
 positive effects of, 224
 promoting, 223
 in trust, 98
 in trustworthiness, 93
Constructive conflict, 223
Consultants, external, 362
Consumerism, 302
Contagion effect, 103–104, 106
Contemporary organization, self-concept in, 49–58
Continuous improvement, on diverse teams, 354
Contradictions, cultural orientation toward, 283
Control
 in success, 16*b*
 need for, 49
 sense of, 330
  happiness and, 393
  in feeling of flow, 396
Convers, John, 395
Conversation, active listening in, 116–117
Cook, John, 89
Cooperation
 across teams, 331
 in teams, 344
 rewarding, 333
Coordination
 of distributed teams, 376
 of diverse teams, 356–357
Coping
 multiple roles in, 409
 self-concept and, 48
Core values, defining, 223, 225*b*
Corning, discrimination in, 287–288
Coughlin, Paula, 301
Counterdependent relationships, 215–216
Country Individualism Index, 43*t*
Courage, 296
Covey, Steven, 33, 116–117, 282
Cox, Marcelene, 394
Cox, Taylor, 285, 286–287
Craig, Holly, 130
Creative intelligence, 12, 14
Creative self-deceptions, 398
Creativity
 diversity and, 353–354
 feeling of flow in, 396
Credibility, in storytelling, 138

Credibility (Kouzes, Posner), 399
Crisis
 organizational, positive emotions and, 102–104
 trust in surviving, 88
Critical evaluator role, 333*b*
Critical thinking, 16, 20–21, 199
 encouraging, 194
Criticality, 191, 193*f*
Criticism, positive feedback and, 121
Crocker, Jennifer, 36
Cross Cultural Adaptability Inventory, 293
Cross-cultural mentoring relationships, 241–242
Cross-gender mentoring relationships, 241–242
Cross-race mentoring relationships, 241–242
Crowd, following, 177–178
Csikszentmihalyi, Mihaly, 393, 395–396, 397, 398*b*
Cultural beliefs
 in diverse team, 359–360
 in self-concept, 38–43, 68
Cultural diversity, managing, 269–304
Cultural-general skills, 304
Cultural-identity group, 271–273
Cultural perspective, 41–43
Cultural preferences, 276*b*
Cultural synergy, creating, 297–302
Culture-general skills, 293, 295–296
Culture-specific skills, 293, 294–295, 304
Cultures
 changing, 43
 communicating across, 128–132, 148
 definition of, 270–273
 differences in, 285
 dimensions of, 273–285
 in self-identity, 274–278
 interaction among, 302
 interdependent, 40–41
 language and, 130–132
 low- versus high-context, 278–280
 norms of in obedience to authority, 230
 time perception in, 280–282
 transitioning between, 62
Currall, Steven, 366
Customer focus, 224, 225*b*
Cyberspace, identity and, 54–56
Cyclical thinking, 282

D

Daily, Bill, 132, 133*t*
Dalton, Maxine, 296

Danko, William, 394*b*
Darwin, Charles, 1
Davis, Benjamin, 217
Davis, Melinda, 65
Dawes, Robyn, 100
Day, David, 66
Day care
    impact of, 411
    quality of, 416–417
De Frantz, Anita, 249
de Rothschild, Baron, 255
"De-storying," 136
The De-Voicing of Society (Lock), 367
Deborah, Ancona, 335*f*
Decentralization, 23
Decentralized organization, 17
Decision-making
    computed-mediated technologies in, 369–370
    diversity and, 286
    limited resources for, 160
    participation in, 98
    rational, 159–160
    rationality in, 196
    self-concept and, 48
Deductive reasoning, 282–283
Defensive pessimism, 102
Deinard, Caitlin, 249–250
Dekker, Wisse, 288
Delegating style, 220
Delusions, 398
Deming, W. Edwards, 14
Demographic categories, 270–271, 303
    base on cultural meaning systems, 271–273
    natural versus social constructed, 273*t*
Demographics, workforce, 410–413, 423
    shifting, 288
Denison, Daniel, 219, 221–222, 225*b*
Denison Leadership Development Model, 219,
    221–223, 257–258
Denny's Restaurants, discriminatory lawsuit
    against, 287
Dependent relationships, 215
Depersonalized trust, 100, 106
Derailment, 3, 25
    reasons for, 3–9
Descriptive feedback, 121
Detachment, 355
Developmental opportunities, 40
Developmental relationships, network of, 243
Diener, Ed., 391–392, 393
Difficult Conversations (Stone), 117

Digital Storytelling, The Center for, 140*b*
Dilbert cartoon, 227*f*
Dilbert Web site, 146*b*
Dillard, Ann, 391
Directing, 220
Direction giving, 125
Direction-giving language, scale for, 126*b*
Discretion, 128
Discrimination, 290
Disney teams, 318*b*
Disney World, story of, 139
Distinctiveness theory, 249
Distributed teams
    versus co-located teams, 363–364
    expressing minority opinions in, 369–370
    managing, 371–379
    social dynamics in, 364–371
Diverse teams, 379–380
    dilemma of, 351–352
    distorted communication in, 355–356
    factors to consider in, 357–358
    hurdles for, 355–357
    leading, 358–361
    potential advantages and disadvantages of,
        352–354
Diversity, 2
    acceptance of, 40
    as competitive advantage, 286–289
    competitive advantage of, 303
    cultural, 285
    differential impact of on team members,
        357–358
    dilemma of, 351–352
    effects of on team process and performance,
        353*f*
    management of in your company, 298
    managing, 269–304
    mentoring and, 241–242
    of networks, 247, 248–251, 258
    in organizational relationships, 22–23
    progress in, 289–291
    promoting, 303
    relevance of to task, 357
    of workforce, 17
    on teams, 351–361, 380
Diversity training programs, 291, 300
Dixon, Dr. Nancy, 18–20
Doan, Robert, 58–59, 61
Doing-being dimension, 275
Doing Business Internationally, 275
Doppelt, Gabe, 363

Dostoyevsky, F., 127
Dowd, Ann Reilly, 247
Drake, Karen, 316
Drama, 138
Drath, Wilfred, 32, 67
Dressing for success, 255
Driver style, 164
   characteristics of, 165*t*
   influence strategies for, 168*t*
   potential behavior under stress for, 167*t*
   potential strengths and weaknesses of, 166*t*
   weaknesses perceived by others, 167*t*
Dropping, skill at, 16*b*
Drucker, Peter, 235*b*
Dubinsky, Donna, 242
Dubois, W. E. B., 62
Dumaine, Brian, 395
Dunifon, Rachel, 50*b*
Dweck, Carolyn, 5
Dynamic cues, 365, 366*f*
Dysfunctional organizational politics,
   minimizing, 192–194, 199

E

E-mail
   communication via, 142–145, 148–149, 366
   system crash, 115*b*
   use of, 141–142
Eastern society, interdependence in, 41
Eby, Lillian, 10
Eccles, Robert, 21
Education
   in empowerment, 226
   encouraging, 300
   level of, 410
   of working parents, 417
Effective people, characteristics of, 2
Effectiveness criteria, team, 314–316
Ego expansion, 116
Ego surfing, 54
Einstein, Albert, 397
Eisenhower, Dwight D., 239
Electronic Communications Privacy Act, 145
Electronic meetings, 373
Ellet, Bill, 146*b*
Elsbach, Kimberly, 139
Ely, Robin, 286, 289–290
Emerson, Ralph Waldo, 412
Emotional intelligence, 12, 14

Emotional resilience, 296
Emotions
   in feedback, 121
   negative, 14
   neutral versus expressive displays of, 279
   positive, 13–15, 101–104
Empathic language, scale for, 126*b*
Empathy, 40
   for abrasive boss, 239
   lack of, 10*b*, 236
   listening with, 117–118
Employee readiness, 219
Employees
   control of work by, 98–99
   developmental needs of, 219–220
   language to motivate, 125
   performance measures for, 220–221
   resistance of through communication, 146*b*
   undermining trust, 99
   willingness of, 221
Empowerment, 17, 224–227, 258
   conditions inspiring feelings of, 226
   culture and, 42
   encouraging, 223
Empty suits, 32
Emrich, Cynthia, 134–135
Encouragement, feedback, 121
Enemy, common, 334
Enriching environments, 37
Enrico, Roger, 2
Environment, cultural relationships toward,
   283–284
Equal employment opportunity, 300
Equal Employment Opportunity Commission
   (EEOC), 287
Equilization phenomenon, 370–371
Ethical persuaders, 197–198
Ethical power
   foundations of, 159–162
   gaining and using, 157–203
Evaluative language, 121
Expansive executives, 32
Expectations
   clear, 331
   of other people, 46
   realistic, 242
Expertise, backfiring, 189*f*
Experts, reliance on, 176
Explanatory styles, 400–401

Expressive emotional display, 279
Expressive style, 164
    characteristics of, 165*t*
    influence strategies for, 168–169*t*
    potential behavior under stress for, 167*t*
    potential strengths and weaknesses of, 166*t*
    weaknesses perceived by others, 167*t*
Extroversion, tendencies of, 74*b*
Eye contact, cross-cultural meaning of, 128

F

Face-to-face communications, 147*b*
Face-to-face meetings, 372
Failure
    admitting, 16*b*
    early success leading to, 6–8
Fair Share Program, 288–289
Fairness, 290
    in trustworthiness, 93
Faith, happiness and, 393
Fallon, Thomas, 176
Family
    integrating work and, 408–420
    self-concept and, 44–46
Farmer, James, 297
Favor, obligation to repay, 183
Feedback, 25, 148
    360-degree, 123–125, 256
    accuracy of, 121
    in communication, 156
    creating work environment for, 120
    in feeling of flow, 395
    followup on, 121
    giving, 120–122
    giving and receiving, 114, 119–120
    honest, 128
    institutionalizing, 120
    lack of, 33
    to motivate employees, 125
    multirater, 123–125
    negative, 125–128
    obtaining, 17
    ongoing positive, 360
    receiving, 122–123
    seeking, 14, 85
    from team members, 328
    for teams, 314
Feedback-friendly work environment, 120
Feelings, describing, 121
Feelings conversation, 117

Ferrari, Enzo, 175
Ferris, Gerald, 10*b*
Finch, Miriam, 132, 133*t*
Fine, Gary, 91
Finklestein, Sydney, 4
Finley, Joycelyn, 291
*The First 90 Days: Critical Success Strategies for
    New Leaders at All Levels* (Watkins), 188
Fisher, George, 286
Fitzgerald, F. Scott, 18
Fitzgerald, Thomas, 292
Flattery, 256
    likeability and, 180, 183
Flaws, in derailment, 8–9
Fletcher, Joyce, 302
Flexibility, 70*b*, 295
    in coalitions, 192
    developing, 297
    interpersonal, 162*f*, 163–169
    promoting, 333
Flow
    happiness and, 395–397
    work's potential for, 398*b*
Follett, Mary Parker, 286, 301, 318
Foot-in-the-door technique, 178
Ford, Gerald, 240
Foreign languages, learning, 294
Forgiveness, 97–98, 105
Formality, 278
Framing, 60
Frankel, Lois, 6
Frankl, Viktor, 271, 397, 421
Fraser, George, 395
Fraser, Simon, 64
Fredrickson, Barbara, 14, 101
French culture, attitudes toward work in, 285
Frensch, Peter, 6–7
Freud, Sigmund, 393, 415
Friedman, Ray, 366
Friedman, Raymond, 249–250
Friedman, Sarah L., 414
Friedman, Stewart, 418*t*
Frisch, Max, 368
Fromm, Erich, 172
Fudge, Ann, 44–45, 116
Future-focused culture, 281–282

G

Gabarro, John, 235*b*, 244
Gaddis, William, 158

Galinsky, Ellen, 417, 418–420
Games Mother Never Taught You (Harragan), 292
Gandhi, Mahatma, 23, 97, 296
Gangestad, Steve, Self-monitoring assessment of, 77–78*b*
Gardenswartz, Lee, 280
Gardner, Randy, 178
Gatekeepers, 344
Gatekeeping roles, 334
Gates, Bill, 8, 140
Gauthier, Alain, 327
Gender
  in communication styles, 130, 280
  culture and, 270–271
Gender-inclusive language, 131–132, 148
  guidelines for, 133*t*
Genetic programming, 37
Gergen, Kenneth, 50–51
Gersick, Connie, 340–341
Giamatti, A. Bartlett, 392
Gibran, Kahlil, 236
Gide, Andre, 116
Gilligan, Carol, 48
Gilmore, Allan, 291
Ginette, Robert, 100
Glass ceiling, breaking, 298–299
Global distributed teams, managing, 369*b*
Global environment, relationships in, 22–23
Global markets, emerging, 288
Global Solutions for Teams (Odenwald), 355–356
Globalization, 2, 285
  new rules in, 17
  virtual teams and, 362
Goals
  clear, 98, 194
  common, 223
  in feeling of flow, 395
  focusing on, 222
"Golden Boy" syndrome, 9
Goldman, Emma, 355
Goldman, Jack, 326
Goldsmith, Oliver, 37
Goldstein, Noah, 184
Goleman, Daniel, 12
Good news
  exaggerating, 127
  managing, 147*b*
Graduate Management Admissions Tests, high scores on, 4

Gratification, postponing, 399
Gratitude, debt of, 172–173
Greenberger, Ellen, 417–418
Greene, Graham, 419
Gretzky, Wayne, 7
Griggs, Lewis, 351
Grothe, Marty, 214, 239
Group cohesion, 40
  of distributed teams, 374–375
  diversity and, 352
  excessive, 331
  reduced, 355
  in virtual teams, 367–368
Group development theory, 336–342
Group dynamics
  dysfunctional, 351–352
  in obedience to authority, 230
  understanding, 327
Group membership, 46–47
Groupthink, 343
  symptoms and solutions of, 332–333*b*
Growth, 67–68, 69
Guard role, 335*f*
Guest, Judith, 255
Guilt by association, 240
Gupta, Rajat, 44
Guru, management, 57–58

H

Habitual behavior, 70*b*
Habitual routines, changing, 60
Hackman, Richard, 314–316, 326, 342
Hallowell, Edward, 367
Hand motions, cross-cultural meanings of, 128–129
Hannah, David, 64
Happiness, 391–393, 422
  wealth and, 392, 394*b*
  work and, 394–397
Harmony
  with environment, 283–284
  interpersonal, 40–41
Harquail, Celia, 48
Harragan, Betty Leehan, 292
Harrington, Michael, 371
Hart, Frances Noyes, 405
Hartzler, Meg, 377–379*b*
Hawkins, Jeff, 373
Haywood, Martha, 349, 368, 375, 377–379*b*

Health
  optimism and, 401–402
  work and, 402–408
Heidrick and Struggle International, 188
Heilbrun, Carolyn, 139
Heller, Joseph, 86
Helps, Sir Arthur, 224
Hemingway, Ernest, 23
Henry, Jane E., 377–379*b*
Heroes, creating, 61
Hersey, Paul, 219–221
Heterogeneous groups, performance of, 287
Hierarchy
  authority relationships in, 214–215
  versus equality, 42
  flattening, 23
  personality and place in, 216–217
  receiving bad news in, 127
Higgins, Monica, 240
High-involvement work culture, 223
High-performing teams
  bottom line in, 342
  characteristics of, 315*f*, 389
  creating context for, 325–336
  foundations of, 316–325
High-power distance cultures, 277
High self-complexity, 62–63
High-trust organizations, 105
Hildebrant, Herbert, 133*t*
Hill, Linda, 20, 64–65, 87, 158, 214, 240
Hirschfield, Lawrence A., 270
Hitler, Adolf, followers of, 227
Hochwarter, Wayne, 10*b*
Hofstede, Geert, 41, 277
  country individualism index of, 43*t*
Holland, Jimmie, 401–402
Holland, Robert, 114
Holmes, Sherlock, 7
Holtom, Brooks, 250
Holyfield, Lori, 91
Homo narratus, 61
Homogeneous groups, performance of, 286–287
Honesty, 183–184
  in ethical persuasion, 197–198
  in minimizing organizational dysfunction, 192
Hong, Yin-Yi, 6
Hooks, Bell, 116
Hosmer, LaRue, 104
Howard, John, 172–173
Hubris, 9
Huey, John, 290

Hughes, Maryfran, 318
Humility, 95
Humphrey, Hubert H., 419
Hurston, Zora Neale, 136, 299
Hurtado, Aida, 62, 63
Huxley, Adolf, 61

I

"I Have a Dream" speech, 134–135
Iacocca, Lee, 138, 212
Ibarra, Herminia, 64, 65
Identity
  in age of Internet, 54–56
  common, 301–302
  cultural, 274–278
  of diverse team, 359–360
  mass media and celebrities in, 56–58
  in success, 16*b*
Identity conversation, 117
Impact, employee belief in, 225
Impression management, 254–257, 258
In-group identification, excessive, 331
Independence, 41
Independence-interdependence dimension, 41,
    274–275
Independent self-concept, 39–40, 76*b*
  versus interdependent self-concept, 42*t*
Independent thinking, 128
Individualism, 274–275
Individualistic cultures, 39–40
Inductive reasoning, 282–283
Industrial age, managerial self-concept in, 59*t*
Inequity, attention to, 296
Influence
  foundations of, 159–162
  gaining and using, 157–203
  precautions against, 171
  six universal forms of, 162, 169–184
Influence: Science and Practice (Cialdini),
    169–170
Influence networks, 191–192
Influence skills, 162*f*
  need for, 159–162
Influence strategies
  for each social style, 168–169*t*
  implementing, 163*t*
Informality, 278
Information
  access to, 226
  in power, 161

Information processing, lazy, 150–160
Information technology, 361–363
Ingratiation strategies, 255, 258
Innovation, 300–301
  rewarding, 224
Inspiring language, 134–135
Institutionally based trust, 92*f*
Instrumental support, 239
  network for, 248–249
Integration, 290
  promoting, 303
Integration-and-learning perspective, 359
Integrity
  in power, 162
  in trustworthiness, 93
Intellective tasks, 352
Intelligence
  beliefs about, 5–6
  cognitive, 4–6
  common sense versus, 7
  creative and practical, 12, 14
  emotional, 12, 14
  fluid versus fixed, 5–6, 9–10
Intensity, listening with, 117
Interactions, technical versus human aspects of,
  229
Interdependence, 215
  common vision in, 331
  of diverse team, 359–360
  mutual, 160
  in team forming stage, 338–339
Interdependent self-concept, 40–41, 76*b*
  versus independent self-concept, 42*t*
Intergroup conflict, 329–330
Intergroup sensitivity, 39
Internet
  growing use of, 141–142
  identity and, 54–56
Interpersonal cues, sensitivity to, 65–67
Interpersonal flexibility, 162*f*
Interpersonal power, 163–169
Interpersonal relationships, 244–246
Interpersonal trust-building strategies, 94–98
Interpersonally based trust, 92*f*
Interpretation, self-concept and, 48
Interventions
  managing types and timing of, 335–336
  type and timing of, 344
Intimacy, 3
  satisfying needs for, 23
Intimidation, 255, 258

Introversion, tendencies of, 74*b*
Involvement trait, 225*b*
Invulnerability, illusion of, 332*b*
IQ tests, 4–5
Isabella, Lynn, 239
Isen, Alice, 101
Isolation, social, 331
Iyengar, Shenna S., 39

J

Jackson, Bradley, 57
Jacobson, Lenore, 46
James, Jennifer, 20, 360
James, William, 132
Janis, Irving, 332*b*
Japanese culture
  business practices in, 294
  communication style in, 129
  fixed-time orientation of, 281
  interdependence in, 40, 41, 274–275
Japanese market, Merck's entrance into, 173
Jarvenpaa, Sirkka, 368
Jen, Gish, 271
Jensen, Robert, 94
Job expectations, clear, 98
Job satisfaction, 246
Job transitions, provisional selves and, 64
Jobs, Steve, 114, 327, 394
Johansen, Robert, 354, 368
Johnson, Philip, 397
Johnson, Sonia, 125
Johnson, Spencer, 120
Jones, John E., 335*f*
Judging, tendencies of, 74*b*
Judgmental decision-making tasks, 353–354
Judgments, influencing, 254–255
Justification, in success, 16*b*

K

Kahn, William, 215–216
Kallath, Thomas J., 425–426*b*
Kanter, Rosabeth Moss, 157
Kaplan, Robert, 32
Karma Yoga, 44
Katzenbach, Jon, 338
Kaye, Walter, 246
Kearney, A. T., 299
Kelleher, Herb, 58, 89
Kelly, Colleen, 293

Kelly, Jack, 9
Kerrigan, Pat, 218
Kiechel, Walter, 32, 125–127
Kiesler, Sarah, 363, 370
Kilbourne, Jean, 171
Kilduff, Martin, 66, 247–248, 249
Killer phrases, 119*b*
Kim, Heejung S., 40
Kimberly Clark, Huggies Pull-Ups of, 135
King, Martin Luther, Jr., 114, 130, 134–135
Kinko's, founder of, 218
Kirkpatrick, Helen, 298
Kitayama, Shinobu, 37, 41
Kiyosaki, Robert, 12, 23
Klaus, Peggy, 34
Klein, Beth, 234
Knight, M., 61
Knowledge workers, empowered, 17
Kofodimos, Joan, 32, 405–406
Kopf, Jerry, 126–127*b*
Korn/Ferry International executive search firm, 186
Kossek, Ellen, 413
Kotter, John, 4, 116, 187–188, 235*b*, 350, 358
Kouzes, James, 399
Kozlowski, Dennis, 8
Krackhardt, David, 247–248
Kram, Kathy, 215–216, 239, 240, 243
Kramer, Rod, 8, 99–100
Krause, Neal, 98
Krishnan, Ramkumar, 390
Kunda, Ziva, 56

L

Labich, Kenneth, 312
Laitala, Lynn Maria, 290
Laliberté, Guy, 175
Lancaster, Hal, 2, 115
Langer, Ellen, 47, 170
Language. *See also* Body language
    cross-cultural meaning of, 128–129
    culture and power in, 130–132
    gender-inclusive, 131–132, 133*t*, 148
    influential, 148
    inspiring, 134–135
    paying attention to, 301
Lao-Tse, 32, 342
Latin American cultures, fluid-time orientation of, 281
Laube, Sheldon, 375

Laurent, Andre, 294
Lazare, Aaron, 96, 97
Lazy information processors, 159–160
Leadership
    in avoiding groupthink, 332–333*b*
    communication in, 114
    communication rules of, 147*b*
    of diverse teams, 358–361
    diversity in, 289–291
    of high-performing teams, 314, 325–336, 389
    models of, 218–223, 257–258
    optimism of, 399
    perceptual biases of, 357
    styles of, 219
The Leadership Moment (Useem), 173
Learning
    enhanced, 354
    lifelong, 18–20, 25–26
    ongoing, 3
    punishment affecting, 176
    sharing, 224
Learning goal assessment, 13*b*
Learning goal orientation, 11–12
Leavitt, Robert Keith, 135
Leavitt, Theodore, 326
Lechter, Sharon, 12, 23
Lee, Will, 318*b*
Legal costs, diversity management and, 287
Legal environment, 298
Legitimacy, 290
Legitimacy, trappings of, 229
Leidner, Dorothy, 368
Lentz, Richard, 133*t*
Lepper, Mark, 39, 284
Lesage, Alain-Rene, 401
Levin, Ira M., 135
Levine, James, 413
Levine, Robert, 160, 171, 183
Levinson, Harry, 236, 239
Levy, Becca, 397
Lewicki, Roy, 96
Lewin, Marcia, 246
Life, balanced, 390–426
Life on the Screen: Identity in the Age of the Internet (Turkle), 54–55
Likeability, 10*b*
Liking, 169, 170
Liking rule, 179–182, 184*f*, 197
    leveraging, 183
    resisting, 183
Linear thinking, 282

Lipnack, Jessica, team stage theory of, 336–342, 361, 374
Listening. *See also* Active listening
  being yourself in, 118
  in building power, 196
  complete information in, 118
  demonstrating acceptance in, 118
  with empathy, 117–118
  with intensity, 117
  in powerful people, 161
  in social style, 165–167
  to storytelling, 139–140
  in success, 16*b*
Litvin, Deborah, 271
Lobel, Sharon, 286–287
Lock, John, 367
Lockheed Martin, e-mail system crash of, 115*b*
Lockwood, Penelope, 56
Lombardo, Michael, 235
Long-term planning, 282
Longevity
  factors in, 406–407*b*
  optimism and, 401–402
Loss, early, 45
Louw, Lente-Louise, 351
Low-power distance cultures, 277
Loyalty, organizational, 102–103
Luk, Vivienne, 409

M

Maccoby, Michael, 238
Machiavellianism scale, 47
Mackinnon, Catherine, 131
MacLean, Tammy, 355
Mahone, Paula, 316
Management
  new ideal of, 18
  trends influencing, 18, 19–20*t*
Management gurus, 57–58
Management skills, 25
Management styles
  variety of, 218–219
  video case of, 268
Manager
  challenges for, 50–51
  cognitive and behavioral complexity of, 257
  cultural competence of, 269–304
  derailment of, 3–9, 25
  growth and development of, 67–68
  importance of, 1

management gurus and self-concept of, 57–58
  multiple self-concepts of, 62–65
  new rules for, 17–23
  trustworthiness of, 87–88
Managerial coaching, 33
Managing Diversity (Gardenswartz, Rowe), 280
Marcic, D., self-assessment personality inventory of, 72–75*b*
Marginalism, 62
Marginalization, 352
Markus, Hazel, 37, 41, 56–57
Marmot, Michael G., 403
Marriage, quality of, 417
Martin, Gregg D., 425–426*b*
Martin, Joanne, 137
Martyna, Wendy, 131, 132
Mary Kay cosmetics, 180
Maslach, Christina, 232*b*
Mass media, identity in age of, 56–58
Mastery, 3, 32
  satisfying needs for, 23
Materialism, 392
Mattel, earnings decline in, 116
Maturity, interdependence and, 40
Maximizer, 393
Mayfield, Milton Ray, motivating language scale of, 126–127*b*
MBA degree programs, 300
McCall, Morgan, 235
McLeod, Poppy, 286–287, 369–370
McNealy, Scott, 363
Me-first thinking, 199
Mead, Margaret, 192, 271, 416
Meaning, 328
  in job, 224
  management of, 60–61
  need for, 49
  teams and, 330
Meaning-making language, 125
  scale for, 126–127*b*
Meaningful life, crafting, 22–23, 26
Meetings
  calculating cost of, 324*b*
  managing, 324–325*b*
  teleconference and videoconference, 377–379*b*
Mehra, Ajay, 249
Memory, self-concept and, 47
Memos, confidential, 115*b*
Menaghan, Elizabeth, 417–418
Mentor-protégé relationships, 258
  managing, 239–244

Mentoring
  bad, 240
  diversity and, 241–242
  dos and don'ts of, 245*t*
  dysfunctional, 243
Mentors, advice for, 244
Mercer, Graham, 372
Merck, in Japanese pharmaceutical market, 173
Messenger, shooting the, 128
Meyers, Judith, 293
Meyerson, Debra, 99–100, 302
Micromanaging, 93
  by abrasive boss, 236
Milgram, Stanley, 176, 227–230, 231–232
Miller, Henry, 422
Milton, John, 101
Minority groups, networks of, 248–250
Minority opinions, expressing, 369–370
Mintzberg, Henry, 1, 23
Mishra, Aneil, 88
Mission, clear and engaging, 221–222
Mission trait, 225*b*
Mistakes, learning from, 9
Mistrust, mutual, 91
Mitsubishi Motor Manufacturing of America,
  sexual harassment suit against, 287
Mobility, independent self-concept and, 40
Mobilizing action, 132–140
Mock jury experiment, 176
Moldoveanu, Mihnea, 47
Money, happiness and, 391–392
Monitoring, self, 65–67, 69
Montovani, Guiseppe, 370–371
Moore, Darla, 15
Moral decision making, 48
Morgan, Gareth, 60, 132
Morita, Akio, 67
Morrison, Ann, 235, 289
Morrison, Tony, 328
Mothers
  working, 423
  working versus stay-at-home, 409–410
Motivating language, 125
  scale for, 126–127*b*
Motivation, relationships in, 268
Multicultural competence
  developing, 296–297
  enhancing, 292–297
  personal, 304
  skills for, 293*f*
Multicultural managers, effective, 303–304

Multiple selves, 61–65
Multirater feedback, 123–125
Multiuser domains (MUDs), 55
Munter, Mary, 372
Murphy, Herta A., 133*t*
Musgrave, James, 38
Mutual trust, in temporary groups, 100
Myers, David, 391–392, 393
Myers-Briggs Assessment, 70–71*b*
Myers-Briggs Type Indicator, 74*b*

N

Nadler, David, 325
Naisbitt, John, 141
Narcissism, 36
NASA Orbiter miscommunication, 115*b*
Nathan, John, 67
National Association for the Advancement of
  Colored People (NAACP), 288–289
National Institute of Child Health and Human
  Development
  data of, 410, 411
  study of, 414–416
Navy, U.S., organizational rites and rituals of, 301
Neale, William, 222*f*, 225*b*
Needleman, Jacob, 171
Needs, fundamental, 49
Neel, Roy, 414
Negative emotions, 14
Negative feedback
  in minimizing organizational dysfunction, 192
  receiving, 122
  sensitivity to, 121–122
Negative thinking, power of, 408*b*
Network organization, 21–23
Networking, 244–247, 258
  advice for, 251
  assessing skills for, 252–253*b*
  definition of, 246
Networks
  broad and diverse, 354
  diversity and, 248–251
  diversity of, 247
  effective, 247–248
  environment of, 26
  informal, 249–250
  status of people in, 247–248
  steps in developing and nurturing, 254*b*
  strong, 213
  strong and weak ties in, 248

New behavior, overlearning, 17
Nohria, Nitin, 21
Norem, Julie, 102, 402, 408*b*, 421
Norms
   clear, 319–320
   in diverse team, 360
   for effective teams, 319–322
   explicit, 320–321
   implicit, 320
   in obedience to authority, 230
   predictable, 375
   for teams, 340
Northcraft, Greg, 122
Nurius, Paula, 56–57
Nursing homes, 411
Nutt, P., self-assessment personality inventory
   of, 72–75*b*

O

Obedience, factors affecting, 229–230
Objectives, focusing on, 222
Odenwald, Sylvia, 355–356
O'Hara-Devereaux, Mary, 354, 368
Olsen, Ken, 140
The One-Minute Manager (Johnson,
   Blanchard), 120
One-size-fits-all approach, 4
Online shopping, 141–142
Open-ended questions, 121
Openness, 118
   setting tone of, 120
Operating costs, diversity management and,
   287–288
Opinion conformity, 256
Optimism, 397–402, 422–423
   explanations in, 400–401
   happiness and, 393
   leading to self-fulfilling prophecies, 399–400
   longevity and, 407*b*
   overrated, 401–402
   well-being and, 101–102
Order, sense of, 50*b*
O'Reilly, Charles, 4
Orfalea, Paul, 218
Organizational capability, developing, 223
Organizational communication, 114
Organizational crises, 102–104
Organizational culture
   effective, 221–227
   high-involvement, 223

   impact of team diversity on, 358
   inspiring high performance, 225*b*
Organizational effectiveness, positive emotions
   in, 102
Organizational learning, promoting, 224
Organizational life, storytelling and, 61
Organizational politics, 198–199
   political savvy in, 184–194
Organizational socialization, 367–368
Organizational stories, powerful, 136–140
Organizational structure
   authority relations and, 214–215
   fluid, 21–23
   positive emotions and, 106
   swift trust and, 99–100
Organizational symbolism, paying
   attention to, 301
Organizational trust-building strategies, 98–100
Organizational values, defining, 223
Organizations, self-concept in, 49–58
Others' needs, adapting to, 213
Overlearning, 17
The Overworked American (Schor), 285

P

Pacht, Asher, 403, 404
Packwood, Robert, 97
Panic emotions, 175
Paraphrasing, 118
Parcel, Toby, 417–418
Parental style, 44–45
Parents
   balancing work and family, 409–420
   organizational impact of, 413
   personality and characteristics of, 417
   work experience of, 417–418
   working, 423
Park, Lora, 36
Parsons, Richard, 329
Participating or supporting style, 220
Participative unit climate, 226
Particularism, 277
   versus universalism, 278*t*
Past-focused culture, 281–282
Patagonia, product design of, 135
PC games, 55
Peale, Norman Vincent, 95
Peer behavior, ethical framework and, 231
People's Express Airline, 7
Perceiving, tendencies of, 74*b*

Perception
  in developing trust, 90–91
  skills for, 295
Perfectionism, 403–404, 423
  Type A behavior and, 405–406
Performance
  clear, measurable standards for, 98, 120
  focus on, 121
  linking culture and leadership to, 222*f*
  measures of, 98, 220–221
Performance goal orientation, 12, 317
Performance reputation, 247–248
Perlow, Leslie, 396
Perot, H. Ross, 316
Personal change, steps toward, 16–17
Personal development, investing in, 326–327
Personal grounding, 296
Personal growth, 67–68, 69
  teams promoting, 315
Personal power, 198
  in increasing political power, 193*f*
  political savvy in, 187–188
Personal responsibility, abdication of, 229–230
Personal Responsibility and Work Opportunity
    Reconciliation Act, 412
Personal style, assessing, 17
Personality
  authority relations and, 215–217
  in obedience to authority, 230
  styles of, 71*b*
  trust and, 91–93
  of working parents, 417
Personality and Social Psychology Bulletin, 178
Personality assessment, 70–71*b*
Personality-based trust, 92*f*
Personality inventory, 72–75*b*
Personality scale, proactive, 11*b*
Personality types
  defining, 72–73*b*
  Type A, 423
  well-being and, 404–406
Personalization, 401
Persuading or coaching style, 220
Pessimism
  defensive, 402, 408*b*, 422–423
  explanatory styles in, 400–401
Peters, Tom, 58
  on building brand, 34–35
Pink, Daniel, 140*b*
Pittinsky, Todd, 413
Plateauing, 67
Platinum rule, 167, 295

Playing dumb, 256
Political power, techniques to increase, 193*f*
Political savvy, 162, 195, 198
  characteristics of people with, 186–192
  developing, 184–186
  in minimizing dysfunctional organizational
      politics, 192–194
Pollard, C. William, 292
Polychronicity Scale, 425–426*b*
Position power, 191, 193*f*
Positive deviance, 104
Positive emotions, 13–15, 105
  cultivating in workplace, 104
  expression of, 104
  organizational crises and, 102–104
  in organizational effectiveness, 102
  success and, 101–104
Positive experience, 181
Positive feedback
  giving, 121
  opportunities to give, 120
Positive illusions, 398
Positive interactions, likeability and, 180
Positive thinking, 422–423
Posner, Barry, 399
Post, James, 147*b*
Postmodern manager, 68–69
  promise and perils of, 58–67
Pound, Ezra, 128
Powell, Colin, 127
Power
  characteristics of, 195
  characteristics of people with, 160–162
  corruption of, 158
  definition of, 159, 195
  in distributed teams, 370–371
  language and culture in, 130–132
  multiple bases of, 192, 198–199
  need for, 159–162
  personal, 187–188
  relational, 188–190
  relationships in, 268
  structural, 190–192
  sustainable, ethical, 159–204
Powerlessness, 158
Praise
  in employee empowerment, 226–227
  likeability and, 183
Predictability, in trust, 98
Present-focused culture, 281–282
Preston, Jim, 353–354
Prison abuse experiment, 232–233*b*

Privacy, Internet and, 142
Private self-concept, 39, 76*b*
Proactivity, 10–11
*Problem Bosses: Who They Are and How to
    Deal with Them* (Grothe), 214
Problem-solving
    diversity and, 286
    positive emotions and capability for, 102
*The Productive Narcissist: The Promise
    and Peril of Visionary Leadership*
    (Maccoby), 238
Professional development, 67–68, 69
Promotions, providing clear guidelines for, 194
Protégés
    advice for, 242–244
    diversity of, 241–242
    relationship with, 239–244
Prothro, Tommy, 313
Provisional selves, 64
Proximity, 180, 181
Pseudo relationships, 338
Pseudoapologies, 97
Psychological well-being, networks in, 246
Psychosocial support, 239, 248–249
    networking in, 251
    of protégés, 241–242
Public self-concept, 76*b*
Publicity, positive, 286
Punctuality, 281
Punishment, effect of on learning, 176
Purpose, clear and engaging, 316–317

Q

Quick fixes, 2
Quinn, Robert, 237

R

Racial diversity, mentoring and, 241–242
Randall, Iris, 235*b*
Rapport talk, 280
Rationality, bounded, 159–160, 196
Reagan, Ronald, 405
Reardon, Kathleen Kelly, 161, 163, 185, 187,
    188, 190, 234
Reasoning, inductive and deductive, 282–283
Reciprocation rule, 40, 169, 171–174, 184*f*,
    197, 257
    versus attractiveness, 181
    leveraging, 174
    resisting, 174

Reciprocity, principle of, 243
Recognition, in employee empowerment,
    226–227
Recordkeeping, careful, 238
Regan, Dennis, 172
Reich, Robert B., 246
"Reindeer games," 299
Relational influence, increasing, 193*f*
Relational power, 188–190, 198
Relationship-focused behavior, 219, 220
Relationship network, 213
Relationship-oriented culture, 275
Relationship skills, 21–23
Relationships
    building, 125, 213
    culture and, 277–278
    diverse network of, 26
    happiness and, 393
    high-quality, 257
    language in building, 125
    managing, 212–258
    power of, 246
    self-monitoring behavior and, 66–67
    trust in, 88, 90–91
    video case of, 268
    in virtual teams, 367–368
    of working parents, 417
Reliability, 93
Replacement activity, skill with, 16*b*
Report talk, 280
Resignation, from bad employment situation,
    238–239
Resources
    limited, 160
    for teams, 314, 328–329
Respect, 257
Responsibility, abdication of, 229–230
Responsiveness, high/low dimensions of, 164,
    196–197
Results, measuring, 302
Results-driven processes, 319–322
Results-oriented professionals, 189*f*
Rewards, 194
    for cooperation, 333
    for high-performing teams, 329
    for progress in diversity, 302
Rich Dad, Poor Dad, 23
Richardson, John H., 397
Riding the Waves of Culture (Trompenaars),
    283–284
Riftin, Jerry, 142

Risk, trust and, 90
Rites, organizational, 301
Rituals, organizational, 301
Robinson, Sandra, 90–91
Roche, Gerry, 188
Roddick, Anita, 135–136, 399
Rodin, 12
Rogers, Carl, 116
Role ambiguity, low, 226
Role-modeling
  of behavior you want, 297–298
  for diverse team members, 360–361
Roosevelt, Eleanor, 9, 216
Roosevelt, Theodore, 22
Rosenthal, Robert, 46
Rothbard, Nancy, 64
Rowe, Anita, 280
Rowley Mayfield, Jacqueline, motivating
  language scale of, 126–127b
Ruderman, Marian, 64
Rules
  bending and breaking, 8
  new, 17–23
Runbeck, Margaret Lee, 96

S

Sanchez-Burks, Jeffrey, 279–280
Sandler, Debra, 395
Sapir, Edward, 130
Satisficer, 393
Saturated life, day in, 52–54
*The Saturated Self: Dilemmas of Identity in
  Everyday Life* (Gergen), 50–51
Scarcity rule, 169, 170, 174–175, 184f, 197
  leveraging, 175
  resisting, 175
Schedules, time orientation and, 281
Schmidt, Benno, 116, 118
Schor, Juliet, 285
Schwartz, Barry, 393
Scott, Walter, 125–127
Scout role, 335f
*The Secret Handshake: Mastering the Politics
  of the Business Inner Circle* (Reardon),
  161, 163
The Secret Handshake (Reardon), 187, 234
Self-assessment, 70–71b
Self-assessment 20 questions, 75–76b
Self-assessment personality inventory,
  72–75b

Self-awareness, 3
  barriers to, 33
  development of, 21, 26, 31–78, 71b
  in effective team leadership, 326–327
  investing in, 295
  limited, 4
  obedience to authority and, 230
  success and, 68
  video case of, 85
Self-brand, 34–35
Self-concept, 35, 68
  in contemporary organizations, 49–58
  cultural influences on, 38–43
  defining, 37
  family influences on, 44–46
  group influences on, 46–47
  importance of, 47–48
  independent, 39–40
  influences on, 38f
  interdependent, 40–41
  interpreting, 75–76b
  management gurus and, 57–58
  other's expectations and, 46
  promise and perils of, 58–67
  social influences on, 43–47
  updated, 59
Self-confidence, 49
Self-deprecation, 255–256, 258
Self-determination, 225
Self-efficacy motive, 49
Self-enhancement, 255, 258
  techniques in, 256
Self-enhancement bias, 39
Self-esteem
  happiness and, 392
  high, costs of, 35–36
  of working parents, 417
Self-handicapping strategy, 255–256, 258
Self-monitoring, 65–67, 69
Self-monitoring assessment, 77–78b
Self-promotion, 32, 256
Self-protective strategies, 234
Seligman, Martin, 401
Senge, Peter, 327
Sensing-intuition tendencies, 74b
Sensitivity overload, 291
Sentry role, 335f
Separateness, 38
Separatism, perceptions of, 251
Sethi, Sheena, 284
Settles, Iris, 63

Seven Habits of Highly Effective People (Covey), 116–117
The Seven Habits of Highly Effective People (Covey), 33
Sex bias, in language, 131–132
Sexton, Anne, 418
Sexual harassment suits, 287
Shaw, Robert Bruce, 86
Sheehy, Gail, 61
Shellenbarger, Susan, 103, 238–239, 414
Shostake, Linda, 45
Similarity, perceived, 180, 181–182
Similarity-attraction hypothesis, 248–249, 352, 380
"The Sims," 55
Sinclair, Amanda, 312–313
Situation analysis, 237–238
Situational cues, 365, 366*f*
Situational Leadership model, 219–221, 257
Situational pressures, 230–232
Sitwell, Edith, 256
Skill-based training, 300
Sleep deprivation, 407*b*
Sloan, Alfred, Jr., 333*b*
Smiling, 180
Smircich, Linda, 60, 132
Smith, Douglas, 338
Smith, Kenwyn K., 214
Smith, Orin, 273–274
Snyder, Mark, Self-monitoring assessment of, 77–78*b*
Social behavior, 415
Social change
  challenge of, 50–51
  self-awareness and, 85
Social context
  in communication style, 278–280
  understanding, 294–295
Social cues, 365
  missing in virtual teams, 365, 366*f*, 381
  sensitivity to, 65–67
Social disapproval, 369
Social dynamics
  in success, 16*b*
  of virtual teams, 380–381
Social groups, categorizations into, 330–331
Social harmony, 40–41
Social influences
  on self-concept, 43–47
  in virtual teams, 368–370
Social lubricant, 88

Social networks, 190–191
Social proof rule, 169, 170, 177, 184*f*, 197
  leveraging, 177–178
  resisting, 178
Social relations, self-concept and, 48
Social rituals, 130
Social saturation, 50–51, 52–54
Social skills
  lack of, 10*b*
  in success, 212
Social stimulation, increasing, 51
Social styles
  characteristics of, 165*t*
  influence strategies for, 168–169*t*
  potential behavior under stress for, 167*t*
  potential strengths and weaknesses of, 166*t*
  weaknesses perceived by others, 167*t*
Social Styles model, 163–169, 196–197
  assessment of, 200–203
Social support, networking in, 251
Society, categorizations in, 330
Socioeconomic trends, 2
Sociopolitical support, 226
Something Happened (Heller), 86
Sony: The Private Life (Nathan), 67
Southwest Airlines, founder's people skills in success of, 89
Sowell, Shaunna, 319
Spreitzer, Gretchen, 88, 224–227
Sproull, Lee, 363, 368, 370
Staffing, appropriate, 327–328
Stamps, Jeffrey, team stage theory of, 336–342, 361, 374
Stanley, Thomas, 394*b*
Starbucks, cultural identity and, 273–274
Static cues, 365, 366*f*
Status
  culture and, 275
  in distributed teams, 370–371
Stein, Gertrude, 372
Steinam, Gloria, 114
Stereotyping
  blocking active listening, 116
  breaking down, 181–182
  diversity and, 285
  negative, 331
  of outsiders, 332*b*
Sternberg, Robert, 4–5, 6–7, 186
Stewart, Martha, 9
Stone, Douglas, 117

Story, creating, 136–138
Storytellers, 61
Storytelling, 135–139, 138–139, 148
  digital, 140*b*
  listening to, 139–140
Strange, John Stephen, 66
Strategic visits, 188–190, 193*f*
"Street smarts," 5
Strengths, overcoming, 6–7
Stress
  behavior of different social styles
    under, 167*t*
  coping with, 406*b*
  in diverse teams, 355
  optimism and management of, 399
  self-concept and ability to cope with, 48
Strong ties, 248
Strube, Michael J., 425–426*b*
Structural barriers theory, 352, 380
Structural influence, increasing, 193*f*
Structural power, 190–192, 198
Subordinates
  attitudes to authority of, 231
  management of, 217–227
  managing boss, 233–239
  relationships with, 257
  self-protective strategies of, 234
Success
  behaviors predicting, 14*f*
  characteristics of, 9–15, 25
  early, 6–8
  intelligence and, 4–6
  optimism and, 397–402
  orderliness and, 50*b*
  predictors of, 1–27
  trust and positive emotions in, 101–104
Sulloway, Frank, 45–46
Sun Microsystems, virtual teams of, 363
Superstars, 56–57
Supervisors, commitment to, 213
Support, 220
Support groups, endorsing, 299
Swift trust, 99–100
Sybil syndrome, 65
Symbolic separation, 250–251
Symbolism, organizational, 301
Syngery, of high-performing teams, 343
Szulanski, Gabriel, 94

T

Taboos, learning, 294
Tacit knowledge, 5
Tailhook scandal, 301
Talent, recruiting and retaining, 286
Tannen, Deborah, 130, 280
Task cohesion, 368
Task-focused style, 219, 220, 268
Tasks
  characteristics of, 219
  networking in accomplishing, 251
  well-designed, 328
Taylor, Jim, 56
Taylor, Shelly, 397–398, 399
Team ideology, tyranny of, 312–313
Team leader
  in adjourning stage, 341
  in forming stage, 338–339
  in norming stage, 340
  in performing stage, 341
  roles of, 343–344
Team members, 318–319, 343
  different backgrounds of, 350
  misperceptions about performance of, 357
  style preferences of, 356*b*
Team orientation, building, 223
Team performance, enhanced, 286–287
Team review, guidelines for, 323*b*
Teams
  adjourning stage of, 341–342
  attention to process of, 354
  attitudes toward, 311
  autonomy of, 313
  beyond hype of, 312–313
  boundaries of
    clear, 313
    managing, 329–335
  bridging boundaries in, 335*f*
  building, 389
  characteristics of, 343, 389
  clear, engaging purpose of, 316–317
  co-located and distributed, 363–364
  common tasks of, 313
  criteria for effectiveness of, 314–316
  definition of, 313–314
  detachment from, 355
  differentiated member roles in, 313

distributed
    managing, 371–379
    social dynamics in, 364–371
diverse, 351–361
faith in, 311–312
first meetings of, 359
forming stage of, 336–339
gatekeeping roles in, 334
goals of, 3
high-performing, 311–344
homogeneous versus heterogeneous, 350
life cycle of, 336–342
managing differences and distances in,
    349–381
managing interventions in, 335–336
norming stage of, 340
norms for, guidelines for creating, 321–322b
performance goals and measures, 317
performing stage of, 340–341
preparation and practice for, 323–325
providing direction, structure, and resources
    for, 327–329
redefining boundaries of, 334
relationship management in, 335f
results-driven processes of, 319–322
sharing time together, 334
storming stage of, 339
swift trust in, 100
synergy of, 343
temporary, 106
virtual, 361–381
Technological environment, managing, 373–374
Technology, 2
    in communication, 140–145, 148–149
    in performing team tasks, 372–373
    privacy and, 142
    self-concept in, 58–67, 68
    in virtual teams, 361, 381
Tejada, Wilfredo, 413
Telecommuting, 413
Teleconference, tips for, 377–379b
Telling or directing style, 220
Temperament
    happiness and, 392
    performance and, 402
Temporary groups
    swift trust in, 100
    trust in, 106
Tharenou, Phyllis, 414
Thinking, critical, 20–21, 194

Thinking-feeling tendencies, 74b
Thomas, David, 244, 286, 289–290
Thomas, R. Roosevelt, Jr., 269
Tichy, Noel, 226
Tillich, Paul, 229
Time
    fixed versus fluid, 281
    linear versus cyclical, 282
    monochronic versus polychronic, 281
    perception of, 280–282
Time Warner, intergroup conflict in, 329–330
Tinkering, 60, 65
Tournier, Paul, 115
Traditional boundaries, breaking, 60
Training, 194
    work-related, 226
Transnational teams, managing, 349–350
Transparency, 194, 199
Triandis, H. C., Self-assessment 20 questions of,
    75–76b
Triggers, 170, 197
Trompenaars, Fons, 275, 283–284
True calling, 65
Trust, 257
    definition of, 89–91
    framework for understanding antecedents
        and consequences of, 92f
    importance of, 86–89
    inspiring, 105
    interpersonal strategies for creating, 94–98
    optimum, 94
    organizational strategies for creating, 98–100
    personality and, 91–93
    positive emotions and, 101–104
    rebuilding, 99
    repairing, 96–97
    roots of, 91–94
    in success, 16b
    in team cohesion, 374–375
    too much, 106
    willingness to, 105
Trust-mistrust tendency, 91–93
Trust-sustaining mechanisms, 98–99
Trusting relationships, 213
Trustworthiness
    assessment of, 93
    building reputation for, 127–128
    personal reputation for, 95
Truth, cultural attitudes toward, 282–283
Tunnel vision, collective, 313

Turk, Carolyn, 6
Turkle, Sherry, 54–55, 60
Turner, Ted, 394
Twain, Mark, 4
Tyco, confidential memos of, 115*b*
Type A behavior, 404–406, 423

U

Uncertainty, 160
   high and low avoidance of, 284
   reducing, 125
   trust and, 90
Uncertainty-reducing language, scale for, 126*b*
Understaffing, optimal, 327–328
Unethical behavior, 227–233
Uniqueness bias, 39
Universalism, 277
   versus particularism, 278*t*
Useem, Michael, 173, 319

V

Vaill, Peter, 229, 231
Values, job aligned with, 224
Van Norstrand, Catherine Herr, 297
Vande Walle, Don, 11–12, 13*b*
Video games, 55
Videoconference meetings, 361
   tips for, 377–379*b*
Virtual community, 54–56
Virtual teams
   co-located versus distributed, 363–364
   distributed, 364–379
   social dynamics of, 380–381
   success of, 363
   trend toward, 361–363
Virtuous organizations, 102
Visibility, 190
Vision, 135–136
   common, 331
   shared, 222, 225*b*
Visiting people, strategic, 188–190
Voice mail, managing, 145*b*
Voluntary commitment, 178–179
Vonnegut, Kurt, Jr., 65

W

Wacker, Watts, 56
Wagner, Jane, 31, 401

Waitresses, liking rule and earning tips, 180
Wal-Mart sex discrimination suit, 287
Walker, Alice, 64, 215, 403
Walker, Danielle, 275
Walker, Thomas, 275
Wall, Toby, 89
Wallace, Harry, 36
Walsh, Bill, 323
Ward, Patricia, 336
Ward-Biederman, Patricia, 328–329
Watkins, Michael, 188, 190
Watson, Tom, Jr., 136–137
Weak ties, 248
Wealth, happiness and, 394*b*
Weick, Karl, 15, 16b, 60, 99–100
Weiss, Robert, 394
Welch, Jack, 44
Well-being
   of children of working parents, 418–420
   negative impact of work behaviors on, 424*b*
   optimism and, 399–400
   personality type and, 404–406
   positive emotions and, 101–102, 105
   work and, 402–408
Wellstone, Paul, 410
West, Candace, 271
What happened conversation, 117
Why Smart Executives Fail (Finkelstein), 4
Why Smart People Do Stupid Things
   (Sternberg), 186
Whyte, William, 291–292
Wick, Judith M. Bard, 405
Wicks, Andrew, 94
Williams, Michele, 90
Willingness, assessment of, 221
Wilson, Meena, 296
Win-win solutions, 223
Winfrey, Oprah, 393
Winnick, Gary, 45
Wins, small, 328
Winterson, Jeanette, 294
Wisdom, in listening to stories, 139–140
Wiseman, Dr. Richard, 7
Witt, L. A., 10*b*
Women
   balancing work and family, 409
   diverse networks of, 248–249
   multiple roles of, 64
   role models for, 241–242
   working versus stay-at-home, 409–410, 423

Work
   cultural orientation toward, 284–285
   enhancing distributed team performance, 374
   happiness and, 394–397
   health and, 402–408
   integrating family and, 408–420
   learning norms of, 294
Work behaviors, negative impact of, 424*b*
Work-life balance, achieving, 390–426
Work-related cultural preferences, 276*b*
Workforce
   demographics of, 410–413, 423
   diversity in, 303
Workplace
   bringing out best in people, 26
   changing physical layout of, 334
   cultivating positive emotions in, 104
   getting best performance in, 22
   obedience to authority in, 230–233
Wright, Stephen, 392

X

Xerox, Black Caucus Group at, 249–250

Y

Ybarra, Oscar, 22
*You Just Don't Understand: Women and Men in
   Conversation* (Tannen), 280
Young, Mary, 147*b*
Youthfulness, 180

Z

Zand, Dale, 90
Zimbardo, Philip, 232–233*b*
Zimmerman, Don, 271